THE SECOND INTERNATIONAL
PART I

By the same author

A HISTORY OF SOCIALIST THOUGHT
I. THE FORERUNNERS, 1789-1850
II. MARXISM AND ANARCHISM, 1850-90
IV. COMMUNISM AND SOCIAL DEMOCRACY, 1914-31.
PARTS I AND II
V. SOCIALISM AND FASCISM, 1931-39

*

ATTEMPTS AT GENERAL UNION, 1818-34
CHARTIST PORTRAITS
THE CASE FOR INDUSTRIAL PARTNERSHIP
INTRODUCTION TO ECONOMIC HISTORY, 1750-1950

A HISTORY OF SOCIALIST THOUGHT: Volume III, Part I

THE SECOND INTERNATIONAL
1889-1914

G. D. H. COLE

MACMILLAN

LONDON · MELBOURNE · TORONTO

ST MARTINS PRESS

NEW YORK

1967

———

*First Edition 1956
Reprinted 1960, 1963, 1967*

MACMILLAN AND COMPANY LIMITED
*Little Essex Street London WC2
also Bombay Calcutta Madras Melbourne*

THE MACMILLAN COMPANY OF CANADA LIMITED
70 Bond Street Toronto 2

ST. MARTIN'S PRESS INC.
175 Fifth Avenue New York NY 10010

PRINTED IN GREAT BRITAIN

PREFACE

THIS volume has been difficult to write because of the extension of Socialism to so many countries and of the paucity of material for many of them in languages I can read. I cannot hope to have avoided making many mistakes, or faulty judgments, though I hope I have got most of the essentials broadly right. Where I could, I sought help and advice from specialists who were known to me, and their kindly answers have enabled me to correct a number of errors. My deepest thanks are due to Mr. H. N. Brailsford, who has again read through the whole volume and helped me greatly, and to Mr. Julius Braunthal, Secretary of the Socialist International, who has not only read the whole but also loaned me a number of books and reports which I should have found it very difficult to consult elsewhere. For loans of books I am also deeply indebted to Mr. Raymond Postgate, Mr. H. L. Beales, Mr. C. A. Macartney, Mr. K. J. Scott of New Zealand and Miss Florence Bradfield. My wife has read some of the chapters and made valuable comments.

My numerous other debts are for information and help with particular chapters — especially with data and biographical particulars. I have to thank Mr. James Joll for help with the section dealing with the Second International ; Mr. J. F. Horrabin, Mr. Maurice Reckitt, Mrs. A. J. Penty, Professor Michael Oakeshott, and Mr. John Mahon (Great Britain) ; M. Maurice Dommanget and M. Michel Crozier (France) ; Mr. Julius Braunthal and Frau Gertrude Magaziner (Austria) ; Mr. Thomas Balogh and Mr. K. Szigeti (Hungary) ; Dr. H. G. Schenk (Bohemia) ; M. Charles Barbier, Professor Max Weber, Mr. Hans Handschin, and the Verband Schweiz Konsumvereine (Switzerland) ; M. René Renard (Belgium), Dr. von Wiessing, Professor A. C. Rüter and the International Institute for Social History (Holland) ; Mr. Poul Hansen (Denmark) ; Mr. Gostar Langenfelt, Baron Palmstierna, and Dr. J. W. Ames (Sweden) ;

v

Mr. B. Hindahl (Norway); Mr. R. H. Oittinen (Finland); Signor L. Valiani (Italy); Mr. L. Popov (Bulgaria); Mr. V. Tunguz (Yugoslavia); Miss Marjorie Plant, Mr. Isaiah Berlin, Mrs. Kuskova-Prokopovitch, Dr. Rudolf Schlesinger, and Mr. Henry Collins (Soviet Union); Dr. H. W. Laidler (United States); Mr. C. A. Fleming, Mr. E. M. Higgins, Mr. N. S. Lynravn, and Mr. Lloyd Ross (Australia); Professor Iwao Ayusawa (Japan); His Excellency Señor Francisco A. de Icaza (Mexico); and Mr. Desmond Crowley, Mr. K. J. Scott, and Miss E. G. Simpson (New Zealand). Mr. Crowley, in particular, was kind enough to lend me his own unpublished book on the Labour movement in New Zealand, which I found very helpful indeed. Mr. Higgins also lent me unpublished material about Australia.

Finally, I have to thank two secretaries, Mrs. Rosamund Broadley and Mrs. Audrey Millar, who have successively borne the burden of my handwriting and helped me in countless other ways.

G. D. H. COLE

OXFORD
September 1954

CONTENTS

PART I

SOCIALIST THOUGHT

THE PRINCIPAL CHARACTERS

[1] Discussed in Volumes I and II.
[2] Also discussed in Volume II.   [3] Discussed in Volume II.

SOCIALIST THOUGHT

INTRODUCTION

IN the second volume of this study I described the development of Socialist thought and action from the middle of the nineteenth century — that is, from the defeat of the European Revolutions of 1848 — to about 1890 — by which time Social Democratic or Labour Parties had been established in most European and in a number of non-European countries. The present volume carries on the record from the foundation of the Second International in 1889 — the centenary year of the great French Revolution — to the outbreak of European War in August 1914. During the period covered by Volume II the struggle between Marxism and Anarchism furnished the central theme. That struggle had not ended in 1889; but it had ceased to occupy the centre of the stage, and both combatants had undergone a considerable transformation. Marxism had been reshaped throughout Western Europe as Social Democracy and had become organised in a series of national parties which were either active in the electoral field and seeking to build up their parliamentary strength by constitutional means or, where the franchise was too narrow to give them a chance of electoral success, were agitating and demonstrating for manhood, or even for adult, suffrage in order to be able to follow the same course. Anarchism meanwhile was being deeply affected by the growth of Trade Unionism, and was being reincarnated in part as what came to be called first Revolutionary Syndicalism and later simply Syndicalism, on the basis of an exaltation of the rôle of Direct Action, with the general strike as a weapon, as against Parliamentary action. The general strike was also proposed, and used, by Social Democrats as a weapon for the enforcement of franchise reform; and in Russia it was the form in which the Revolution of 1905 actually began. But the general strike as used in Austria and Belgium as a means of extorting franchise reform was something quite different from the 'social' general strike of the Anarchists and Syndicalists and of the Russian revolutionaries: it was meant, not to usher in violent revolution, but to win a limited constitutional reform and thus clear the road for effective parliamentary action, and it was accordingly to be a disciplined affair, ordered by the Social Democratic Party, and not a spontaneous mass movement in which the militants would draw the main body of the workers into revolutionary action. Even in this limited form, it was rejected by the German Social Democrats, who possessed by far the strongest and best-organised Socialist Party and had behind them the greatest prestige, both as the reputed guardians of the Marxist tradition and because of the success with which they had held out against Bismarck's attempt to destroy them by means of the Anti-Socialist Laws. These laws were still in force when the Second International was born ; but they lapsed the following year, and the German Party was set free to rebuild its organisation legally on German soil and to adopt its new Erfurt Programme of 1891, which had a great influence on the policy of the Socialist Parties of other countries.

The German Social Democratic Party, fully unified and in effective command of the German Trade Union movement, which, though nominally independent of it, obediently followed its lead, was by far the most powerful single force in the new International and in the world Socialist movement. Next to the Germans in influence and power stood the French ; but in 1889 the French Socialist and Labour movement was split up among a number of contending factions. There were in France not only rival Socialist Parties but also rival Trade Union movements ; and even when the rival Parties had been unified under international pressure in 1905, the Trade Union movement was by no means prepared to follow the lead of the Socialist Party. In the Congresses of the Second International the French delegations were always sharply divided, whereas the Germans almost always presented a solid front.

Next in importance to the Germans and the French stood the Russians, though they had no mass organisation comparable with that of the countries in which the work of organisation could be openly and lawfully carried on. Indeed, until 1905 the Russians played no large part in the International's affairs ; and even thereafter they continued to be sharply divided, not only between Social Democrats and Social Revolutionaries but also within the Social Democratic fraction between Bolsheviks and Mensheviks. The Russians, however, had this in common : they were all revolutionaries, because there was no other course open to them in face of the autocratic Czarist régime. After the defeat of the Revolution of 1905 there was indeed a sort of Parliament — the Duma ; but the conditions of its election denied the Socialists all chances of winning any substantial representation in it, and in any case its powers were very narrow. There was in Czarist Russia no possibility of building up a primarily parliamentary Socialist Party on the German, or on any Western, model ; and though the Russian Social Democratic delegates at International Congresses continued to regard the German Social Democratic Party as the leading exponent of the Marxist creed, their own situation was so different from that of the Western countries which dominated the International's proceedings as to make it difficult for them to take much part in many of the discussions. Their most important intervention was at Stuttgart in 1907, when Lenin and Rosa Luxemburg managed to amend the resolution defining the attitude to be taken by Socialists in the event of international war.

The British Socialists' part in the International was small in relation to the world position of Great Britain because they were both divided and late in developing a powerful political movement. The British Trades Union Congress, though it sent delegates to the International, played no large part in its affairs and hardly treated its participation seriously ; nor did the Labour Party, when it joined the British Section, count for a great deal. The Social Democratic Federation and Keir Hardie's Independent Labour Party carried their quarrels from the national into the international field, and between them dominated the British delegation. Keir Hardie's advocacy of the general strike against war made him a leading figure after 1905 ; but no other British delegate made any deep impression. Hyndman's strong views on the German menace prevented him, despite his Marxism, from playing a leading rôle. The British were continually taken to task in the International for their failure to create a powerful unified Socialist Party and for the backwardness of their Trade Union movement in international loyalty to the class struggle.

Among the lesser Parties the Austrians and the Belgians

played the most active part. Victor Adler and Émile Vandervelde were outstanding international personalities. The
Austrians in the main followed the German lead, but were much
more conciliatory to the opposition : the Belgians were best
placed for acting as mediators between the Teutons and the
Latins, especially when it was a question of the place of Trade
Unions and Co-operative Societies in relation to the political
parties. The Italians were always divided among themselves,
like the French ; and so were the Dutch. The Scandinavians
had not yet risen to the position of importance they occupied
after 1918. The Spaniards were represented only by the small
Marxist Party of Pablo Iglesias, which faithfully followed the
German Social Democratic lead. The Balkan countries had
only small and for the most part heavily persecuted Socialist
Parties — the most important group, the Bulgarians, being
sharply divided into rival sects. The Americans, too, were
divided, between De Leonites and moderate Social Democrats ;
but neither faction commanded a large or influential following.
Other non-European countries made only intermittent appearances and exerted very little influence on the International's
affairs. Usually the Germans, the French, the Austrians, and
the Belgians dominated the debates, with British, Italians, and
Dutchmen playing a substantial secondary part, and Russians
intervening with occasional effect.

Inevitably, this third volume is made up largely of accounts
of Socialist developments in particular countries ; for during
the period between 1889 and 1914 Socialist thought and action
developed chiefly along national lines. Each Socialist Party and
each Trade Union movement, as it strengthened its position
and achieved some measure of success and organisation, found
itself faced with its own peculiar problems, and set out to respond to the needs and interests of its own potential supporters.
This was indeed a necessary condition both of electoral success
and of the consolidation of Trade Unionism as a bargaining
force ; and the leaders of the International, albeit sometimes
with reluctance, recognised the need to allow each national
party wide scope to shape its policy and programme in accordance with the conditions under which it was called upon to
work. The Second International was throughout its career
only a loose federation of national groups, with only a very

limited power to bind its constituent elements. It could indeed lay down mandatory decisions on matters of policy only when there was a large measure of agreement; and it always took care so to shape its resolutions, where they called for positive action, as to secure the assent of at least the leading delegations. In particular, it could venture nothing against the solid vote of the Germans, whose disciplined unity gave them in practice an almost unlimited veto, though not the power always to get their own view endorsed.

During the earlier years of the International, discussions ranged over a wide area, with no one question standing out above the rest. Then came the sharp dispute provoked by the *affaire Millerand*, itself an outcome of the Dreyfus case, concerning the legitimacy of Socialist participation in bourgeois Ministries; and a split was averted by Kautsky's dexterous drafting of the resolution known by his name. The centre of interest then passed to the attempt to promote Socialist unity, above all in France; and when the French parties had been induced to join forces in 1905, and the Russian Revolution of that year had been beaten down, the International turned its main attention to the growing danger of war between the great imperialist powers. That question continued to occupy it right up to 1914, when the hollowness of its pretensions to override the national loyalties of the workers in the key countries was finally exposed and its structure broken in pieces by the outbreak of the war in Europe.

Then came, as an outcome of the war, the Russian Revolution of 1917; and with the establishment of Communism in Russia the possibility of recreating a common Socialist International disappeared. For Communism, in its new form, involved an entire repudiation of the loose federal structure which had made it practicable for widely divergent groups to co-exist within a single international organisation on a basis of live and let live. The new creed of democratic centralism, not merely within each country but internationally, was wholly incompatible with the type of parliamentary Socialism which had been developed by the national Social Democratic and Labour Parties of the liberal-democratic countries of the West; and these parties, emerging from the war for the most part with greatly increased electoral strength, were not at all minded to abandon their pursuit of parliamentary power for that of world revolution under Communist leadership. Accordingly, while the Russians were establishing a Third International as the instrument of world revolution, the Social Democratic and Labour Parties set to work to re-establish an International modelled on that which had broken down in 1914. It was no accident that the attempts of the Austrians and their associates in the so-called 'Two-and-a-half' Vienna International to bring the adherents of the Second and the Third into a common organisation were ineffective. Only a centrally disciplined International could suit the Communists : only a loosely federal International could be made compatible with the needs of Socialist Parties aiming at a constitutional conquest of parliamentary power. For the wooing of a mass electorate involves giving pride of place to programmes of immediate demands carrying the widest possible appeal, and these demands are bound to vary widely from country to country and, where a wide franchise and responsible parliamentary government both exist, are most unlikely to assume a revolutionary character. Parliamentary Socialist Parties find themselves, where these conditions exist, impelled irresistibly towards the development of the 'Welfare State' rather than towards outright social revolution. Nor can they afford to be more internationalist than the main body of the electors whose votes they must win in order to get power.

All this has become much more evident to-day than it was forty or fifty years ago, when revolutionists and reformists were able to act within a common International. Before 1914 the number of countries which possessed both wide electorates and fully responsible parliamentary government was very small. It included Great Britain, France, Belgium, Switzerland, the United States, Canada, Australia, and New Zealand, and not many more. The Germans and the Austrians had a wide franchise, but not responsible government. The Russians had neither. In Italy the franchise had been widened only just before 1914. In Spain and in a number of other backward countries, electoral rolls and even votes could be rigged by the authorities. In these circumstances the line between revolutionists and reformists could not be clearly drawn. In Russia even moderates had to be revolutionists ; and neither Germans nor Austrians could be simply constitutionalists, because they had in both cases to face autocratic régimes which could not be got rid of by purely constitutional means. Reformist though both the German and the Austrian Party were in practice, each continued to proclaim its faith in the Socialist Revolution. Only with the Bolshevik Revolution and the fall of the Hohenzollern and Hapsburg monarchies did the dividing line between revolutionists and reformists come to be clearly drawn and to divide the world working-class movement into two irreconcilable elements — thus opening the door to Fascism rather than to the World Revolution without which the Bolshevik leaders believed their own Russian Revolution was doomed to defeat.

I have pondered long about the title to give to this volume. In the end I decided to call it 'The Second International' because I could find no really satisfactory name. 'Social Democracy *versus* Syndicalism' seemed too narrow, though I should have liked to get the theme of Direct Action as against parliamentary action into the title. 'Revolution or Reform?' would not do because, as I have said, up to 1914 the line between revolutionists and reformists could not be clearly drawn. The name I have chosen is unsatisfactory because it puts all the emphasis on the Parties which made up the International, to the exclusion of the Trade Unions and the other elements which go to the making up of the whole working-class movement. It is, however, the best I can find; and it does at any rate accurately delimit the period I have attempted to cover — though in a few cases I have found it necessary to go back beyond 1889 or to carry the story of a particular movement on beyond 1914. My next volume, if I live to write it, will probably continue the record up to 1939.

CHAPTER I

THE SECOND INTERNATIONAL:
EARLY YEARS

B Y the end of the 1880s Social Democratic parties, modelled largely on that of Germany, existed, at least in embryo, in a number of European countries; and the time seemed to have come for them to join forces in a new International. After the split at the Hague Congress in 1872 what was left in Europe of the First International had passed into the hands of the Federalists, who repudiated Marx's authoritarian leadership. But, as we have seen, the Federalist (often called the 'Anarchist') International had gradually petered out during the 'seventies. It had held its last Congress at Verviers in Belgium, in 1877, immediately before the Ghent Socialist Unity Congress of the same year, called with the purpose of re-establishing an inclusive International. At Ghent, the familiar battle between Anarchists and advocates of political action had been resumed. The out-and-out Anarchists had been out-voted; and it had been decided to set up an International Correspondence and Statistical Office at Verviers open to organisations of all shades of opinion. But this body never came into existence. In face of the irreconcilable differences of attitude manifested during the Congress the majority which favoured political action called a meeting of their own, without the Anarchists, and set up a Federal Bureau, with instructions to summon a further Congress. The decision to do this, and to break with the Anarchist group, was signed, among others, by César de Paepe, who had been a leading figure in the Federalist International, as well as by Wilhelm Liebknecht, who represented the German Party. Other signatories included Herman Greulich, the Zürich Social Democratic leader, Louis Bertrand and several other Belgians, T. Zanardelli of Milan, who had broken away from his fellow-Italians, Leo Fränkel of

Hungary, André Bert of France, and the English delegates, John Hales and Maltman Barry.

In this development was foreshadowed the coming of the Second International. But, though the Ghent Bureau did succeed in holding a further International Congress at Coire, in Switzerland, in 1881, there the matter ended. Liebknecht and Louis Bertrand went to Coire as representatives of the German and Belgian Parties ; and representatives also appeared from the French Parti Ouvrier (Benoît Malon and Jules Joffrin, both ex-Communards) and from the American Socialist Labor Party (P. J. McGuire, Secretary of the Brotherhood of Carpenters). But for the most part the Congress consisted of German-Swiss delegates, including the faithful veteran, J. P. Becker, of Geneva. Paul Axelrod, of Russia, came as a fraternal delegate ; and there were a few Poles, representing groups of exiles. No one came from Great Britain or Holland, or from Spain or Italy. The Anarchists, who were not invited, were busy with their own Congress in London, at which the formation of a definitely Anarchist International was proposed.

The Coire Congress, though its debates covered a wide ground, came to the conclusion that the time was not ripe for setting up a Socialist International. Nowhere except in Germany was there as yet a fully constituted Socialist Party, though Belgium was already well on the way to one. Germany, with the Anti-Socialist laws in force, could not take the lead in international action. In France, Jules Guesde's Parti Ouvrier was only in course of formation. The Ghent Congress, in one of its few moments of agreement, had decided that a Trade Union International ought to be formed, and that an International Trade Union Congress ought to be summoned for this purpose ; but no one had undertaken to convene it. Nor was it what the Germans wanted ; for it would have been impossible to keep out either the Anarchists or the moderate Trade Unionists who rejected the idea of independent working-class political action. Accordingly, the Coire Congress had no successors, and the idea of a new Socialist International, though never abandoned, was postponed to an uncertain future.

The attempt to revive the International was, however, soon renewed, with the French taking the lead. The French working-class movement was making a rapid recovery in the early 'eighties, but was divided among many rival groups. By 1882 Guesde's Parti Ouvrier was fully established and was gaining a considerable ascendancy over the Trade Union movement. But against Guesde and his Marxists were ranged the Possibilists, headed by Paul Brousse, who formed the Parti Ouvrier Socialiste Révolutionnaire in 1882 and had their own substantial Trade Union following. In 1883 the Possibilists made their first attempt to call an International Labour Congress in Paris. This, like most of the Congresses of French Labour called during the decade, was a mixed affair, open to a variety of bodies, industrial as well as political, and representing different tendencies. Its significance lies, not in anything it accomplished, but simply in the fact that it was called as a response to the feeling that the developing working-class movements of the different countries ought to co-ordinate their demands for the improvement of industrial conditions, and especially for the shortening of the working week. This objective was much more clearly formulated at a second International Congress, summoned under the same auspices, which met in Paris in 1886. By this time the main question had become that of simultaneous action in as many countries as possible for the achievement of the eight hours' day. The agitation for the eight hours had already been in progress for a considerable time in the United States. In Australia the Melbourne skilled workers, profiting by the labour scarcity that followed the 'gold rush', had won the eight hours' day as early as 1856 by threatening a general strike, and the concession had spread before long to other States, but, in the absence of legislative sanction, had not become universal.[1] During the late 'seventies there had been an agitation for its general enforcement ; and in 1885 legislation making it mandatory for women and children had been passed. The presence at the Paris Congress of an Australian delegate, John Norton, made the Congress aware of these achievements ; and developments in the United States were also being eagerly followed. There, the Eight Hours' Leagues organised under the influence of Ira Steward in the 1860s and early 1870s had collapsed during the ensuing depression ; but in 1883 the Knights of Labor had made the eight hours' day a plank in their immediate programme, and in 1885–6 there had been

[1] See p. 855 f.

3

many local strikes for its enforcement. At Paris, the Broussist Victor Dalle presented a report putting forward the demand for international labour legislation to implement the demand and was strongly supported both by his fellow-Possibilist, Simon Dereure, and by Édouard Anseele and César de Paepe, who were present as delegates from the Belgian Socialists. These two proposed the setting up of an international labour organisation with the eight hours' day as its first objective and urged that a further International Congress should be held in 1889, as part of the celebration of the centenary of the French Revolution, in order to bring it into being. This proposal was adopted, and the French Possibilist Party was given a mandate to act as the organising body. The only opposition to the proposal came from the British delegates, who did not question the desirability of shortening the hours of labour, but were opposed to legislation for that purpose, and abstained from voting on the main resolution. The French delegates went on immediately from the International Congress to their own Labour Congress at Lyons, where the lead for the eight hours was taken by Raymond Lavigne (1851–1930) and Antoine Jourde of Bordeaux, aided by the oratory of Jean Dormoy. At Lyons the agitation for the eight hours' day came into connection with the Anarchist advocacy of the general strike. It was urged that, if Governments or employers refused to concede the eight hours, the workers should resort to a general strike for its enforcement. This policy did not receive full endorsement: the majority preferred to begin with a series of simultaneous demonstrations which would present the claim to employers and public authorities, ceasing work for a single day for this purpose; whereas the minority insisted that nothing was to be expected from Governments and that the demonstrations could be of use only in as far as they served to educate the workers for more militant action.

Thereafter, as we shall see in a subsequent chapter,[1] the French Trade Unions concerned themselves to an increasing extent with the idea of preparing for a general strike, thought of by some as the opening move in a workers' insurrection and by others as a weapon for extorting economic concessions without resort to the 'capitalist' State. By 1888 the movement,

[1] See p. 329 ff.

4

clearly linked to the demand for the eight hours' day, had won widespread support, and preparations were in full swing for simultaneous one-day stoppages early the following year.

In the meantime a further International Labour Congress had been arranged. It met in London in 1888, and was attended by representatives of the British Trades Union Congress, as well as by Socialists, including John Burns, Annie Besant, Tom Mann, and Keir Hardie. The Trades Union Congress had been represented at the International Congresses of 1883 and 1886, despite the resistance of the Parliamentary Committee, which had to bow to the wishes of the main body of delegates. When requested by the French to undertake the organisation of the 1888 International Congress, the Parliamentary Committee at first insisted on referring the question back to the full Trades Union Congress, and issued a pamphlet strongly critical of the instability and unreliability of the continental Trade Unions. When, despite their objections, the delegates instructed them to organise the international meeting, they drafted rules designed to exclude Socialist bodies, so as to convert it into a purely Trade Union affair. This prevented the Social Democratic Federation and the Socialist League, as well as the continental Socialist Parties, from being represented ; but it did not avail to exclude Socialists who could procure mandates from industrial bodies. The Germans were effectively excluded ; but Belgians, French and Dutch appeared in force, together with two Danes and a single Italian, Costantino Lazzari of Milan. The sessions were tumultuous ; and in the absence of proper reports it is not easy to discover exactly what occurred. There is, however, no doubt that the main resolution, in favour of an international agitation for the enforcement of the eight hours' day by legal enactment, was carried, and that it was decided to hold a further Congress in Paris the following year, during the International Exhibition, in order to set up a definite international organisation.

The London Congress of 1888 was out of step with its predecessors because of the insistence of the British Trades Union Congress leaders on making it, as far as they could, non-political. This naturally annoyed the continental Socialists, especially the Germans and the French Guesdists, and also the Belgians. The consequence was that the German Social

5

Democrats, in conjunction with their allies, set to work to organise an International Socialist Congress of their own, to meet in Paris the following year, while in France the Possibilists sent out their invitations to the International Labour Congress which had been decided upon in London, but were no longer limited by the rules the British Trade Union leaders had imposed. Consequently there was a great deal of confusion. A meeting, called by the Dutch and Belgians, was held at the Hague in the hope of uniting the rival Congresses; but the negotiations broke down in face of sharp quarrelling between Marxists and anti-authoritarians, and in the event both were held, and both passed practically identical resolutions on the question of the legal eight hours' day. This uniformity of action was due largely to American influence. Two United States delegates, both printers, took part in the Congress called by the Possibilists; and, though no American delegates were mandated to the Marxist Congress, Hugh MacGregor, later Secretary of the Seamen's Union, was present as an observer, and transmitted a message from the Americans which served as the basis of the resolution finally adopted.

By this time, in the United States, leadership in the eight hours' movement had passed from the Knights of Labor to the American Federation of Labor, which was being built up into a powerful body by Samuel Gompers. In 1888 the A.F. of L. had decided to launch a new campaign for the eight hours; each year, simultaneous strikes for the eight hours' day were to be launched all over the country in a single industry, the strikers receiving financial aid from the trades which remained at work, until each industry had had its turn and the concession had thus been universally secured. The idea of making May Day the occasion for launching a forward workers' movement was not novel; but it appears to have come on this occasion from the United States and to have been written into the resolutions proposed at the two Paris Congresses as a direct result of the action the A.F. of L. had already decided to take. Actually, before the Congresses met, the French workers had carried out, in February 1889, the first of their simultaneous eight hours' demonstrations, which had been enthusiastically responded to in most of the industrial centres. At Paris it was decided that, for the future, May 1st should be Labour Day, and that the eight hours' day should be given pride of place as an immediate demand. There had been fears, during the abortive unity discussions at the Hague, that the Germans, fearful of further repressive measures from Bismarck, would refuse to fall in with the proposal; and their spokesman Wilhelm Liebknecht, did in fact insist that each national movement must be left free to adapt its action to national conditions, and that there must be no pledge to undertake strikes in every country. This conceded, the Germans accepted the resolution.

The two Paris Congresses of 1889 were both numerously attended, and at both the French were in an overwhelming majority. The Possibilist gathering in the Rue Lancry was the more numerous with over 600 delegates, of whom more than 500 were French. The Marxist Congress in the Salle Pétrelle mustered 391, of whom 221 were French. It had the larger international participation, with 81 Germans, 22 British, 14 Belgians, 8 Austrians, 6 Russians, and smaller delegations from Holland, Denmark, Sweden, Norway, Switzerland, Poland, Rumania, Italy, Hungary, Spain, Portugal, Bohemia, and Bulgaria, *plus* visitors from the United States, the Argentine, and Finland. Some of the smaller delegations were doubtless hardly more than nominal, consisting of exiles mandated by tiny groups of expatriates. Nevertheless, the Congress assembled a goodly array of leaders of the emergent Socialist Parties of Europe. Among the Germans were Wilhelm Liebknecht and August Bebel, already veterans; Eduard Bernstein, not yet known as a 'revisionist' but with great journalistic services to his credit; Karl Legien, the chief organiser of the Trade Unions; Georg Heinrich von Vollmar, the Bavarian leader; Hermann Molkenbuhr, already the Germans' specialist in labour legislation, and Clara Zetkin. The French included Jules Guesde, Édouard Vaillant, Charles Longuet, and Paul Lafargue — both sons-in-law of Marx — Zéphirin Camélinat, Raymond Lavigne, and Victor Jaclard. Sébastien Faure was also present, as spokesman of the French Anarchists.

The Belgians were headed by César de Paepe and Édouard Anseele, the principal founder of the famous Co-operative Vooruit of Ghent. Victor Adler led the Austrians and Leo Fränkel the Hungarians; Pablo Iglesias and José Mesa came from Spain, and S. Palmgreen from Sweden; Peter Lavrov and G. V. Plekhanov represented the Narodnik and Marxist tendencies among the Russians. From Holland came Domela Nieuwenhuis, soon to go over to Anarchism. Some of the Italians, however, including Andrea Costa and the Old Garibaldian and Communard, Amilcare Cipriani, put in an appearance at both Congresses. So did Émile Vandervelde, the rising hope of the Belgian Labour Party. The principal absentee was the British Social Democratic Federation, which found itself incongruously, but to Engels's great satisfaction, in the opposing camp.

The British delegation at the Salle Pétrelle was a strange one. In the quarrel between the S.D.F. and the Socialist League Engels had supported the League and had seen to it that the main part of the British representation came from this source. Consequently, William Morris, the principal delegate, found himself at the head of a group for the most part opposed to the parliamentary methods to which the Marxists were committed. Among them were Anarchists such as Frank Kitz and Arthur Tochatti; Marx's third son-in-law, Edward Aveling, and his wife Eleanor Marx Aveling; and, to diversify the views, R. B. Cunninghame Graham and Keir Hardie from the recently established Scottish Labour Party.

At the rival Congress in Rue Lancry there were no Germans, and the French were the predominant group in personalities as well as numbers. H. M. Hyndman and John Burns were the outstanding figures in the British delegation. F. S. Merlino, as well as Costa and Cipriani, represented Italy; among the French were Paul Brousse, Jean Allemane, J. B. Clément, Victor Dalle, and Joseph Tortelier, the notable orator of the Anarchists. The names of a number of the foreign delegates were not disclosed, for fear of police attentions when they returned to their own countries. Among those who are known and played a leading part were Bolesław Limanowski from Russian Poland, the Dane Harald Jensen, the Dutchman Willem Hubert Vliegen, F. V. de Campos from Portugal, and the Americans, W. S. Wandly and P. F. Crowley.

The Marxist Congress was, then, much the more distinguished gathering, and fairly beat its rival out of the field. In consequence, the earlier International Congresses which helped to prepare the way for the Second International have been largely forgotten, and with them the close connection of the entire movement in its early stages with the struggle for the eight hours' day and with the American initiative in this respect. What in effect happened was that the drive towards a new International, largely American and French in origin and at least as much Trade Unionist as Socialist, was taken over by the German Social Democrats and given an essentially different character as a move towards international federation of Socialist Parties which accepted the primacy of political action and set out, wherever circumstances allowed, to fight their main battles on the parliamentary plane. This was able to happen all the more because the German initiative came on the eve of the repeal of Bismarck's Anti-Socialist Laws and of the resounding successes of the German Social Democratic Party in the Reichstag elections of 1890.

The actual resolution adopted on the final day at the Salle Pétrelle, dealing with the action to be taken as an outcome of the Congress, was as follows :

> A great manifestation will be organised on a fixed date, in such a way that, simultaneously in all countries and in all towns, on the same agreed day, the workers will call upon the public authorities to reduce the working day by law to eight hours and to put the other resolutions of the Congress of Paris into effect.
>
> In view of the fact that a similar manifestation has already been decided on for May 1st, 1890, by the American Federation of Labor at its Congress held at St. Louis in December 1888, this date is adopted for the international manifestation.
>
> The workers of the various countries will have to accomplish the manifestation under the conditions imposed on them by the particular situation in each country.

The final paragraph of this resolution was inserted at the request of the German delegation, which would not pledge itself to strike action, or indeed to anything likely to provoke a renewal of the Anti-Socialist Laws, which were due to expire in 1890 unless the Reichstag agreed to their renewal.

As we saw, the Congress in the Rue Lancry passed a resolution in much the same terms, putting the demand for 'a maximum day of eight hours, fixed by an international law', at the head of its immediate programme. But, curiously enough, the official report of the Salle Pétrelle Congress, which was edited and published in German, though it gives the text of the resolution and says that it was moved by Raymond Lavigne on behalf of the French National Federation of Trade Unions, does not report the debate or assign any particular importance to the decision. Clearly the Germans regarded the eight hours' day and the decision to take simultaneous action on May 1st, 1890, as a comparatively minor matter.

Nevertheless, May 1st, 1890, was a remarkably impressive occasion. Great demonstrations for the eight hours' day were held in many countries and in many cities within them, and there were extensive stoppages of work not only in France but also in Austria, in Hungary, in parts of Italy and Spain, in Belgium and Holland, and in the Scandinavian countries, as well as in the United States. The British Trade Unions, however, contented themselves with great meetings on the first Sunday in May, so as to avoid any stoppage of work. In some places the workers limited themselves to orderly demonstrations and meetings ; but in France, Spain, and Italy, where the Anarchists were to the fore, there were some serious clashes with the police and the soldiers. Even before May 1st there had been many arrests of journalists and militants who were accused of incitement to violence — especially of Anarchists and near-Anarchists. In France, particularly, there were strong disagreements. The right wing of the Possibilists and their Trade Union supporters opposed any stoppage of work, and urged their followers to rest content with peaceable processions to present petitions to the public authorities ; whereas the left wing, headed by Jean Allemane, demanded a general cessation of work. This was one of the causes of the split in the Possibilist Party and of the formation of Allemane's new left-wing Revolutionary Socialist Party by the dissident groups.

Only in the United States did the movement of May 1st, 1890, achieve immediate practical successes. Considerable bodies of workers — especially carpenters — won the eight hours' day ; and many more were successful during the next few years, as the American Federation of Labor followed the policy of throwing a particular type of worker into the fray each spring. In other cases the nine though not yet the eight hours' day was secured.

Indeed, the international workers' demonstrations begun in 1890 developed into a regular annual affair — by far the most impressive manifestation of international working-class solidarity that had ever been made. The Conference called by the German Emperor in 1890 to consider the question of 'international labour legislation' and the Papal Encyclical (*Rerum Novarum*) of May 1891 are both clearly connected with the rapid spread of the demand for social legislation — especially the eight hours' day and the prohibition of insanitary or dangerous conditions of employment. The German Emperor's initiative yielded no practical results; for the inter-governmental Conference at Berlin failed to reach any agreement. But the early 1890s were a period during which the 'social question' was brought vividly before public opinion, and the foundations of the older, *laissez-faire* economic liberalism were seriously shaken.

The working-class movement of these years was deeply stirred by a conflict of ideas which by no means simply divided the right from the left — or both from a body of central opinion. There were a number of battles simultaneously in progress, about both strategy and objectives. One battle was over political action, not only between Marxists and Anarchists, but also between reformist politicians and those who put their faith in industrial conciliation without appeal to the State for legislative action; and another, connected with it but by no means identical, centred upon the attitude which workers' movements ought to take up towards capitalist States and Governments. The Marxists, as we have seen, were determined advocates of highly disciplined political action through centralised parties using Trade Unionism as a recruiting agency and an electoral auxiliary, but taking care to keep the control of policy in the hands of the party leadership. They wanted to capture control of the national legislatures by electoral organisation and propaganda; but they did not as yet, for the most part, regard electoral success, even to the extent of winning a parliamentary majority, as carrying with it any change in the essential character of the State. They still thought of electoral victories as only preparing the way for some sort of revolution, as an outcome of which the existing State would be overthrown and a new Workers' or People's State would come into being in its place.

They had indeed their programmes of immediate demands, including, to an increasing extent, demands for industrial legislation. But they still mostly thought of these reforms as needing to be snatched from a hostile State, rather than as instalments in the process of the State's transformation into an instrument of democracy. Over most of Europe, Marxists as well as other men, when they thought of 'the State', instinctively regarded it rather as an executive than as a legislative authority. In Germany as much as in Russia, and indeed to a considerable extent almost everywhere save in Switzerland and perhaps Denmark, 'the State' meant the Government, and the Parliament, where one existed, was thought of as a limiting factor upon the State, rather than as its supreme organ of power. This was largely true even in France, where the Third Republic had inherited much of the tradition of the Napoleonic Second Empire and it was not easy to look to the Chamber or the Senate as a source of social regeneration.

This attitude to the State, as we shall see further in the chapter in which the orientation of German Social Democracy after 1890 will be considered,[1] effectively prevented the German Socialists from formulating their programmes in terms of the nationalisation of the means of production by parliamentary means. National control, with the State as it was, would mean, in the view of Kautsky or Liebknecht, not socialisation, but the handing over of more economic power to an executive authority representing the capitalist bourgeoisie in alliance with feudalism and autocracy. Not until the State had been remade by the revolution would it become an instrument through which the workers' cause could be advanced through democratic administration of the people's estate. It followed that the great workers' party must be built up in entire independence of all other parties, and that it was wrong for Social Democrats to contemplate, even for the purpose of getting some of their immediate demands met, any sort of coalition or governmental collaboration with any bourgeois party. These views were, indeed, soon to be challenged, within German Social Democracy, by such heretics as Vollmar and Bernstein; but in 1889 this challenge had barely been made, and even when it was made, the whole Marxist tradition was there to meet it.

[1] See p. 275 f.

In France the situation was different, because France was to a substantially greater extent a country under parliamentary government. The Republic, unlike the German Empire, was a political structure which many Socialists felt under an obligation to uphold against any renewal of Caesarism or monarchist reaction. This was to become a vital issue in the critical years of the *affaire Dreyfus* and the *affaire Millerand*, which directly raised the question of Republican defence, and split the French Socialist movement into rival factions.[1] The Germans had no Republic to defend, and no real parliamentary system. The French had ; and even those who held the Parliament in low esteem were not equally deaf to the call of the Republic. Nevertheless, the French Marxists, at the height of the Dreyfus danger, refused to be led into collaboration with the republican bourgeoisie, and were even inclined to say that the squabbles of the bourgeois politicians were no affair of theirs. The Blanquists naturally agreed with them : Jaurès, Malon, and the Independents emphatically disagreed ; the Broussists, or Possibilists, split into two rival factions.

The conflict in the French working-class movement was, however, a good deal more complicated than these divergences suggest. In Germany the Anarchists had been practically eliminated as an influence on mass-opinion, though they could provide a few would-be assassins during the Anarchist revival of the 1890s, and there was always a small anti-parliamentarian group on the extreme left. The Trade Unions, except the relatively small groups under Christian or Liberal (Hirsch-Duncker) auspices, were firmly disciplined under Social Democratic leadership. But in France Anarchism, in many forms ranging from 'propaganda by deed' to Anarcho-Syndicalism, was a lively force ; and the Guesdists' attempt to bring the Trade Unions to heel behind the party had achieved only a precarious and partial success. Paul Brousse, the leader of the Possibilists, had begun as an Anarchist, and continued as the enemy of centralisation ; but he had passed from Anarchism to the advocacy of municipal Socialist action, and his following had come to include a high proportion of moderates who were equally hostile to Marxism and Blanquism on the one hand and to the growing movement of revolutionary Syndicalism on the

[1] See p. 342 ff.

other. When Jean Allemane led the left-wingers out of the Possibilist Party, it turned into a party of the Socialist right, but retained a number of its Trade Union connections. The Independent Socialists, with whom it then found itself allied, differed from it in being primarily a parliamentary group of leaders rather than a movement with any substantial local organisation behind them.

During the years before the Dreyfus affair and the threat to the Republic brought the question of collaboration with the bourgeois Republicans right to the front, the great issue dividing the French was that of the relative rôles of political and industrial action. The Guesdists and Blanquists could combine with the other groups in demanding the eight hours' day and in wishing the workers to use May Day for demonstrating their national and international solidarity ; but there was no real agreement about either the right way of demonstrating or the immediate objective to be pursued. Broussists, Marxists, Blanquists, and Syndicalists might all agree to demand industrial legislation — though the out-and-out Anarchists demurred even to this. But, whereas the Broussists wanted only peaceable processions and deputations to the public authorities, and the Guesdists were chiefly intent on using the occasion to win support for the Marxist party, the Blanquists, or at any rate some of them, were still dreaming of turning the demonstrations into an insurrection, while the Syndicalists looked on each May Day as primarily a rehearsal for the great strike which would usher in the transformation of society as soon as the minds of the workers had been sufficiently prepared. All this, of course, puts the state of opinion too crudely : there was in fact much confusion of ideas in all the rival groups. But it remains true that in France, unlike Germany, there were always powerful forces which were unready to accept political leadership from any source — right, or left, or centre — and looked for inspiration to Trade Unionism rather than to any political party. These groups were hostile to the State, not as the Germans were, because it was the State of the bourgeoisie, almost due to be superseded by the centralised State of the proletariat, but because it was *the* State, and therefore the enemy of the people as long as it existed at all. They regarded it, at best, as a body from which the workers could hope to exact concessions by using their organised class-power, but not, even remotely, as an institution which they could in due course transform to serve as the expression of their collective will.

What, then, was the purpose of the May Day demonstrations ? To petition the public authorities and to assert the solidarity of the working class ? That was one view. To enforce, by strike action, concessions from both private employers and public authorities ? That was a second view — and, incidentally, that of the American Federation of Labor, which had so greatly influenced the immediate course of events in Europe. To rally the workers behind the Socialists, until they were able to win a parliamentary majority and to take the State into their own hands and refashion it as a workers' State ? That was a third view, held by the French Marxists under the influence of their German inspirers. To prepare the workers for strike action on an ever larger scale, and in the meantime, by striking, to win concessions from private employers, from municipal authorities, and even from the State itself without the need to engage in parliamentary action, or to get lost in the manœuvrings and compromises of Parliament ? That was a fourth view, held by the growing body of Syndicalists. Or, finally, to promote clashes with the police and the military, to train the workers not merely to strike but to become out-and-out revolutionaries, and thus to prepare the way for the insurrectionary general strike in which the State would be destroyed and the free society of the future would be brought to birth ? That was a fifth view - - the Anarcho-Syndicalists'. Or, finally, simply to stir up as much trouble and to generate as much destructive fury as possible, in order to achieve — what ? Anarchism in its most unqualified shape, involving an entirely non-governmental society free even from Trade Union tyranny, and the utter annihilation of bourgeois morality as well as of bourgeois rule. This last attitude was, of course, held only by a few ; but it *was* held, and it linked, in a few Anarchist strongholds, the advocates of May Day demonstrations to the tiny underground groups which put their hopes in 'propaganda by the deed'.

No International Socialist Congress was held in 1890 ; but the 337 delegates from 15 countries who assembled at Brussels in August 1891, greatly encouraged by the success of the May demonstrations of 1890 and 1891, decided to make the celebration of May Day an annual affair, and to consecrate the celebrations to three objects — the demand for the eight hours' day, pressure for the development of international labour legislation over a wider field, and the affirmation of the will of the workers of all countries for the maintenance of the peace of nations. The Congress further resolved that the workers should abstain from work on May Day 'everywhere except where it is impracticable'.

This seems to have been the first occasion on which 'Labour Day' was definitely associated with the demand for peace. This new object was introduced, mainly on German initiative, as the German Social Democrats wished to give May Day a political rather than a purely economic character and to use it for emphasising the internationalism of the workers' movement and its antagonism to imperialist war-mongering. The Germans told their fellow-workers with pride how they had protested against the annexation of Alsace-Lorraine, and would continue to protest; how they voted against the imperialist budget of Germany, and how they wished to make common cause with the Socialists of France and of other countries. They were also, no doubt, hopeful that, if May Day could be diverted to this purpose, they might be able to escape being committed to strike action for the eight hours, for which they felt unprepared and which might, they feared, bring back the legal repression so recently lifted from their country.

The Germans, indeed, were exceedingly reluctant to enter into any undertakings that might involve them in strike action. As we saw, they had insisted on the inclusion in the resolution of 1889 of a clause which left each country free to decide what form its participation in the international May Day manifestations should be given. At Brussels they joined hands with the British delegates in a proposal to shift the entire celebration from May 1st to the first Sunday in May. This would have meant that there need have been no strikes, and would of course have been a complete abandonment of the plan originally put forward by the American Federation of Labor, which involved strike action designed to enforce the concession of the eight hours — striking, that is, not merely for one day but for as long as might be needed to achieve success. This American plan, however, had never been adopted by the European movements. It was based on choosing each year a particular industry to which the immediate demand would be confined, and supporting the strike by help from the trades that remained at work. As against this, the European plan, hatched mainly in France, had been for a general strike limited to a single day, and used in the first instance mainly for mass-demonstrations directed at the public authorities. This too involved a cessation of work — indeed, a much more extensive cessation, though only for one day — and it thus opened the way to dismissals and to legal reprisals where the right to strike was in any way restricted by law — as it was in most countries. It was, in the eyes of the French protagonists, one of the plan's merits that it called on the workers to defy the unjust laws to which they were subject.

The Germans, on the other hand, and also the British Trade Union leaders, were far from wishing to incite the workers to flout the law, and would have preferred to make May Day a simple, fully lawful and peaceable demonstration of Labour solidarity, to be carried through without any disturbance of industry and without any breach of contracts or collective agreements. But they were unable to convince either the French or the Austrians, or indeed most of the other delegations. In France the demonstrations of 1891 had involved very serious clashes with the police in a number of places,[1] and there had been similar events in other countries — in Austria, Italy, Spain, and Belgium, for example. Where such conflicts had occurred, the workers' blood was up, and they were mostly more determined than ever not to give way by abandoning May 1st as the day of manifestation. They made to the Germans and the British the concession that strike action should be required only where it was not deemed to be 'impracticable' — deemed, that is, by the leaders in a particular country. But they stuck firmly to May 1st, and insisted that, in general, the demonstrations should include abstention from work on the chosen day.

The Brussels Congress was severely critical of the failure of the Inter-governmental Conference on Labour Legislation held

---

[1] At Fourmies, near Avesnes, soldiers and gendarmes shot at a crowd of demonstrators in the square and killed ten, wounding many more, including women and children.

the previous year in Berlin. It took the failure as evidence of the essentially reactionary character of the capitalist States and as a warning that the working class would have to rely on its own efforts to improve its position. But, of course, that left open the question whether the main instrument was to be industrial action or the winning of parliamentary victories ; and on this issue opinion remained as divided as ever. The sprinkling of Anarchists who were present at the Brussels Congress as delegates from Trade Union groups were voted down ; but that was not by any means the last of them. In any case, there were differences enough without them between the Marxists, who put their entire faith in the power of a solidly organised party, and those who assigned an important creative rôle to the Trade Unions and were attracted by the possibilities of the general strike as the highest expression of working-class solidarity.

The Brussels Congress spent a great deal of its time in controversy between Social Democrats and Anarchists, with a good number of delegates expressing impatience at the waste of so many precious hours by participants who had travelled a long distance to the meeting, at high expense to their organisations, and wanted to have practical results to report to their constituents. The same thing happened at the Zürich Congress of 1893, and yet again at the London Congress of 1896. All these early Congresses, as we have seen, were of uncertain composition. They were commonly described as 'Socialist Workers' Congresses', but sometimes, as in 1896, as 'Socialist Workers' and Trade Union Congresses', and it was not questioned that Trade Unions, as well as Socialist Parties and societies, had a right to be represented at them. In Germany the Trade Union problem gave rise to no difficulty, because the Trade Unions, under Karl Legien's leadership, were firmly allied to the Social Democratic Party, and their representatives formed in effect part of the Socialist delegation. The Germans' troubles, such as they were, came from a semi-Anarchist left wing led by Gustav Landauer, the editor of the Berlin *Socialist*, and H. Werner, who got their chance only in the opening stages, before the delegates' credentials had been verified. Under the arrangements of these Congresses the verification of credentials was primarily a matter for each national delegation, which presented to a full session a report showing whose claims it had accepted or disallowed. This report could be challenged on the floor of Congress, but was usually, though not always, accepted. The Germans had a firm way of dealing with inconvenient minorities, by refusing to allow them to sit. Other delegations could not carry matters with so high a hand. The French, for example, were always sharply divided, and on critical issues the division was apt to be nearly equal, not because there were only two groups — for there were many — but because in the last resort it was always an issue between reformists and revolutionaries. This was not the same as the division between political and industrial actionists, for the politicians themselves were sharply divided. Blanquists and Guesdists were against Possibilists and the mainly parliamentary group of Independents, headed by Jaurès and Millerand, and the Allemanists were breaking away more and more from the Possibilist to the revolutionary camp. Trade Unionists, too, were divided into at least three main groups — moderates, Guesdists, and Syndicalists — and there was a considerable Anarchist element, some of whose members came with Trade Union credentials and others as the nominees of various groups bearing Socialist titles. Among the French the situation was always confused, and the voting close. There was no compact majority that could venture to refuse its opponents' credentials. At the London Congress of 1896 the French were reduced to meeting as two separate delegations, each demanding recognition from the full session ; and there was a tremendous squabble about the admission of Jaurès, Millerand, and Viviani, who came as delegates from the Independent Socialist group in the Chamber of Deputies, and refused to submit their credentials to anyone except the full Congress — which in the end admitted them.

The British were in no less difficulty. The Social Democratic Federation had indeed found its way into the Congresses after the fiasco of 1889 ; but it was never in a position to take the lead as the German S.D.P. could do. The Trades Union Congress had been pushed into the lead in organising the London Congress of 1888, when the eight hours' day was already becoming the principal issue ; and, lukewarm though its Parliamentary Committee was, it was clearly by far the most representative organisation of the British workers, and was bound to be offered an important place as long as the Congresses were concerned mainly with such matters as the eight hours' day and international labour legislation. Above all, when the International Congress met in Great Britain, the responsibility of organising it and of sending out the invitations was bound to fall largely on the T.U.C. But, of course, at this stage, neither the Parliamentary Committee nor the T.U.C. itself — any more than the American Federation of Labor — could be regarded as Socialist. The delegates who went to the various International Congresses as representing the T.U.C. or such of its affiliated Unions as chose to be represented included a few Socialists; but most of them were Trade Unionists of the 'Liberal-Labour' persuasion, and found the discussions little to their taste and often quite outside their comprehension. When it was a question of being for or against 'political action', they voted for it; but they meant something quite different from what was meant by the Germans or the Austrians or the French Marxists and Blanquists, who insisted that 'political action' must take the form of action by an independent working-class party, entirely free from entanglements with the bourgeois parties. The British Independent Labour Party, of course, also took this line, as well as the Social Democratic Federation; but it was not established until 1893, and before then there were only a number of local 'Independent Labour' bodies, including the Scottish Labour Party set up in 1888–9. From 1893 onwards, with the Socialist League gone over to Anarchism and dying away, there were three main constituents of the British delegation — the S.D.F., the I.L.P., and the T.U.C., with the Fabians and a few minor bodies making up the rest. In this confusing situation the British delegates usually took the side of tolerating nearly all claims when it was a question who should be admitted; but on the substantive issues most of them voted with the 'politicals' against the exponents of industrial action, and divided right and left, like the French, when the issue of reform versus revolution was raised.

Of the other large delegations the Austrians, who had organised their Social Democratic Party nearly on the German model at their Hainfeld Congress of 1889, usually presented an almost solid front, though they admitted the Czech Social Democrats as a distinct group within their delegation. Dr.

Victor Adler was already their principal spokesman ; Karl Kautsky, who was Austrian by birth, had played a large part in the drafting of their programme, and his wife, Luise Kautsky, was an outstanding leader among the Viennese women. Hungary (with a Croatian contingent) had a separate delegation headed by Leo Fränkel, formerly active in the First International and the Paris Commune, and firmly Marxist. The Swiss were less fully unified ; but the Anarchists and near-Anarchists had lost their former predominance, and the two main organisations — the Grütli Union and the Gewerkschaftsbund — worked on good terms with the developing Social Democratic Party. The outstanding figures were the veteran, Karl Bürkli and the younger Herman Greulich, both of the Grütli Union and the latter active in the party as well, and Robert Seidel, of the Social Democratic Party. August Merk was the most prominent of the delegates from the Gewerkschaftsbund ; and old Dr. Pierre Coullery, the long-standing opponent of the Jura Anarchists, also reappeared as a delegate.

The Belgians, in process of consolidating their Labour Party, with its close links with the Trade Unions and the Co-operatives, had ceased to lean to the 'Federalist' side. Their newer men — Édouard Van Beveren, Édouard Anseele, and Émile Vandervelde, with Louis Bertrand as their chief representative in Parliament — had their own views, and were by no means faithful satellites of the Germans ; but they were firm believers in political action, even though the narrow Belgian franchise gave them little chance of parliamentary victories. They believed in giving Trade Unions and Workers' Co-operatives a position of independent influence within the party, and had a much less 'State Socialist' outlook than the orthodox Marxists. There remained Anarchist and semi-Anarchist groups, especially in the coalfields ; but these had lost much of their influence. In Holland, on the other hand, Anarchist or near-Anarchist tendencies were still predominant, with Domela Nieuwenhuis and Christiaan Cornelissen as the outstanding figures in the Dutch Socialist League. At the London Congress of 1896, the majority of the Dutch delegates, headed by these two, finally withdrew when a definite pronouncement had been made excluding Anarchists. They left behind the five delegates of the Dutch Social Democratic

Labour Party, which they accused of being a mere satellite of the Germans. Its leading figures were H. H. van Kol, P. J. Troelstra, and W. H. Vliegen.

The Swedes were Social Democrats, mainly on the German model, but with greater influence in the hands of the Trade Unions. They did not send any delegation to Zürich in 1893 ; but in 1896 Hjalmar Branting, already in Parliament, and the Trade Union leader, Charles Lindley of the Transport Workers, could speak for a rapidly growing Social Democratic movement. The Norwegians usually contented themselves with a single delegate, from the Social Democratic Labour Party. The Danes, on the other hand, were well represented, by a Social Democratic Party closely allied with the Trade Unions, with whom they shared their delegation on amicable terms. J. Jensen, from the Trade Unions, and P. Knudsen from the Social Democratic Party, were their leading spokesmen.

At the other end of Europe the Italians were still quarrelling furiously among themselves. They usually sent a large delegation, including many different tendencies. In 1889, as we saw, they hovered between the rival Congresses. Andrea Costa, who had broken with the Anarchists and founded a Socialist Party in the 1880s, joined forces in 1892 with a number of other groups to form an United Socialist Party ; and new men, Filippo Turati of Milan and Professor Enrico Ferri of Rome, reinforced Costantino Lazzari and the Marxist scholar, Professor Antonio Labriola. But against these political Socialists were ranged still powerful Anarchist bodies, with a following in the Trade Unions and connections ranging across France to Barcelona. The principal spokesman of the latter group was Amilcare Cipriani, who appeared sometimes as an Italian and sometimes as a French delegate. He claimed to speak in the name of a Latin Section of a General League of Peoples, and protested again and again when the Socialist Congress tried to rid itself of the Anarchists. The greatest of the Italian Anarchists, Errico Malatesta, was outside the new International from the first, though he put in at least one appearance at it.

Spain sent but few delegates. The political leader was Pablo Iglesias, founder of the Spanish Socialist Workers' Party on the Marxist model ; and with him usually came at least one delegate from the General Union of Spanish Workers, which was associated with the party. The Spanish Anarchists mostly kept away.

Russia, as we saw, had representatives of several tendencies at the Paris Congress in 1889 — ranging from Peter Lavrov, the Narodnik theorist, and Jusef Beck, of the People's Will Group, to George Plekhanov, the leading exponent of Marxism in Russia. Plekhanov was sole Russian delegate at Zürich in 1893 ; but at London in 1896 there were seven Russians, including, as well as Plekhanov and his wife, Rosalie, the Social Democrats Paul Axelrod and Vera Zasulich. There were troubles over the acceptance of other delegates — Tchaikovsky and Felix Volkhovsky, for example — who were rejected by the Marxist groups. Plekhanov was able to report the rapid growth of the underground Social Democratic movement in Russia, and to sweep aside the Narodniks as survivors from a past epoch.

Poland always had its delegation. In 1889 it was headed by Felix Daszyński, Stanisłas Mendelssohn, and Marie Joukowska, with Leo Winiarski from the Polish Section of the Slav League. At Zürich Daszyński and Mendelssohn were reinforced by Stanisław Grabski and a number of others ; and at London, in 1896, there were thirteen in all, including besides Daszyński three important newcomers, Józef Pilsudski and J. Moscicki of the Polish Socialist Party, and Rosa Luxemburg, representing the Poles of Posen and Breslau. These Polish delegations came as representing all parts of Poland — Russian, Austrian, and German : they were already sharply divided between those who looked eastward to Russia and those who looked rather to Germany, and also between Marxism and a more nationalist brand of Socialism, of which Pilsudski was to become a notorious exponent. A number of them were exiles, sent by Polish groups in America as well as in London and Paris. They did not play any large part in the early debates of the International, and for the most part did not place themselves easily in relation to the quarrels of the leading delegations.

From the Balkan countries Roumania had always its contingent, mainly from the Social Democratic Party. The Bulgarians had already their rival factions, represented in 1893 by Christian Rakovsky and N. C. Gabrowsky ; but in 1896 at London Rakovsky headed a single delegation. Serbia, too, had a single delegate at Zürich, but none in London. An Australian Social Democrat appeared in 1893; but in 1896 Edward Aveling was asked to serve as the Australian delegate. There were no real representatives of the Trade Unions or Labour Parties of Australia, and none even purporting to represent New Zealand.

Finally, we come to the Americans. As we saw, a couple of American Trade Unionists attended the Possibilist Congress of 1889, and a third was a visitor at the Marxist Congress, at which there were also delegates from some scattered foreign groups in the United States; but the American Federation of Labor, though messages were delivered on its behalf to both Congresses, was not officially represented at either. At later Congresses there were always American delegates; but they did not come from the main body of American Labour. The outstanding figure from the United States was the Marxist, Daniel De Leon, of the Socialist Labor Party. With him came to Zürich Louis Sanial, of the New York Central Labor Federation, and Abraham Cahan, from the Jewish Trades of New York. Sanial was present again in 1896, representing this time the De Leonite Trades and Labor Alliance; and with him were Mathew Maguire of the S.L.P. and five others representing scattered Trade Union groups, some of whose claims were disputed. The S.L.P. was by then rent by internal struggles: the new American Socialist Party had not yet emerged.

At all these early Congresses of the Second International the Social Democrats, who knew what they wanted and acted closely together, had the last word. Again and again they voted down the Anarchists, told them to get out, and asserted that they had nothing in common with them. But they could not get rid of them; and, though a good many of the out-and-out Anarchists shook the dust of the International from their feet, there were always others who came back, protesting that they too were men and brothers and asked only for a 'Free' International, open to all the enemies of capitalism who were attempting to rally the working class in order to compass its downfall. There were always in addition, said the Marxists, sentimental idiots who fell for the Anarchist affirmations of brotherhood and wanted everyone to be free to speak his mind; and there were also persons who were not Anarchists, but had no use for the disciplined party or the electioneering in which the Social Democrats put their trust. It was difficult to rally a majority for the expulsion of these middle groups : nor did the Social Democrats wish to expel them *en masse*. They hoped to win some of them over, and to deal with the rest, nationality by nationality, as they gained enough control of each national delegation and of the movements behind it. Their tactics were to keep on passing Congress resolutions committing the International to political action as a necessary weapon, and to seize every chance that offered of showing any awkward group of their opponents the door.

There was, however, the very grave difficulty that, even if the Anarchists' credentials could be rejected when they came from openly Anarchist organisations or from thinly camouflaged Socialist bodies, there was still nothing to prevent the Anarchists from coming back again and again when they could get Trade Union nominations. This difficulty did not arise where there was an effective central Trade Union organisation closely allied with, or subordinate to, the Social Democratic Party, or to a Labour Party of similar outlook. But in most countries no such organisation existed. In France there were rival Trade Union groups standing for different tendencies, as there were in Italy, in Spain, and in the United States. In Great Britain the Trades Union Congress united the Unions, but was itself a battleground of rival tendencies — the Old Unionism and the New : nor was there any united Social Democratic Party to bring the Trade Unions to heel. For the Congresses of the 'eighties delegates had been accepted from individual Trade Unions, as well as from national centres, even where such centres existed ; and nobody knew how to find any internationally applicable definition of a Trade Union that was *bona fide* enough to have its credentials accepted. In the struggle for the eight hours' day it was plainly indispensable to secure the widest possible Trade Union support, and to give the Trade Unions an important place in the successive Congresses. But this could not be done without letting in on the one hand British Lib-Labs who opposed the creation of a Socialist or Labour Party and on the other Syndicalists and Anarchists who denounced parliamentary action as a fraud and a betrayal.

Thus, the Social Democrats were in a perpetual dilemma.

They could not go all out for a purely Marxist, Social Democratic International without forfeiting a large part of the Congresses' Trade Union support; but they could not easily stomach having them used as platforms for Anarchist or Syndicalist propaganda. Indeed, they could stomach this the less, as a fresh wave of Anarchist violence spread over Europe, and as reactionaries everywhere seized every chance to identify the Socialists with the dynamiters and assassins. Some Anarchists could not be prevented from coming; and, if they came, the outraged Social Democrats could not be stopped from consuming the time of Congress in endeavouring to dissociate themselves from their revolutionary utterances. So the wrangling went on, exasperatingly, from one Congress to another.

At Zürich, in 1893, the outcome of the dispute was the passing of a resolution which reads as follows in the English text:

> All Trade Unions shall be admitted to the Congress: also those Socialist Parties and Organisations which recognise the necessity of the organisation of the workers and of political action. By 'political action' is meant that the working-class organisations seek, in as far as possible, to use or conquer political rights and the machinery of legislation for the furthering of the interests of the proletariat and the conquest of political power.

There were disputes later about the meaning, and indeed about the correct text, of this resolution. It was clearly meant to rule out non-trade union organisations which did not support political action designed to conquer political power and to secure parliamentary representation; but this test could not be applied to the Trade Unions. If, however, *all* Trade Unions were to be admissible, the door was left wide open, not only to anyone who could get nominated by an existing Trade Union, however small, but even to nominees of Trade Unions formed simply for that purpose. It was accordingly argued, both by the Social Democrats and by the organised national Trade Union Centres, that only *bona-fide* Trade Unions could be meant; but what was a *bona-fide* Trade Union? A number contended that it must be a Trade Union which was committed to political action, if only to the extent of advocating labour legislation, on the ground that no Trade Union which did not go as far as that could have any concern with the International's affairs. But even that was not acceptable : the British Trades Union Congress Parliamentary Committee was not prepared to see excluded those of its members who were opposed to the legal eight hours' day. It remained uncertain what 'all Trade Unions' meant ; and a number of suspect delegates were able to creep in through the gap.

Take, by way of illustration, the composition of the numerous British delegation at the London Congress of 1896. No fewer than 159 out of the 476 came from Trade Unions, another 26 from local Trades and Labour Councils, 2 from the Women's Trade Union League, and 3 from the Women's Industrial Council. The Social Democratic Federation sent 121, the Independent Labour Party 117, and the Fabian Society 22. Three came from William Morris's Hammersmith Socialist Society, 3 from local Socialist Societies in Bristol, Oxford, and Berkshire, and 3 from John Trevor's Labour Church Union. The only disqualification recommended by the delegates was that of the Berkshire Socialist Society, which had only 4 members, of whom it had sent 2. The British delegation allowed it 1, and rejected the other.

This was, of course, a swollen delegation, because the Congress was meeting in London. At Zürich in 1893 the British delegates had numbered 64, and had been considerably more miscellaneous in origin. The S.D.F. had sent 8, the I.L.P., still barely formed, 5, and the Scottish Labour Party 2. The Fabians had 5 and various local Socialist Societies another 5. One came from the London Communist Club, mainly foreign in its composition. One came from a Co-operative Producers' Society of Socialist outlook, and 1 from a Jewish Trade Union and Socialist Society. On the Trade Union side the Trades Union Congress Committee and the Miners' Federation each sent 4, and the Durham Miners 2 on their own. The Gasworkers' Union had 3, and other Trade Unions 16 in all. Local Trades Councils sent 6 and the Women's Trade Union League 2. One or two Anarchists — for example, C. W. Mowbray — got in as Trade Union delegates.

This was as nothing in comparison with the complexity of the French and Italian delegations, whose members were apt to come each with credentials from several bodies, so that if one were rejected another might serve. The Frenchmen came from rival Socialist Parties and from rival national Trade Union Federations; from Student groups and local Chambres Syndicales; from Socialist journals; from local Syndicats and from national Fédérations de Syndicats; from Bourses du Travail and from propagandist societies; and, in 1896, also from the parliamentary group of the Independent Socialists. The delegates simply cannot be classified so as to show what bodies they predominantly represented, or in whose name they spoke.

The Zürich resolution came up as first business at the London Congress of 1896. Tom Mann and Keir Hardie both pleaded for wide toleration of differences, with Jaurès and Hyndman taking the opposite view. Nieuwenhuis of Holland questioned the validity of the Zürich resolution and maintained that Anarchist-Communists, such as Kropotkin, were good Socialists, even if some Anarchists were not. James Mawdsley, of the British Cotton Spinners' Amalgamation, who was soon to stand for Parliament as a Conservative candidate, said that the British Section would uphold the Zürich decision. Then came the voting, by nationalities. Australia, Austria, Belgium, Bohemia, Bulgaria, Denmark, Germany, Hungary, Poland, Portugal, Rumania, Russia, Spain, Sweden, Switzerland, and the United States voted solidly for the reaffirmation of the Zürich resolution. France voted against, by 57 votes to 56, and Holland, by 9 to 5. The Italians, being equally divided, abstained. The British voted for the resolution, by 223 votes to 114. This was prior to the verification of credentials, so that anyone who claimed to be a delegate could vote. The national delegations then met to verify the standing of those present; and a few exclusions were made. There was a wrangle, already mentioned, about the position of the French Independent Socialists, and another about a rejected Pole. Yet another occurred over the Italian report. Louise Michel claimed to be holding an Italian mandate, whereas Malatesta was sitting among the French delegates. The President of the session, Hyndman, ruled that it had already been decided to exclude Anarchists, and several, after protesting, withdrew. The Dutch, who had a near-Anarchist majority, finally announced that they had agreed to accept the parliamentarian minority.

The French put forward their claim to divide into two separate sections, and Millerand was allowed to speak in favour of it. After it had been made clear that the two French groups would share equally the French quota of Commission members their proposal was accepted on a division, the French majority voting against. Four sessions had gone by, with no constructive business done ; but the Commissions on matters of policy into which the Congress had agreed to divide were not yet ready to report — so perhaps the waste of time did not much matter.

Most of the Commission Reports, when they were ready, did not amount to a great deal. There was no time to straighten out the complications involved in applying proposals to the varying circumstances of the different countries ; and the result was that in most cases only generalities got endorsed, and specific proposals were brought forward as Minority Reports, and mostly voted down almost without discussion. Thus, the Agrarian Commission declared that the land should be socialised, but confessed its inability to make any agreed proposal as to the means. It could only recommend active steps to organise the agricultural proletariat and leave to each country the duty of working out its own programme. The Political Action Commission, whose reporter was George Lansbury, then of the S.D.F., declared for working-class political action for the conquest of political power, and for the use of legislative and administrative means towards working-class emancipation. It described these means as directed towards the establishment of 'the International Socialist Republic', demanded 'independence of all bourgeois political parties, universal suffrage, including the emancipation of women, second ballot, the referendum and the initiative, full autonomy of all nationalities, and the destruction of colonial exploitation'. It called upon the workers in all countries subject to militarism and imperialism 'to fall into line, side by side with the class-conscious workers of the world, to organise for the overthrow of international capitalism and the establishment of International Social Democracy'.

This brought up the French Anarchist, Tortelier, who held a Trade Union credential, and then Vaillant and Jaurès on the other side. Then came the British Lib-Labs, protesting against the demand for political independence, and Pete Curran of the I.L.P. defending it. Bebel followed as the spokesman of the

German Party, and Ferri for the Italians — both for independence. After the British Lib-Lab amendment and some others had been defeated, the report was accepted *nem. con.*

At the next session Sidney Webb produced the report of the Education Commission, summed up in seven resolutions, which went much more into detail than most of the reports. They demanded that the 'public administration' in each country should provide 'a complete system of education under democratic public control', 'extending from the kindergarten to the university'. School meals were to be provided for all children ; the minimum school-leaving age was to be sixteen, with half-time education up to eighteen ; scholarships and maintenance allowances were to be made available ; and there were to be strict limitations on children's employment and a strict international code of factory legislation. All this was somewhat utopian, even for the more advanced countries ; but it was not seriously challenged. Keir Hardie scented in it a concealed intention to favour the clever children at the expense of the rest ; and Clara Zetkin answered that the Commission certainly did not intend that all children, irrespective of their capacity, should receive a university education — which Hardie thereupon denied having meant. There was a wrangle about alleged discrepancies between the English, German, and French texts of the report ; and an amendment by Hardie to delete a reference to 'scholarships' — which apparently had a bourgeois connotation in many minds — was carried. Then, on a French motion, the entire clause dealing with school meals and maintenance was deleted, on the plea that it was unnecessary to go into detail and that the Brussels Congress of 1891 had already declared it to be the State's duty to do everything needed to provide education for all children. Mrs. Pankhurst succeeded in getting Webb's word 'gradually' struck out, and 'as quickly as possible' substituted ; and then the report was adopted.

Next came the report of the Organisation Commission, introduced by C. A. Gibson of the S.D.F. This proposed that the Congress should establish itself as a permanent organisation, by setting up a permanent International Committee, with a responsible secretary and a fixed seat. It wanted the Congress to appoint a Provisional Committee to draw up a full scheme and report to the ensuing Congress. In addition, it proposed the establishment in each country sending out or receiving emigrants of special bodies to ensure that they were not lost to the working-class movement, with a particular proposal to distribute informative tracts to them before they left their own countries, and to arrange for them on arrival a reception by the working-class organisations of the receiving countries — especially across the Atlantic. London was approved as the seat of the International and the report was accepted ; but the Congress dispersed in the end without taking any step to set up the proposed Committee ; and nothing happened. The discussions were interrupted for the reception of the report of the Commission on War, which led to so prolonged a debate that the Organisation Commission's proposals were never properly debated.

The War Commission began by affirming that economic and not religious or national antagonisms were the chief cause of war under capitalism. It said that the workers in all countries must win political power in order to deprive Governments 'which are the instruments of the capitalist class' of the means of war-making. It demanded the 'simultaneous abolition of Standing Armies and the establishment of a National Citizen Force' ; the establishment of Tribunals of Arbitration to regulate international disputes ; and that 'the final decision on the question of War or Peace should be vested directly in the people in cases where the Governments refuse to accept the decision of the Tribunal of Arbitration'.

In the discussion, Dr. R. M. Pankhurst moved to delete the reference to a 'Citizen Force', but was defeated. Belfort Bax moved to add that the decision of Tribunals of Arbitration should be final ; and this was agreed, though Sanial declared that arbitration was 'all middle-class molasses'. Bax then tried to delete the demand for reference to the people ; but Greulich of Switzerland spoke strongly for its retention, and carried the day. Finally the amended report was unanimously adopted.

Next came the report of the Economic and Industrial Commission, which covered a very wide ground. It began with a comprehensive declaration in favour of the universal 'Socialisation of the means of production, transport, distribution, and exchange, the whole to be controlled by a completely democratic organisation in the interests of the entire community'. This,

SOCIALIST THOUGHT

it was urged, was becoming daily more necessary because of the
growth of monopolies, which 'cannot be effectively countered
by ordinary Trade Unions or isolated political action'. The
Commission advocated the establishment of some international
agency to keep watch on trusts and combines and their political
intrigues, and to work for their socialisation 'by national or
international enactment'. It then went on to attribute crises
and unemployment to capitalist obstruction of the full use of
mankind's rapidly increasing productive power, and to record
its view that coal mines, iron and chemical works, railways, and
the larger factories 'have all reached the stage when their
nationalisation and socialisation present no difficulty from the
economic point of view'. The workers of the world were therefore called upon 'to proceed at once to urge definite measures
of socialisation, nationalisation, and communisation in their
respective countries'.

The next section discussed the functions of Trade Unions.
These, it was said, were indispensable for defending and
improving the workers' conditions; but by their struggle 'the
exploitation of labour will be only lessened, not abolished'.
Abolition required the conquest of political power, and its use
for legislative purposes. The Trade Unions should help in
this: 'the organisation of the working class is incomplete and
unfinished as long as it is political only'. But the economic
struggle also calls for political action by the labouring class.
'Whatever the workers gain from their employers in open disputes must be confirmed by law in order to be maintained,
while conflicts may in other cases be rendered superfluous by
legislative measures.'

From these more general propositions the Commission went
on to more detailed proposals. It called for 'the abolition of all
tariffs, duties on articles of consumption, and exportation
premiums', and for international legislation for the protection
of labour. In respect of the latter, it recommended limiting
the immediate 'palliative agitation' to three specific demands,
headed by the eight hours' day, and including full rights of
combination and the abolition of sweating. The Commission
then recited eight demands for international labour legislation
adopted at the Paris Congress of 1889, and, returning to the
question of Trade Unions, urged the workers 'to organise in

national Trade Unions in their respective countries, thus
avoiding waste of power by small independent or local organisations'. It laid down that 'difference of political views ought not
to be considered a reason for separate action in the economic
struggle : on the other hand, the nature of the class-struggle
makes it the duty of the labour organisations to educate their
fellow-members up to the truths of Social Democracy'. The
Trade Unions were then called upon to admit women and to
secure 'equal wages for the same kind and amount of work'.
Finally, as a basis for international organisation, it was proposed
that 'a Central Trade Union Commission should be constituted
in every country', and that 'in cases of strikes and lock-outs
and boycotts, the Trade Unions of all countries should assist
one another according to their means'.

This was the Majority Report of the Economic and Industrial Commission. Its adoption was moved by Harry Quelch of
the S.D.F. after it had been introduced by the German,
Molkenbuhr. The Minority Report, which was brief, drew
attention to the declarations of a succession of French Labour
Congresses — Marseilles (1892), Paris (1893), Nantes (1894),
and Limoges (1895) — in favour of the general strike, and called
upon the workers in all countries 'to study this important
question, which should be decided at the next Congress'. Thus
began the great debate about the general strike, which was to
occupy so much of the time of the Second International in
subsequent years. It should be noted that, in the form in
which it came up in 1896, it had no specific reference to the
prevention of war. It was part of the Economic Commission's
minority report, and was advanced as 'a method of emancipation'. This Minority Report was rejected at the London
Congress almost without discussion, and the Majority Report
was accepted with only a few minor amendments, of which the
most important, moved by Dr. Pankhurst, laid down that
'wherever private employment fails, public employment should
be provided at reasonable wages'. A further amendment,
moved by Edward Aveling as representing Australia and adopted,
called upon workers' organisations not to ask for restrictive
legislation against the immigration of aliens ; and yet another,
moved by A. Fauquez of Switzerland, reaffirmed the decision
to continue May Day manifestations, having 'as their chief

objects the obtaining of the legal eight hours' day and protests against militarism'.

Last came the Report of the Miscellaneous Commission, presented by J. Bruce Glasier, of the British I.L.P. This affirmed 'the fundamental right of liberty of conscience, of speech, and of the press, and the right of public meeting and combination, both locally and nationally'. It demanded an amnesty for political prisoners and protested against the system of police provocation. Further, it demanded the suppression of private employment exchanges and the general introduction of free exchanges conducted by municipalities or Trade Unions. Finally, it said that it was not in a position to present a report on the question of an international language, which had been referred to it; but it invited the Congress to declare 'which of the languages, English, French, or German, it would prefer to adopt'. This the Congress did not find time to do.

The Congress turned last to the arrangements for the next Congress. Liebknecht, for the Bureau, moved a resolution in the following terms:

> The Standing Orders Committee of the Congress is entrusted with the duty of drawing up the invitations for the next Congress by appealing exclusively to:
> 1. The representatives of those organisations which seek to substitute Socialist property and production for capitalist property and production, and which consider legislative and parliamentary action as one of the necessary means of attaining that end.
> 2. Purely trade organisations, which, though taking no militant part in politics, declare that they recognise the necessity of legislative and parliamentary action: consequently Anarchists are excluded.

There followed a paragraph proposing the setting up of a Credentials Commission, to which appeals could be made from the decisions of a National Commission. The S.D.F. tried to amend Liebknecht's draft to make the Congress even more a gathering of representatives from Social Democratic Parties, but was voted down. A British Trade Union delegate, W. Stevenson of the Builders' Labourers, protested that the Trade Unions had been brought to the Congress on false pretences, outvoted in the British delegation, and made to listen to a lot of 'disquisitions on an ideal society which is as far off as the millennium'. After a few formalities, and the adoption of Liebknecht's report, the Congress ended.

I have recorded rather fully the proceedings of the London Congress of 1896 in order to give an idea of what went on in these early gatherings of the Second International, while it was still only taking shape as essentially a political gathering based on the emergent Socialist Parties.

It will be seen that almost all the big issues that were to divide the International up to 1914 had already been raised during these early Congresses. Apart from the struggle to exclude the Anarchists, which was almost over after 1896 — though the battle between the 'politicals' and the Syndicalists remained very much in being — the questions under debate in 1896 were still being debated in 1914 — or would have been, had not the Congress summoned for that year been prevented from meeting by the outbreak of war. The greatest difference between the earlier and the later Congresses was that, from 1900 onwards, the question of war and peace occupied an ever-increasing place in the International's debates and tended to thrust rather into the background the question of industrial legislation that had been in the forefront during the early years. There was also a difference arising from the fact that in a number of countries changes in the franchise after 1900 made possible the winning of enough seats in the Parliaments to convert the Socialists from small groups into powerful parties to which the Parliaments had in varying degrees to adapt their procedure. There were still in 1914 countries represented in the International that were unable to establish such parties and had still to conduct the greater part of their political activities from outside Parliament. But in general Socialism had assumed by 1914 a much more parliamentary complexion than it had in the 1890s.

With this change went, of course, a decline in the revolutionary intransigence of the Socialist movements of the countries affected by it, and therewith a sharper division between these countries and those which remained subject to absolute rule. Up to 1896 Reformism, though it clearly existed as a tendency, had not been clearly formulated as a body of doctrine challenging Marxism in such a way as to lead to a sharp confrontation of the rival attitudes on an international basis.

Fabianism was a British doctrine, Possibilism a French: German Revisionism had not yet taken shape, though South German Reformism had. Internationally, Marxism held the field by virtue of its victory over the Anarchists. The battle with the Syndicalists was only beginning.

CHAPTER II

THE SECOND INTERNATIONAL:
LATER YEARS
(i) 1900 — PARIS

THE Paris Socialist Congress of 1900 was chiefly notable, on the surface, for three things — its handling of the crisis arising out of the Millerand affair, its decision to set up an International Socialist Bureau, and its apparent solidarity on a number of issues that were before long to arouse acute dissensions. It was held at a time when the Revisionist controversy was already being carried on with great vehemence among the Germans, but had not yet fully presented itself as an international issue, or rather had not been separated internationally from the issue of Socialist participation in non-Socialist Governments, which raised some of the same questions of ideology and practical policy, but did so in such a way as to produce an artificial majority for the left by ranging the centre firmly with the revolutionaries against the participationists. In the struggle against Reformists of the Millerand type, those Social Democrats who set their hopes on building up parties which would presently become strong enough to dominate the Parliaments of their countries, tended naturally to side with the revolutionary left wing because they saw coalition with the bourgeois Radicals as an obstacle to the electoral growth of Social Democracy. Coalitions might no doubt be in a position to secure legislative advances which Socialist Parties could not hope to win as yet by standing alone; but if there was a real prospect of getting, at some not too distant date, a clear Social Democratic majority it seemed to be folly, as well as even betrayal, to throw away that chance by entering into coalitions with the bourgeois left, or even into electoral alliances except in the form of second ballot arrangements — if even at that stage. In the view of the majority of the Germans the great task was to build up the party as a mass electoral force, and all other considerations needed to be kept subordinate to that task. The immense prestige and influence of the German Social Democratic Party gave its insistence on this point a great deal of weight; and among the Germans this was the view not only of the left and centre, but also of many of the Revisionists who followed Bernstein, though not of the South German Reformists from Bavaria and Baden. Revisionism and Reformism in Germany, though they were allies in the fight against Bebel and Kautsky, were not the same: it was fully possible, and indeed common, for a Revisionist to be as strongly opposed to Millerandism as Kautsky was, because participationism might prevent the party from taking the course that would, in time, bring it a majority of its own. Just as, in the 1930s, the British Labour Party would have nothing to do with the attempt to build up a 'Popular Front' against Fascism, because it hoped to win political power for itself in due course, so most of the Germans in 1900 were dead against participation. It is pertinent to observe that they were not themselves practically faced, in Reich politics, with any such issue; for there was no immediate prospect of anyone asking them to join a Reich Cabinet. The issue did, however, face them practically in some of the Laender; and Reformism, as distinct from Revisionism, drew its strength from the politics of the Laender rather than of the Reich.

In most of the other countries represented at the International the Socialist Parties had much less prospect or even hope than in Germany of winning the support of a majority of the electorate or, even if they did, of getting a majority of the seats, even in the popular Chamber. But many of them were under the spell of the Germans' success in continuously increasing their votes and seats and were disposed to accept the German electoral policy as a model, in the hope that in the long run it would enable them to achieve what German Social Democracy seemed to be well on the way to achieving. For many of them the first task appeared to be the winning of universal suffrage, which, as far as Reich elections were concerned, the Germans had had handed to them by Bismarck without any need to struggle for it. They could, indeed, hope to secure this constitutionally only with the aid of the bourgeois parties, and they were bound therefore to back up the bourgeois reformers who were working for it inside Parliament. But in

most cases they were not tempted by this necessity into favouring coalition with the bourgeois parties because they thought of
the struggle for franchise reform as having two distinct aspects.
Inside the Parliaments the bourgeois parties would be bound to
take the lead because, under the existing franchise, they held
most of the seats. But the prospect of getting electoral reform
depended, in Socialist eyes, mainly on the vigour with which
the campaign for it was carried on outside Parliament, by constant agitation, mass demonstrations, and, where practicable,
demonstration general strikes of short duration. The chances
of getting the franchise widened would not be appreciably
improved, in most countries, by the Socialists joining bourgeois-
dominated Coalition Governments even if they were asked.
They would do better by voting for the most advanced measures
the bourgeois parties could be induced to put forward under
pressure from outside — not by joining coalitions in which they
would have to become actual parties to compromises that would
take the edge off their own extra-parliamentary campaigns.

It was thus fully possible to rally a good majority against
participationism. Nevertheless, because the possibility of
building up Socialist parties capable of winning, some day,
clear majorities evidently depended on complete, or nearly
complete, unity of the Socialist forces, it was undesirable to
press the opposition to participationism to an extreme point for
fear of causing right-wing secessions. Accordingly, the object
of the majority of the International's leaders was to devise a
resolution which would at one and the same time record
opposition to Millerandism and to almost all possible kinds of
coalitionism, and yet not actually and finally bang the door.
There was no need to placate Millerand, who had clearly
transgressed the permissible limits by acting without even
consulting his party ; but there was need to placate Jaurès, who
had supported him, albeit with reserves, if the French Socialist
movement was not to be most dangerously split. It was
Kautsky's task to devise a form of words that would satisfy the
centre and disarm the extreme Left without driving the right
wing out of the International, and without making Jaurès's
position impossible.

This is how Kautsky did it, in the resolution which was
eloquently moved by Émile Vandervelde at the Paris Congress :

The winning of political power by the proletariat in a modern democratic state cannot be the result of a *coup de main*, but can come only as the conclusion of long and patient activity for the political and industrial organisation of the proletariat, for its physical and moral regeneration, for the gradual winning of seats on municipal bodies and legislative authorities.

Where, however, government power is centralised, it cannot be won in this piecemeal fashion. The entry of a single Socialist into a bourgeois Ministry cannot be considered as the normal beginning for winning political power : it can never be anything but a temporary and exceptional makeshift in an emergency situation.

Whether, in any given instance, such an emergency situation exists is a question of tactics and not of principle. The Congress does not have to decide that. But in any case this dangerous experiment can only be of advantage if it is approved by an united party organisation and if the Socialist Minister is, and remains, the delegate of his party.

Whenever a Socialist becomes a Minister independently of his party, or whenever he ceases to be the delegate of that party, then his entry into the Government, instead of being a means of strengthening the proletariat, weakens it, and, instead of being a means to furthering the winning of political power, becomes a means of delaying it.

The Congress declares that a Socialist must resign from a bourgeois Government if the organised party is of opinion that the Government in question has shown partisanship in an industrial dispute between capital and labour.

This resolution was finally carried by 29 votes to 9, the voting being by national delegations and not by individual delegates, each delegation having two votes. Only two delegations — Belgium and Ireland — voted solidly against it. France, Italy, Russia, Poland, and the United States were divided and cast one vote for and one against. The other delegations voted solidly for the resolution, though, of course, there were individual dissidents within their ranks. In the debate the main speakers for the resolution were Vandervelde, Jaurès, Anseele, and Auer, and against it Ferri, Guesde, and Vaillant. The Italian Ferri, then on the Left, moved an amendment drafted by Guesde in the following terms :

The Fifth International Congress at Paris declares again that the winning of political power by the proletariat, whether

40

it takes place by peaceful or by violent means, involves the political expropriation of the capitalist class.

Consequently it allows the proletariat to participate in bourgeois government only in the form of winning seats by its own strength and on the basis of the class-struggle, and it forbids any participation whatsoever by Socialists in bourgeois Governments, towards which Socialists must take up an attitude of unbending opposition.

Language apart, the Guesde-Ferri amendment did no more than lay down the policy which had been almost taken for granted by most Social Democrats up to the time of the Millerand affair. But, in effect, until that affair occurred, the issue had hardly arisen in a practical form. When it did arise, it split the French Socialists not mainly on the question of revolution versus reform, or even of the expediency of bourgeois-Socialist coalitions in general, but rather on that of defending the Republic, which was felt to be in danger as a consequence of the Dreyfus case. Millerand himself no doubt favoured participation in a Radical Ministry for the sake of the social reforms he hoped to get by it; but only a few others followed this line. Jaurès, though he began by defending Millerand, based his defence on the need for Socialists to rally round the Republic in its hour of peril; and as the discussion proceeded he in effect threw Millerand overboard while continuing to defend participation in the Republican cause. In taking this line he had a strong case against the Guesdists, who took up the remarkable attitude that the Dreyfus affair was nothing to Socialists, and that it could not really matter what kind of non-Socialist régime they had to deal with. It would, however, have been possible to rally to the defence of the Republic by supporting the Radical Government from outside, without actually joining it. Indeed, this is in effect what the followers of Jaurès and Brousse actually did. The Socialist Congress, however, never came to grips with the question whether this was the correct line to take. It got into an argument which was concerned, on the face of the matter, solely with the question of participation in a bourgeois Ministry.

On this issue, it could safely condemn Millerand without fear of causing a split in its ranks. But it could not go so far as to condemn participation in all its forms. Such a condemnation would have made it quite impossible to establish a united party in France and would probably have caused a good deal of trouble elsewhere — for example, in Belgium and in Great Britain. The door had to be left open to possible participation in a serious emergency, and not only to possible support of a bourgeois Government from outside. But, in order to carry the central body of opinion, it was necessary to leave the door leading to actual participation as little ajar as possible, by attaching stringent conditions ; and in order not to widen the area of dispute it was expedient to say nothing at all about the legitimacy of the policy of non-participant support. It can hardly be supposed that anyone believed that the conditions on which a Socialist was to be allowed, in an emergency, to become a member of a bourgeois Government could be literally workable; for they cut clean across the established methods of Cabinet government and would have put any Socialist Minister in a quite impossible position in relation to his colleagues. Nor can the delegates have thought that it could be easy to interpret the clause — inserted at Plekhanov's insistence — requiring any Socialist Minister to resign if the Government showed itself less than impartial in connection with industrial disputes — for who was to decide whether it was being ·impartial or not ? These conditions were not meant to be workable : they were designed to go as far against participationism as the International could go without serious danger of a split. The majority of the German Party, which carried the greatest weight, was definitely anti-participationist ; but the need for unity took precedence for it over the unequivocal expression of its view.

Having disposed of the Millerand affair, the Paris Congress turned to the question of colonial imperialism. The resolution, moved by the Dutchman, van Kol, committed the International not only to fight by every possible means against the colonial expansionist policies of the capitalist powers but also to promote the formation of Socialist parties in the colonial and semi-colonial countries and to collaborate with such parties to the fullest possible extent. It is interesting to observe that this unequivocally anti-imperialist resolution was carried unanimously. British delegates from both the S.D.F. and the I.L.P. took the occasion to denounce British imperialism as manifested in the South African War. A few years later, colonialism was to find defenders in the ranks of the German Social Democrats,[1] the Belgians were to be sharply divided on the question of accepting responsibility for the Congo Free State,[2] the Dutch Socialists were to fall out in connection with the East Indies, and such conflicts of opinion were to be echoed in the debates of the International. But in 1900 these disagreements had not been forced to the front by the growing imperialist rivalries of the leading powers, and it was still possible for Socialists to join almost unanimously in whole-hearted denunciation of colonialism.

Next came, at Paris, the great debate concerning anti-militarism, with Rosa Luxemburg as the mover. The Galician delegation, headed by Daszyński, once more challenged Rosa Luxemburg's mandate to represent Poland ; but the Congress upheld her claim. Rosa Luxemburg's speech was notable chiefly for her emphasis on the probability of the final crisis of capitalist society being precipitated, not by economic collapse, but by the imperialist rivalries of the great powers. Speaking at a time when, in a purely economic sense, capitalism was making very rapid advances, above all in Germany and the United States, she clearly did not expect that it would speedily meet its death as a consequence of internal collapse or of the 'increasing misery' of the proletariats of the advanced capitalist countries. Indeed, she said that the rule of capitalism would 'perhaps endure for a long time', but that sooner or later its hour would strike, most likely as the result of war between the great exploiting States, and that it was essential for the workers to prepare for that decisive moment by continually engaging in international action. The resolution accordingly urged the Socialist Parties to undertake a joint struggle against militarism and colonialism, the methods proposed including, first, the organisation and education of the youth in all countries for the carrying on of the class-struggle ; secondly, the casting of the Socialist vote in the Parliament of every country against all military or naval estimates and against all forms of expenditure on colonial ventures ; and, thirdly, the organisation of simultaneous protests and demonstrations against militarism in all countries, whenever an international crisis threatened to develop.

[1] See p. 70.   [2] See p. 635 ff.

This resolution, too, was carried with unanimity, so little had the Socialists for the most part realised how soon they were going to be faced with a sharp conflict between the calls of national and international solidarity. The delegates at Paris were still trying to exorcise with fine sentiments a threat which had not yet become imminent enough to compel them to discover where their ultimate loyalties lay. They went on to pass a resolution denouncing the Hague Peace Conference of 1898 as a barefaced swindle, on the ground that it had consisted of representatives of the very Governments which were openly pressing imperialist aims, and that it was nonsense for capitalist and militarist exploiters to talk of disarmament, arbitration, and the humanisation of the laws of war.

In the closing session, the Paris Congress began upon the debate concerning the general strike against war that was there-after to occupy so much attention. The Paris discussion was brief, for lack of time ; but it gave Briand, then on the extreme left, his chance to make a flamboyant speech in favour of the general strike, and Legien his chance to assert strongly the opposition of the German Trade Unions and to predict the certain failure of the attempt, if it were ever made. Briand argued for the general strike on this occasion not merely as a means of preventing war but chiefly as the beginning of a revolution that would enable the proletariat everywhere to seize the means of production and to establish a new society based on their lasting appropriation. The French, Italian, and Spanish left wings, and the Russian Social Revolutionaries supported him ; but the great majority preferred to adjourn the whole question for fuller discussion within the national parties before reaching a collective decision.

The remaining important resolution of the Paris Congress was that which led to the establishment the following year of an International Socialist Bureau with its seat in Brussels and the Belgian, Victor Serwy, as its first secretary. The Bureau was to have two main organs — an International Committee consisting of delegates appointed by the national sections, and also an Inter-parliamentary Commission to co-ordinate action between the national parliamentary groups. It was to include a Secre-tariat, elected by the International Committee, which was to act between Congresses as the voice of the International and was to take any requisite action on resolutions passed at Congress. It was not, however, armed with any power to order the national parties to undertake any particular action : indeed, it could not be, when the Congress itself had no coercive authority over them and could only seek to persuade them to comply with its resolutions. It was, however, a development of considerable importance and, as far as it went, a real attempt to bring the national sections into closer and more continuous contact. Thereafter, the International Socialist Bureau played an important part in influencing Socialist policy at each of the recurrent crises up to 1914; but closer contact could not resolve fundamental differences of attitude and policy, and the fear of doing anything that might provoke a split was always present to restrict positive action within the limits of agreed compromise. The Inter-parliamentary Commission was even less effective; for the organised party in each country claimed the last word in settling policy as against the parliamentary group, and each group tended to be influenced, even more strongly than the party as a whole, by tactical considerations which varied widely from country to country.

Thus, apart from the setting up of the International Socialist Bureau and the compromise concerning 'participation', the Paris Congress was chiefly notable for the passing of a series of resolutions which made it appear a good deal more militant than it really was. When the Kautsky resolution had been steered through to success, the delegates were allowed to have their heads about colonial and militarist issues, and were stopped only when it came to the practical question of authorising the general strike as a revolutionary weapon. The main issues raised by the German Revisionists were not yet ripe for international discussion, being still mainly a domestic affair among the Germans. They were to come to the front only at the next Congress, held at Amsterdam in 1904.

(ii) 1904 — AMSTERDAM

By the time the next International Socialist Congress assembled at Amsterdam in 1904, Revisionism had replaced Participationism as the main issue. From the publication of Bernstein's opening articles up to the Dresden Congress of the Social Democratic Party in 1903 the conflict raged, getting mixed up with the debates arising out of the *affaire Millerand*, but transcending them in importance in German eyes. After the mild censure passed on Bernstein's activities at the Hanover Congress of 1899[1] came the rather less equivocal condemnation of them by the Lübeck Congress of 1901, embodied in a resolution which carefully refrained from pronouncing judgment on Bernstein's conclusions, though it criticised his methods. Only at Dresden in 1903 did the German Party finally and explicitly condemn Revisionism; and even then it did so in a resolution passed by an overwhelming majority, which included most of the leading Revisionists. When it came to a final show-down, such men as Ignaz Auer, Wolfgang Heine, and Hermann Südekum, who had been prominent on the Revisionist side, voted among the 288 who supported the official resolution; and only a handful — a mere eleven — voted against it. So powerful was the appeal to unity — to the acceptance of majority decisions by minorities, provided that the majority was prepared to stop short of expelling the minority, or of rendering its continuance within the party impossible. At Dresden the vote was taken openly, each delegate giving his name as he voted. This was done in order to give the resolution the character of a solemn declaration, which the entire party was called upon by its leaders to accept.

The Dresden resolution, which was soon to become well known outside Germany after it had been endorsed by the French Guesdists and referred by them to the International for approval as a basic principle of Socialist action, was carefully drafted in terms which, while they clearly condemned Revisionism, left the door just open for the Revisionists to remain within the party. The attempts of Rosa Luxemburg and the left wing, begun in 1899 and kept up throughout the controversy, to get the Revisionists and Reformists expelled, met with no success. Bebel was quite ready to make fiery and eloquent speeches against the right wing, and to proclaim that the German Social Democratic Party stood fully by its revolutionary faith. He was ready to quote the more intransigent utterances of the recently dead leader, Wilhelm Liebknecht, from his

[1] See p. 273.

famous pamphlet, *No Compromise!*, and to declare that any concession to the Revisionists would be fatal to the prospects of Socialism. Indeed, he had to make a thoroughly revolutionary impression on his audience in order to isolate the extreme left as well as the right, and to prevent Rosa Luxemburg and her group from splitting the party. His speeches ensured that, if a split did occur, only a fairly small group on the extreme left would break away and would be regarded as unreasonable in doing so by the great majority of the party rank and file. The right wing, he knew, would not split off; and he set out to make it impossible for the left wing to do so either, without losing most of its influence. In 1903 Bebel reached the height of his reputation as a Marxist and a revolutionary; so that he came to the Amsterdam International Congress the following year with the laurels of Dresden covering his brow and was able there to repeat his triumph.

I am not suggesting that in taking this line Bebel was being dishonest, any more than Kautsky was. They did both quite sincerely disapprove of Bernstein's attitude and were quite sincerely opposed to the Reformist tendencies within the German Social Democratic Party. Bebel quite honestly believed that the correct policy for the party was to reject all compromise with the established German régime and all coalition with the bourgeois Radicals, in order to build up in opposition a clear majority of Social Democratic voters, and, in the Reichstag, a strong enough position to make the continuance of irresponsible imperial government impracticable. He did quite honestly hold that this was the way to make the German Revolution, by confronting the Kaiser and the ruling classes with a body of Socialist opposition plainly too strong to be resisted except by an appeal to naked force. What would happen when this had been done he did not profess to know. If the Kaiser and the ruling classes decided to fight, the Socialists would have to fight back; but I think he clearly entertained the hope that, when the time came, they would not dare to appeal to force and would allow the Revolution to happen by constitutional, or at any rate by non-violent, means. Whether or no, he saw no inconsistency at all between calling himself a revolutionary and concentrating all the party's energy on the struggle to win a majority by parliamentary means; and this was the policy he invoked in order to defeat both Bernstein and Rosa Luxemburg and to rally the main body of the party behind him in the name of Marxism and revolution.

The resolution adopted at the Dresden Congress opened with an explicit condemnation of the whole Revisionist position.

> The Congress most decisively condemns the Revisionist endeavour to alter our twice-tested and victorious tactics based on the class-struggle. The Revisionists wish to substitute for the conquest of political power through the overcoming of our enemies a policy of meeting the existing order of things half-way. The consequences of such Revisionist tactics would be to transform our party. At present it works towards the rapid conversion of the existing bourgeois order of society into a Socialist order : in other words it is a truly revolutionary party in the best sense of the word. If the Revisionist policies were adopted it would become a party content with merely reforming bourgeois society.
>
> Further, our party Congress condemns any attempt to gloss over the existing, ever-increasing class-conflicts for the purpose of turning our party into a satellite of bourgeois parties.

This seemed plain language — plain enough to make it very difficult for the Revisionists to vote for their own condemnation. What made it possible for them to do this was that, though they were condemned, they were not excluded or even silenced : so that it remained open to them to try again, if not under the banner of Revisionism, at any rate by advancing most of its ideas and proposals without using the name — which, indeed, many of the Reformists never had used. Auer and Südekum and the rest who voted for the Dresden resolution could say that they had never called themselves 'Revisionists' — the label had been bestowed on them by no act of theirs. Reformism, as distinct from Revisionism, had no doubt been implicitly condemned ; but it had not been banned explicitly, and it had been made perfectly clear that Bebel did not want to drive its exponents out of the party if they were prepared to conform in action to the decision of the majority. The only threat Bebel uttered was when he was insisting that the Party Group in the Reichstag must accept the instructions of the Congress and renounce any claim to follow a line of its own against the Congress's declared will. He did tell the right-wing spokesman

Wolfgang Heine that, unless he was prepared to toe the line in this respect, he would be expelled. But he was well aware that the fairly numerous right-wing faction among the Reichstag deputies would not dare to defy party discipline, as they would be in no doubt that, if they did so, the party machine would soon see to it that most of them lost their seats. The only hope for the 'Reformists' after 1903 was to avoid the use of the word 'Revisionist' and to go on working away quietly inside the party on particular issues as they arose, in the well-founded expectation that the party would presently come round in detail to a good part of what it had rejected when it was put forward in a lump and labelled as doctrinally heterodox. The right wing, as much as Bebel and Kautsky, saw the need for unity ; and it also saw, more clearly than either Bebel or Kautsky, that in the long run unity would mean moderation, and would mean putting off anything really revolutionary to an indefinite future.

Bebel and Kautsky, then, arrived at the Amsterdam Socialist Congress of 1904 with the reputation of having gloriously rescued German Social Democracy from the Revisionist danger, and of having it behind them as the exponent of a revolutionary policy directed against every sort of participationism and reformist compromise. They arrived, however, quite as determined not to split the International as they had been not to split their own party, and not quite so sure of being able to induce their international comrades who were of some sort of Reformist persuasion to vote against themselves in the name of unity. This, none the less, was what they wanted to get as near to as they could without risking a split ; but they were well aware that the passions that had been stirred up by the *affaire Millerand* would not be easily laid, and that there would be not a few delegates from France and other countries who would not be easily satisfied with any compromise that would leave their opponents free to practise Reformism under the International's aegis. Bebel had, indeed, to attempt at Amsterdam to achieve two almost irreconcilable objects — to get the Socialist Congress to reaffirm its revolutionary faith, and at the same time to persuade the contending factions, above all in France, to unite into unified national parties broad enough to include them all. He had somehow to reconcile Guesde and Jaurès, as well as to persuade all the Socialists of the world — or nearly all — to take the German Social Democratic Party as their model — doctrine, policy, and all.

This task was not, in practice, quite so difficult as it appeared. There were, at any rate, two parties of major standing in the International that could be relied on to set their faces firmly against a split, and at the same time to be ready to go a longish way towards endorsing the German attitude. These were the Austrian and Belgian Parties, led respectively by Victor Adler and Émile Vandervelde, both already outstanding figures in the International. Of these two, Vandervelde was likely to feel most sympathy with the Reformists, not only because he was temperamentally inclined that way, but also because the situation of the Belgian Party, especially in 1904, when it had recently emerged from defeat in a general strike for electoral reform,[1] induced it to consider seriously the prospects of electoral collaboration, if not of actual coalition, with the Liberals. In Austria, this issue did not arise in anything like the same form;[2] but Adler was by nature a conciliator, and would be certain to put the claims of unity higher than those of affirming revolutionary faith at the cost of provoking a split. Of the other important delegations, the British, as well as the French, were certain to be divided — they always were. The Spanish Social Democrats would probably follow the Germans; and so probably in this case would Plekhanov and the Russians. The danger was that some of the smaller parties would be too intent on affirming their revolutionary faith to know where to stop, and would be unmoved by the danger of their intransigence causing a split. They would need careful management and the solace of as much revolutionary phraseology as the right wing could be induced to put up with.

The German delegates arrived at Amsterdam with more than the Dresden resolution to offer to the Congress as a sign of their success. At the Reichstag elections of 1903 they had increased their vote from 18 to 24 per cent of the total and their seats from 32 to 55. This, to be sure, left them still with a very long way to go before arriving at the constitutional conquest of political power; but it was very encouraging to those who believed that this was the right way to proceed towards Socialism, and other delegations were no doubt impressed. Jaurès,

[1] See p. 634.   [2] See Chapter XII.

however, who was the most important antagonist they had to face at Amsterdam, refused to bow down and worship. He was well aware that his own policy stood no chance of being accepted by the Congress and that the main struggle would be between those who wished to force through the Dresden resolution and those who wished merely to soften it down. But he saw no good reason why he should not speak his mind; and, while paying tribute to the solidarity of the German Socialists and to their recent electoral success, he told them bluntly that they had no real policy and that, far from being, in fact, the most powerful Socialist Party in the world, as they believed themselves to be, they were among the most impotent. He accused them of impotence because, placing all their hopes in a future victory, they failed to do anything to improve actual conditions of living for the German workers or to lessen their oppression within the capitalist system. He accused them of having, in the Dresden resolution, masked with revolutionary phrases their incapacity for present action. He went on to trace their impotence to the lack of any revolutionary tradition among the German proletariat, reminding the Germans that they had not even won universal suffrage, as the French had and as other people were on the road to winning it, by unremitting struggle, but had been handed it from above; and he suggested that what had been got without struggle could be taken away by the hand that had given it, as the unresisted abrogation of the popular franchise in 'Red' Saxony had clearly shown. The revolutionism of the Germans, he asserted, was a revolutionism of phrases, not of deeds, and its unreality was matched by an equal failure to understand the conditions of successful parliamentary action, in the sense that obsession with revolutionary phrases prevented the German Party from extracting any real benefits from its growing parliamentary strength. The Germans, Jaurès argued, were attempting with their Dresden resolution to put Socialists throughout the world into the strait-jacket of a self-contradictory policy which was stultifying even their own action. The conditions governing tactics and policy, he contended, must differ widely as between countries which, to a substantial degree, already possessed democratic institutions as a reward for past struggles and countries still subject to autocratic rule. It was altogether wrong, he said, to treat all

non-Socialist parties in the former group of countries as constituting a single reactionary mass, when, in fact, some of them
were prepared to support a considerable part of the measures
which constituted the Socialists' immediate programme. For
France, with its great revolutionary tradition, for Belgium with
its special problems of national and religious divisions, for Great
Britain with its long tradition of parliamentary government, he
held the prescription of the Dresden resolution to be wholly in-
apposite. He did not suggest that what suited these countries
would suit Germany or Russia : he was maintaining the need
to allow each country to work out its strategy and tactics to suit
its own conditions. He was calling on the Germans, not to do
as he wished the French to do, but to show more fighting quality
in their actions as well as in their words, and to recognise that
the mere winning of a Reichstag majority — if they ever did
win one — would not suffice to make them masters of the
German State. The Germans had accused him and those who
agreed with him of abandoning the class-struggle : he threw
the charge back at them, contrasting the substantial real
achievements that had been won in France by rallying to the
defence of the Republic with the Germans' failure to defend in
Saxony even what they had previously won. In France, he
said, the schools had been set free from church control and
laicité established as the basis of the Republic ; chauvinists and
colonialists had been defeated, and the cause of peace advanced ;
and some real progress had been made in social and industrial
legislation. He strongly attacked the Guesdists who had refused
to lift a finger in the Republic's defence during the Dreyfus
affair and accused them of clinging to an obsolete Blanquism
instead of upholding the workers' day-to-day struggles.

Jaurès's speech was a magnificent tour de force. It was
answered by Bebel, in a speech by no means its equal in eloquence, but more in tune with what the majority of the delegates
wanted to hear. Bebel began by asserting that the German
Government was the worst in Europe — a sentiment which he
presently modified by excepting Turkey and Russia — and
that the German Socialists were, of course, Republicans and
envied the French their Republican institutions. They were,
however, Socialist Republicans ; and they did not propose
'to get their heads broken' for the bourgeois Republic. He went

on to refer to the bad record of the Republics — of the United States as well as of France — in using the powers of the State to break strikes and to shoot down strikers. The bourgeois Republic, he said, could always be relied on to defend capitalist interests. As for immediate benefits, he said that France was more backward than Germany in social legislation and had a much more reactionary tax system. He denied that the Germans had failed to act in co-operation with bourgeois parties when it was a matter of voting for useful palliative legislation, and claimed that the sole credit for such legislation as had benefited the workers belonged to the Socialists and that reforms had been granted because of the fears aroused by their growing power. The German Socialists, he contended, did not object to voting for good laws, whoever proposed them : their objection was to any alliance with non-Socialist parties that went beyond such voting. Bebel argued that the Dresden resolution furnished correct guidance for Socialists in all countries and in all circumstances, irrespective of local differences, because it stressed the fundamental antagonism between the proletariat and the capitalist State. Jaurès's policy, on the other hand, would corrupt the proletariat and confuse the issue. Jaurès had maintained that the Dresden resolution was inconsistent because it led to a negation of policy and to a frustrating attempt to combine revolutionary phrases with parliamentary methods. Bebel denied this : he held that it did just what was needed by sanctioning palliative activities only in proper subordination to revolutionary objectives. He did not attempt, save by implication, to answer Jaurès's point about the failure to resist the taking away of the vote in Saxony ; but he in effect met it by enquiring whether Jaurès meant that the German Socialists should have resorted to insurrection while they were still in a minority, and said he could not see what Jaurès thought they should have done to make their power more effectively felt after their recent electoral victories. The Socialists, he said, could afford to wait until they had conquered electorally ; and he stressed, for its bearing on their prospect of winning a majority, the fact that they had not expelled a single person, even among the extreme Revisionists. All they had done was to insist on the minority accepting the discipline of the majority. They wanted unity, not expulsions ; but unity must involve discipline in action, or the party's programme would be effectively stultified.

After Bebel came Victor Adler, as the proposer of a compromise amendment agreed upon with Vandervelde, and supported by the Austrian and Belgian delegations. The Adler-Vandervelde amendment differed from the Dresden resolution chiefly on two points : it omitted the explicit rejection of Revisionism in all its forms and substituted a positive declaration of the need to maintain unmodified the present tactics based on the class struggle and opposition to the bourgeoisie, with the winning of political power as its objective; and instead of pronouncing a complete ban on participation in government within 'bourgeois society', it limited itself to re-affirming the warnings against the dangers of such participation that had been contained in the Kautsky resolution of 1900. Adler, in moving the amendment, stressed the dangers of attempting to impose any international discipline on the parties in the various countries. The national movements, he said, had enough on hand in disciplining themselves.

When the vote was taken there were 21 votes for the Adler-Vandervelde amendment, and 21 against. The amendment, therefore, failed to pass. On the slightly altered Dresden resolution the voting was 25 for and only 5 against, with 12 abstentions. The voting was of course by countries, each country having 2 votes. Only Australia cast 2 votes against the resolution, 1 French, 1 Norwegian, and 1 British delegate making up the rest of the minority. The abstentions included the Belgians, the Swiss, the Swedes, the Danes, and the Argentinians.

The voting on the amendment (see p. 55) gives a better idea of the real division of opinion.

Before voting on this controversial matter the Amsterdam Congress had passed unanimously a resolution declaring it to be indispensable that in each country there should be only one Socialist Party, 'as there is only one proletariat', and affirming it to be the fundamental duty of all Socialists to work for this unity 'on the basis of the principles laid down by the Congresses of the International and in the interests of the international proletariat'. It had thus been made clear, before the controversial votes were taken, that there were to be no exclusions —

at any rate, unless any group refused to accept the Congress's verdict on the Dresden resolution. In fact, the strong phrases used in the Dresden resolution did not prevent the French parties from joining forces the following year under the leadership of Jaurès, who had been its principal opponent. For the time being the question of participation was out of the way. When John Burns joined the British Liberal Cabinet in 1905 there was no question of disciplining him; for he had put himself outside the jurisdiction both of the International and of

VOTING ON THE ADLER-VANDERVELDE AMENDMENT

FOR		AGAINST	
Argentina, 2	France, 1	Bulgaria, 2	France, 1
Australia, 2	Norway, 1	Germany, 2	Norway, 1
Austria, 2	Poland, 1	Hungary, 2	Poland, 1
Belgium, 2		Italy, 2	
Denmark, 2		Japan, 2	
Great Britain, 2		Russia, 2	
Holland, 2		Spain, 2	
Sweden, 2		U.S.A., 2	
Switzerland, 2		Others, 2 *	

* Presumably Serbia and Armenia, each represented by a single delegate.

its British affiliates. The revolutionary phrases of the Dresden-Amsterdam resolution were on record ; but they were singularly ineffective in preventing a continued drift in a Reformist direction, either in Germany or elsewhere.

The Amsterdam Congress had other important issues before it besides those arising out of the Revisionist-Reformist dispute. In particular it received from Henriette Roland-Holst, on behalf of the Dutch delegation, a report on the general strike as a weapon in the proletariat's struggle. She presented with her report a resolution embodying its main points. The resolution argued that a really complete general strike would be impracticable because it would starve the workers as well as everyone else, and that the necessary conditions for the success of any widespread strike must be strong organisation and voluntary discipline among the proletariat. It went on to say that no such sudden effort could result in the emancipation of the working class, but that an extensive strike of the key industries might prove to be a supreme method of bringing about very important social changes or of defence against reactionary attacks on working-class rights. The resolution then uttered a warning against Anarchist propaganda for the 'General Strike', with its tendency to distract the workers from the true and unceasing struggle — that is, from political, Trade Union, and Co-operative action. It called on the workers to develop their class organisation and to reinforce their unity, because on these conditions depended the success of the political strike, should this be found some day to be necessary and advantageous.

The debate that followed Henriette Roland-Holst's speech was mainly a French affair, with two contradictory contributions from Germans. Dr. Freideberg of Berlin, on behalf of the seldom articulate German industrialist minority, moved a resolution deploring the undue stress laid on parliamentary action and asserting the primacy of direct working-class action in the industrial field, above all on account of its effect on working-class psychology. He deplored the Dutch resolution as tending to widen the breach between Socialists and Anarchists, and called for the abandonment of parliamentary methods and the concentration of effort on 'the intellectual and moral elevation of the proletariat and on the economic struggle'. This resolution, moved in the name of the 'Free Federation of German Trade Unions', got no support. It was replied to by Robert Schmidt, also of Berlin, who described it as a 'soap-bubble', and, while affirming that the German Trade Unions had won many useful concessions, said that they were opposed to being dragged by the general strike into politics, 'which is not their place'. For some time past, he said, only a small group in Germany had favoured the general strike. Freideberg had no title to speak for more than this insignificant minority.

Among the French Jean Allemane, Albert Wilson, Adrien Meslier, and Aristide Briand supported counter-resolutions favouring the general strike, or at the least calling for fuller enquiry into its possibilities. Ustinov, for the Russian Social Revolutionaries, was on the same side, and described the Dutch report as 'utopian and illusionist' in its reprobation of the use of force. W. H. Vliegen, from Holland, supported the Dutch resolution, observing that all the speakers for the general strike appeared to have a contempt for parliamentary action, and that its advocates were to be found in the countries in which working-class organisation was weak, and not where there were strong Trade Union movements. Briand, in a careful speech, limited himself to asking for further enquiry, asked what other weapon than the general strike Socialists proposed to use if reactionary Governments attempted to deprive them of the vote or to suppress their movements, and adjured them not to cut themselves off from working-class sentiment by renouncing a weapon for which there was strong psychological support. Heinrich Beer of Austria emphasised the need to oppose the Anarchist notion of the general strike, without discarding it as a political weapon, and the necessity for strong organisation and careful preparation for its political use, and held that there was no need for any further study. When the vote came, the main French resolution was rejected by 34 votes to 8 and the Dutch resolution carried by 36 to 4, with 3 abstentions.

Of the rest of the proceedings at Amsterdam not much needs to be said. Molkenbuhr, the German Socialists' expert on social services and industrial legislation, presented a report embodying demands for insurance against unemployment, sickness, accident, old age, and other contingencies. The report urged that these services should be paid for out of taxes levied on large incomes and on inheritance, and that their management should be entrusted to organisations representing the insured. James Sexton, of the Liverpool Dock Labourers, tried in vain to get acceptance for an amendment excluding workers' contributions. Vliegen of Holland accused Molkenbuhr of devoting most of his report to praise of the German system, which outside Germany found favour chiefly among anti-Socialists. But all proposed amendments were rejected, and the report was approved, the British, the Americans, the Spaniards, and one of the French factions voting against it.

There was also a discussion on colonial and imperial questions. Van Kol, of Holland, moved a comprehensive resolution committing the Congress to uncompromising opposition to all imperialist or colonial measures, and to all expenditure on them. The resolution went on to declare against all concessions or trade monopolies in colonial areas, to denounce the oppression suffered by subject peoples, and to advocate measures for improving the condition of such peoples through public works, health services, and schools free from missionary influence. It demanded 'the greatest amount of liberty and autonomy compatible with the state of development of the peoples concerned, with complete emancipation as the end to be sought'. Finally, it called for parliamentary control over the exploitation of subject territories. This resolution was carried unanimously, and on the motion of the Italian, Rossi, Congress decided to set up a Colonial Bureau in connection with the International Socialist Bureau at Brussels.

Among those present at Amsterdam was the Indian leader, Dadhabhai Naroije, a founder and President of the Indian National Congress, who was invited to speak after S. G. Hobson, representing the Fabian Society, had moved a resolution strongly denouncing the British pillage of India as mainly responsible for the great famines to which that country was subject, and calling on the British workers to insist on self-government for the Indian people under British sovereignty. Dadhabhai Naroije fully endorsed what Hobson had said and accused Great Britain of breaking its promise to treat the Indians as fellow-nationals, and of burdening them with a host of officials and an unbearable toll on their natural resources. He called on the delegates to express their sympathy with the Indian people in their struggle for freedom. Hobson's resolution was carried with enthusiasm, and the Chairman, van Kol, emphasised from the chair that British imperialist policy had been unequivocally condemned by the International.

The only remaining incident of the Congress that is worth recording had to do with the war that had recently broken out between Russia and Japan. Sen Katayama, who was present as Japanese delegate, appeared on the platform with Plekhanov, and the two solemnly shook hands in order to affirm the solidarity of their respective working classes against the autocratic Governments of the two empires.

The Amsterdam Congress has often been described as the high-water mark of the Second International, on account both of its repudiation of Revisionism and of its lead towards Socialist unification within each country. These two much-acclaimed decisions were, however, in fact quite inconsistent. The insistence on unity within each country meant, as we saw, that no substantial body of Socialist opinion could be expelled or left outside — though out-and-out Anarchists could be excluded because they did not belong to political parties in any event. But it was impossible to silence the Revisionists and Reformists while keeping them within the national parties ; and accordingly the Dresden resolution could be only declaratory, and could not be enforced. What Amsterdam did bring about was more unity, not more discipline. The French parties came together in 1905, and stayed together with Jaurès as leader and Guesde, the promoter of the Dresden resolution, as a grumbling second-in-command. The British formed their numerous separate bodies into a single British Section of the International, which managed to work together without too much friction. The Bulgarians, indeed, firmly resisted unification ; and so did the Russians, save to a limited degree during the actual Revolution of 1905-6. But, in general, the policy of Socialist unity made headway, at the expense not of the Reformists but of the self-styled Revolutionaries, who were soon to split into rival factions of Left and Centre, with the erstwhile Revolutionaries of the Centre leaning more and more on the Right for support.

(iii) 1907 — STUTTGART

Three years passed between the Amsterdam International Congress and the next Congress, held at Stuttgart in 1907. Between the two meetings the first Russian Revolution had broken out and gone down to defeat, and the immense excitement aroused by its occurrence had had time to die down. The events in Russia had given fresh actuality to the discussions concerning the general strike ; for mass strikes had played an outstanding part in the Russian revolutionary movement and had led, especially in Germany, to urgent demands from the left that consideration should be given to the use of the general strike as a political weapon, or even as the opening phase of a German Revolution. In this campaign Rosa Luxemburg, in her dual capacity as an active leader of the German Left and of the Polish Social Democrats who were allies of Russian Bolshevism,[1] had played a very prominent part ; and by 1907

[1] See p. 493 ff.

59

the disintegration of the Amsterdam Anti-Reformist majority was already setting in as a consequence of the increasingly cautious attitude of the German Trade Unions. In France, Jaurès had established his position as leader of the Unified Socialist Party, and the Trade Unions, led by Victor Griffuelhes, had embarked on their great period of militant industrial action. In Great Britain the Labour Representation Committee, previously insignificant, had emerged under its new title of Labour Party, as a substantial electoral force, with a contingent of 30 M.P.s : so that for the first time the British counted as a major working-class party, though not on a definitely Socialist basis. In 1907 the Austrians won their great franchise extension, which enabled them to send 87 delegates to the Reichsrath. As against this, the German Social Democrats, instead of following up their electoral triumph of 1903 with a further advance towards their goal of a Reichstag majority, had experienced in 1906 a serious setback in seats, though not in votes, as a consequence of the defection of middle-class supporters when von Bülow had manœuvred them into the position of appearing as enemies of national expansion in connection with the international crisis of 1905–6.

Indeed, from the point of the Moroccan crisis which was patched up by the Algeciras Treaty of 1906 the international outlook in Europe had become much more threatening, and at Stuttgart the affairs of the Second International began to be dominated by the threat of war between the great European powers, and especially between Great Britain and Germany — the chief imperialist rivals. Russia was for the time being out of action as a consequence of the defeat at the hands of Japan and of the dislocation caused by the Revolution ; but France and, to a less extent, Great Britain had come to the rescue of Czardom with money for Stolypin's programme of economic development, and the confrontation of forces between the Triple Alliance and the Triple Entente, that was to become actual in 1914, was already foreshadowed. In these circumstances, the Stuttgart Congress was already less concerned than its predecessors with theoretical differences of doctrine and more concerned with the practical question of Socialist action to prevent war, or to face the very difficult situation that would confront its component parties should war actually break out despite its efforts. This question could not of course be dissociated from the dispute about doctrines ; for the issues of war and peace, of nationalism and internationalism, and of reformism and revolutionism were all closely intertwined. But, in face of the war danger, they had all to be approached from a new angle. It was no longer mainly a matter of debating the respective merits of Bernstein's and Kautsky's theories, or of industrial and parliamentary action as means of waging the day-to-day class-struggle, or of winning piecemeal improvements. It had become apparent that international Socialism might be called on at any time to face a great immediate crisis and that the discussions about Revisionism and Reformism had left it without any clear policy to guide its conduct in such an event.

The agenda for the Stuttgart Congress gave a plain indication of the change in the situation which the Socialists had to face. It had been intended that it should deal largely with the problems of the correct relations between the Socialist Parties and the Trade Unions ; but when the time came this issue, though it was debated, was relegated to a secondary position and the main debates turned on the issues of colonialism and war. The Socialists had to make up their minds whether their declared hostility to the capitalist States was so deep as to absolve them from all obligations to defend their national territories if they were attacked, or whether they recognised an obligation of national defence as transcending their opposition to the Governments under whose auspices it would in practice need to be conducted. They had to make up their minds whether they were prepared to co-operate with bourgeois pacifists in attempts to prevent war ; whether they should support bourgeois projects of international arbitration and agreed reduction of armaments ; and whether they should be prepared to assign degrees of guilt to the rival imperialist powers in the event of a threatened or actual conflict. They had to consider whether to distinguish between wars of offence and of defence, and whether to treat the outbreak of a great war as the signal for international proletarian revolution or for a cessation of internal conflicts within each nation. They had also to decide whether they really disapproved of 'colonialism' in all its forms, or were prepared to condone, or even to support, the claims of the 'have-not' powers to a share in the spoils, or advantages, of colonial expansion.

It was a matter of some significance that the Stuttgart Congress met on German soil. On all previous occasions Germany had been regarded as an unsuitable rendezvous for a Socialist international gathering because of the police powers of the German State and of the danger of delegates being arrested and perhaps handed over to their own Governments, and of the proceedings being suppressed by fiat of the authorities if the less accommodating delegates were freely to speak their minds. But by 1907 the Germans were prepared to venture an assembly, not indeed in Prussia, but in the less illiberal atmosphere of Württemberg; and the International Socialist Bureau had made up its mind to take the risk. In the event one delegate, Harry Quelch of the British Social Democratic Federation, did get into trouble with the police and was deported out of Germany despite the protests of the Congress for alleged insulting references to the German Government; but, apart from that one incident, the Congress was unmolested. Indeed, the German authorities may possibly have been not displeased at its proceedings, which seemed to point to the likelihood of a good deal more trouble from the French and Russian than from the German working classes in the event of war.

The main debate at the Stuttgart Congress turned on the question of militarism and war, and ended with the almost unanimous adoption of the celebrated resolution defining the duty of Socialists and of the Socialist movements of the various countries in face of a threatened and of an actual outbreak of war. This near-unanimity was the outcome of the labours of a special sub-commission set up after the Congress had found itself confronted with no fewer than four rival resolutions and with a number of proposed amendments. The four main resolutions emanated respectively from Bebel, on behalf of the Germans, from Vaillant and Jaurès, on behalf of the majority of the Unified French Socialist Party, from Guesde on behalf of the second French group, and from Gustave Hervé on behalf of the extreme anti-patriotic fraction. Hervé's resolution was a short, straightforward incitement to the working classes of all countries to repudiate all forms of 'bourgeois and governmental patriotism, which lyingly asserts the existence of a community

of interests among all the inhabitants of a country'. It called
on the workers to carry on a united struggle against international capitalism, and to refuse to fight except for the establishment of the collectivist or communist system, or for its
defence after it had been established, and it invited every
citizen to respond to any declaration of war, from whatever
source it might come, by the military strike and insurrection.

From a quite different point of view Jules Guesde's resolution expressed opposition to any special campaign against
militarism, as calculated to divert the working class from its
essential task — the taking of political power for the expropriation of the capitalists and the social appropriation of the means
of production. It argued that campaigning specially against
militarism would hamper propaganda and recruitment for
Socialism, and that the only form of anti-militarist campaign
that was not either utopian or dangerous was a campaign for
the organisation of the workers of the world for the destruction
of capitalism. It then went on to declare that, in the meantime,
Socialists should work for the shortening of the period of
military service, and should vote against all credits for the
armed forces, and for the arming of the whole people in substitu-
'tion for standing armies as means of preventing international
conflicts.

The resolution proposed by Vaillant and Jaurès began by
declaring that militarism and imperialism were in effect the
organised armament of the State for keeping the working class
under the economic and political yoke of the capitalist class.
It then proclaimed that one nation could not threaten the
independence of another without attacking that nation, its
working class, and the international working class ; that the
nation attacked and its working class had the imperative duty
of guarding their independence and autonomy against such an
attack, and therewith the right to count on the support of the
working class of all other countries ; and that the purely
defensive anti-militarist policy of the Socialist Party required it
to seek, to this end, the military disarmament of the bourgeoisie
and the arming of the working class through the general
arming of the people. The resolution, in its second part, went
on to lay down international solidarity as the first duty of the
proletarians and Socialists of all nations, to remind them that

they celebrated this solidarity every May Day, and therewith proclaimed, as its first necessary consequence, the maintenance of international peace, and to recall the action taken by the International Socialist Bureau and the Inter-parliamentary Socialist Conference in face of the Russian Revolution and of the help given to Czardom by its imperialist neighbours in quelling it. It then called upon the workers to render these decisions effective by the national and international Socialist organisation of a well-prepared, ordered, and combined action that would in each country, and first of all in the countries affected, direct the entire energy of the working class and of the Socialist Party to the prevention and hindering of war by all means, from parliamentary intervention, public agitation, and popular manifestations to the general strike and to insurrection.

Finally, Bebel's resolution began by asserting that wars between capitalist States were generally the consequence of rivalries in the world market, each State seeking new markets and following a policy of enslaving foreign peoples and confiscating their territories. Wars, it said, were favoured by the prejudices of one people against another, and such prejudices were deliberately fostered among civilised nations in the interests of the ruling classes. Wars were of the essence of capitalism, and would cease only when the capitalist system was brought to an end or when the magnitude of the sacrifices of men and money, called for by the development of military techniques, and the revolt provoked by armaments, drove the peoples to renounce this system. The working class was the natural antagonist of wars, both because it bore the brunt of them and because they were in contradiction to its aim of creating a new economic order based on Socialist conceptions and destined to translate the solidarity of the peoples into reality. The resolution then asserted that it was the duty of all workers, and particularly of their parliamentary representatives, to fight with all their strength against land and sea armaments, stressing the class-character of bourgeois society and the motives which impelled it to maintain national antagonisms. They should refuse all financial support to such policies. Next, the resolution declared in favour of the democratic organisation of the defence system, including all citizens capable of bearing arms, as a real assurance, rendering wars of aggression impossible and furthering the disappearance of national antagonisms. The final paragraph laid down that, should war threaten to break out, the workers and their parliamentary representatives in the countries affected were under an obligation to do all they could to prevent its outbreak by using the means which seemed to them most effective, and, should it break out despite their efforts, to bring it rapidly to an end.

These four resolutions are of interest both in their disagreements and in the points on which they agree. All except Hervé's demanded some sort of citizen army, or armed people, in place of a standing army, and appeared to regard this as a safeguard against war, or at any rate against wars of offence. The British and American delegates objected to this proposal, because of their hostility to any form of conscription. They failed to get it deleted from the resolution finally approved, but received a verbal undertaking that it was not meant to compel them to support compulsory citizen service in their own countries.

The Vaillant-Jaurès resolution, as well as Hervé's, referred to the general strike (in Hervé's case the 'military strike') and to insurrection as possible means of combating war, whereas neither Guesde's resolution nor Bebel's made any mention of either of these weapons — except, in the case of Guesde, to deny their value. Guesde's weapon of last resort was 'social revolution' — not further defined ; but this was not to be directed specifically against war. Bebel's resolution simply spoke of 'doing everything possible', without any specific reference to means, but went out of its way to emphasise twice the particular rôle of the parliamentary representatives of Socialism in opposing war, and thus seemed to imply that the anti-militarist struggle would take mainly a parliamentary form.

Only the Vaillant-Jaurès resolution affirmed the right and the duty of national defence against aggression from without, coupling with it the duty of the workers of other countries to rally to the support of the nation attacked. Only Hervé's resolution explicitly denied these duties. Bebel's implicitly recognised national defence as a duty, and drew a distinction between aggressive and defensive war. Guesde's drew no such distinction.

Bebel's resolution went furthest in asserting the source of

wars to lie mainly in capitalist economic rivalries. Guesde's also stressed the connection between capitalism and war and declared that wars would continue until capitalism had been abolished. The Vaillant-Jaurès resolution was silent on this issue, except that it confirmed the resolutions of previous Congresses, in which the point had been made. Hervé too said nothing about the causes of war, and simply called on the workers to refuse to fight, save in a class-war insurrection.

Next to Hervé's, the Vaillant-Jaurès resolution was the most explicit in its proclamation of international working-class solidarity, though this was implied in Guesde's resolution. Bebel's said nothing about it.

Except Hervé's, none of the resolutions gave very clear guidance to action. The Vaillant-Jaurès resolution recommended all means, without laying particular emphasis on any one. It did not so much recommend the general strike as refuse to rule it out. Bebel's resolution had nothing explicit to say about methods beyond recommending parliamentary opposition. On the other hand, only Bebel's resolution dealt explicitly with the duty of Socialists in the event of war actually occurring despite their efforts; and his only told them 'to act so as to bring it rapidly to an end' — which was by no means clear advice. The Vaillant-Jaurès resolution told them to 'hinder' the war, but it was not clear whether this referred to the situation after, or only before, the actual outbreak.

All four resolutions, then, had serious weaknesses. Hervé's could, in effect, be ruled out as quite impracticable. At the Congress practically no one supported it. Guesde's was of the 'head in the sand' type to be expected from its author : it was of a piece with his refusal to see in the Dreyfus case anything about which Socialists need get excited, or take any action. It was, indeed, the usual Guesdist doctrinaire parody of the Marxist gospel. The Vaillant-Jaurès resolution was notable for its unequivocal affirmation of the duty of national defence — a matter about which the Germans were in full agreement, but preferred to say nothing. Its weakness lay in the fact that, in recommending all methods, it in effect recommended none ; and it was calculated to antagonise the German delegates by the conditional endorsement which it gave to the general strike. Finally, Bebel's resolution had as its central core the assertion that wars arose mainly out of imperialist rivalries, but, having said this, was exceedingly unhelpful about the means to be used in preventing them.

After a long debate, begun by Bebel, who was followed by Hervé, Troclet, Vaillant, Jaurès, Vollmar, Vandervelde, Victor Adler, Rosa Luxemburg, Russell Smart, Franz Weiss of Italy, Branting, Scheu, Costa, Jeppesen of Norway, Gudelevsky of the Argentine, Henriette Roland-Holst, and E. E. Carr of the United States, it was decided to appoint a sub-commission to draw up, if possible, an agreed resolution. This was made up of Vandervelde, as chairman, Bebel and Vollmar (Germany), Adler and Skatula (Austria), Jaurès and Guesde (France), Andreas Scheu and T. Russell Smart (Great Britain), Ferri and Costa (Italy), Rosa Luxemburg, and Bystrenine — the latter for the Social Revolutionaries (Russia), Johann Sigg (Switzerland), and Branting (Sweden). During the debate a message had been received from Karl Liebknecht replying to certain statements made about him by Vollmar and urging strongly the need for special anti-militarist propaganda, including propaganda among the soldiers. Karl Liebknecht was at this time subject to trial for his well-known anti-militarist pamphlet.[1] At the end of the debate Rosa Luxemburg, Lenin, and Martov, on behalf of the Russian Social Democrats, handed in certain amendments to Bebel's resolution. The purport of the more important of these amendments was first to complement Bebel's reference to the source of wars in capitalist economic rivalries by adding a reference to the militarist competition in armaments ; secondly, to stress the need for the education of youth in the ideas of Socialism and fraternity of peoples and in class-consciousness ; and, thirdly, to rewrite Bebel's final paragraph, so as to give much more explicit guidance, in the following terms :

> If a war threatens to break out, it is a duty of the working class in the countries affected, and a duty for their parliamentary representatives, to make every effort to prevent the war by all means which seem to them appropriate — means which vary and develop naturally according to the intensity of the class-struggle and to the political situation in general. Should war none the less break out, it is their duty to

[1] See p. 314.

intervene in order to bring it promptly to an end, and with all their strength to make use of the economic and political crisis created by the war to stir up the deepest strata of the people and precipitate the fall of capitalist domination.

From the unreported debates of the sub-commission emerged the well-known Stuttgart resolution in its final form. It was, as Vandervelde said in introducing it, much too long; for in an attempt to incorporate agreed passages from all the drafts, except Hervé's, and to meet objections it had swollen to an inordinate volume. It began by confirming the resolutions of previous Congresses and then went on to include Bebel's reference to the economic causes of war, with the Russian addition concerning militarist rivalries, and his remarks about nationalist prejudices. It said that wars were of the essence of capitalism and would cease only when it ended, or when the burdens and sacrifices they involved caused the peoples to renounce them. It kept the paragraph about the workers being the chief sufferers by war and its natural antagonists, and the following paragraph about the duty of the workers and their parliamentary representatives to oppose armaments and the money grants required for them . . . and at this point it tacked on the Russian sentence about the education of youth. Then came the paragraph urging the substitution of national militias for standing armies, and the statement that these would serve as a safeguard against aggressive wars.

Next a paragraph was inserted affirming the impracticability of 'shutting up within rigid formulae' the action to be taken, as this would necessarily vary with the occasion and with the background of the different parties. An account was then given of what the proletariat had actually done since the Brussels Congress to combat militarism and war, with particular reference to Anglo-French relations after the Fashoda Incident, to Franco-German relations during the Moroccan crisis, to Austro-Italian relations and to the Trieste Austro-Italian Socialist Conference, to the Swedish Socialists' help to Norway at the time of the separation between the two countries, and to the international aspects of the Russian Revolution of 1905. Attention was drawn to the need for stronger co-ordination by the International of the activities of the national parties and the preliminary paragraphs came to a close by asserting that, under pressure from the proletariat, the serious practice of international arbitration could be substituted for the pitiable approaches to it by the bourgeois Governments, and that in this way the peoples could be given the benefit of general disarmament, so that the immense resources devoured by armaments and wars could be devoted instead to the progress of civilisation.

Last came the two paragraphs laying down the duty of the workers in face of the threat, or of the actual outbreak, of war.

> If a war threatens to break out, it is a duty of the working class in the countries affected, and a duty for their parliamentary representatives, with the aid of the International Bureau as an active and coordinating power, to make every effort to prevent the war by all means which seem to them the most appropriate — means which naturally vary according to the intensity of the class-struggle and to the political situation in general.

> Should war none the less break out, it is their duty to intervene in order to bring it promptly to an end, and with all their strength to make use of the economic and political crisis created by the war to stir up the deepest strata of the people and precipitate the fall of capitalist domination.

Thus, in the final operative paragraphs the Russian Social Democrats got their way, and the parties of the International were formally pledged not merely to do their best to prevent war, but also, should it occur, to do their best to end it at once and to use the occasion for action to bring about the fall of capitalism. In the final resolution nothing was said about the general strike, or about insurrection — the Germans saw to that; but thanks to the Russian addition the prescription for action went a long way beyond the mere parliamentary protests which alone had been explicitly set forth in Bebel's draft. The general strike was not ruled out — it was passed over in silence; and the same can be said of insurrection, which can indeed be regarded as implicit in the final paragraph.

The resolution, in its ultimate shape, seems to have satisfied everybody. Even Hervé voted for it, leaping on a table to mark his enthusiasm. The delegates felt sure that they had done something almost heroic, while stopping short of incommoding the German comrades by any awkward references to insurrection that might have got them into trouble with the German

Government. The remaining proceedings at Stuttgart, however, throw some doubt on the reality of the unanimous endorsement of the main resolution the Congress was called upon to pass. In particular, the debate on the colonial question brought out differences of attitude which were evidently liable to lead to serious trouble in face of an actual threat of war. Van Kol of Holland, acting as *rapporteur* for the Colonial Commission of the Congress, strongly urged the need for a positive Socialist colonial policy, saying that the negative anti-colonialism of the resolutions passed at previous Congresses had been most unhelpful and that Socialists were required in practice to recognise the unavoidable existence of colonial empires — which, he said, had existed throughout human history — and to bring forward concrete proposals for improved treatment of the natives, development of natural resources, and the utilisation of these resources in the service of the whole human race. He enquired of the opponents of colonialism whether they were truly prepared, as things were, to do without the resources of the colonies, however much these might be needed by their peoples. He quoted Bebel as saying that there was nothing wrong in colonial development as such,[1] and referred to the success of the Dutch Socialists in bringing about improvements in the conditions of the natives.

In opposition to this view, Georg Ledebour, as spokesman for the minority of the Commission, attacked colonialism root and branch and stressed the absurdity of asking the imperialist powers to become the exponents of a policy favourable to native interests. This issue sharply divided the Germans, Eduard David and Bernstein, among others, coming forward in support of van Kol. When the matter came to a vote in the full Congress, the minority narrowly defeated the majority — by 127 votes to 108 — and the International thus went on record against colonialism, declaring that 'capitalist colonial policy, by its very essence, necessarily leads to enslavement, forced labour, and the destruction of the native peoples under the colonial régime'. It declared that the 'civilising' mission proclaimed by capitalist society was but a pretext to cover its thirst for exploitation and conquest, and that, far from expanding the productive powers of the colonies, it destroyed their

[1] At the Amsterdam Congress, I think.

natural riches by the slavery and poverty to which it reduced their peoples. The resolution said that colonialism increased the burden of armaments and the danger of wars ; and it called upon Socialists in all Parliaments to offer unremitting opposition to the serfdom and exploitation prevalent in all existing colonies, to demand reforms to improve native conditions, to be vigilant on behalf of native rights, and to work, by all available means, for the education of the native peoples for independence.

The resolution, in this intransigent form, was finally adopted without dissent, only the Dutch abstaining ; but it represented a serious defeat for the colonialists. In the voting on the amendment, the defeated side included the Germans (who voted solid despite sharp disagreement), the Dutch, the Danes, the Austrians, the Swedes, the Belgians, and the South Africans. On the winning side were the Russians, the Poles, the Hungarians, the Serbs, the Bulgarians and the Rumanians, the Spaniards, the Australians, the Japanese, the Americans, the Argentinians, the Finns, and the Norwegians. The French, the British, and the Italians were divided. The Swiss abstained.

These debates showed a dangerously close division of opinion. The crucial question was whether the Congress should go on record as opposing colonialism in principle, or should say that, while opposing the actual colonial policies of the imperialist powers, it did not 'condemn in principle and for all time all colonial policy, which might, under a Socialist régime — be a task of civilisation'. David wished to go a good deal further, and to lay down that 'the Congress, affirming that Socialism needs the productive powers of the entire world, which are destined to be placed at the service of humanity, and to raise the peoples of all colours and languages to the highest culture, sees in the colonialist idea envisaged in this connection an integral element in the universal aims of civilisation which the Socialist movement pursues'. But David's proposal found only a few supporters : the majority of the Commission wished only to stop short of a complete condemnation of colonialism in all its forms.

Three other Reports remained to be dealt with at the Stuttgart Congress — on the relations between Socialist Parties and Trade Unions, on Women's Questions, and on Migration. The debate on the relations between the Parties and the

Trade Unions turned formally, for the most part, on the question whether there should or should not be organic links between the two central organisations in each country. Apart from a few dissentients led by Daniel De Leon, who insisted on the priority of the economic over the political struggle, there was general agreement that the Trade Unions must be free to conduct the day-to-day economic struggle without interference from the Party, and that the Party must have a similar autonomy in the political field. It was also agreed that while it was necessary for the Trade Unions to rise above corporate craft egoism and to conduct their affairs in the spirit of the class-struggle, unity was indispensable in the economic field and it was therefore imprudent to impose any political tests upon Trade Union membership or to insist on Trade Unionists belonging to the Party as individuals. At the same time, some delegations, including the Belgians and the Swedes, favoured a system under which the Trade Unions were collectively affiliated to the Party, whereas others — especially the Germans — were opposed to such formal affiliation and believed in close *de facto* personal co-operation without formal links. The majority of the French delegation could not accept either of these solutions, and held to the principle of complete independence of the Trade Unions in accordance with the policy of the Confédération Générale du Travail. They too believed in the need for the Trade Unions and the Party to work together for Socialism, but accepted that in France this had to be done in such a way as to respect the Syndicalist outlook of the C.G.T.

Behind these differences there lurked a deeper difference concerning the functions of Trade Unionism. Louis de Brouckère of Belgium, who presented the report on the whole question, argued that, while both Parties and Trade Unions had separate tasks of their own which they must autonomously direct, there was also between them a large and growing sphere of action which could not be assigned exclusively to either, and that this common sphere included particularly the grand task of creating a Socialist Society. This view was immediately attacked by the Germans and Austrians, who contended that the Trade Unions had to do only with the economic struggle, and that the establishment of Socialism was essentially a matter for the Party. On this issue, of course, the French majority was at one with de Brouckère. To a great extent, what the disputants were arguing about was the general strike, though other matters came in as well. The German Trade Unions had just rejected the general strike as a Trade Union method at their own Congress, and had laid down that, if it were to be used at all, the responsibility for calling it must rest with the Party and not with the Trade Unions, on the ground that it was essentially 'political'. The French majority, on the other hand, with the Guesdists dissenting, regarded the general strike as an economic as well as a political weapon, and the C.G.T. held that its use in both aspects came within its legitimate sphere. De Brouckère, faced with the refusal of the Germans and Austrians to accept his draft, withdrew the controversial passages, and compromised on an innocuous resolution which stressed the need for permeating the Trade Unions with the spirit of Socialism, without going so far as to prevent their unity, and pronounced in favour of Trade Union autonomy in the economic field, and for cordial relations between the Party and the Trade Unions, without declaring either for or against any form of organic unity. On this basis an agreed resolution (except for the De Leonites) was passed, after the French majority had read a declaration expressing their adherence to the principle of complete Trade Union independence. But the differences remained, not only between the French and the rest, but also between the Germans and the Belgians; and the resolution did more to cover up a fundamental divergence than to achieve any real agreement. For the vital question at issue was whether Socialism was essentially a matter for the Party alone, and Trade Unionism only a means of protecting working-class interests under capitalism, or whether Party and Trade Unions were to be regarded as equal partners in the building of a Socialist society.

The Stuttgart debate on the question of Votes for Women took place as the sequel to an International Socialist Women's Conference which prepared a resolution for the full Congress. The matter at issue was not whether women should have votes — on that all delegations were agreed and previous Congresses had passed unequivocal resolutions. The main question was whether the Parties of the International should launch within each country campaigns for Universal Suffrage, including Votes for Women, or whether it was legitimate, on grounds of tactics, to give priority, as the Austrians had just done in a notable campaign, to the demand for Manhood Suffrage. There was also the secondary question whether proposals to confer limited voting rights on women, subject to property or other qualifications, should be accepted as an instalment of social justice or rejected as favouring the female bourgeoisie against the working women. On this latter issue all except a section of the British delegation favoured opposition to all proposals for a limited franchise. Clara Zetkin, who introduced the resolution passed at the Women's Conference and also later the agreed resolution of the Commission, demanded that in future any Socialist Party conducting a campaign for franchise reform should claim the vote for women as well as for men, and on identical terms. Victor Adler defended the action of the Austrian Party in not advancing this claim in its recent campaign ; and the Congress accepted an amendment recognising that it was impracticable to fix a definite date for the beginning of a general campaign for franchise reform, but insisting that, when such a campaign was launched, the demand should be made on behalf of both sexes and on a universal basis.

Finally, the Stuttgart Congress dealt with the problem of immigration. The main difficulty in this connection arose out of the wish of the Australians, the one South African, and some of the Americans to exclude coloured immigrants on the ground that they would be used to bring down the living-standards of white workers. The other delegations, while they appreciated the force of this argument, were not prepared to accept any exclusion of immigrants on grounds of race or colour. They were, however, quite prepared to take a stand against the deliberate importation of bodies of immigrants for the purpose of undermining the standards of living of the workers in the countries of immigration, and to press for public regulation of immigration with this end in view, as well as for the improvement of conditions on vessels carrying migrants and for the prevention of misleading propaganda in favour of immigration by shipping companies and commercial agencies. The resolution carried by the Congress stressed the need for the education and organisation of immigrant workers and for the extension to them of the same wages, working conditions, and social and economic rights as were accorded to indigenous workers.

It will be seen that the Stuttgart Congress covered a wide field and got through a great deal of work. No part of its labours, however, greatly advanced matters from the standpoint of international Socialist policy, except the one resolution dealing with the problem of militarism and war. On that question the Congress did arrive at a momentous agreement, though when in 1914 the time came for acting on its brave words, its apparent unanimity proved to be void of both the will and the power to act up to its declarations. It had, in effect, allowed Rosa Luxemburg and Lenin to commit it to a great deal more than it was really prepared to do. In transforming the letter of Bebel's original resolution the Russian leaders had no power to transform the real attitudes of the Parties which nominally endorsed their policy.

(iv) 1910 — COPENHAGEN

The International Socialist Congress that met in Copenhagen in 1910 was notable chiefly for the recurrence of the question of the general strike against war, which the Germans at any rate hoped they had finally disposed of at Stuttgart. The agenda had been arranged to give pride of place to a discussion of relations between the Socialist Parties and the Co-operative movement, parallel to the Stuttgart discussion of relations with the Trade Unions. It had also been decided to give an important place to the consideration of the whole question of industrial and social legislation, including the provision to be made for the unemployed. These were the main new subjects on the agenda. In addition, there were to be debates on the steps taken and to be taken to carry out the terms of the Stuttgart resolution on militarism and war; and the question of the Trade Unions was to be further considered with a view to the implementation of the recommendations made at Stuttgart. There was also an exceptionally large crop of resolutions dealing with particular matters sent in by affiliated parties or groups; and the Copenhagen Congress divided itself into five Commissions, one for each of the main issues and one to deal with the miscellaneous resolutions that had been received. As at Stuttgart the Congress was preceded by a special Women's

Conference and by a meeting of the Socialist Interparliamentary Commission. Of the outstanding personalities of the International, August Bebel was absent, seriously ill; and the leadership of the German delegation was shared between Ebert and Legien.

Between Stuttgart and Copenhagen a good deal had happened. The great powers had continued to increase their armaments, and in particular the race between Great Britain and Germany in naval armaments had developed to a serious extent. The Moroccan crisis had bubbled up again : there had been 'incidents' between France and Germany, which were referred to the Hague Court; and the Spaniards had engaged in a full-scale colonial war. There had also been continued fighting in the areas under French control. In Eastern Europe, the Austrians had provoked a crisis by annexing Bosnia and Herzegovina; and the rivalries of Russia, Austria-Hungary, and Germany in the Near East had become more menacing. In Russia, French help and Stolypin's policy of economic development had re-established the Czar's authority for the time being; but the revolutionary forces were gathering for a fresh attempt. Turkey and Persia had experienced actual revolutions; and in China the revolution was on the eve of breaking out.

In the world of Labour the outstanding event had been the Swedish general strike of 1909, in which the Swedish Trade Unions had been defeated by the consolidated power of the large capitalist concerns. There was much discontent at the inadequacy of the help given to the Swedes in their struggle, especially by the British Trade Unions; and a large part of the discussion of Trade Union matters at Copenhagen was devoted to considering how the Trade Union movements of the various countries could be not only consolidated internally but also put in a position to help one another more effectively in big industrial disputes. Much was said about the growth of capitalist trusts and combines, national and international, and about the growing tendency of the capitalists to create powerful central organisations for combating the Trade Unions. These were regarded as signs of the increasing intensity of the class-struggle and as calling for counter-measures from the Trade Union side. There was dissatisfaction with the International Trade Union

Secretariat, as being no more than an information bureau and as failing to take any steps towards the international consolidation of the industrial forces of Labour. It was not, however, easy to see what the Socialist International could do to improve the position, unless the Trade Union International was prepared to act; and of that there appeared to be scant prospect in view of the sharp division of opinion between the Germans and the French concerning the functions of Trade Unions and the methods it was proper for them to employ. There was also serious trouble over Trade Union affairs in Austria,[1] where a section of the Czechs had insisted on setting up their own national Trade Union movement, breaking away from the multi-national Trade Union structure which the Austrians had so far maintained, even after their Socialist Party had begun to break up into a series of national Parties representing the various nationalities of the Austrian Empire. Despite Antonín Němec's impassioned pleas on behalf of the Czechs' independence, in Trade Union as well as in political affairs, the Copenhagen Congress came down practically solidly against him, with a strong denunciation of all attempts to break up the Trade Unions within a State, however diversified, into separate national movements. Any such divisions, it was argued, would disastrously weaken the economic position of the workers in their day-to-day struggles; but, over and above this, there was a powerful sentiment against anything that would tend to strengthen the hold of nationalism in the working-class movement.

The debates on the Trade Union question had no substantial result. Once more, the delegates put on record their belief that there should be, in each country, only one Trade Union movement, as well as but a single party, to stand as the champion of working-class unity. They told the International Socialist Bureau to give any help it could in promoting national and international Trade Union consolidation; but nothing much came of the Bureau's efforts. Undoubtedly, the Socialists were disposed to exaggerate the extent of consolidation on the employers' side, in respect of both anti-Trade Union combination and trustification. It was a firm conviction among the German orthodox leaders — Kautsky above all — that capitalist

[1] See p. 533.

trustification and large-scale enterprise were rapidly preparing the way for Socialism ; and the Socialists were apt to speak at one moment of the development of international capitalism as a growing menace to the workers' claims and at the next of the increasing rivalries between national capitalist groups as the principal danger to world peace.

The full-dress discussion at Copenhagen of the relations between the Socialist Parties and the Co-operative movement was also somewhat inconclusive. The main issue was whether the Socialists should set to work to build up their own partisan Co-operative Societies as agencies for helping the Trade Unions in their industrial struggles and the Socialist Parties by providing meeting places and financial help. If this were done, as it was to a great extent in Belgium, in Northern France, and in parts of Italy, there were bound to be rival Co-operative Societies conducted under other auspices, Christian, Liberal, or neutral. This the Congress was not prepared to face. It seemed clear to most of the delegates that, just as there should be one unified Socialist Party and one comprehensive Trade Union movement, so there should be in each country a single Co-operative movement open to all as the expression of working-class unity. The Socialists wanted this movement to be animated by Socialist ideas, or at any rate by the spirit of class-struggle. They wanted it to be autonomous, in the same way as they accepted the need for Trade Union autonomy in the economic field ; but they also wanted it to act in close harmony with both the Parties and the Trade Unions in the various countries. They were, in effect, trying to have matters both ways — to prevent the growth of Christian and other rival Co-operative movements, and yet to make the unified Co-operative movement an ally in the working-class campaign.

This, of course, could not really be done. The Belgians, and those who thought with them, were no more prepared to give up their Socialist Co-operative Societies than their Socialist Trade Unions ; and in France the Guesdists were strong believers in the virtue of Socialist Co-operation. On the other side, the advocates of unity were no less determined. There was, however, at the time, no possibility of Co-operative unity except on a basis of political neutrality, of a kind inconsistent with the Socialist claim that the Co-operatives should regard themselves as the partners of Socialism and Trade Unionism in a common working-class struggle. Here again, the Germans had their distinctive point of view. Just as they took a strictly limited view of the functions of Trade Unionism, they tended to regard Co-operation as a movement concerned with immediate working-class interests rather than with the task of transforming society — a function which they reserved exclusively for the Social Democratic Party. They were thus able to renounce the ambition to make the Co-operatives explicitly Socialist, or to make any political use of them, though they did wish to employ them on occasion as allies of the Trade Unions in industrial disputes. In practice, the German Co-operative Societies consisted largely of supporters of the Social Democratic Party, and relations with them were good. This broadly satisfied the German Socialists ; and, as usual, they were able, with von Elm[1] as their chief spokesman, to impress their view on the Congress to the extent of ensuring that nothing inconsistent with it should appear in the resolution finally passed.

What has been said in the preceding paragraph applies mainly to Consumers' Co-operation, in which the delegates were mostly interested. In relation to Producers' and to Agricultural Co-operation the situation was somewhat different. With the Agricultural Co-operatives, still mainly concerned with the provision of credit, the Socialists had very little contact ; and their position was hardly discussed. Producers' Co-operation was of much closer concern to the Trade Unions, if not to the Socialist Parties. In many countries — and especially in France and Italy — there was a substantial Producers' Co-operative movement, in many cases closely allied to the Trade Unions and including a number of societies conducted under Trade Union auspices. In this field, it was much less likely that rival movements would appear on any considerable scale under other auspices ; and the problem of unity was therefore of less importance. But the question of Producers' Co-operation was not much considered at Copenhagen : it was mainly Consumers' Co-operation that the Congress had in mind.

It is true that the resolution passed at Copenhagen included among the functions assigned to the Co-operative movement that of 'educating the workers for the fully independent

[1] See p. 313.

management of their own affairs, and thus helping them to prepare the democratisation and socialisation of the powers of exchange and production'. This clause in the resolution brought Lenin to his feet with an amendment proposing that recognition should be given to the socialising and democratising rôle of the Co-operatives only as something that would develop after the expropriation of the capitalists. Lenin's proposal was rejected by a large majority. The resolution in its final form eliminated Guesde's hostile criticisms of 'neutral' Co-operation: it also eliminated all direct reference to Producers' Co-operation and to Agricultural Co-operation, to which the French had wished to give special recognition. After asserting the insufficiency of Co-operation by itself to realise the aim of Socialism — the collective ownership of the means of production — and warning Socialists against Co-operators who took the opposite view, the final resolution was devoted chiefly to urging that trading surpluses should not all be distributed in dividends on purchases, but should be devoted in part to developing Co-operative production and to education, and to stressing the need for agreement with the Trade Unions concerning Co-operative wages and conditions. It then laid down that it was the affair of the various Co-operative Societies in each country to decide whether and how far to give direct help out of their resources to the political and Trade Union movements. All Socialists and Trade Unionists were urged to take an active part in the Co-operative movement 'in order to develop the spirit of Socialism within it and to prevent the Co-operative Societies from defaulting on their task of working-class education and solidarity'.

In the Commission on Industrial and Social Legislation discussion began with the question of unemployment. It was opened by Molkenbuhr in a remarkably reactionary speech, in the course of which, while advocating a state system of unemployment relief, he rejected the idea of the Right to Work. This provoked protests from Ramsay MacDonald and Harry Quelch; but Braun of Austria supported Molkenbuhr by saying that the Right to Work at fair wages was a demand unrealisable under capitalism. 'Not the Right to Work, but the suppression of capitalism, will cause unemployment to disappear.' There was a good deal of argument about the best way of meeting the cost of maintaining the unemployed, some arguing that it ought to be borne wholly by the employers, in whose interest the 'reserves of labour' were kept idle, while others wished a part or the whole of the cost to fall upon general taxation. The final resolution demanded 'from the public authorities a general system of compulsory assurance, the administration of which should be entrusted to the workers' organisations and the costs borne by the proprietors of the means of production'. It also called for exact and regular statistics of unemployment ; for an adequate development of public works, with standard wages for those employed on them ; for special subsidies to unemployment funds at periods of crisis ; for the retention of full political rights by those receiving benefit ; for the establishment of employment exchanges conducted either by the Trade Unions or jointly with the employers ; for the reduction of hours of labour by law ; and for subsidies to Trade Union unemployment benefits pending the establishment of a general compulsory system. In the course of the discussion it was proposed that public works should be so timed and distributed as to offset fluctuations in the demand for labour.

From unemployment the same Commission went on to discuss industrial and social legislation in general. The resolution stressed the inadequacy of existing legislation in all countries, and proceeded to formulate a series of demands. These included the legal eight hours' day ; the prohibition of child labour under 14 years and of night work, save in special cases ; a continuous rest period of at least 36 hours each week ; the abolition of truck ; the assurance of the right of combination ; and inspection of both industrial and agricultural work with the collaboration of representatives of the workers. The resolution then dwelt on the meagreness of the results achieved through the governmental conferences on international labour legislation, and went on to demand the establishment in all countries of 'institutions, assuring adequate means of subsistence to the sick, the injured, the incapacitated and the aged, adequate help to women before and after childbirth and to their infants, and protection for widows and orphans as well as for the unemployed against destitution'. Attention was then drawn to the specially unprotected state of the workers in agriculture and forestry. Finally, the workers in every branch of economic activity were adjured to conduct ceaseless propaganda and to establish powerful political and economic organisations in order to overcome the resistance of the possessing classes to the enactment of effective legislation for the protection of their rights.

All this was straightforward Reformism, uninhibited by fears of adding to the powers of the capitalist State. Of course, there was nothing new in the demands themselves, many of which had formed part of the programme of the International since its inception. Moreover, their advocacy was still conjoined with assertions that they could never be fully achieved while capitalism remained in being. There was, nevertheless, a noticeable shift in emphasis. The spokesmen of the International were thinking more in terms of their immediate demands upon capitalism for reforms, and a good deal less in terms of revolutionary hostility to the capitalist State. At any rate, this was the case with the Germans, though hardly with the French. It was somewhat curious to find the British more critical than the Germans appeared to be of the dangers of gifts proffered by bourgeois Governments.

We come now to the most important debate of the Copenhagen Congress, dealing with the problem of war. The discussion was meant to turn chiefly on the positive steps to be taken to follow up the resolution passed at Stuttgart, and particularly on the attitude to be adopted towards arbitration and disarmament. It is worthy of note that at Copenhagen there was overwhelming support for the demand that all disputes between States should be referred to international arbitration and that standing machinery for this purpose should be set up. There was also general agreement that the International should press, both through its parliamentary representatives and by mass agitation, for an agreed reduction of armaments by the great powers. Much was also said about the need, while relying chiefly upon the working-class movement, to make use of such support as could be found among the bourgeoisie for these proposals. Special stress was laid on the need to bring about an agreed reduction of naval armaments — primarily between Great Britain and Germany ; and the Germans, in a special report to the Congress, gave an account of their challenge on this matter in the Reichstag, and of the rejection by the German Government of Asquith's proposal of a conference on the question of reducing naval expenditure. As against this German refusal, many delegates set the refusal of Great Britain to renounce the right of seizure of merchant vessels in time of war ; and the Congress showed itself a strong supporter of the abandonment of this claim. The Italians, whose spokesman was Morgari, pressed for concentration on a single issue, and tried to persuade the Congress to adopt a resolution calling upon all the parliamentary Socialist Parties to. propose in their several Parliaments a reduction of all armaments by 50 per cent, the appeal to be backed up by popular demonstrations and to be repeated annually until it achieved success. The delegates, however, rejected this plan.

The great disagreement arose on the amendment moved jointly by Vaillant and Keir Hardie, with the support of the British Labour Party as well as of the I.L.P. and the French Socialist Party. This amendment ran as follows :

> Among all the means to be used to prevent and hinder war the Congress considers as particularly effective the general strike of workers, especially in the industries which supply the instruments of war (arms, munitions, transport, etc.), as well as popular agitation and action in their most active forms.

This raising afresh of the issue of the general strike was annoying for those who had hoped it had been finally disposed of at Stuttgart. Keir Hardie, in his opening speech, made it clear that he was not proposing unilateral action by the workers of a single country, and that what he was envisaging was a simultaneous stoppage by the workers in the belligerent countries. He also stated that he was concerned not with a general strike of all workers, but rather in the first instance with a stopping of war supplies by a refusal to produce munitions or to transport either troops or equipment. He said nothing about the kind of strike he advocated being the prelude to insurrection, nor did he speak as if he had anything of this sort in mind. In illustrating his argument he said that a strike of the British coal-miners would suffice by itself to bring warlike activities to a stand. His proposal in this modified form was no more pleasing to the opponents of the general strike than the more extreme projects of the French or of Rosa Luxemburg. Ledebour, though he belonged to the German left, was no more prepared to consider it than Legien. The German view, supported by a number of other delegations, was that nothing must be included in a resolution of the Congress unless it commanded something near to general assent, as the Congress had no authority to issue orders to the national parties without their consent. The course of the discussion, however, made it plain that the Hardie-Vaillant amendment could not be rejected outright without causing a great deal of discontent; and Émile Vandervelde presently came forward with a proposal that it should be held over for further consideration at a subsequent Congress. The opposition accepted this, and the main resolution was carried unanimously, without any reference to strike action as a means of preventing war. There were, however, objections even to this compromise, though in the end the objectors were persuaded to give way. German and Austrian delegates argued that to make any reference to strike action in face of war, even by mentioning it as a matter which the International had undertaken to consider, might lead to prosecution of the Social Democratic Parties of those countries for treasonable practices and might give the Governments an opportunity to suppress them and to confiscate their resources. The Social Democratic leaders were by no means prepared to face such a crisis in connection with the policy to which they were altogether opposed; but they were finally induced to accept the view that a mere undertaking to consider the question at a future Congress could hardly bring these perils upon them, especially in view of the fact that it had actually been debated already on more than one occasion. They consented reluctantly to Vandervelde's suggestion, not with any intention of modifying their opposition to the Hardie-Vaillant proposal, but because they did not want to drive the French and British delegates into pursuing it independently of the International.

Shorn of any reference to strike action, the resolution passed at Copenhagen put the main duty of combating war on the Socialists in the various Parliaments. It called upon them to vote against all military and naval appropriations, to demand the acceptance of compulsory arbitration in all international disputes, to work for general disarmament and, as a step towards it, for conventions limiting naval armaments and abolishing the right to seize merchant vessels, for the abolition of secret diplomacy and the publication of all international treaties, present and future, and, finally, for the autonomy of all peoples and their defence against all warlike attacks and all oppression. Most of this was almost identical with the pro-grammes of non-Socialist peace movements, except perhaps the final recommendation about autonomy for all peoples.

The Copenhagen resolution then proceeded to reaffirm the two key paragraphs of the Stuttgart resolution, defining the duty of the working class in face of the threat and of the actual outbreak of war. It instructed the International Socialist Bureau to promote common action between the parties of the countries concerned in any threat of war and, should there be delay or hesitation by any such party, to convene an emergency meeting of the Bureau and the Inter-parliamentary Commission.

Having disposed of this issue, the Copenhagen Congress had still to deal with a number of resolutions mostly arising out of recent events. It passed a strong resolution demanding the abolition of the death penalty and accusing the bourgeois parties of having abandoned the campaign against it and of invoking it to an increasing extent as a weapon against the workers in the class-struggle. In connection with this, it also passed a resolu-tion protesting against recent violations of the right of asylum, above all by Russia, but also by other countries, including Great Britain. It protested against the behaviour of the oligarchy in the Argentine in falsifying the operation of universal suffrage and stirring up 'factional revolts' in the interests of native and foreign capitalism. It condemned in strong terms the persecution of Socialists in Japan. It recorded its deep sympathy with the Spanish Socialists and with the workers of Catalonia for the barbarous repression they had suffered on account of their opposition to the Moroccan adventure, pro-tested strongly against the execution of Ferrer, and congratu-lated Iglesias on his election to the Cortes. It vigorously condemned the repressive policy towards Trade Unions of the Young Turks, welcomed the beginnings of a Socialist movement in Turkey, and called for radical democratic reforms in the Balkan countries and for a close understanding between them as the best means of combating the capitalist colonial policies which the great powers were pursuing in the Balkan region. It severely condemned the oppressive policy of the Russian Government in Finland, and accused the great powers of cynical support for Czarism in its violation of the pledges given to the Finns. Finally, it accused the Russian Government of armed intervention against the Persian Revolution, and also in Turkey, and called on the European Socialist Parties to use every means in their power to put a stop to the reactionary proceedings of Czarism.

This crop of resolutions is enough to show how widespread by 1910 were the conflicts with which the International felt itself to be intimately concerned. It was also conscious that the mere passing of resolutions of protest did not greatly advance matters, and that its power to induce even the parliamentary Socialist Parties to act energetically on its decisions was small. Each country was apt to be preoccupied with its own affairs and to be reluctant to take up issues which were felt to be unlikely to arouse much popular support, or even liable to antagonise it. Accordingly, the Copenhagen Congress put on record its view of the duty falling on the national parties in respect of Congress resolutions, in the following terms :

> The Congress, recognising that it would be difficult to formulate a model instruction for the carrying out of the resolutions of International Congresses, declares that it is necessary to leave to the national parties the power to choose the form of action and the opportune moment.
>
> It nevertheless insists strongly on the parties' duty to do their utmost to carry out the resolutions of International Congresses.
>
> The International Socialist Bureau will prepare, before each International Congress, a report giving an account of the action taken by the national parties to carry out the resolutions of the Congresses.

The Copenhagen Congress, taken as a whole, clearly meant a move towards the right. Although it reaffirmed the essential clauses of the Stuttgart resolution on war, it did nothing to clarify them or to indicate that there was any real intention of acting upon them beyond parliamentary protests. It came much nearer than the Stuttgart Congress had done to identifying itself with the bourgeois Peace movement; and its discussions on industrial and social legislation and on unemployment had a markedly more reformist tone than those at earlier Congresses. It did little towards defining a clear policy towards the Co-operative movement ; and in its resumed discussion on Trade Unionism and on Socialist politics it did no more than reassert its belief in the need for a single Party and a single Trade Union movement in each country. To the student of its proceedings forty-five years after the event, it gives the impression of a movement conscious of being faced with a mounting crisis in many parts of the world and highly uncertain of its power to confront the situation with success. Despite brave words, it was already clear in 1910 that, should the threatened European War break out, no effective opposition was to be expected from the German Socialists, though they would in all probability do their best to carry out the policy of the International up to the point of the actual outbreak. The attitude of the French and of the British was still more difficult to foresee. But in the industrial field the militancy of the French Trade Unions had already passed its peak, and in Great Britain it was a moot point whether Keir Hardie enjoyed enough popular backing to make his anti-war policy effective. Already Blatchford and Hyndman had fallen foul of the main body of British Socialists and had begun crusading for armament against the German menace ; and though the Labour Party appeared to be on Hardie's side, the extent of his backing among the Trade Unions was, to say the least, doubtful. It was not difficult to foresee, even in 1910, that, if war did come, the International would collapse ; but there was still some hope that its influence might count for something in staving off the danger.

(v) 1912 — BÂLE

The emergency Socialist Congress which met at Bâle in November 1912 was in reality not so much a Congress as a demonstration. The 555 delegates who assembled for it came, not to argue, but to present a united Socialist front against war. The occasion was the actual outbreak of war in the Balkans, where Bulgaria, Serbia, Greece, and Montenegro had combined their forces to destroy what was left of the Turkish Empire in Europe and to partition it among themselves. By the time the Congress met, the outcome of the war was already decided. The Turkish forces had been routed in Thrace by the Bulgarians, in Macedonia by Serbs, Bulgarians, and Montenegrins in combination and, from the west, by the Greeks, whose navy had made it impossible for the Turks to reinforce their armies of occupation with troops from Anatolia. The process of partitioning the provinces of European Turkey among the victors was already well on the way.

The war had been waged without direct intervention by any of the major European powers. But these powers would certainly not disinterest themselves in the settlement, and there remained the danger of war spreading if any of them considered its interests seriously threatened. The fear of this was uppermost in the minds of the delegates at Bâle and gave them a strong concern in working for a settlement that would allow the peoples of the Balkan States to live together on friendly terms in the future. The Socialist leaders realised that the best hope of preventing the turmoil in the Balkans from opening the way to intervention by rival great powers pursuing their several interests lay in persuading the Balkan countries to join hands in a common federation, and to sink their mutual enmities in a united resistance to encroachment by any outside power. At an earlier stage, before the war actually broke out, the International had been pressing federation on the Balkan States, and urging them to oppose the war policy of their Governments for fear of stirring up a general conflagration; and Sakasov, the leader of the 'Broad' Socialist Party in Bulgaria, had from the first taken a courageous line against the Bulgarian expansionists, and had made himself the champion of the policy of Balkan Federation. In all the Balkan States the Socialists were far too weak to exert any significant influence on the course of events : they could only protest — and even protest was very dangerous in face of the ebullition of popular nationalism.

Vandervelde, who presided over the International Socialist Bureau, was ill at the time of the Bâle Congress, and his place in the chair was taken by Édouard Anseele. With that exception, the Congress was a gathering of all the talents — an occasion for eloquent speech-making, in which all the leading orators took part. The war resolution passed at Stuttgart and reaffirmed at Copenhagen was passed yet again, with every sign of enthusiasm ; and the delegates were told that every Socialist Party had acted up to it by making vigorous pronouncements in favour of peace and by doing its utmost to prevent the war from spreading. The Congress told them to go on with the good work, using 'all appropriate means'. It asserted that 'the governing-class fear of proletarian revolution has been an essential safeguard of peace' — by which was presumably meant that it had contributed to prevent the great powers from intervening actively in the conflict. It can reasonably be doubted whether this fear in fact counted for a great deal ; but it was encouraging for the Socialists to believe that it had. Naturally, in view of the weakness of the working-class movements in the Balkan countries there had been no question of their attempting to stop the war by strike action or insurrection ; and no one had suggested that the workers of other countries should strike in order to compel them to make peace or to cut off supplies. All the International could do was to adjure the Socialists of France, Germany, and Great Britain to take a strong line in order to prevent their Governments from giving any help to either Austria or Russia — the two powers that were obviously the most likely to intervene in the conflict. No Socialist really wanted to prevent the Balkan States from carving up European Turkey, or regretted the collapse of the Turkish resistance. What the Socialists wanted was to prevent the Balkan War from being turned into a general European War. Although the most obvious danger was that Austria and Russia might become directly involved, the greatest fear in the Socialists' minds was that, if this occurred, France, Great Britain and Germany would be drawn in. Most of all did they fear that the effect of Anglo-German rivalry might be to bring in these two on opposite sides ; and the Congress accordingly called on the British and German Socialists to make common cause in order to bring about a *détente* between these two.

The Balkan struggle was still in its first phase when the Bâle Congress met. Only after it had dispersed did the victors fall out over the distribution of the spoils and, instead of establishing the Balkan Federation favoured by the International, fly at one another's throats in the Second Balkan War of 1913. Even then, direct intervention by the great powers did not occur. Peace was made, with Serbia, Montenegro, and Greece, reinforced by Rumania, despoiling the Bulgarians of a part of the fruits of victory and allowing the Turks to regain a little of what they had lost. But though world war was staved off in 1912 and 1913, the respite was brief, and it is doubtful if the Socialist stand for peace had much to do with procuring it. The Socialist Parties, both in and outside Parliament, did their best in the way of protests and demonstrations ; but they had in plain truth no power to avert the disaster. In the western countries they had neither the power nor the will to prevent war by the only means that could have prevented it — revolution ; and even in Russia the Revolution came, not to prevent war, but as its aftermath.

(vi) 1914 — VIENNA AND PARIS. THE COLLAPSE OF THE SECOND INTERNATIONAL

A full Congress of the Socialist International was due to assemble in Vienna in August 1914. But on June 28th the Archduke Franz Ferdinand, heir to the Austrian throne, was assassinated at Sarajevo, the capital of Bosnia. After various diplomatic comings and goings, the Austrian Government, on July 23rd, delivered to Serbia an ultimatum in terms so extreme as to exclude the possibility of its acceptance ; and five days later the ultimatum was followed by a declaration of war. The Austrians would not have acted as they did without assurance of support from Germany should the Russians come to Serbia's aid — as they were practically bound to do. If Germany joined Austria-Hungary against Russia, it was hardly possible for France to stay out ; and France in turn would expect Great Britain to come to its aid. In fact, on August 1st, Germany declared war on Russia and, the following day, sent an ultimatum to the Belgian Government demanding permission for the German army to march through Belgium for the invasion of France. The Belgians, standing on their guaranteed neutrality and reinforced by an understanding with France and Great Britain, refused. The German Government thereupon declared war on France, on August 3rd, and launched its invading force on Belgian territory. On the following day,

August 4th, Great Britain, on the plea that Belgian neutrality had been violated, declared war on Germany. On the 5th Austria-Hungary declared war on Russia; France, on the 10th, declared war on Austria-Hungary; and Great Britain followed suit two days later. The Germans had entered Belgium on August 4th, and British troops had begun to land in France on the 9th. The Austrians invaded Serbia on the 13th, and the Russians East Prussia on the 16th. On the 20th the Germans occupied Brussels, and on the 26th began the battle of Tannenberg, in which they decisively defeated the Russians. The Austrians were temporarily thrown back in Serbia; but by September 5th the Germans were within ten miles of Paris, only to be halted there just in time. The great war had begun on many fronts; and the international Socialist movement, instead of making any concerted attempt to stop it, had been broken into warring fragments.

Before the actual outbreak, the Vienna Congress of the International had been first transferred to Paris and then definitely abandoned. But on July 15th and 16th a special Congress of the French Socialist Party met in Paris and was attended by a number of leaders from other countries — among them Plekhanov and Rubanovich from Russia, Anseele and Wauters from Belgium, Vliegen from Holland, and Karl Liebknecht from Germany. Conscious of the imminent danger, Vaillant, supported by Jaurès, reiterated his demand for an international general strike to prevent war. Marcel Sembat agreed with them: Guesde and his followers were, as ever, most strongly opposed to it. The effect, Guesde said, would be to expose to disaster the country that was most socialistic and to make certain the crushing of Socialism and of civilisation. Gustave Hervé, previously the leader of the extreme anti-militarists, surprised the world by supporting Guesde, on the ground that there were no means of ensuring concerted strike action in the various countries. Despite these critics, the Congress gave its approval by a small majority to 'the general strike, simultaneously and internationally organised in the countries concerned'.

A few days later, on July 29th, when Austria had already declared war on Serbia, the International Socialist Bureau held an emergency meeting at Brussels. It was attended, among

others, by Jaurès, Guesde, Vaillant, Sembat, and Jean Longuet
from France ; by Victor and Friedrich Adler from Austria ; by
Burian and Němec from Hungary and Bohemia ; by Rubanovich from Russia ; by Vandervelde from Belgium ; by Morgari
from Italy ; and by Keir Hardie, Bruce Glasier, and Dan
Irving from Great Britain. Hugo Haase, Chairman of the
Social Democratic Party and of its Reichstag group, came alone
from Germany ; but Rosa Luxemburg attended as representative of Poland. It was at this meeting the decision was taken,
on Haase's motion, to summon a special session of the International Congress, which was due to meet at Vienna on August
23rd, to assemble in Paris on August 9th. At the Bureau
meeting, Victor Adler declared, with the concurrence of Němec,
that the war against Serbia was very popular in Austria and
that it would be most difficult for the Austrian Socialists to
take any action against it, though they had protested against the
extreme wording of the ultimatum to Serbia. It was already
foreshadowed plainly that the leaders of Austrian Socialism
would do nothing to oppose the war against the Serbs, and that
what they wanted from their fellow-Socialists was action to
limit the conflict, especially by preventing Russian intervention.
These intimations were ill-received ; and the members of the
Bureau turned to Haase for a declaration of the German
Socialists' intentions. Haase, who was soon to be displaced
from his position of leadership in Germany, gave an account of
the steps his party had already taken to oppose Germany's
entry into the war and to protest against the intransigent
attitude of the Austrian Government. He gave his fellow-
members of the Bureau to understand that the German Socialists would oppose German intervention even if the Russians
declared war on Austria, and that they would refuse to vote war
credits despite overtures already made to them on the Government's behalf. At a great public demonstration held immediately after the victory of the Bureau Haase publicly repeated
these statements and spoke of the great anti-war demonstrations
that were taking place in Germany. He received an ovation.

The resolution passed by the International Socialist Bureau
called upon all the workers' movements in the countries concerned not merely to continue but to intensify their demonstrations against war and to insist on the settlement of the

Austro-Serbian dispute by arbitration. It proclaimed that the French and German workers in particular would bring all possible pressure to bear on their respective Governments, the one in order to induce the French Government to prevent Russian intervention, and the other to induce the German Government to exert a moderating influence on Austria-Hungary.

The Bureau dispersed after a further meeting on the morning of July 30th, and the delegates returned to their own countries to report on what had been decided. The following day the French leaders, headed by Jaurès, who remained confident that the peace would be saved, attempted to see the French Prime Minister, the former Socialist Viviani, in order to urge him to take further steps to restrain Russia. Viviani did not see them ; and the Under-Secretary of State who received them in his stead was entirely unhelpful. The same evening Jaurès, still hopeful, was assassinated by a young reactionary at a restaurant where he had been dining with several of his colleagues on the staff of *Humanité*.

The death of Jaurès, the outstanding orator and intellectual leader of the Socialist movement, came as a terrific shock to Socialists, not only in France but everywhere. Despite sharp disagreements with the German Social Democrats and with their admirers in other countries he had been almost universally respected and admired. Even Rosa Luxemburg, who had opposed him fiercely, was a great admirer and a close personal friend. In France he had towered above the other political leaders and had been on good terms with the leaders of the Confédération Générale du Travail, whom he had taken great pains not to offend. He had, indeed, in the International, upheld strongly the right and duty of national defence against foreign aggression ; but he had been also among the foremost advocates of friendship between the French and the German working classes, and had worked his hardest to improve Franco-German relations and to advance the cause of international arbitration. His sudden end left the French Socialists leaderless ; for neither Guesde nor Vaillant was big enough to take his place.

It could, in all probability, have made no difference to the immediate international situation if Jaurès had survived. The current was already set strongly towards a war in which the five greatest European powers would be involved. The

Russians had already decided to intervene against Austria;
and the German Government had already made up its mind to
declare war on Russia — which it did on the day immediately
following his death. Despite Haase's brave words at Brussels
there was no real prospect of the German, any more than of the
Austrian, Socialists offering effective opposition to their Government's plans. The difference Jaurès might have made would
have been, not in preventing the war but in guiding the conduct
of the French Socialists, and perhaps in influencing that or
others, after it had broken out. It has often been said that
Jaurès, had he lived, would have rallied to the cause of national
defence against Germany, as Guesde and Vaillant both actually
did. This view is probably correct; but it is also probably the
case that he would have shown greater wisdom than they did
in working for a negotiated peace. His chance for this could
have come only later, after Germany had failed to achieve a
rapid victory. But it would have come; and in the situation
after 1916 his presence might have made a real difference.

For the moment, the effect of his death was to paralyse the
French Socialists till after the Germans had marched into
Belgium for their drive on Paris. But it was not yet evident, on
the night of July 31st, that the die was irrevocably cast. The
British Government was still trying to hold back the Russians;
and the German declaration of war on Russia, though decided
on, had not been actually made. There were still discussions
to take place between the Socialists of the countries so soon to
be locked in combat.

On August 1st, the day after Jaurès's murder, Hermann
Müller arrived in Paris as the emissary of the German Social
Democratic Party. He came, accompanied by the Belgian,
Henri de Man, not to make any definite proposal, but to
exchange information. Müller told the French Socialists that
the German party had reached no decision concerning its
attitude towards voting on the war credits. He said the party
would certainly not vote for them, but that there was a tendency
towards abstaining. He made it clear that for many of the
Germans the coming war appeared mainly as a German struggle
against Russian barbarism; and he insisted that the blame, if
war did break out, would rest not mainly on Germany, but on
the governing classes of all the imperialist powers. This, of

course, was before the German Government had demanded formally the right to march through Belgium ; but it was only the day before. The evening of the day following Müller's conversations in Paris, the German ultimatum to Belgium was received, and only twelve hours were allowed for an answer. The effect was to rally the Belgian Socialists practically solidly to the cause of national defence and, two days later, to bring Great Britain into the war on August 4th.

On this same day the vote on war credits was taken in the German Reichstag ; and the German Social Democrats voted solidly in favour of them. This did not mean that they were all agreed : in the party meeting 14 out of the 111 Socialist deputies had cast their votes against the credits. But the minority, headed by the party leader, Haase, had bowed to party discipline ; and it fell to Haase, whose offer of resignation was not accepted, to make the official speech in favour of the policy to which he was personally opposed. Even Karl Liebknecht, who was very soon to defy the discipline of the party, yielded to it on this occasion.

It can be said for the Germans that up to the time when it became clear that the Russians meant to go to war with Austria-Hungary in support of the Serbs they had done what they could, within constitutional limits, to prevent the extension of the area of conflict. Their press had taken a strong line against German intervention ; and they had held monster meetings and demonstrations in favour of peace. But at no stage had they shown any sign of going beyond constitutional protest. They had always been strongly hostile to proposals to meet the threat of war by strike action and to all ideas of insurrectionary protest ; and they had made this abundantly clear at successive Congresses of the International. But in the situation which existed in July 1914 mass demonstrations were bound to be futile. The Austrian Government had undoubtedly sounded the Germans before delivering its ultimatum to Serbia, and had received promises that, if Russia came in, Germany would too. The German Government, in estimating the probable reactions of the German working class, was able to reckon on the strength of anti-Russian feeling among both leaders and rank and file, and could feel fairly sure that, at the worst, the main body of Social Democrats would only protest and would neither rebel nor strike so as to hold up mobilisation or impede war supplies. In defence of its action against Belgium it could argue that, if the Germans did not march into that country, the French would, as their easiest road to Germany; and this argument, even if it was incorrect, had some backing from the discussions which were known to have taken place between Belgian, French, and British military leaders. This does not justify the German action; but it helps to explain, though by no means to justify, the German Socialists' acquiescence. The French, for their part, confronted with the prospect of almost immediate invasion when the German armies had swept the Belgians aside, had little choice. Most of them rallied at once to the cause of the nation.

In Russia during July there had been great strikes and demonstrations against war. But the Russian Socialists, even if they had been united, were in no position in 1914 to offer effective resistance to Czarist war policy. In fact, they were not united. When the Russian Government decided to support Serbia against the Austrians, there was a wave of pro-Slav feeling which became much stronger when Germany declared war on Russia. Not only many of the Social Revolutionaries, but also Plekhanov, the doyen of Russian Marxism, became converts to Russian patriotism. Most Social Democrats, both those inside Russia and those who, like Lenin, were in exile, remained unshaken in their hostility to the war; but only a small minority agreed with Lenin in seeing in it the means to Russian and to world revolution, or were prepared to adopt his policy of defeatism as part of their revolutionary creed.

In Austria, as we have seen, Victor Adler had held, almost from the moment of the Sarajevo murder, that mass-opinion was too hostile for the Socialists to be in a position to put up an effective opposition to the Government's policy. The Austrian Socialists had, indeed, protested against their Government's intransigence, and had demanded that the dispute with Serbia should be settled by arbitration. But they had said from the first that Austria had a right to require guarantees and repara-tions from Serbia, and had opposed their Government only on the ground that it had gone too far. There remained in Austrian Socialism a small minority, headed by Friedrich Adler, that opposed the war even when other countries had been drawn in. But for the time being this minority was helpless.

As for Great Britain, the last of the five great powers to enter the struggle, the question of positive action to prevent participation was finally swept aside by the German invasion of Belgium. The British leaders, on their return from the Brussels meeting of the International Socialist Bureau, were able to persuade the British Section of the International to organise anti-war demonstrations, addressed among others by Keir Hardie and Arthur Henderson. But there was never any real question of going beyond demonstrations : Keir Hardie's notion of strikes to prevent the movement of troops and war materials — which he had, in fact, advocated only as part of a concerted international movement — was never even considered. Some hopes were set on the British Government's attempts to dissuade Russia and Germany from intervening ; and there was a minority that wished Great Britain to stand aside even when they had intervened in arms. But it was only a small minority, based on the Independent Labour Party and on a section of the British Socialist Party. Hyndman, the B.S.P. leader, had long been preaching armament against Germany ; and the Trade Unions, which in the last resort controlled the Labour Party, rallied by a vast majority to the support of the war when they were faced with the fact of the German army on its road through Belgium to France. Probably they would have taken the same line even if there had been no violation of Belgium's neutrality ; but that came too speedily for the question to be effectively discussed.

Thus, in none of the five leading States which went to war in 1914 did the existence of an international Socialist movement pledged to use its utmost endeavours to prevent war make any substantial immediate difference, or restrain the Governments from pursuing policies that committed them to war. It can be argued with much force that the blame for this rests mainly on the German and Austrian Socialists because their Governments were thoroughly in the wrong — the Austrian for allowing no room for a negotiated settlement with Serbia, and the German first for promising the Austrians its support and subsequently for violating Belgium's neutrality. Immediately, it is clear that Austria and Germany were the aggressors and that, if the policy

of the International was to be taken seriously, the obligation to
stop them rested on the Austrian and German Socialists, who
alike wretchedly failed to act up to it. No doubt, the Czarist
Government, too, showed an intransigent spirit; but in Russia,
where Socialism was still an underground movement of revolt,
the Socialists were not in a position, in 1914, to do more than
they had been doing all along. Nothing short of actual revolution could stop the Czarist Government; and revolution was
beyond their power until the way to it had been opened up by
the strains and disasters of war. As for the French and British
Socialists, what could they be expected to do during the fatal
days of July and early August? Their Governments, whatever
their sins over a longer period, had no responsibility for the
crisis: all they could be called on to do, during the critical
fortnight, was to exert as much restraining influence as they
could on Germany and on Russia, in order to localise the conflict
and compel the Austrian Government to accept arbitration or
mediation.

But, of course, the whole situation needed to be looked at
not as if it had all started with the Sarajevo murder, but as the
latest phase in a complex international cold war that had been
going on, and getting almost continuously worse, for many
years, and had been studied for a long time with growing alarm
by the Socialist leaders. Behind the Austro-Serbian dispute
lay the long history of imperialist rivalries in the Balkans,
involving not only Russia as well as Austria-Hungary, but also
Germany and Great Britain. Behind it lay, too, the almost
world-wide struggle for colonial influence between Great
Britain — the great 'have' — and Germany — the great 'have
not'. To these must be added, in Western Europe, the legacy
left, in Alsace-Lorraine, by the war of 1870. The German
Socialists, when they were attacked for supporting the aggressive
policies of the German Government, were apt to retort that in
the existing situation in Europe, the phrases 'aggressive war'
and 'defensive war' had lost their meaning, and that the blame
rested, not on the immediate 'aggressor', even if one could be
named, but on the imperialist policies of all the great powers,
which had reduced all talk of international morality to sheer
humbug. Much was made of Great Britain's refusal to agree
to modification of naval rights of blockade, of the alliance of

France and Great Britain with reactionary Russia, and of Germany's legitimate claim to a 'place in the sun'. These contentions failed to convince a substantial minority among the German Socialists themselves; but there was enough in them to give the counter-contention that Great Britain had entered the war simply for the defence of 'brave little Belgium' a distinctly hypocritical ring.

It thus came about that the leaders of the British Independent Labour Party, who had for years been denouncing the foreign policy of Sir Edward Grey and the alliance with Russia as a menace to peace, found themselves in 1914 deeply suspicious of British policy, as having practically committed the country to war behind the backs of the people. They called on the British Government to remain at peace, even if Russia and France were drawn in, and to stand ready to act as mediator at the earliest opportunity. But in face of the German attitude and of the failure of the German Socialists to stand out against it, they had but little chance of carrying with them the main body of British Labour. The Labour Party and the Trade Unions, as distinct from the I.L.P. and the other Socialist societies, had been only marginal participants in the International, and had taken little part in its great debates on the issues of war and peace. The Labour Party did not at that time even pretend to be a Socialist party: Great Britain had always been regarded in the International as a politically backward country, and the German Socialists had been held up to it again and again as a shining example. Despite Keir Hardie's advocacy of the general strike against war, no one on the Continent — or for that matter in Great Britain — had seriously expected the British workers to resort to it; and the Labour Party's position in Parliament was evidently too weak for it to achieve much there, even if it had been united. There remained only the resort to mass demonstrations; but from the moment when the German armies began to march the Socialists who were still against war lacked all power to bring the masses out on the streets. In practice, the question they had to face from that moment was whether, being few, they were prepared to go on opposing the war effort in face of an overwhelmingly hostile public opinion, or whether, with Great Britain actually at war with an aggressive Germany, they should rally to the national cause, at any rate to the extent of doing their best to prevent a German victory.

On this issue the I.L.P. itself was not united. A part of its membership, headed by J. R. Clynes, its chief Trade Unionist figure, went over to full support of the war effort. The main body, headed by Philip Snowden, maintained its opposition, but could for the time being do little about it. Of its two outstanding figures, Keir Hardie, broken-hearted at the collapse of his hopes, fell ill and died in September 1915 ; while Ramsay MacDonald, after resigning his leadership of the Labour Party in favour of Arthur Henderson, combined his attack on Grey's foreign policy with an affirmation that the war, once started, had to be won, or at any rate not lost, and accordingly refused to oppose the recruiting campaign.

Meanwhile in France, on August 26th, two Socialists — Jules Guesde and Marcel Sembat — had become members of Viviani's reconstituted Cabinet. In Belgium Émile Vandervelde had already joined the Cabinet on August 4th. In Great Britain, Labour's entry into the Cabinet came only in May 1915, when Arthur Henderson, who had been made a Privy Councillor in January, became President of the Board of Education, while two others — William Brace and G. H. Roberts — were appointed to minor office. In the other belligerent countries, Socialist entry to the Governments came only through revolution — in Russia in 1917 and in Germany and Austria at the conclusion of the war.

After the Brussels meeting of July 1914 the Second International ceased to function as a collective expression of international Socialist policy. Its continuance in any form on Belgium soil was out of the question : what was left of it had to seek refuge in a neutral country. Its secretary, the Belgian, Camille Huysmans (b. 1871), transferred its headquarters to Holland, and from this point of vantage tried to maintain relations with the affiliated parties in the belligerent as well as in the neutral States. As early as September 1914 the American Socialists wrote to the International Socialist Bureau proposing the convocation of an International Conference ; and soon afterwards suggestions were received from Italy and from other neutral countries. In January 1915 a Conference of neutral Socialists met at Copenhagen and called upon the Bureau to convene an International Conference 'as soon as conditions allow and, in any case, not later than the opening of negotiations for peace'. The following month the first of a series of Conferences of Allied Socialists met in London ; and a Conference of Socialists of the Central Powers was held in Vienna in April 1915. A second Conference of Neutrals took place in July 1916 at The Hague, and called for a meeting of the International Socialist Bureau. Meanwhile, in September 1914 an Italian-Swiss Socialist Conference had been held at Lugano, and the Swiss Socialist, Robert Grimm, had begun his efforts to bring together an international gathering of Socialists opposed to the war. In March 1915, largely under Clara Zetkin's impulsion, an International Socialist Women's Conference assembled at Berne and published resolutions calling for the immediate ending of the war. At this meeting, under Lenin's influence, the Russian Social Democrats broke away, demanding a complete break with 'Social Chauvinism' and the establishment of a new International. Meanwhile, Grimm, in conjunction with Morgari, of the Italian Socialist Party, continued his efforts to persuade the leaders of the Second International to call its parties together ; and, on their refusal, the Italians decided to act without them, and to summon a Conference with the object, not of forming a new International, but of re-establishing international relations and promoting common action for peace. Out of this move arose the Zimmerwald Conference of September 1915, commonly regarded as the precursor of the Third International. Lenin there proposed that the new International should be set up at once, but failed to carry his point, either at Zimmerwald or at its successor, the Kienthal Conference of April 1916. Both these gatherings, though they were made up of opponents of the war, were a mixture of revolutionary and pacifist elements : they ranged from those who, with Lenin, hoped to turn the war of nations into a revolutionary civil war between capitalists and workers to those who wished only to bring the warring nations together in a negotiated peace, and between these extremes were Syndicalists and left-wing Socialists of various shades. At Zimmerwald the French and German representatives — Merrheim and Bourderon of the French C.G.T. and Georg Ledebour and Adolf Hoffmann of the German minority — signed a joint

declaration of fraternity, including a denunciation of the violation of Belgium (written by Ledebour himself). Trotsky, with
Grimm and Henriette Roland-Holst of Holland, drafted the
Zimmerwald Conference's main declaration, which Lenin
signed after his own proposal had been rejected by 19 votes to 12.

Thus, before the Russian Revolution of 1917 had dramatically changed the situation, two rival movements for the return
to international Socialist action had already begun to take shape
— one under the auspices of the neutrals who had remained
in touch with the International Socialist Bureau, and the other,
sponsored by a Swiss-Italian group, among the parties and
minorities that had adopted an anti-war attitude. The first of
these, in the hands of a Scandinavian-Dutch Committee
headed by Hjalmar Branting of Sweden and Pieter Troelstra of
Holland, was to lead to the attempt, after the first Russian
Revolution, to convene at Stockholm, with the aid of the
Russians, a Socialist Peace Conference in which it was hoped
that the Socialist parties of both belligerent groups would take
part. The second, after shedding its pacifist elements, was to
prepare the way for the Bolsheviks to found the Third International on the morrow of their victory in Russia. The account
of these developments must be held over for the next volume
of this work.

At this stage it remains only to observe that the collapse of
the Second International in 1914, though it brought consternation to many Socialists at the time, could have been foreseen —
and, no doubt, was foreseen by the Governments of the great
powers which went to war without taking much notice of the
Socialists' threats. It had been plain enough both at Stuttgart
and at Copenhagen that the International had no concerted
policy that was likely to be effective in stopping war unless the
Governments of the great powers could be bluffed into mis-
taking demonstrations for a positive will to resist. In all the
countries concerned, except Great Britain, compulsory military
service was in force, and even before hostilities began a large
proportion of the Socialists were liable to be recalled suddenly
to the colours. Effective resistance to war could have been
offered only if the Socialist parties had been prepared to counsel
their members to refuse to answer this summons. But this
vital issue was never even discussed, except by Hervé and a

few extremists. It was taken for granted that the reservists would obey the call. But, once they had obeyed, the rest of the workers, if they attempted to hamper the war effort, would be open to the charge of letting their own comrades down: they would be helpless, unless and until the conscripts in arms were ready to rebel. In face of the known attitudes of the main parties the resolution passed at Stuttgart and reaffirmed at Copenhagen and at Bâle, even apart from its vagueness, did not make sense.

CHAPTER III

GREAT BRITAIN—
SOCIALISM BEFORE THE LABOUR PARTY

(i) THE BEGINNINGS OF FABIAN SOCIALISM

IN the second volume of this history the story of Socialist developments in Great Britain was carried up almost to the end of the 1880s, except that the account of the Fabian Society was deferred to the present volume. The reason for this is that, though the Fabian Society was founded at the beginning of 1884, actually before the Social Democratic Federation had adopted a definitely Socialist programme, its influence was small until the publication of *Fabian Essays in Socialism* at the end of 1889, and its impact on Socialist thought belongs to the period which had begun about then with the emergence of the New Unionism in the London gasworkers' and dockers' strikes. Fabian Socialism became a distinctive body of doctrine only with the appearance of *Fabian Essays*: it has to be studied in connection not with the Social Democratic Federation or William Morris's Socialist League but with the Independent Labour Party, founded under Keir Hardie's chairmanship in 1893, and with the New Unionism of which John Burns, Tom Mann, and Ben Tillett were the outstanding leaders.

There was indeed in the Fabian Society's earliest days nothing at all to indicate that it was likely to become important. It was, no doubt, significant that in the winter of 1883 a group consisting almost entirely of middle-class intellectuals, mostly with but few contacts with the workers, should decide to establish a society committed to a Socialist attitude ; and it is no doubt true that only a group of this sort could have developed into the type of society the Fabians actually became. But there was at the outset nothing to show either what the distinctive Fabian outlook and policy were to become, or that the Society was more likely to survive than other almost chance gatherings of a few unknown individuals who were dissatisfied with the existing basis of society and met in the hope of groping their way towards means of social improvement. Actually, the original intentions of the group out of which the Fabian Society emerged had almost nothing in common with the Fabianism that developed out of them; and the Society was the outcome of a breakaway from the original plan. The affair began when Thomas Davidson, known as 'The Wandering Scholar', settled for a time in London in 1883 and, after his wont, gathered round him a group of disciples, mostly young men and women, to whom he proposed the foundation of a 'Fellowship of the New Life'.

Thomas Davidson (1840–1900), elder brother of the John Morrison Davidson who wrote *Annals of Toil* and played a part in the Scottish Labour movement, was born of crofter parents and became a schoolmaster in his native village and later at Oundle and Aberdeen. Resigning his post in search of a philosophy, he took to wandering. At Rome he had a long interview with the Pope, to whom he proposed a new edition of the works of Aquinas; and he set to work to edit and translate the works of Antonio Rosmini (1797–1855), the founder of the Institute of the Brethren of Charity. Moving to America, he became a pioneer of the summer school movement, organising regular annual summer camps for the study of philosophy, religion, and social questions. His strongly idealistic philosophy was confused and confusing, and cannot be summarised. It included the view that social advance depended on individual regeneration, and that the way to bring the world to a better way of life was for groups of individuals to pledge themselves to live in accordance with a high ideal of love and brotherhood, establishing when and as they could communities for this purpose, but, short of that, practising their ideals while they continued to follow their ordinary avocations. The purpose of the Fellowship of the New Life was to explore the possibilities of a communal way of living, and in the meantime to study the conditions of the good life. Davidson left for the United States, where he established a similar body, before his London Fellowship was even fairly launched; and, with his dynamic personality removed, the members of the group soon decided to go their several ways. One section, headed by Percival A.

Chubb, later well known as an Ethical Church leader in America, but at this time a clerk in the Local Government Board, went on with the Fellowship of the New Life, which lasted until 1898 and published throughout its life a monthly journal, *Seedtime*. Among its members were several notable figures — Havelock Ellis (1859–1939) the psychologist, Henry S. Salt (1851–1939) the humanitarian, Edward Carpenter (1844–1929), John Francis Oakeshott (1860–1945) and also James Ramsay MacDonald. The other group, which included Edward R. Pease, Frank Podmore (1856–1910), Hubert Bland (1856–1914), Frederick Keddell, and John Hunter Watts (d. 1924), split away and at the beginning of 1884 founded the Fabian Society. Sceptical of Davidson's idea of founding communities and wanting a more specific programme of social reformation, the members of this second group, who numbered at the beginning fewer than a dozen, admitted their uncertainty about the course to be pursued, and decided that they needed time for discussion and reflection before they could be ready to formulate a policy. They took, at Podmore's suggestion, the name 'Fabian' in order to indicate their wish to look more closely before they leapt. Perhaps they had in mind John Gay's lines

> Let none object my lingering way :
> I gain, like Fabius, with delay,

but they chose later for their motto, not these verses, but two alleged prose quotations — which, it appears, were actually Podmore's invention.

> Wherefore it may not be gainsaid that the fruit of this man's long taking of counsel — and (by the many so deemed) untimeous delays — was the safeholding for all men, his fellow-citizens, of the Common Weal.
>
> For the right moment you must wait, as Fabius did most patiently, when warring against Hannibal, though many censured his delays ; but when the time comes you must strike hard, as Fabius did, or your waiting will be vain, and fruitless.

Thus, the use of Fabius's name indicated, at the outset, not an anticipation that Socialism itself would need to be achieved gradually, by stages, but rather a will to take time in working out the right method and policy. Gradualism was an easy graft upon this initial notion, but formed no part of it. It seems in fact to have come into the Society well after its foundation, as the distinctive contribution of Sidney Webb.

There was no necessary antagonism between the Fabians and the Fellowship of the New Life. Indeed, a few of the original group went on belonging to both — among them William Clarke, who contributed to *Fabian Essays*, Havelock Ellis, and J. F. Oakeshott, who was for many years active on the Fabian Executive. But the two bodies went their separate ways, each attracting its own recruits. The Fabian Society soon produced its first Tract, *Why are the Many Poor?*, written by the only workman then in its ranks, the house-painter W. L. Phillips. Its second tract, *A Manifesto*, also published in its first year, was by a brilliant new recruit, George Bernard Shaw (1856–1950), who soon brought with him another, Sidney Webb (1859–1947). These two arrivals made the vital difference. Between them, Shaw and Webb proceeded to turn the Fabian Society from a not very notable little group of earnest seekers after truth into a powerful intellectual force armed with a new and eminently practical social gospel.

In 1884 Shaw was 28 and had already been eight years in London, mainly writing novels which no one would publish and living by casual journalism. He had turned Socialist in 1882, inspired partly by hearing Henry George lecture, and he had soon begun to lecture and to speak at street corners himself. At this stage he was attracted to Anarchism and had connections with the Social Democratic Federation, which had not yet shed its anti-Marxists. He was studying Marx, and had no clearly settled Socialist attitude, though he was already full of ideas. It took a little while for Sidney Webb to lead him captive to the gradualist Socialism which that indefatigable apostle soon implanted in the almost virgin soil of Fabian zetetic enthusiasm.

Sidney Webb was 25 when he joined the Fabians in 1884. He was a clerk in the Colonial Office, with a very orderly mind, a prodigious memory, and a passion for social justice. Of the rest of the group, Edward R. Pease was 27, Frank Podmore 28, Sydney Olivier 25, and John Francis Oakeshott 24. Graham Wallas was 28 when he joined in 1886. Some older men and women came in later ; but the chief makers of the Society were young men in their twenties — young men deeply interested in Socialism, but still (with the notable exception of Sidney Webb) not at all certain what it meant.

The year of the Fabian Society's foundation was also that of the Reform Act which extended the widened urban franchise of 1867 to cover the whole country, raising the British electorate (exclusive of Ireland) from three to five millions. It was moreover the year of the great split in the Social Democratic Federation, from which William Morris and a majority of the Executive broke away to form the Socialist League. Up to the split, a number of the Fabians belonged to the S.D.F.; and a few stayed in it. But the Fabian Society in 1885 joined in the outcry against the S.D.F. when the fiasco of its candidates financed by 'Tory gold' was brought to light;[1] and Bernard Shaw, though he continued to lecture to S.D.F. branches, was much closer to William Morris than to Hyndman. In 1885 the Society published nothing except a squib by Shaw: the following year it issued a twelve-page tract, *What Socialism Is*, in which were presented for the information of readers two rival views of Socialism. Kropotkin's collaborator, Mrs. Charlotte Wilson, who remained in the Fabian Society for many years as the almost solitary exponent of Anarchism, expounded the 'Free Socialism' of the Anarchist-Communists, while Collectivist Socialism was presented in a translation from August Bebel, the German Social Democratic leader. The two contrasting views were introduced by an historical account of the rise of capitalist society; but no attempt was made to come down definitely on either side. The general impression left on the reader was that the British Socialist movement was still unformed, but that in due course there were likely to emerge from it two great parties, the one Collectivist and the other Anarchist-Communist, reproducing the divisions which had long set continental Socialists by the ears. As between these tendencies the Society had not yet taken up a position: the pamphlet was designed to impart information, rather than to supply a conclusion.

During the same year the unemployed agitation was already beginning, with John Burns as its effective leader. The Fabians took little part in it; but they did set up a committee, with Webb and Podmore as its most active members, to produce

[1] See Vol. II, p. 403.

a report. The outcome was the highly contentious report on *Government Organisation of the Unemployed* to which I made reference in the second volume of this history.[1] This report, with its curious proposals, including conscription as a possible remedy, led to the first serious storm inside the Society. The report was issued to members; but a meeting of members rejected the proposal to publish it as a Fabian tract. There may well have been more than one reason for its rejection : the project of State tobacco cultivation may have offended some, and the favourable references to compulsory service undoubtedly antagonised others. But there was also in the whole document a strong reformist and gradualist outlook which the Society was not yet ready to accept. Sidney Webb's first piece of writing for the Fabian Society thus met with a rebuff; but his influence was strongly reasserted the following year, when he produced *Facts for Socialists*, the first of the long series of informative propagandist tracts which did much to establish the Society's reputation for solid work. The significance of *Facts for Socialists* in its original form lay less in the telling statistics of riches and poverty which Webb assembled in it than in its attempt to build the case for Socialism largely on citations from non-Socialist authorities and to represent Socialism not as a revolutionary movement aiming at the overthrow of existing society but rather as a logical and necessary development of tendencies already at work within capitalism. Already in this remarkable tract Webb's characteristic approach was fully present : Socialism was regarded as a fulfilment, and not as a violent reversal, of existing trends, and it followed that its advent was to be expected as an outcome not of sudden revolutionary change but rather of an evolutionary process of adding reform to reform, with no violent break at any point. In *Facts for Socialists* this conception was only implicit, and not formally stated; but the implication was clear.

On this first really distinctive Fabian publication followed, two years later, *Facts for Londoners* and *Figures for Londoners*, both written by Webb at the time of the establishment of the London County Council and designed as propaganda for the Progressive candidates. But before this, in 1887, Bernard Shaw had written *The True Radical Programme* as a retort to

[1] See Vol. II, p. 405.

the inadequacies of the new programme recently adopted by the Liberal Party. In this tract the Fabians demanded adult (including women's) suffrage, payment of M.P.s, taxation of unearned incomes, the eight hours' day, and railway nationalisation, as constituting a sufficient set of immediate demands 'to fill the hands of the True Radical Party, the New Labour Party — in a word, the Practical Socialist Party'.

This Shavian pamphlet was issued under the auspices of a specially constituted body — the Fabian Parliamentary League — and not of the Society as a whole. This was done because there were still in the ranks of the Fabian Society persons who were opposed to parliamentary action — either as Anarchists or as revolutionaries who regarded parliamentary contests as calculated to corrupt. Thus, despite *Facts for Socialists*, the Society still treated the whole question as open ; but it soon became apparent that the great majority of the members were on Webb's side, and the Parliamentary League was quietly dropped — or, rather, merged in the general work of the Society.

The following year, 1888, Sydney Olivier (1859–1943) drafted for the Fabians their first essay in theoretical economics — the tract entitled *Capital and Land*. This was in the main an attack on the followers of Henry George, designed to show that capital equally with land was a form of anti-social monopoly by means of which 'rent' was extracted from the producers. This was, of course, already a familiar Socialist contention : it had been brought forward by Hyndman and other S.D.F. leaders on many occasions. But whereas the S.D.F. argued the case in terms of the Marxist concept of 'surplus value', the Fabians simply made use of the Ricardian theory of rent, and extended Henry George's application of that theory from land to other capital goods as equally productive of a rent which the owner was able to extract from the labour of the people. Just as Webb, in *Facts for Socialists*, had cited Mill and Jevons as witnesses to the truth of the Socialist arguments, so Olivier cited Ricardo and his successors.

The Fabian Society's next essay in 'Practical Socialism' was a tract, written by Sidney Webb, containing the full draft of *An Eight Hours Bill*. This appeared in 1889 ; and at the end of the same year the Society published its first book, the collection of *Fabian Essays in Socialism*, edited by Bernard Shaw.

This volume, which has continued to be reprinted at intervals right up to the present time, first gave the Fabian Society a really wide public and established it as the advocate of a particular kind of Socialism sharply different both from the Marxism of the Social Democrats and from the semi-anarchist 'Free Communism' of William Morris and the Socialist League. It was based on a series of lectures given by the seven essayists in the autumn and winter of 1888. The general line of the lectures was worked out by the seven in close consultation, and the book was edited by Bernard Shaw, who suggested numerous changes to most of his fellow-authors, and contributed two of the essays himself. The seven authors were Shaw, Sidney Webb, Graham Wallas (1858–1932), Annie Besant (1847–1933), William Clarke (1852–1901), Sydney Olivier, and Hubert Bland.

The volume was divided into three sections. In the first section, on 'The Basis of Socialism', Shaw wrote the essay headed 'Economic', Webb the 'Historic' essay, Clarke the 'Industrial', and Olivier the 'Moral'. The second section, 'The Organisation of Society', was made up of two essays — 'Property under Socialism', by Wallas, and 'Industry under Socialism', by Annie Besant. Finally, under the heading 'The Transition to Socialism', came Shaw on 'Transition' and Hubert Bland, already known, under the name 'Hubert', as a lively political journalist on the *Sunday Chronicle*, who wrote on 'The Outlook', and was highly sceptical about the possibilities of 'permeating' the Liberal Party. It is a remarkable fact that the word 'permeation', making its appearance under Fabian auspices in Bland's essay, is used in a pejorative sense.

Edward Reynolds Pease (1857–1955), who was secretary of the Society from 1890 to 1913, served on its executive from 1884 to 1939, and was the last survivor of the original group, in his *History of the Fabian Society*, stakes out the claims of the *Essays* in the following terms :

> *Fabian Essays* presented the case for Socialism in plain language which everyone could understand. It based Socialism, not on the speculations of a German philosopher, but on the obvious evolution of society as we see it around us. It accepted economic science as taught by the accredited British professors ; it built up the edifice of Socialism on the

foundations of our existing political and social institutions ; it proved that Socialism was but the next step in the development of society, rendered inevitable by the changes which followed from the industrial revolution of the eighteenth century.

Thus the Fabian essayists, equally with Karl Marx, proclaimed the inevitability of Socialism and based their confident prophecy on a theory of economic evolution. The Fabian interpretation of history was no less economic than Marx's, and laid as much stress on the tendency towards the concentration of economic power. Bernard Shaw's and William Clarke's contributions to *Fabian Essays* are full of references to this tendency — to the rapid advance of trusts and combines, the obsolescence of the small-scale producer, and the logical outcome of capitalistic centralisation in the socialisation of the means of production, distribution, and exchange, thus made ready by the unwitting capitalists for transfer to the common possession of the peoples. The difference between the Marxists and the Fabians was not that one party accepted, while the other rejected, the conception of an inevitable advance to Socialism under stress of economic forces, but that, whereas Marx had treated social revolution as the necessary form of the transition, the Fabians held that Socialism was destined to come into being as the culmination of an evolutionary process which had already advanced a considerable way, and would continue to advance under the increasing pressure of a democratic electorate that was becoming more and more aware of its ability to manage its own affairs and to dispense with the private landlords and capitalists whom it had hitherto allowed to extract various forms of 'economic rent' as the reward of mere ownership.

In the Marxist theory of history there were, as we have seen, two distinct elements, which were combined to form a single doctrine. At the basis of the entire process of social change lay the developing 'powers of production' — that is, the material resources which men used to create wealth with the aid of their knowledge of the productive arts. For the exploitation of these 'powers of production' there had to be social arrangements ; and at each stage in their development a particular economic structure emerged as the most appropriate for the full use of the available resources and knowledge. This economic structure had, in its turn, to be maintained and defended by the use of enough force to ensure obedience to the rules laid down by those persons who were marked out as the directors and principal beneficiaries ; and the political structure of society, with its laws and its coercive agents — judges, policemen and, in the last resort, the armed forces — constituted this mechanism for the upholding of the economic order. The State was thus, according to Marx, essentially an instrument of the ruling economic class for the coercion of its subjects ; and as no ruling class would ever yield up its authority except to superior force, the only means of changing the system of class-rule embodied in the State was forceful revolution from below, resulting in the victory of a new ruling class and in the creation of a new State made in its image for the defence of a new economic order embodying its aspirations. Of course, in Marx's view, such a revolution could occur only when the underlying economic conditions — the advance in the 'powers of production' — had rendered the old economic system obsolete ; and the new ruling class would be the class that was designated to assume authority by its superior fitness to organise the economic life of society. The new class would win, not because it had aspirations, but because the material conditions of production had made its victory necessary. Thus, the second element in the Marxist doctrine was the assertion that history was made up of a series of class-wars, and that every transition from one epoch to another was necessarily marked by a revolutionary shifting of class-power.

This second part of the Marxist doctrine the Fabians rejected as completely as they upheld the other part. They did not, indeed, formulate, as Marx did, any universal theory of history. They concerned themselves only with the phase that had begun with the rise of modern capitalism, and principally with the period since the Industrial Revolution ; and they took the greater part of their arguments and illustrations from the history of British capitalism, making the broad assumption that what had been occurring in Great Britain, as the pioneering country, was also occurring, or was destined to occur, in other capitalistic societies. They were as convinced as Kautsky and the rest of the German Social Democrats who drafted the Erfurt Programme of 1891 that the private business was destined to be crushed out by the advance of the great capitalist combines and that the advent of trustified capitalism was preparing the way for Socialism by easing the path to public ownership. But whereas the Marxists of the time assumed that the process of socialisation would involve political revolution and that the victory of the working class would mean the establishment of a new kind of State embodying the class-power of the victors, the Fabians envisaged the process of social and economic transformation in terms not of class-war or revolution, but of the gradual and progressive modification of the system by democratic means, as a result of pressure from a popular electorate that would grow more and more insistent on the claims of social justice and would become convinced that nothing short of the socialisation of the means of production would suffice to ensure their use to achieve the highest practicable level of general well-being.

The Fabians, in effect, thought of the advance of Socialism in terms mainly not of power alone, but of power animated by rational conviction and inspired by the ethical impulse to achieve social justice. They did not disdain power; but they did not, as Marx did, envisage it as a sheer force of economic necessity, to which ideals could make no practical contribution. They thought of it in terms of popular electoral pressure and of the influence of informed opinion rather than in terms of class; and they regarded the efficacy of these forms of pressure as sufficiently proven by the actual progress made in social legislation and in the progressive transformation of opinion. This progress they no doubt regarded as having been made possible only by the development of industrialism; and in this they were fundamentally at one with the Marxist diagnosis. But they denied altogether that the catastrophism which formed an integral part of Marxism really followed from, or was even consistent with, an economic interpretation of history. Capitalism, they argued, had become the dominant force in advanced societies not by suddenly and violently overturning feudalism and setting up a new class State in place of it, but rather by a long and gradual process of infiltration into the old order, so as to transform it by stages into something essentially different and in conformity with the economic requirements of an industrial society. Was it not to be expected that Socialism would develop in the same way? Was it not, indeed, already and evidently doing just that?

This line of argument was advanced most clearly in the chapter which Sidney Webb contributed considerably later (in 1910) to the volume of the *Cambridge Modern History* which dealt with nineteenth-century trends — a chapter which the Fabians reprinted as a pamphlet under the title *Towards Social Democracy*. But the doctrine set forth in this chapter was essentially one with that of *Fabian Essays*. It involved, fundamentally, an identification of Socialism with collective control and planning under the auspices of a democratic parliamentary system. It brought together into a single doctrine the political tendency towards the control of society by a government responsible to a democratic electorate and the economic tendency towards the centralised planning of production, distribution, and exchange; and it welcomed these two tendencies as flowing together towards an outcome which could be best described as Socialism.

The Fabians, however, did not, as is often supposed, put their emphasis on nationalisation as the essential of Socialism. Pride of place was given rather to the social appropriation of 'rent' in all its forms, with taxation as the principal instrument for effecting the transfer. Although for a very long period the Fabian 'Basis' — the brief statement of Socialist doctrine to which new members were asked to subscribe — declared formally against payment of compensation for capitalist property taken over by the public, Shaw was already, in *Fabian Essays*, stating quite clearly the case for compensating each individual owner whose property was taken away. It would be unfair, he argued, for the State to take one man's property, or part of it, without compensation while leaving others in possession; and British opinion would never stand for such a proceeding. If Socialism was to come in by gradual stages it followed that the right course was to compensate the expropriated individual; but the sums needed for this should be raised by a tax levied on the whole body of property-owners, so that there would be a real gain to the public and not a merely nominal transfer of ownership that would leave the public saddled with a continuing charge for interest. Such compensation would cost the public nothing: it would merely spread the confiscation of 'rent' evenly over the entire owning class.

Starting out from Henry George's 'single tax' proposals and contending that other forms of capital, equally with land, yielded a 'rent' extracted from the producers, which it was both just and expedient to transfer to public enjoyment, the Fabians nevertheless continued to think of the rent of land as the outstanding form of 'unearned income' calling for public appropriation. They did not, however, wish to 'nationalise' the land, in the sense of handing it over to State ownership and control. Wherever the question was discussed in *Fabian Essays* it was argued that the land should pass into the possession of local or regional, rather than of national, public agencies, and that no great advance towards Socialism could be made without the aid of a powerful and fully democratic local government machine. *Fabian Essays* were actually written in the year — 1888 — in which a Conservative Government set up elected County Councils to replace the undemocratic county jurisdiction of the justices of the peace; and one essayist after another acclaimed the County Councils Act as providing an essential part of the foundations for a Socialist society. The new County Councils and the County Borough Councils, which between them covered the whole country, were regarded as the appropriate bodies to receive the proceeds of a tax on 'rent' and presently to become the owners of the land, both rural and urban. Moreover, the taxation of rent would place in the hands of these Councils vast sums which they would need to use not only for meeting the costs of local government and social services but also for replacing private investment in both agriculture and industry as such investment necessarily declined. The County and County Borough Councils would thus become by stages, as the taxes on rent were pushed nearer and nearer to 100 per cent, the principal providers of the capital needed for every form of economic development.

There were, indeed, certain industries and services which the Fabians wished to transfer to State ownership and control — for example, the railways and such other services as required, on technical grounds, to be operated as national monopolies. In addition, it was argued that where under capitalism an industry had passed into the hands of a great private trust, the State should simply take it over and continue to work it as a national monopoly under public control; and the essayists sometimes talked as if they expected such trustification to advance at a prodigious pace. Nevertheless, they clearly thought that the great majority of industries would pass by stages into the hands of local or regional, and not of national, public bodies; and they laid great stress on the need for the County and other Councils to set up new productive enterprises in direct competition with the capitalists, whom they expected to see driven rapidly from one field after another by the greater efficiency of the publicly directed concerns. These latter, they argued, being free from all charges for rent or interest, would be able easily to undercut their profit-seeking rivals; [1] and they would be in a position to offer minimum wages and conditions of work that would drive away from private industry all the better labour, and would finally leave the profit-seekers unable to command any labour at all. All this was a resuscitation of Louis Blanc's ideas in the 1840s, and of Lassalle's in the 1860s. Except in the case of the basic services, such as the railways, and of industries dominated by private trusts and combines, the essayists envisaged the process of socialisation in terms less of the taking over of existing enterprises than of the establishment of new ones with public capital derived from the progressive confiscation of 'rent'. They were insistent that a large part of the proceeds of the taxes on 'rent' must be treated as capital for public investment rather than as spendable income that could be applied to consumption.

These arguments in favour of county and municipal enterprise were closely linked in the minds of the essayists with the contemporary Socialist demand for the 'right to work' and with the unemployed agitation of the middle 'eighties in which this demand had taken pride of place. Here, again, the connection was close with Louis Blanc, who had also put forward his idea of 'national workshops' in close connection with the demand for the 'right to work'.[2] The essayists called on the new County Councils to provide work for the unemployed, first by developing public works — roads, bridges, schools, hospitals, housing, and public utility services — and thereafter by establishing their own farms and factories. They denounced 'relief works', in which unemployed workers were engaged

---

[1] This idea reappears in Hertzka's *Freeland*. See p. 559 ff.
[2] See Vol. I, Ch. xv.

regardless of skill or suitability, simply in order to give them work to do in preference to mere relief. They insisted that the Councils must provide jobs to suit the qualifications of the workers who were out of jobs, and must train them where new qualifications needed to be acquired. There was, moreover, in *Fabian Essays*, a revival of the proposal to establish rural communities for the practice of collective farming with the aid of the most modern machinery and techniques, and for the building up round these Council farms of auxiliary industrial enterprises and communal services — a proposal which harked back to Robert Owen and Fourier and also owed something to Peter Kropotkin's conception of reintegration of agriculture and industry in rural settlements based on the general availability of electric power.

Where industries or services did need, for technical reasons, to be conducted under national rather than local auspices, *Fabian Essays* favoured the entrusting of the actual administration to public boards or commissions very similar to the public corporations of the present day. Mrs. Besant, in her essay on 'Industry under Socialism', rejected the idea that the workers should be given control of their industries or the choice of managers, and advocated control by the elected public authorities, which should nominate the boards and, directly or through them, the actual managers and supervisors. The whole weight was put on the need to make industry the property and the business of the whole body of citizens, rather than of any section ; and the notion of 'industrial democracy' was brusquely dismissed. But it has to be borne in mind that national administration was thought of as exceptional, and that for most types of industry the Fabians envisaged control by the municipality or the County Council (or by smaller local authorities in some cases) rather than by a national board or department. Their model Socialist employer was to be a local or regional administrative body, popularly elected ; and they tended to think even of Parliament as destined to become more and more like a local Council in its method of working as it took on more functions of economic administration and control. The notion that the early Fabians were essentially nationalisers who wished to bring all industries under the centralised rule of government departments is entirely wrong. They had, indeed, no objection to centralisation where the technical conditions or the actual trustification of an industry under capitalism seemed to them to demand it; but they took it as a matter of course that democracy required for its successful working a strong foundation in local self-government and that land ownership and the responsibility for most forms of industrial enterprise would be taken over by local or regional public agencies.

There is, in retrospect, something rather comic about the immense hopes which the Fabians of 1889 rested on the newly established County Councils as the principal instruments for the advance towards Socialism. It has, however, to be borne in mind that the Fabian essayists were a group of Londoners, and that a large part of their hope rested on the new London County Council, on which they were immediately to play an important part in the policy-making of the Progressive Party. The Fabians did not originate London Progressivism, which had developed in connection with the London Radical Reform movement long before the County Council was set up. But they threw themselves into this movement; and the policy of 'permeation' which came to be regarded as their characteristic political doctrine was in fact worked out largely in relation to metropolitan affairs. Their conception of gradualism, and of Socialism as a tendency already in active operation and possessing a powerful momentum of its own, derived from the necessary processes of economic and technical evolution, inclined them to endeavour to manipulate existing agencies rather than to create new ones; and in the London Reform movement they thought — or at any rate most of them did — that they saw an instrument ready for use and much more likely to yield positive results than either the Marxist Social Democratic Federation or any other body which cut itself off from contemporary trends and set out to work for revolution rather than for evolutionary change. It has always to be borne in mind that *Fabian Essays* was written and Fabian policy mainly worked out before the gasworkers' and dockers' strikes of 1889 had given birth to the New Unionism, and before the movement for independent Labour representation had taken shape, except here and there. Fabianism might have taken a different turn had the Fabian Society been founded, say, in 1890 rather than in 1884. As matters were, the rise of the New Unionism and of the political movements which drew together in 1893 in the Independent Labour Party found the Fabian leaders fully committed, in London, to the Progressive alliance on the County Council, and therefore instinctively hostile to any action which threatened to disrupt this alliance by attempting to set up an independent Labour Party in the London area. At the same time, they could not, as Socialists, dissociate themselves from a movement which was setting out to preach an undogmatic Socialism closely resembling their own : nor could they ignore the fact that the Progressivism which was flourishing in the London area had no analogue in the greater part of the country. For example, in most of the northern and midland industrial towns and in Scotland the Liberals were by no means minded to enter into any sort of municipal partnership with the Socialists and a fierce battle was being waged between the old-fashioned 'Lib-Lab' Trade Unionists and Co-operators on the one hand and the New Unionists and Socialists on the other; and as the influence of Fabianism spread into the provinces after 1889 the provincial Fabian Societies, however ready to endorse the rest of the essayists' doctrine, could not stomach that part of it which involved coalition with the Liberals in municipal affairs. That was why the numerous local Fabian Societies which came into existence after 1889 mostly disappeared within a few years, merging themselves into the Independent Labour Party, there to fight the battle against capitalist Liberalism to their hearts' content. Meanwhile, the parent Fabian Society followed in politics an ambiguous line, as the ally of the Progressives on the London County Council and at the same time as a lukewarm supporter of the I.L.P. in the country as a whole. Indeed, throughout the 1890s the Fabian leaders mostly regarded it as their mission to 'permeate' the I.L.P., just as they were seeking to permeate the Liberal Party, without positively throwing themselves into the movement for independent Labour representation.

In London, where Sidney Webb was very active as a Progressive member of the London County Council from 1892, the Fabians made their impact chiefly in the field of education, first through the Technical Education Board and later, after the Education Act of 1902, on the Local Education Authority which replaced the London School Board. In the 'nineties, as far as I can discover, they made no special attempt to press for municipalisation : certainly they did not fall out with the Liberal Progressives over this issue. Indeed, save in the field of education, the Fabians on the L.C.C. appear to have made, and to have attempted, little that had not been already advocated by the London Radicals, under the leadership of J. F. B. Firth (1842–89), before they appeared on the scene. They were, in relation to the whole membership of the Council and of the Progressive Party upon it, always a very small group — none at all on the first Council and only about half a dozen on the Council after 1892. They would not have found it easy to persuade the Progressives to adopt an advanced policy of municipalisation, however hard they had tried. But it does not appear that they did try. Of course, they advocated a form of municipal ownership for a number of services — water-supply, tramways, docks, and so on ; but so had Firth and the Radicals before them, and they were always careful to state their case by pointing out that these and similar services had already been municipalised in one way or another in other big towns which had not had to wait so long as London to be equipped with workable local government institutions. Webb's chief activities on the L.C.C., outside the educational field, were in matters of financial reform and in connection with the discussions which led up to the establishment of the Metropolitan Borough Councils in 1899. In general, the Fabians on the L.C.C. behaved rather as Radicals than as Socialists : they were more interested in the development of education and in the reform of the rating system than in municipalisation ; and even where they did favour public ownership they tended to prefer the establishment of the Metropolitan Water Board to the direct administration of the water-service by the L.C.C. Webb's book, *The London Programme* (1891), was not much ahead of what Firth had written in numerous tracts issued by the Municipal Reform League in the 'seventies and 'eighties ; and the London Reform Union, formed in 1892 as the propagandist agency of the Progressive Party, though it had Tom Mann as its Secretary from that year until 1898, for the most part only repeated what Firth and his group had been advocating for a long time past. The Fabian emphasis in London politics was less on municipalisation as such than on the improvement of metropolitan services (which might involve it) and on a fairer distribution of the burden of paying for them. As in national affairs, it was 'rent', rather than administration, that they set out to socialise in the first instance. This is not necessarily a criticism : indeed, Webb's work for London education was quite outstanding. But it does run counter to the legend that the Fabians were the principal inspirers of London's progressive social policy.

We saw earlier that *The True Radical Programme*, the tract issued in 1887 by the Fabian Parliamentary League, proposed nationalisation of railways, but did not include any further proposals for public ownership. Its main demand in the economic field was for the taxation of unearned income on a rising scale. The Fabian 'Basis', adopted earlier in the same year, declared for 'the emancipation of Land and Industrial Capital from individual and class ownership, and the vesting of them in the community for the general benefit'. It went on to say that 'The Society further works for the transfer to the community of the administration of such industrial Capital as can conveniently be managed socially'. But it said nothing about the forms which social administration of such capital was to take, or about how the land and other kinds of capital would be dealt with after their ownership had been vested in the community. It was left open whether social ownership was to be local or regional or national. The emphasis was not on social administration, but on the transfer to the community of the surplus to which the Fabians gave the general name 'rent', in preference to the Marxist term 'surplus-value'. The Basis laid down explicitly that 'The Society . . . works for the extinction of private property in Land and of the consequent individual appropriation, in the form of Rent, of the price paid for permission to use the earth, as well as for the advantage of superior soils and sites'. This sentence, taken by itself, sounds like a direct echo of Henry George, or perhaps rather of the Land Nationalisers with whom he was largely identified in his earlier propaganda.[1] But the sentence came, in the Fabian Basis, in between the opening declaration in favour of public ownership of 'Land and Industrial Capital', and the less decisive phrases concerning the administration of 'such

[1] For Henry George's attitude to land nationalisation see Vol. II, p. 373.

industrial Capital as can conveniently be managed socially'. The Fabians, in 1887, were clear about land *ownership*, as the key to the appropriation of 'rent' in the ordinary sense of the word. They were also clear in regarding other forms of Capital, equally with Land, as yielding to their owners what could properly be called a 'rent' — what Marshall a little later called a 'quasi-rent'. But they were vague about, or at any rate prepared not to erect into an article of faith, any statement concerning the administration of the land when it had become public property; and they were much more hesitant than Shaw was in his opening contribution to *Fabian Essays* in asserting that Land and Capital were quite on all fours as sources of universal tribute levied on the community by their possessors. In relation to Capital, as distinct from Land, the words used in the Basis were that 'Owing to the monopoly of the means of production in the past, industrial inventions and the transformation of surplus income into Capital have mainly enriched the proprietary class, the worker being now dependent on that class for leave to earn a living'. Moreover, the following paragraph went on to say that if the proposed measures of transfer to public ownership were carried out, 'Rent *and Interest* will be added to the reward of labour, the idle class now living on the labour of others will necessarily disappear, and practical equality of opportunity will be maintained by the spontaneous action of economic forces with much less interference with personal liberty than the present system entails'. Thus, in the Basis, the word 'Rent' was used in relation to Land only, and in relation to Capital the Fabians spoke of 'Interest'. But by the time *Fabian Essays* were written, the near-identity of land-rent and of the return on capital as species of a wider genus, 'Rent', was unequivocally asserted. 'Colloquially', Bernard Shaw wrote in his exposition of Socialist economics, 'one property with a farm on it is said to be land yielding rent; whilst another, with a railway on it, is called capital yielding interest. But economically there is no distinction between them when they once become sources of revenue.' Shaw does indeed, elsewhere in the same essay, draw a distinction between rent in general and pure economic rent which corresponds to differential advantages of fertility and situation. The latter — rent in the strictly Ricardian sense — must, he says, be taken by the public and used to provide the resources for economic development; whereas all the rest, he says, is available for adding to the incomes of the producers. But this sharp distinction did not come to form a part of the essential Fabian doctrine.

It will have been noticed that the Fabians, in the passage just quoted from their 'Basis', spoke of 'equality of opportunity', maintained 'by the spontaneous action of economic forces', as the state of affairs that would prevail when the unearned incomes of landlords and capitalists had been sequestered. This sounds very much as if they envisaged a future in which competitive enterprise would continue but would be rendered fair by the elimination of the monopolistic privileges attaching to private ownership of the means of production. But it is not clear how far they did mean this : probably they had rather in mind that, given public ownership of land and capital, each individual would tend to be rewarded in accordance with his capacity and service — that is to say, a state of affairs closely resembling that which Marx, in the *Critique of the Gotha Programme*, had envisaged as appropriate to the period of transition from a capitalist to a fully socialised economy.

At all events, the Fabian essayists made it perfectly clear that, during the transition to Socialism, public boards, national or local, in charge of enterprises carried on for the general benefit, would need to pay their managers and administrators salaries high enough to attract the best men. At the outset this would mean outbidding capitalist enterprises, or at least paying whatever was necessary to make positions in the public service as desirable as anything private enterprise could offer, after making allowance for differences in risk and security of tenure. The Fabians held, however, that as public enterprise showed its greater efficiency, capitalist businesses would be able to offer less and less, so that the need for high salaries would be progressively reduced. We saw that they expected public enterprises to be able, because of their freedom from charges for capital, to offer better wages than the capitalists could afford and none the less drive them progressively out of business. Similarly, public enterprise would be able to afford high salaries for good administrators and technicians, as long as this continued to be necessary.

The assumption underlying this idea of the ability of public to outbid private enterprise was, then, not only that public enterprise would prove itself superior in efficiency, but also that capital for it would be available free of interest out of the yield of the taxes on land-rent and other unearned incomes. The process of socialisation which the Fabians envisaged at this stage was in the main not the buying out of the existing owners on terms which would leave them as bondholders receiving unearned incomes from the public authority, but the setting up of new public enterprises capitalised out of the new taxes on property-incomes, without any interest being payable on the capital thus invested. Where particular enterprises were bought from their private owners, Shaw did advocate the payment of compensation to the particular owner who was bought out. But this compensation was to be paid, not by the creation of public debt, but out of the same tax fund as was to supply the capital for founding new public enterprises. When the Fabians asserted, in their 'Basis', that the acquisition of Land and Capital was to be 'without compensation, though not without such relief to expropriated individuals as may seem fit to the community', they appear to have had in mind, not the refusal of compensation to the individual capitalist who was singled out for early expropriation because the acquisition of his business was given a high priority on grounds of public interest, but rather that the main form of expropriation would be an increasing tax on the incomes derived from ownership, plus the progressive driving out of capitalistic businesses by the successful competition of the new public concerns. The capitalist was clearly to receive no compensation for being more and more highly taxed ; and equally he was to receive none for having his profits destroyed by the competition of the interest-free enterprises started under public ownership or for having his workers drawn away by the superior attractions of public employment.

There remain two paragraphs of the Fabian 'Basis' of which, so far, no mention has been made. The first of these, set out at the head of the whole document, consisted of a single brief statement. 'The Fabian Society consists of Socialists.' The other, the concluding paragraph, laid down that 'for the attainment of these ends' — i.e. of the objects set forth in the intervening paragraphs, 'the Fabian Society looks to the spread of Socialist opinions, and the social and political changes consequent thereon. It seeks to achieve these ends by the general dissemination of knowledge as to the relation between the individual and Society in its economic, ethical and political aspects.' Thus, the Fabians proclaimed both their faith in democratic methods and in political and social education and their recognition of ethical and political aspects as standing on all fours with economic aspects. They regarded the advent of Socialism as needing to be brought about by persuading men to adopt Socialist opinions, as well as by the historic forces making for socialisation on the basis of developing productive and administrative techniques. Like the Marxists, they saw no inconsistency in regarding Socialism both as an inevitable tendency and as a cause to be advanced by educational and propagandist effort. The difference from the Marxists was that their interpretation of history was gradualist rather than revolutionary, so that they expected Socialism to be achieved by gradual and progressive stages rather than by any sudden victory of one class over another, and by spreading democratic conviction rather than by force.

It is a rather astonishing fact that the Fabian 'Basis', drawn up in 1887, apparently without much discussion or controversy, remained entirely unchanged until 1905, when it received a single amendment, and thereafter up to 1919, when a more substantial revision was made by the Executive Committee and approved at the Annual Meeting on the motion of Sidney Webb. The amendment of 1905 arose out of the feminist agitation of that period, and simply committed the Fabian Society to pursue 'the establishment of equal citizenship for men and women'. Sex equality had in fact been accepted as an objective by the Society from its early years; but as a matter of practical politics the early Fabians had been prepared to demand manhood suffrage in the first instance, leaving adult suffrage to follow at a later stage when public opinion had been better prepared to accept it. In the new century this attitude was no longer acceptable to the feminists, many of whom were determined to oppose any further enfranchisement of males unless women were enfranchised as well. The Fabian Society yielded to the feminist attack; but in all other respects attempts to alter the 'Basis' met with defeat, not so much because the wording was regarded as fully satisfactory as because every proposal to change it ended in failure to agree on a revised formulation. Even the revision of 1919 left the essentials unchanged, the main alteration of substance being a commitment to support the Labour Party and the Socialist International; and after 1919 no further changes were made for another twenty years. Finally, in 1939, when the Fabian Society merged with its offshoot of 1930, the New Fabian Research Bureau, the 'Basis' disappeared, and was replaced by a very simple statement of Socialist faith incorporated in the Rules of the reorganised Society.[1]

Up to 1890 the Fabian Society was a small but active body consisting mainly of Londoners, though it had scattered members in a number of provincial towns and in Scotland, and a few living abroad. The total membership in 1890 was only 173; but by the spring of 1891 it had risen to 361, and in addition a number of local Fabian Societies had been established as independent bodies, whose members were not automatically attached to the parent Society. The following year the Society itself had 541 members, and in 1893 there was a further rise to 640. By this time there were also no fewer than 74 local Fabian Societies, in addition to a number of local groups in the London area. Of the local Societies 24 were in Lancashire and Cheshire — largely the outcome of a propagandist lecturing campaign — 14 were in Yorkshire, and 7 in the four Northern counties. The Midland counties accounted for 8, Wales and Monmouthshire for 4, Scotland for 3, and Ireland for 2. The rest were widely scattered over England, except 1 in Australia

---

[1] In 1954, the relevant Rule (Rule 2), which had remained unchanged since 1939, ran as follows : 'The Society consists of Socialists. It therefore aims at the establishment of a Society in which equality of opportunity will be assured and the economic power and privileges of individuals and classes abolished through the collective ownership and democratic control of the economic resources of the community. It seeks to secure these ends by the methods of political democracy. The Society, believing in equal citizenship in the fullest sense, is open to persons, irrespective of sex, race or creed, who commit themselves to its aims and purposes and undertake to promote its work. The Society shall be affiliated to the Labour Party. Its activities shall be the furtherance of Socialism and the education of the public on socialist lines, by the holding of meetings, lectures, discussion groups, conferences and summer schools, the promotion of research into political, economic and social problems, national and international, the publication of books, pamphlets and periodicals, and by any other appropriate methods.'

and 1 in India. The parent Society took no responsibility for their doings, though it recorded their existence and held, in 1892, a solitary conference to which 14 of them, representing about 1100 members, sent delegates.

This spread of Fabian activity into the provinces was short-lived. By 1894 there were only 53 local Societies, though quite a number of new ones — including 1 in Ottawa — had been set up; and in the following year the Annual Report stated that 'only a few of the local Societies now possess much more than a nominal existence'. In 1896, at the International Socialist Congress held in London, 13 local Fabian Societies were represented; but the number continued to fall away, and by 1900 there were only 8, including 4 University Fabian Societies at Oxford, Cambridge, Glasgow, and Aberystwyth. The only important local body was at Liverpool: in all the other big towns the local Societies had ceased to exist. Meanwhile, the membership of the parent Society had risen to a peak of 861 in 1899 and thereafter, with some oscillations, tended for some years to decline, mainly because it became stricter in striking off defaulters. In 1904, just before the revival described in a subsequent chapter,[1] its membership was 730.

The rapid rise and fall of the local Fabian Societies is easily explained. Their rise followed hard on the publication of *Fabian Essays* and was part of the rapid spread of Socialist opinion after the London dock strike and the development of the New Unionism. Their decline was the direct outcome of the establishment in 1893 of the Independent Labour Party, which became the political representative of the new trend, and either swallowed up the local Fabian Societies or reduced them to inactivity by taking over most of their members. The parent Society in London, which had done little to bring them into being, did nothing at all to sustain them when the I.L.P. appeared to offer a more attractive rallying point for provincial Socialism. The leading Fabians expressed no regrets when their local followers deserted to the I.L.P. They may indeed even have been relieved, because they were set free almost without opposition to pursue their policy of 'permeation' and to collaborate with the Liberal Progressives on the London County Council — a policy to which, as we saw, many of the

[1] See p. 201 ff.

provincial Societies were opposed. After 1893, though the Fabian Society continued to give valuable service to the I.L.P. as a formulator of social projects and a supplier of Socialist tracts and lecturers, the main work of building up the new reformist Socialism as a national movement passed into the hands of the Independent Labour Party. To that body we must accordingly now turn our attention, and come back to the Fabians when we have attempted to assess the nature and strength of the forces which rallied under Keir Hardie's leadership to give political expression to the aspirations of the 'New Unionism' and found in Robert Blatchford's *Clarion* an inspiration to comradeship fully as important in the making of a distinctively British type of Socialist movement.

(ii) The New Unionism and its Background

At the time when Henry Mayers Hyndman launched his Democratic Federation [1] the time was still unripe for the emergence in Great Britain of a considerable Socialist Party, or even of a Labour Party devoted to the advocacy of immediate working-class claims. The Trade Unions, after the sudden expansion of the early 1870s, in which Joseph Arch and the agricultural labourers had played a memorable part, had shrunk up in the later 'seventies into merely defensive agencies of a skilled minority, well content if they could hold their own in face of unemployment and falling prices. The British following of the First International had melted away, leaving hardly a trace. The political leadership of the 'left' had passed into the hands of Joseph Chamberlain and Charles Dilke, who were doing their best to radicalise the Liberal Party and were preaching not only Radical politics but also Radical economics, including both social reforms to be brought about largely by municipal action and progressive taxation of the rich. Falling prices, though they penalised certain groups of workers — notably the coal-miners, whose wages were linked to coal prices — and though they caused distress through unemployment, brought to the employed workers the compensation of cheaper food. There is little doubt that, on the average, the standard of

[1] For the Social Democratic Federation see Vol. II, p. 390.

living was actually rising, at any rate for the more skilled workers. The result was that the areas of acute discontent were limited. There was unrest in the coalfields, in the slums and lower working-class quarters inhabited by the less skilled workers, and in any area that was particularly hit by unemployment; but there was no general working-class temper of revolt and no inclination on the part of the Trade Unions of craftsmen to put themselves at the head of any movement showing such a temper. In the absence of any movement exerting a mass-appeal, the individual malcontents among the workers tended to attach themselves to Charles Bradlaugh's atheist Republicanism or, if they were less extreme, to the Radical Clubs which supported Chamberlain and Dilke in their efforts to democratise the Liberal Party by doing battle with the Whigs.

In 1881, when the Democratic Federation was started, though average money wages had fallen a few points below the level reached in the first half of the 'seventies, real wages had actually risen for those in full employment. Nor was unemployment, at 3 or 4 per cent, at all severe among the skilled workers. No doubt conditions among the less skilled workers were appallingly bad, especially in the slum districts of the bigger towns; but they were certainly no worse than they had been ten years before, or indeed at any time within living memory. With prices — especially food prices — falling and enough unemployment to make the Trade Unions wary of courting trouble, political rather than industrial action appeared to offer favourable prospects, with municipal action coming a good second. Chamberlain's appeal was therefore very strong, especially to the unenfranchised, on whose behalf he was demanding an extension of the household suffrage, won for the townsmen in 1867, to the country districts, including, of course, the great mining areas and also many industrial centres outside the corporate towns. Moreover, Chamberlain was the leader of the municipal reform movement as well as of the political Radicals, and could thus appeal effectively to the workers in the boroughs as well as in the counties.

Within a few years, however, the situation was entirely transformed. Chamberlain, having carried through the Reform Act of 1884 and thus largely democratised the county electorate, fell out with the Liberal Party over Home Rule at the very moment when the same Reform Act had given the Irish Nationalists complete command of the Irish constituencies outside Ulster and had thus brought to Westminster a powerful Irish Party without whose support the Liberals could scarcely hope to maintain their power, even if their Whig and Radical sections remained united. But there were Whigs as well as Chamberlainites who could not stomach Home Rule ; and the Liberal-Unionist secession over this issue wrecked the entire prospect of the emergence, on the basis of the widened franchise, of a united Liberal Party drawn towards Radicalism under Chamberlain's leadership, and created a confusion which prepared the way for the advent of an independent working-class party. For what was a good working-class Radical to do when the effective leader of political Radicalism, in company with a number of reactionary Whigs, left the Liberal Party on the Irish issue and thus removed from it a great deal of the driving force towards a Radical policy ? To follow Chamberlain into Liberal Unionism meant abandoning Liberalism in favour not of a purer Radicalism but of an anti-Irish alliance with the Tories, whereas support of Irish Nationalism was part of the traditional Radical creed. On the other hand, to remain with the Liberals meant carrying on with the attempt to radicalise the Liberal Party under much less favourable conditions than had existed under Chamberlain's forceful leadership ; and the dilemma was made much more difficult when the only alternative leader of Radical Liberalism — Charles Dilke — was removed from the political scene in 1886 by implication in a divorce suit. Puritan England could not at that time even contemplate the possibility of being led by a person to whom such things could happen. The Liberal-Radicals were left leaderless, or at any rate without any leader capable of exerting a really popular appeal. For the time being most of them clung to their Radical Clubs : and most of the leaders of the old Trade Unions continued their attempts to induce the Liberal Party to adopt a programme advanced enough to attract the organised workers ; but their scant success exposed them to more and more devastating criticism from the small but growing body of Socialists, Anarchists, and unattached left-wingers who denounced the Liberal Party as the party of capitalism and inveterate belief in the virtues of *laissez-faire*.

The other great factor in the transformation that took place in the middle 'eighties was the recurrence of serious unemployment. The Trade Union percentage of unemployed — that is, mainly of skilled workers out of jobs — rose from 2·3 per cent in 1882 and 2·6 per cent in 1883 to 8·1 per cent, 9·3 per cent, and 10·2 per cent in the three following years. It then fell back to 7·6 per cent in 1887, 4·9 per cent in 1888, and 2·1 per cent in 1889 and 1890. Thus from 1884 to 1887 there was heavy unemployment — much heavier among the less skilled workers than these figures suggest; and the trade recession coincided in time with the great extension of the franchise in the first of these years and the rift in the Radical movement caused by Chamberlain's defection and Dilke's sudden eclipse. The members of the Social Democratic Federation and of the Socialist League who put themselves at the head of the unemployed agitation did not make a great many converts to their rival brands of Socialist doctrine; but they did accomplish between them a considerable diffusion of socialistic ideas. Charles Bradlaugh's vigorous hostility to Socialism helped rather than hindered this development; for it was excellent publicity, and attracted large audiences whom the Socialist gospel would not have easily reached without its aid. The Bradlaughites and the Socialists found themselves allies in upholding the rights of public meeting and procession, not only in London, but also in other towns; and police attempts to stop demonstrations cemented the alliance and inclined many of Bradlaugh's followers to lend a friendly ear to Socialist orators who, in appealing to the unemployed, modified their dogmatism and addressed themselves to immediate grievances. John Burns (1859–1941) played at this stage a leading part in preaching a forthright, simple Socialist sermon without much Marxist jargon: Annie Besant, who had been Bradlaugh's principal collaborator, was converted to Socialism and drew many Radicals after her. The hue and cry after Dilke disgusted many who had previously adhered to some sort of Nonconformist belief, and reinforced the mistrust of Liberal capitalists who were busy cutting wages in view of the depression. The sufferings of the unemployed, the harsh administration of the poor law, and the Government's failure to respond to the demand for adequate relief aroused the social conscience of many members of the middle classes who had previously shown little awareness of the 'social question'. Among these were ministers of religion, novelists such as Walter Besant, and, most important of all, a growing number of popular journalists, headed by a certain contributor to the sporting press who went by the name 'Nunquam Dormio' (I never sleep), and whose real name was Robert Blatchford.

Indeed, Blatchford and his friend A. M. Thompson were themselves among the converts to the Socialist cause who were brought into politics by the unemployed troubles and by the experiences of working-class misery which these troubles helped not a little to make known. The Fabians, though they were too few to play any substantial part in the unemployed agitation, contributed a stream of facts and figures about riches and poverty which speakers and journalists could turn to effective use. The new social thinking and feeling that went into the making of the new British Socialist movement of the 1890s were already well on their way before the depression ended, and the trade revival cleared the road for the great Trade Union outburst of 1889.

The 'New Unionism' of that year was indeed the child of Socialism out of unemployment, with the distraught Liberal Party as midwife. All over the country the revival of trade released forces which had been steadily gaining strength during the depression. Ben Tillett (1860–1943) had begun to organise his London Tea-porters' and General Labourers' Union at the docks in 1887, while trade was still bad. Annie Besant had put herself at the head of the London match-girls' strike, which she had unwittingly provoked, in 1888; and in the same year a considerable section of the miners, tired of having wages cut again and again under the sliding-scale system which linked them to the price of coal, had founded the Miners' Federation of Great Britain on the basis of a breakaway from the sliding-scale and a demand for a living wage. There was a harking back to the great days of the early 1870s, when for a brief period Trade Unionism had spread considerably among the less-skilled urban workers, as well as among the agricultural labourers, only to be almost annihilated among these groups when the boom ended. But the new movement differed from its predecessor in that the new men who appeared as its leaders were mostly Socialists, at least to the extent of calling upon the Government to make itself responsible for the concession of the 'right to work'. Most of them demanded in addition a legal minimum wage and a legal eight hours' day — the latter called for the more urgently because it was widely regarded as a means of spreading the available employment more evenly among those looking for work.

In 1885 the membership of the Trade Unions affiliated to the Trades Union Congress was only half a million. By 1890 it was nearly 1,600,000 and the total affiliated membership, including Trades Councils, had risen from 631,000 to 1,927,000. Part of this was a mushroom growth : within another year there had been a very sharp fall. But the Trade Union awakening of 1889 left the strength of Trade Unionism lastingly doubled, with a great influx of members into the older Unions as well as the establishment of numerous new Unions which, though they lost members, managed to survive the ensuing recession.

These new Unions were essentially bargaining organisations, and not friendly societies as well. They catered mainly for workers who could not afford high weekly contributions ; and they were accordingly unable to offer many benefits. Many of them made a virtue of this necessity, denouncing the friendly benefit activities of the older Unions as the principal cause of their lack of militancy and failure to pay any attention to the claims of the less skilled. The orators of the Social Democratic Federation and the Socialist League had long been eloquent on this theme. The Hyndmanites had attacked the craft Unions as monopolists bent on defending exclusive craft interests against the working class as a whole, and regarded them as the worst enemies of those who were seeking to organise the workers politically into a class party. The Socialist Leaguers had shown more disposition to throw their weight on the side of the Trade Unions, wherever they were engaged in industrial struggles — for example, the Unions in the north-eastern coalfields and the engineers and textile workers in Yorkshire. But they too had been vehement in denouncing the existing leadership of the Unions, and had in effect differed from the S.D.F. mainly as disbelievers in the virtues of fighting elections and of a disciplined party machine. The fact that most of the leaders of the old Unions were still trying to radicalise the Liberal Party, despite Chamberlain's defection, furnished a further ground of hostility between the Old Unionism and the New, which was led mainly by men who had either broken away already from Liberal Radicalism or had become active only when it had been already disrupted by Chamberlain's defection.

The New Unionism, however, was not a single or a united force. The new Unions of dockers, gasworkers, navvies, and other previously almost unorganised groups were organised and led almost exclusively by men who were either already Socialists or ready to accept the gospel of 'Labour independence' which the Socialists among them preached. Among the miners and textile workers, on the other hand, Trade Unionism was already strongly entrenched; and the inflow of new members and the adoption of new policies did not carry with it a displacement of the old leaders. The Miners' Federation had a new policy — minimum wage, no sliding-scale, the eight hours' day — but for the most part the old leaders accepted the new policies without changing their political allegiance. Similarly, the cotton operatives came out with stronger demands for improved factory legislation, but remained wedded to craft Unionism and to their old leaders. In Yorkshire, on the other hand, where Trade Unionism had been very much weaker, the woollen and worsted operatives did enter the field with new Unions under new leaders who were much readier to accept the political implications of the new working-class gospel. In some coalfields, notably in West Scotland and parts of South Wales, Trade Union weakness made it easier for new men and new ideas to take the lead. But Keir Hardie could not bring the Miners' Federation round to either Socialism or independent Labour political action, even though they were calling on the State to legislate on their behalf. Nor could the Lancashire Socialists convince the majority of cotton operatives that their demand for factory legislation logically involved their defection from the Liberal Party in which their employers were so strongly entrenched.

Coal and cotton, in effect, came to occupy a place between the Old Unionism and the New. Except the Unions of skilled coal-hewers in Durham and Northumberland, most of the miners were supporters of the legal eight hours' day and of the minimum wage; but they continued to send their leaders to Parliament as 'Lib-Labs' and to vote for Liberal candidates who were prepared to give some support to their economic claims. The cotton operatives were more divided; but on the whole they followed leaders who remained attached to Liberalism and combined their demands for legislation with a policy of exceeding moderation in the industrial field. Miners and cotton operatives favoured, in the main, increasing State intervention in the regulation of industrial conditions; but they did not become easy converts to any kind of Socialism.

Thus, the New Unionists who rallied to the cause of Socialism and Independent Labour representation were for the most part either very new Unionists, belonging to Unions but recently established, or were in a minority in older Unions still mainly led by men who cherished the hope of bringing the Liberal Party over *en masse* to support of a moderate working-class programme, as well as of further instalments of political Radicalism. Some of the new men had served their apprenticeship in the S.D.F. or the Socialist League, or in the unemployed agitations of the middle 'eighties. Some of them had been followers of Bradlaugh and Annie Besant in the Secularist movement, or had been active in such bodies as the Land Restoration League. A few had been influenced by Stewart Headlam or other exponents of Christian Socialism. But most of them, including some of the foremost, were new men, who had taken no active part in any previous movement, but had felt the stirring of the times and had awakened to social consciousness just as the new movement of Labour independence was taking shape. These men and women, mostly young and eager, did not need to be detached from Liberalism, to which they had never owed allegiance. But many of them did badly need a sense of fellowship and of adventure in a new way of living that was much more than an acceptance of the call to work together for merely economic ends or even for economic and political ends.

The men and women who made the new Socialism of the years after 1889 wanted a new way of life, and not merely an economic or political creed. But the form of this want was by no means the same for all of them. There were in the new gospel two interwoven threads — one Puritan, deeply serious,

and apt to be censorious ; the other, in revolt against the drabness and misery of the contemporary world, desperately
determined to be jolly, and by no means ill-pleased when the
Puritans looked down their noses at its goings-on. Keir Hardie
and Philip Snowden, though they differed greatly in temperament and attitude, belonged to the first group : they had
been Good Templars and lay preachers before they became
Socialists, and they carried over into their Socialism the
puritanical rigour of their earlier evangelism. Robert Blatchford
and the Clarion Fellowship were the protagonists of the other
group, which was certainly no less moved by moral fervour,
but urged its crusade against suffering rather than against sin,
and set out to make friends with the sinners and enlist them
under the Socialist banner, rather than to call upon them to
repent and become respectable. Personally, the outstanding
leaders of the second group were a singularly unsinful lot —
certainly, no more sinful than the Puritans. But they had a
horror of the 'unco' guid', and of the respectability which they
felt to be withering up the human feelings of their Puritan
fellow-workers, especially when it was a question of helping
the bottom dogs. It made them angry when they heard fellow-
Socialists denouncing the evils of drink and blaming the poor
for their feckless and improvident habits, instead of blaming
their vices on the system and crediting the poor with hearts of
gold. It was no accident that Blatchford became an ardent
determinist, and wrote *Not Guilty* to demonstrate that what
men did amiss was no fault of theirs but the necessary outcome
of their nurture and environment in a world given over to the
evil doctrines of competition and *laissez-faire*. The French
moralists of the eighteenth century had taken the same view ;
and so had Robert Owen, through whom the belief that man's
character is a product of his social environment had been
transmitted to the Secularists and Rationalists of subsequent
generations. Blatchford, though poverty had reduced him to
the working class, came out of the lower ranks of artistic
Bohemia : he became a soldier and a lover of soldiers and of
common people who lived by conventions widely removed
from both church and chapel. He rejoiced in proclaiming his
love for all men and women as they actually were, and not as
they ought to be — which did not prevent him from dissembling

very successfully his love for such of them as were either exploiters or superior persons. But he did not behave in his private life a whit less respectably than the Puritans he so cordially disliked. The Clarionettes were fond of extolling the virtue of having a good time; but in practice they got jolly over tea and coffee much more than over mugs of beer, and denounced the working man's indifference to politics just as roundly as if they had not proved conclusively that it was none of his fault.

Blatchford and Keir Hardie, outstanding leaders respectively of the Clarionettes and of the Independent Labour Party, could never get on together, although both were men of the highest ideals and their ideals had a great deal in common. Blatchford mistakenly thought Hardie a killjoy : Hardie, no less mistakenly, regarded Blatchford as flippant and as a stumbling-block in the way of Socialism, because he antagonised the very people to whom it was most important to appeal. As a matter of fact, Hardie had a considerable sense of humour and liked, as much as Blatchford, to see people enjoying themselves, provided they stayed sober; while Blatchford had in him something of the recluse and had gloomy fits in which he was not even remotely jolly. Nevertheless, the one did stand for the Puritan tradition and the other for the reaction against it. It was of course really necessary, if an effective movement was to be built, to appeal to both types — to Puritans and to those who were in revolt against them. But this could not easily be done by the same methods, or by the same men.

Between the Puritans and the 'Merrie Englanders' was a great mass that belonged to neither group. There were professional blasphemers who liked 'Nunquam's' attacks on religion but, being without a sense of humour, objected to his light way of writing about serious matters almost as much as did those who were shocked by his 'irreligion'. There were old working-class Radicals and old Socialists who shared Blatchford's uncompromising hostility to the 'capitalist parties', but were offended by his hostility to revolution and disbelief in the possibility of a sudden leap to a Socialist way of life. There were groups which shared Blatchford's zeal for education and popular culture, but differed from him in holding that the new culture must be based on a decisive repudiation of bourgeois values. Finally, there were the simple seekers after a new gospel who were neither Puritans nor anti-Puritans, neither abstainers nor drinkers on principle, neither much addicted to fornication nor shocked by it, neither religious nor irreligious, neither revolutionaries nor reformists — in short, the common run of the men and women who were joining Trade Unions for the first time in their lives and listening with approval to the Socialist orators' denunciations of wicked aristocrats, landowners, and capitalists, without either having, or consciously needing, any clear notion of what the orators wished to put in their place.

It must not, however, be overlooked that at the time when the New Unionism and the new Socialism were taking shape, the hold of Nonconformity, and therewith of the Puritan attitude, on a large part of the working classes was still very strong. It was least in London and in the slum districts of other big towns ; and in every large town there was a section of the working people that had broken violently away, and hated the smug Nonconformists worse than it hated the Church. These men were the backbone of Secularism, which had a continuous tradition going back to Richard Carlile and even to the followers of Tom Paine. In the 1880s they became divided into Bradlaughite Republicans, Hyndmanite Social Democrats, and Anarchists or half-Anarchists of the Socialist League or the groups round Peter Kropotkin and Charlotte Wilson. All these groups were fairly small ; but they were active and knew how, on occasion, to get the 'ragged-trousered' slum-dwellers into the streets. They had, on the other hand, but little hold over the main body of the more skilled workers, though many of them were craftsmen and members of the older Trade Unions.

Even in the great towns Nonconformity was strong in the 'better' working-class districts. It was well entrenched in the Co-operative Societies, as well as in the craft Unions. Spiritu-ally, it was of an 'other-worldly' outlook, and the saving of souls from the everlasting fire still took a large place in the work of its chapels, though no longer so often as earlier in the century to the extent of making its devotees largely indifferent to the phenomenon of this-worldly unhappiness. But Nonconformity was at its strongest, not in the big cities, but in the industrial areas outside them — above all in the coalfields, which had

139

been evangelised principally by Methodists of one sort or another. It was in these areas that the chapels counted for most in the formation of political and social opinion, and also as key factors in the whole structure of family and community life. Consequently, the mining districts were the hardest to tear away from Liberal allegiance, which was closely bound up with the chapel communities.

In the towns, too, though in a less exclusive sense, the chapels were centres of community living, as well as of religious worship and politico-social loyalties. The individual or house-hold that broke away from chapel connection was very apt to feel lost and lonesome in a hostile world. Such outcasts — even if they were outcasts by their own act — wanted a sense of 'belonging' and of comradeship in some group small enough for intimate personal relations. Not a few of them wanted in addition that this new group should reproduce, in not too different a form, some of the observances to which they had been accustomed — singing together, listening together, taking part in some form of common service. John Trevor's (1855–1930) Labour Church movement, which caught on chiefly in the 'better' working-class districts of Lancashire and Yorkshire, set out to meet this need in its most exacting form, by organising Labour services, with ethical hymns and readings and addresses which were half-lectures and half-sermons that made the good ex-chapel-goer feel at home, and gave him an alternative centre for making like-minded friends and attending *en famille* on Sundays. But there were many others who wanted a new comradeship, but not a substitute chapel ; and many of these straying sheep found a part of what they needed in the personal intimacy of Robert Blatchford's writings in the *Sunday Chronicle* and later in the *Clarion*, which he founded when the *Chronicle* would no longer let him speak his full mind. The many sociable activities for which the *Clarion* movement was re-sponsible — Glee Clubs, Cycling Clubs, Rambling Clubs, Clarion Scouts, and many more — arose directly out of the very personal relation that Blatchford was able to build up with his host of readers ; and in the *Clarion* movement many of the new converts found the comradeship and the feeling of com-munity that they could not bear to be without.

There were, however, many others for whom the Clarionettes were both too boisterous and, before long, as Blatchford developed his views, too irreligious, too anti-respectable, and politically too extreme. For by no means all the converts to Socialism and Independent Labour either deserted their chapels or lost their faith, even if they cast away some of their old beliefs. For these chapel-going Socialists, the local Labour Unions, Labour Councils, and similar bodies which, in 1893, joined forces under Keir Hardie's leadership to set up the I.L.P., provided a home. Not, of course, that the I.L.P. was composed mainly of chapel-goers, or that most of the chapel-goers who voted Labour ever belonged to it. The I.L.P. aimed at organising on the broadest possible basis anyone who stood for Labour's political independence of other parties and for some kind of Socialism as the goal. But under Hardie's leadership it had a particular attraction for Socialists who had changed their politics without altogether abandoning their religious faith, and had kept a good deal of their Puritanism intact. Hardie's question *'Can a Man be a Christian on a Pound a Week?'* — the title of an address widely circulated as a pamphlet — struck the note such converts wanted. For Hardie Socialism was always the political doctrine of the Sermon on the Mount, a gospel to be preached in God's name and on the assumption that there was a God who cared for all men and would help them if they helped one another. There was not really much difference between their gospel and Blatchford's, except in their ways of putting it. But the way it was put made an enormous difference.

This must not be taken to mean that Blatchford and Hardie were leaders of two sharply separated movements. On the contrary, for some years Blatchford was one of the most active I.L.P. protagonists, and a great many Socialists were connected with both groups. F. W. Jowett of Bradford, for example, distributed his contribution between the two for many years with no sense of incongruity. But Hardie, who had his own organ, *The Labour Leader*, always disliked the Clarionettes; and Blatchford before long dropped out of activity in the I.L.P. when his policy of requiring Socialists never to vote for any candidate who was not a Socialist, even when no Socialist was in the field, was rejected by Hardie and the other principal leaders of the party. The *Clarion* became more and more a free-lance Socialist organ, owing allegiance to none except its own following, and expecting them to follow eagerly wherever Blatchford felt called upon to lead them.

Standing apart from all the groups so far described, but friendly to all, or almost all, was the idealistic Socialist, Edward Carpenter (1844–1929), whose poem in free verse, *Towards Democracy* (1883) had in its day a very wide appeal, not only in Great Britain but also in America and in the East. Carpenter began his career as Fellow of Trinity Hall, Cambridge and curate at Cambridge to F. D. Maurice, the Christian Socialist. But four years later, in 1874, he threw up both his curacy and his fellowship, and became a lecturer for the newly founded University Extension movement. In 1877 he paid his first visit to the United States and met Walt Whitman, who had a deep influence on him. *Towards Democracy* was written in a manner mainly derived from Whitman, and largely reflected his ideas. In 1886 he gave up his lecturing, largely for reasons of health, and settled down near Sheffield as the lodger of a working-class friend, Albert Fernehough, to write *Towards Democracy*. In 1882 his father died and he came into a few thousand pounds, a good deal of which he soon gave away. His money helped the S.D.F. to start *Justice*. He bought a few acres of orchard land in Derbyshire, still near Sheffield, and settled down to fruit-farming, to which he presently added sandal-making. Carpenter had become, after his visit to America, a keen advocate of the 'simple life', a pungent critic of so-called 'civilisation', and a convinced utopian, fully assured that mankind would before long abjure the errors of 'civilised' living and find peace and unity in a simple, communistic way of life, resting on complete social equality. Disease, he was sure, would almost disappear if men returned to a simple way of living in harmony with nature; and love would be purified when men had learnt to dispense with the manifold evils of property and mass-production of unnecessary things.

For the rest of his life Carpenter remained faithful to this ideal, which he expressed in a number of prose works as well as in additions to *Towards Democracy*. Among his best-known books are *England's Ideal* (1885) and *Civilisation, its Cause and Cure* (1889). His later writings dealt mainly with Eastern philosophy and with his thoughts on artistic creation — *From*

Adam's Peak to Elephanta (1892) and *The Art of Creation* (1904) or with the question of sex — *Love's Coming of Age* (1896). He published his reminiscences — *My Days and Dreams* — in 1916. Though he took little active part in the Socialist movement, except through his writings, he made a not unimportant contribution to the new Socialist thought of the closing decades of the nineteenth century. For many years he kept open house to Socialist visitors, especially from Sheffield, and to pilgrims who came to visit him from many countries. No system-maker, he was rather Anarchist than Socialist in his essential ideas : he looked forward to the complete disappearance of coercive government and to the advent of a free society in which every man would be able to find pleasure in the work of his hands and all unnecessary drudgery would have disappeared. He was, doubtless, what is called a 'crank' ; but he was well loved and deeply respected by those who knew him. His starry-eyed idealism, which repelled all doubt, met a need that was strongly felt by many of the new converts to the equalitarian gospel ; and his influence was even greater in India than in Great Britain. With the rise of the Labour Party and the development of Socialism into an organised political movement the mood that had responded to his writings passed, and his influence waned. But for a time, though never a leader, he ranked as a considerable minor prophet.

Even to-day, when few read *Towards Democracy*, Carpenter's Socialist song, 'England, Arise!' continues to be sung at countless meetings and serves to recall the exalted optimism of earlier Socialist days.

The purpose of this section has been to make some analysis both of the forces that led to the outburst of the 'New Unionism' in 1889 and of the states of feeling and opinion that accompanied this outburst and provided a stream of converts to the cause of 'Independent Labour' and of a Socialism essentially different from the 'scientific' Marxism of the continental Social Democrats and of the S.D.F. in Great Britain. There was, however, besides the working-class groups which have been discussed in this chapter, a substantial group of middle-class intellectuals who rallied to the workers' side and were impelled by largely similar emotions. In this group the Fabian Society did not stand alone ; but it came to exert by far the greatest influence, and before we attempt any analysis of the positive content of the new Socialism of the I.L.P. we must pass under review the earlier stages of the working out of the characteristically British doctrine of Fabian Socialism. This was above all the work of Sidney Webb, who by the end of the 1880s had clearly formulated a comprehensive philosophy of Socialism based not on Marx, but on a blend of Benthamite Utilitarianism as reinterpreted by John Stuart Mill, Darwinian Evolutionism, and Jevonian Economics, with a Materialist Conception of History scientifically degutted of its revolutionary parts.

(iii) THE INDEPENDENT LABOUR PARTY

The movement for 'Independent' Labour representation in Great Britain took shape in the Independent Labour Party, founded in 1893, and prepared the way for the Labour Party. It began in a number of separate local movements of opposition to the attempt to build up a Labour group inside the Liberal Party. The origins of this 'Lib-Lab' group went back to the Labour Representation League which was set up after the Reform Act of 1867 and secured its first successes when the two miners' leaders, Alexander Macdonald and Thomas Burt, were elected to Parliament in 1874. These two, with the stone-mason, Henry Broadhurst, Secretary of the Trades Union Congress, were successful at the election of 1880, at which Charles Bradlaugh also was elected, only to be unseated by the House of Commons, and to be re-elected in 1881, 1882, and 1884 in the course of his long struggle for the right to affirm instead of taking the oath. Macdonald died in 1881 ; and his seat was fought and lost. In 1884-5 two Acts extended the suffrage in the county areas and redistributed seats to the advantage of the industrial areas ; and in the ensuing election of 1885 6 miners and 5 other Trade Union leaders were elected, in addition to Bradlaugh and 2 crofters' representatives from the Scottish Highlands. The 11 Trade Union M.P.s constituted a regular group within the Liberal Party, and high hopes were entertained of the Liberals' conversion to a form of Radicalism that would warrant Labour support. At this point, however, came the Liberal split over Home Rule, marked by Chamberlain's secession and the break-up of the Radical alliance. This crisis coincided in time with the unemployed troubles of the middle 'eighties, which greatly increased Socialist influence in the industrial areas. At the General Election of 1886, which arose out of the Home Rule crisis, 5 of the 6 miners held their seats, but 3 of the 5 other Trade Unionists were unseated, and only 2 fresh seats won. This setback caused the Trades Union Congress, which had been voting down resolutions demanding that it should take up the movement for Labour representation, to change its mind, and to set up in 1886 a Labour Electoral Committee on the motion of John Wilson, the Durham miners' leader, who had lost his seat. The old Labour Representation League had faded out after 1881 : the new agency was set up at first as a committee of the Trades Union Congress, but was turned the following year into a separate Labour Electoral Association, designed to work mainly through the local Trades Councils, but empowered to set up local associations of its own where it thought fit.

The L.E.C. was established by the combined vote of all the groups at the Trades Union Congress which favoured working-class political action, whether in association with the Liberals or not. But it became essentially a 'Lib-Lab' body ; for most of the Trade Union leaders were still firmly attached to the Gladstonian party, despite Chamberlain's defection, and the Liberals were naturally making every effort to hold Trade Union support. Indeed, Schnadhorst and the central organisation of the Liberal Party were doing their best to induce reluctant local Liberal Associations to accept Trade Union candidates for seats that would be imperilled without their support. The policy of the Labour Electoral Association was to get a Trade Union candidate put forward by the local Trades Council or by some other Trade Union body, such as a Miners' Association, and then to urge the local Liberal Association to adopt him. If the Liberal Association refused, the L.E.A. next demanded that the names of the Liberals' proposed candidate and of the Trade Union nominee should be balloted upon by the local Liberals, each party giving a pledge to support the candidate who got most votes. If this was accepted, and the Trade Unionist won, he was to become the official Liberal and

Radical nominee. If, on the other hand, the Trade Unionist was beaten in the Liberal ballot, or the Liberals refused to take a ballot, the L.E.A. usually withdrew its candidate in order to avoid splitting the vote and making the Conservative a present of the seat. This meant in practice that 'Lib-Lab' candidates were adopted for a number of constituencies dominated by the mining vote, and for a few others, but that, in face of strong opposition from most of the local Liberal Associations, no great progress could be made. Of the 5 Trade Unionists, apart from the miners, elected in 1885, 3 sat for East London constituencies, 1 for a Birmingham seat, and 1 — Joseph Arch — for the agricultural constituency of North-West Norfolk. In 1886 Broadhurst, ejected from Birmingham because of the Chamberlain split, got in for West Nottingham : the other 3 successful Trade Unionists were all in East London. The Liberals in the northern industrial towns were not ready to yield seats to working men, even as Liberals.

In these circumstances there was naturally a growing hostility to the Liberals and to the Labour Electoral Association among the workers who had been shaken by the Chamberlainite split and were being awakened by the unemployed troubles and by the first stirrings of the New Unionism. In the political field nothing much happened until 1888, when James Keir Hardie (1856–1915), the leader of the Ayrshire Miners and of a movement for uniting the Scottish miners in a single federation, was put forward as miners' candidate at a by-election in Mid-Lanarkshire on the retirement of the sitting Liberal. Hardie's name was proposed to the local Liberal Association, which refused to accept him. Hardie's supporters then demanded a ballot of the Liberal electors, which was also refused. The Labour Electoral Association intervened vainly on his behalf : Schnadhorst, for the Liberal headquarters, arrived on the scene and, failing to move the local Liberals, privately offered Hardie a safe seat elsewhere at the next General Election and a maintenance allowance of £300 a year while he was in Parliament. Hardie refused to withdraw, rejecting the entire offer, despite pressure from T. R. Threlfall, the national Secretary of the L.E.A., to accept. The L.E.A. withdrew its support, and Hardie contested the seat as an independent Labour candidate, polling 617 votes against 3847 for the Liberal and 2917 for the Conservative. This was the beginning of 'Independent Labour', as distinct from 'Lib-Lab' or Social Democratic, politics.

Keir Hardie, at the time when he entered on the Mid-Lanark contest, still regarded himself as a Liberal. He was 31 years old, and had already made his name as a Trade Union leader by his endeavours to build up Trade Unionism among the miners of Western Scotland. This had involved tough struggles against bitter opposition from the coal-owners; and Hardie had tasted boycott and victimisation, and would have fared ill had he not been able to support himself by journalism in the shape of articles chiefly on mining conditions in the Ayrshire papers. In 1886 he had become Secretary of the Ayrshire Miners' Union, at a salary of £75 a year, and in January of the following year he had started his own monthly journal, *The Miner*. In the course of the same year he had become Secretary of the newly formed Scottish Miners' Federation, and had been adopted as miners' candidate for North Ayrshire. In this connection he had carried at the Ayrshire Miners' demonstration a resolution in favour of forming a 'Labour Party' and, when the Liberal Association refused to support him, had followed the Labour Electoral Association's line by demanding a ballot of the Liberal electors. He had also said that he would 'endeavour to have a branch of the Labour Electoral Association formed in every town and village in the constituency'. When, however, the vacancy occurred in Mid-Lanark he accepted the invitation to contest that seat instead.

There is evidence that Keir Hardie, though he was still a Liberal, already regarded himself in 1887 as some sort of Socialist. He was sent to London that year as a member of a deputation from the Scottish Miners and took the opportunity to meet Engels and Eleanor Marx, among others, and to get into touch with the Social Democratic Federation, with the intention of becoming a member. But his Puritan spirit was revolted by the atmosphere of beer and blasphemy which he found among the London Social Democrats. He was a proselytising teetotaller, and had been an active worker for the Evangelical Union; and though he had begun to throw off his theological dogmatism, he remained a Christian as well as a rigid total abstainer. He returned to Scotland without carrying out his intention of joining the S.D.F., or severing his Liberal connections. But in *The Miner* he freely printed contributions from Socialists, land nationalisers, and other rebels; and his own articles were already proclaiming the downfall of capitalism as near at hand.

Out of the Mid-Lanark election developed the Scottish Labour Party, in which men from a number of advanced movements came together. John Murdoch, the crofters' leader, presided at the preliminary meeting; Dr. Gavin B. Clark (1846–1930), one of the crofters' M.P.s, became a Vice-President. R. B. Cunninghame Graham (1852–1936), the 'Socialist laird' who had won a seat in Lanarkshire as a Radical in 1886, became President; the Glasgow Irishman, John Ferguson (1836–1906), a Vice-President; J. Shaw Maxwell (1855–1928), from the Henry Georgeite Scottish Land Restoration League, Chairman of the Executive; the Glasgow Socialist, George Mitchell, Treasurer. Hardie himself was Secretary, adding this office to the many he already held. What was left of the Scottish sections of the Socialist League rallied round under J. L. Mahon's influence. The programme included nationalisation of railways and other forms of transport, a national banking system and a state monopoly of the issue of money, and other socialistic proposals, as well as the more immediate demands for the eight hours' day, the right to work, and so on. Hardie and his group set to work energetically organising branches throughout Scotland.

Meanwhile, Henry Hyde Champion (1859–1928) had quarrelled with the S.D.F. after the rumpus over 'Tory gold', and had become active in the cause of Labour representation. In 1887 he started a paper, *Common Sense*, which soon developed into *The Labour Elector*, and threw himself into the Labour Electoral Association in the London area, trying to bring it over to independence of the Liberals. In London a Metropolitan Radical Federation had been set up in 1886 as a rival to the orthodox London Liberal and Radical Union, and this body had been accepted by the National Liberal Federation side by side with its rival. In 1888 the establishment of the London County Council raised in an immediately pressing form the question whether there was to be a 'Progressive' alliance on the new body. The Fabians and John Burns's followers alike favoured this plan : Burns formed his own Battersea Labour League and left the S.D.F. in 1889, the year of his election to the L.C.C. Champion, though he too was out of the S.D.F., which expelled him in 1888, was hostile to the 'Progressive' alliance, and became an active leader of the London movement for an independent Labour Party. He also took up energetically the question of the eight hours' day. Hardie, who had changed the title of his *Miner* to *The Labour Leader*, found it beyond his power to carry it on, and merged it into Champion's *Labour Elector*, of which he became Scottish correspondent. But in 1890 Champion quarrelled with Burns, Mann, and Tillett, and *The Labour Elector* suspended publication. Its place was taken by Joseph Burgess (1853–1934), with his *Workman's Times*, and Burgess at once set out to make his paper the rallying point for the national movement to bring an independent Labour Party into being. *The Workman's Times* was soon publishing a number of local editions, filled with news of Trade Union and Labour events, and serving as the first widely circulated organ of the new movement.

This was after the events of 1889, which had an immensely stimulating effect on working-class opinion all over the country. The victory of the London gasworkers, followed by the much more resounding success of the London dockers' strike, started the New Unionism on its crusade among the less skilled workers. Will Thorne (1857–1946), the leader of the London gasworkers, and Pete Curran (1860–1910) toured Yorkshire, organising branches of the Gasworkers' Union ; and there was a rapid spread of Trade Unionism into many trades, including the very badly organised woollen and worsted industry. John Andrew (1850–1906), the proprietor of the Lancashire *Cotton Factory Times*, started a *Yorkshire Factory Times* in 1889, with Joseph Burgess as editor ; and out of this the *Workman's Times* developed as a London offshoot the following year. Dock workers' Unions were organised on Merseyside and Tyneside and in other areas, and some of them expanded into Unions catering for a wide variety of less skilled workers. There was a ferment of working-class activity, which soon began to have political repercussions. At the end of 1890 the textile workers' strike at Manningham, near Bradford, led by W. H. Drew, was marked by serious conflicts between the strikers — who had no Trade Union —

and the police ; and out of it arose the Bradford Labour Union, with Drew as President, and with an aggressive policy of political independence. Ben Tillett, the London dockers' leader, and Robert Blatchford were secured as independent Labour candidates to fight seats at Bradford against the sitting Liberals. A few months later a similar Labour Union was founded in the Colne Valley, and Tom Mann was chosen as candidate. The Salford Labour Electoral Association joined the Independents a month later ; and at about the same time the London Trades Council formed its own Labour Representation League. Early the following year, Blatchford and John Trevor took the lead in establishing a Manchester District Independent Labour Party ; and at the same time Burgess launched in *The Workman's Times* an appeal to all supporters of an Independent Labour Party to send him their names in order that those who were willing to help could be put into communication and enabled to start branches of the proposed party in their several areas. This appeal met with a good deal of success : indeed, it set on foot many of the local bodies which sent their delegates to found the Independent Labour Party the following year. In June 1892 the Burgess group set up an Independent Labour Party in London, with Shaw Maxwell as Secretary, and tried to get the London committee accepted as the organising agency for the national party. The Scots and northerners took objection to this, and insisted that the new party should be formed with their full collaboration. They induced Hardie, who was elected to Parliament for a Greater London seat — South-West Ham — in July 1892, to take the lead by calling a preparatory meeting during the Trades Union Congress at Glasgow. It was there decided that a national conference to form an Independent Labour Party should be called to meet at Bradford in January 1893.

At the General Election of 1892 6 miners were again returned as 'Lib-Lab' M.P.s, together with 4 other Trade Unionists of the same persuasion. In Scotland Cunninghame Graham was defeated ; but Dr. G. B. Clark held his seat as a Radical. In Ireland, 3 Labour men, including Michael Davitt (1846–1906), of the Irish Land League, were elected ; but Davitt was unseated. In England, Independent Labour scored its first victories. John Burns won the Battersea seat, and Keir

Hardie was successful at West Ham. The Seamen's leader, Joseph Havelock Wilson (1859–1929), won at Middlesbrough in a three-cornered fight against Liberal and Tory opponents, but at once made his peace with the Liberals. It was thus left to Burns and Hardie to stake out the claim of the new party at Westminster. But Burns hung back. Hardie offered to work under his leadership; but Burns had no love for Hardie, and was deeply committed to the Progressive alliance on the London County Council. It fell to Hardie's lot to represent alone the claims of the rising movement, by standing forth as the champion of the unemployed and of the legal eight hours' day. Many writers have told the story of his arrival at the House of Commons, dressed in working clothes with a cloth cap, on a wagonette filled with dockers, one of whom scandalised the respectables by playing a cornet. This display, which was not prearranged, was somewhat out of character, for Hardie was a most serious person, little inclined to that kind of display, though he was ready enough to make a scene on a serious occasion. He soon did so, in protest against the levity with which the Commons treated a mining disaster; and he was always ready to make another, when he saw no better way of getting publicity for his case. But his scene-making was the outcome of passionate feeling, and not of any taste for flamboyant action. He remained the dour, hard-hitting Puritan he had been from the first; and, though he could on occasion enjoy himself with the best, he felt a keen displeasure at anything he regarded as frivolity or foolish revolutionary froth. Though he gained the reputation of being an extremist, he was throughout really a moderate, determined to concentrate on immediate reforms and impatient of those who believed that Socialism could be introduced suddenly by means of violent revolution.

The men and women who gathered under Hardie's chairmanship in January 1893 to establish the Independent Labour Party formed a heterogeneous gathering. They included delegates from the Scottish Labour Party, which soon merged itself in the new body; from a number of local Labour Unions and similar groups, such as the Bradford Labour Union, the Manchester I.L.P., and the various I.L.P.s which had been formed under the auspices of *The Workman's Times*; from a handful of branches of the Social Democratic Federation; from the London Fabian Society, and from a number of local Fabian Societies which had sprung up since the publication of *Fabian Essays* in 1889. There were a very few Trade Union groups, and one or two miscellaneous bodies, such as Edward Aveling's (1851–98) Eight Hours League. Bernard Shaw, representing the London Fabians, announced at the start that the parent Fabian Society had no intention of merging itself in the new party, as it was determined to carry on its policy of permeating the existing parties with Socialist ideas. The Fabian Society's credentials were challenged, partly on this ground and partly because of their commitment to alliance with the Liberals in London municipal politics, which ran counter to the views of most of the provincial delegates, who were engaged in fighting the Liberals in their own municipal Councils. On this issue, most of the local Fabian Societies outside London took sides against Shaw, and transferred their allegiance to the I.L.P.

At the outset the I.L.P. was intended to be a federation, based mainly on the local Labour Unions, but open to affiliations of Trade Unions and other Labour and Socialist bodies. But the Trade Unions held aloof, and the branches of the S.D.F. refused to desert their old allegiance. Within a few months of its formation, the I.L.P. had turned into a national society with branches, and the local Labour Unions and similar bodies had accepted branch status under the National Administrative Council set up at the Bradford Conference. Thereafter, the aim of converting the Trade Unions to independent Labour politics had to be pursued in other ways, by persuading them to set up a federal party in which Socialist and Trade Union groups could act together. It took seven years' hard work to accomplish this, by persuading the Trades Union Congress to convene the conference which set up the Labour Representation Committee. Meanwhile, the Labour Electoral Association remained in being until 1896, but gradually lost ground as a number of its local groups went over to the I.L.P. or died of inanition. The General Election of 1895 reduced the miners' contingent from 6 to 5 and the rest of the Lib-Lab group from 4 to 3, including Havelock Wilson. Burns and Dr. Clark were re-elected, and so were the 3 Irishmen, including Davitt, who took his seat for South Mayo. But at South-West Ham Keir Hardie was beaten, though no Liberal took the field against him; and thereafter the I.L.P. had no representative in the House of Commons. It fought 28 seats, of which 8 were in Lancashire and Cheshire, 7 in Yorkshire, and 7 in Scotland, but it failed to win even one. The S.D.F. had 4 candidates, and 4 other Socialists fought under various local auspices. But by 1895 the New Unionism had lost a good deal of the ground it had won in 1889 and the following years, and was merely holding on. Despite the establishment of the I.L.P., the cause of Independent Labour was no longer advancing. Many of the older Trade Union leaders, such as George Howell (1833–1910), were predicting the speedy disappearance of the New Unions and a return to the 'Lib-Lab' alliance.

Nevertheless, though the spectacular advances of the early 'nineties had not been held, the new Socialism was gradually permeating the older Trade Unions, and at successive Trades Union Congresses the Socialists were winning an increasing support. In 1895, when the reaction against the New Unionism was at its height, the Trades Union Congress resolved, at the instance of John Burns, by then thoroughly estranged from the new political movement, to expel from membership the local Trades Councils and to restrict the choice of delegates to men actually working at their trades or holding Trade Union office. The reason given for the first of these decisions was that Trades Council membership duplicated that of the affiliated Trades Unions : the real motive was to get rid of the rebels, who were strongly represented among the Trades Council delegates. For a time the change was effective in restoring the power of the old leaders. In 1893 and 1894 the Trades Union Congress had passed Socialist resolutions and had even voted in favour of a fund to be devoted to the support of Trade Union candidates — a decision which the Congress's Parliamentary Committee failed to implement on the ground that there was no effective Trade Union support. From 1895 to 1898 similar resolutions were defeated by large majorities, and even in 1899 Congress voted down a further proposal to institute a central political fund. That year, however, the Socialists at length achieved a come-back by persuading the delegates to vote in favour of the resolution under which the Parliamentary Committee was instructed to call the conference of Trade Unions and other Labour and Socialist bodies that established the Labour

Representation Committee the following year.

The advance made by the new Socialism during the period of apparent setback between 1895 and 1900 was due largely to its successes in the field of local government. Held back in London by the Progressive alliance, the I.L.P. followed in the provincial towns a policy of opposition to both the older parties and was able to obtain a foothold on a number of Councils, using its vantage to press for immediate reforms such as the improvement of schools, the promotion of municipal housing and slum-clearance schemes, the provision of work for the local unemployed, and the raising of the very low wages paid to council employees. This policy of 'practical Socialism' gained it an increasing amount of support, and also served to define its character as the party of reform rather than of revolution, with long-run Socialist aspirations but with an immediate programme that appealed to many who rejected the Marxist gospel of the S.D.F. as much as they were discontented with the half-heartedness of the Liberal Party for the more advanced parts of its Newcastle Programme of 1892. Labour representatives were still at best no more than small minorities on the municipal Councils, and were hardly represented at all on the County Councils set up in 1888. They were even fewer on the Councils of Urban and Rural Districts : rather more numerous on School Boards and on Boards of Guardians in the industrial areas. But in a good many places they were able to exercise an influence out of proportion to their numbers on committees dealing with housing and other social questions ; and this local work made the leading I.L.P.ers known and often paved the way to later successes in parliamentary contests. The Fabian Society, despite its preoccupation in London with the Progressive alliance on the L.C.C., was of considerable help to the Labour members on local authorities throughout the country as a provider of useful statistical information and of pamphlets explaining the powers of the various Councils and working out lines of policy.

The second factor that helped the I.L.P. to gain influence during the later 'nineties was the activity of its branches in helping strike movements. In 1897 much help was given to the Amalgamated Society of Engineers in its unsuccessful resistance to the lock-out declared by the employers over the issue of Trade Union interference in 'managerial functions', and during the following year the help given to the South Wales miners during their strike and lock-out gave the I.L.P. a firm foothold in South Wales, which had been entirely unrepresented at the Inaugural Conference of 1893. Hardie owed his election at Merthyr in 1900 to the great part which he played in this struggle ; and thereafter South Wales soon became one of the movement's principal strongholds.

In local politics the I.L.P., in most areas, was fighting elections against both the older parties, though its representatives, when they had secured election, were often able to work with other progressives in committee work. In national politics the question which immediately faced the new party was that of its attitude in elections where it had no candidate of its own in the field — that is, in the great majority of constituencies. When Blatchford and his group set up the Manchester District I.L.P. in 1892 they included in the constitution a clause which not only required members to sever all connections with other parties, but also forbade them to vote for any non-Socialist candidate in any constituency. This involved requiring most of their members to abstain from voting at all until the movement was in a position to put up its own candidates in the areas in which they lived. At the Bradford Inaugural Conference of the I.L.P., and subsequently, the Manchester men fought hard to get the 'Fourth Clause' — so called from its place in the constitution of the Manchester I.L.P. — accepted as national policy. In this they were unsuccessful : the policy approved at the national level was that I.L.P. members should resign all connections with other parties, and should vote in municipal elections as their branch decided and in parliamentary elections in accordance with the decision of a national party Conference. This last provision was put to the test at the General Election of 1895 ; and on that occasion the national Conference decided in favour of the full rigour of the 'Fourth Clause' policy — though it is said that the decision was widely disregarded, and that many members of the I.L.P. voted for Tories.

The explanation of this policy of abstention except where I.L.P. or other Socialist candidates were in the field is that the I.L.P. was so set on breaking up the old Lib-Lab alliance and on detaching the workers from their traditional allegiance to the old Radicalism as to be ready to forfeit its chance of influencing the elections over most of the constituencies. There was the big risk that if members, or branches, were allowed to vote for the better candidate when no Socialist was in the field the way would be opened for pacts between neighbouring constituencies, whereby the Liberals would recommend their supporters to vote Labour in one place in return for reciprocal favours in another. If this were allowed, it would be impracticable not to vote for Lib-Lab candidates in some places, and the sharp distinction between Independent Labour and Lib-Lab would be in danger of being broken down. There was enough difference of opinion among the I.L.P. leaders to prevent the 'Fourth Clause' from being written into the party Constitution; but in 1895 the 'Fourth Clause' advocates carried the day. I.L.P. members were allowed, and encouraged, to vote for S.D.F. or other independent Socialist candidates; and in 1900 there was even a candidate at Rochdale sponsored by both the I.L.P. and the S.D.F. The 'Fourth Clause' policy and the less rigid policy accepted by the I.L.P. as its official line were both inspired by a determination to have no truck with the Liberals or with those Trade Unionists who ran for election under Liberal auspices.

Despite this electoral intransigence the I.L.P. was from the outset definitely a non-revolutionary party as far as its immediate programme and policy were concerned. Blatchford, the leading advocate of the 'Fourth Clause', was also President of the Manchester Fabian Society at the time when it was drawn up by the Manchester District I.L.P., and was an outspoken critic of the revolutionary notions of the S.D.F. He insisted that a revolution, even if it were practicable, could do no good, because the Socialists were by no means ready to replace capitalism by a complete new social system. He stressed the paramount importance of Socialist education as a preparation for the introduction of the Socialist way of life, and was much less interested in winning parliamentary seats than in conducting outright Socialist propaganda. Indeed, the real division inside the I.L.P. was between those who thought mainly in terms of parliamentary successes and those who were doubtful about the value of getting Socialists into Parliament until there was enough Socialist opinion behind them to prevent them from falling into subjection to parliamentary traditions and the exigencies of electioneering. William Morris, in his Socialist League days, had held a similar opinion, and had regarded the contesting of seats in Parliament as premature. The I.L.P. left did not go to that length, for its members mostly accepted the necessity of a gradualist approach. But they were suspicious enough of parliamentary compromise to insist that their candidates must be firmly pledged against all association with other parties and against all pacts that might involve a derogation from the pure gospel of Socialism. They were, however, much less suspicious of the corrupting influence of municipal politics, though there too they were determined to reject all non-Socialist electoral associations. Fred W. Jowett (1864–1944), for example, the Bradford municipal pioneer, drew a sharp distinction between the procedure of the House of Commons and that of a municipal Council, with its administrative committees on which members of all parties worked together. Far from seeing in the committee system of local government a dangerous tendency to blur party divisions in day-to-day administrative collaboration, he upheld the municipal system as vastly superior to the parliamentary, and demanded that the latter should be reformed in imitation of the former. He was, however, as insistent against inter-party municipal as against inter-party parliamentary pacts. The great task ahead, all the I.L.P. leaders agreed, was to bring the working classes over to the gospel of strict political independence.

At the Bradford Conference of 1893 a section of the delegates, headed by two Scottish representatives, George Carson and Robert Smillie (1857–1940), later the leader of the Miners' Federation and an outstanding figure in the Socialist movement, wished to include the word 'Socialist' in the title of the new party. The proposal was defeated, on tactical grounds; but there was never any doubt that the I.L.P. regarded itself as a Socialist Party. The object of the party was defined at Bradford as 'the collective ownership of all the means of production, distribution and exchange'. The resolution at first read 'collective or communal ownership'; but the words 'or communal' were deleted as savouring unduly of Anarchist-Communism. An attempt by John Lincoln Mahon (1866–

1933) to state the object as being merely 'to secure the separate representation and protection of Labour interests on public bodies', without committing the party to any expression of Socialist doctrine, was heavily defeated. Another resolution committed all I.L.P. candidates, if returned, to act with the majority of the 'Socialist Independent Party in Parliament in advancing the interests of Labour irrespective of the convenience of any political party'.

What did these professions of Socialism mean? They fully committed the new party to general socialisation as a final objective : indeed, such a commitment was felt to be the only way of marking its adherents off sharply from the 'Lib-Labs' and the old-style Trade Unionists. But this profession of faith left the party free to concentrate its immediate endeavours largely on the advocacy of major social reforms — above all others, the eight hours' day, the right to work or maintenance, and the legal minimum wage. The eight hours' day was at the outset the most insistent demand, together with the adoption of public measures to reduce unemployment and to secure better treatment of the unemployed, especially by the municipal and poor law authorities. The demand for housing reform and for better education, with medical treatment and school feeding of the children, also loomed large in the I.L.P.'s local propaganda.

In advocating reforms, as distinct from a catastrophic overthrow of the existing social order, the I.L.P. propagandists of the 1890s often distinguished between those partial reforms which they regarded as practicable 'under capitalism' and those which they regarded as unrealisable except 'under Socialism'. Thus, it was regarded as quite possible for the State, under capitalism, to find work for some of the unemployed, and to maintain the rest under tolerable conditions ; but unemployment itself was regarded as inherent in the capitalist system. It was possible to improve housing by slum-clearance without compensation to slum-landlords, and by municipal building ; but to get rid of the squalor and hideousness of the factory towns as a whole it would be necessary to replace the profit-motive by a system of communal endeavour towards the good life. The line between what was practicable under capitalism and what was not was never at all clearly drawn ; for such clarity was hardly needed while there was so much that could be done to alleviate misery by secondary reforms, and while the Socialists had no early prospect of being able to carry the major structural changes into effect. In these circumstances there was, paradoxically, a revival of Utopianism among the reformists, who drew pictures of a coming Utopia at the same time as they conducted campaigns against particular abuses and for quite moderate measures of legislative or administrative reform.

Although, at the Bradford Conference, socialisation was made the criterion of the Socialist nature of the new party, the inspiration that lay behind it was ethical rather than economic. The stress was on the misery of the poor — the avoidable misery which was inflicted on the weaker members of society. The men and women who formed the I.L.P. had had their indignation stirred by the exposure of the conditions of ill-health, semi-starvation, and squalor in which a large section of the people lived — a story of wrongs and sufferings to which the uprisings of the less skilled workers in 1889 had applied the match to light the fire that illuminated the social scene. The I.L.P.ers were intent to fight on behalf of the 'bottom dogs' much more than of the working class as a whole. They were not very much concerned with the efforts of the skilled workers to better their own conditions, though they of course sided with them when they became involved in strikes or lock-outs. Their main concern was with the underdogs who had flocked into the New Unions and with the much larger class out of which these converts to common action had emerged. They were ready enough to believe the Fabians, who told them how much more efficient socialised industry and agriculture would be and how easily enough for all could be produced by a collective effort in which all took part. But they wanted Socialism, fundamentally, not because it would be efficient but because it would promote social justice.

No doubt the Lib-Labs also wanted social justice, and based their adhesion to the Liberal gospel on ethical grounds. The difference was that the New Unionists approached politics from an angle of vision which threw into prominence the special claims of the less skilled workers, and emphasised at every point the need for State intervention in economic affairs. The Lib-Labs were for the most part representatives of trade groups among which organisation was already well established and a substantial amount of recognition had been secured for the right of collective bargaining. They favoured heavier taxation of unearned incomes, especially of those accruing to landlords and to other rich men who played no active part in the productive process; but their principal immediate objectives were political rather than economic and allied them rather to Radicals than to the supporters of the New Unionism. Both groups wanted fuller recognition of their right to bargain collectively with the representatives of capitalist industry, but the 'Old' Unionists wanted this rather in the interests of the organised workers than as a 'new deal' for the working class as a whole; whereas the 'New' Unionists were impatient of restrictions which denied the less skilled workers' claim to be considered as the social equals of the craftsmen, or at all events to be given special backing on account of their more urgent human needs. At the same time the I.L.P.ers were anxious not to repeat the mistakes of the Social Democratic Federation by antagonising unnecessarily the members of the older Unions, as distinct from their Lib-Lab leaders. They found, indeed, a substantial part of their support among the younger members of the older Unions; and most of them were convinced of the need to bring such established groups as the miners and cotton operatives, who also needed legislation to reinforce their bargaining strength, over to the party of Independent Labour and, if possible, to Socialism. Not a few of the active members of the I.L.P. were connected with the older Unions and were doing battle inside them in the cause of the New Unionism and of independent political action. The aim of these men, even when they helped to start new Unions among the less skilled workers, was not to create a rival Trade Union movement in hostility to the older Unions, but rather to convert the latter to the new ideas and to demonstrate to their members that their real interests lay, not in holding on to their monopoly position in face of technical change, but rather in making common cause with the less skilled in a movement to establish minimum standards of wages and conditions, in the assurance that a higher minimum for the underdogs would bring with it a general improvement in the distribution of the proceeds of industry between workers and capitalists, and that the more the State intervened to prescribe minimum standards, the less would the employers be able to use the unskilled workers to undermine the collective bargaining power of the Unions of skilled workers.

Thus, whereas the S.D.F. had been prone to denounce not only the Lib-Lab leaders of the older Unions, but also the Unions themselves as embodiments of sectional monopoly against the aspirations of the working class as a whole, the I.L.P.ers set out to woo the members of these Unions, while denouncing their leaders, and to offer them a programme which combined the ethical with the economic appeal. In place of doctrinaire Marxism and class-war this programme was concentrated on demands which promised results not merely after 'the revolution', but at once; and such a programme appealed not only to workers but also to middle-class sympathisers who were prepared to rally to their support on grounds of social justice, but not to throw over in favour of Marxist 'materialism' the Christian ethics they had learnt to regard as the basic imperative to social action.

The leaders of the Independent Labour Party in the 1890s were a mixture of workers and middle-class Socialists. Besides Hardie as Chairman, the original National Administrative Council of 1893 included Pete Curran (1860–1910), Edward Aveling (1851–1898), W. H. Drew of Bradford, George Carson of Glasgow (d. 1923), Joseph Burgess (1853–1924), and Katherine St. John Conway (1868–1950), later the wife of James Bruce Glasier and a lifelong worker for I.L.P. Socialism. James Shaw Maxwell (1855–1928) was Secretary. Tom Mann became Secretary in 1894, and Ben Tillett, who soon dropped out, and Fred Brocklehurst of Manchester (1866– ?) joined the Council that year. Dr. R. M. Pankhurst (d. 1898), husband of the suffragist leader, Emmeline Pankhurst, who also played an active part in the I.L.P., was elected to the Council in 1896. That year James Ramsay MacDonald (1866–1937) was the runner-up for a seat, which he won in 1897. In 1898 Mrs. Pankhurst (1858–1928) and James Bruce Glasier (1859–1920) were elected. Philip Snowden (1864–1937) got on only in 1899 and F. W. Jowett (1864–1944) only in 1901. Hardie was Chairman until 1900, when Glasier succeeded him, to be replaced by Snowden in 1903 and by MacDonald in 1906. Mann had ceased to be Secretary in 1897, when John Penny of Preston (1870–1938) took his place. On the whole the middle-class element on the Council increased, and its influence certainly grew much greater with the advent of Snowden and MacDonald. But, of course, most of the local leaders were workers, and workmen and working women preponderated among the Conference delegates. The I.L.P., however, had from the first a substantial body of middle-class supporters, and most of its branches included at least a few. Its tone was strongly ethical: it, rather than the S.D.F., attracted the main body of middle-class Socialists in the industrial areas, whereas the Fabian Society consisted mainly of Londoners and found its recruits chiefly in the professions, rather than in the middle classes as a whole.

It will be seen that neither MacDonald nor Snowden was active in the I.L.P. at the beginning. At the outset Hardie held an almost unquestioned leadership, with Mann and Curran, and for a while Tillett, as his principal lieutenants. In 1893 a large Council had been elected; but for reasons of economy the numbers were cut down the following year, and they remained small until the size was increased again in 1906. Except for the national officers, the elections were by regional divisions; and the divisional machinery played an important part in holding the local branches together. Progress was rather slow during the early years, for the I.L.P. suffered from the decline of the New Unionism which set in just about the time of its foundation. It did, however, succeed in building up, if not a mass membership, at least an influential body of recruits among the younger Trade Unionists and among other young people who had been touched by the spirit of the times; and its influence ran a long way ahead of its numbers.

The I.L.P.'s strongholds, during these early years, were in Lancashire and Yorkshire, on the Clyde, and in the West of Scotland coalfields. It had a few strong groups elsewhere — at Leicester and Nottingham, for example. In London it was not very strong, and it had little following in Wales till the late 'nineties. The S.D.F. rivalled it especially in Lancashire and in London and to some extent in Scotland. But, of course, neither of them ever became a great party comparable with those of Germany or Austria, or even of Belgium or France.

(iv) ROBERT BLATCHFORD AND 'THE CLARION'

The British Socialist movement, unlike the French, has produced few outstanding journalists. Keir Hardie, though he
practised the profession for most of his life, had no great talent
for it : his *Labour Leader* had always a heavy touch, unrelieved
by much humour, and his writing rose above mediocrity only
when he was strongly moved or telling stories of his childhood.
William Morris practised journalism only against his will :
his *Commonweal* contains excellent things, but was never a good
paper. Harry Quelch, in the S.D.F.'s *Justice*, hit hard, but
showed no special *flair*. Joseph Burgess, whose *Workman's
Times* did much to mobilise the feeling for an Independent
Labour Party, was a ragged writer, unable to enlist his readers'
affections. Annie Besant, who had journalistic as well as
oratorical talent, made her main contribution to journalism on
Bradlaugh's *National Reformer*, and, after showing her capacity
for Socialist writing in *The Link*, vanished out of the movement
to become a protagonist of Theosophy and of Indian Nationalism. Unless we are to count Bernard Shaw, who won his place
in journalism mainly as a musical and dramatic critic before he
established his major position as a playwright, the only man
who, in the period with which we are now dealing, made his
mark primarily as a Socialist journalist, and built up a great
political following by the written rather than the spoken
word, was Robert Blatchford (1851–1943), whose *Clarion* first
appeared in 1891 and lasted through many vicissitudes till
1935.

Blatchford's book *Merrie England*, first published serially in
The Clarion, far outsold any other Socialist work of its time.
News from Nowhere and, of course, *Fabian Essays*, had only
minute circulations in comparison with it. In the British
market it sold many more copies even than Henry George's
Progress and Poverty — its nearest rival. An edition published
at one penny was partly responsible for its enormous sale ; but
it had proved its appeal before this edition was thought of.
Indeed, even before *Merrie England* was written or *The Clarion*
appeared Blatchford had made himself a place in popular
journalism that was quite distinctively his own.

In social origin Robert Blatchford came out of the 'un-classed' rather than of either the working or the middle class. His father, who died when he was two years old, was a strolling comedian, and his mother the actress daughter of a theatrical composer of Italian descent who had been in boyhood a mid-shipman at the battle of the Nile. Robert Blatchford's child-hood was passed in travelling round with his mother and his elder brother from theatre to theatre. When he was 11, and his brother Montagu 13, Mrs. Blatchford settled down in Halifax, where she became a dressmaker. At 14 he was apprenticed to brushmaking, and he stayed at the trade till he was 20. Then he ran away to London, lived for a while on odd jobs, and joined the army in 1871. There he remained for six years, rose to the rank of sergeant, and, after a brief interval, got a job as time-keeper at Northwich under the Weaver Navigation Company. That was in 1878. In 1880 he married an old flame from Halifax, Sarah Crossley, to whom he remained devoted for the rest of his life.

Blatchford's army experience was the making of him. He had been a rather dreamy, studious youth, shunning rowdiness and timid in social intercourse. But he loved his army com-rades, with all their drunkenness, fecklessness, and disregard for most of the ten commandments. He came out of the army with a deep belief that common men and women had hearts of gold, and with a passion to enlighten their intellectual darkness without playing the superior person or the prig. Ever after-wards he tended to think of civilians — especially workers — as soldiers in mufti, and to condone the faults of the least respectable among them because he thought of them in that guise. He wrote best, and most naturally, about soldiers and the life of camp and barracks. In his autobiography he showed much more interest in his experiences in the army than in all his work for Socialism. His social origins, his upbringing in poverty, and his life as a soldier combined to give him an intense sympathy for the 'bottom dogs', rather than for the respectable working class. In his private life he was a most respectable person ; but he tended to dislike acutely those who made a virtue of respectability. This gained him a reputation, with straitlaced Socialists of Nonconformist antecedents and ways of thought, for being an apostle of wickedness ; but there was no sin in him, unless it be sinful to sympathise with sinners and to hate self-righteousness.

Blatchford's first attempts at writing were soldier stories and sketches : his first essays in journalism were humorous columns in obscure North of England papers. His chance came through his meeting with the Manchester journalist and play-writer, Alexander Mattock Thompson (1861–1948), who became at once his devoted friend and admirer. Thompson was on the staff of Edward Hulton's *Sporting Chronicle* ; and when Hulton bought the old sporting paper, *Bell's Life in London*, it was through Thompson that Blatchford was offered a job on it, and threw up his position on the Weaver Navigation. Then Hulton started the *Sunday Chronicle*, and Blatchford wrote first leading articles and then the feature articles that made his name. Or rather, the articles made the name of 'Nunquam', by which they were signed. Originally, it had been 'Nunquam Dormio' (I never sleep), and had been taken over from a previous writer on *Bell's Life*. On the *Sunday Chronicle*, which began in 1885, Blatchford moved over from humorous and sporting journalism to social writing, with a strong bent towards the defence of the helpless victims of the social order — above all the slum children, for whom he started his Cinderella Clubs to provide food and entertainment without moralisings to spoil the pleasure. When he began this work he was not a Socialist, and indeed regarded himself as an opponent of Socialism. He became a convert gradually, influenced by his reading of William Morris, of Henry George, and of the S.D.F. and Fabian writings, but much more by visiting the Manchester slums and reacting against the defence of the existing order by Liberal and Tory apologists, and most of all by his friendship with Alexander Thompson and others of the group which presently followed him to establish *The Clarion*. He was in fact travelling a road along which many other men and women were moving with him in the last years of the 1880s ; and his full conversion came just in time to enable him to proclaim his faith amid the excitements of the gasworkers' and dockers' revolts. The following year he came out strongly in support of the Manningham textile strike,[1] and this led to an invitation to contest a Bradford seat as the independent Labour

[1] See p. 149.

candidate of the Bradford Labour Union. With many misgivings he accepted, knowing that he was no speaker, and feeling a strong reluctance to enter the parliamentary field.

Blatchford's connection with the *Sunday Chronicle* ended in 1891, when Hulton, who did not like Socialism, at length rebelled against the intransigence of his principal contributor. Blatchford refused to modify his tone, resigned a lucrative position, and found a temporary refuge on Burgess's *Workman's Times*. Thompson and Edward Francis Fay (1854–1896) — later 'The Bounder' of the *Clarion* group — resigned with him, taking R. B. Suthers (1870–1950), then a clerk but later well-known as a writer of popular Socialist propaganda, along with them. They had hardly any money; for Blatchford had just lost his savings on a play he had written and produced. But with high hopes and very little planning they brought out in December 1891 the first number of *The Clarion*. The circulation, after a bigger start, settled down at about 30,000 — which was much for those days, but not enough to yield large profits. The founding fathers got little out of it: Thompson went on writing plays for a living, and the rest lived partly on his earnings. Early in 1892 Blatchford gave up his parliamentary candidature, on which he could afford to spend neither time nor money, and settled down to editorship just as the I.L.P. was being formed.

It has often been affirmed that Robert Blatchford's *Clarion* made many more converts to Socialism than Keir Hardie's Independent Labour Party, and that *Merrie England*, which first appeared in its columns, is the most effective piece of popular Socialist propaganda ever written. The first of these statements evidently cannot be verified any more than the second: they are both matters of opinion. It is, however, quite beyond doubt that in the 1890s Robert Blatchford was by a long way the most popular writer on the side of Socialism, with a much bigger public than Bernard Shaw or William Morris, whose appeal was mainly to intellectuals or to exceptional workers. Keir Hardie too had a great following, but mainly as a speaker and, from 1892 to 1895, as 'the member for the unemployed'.

Blatchford was no speaker: his platform appearances were saved from failure only because he was a popular hero on account of his writings, and his audiences were well enough pleased to cheer him to the echo whatever he said — even if they could not hear most of it. He had the art of establishing a closely personal relation with his readers, even if they had never seen him ; and because of this merely to see him became a memorable experience. Moreover, though in the group that produced *The Clarion* he was unquestioned cock of the walk, he had the art of inspiring his devoted band of collaborators with his own personal touch ; so that the entire *Clarion* group of writers became friends with their readers, and were felt as a band of brothers whose every move, or even antic, was followed with lively sympathy and delighted interest. Readers as well as writers became partners in a common fellowship : they were never happier than when they were excitedly doing things together and proving to themselves and to the world that Socialists, far from being dismal persons set on restraining personal liberty for the common good, knew better than anyone else how to enjoy themselves and to foreshadow, by their good cheer, the 'Merrie England' which would become the common heritage of all when Socialism had won the day.

Blatchford's appeal as a writer was immense : yet his contribution to Socialist *thought*, in any ordinary sense of the word, was next to nothing. He was neither a theorist nor a planner, and to Socialist doctrine he neither contributed nor sought to contribute any original idea. In such matters he was a populariser, handling other men's ideas so as to make them seem intelligible to ordinary men and women, most of whom could not respond to Bernard Shaw's subtleties or to Sidney Webb's logical marshalling of fact and argument, or even to William Morris's warmer, but still essentially literary and artistic appeal. Blatchford's ideas about Socialism were indeed derived more from Morris, whom he revered deeply, than from anyone else ; but in his hands Morris's conception of the good life turned into something which 'John Smith of Oldham' could much more readily understand. This 'John Smith' was the imaginary workman — decent and well intentioned, but none too well informed or intellectually subtle — to whom he addressed the open letters that told about 'Merrie England' ; and the million copies of the book must have reached a far higher proportion of the 'John Smiths' than had ever been reached before by any sort of written Socialist appeal.

Blatchford's originality lay, not in his ideas about Socialism, but in his conviction that anything that interested him could also be made interesting enough to the John Smiths to make it a practicable task to leaven the whole lump. When he started *The Clarion* he was confident of his ability to convert the British working class to Socialism within a very few years. That, of course, was an overweening hope, even if he had been a much greater and more persuasive writer than he actually was. Yet he did, by striking hard at just the right moment, accomplish a great deal ; and if, thereafter, disillusionment came upon him when he discovered that he could not lead as well as inspire, nevertheless his work stood, however disposed he grew to belittle the best of it and to lament that he had allowed the propagandist in him to overcome the creative artist in words he had hankerings to be.

Yet 'John Smith', though he was not credited with cleverness, was by no means addressed as a person of mean tastes or natural capacities. He was expected to be capable of taking politics seriously, when his attention had been drawn to their bearing on his own life and that of his fellows; and beyond this he was expected to respond to the call of beauty, and to be able to see not only the hideousness of his environment, but also the pretentious fulsomeness of much that was offered to him as beautiful. His love of natural beauty was taken for granted ; and so was his sense of the importance of widening and deepening his intellectual and aesthetic perceptions. Blatchford was indeed the very last person to set out to pander to the vulgarity of popular tastes : he was always seeking to get 'John Smith' to enjoy what he enjoyed for himself and to demand fuller opportunities for such pleasures as a reasonable man might desire. Blatchford's own tastes were literary and speculative : he loved books, and had a taste widely ranging enough to make him a devotee of Henry James as well as of Dickens, of Shakespeare as well as of Browning and Walt Whitman. Indeed, his interests were much more literary than political ; and he became involved in politics much against his personal bent. His private correspondence is filled with lamentations about being compelled to write about politics and economics, instead of developing his talent for story-writing or other more literary forms of composition.

The 'John Smith' to whom he addressed *Merrie England* he conceived of as a man who was capable, like himself, of developing cultured tastes and intellectual interests despite the lack of formal education and of involving himself in politics not because he liked them but because he felt an imperative call to help in setting crooked things straight. This call was that of a plain duty to do away with every eradicable form of human suffering and waste of human quality. It was the call of the idealist, outraged by the wretchedness around him, to the idealism which he believed to be present in every normal man and woman, because he could not think of other people as at bottom much different from himself, or as incapable of responding to what moved him, however strongly he might insist in some of his writings that man's character was sheerly the product of his environment, and denounce the environment of contemporary society as calculated to generate meanness and vice.

Blatchford, when he became a Socialist, joined the Fabians, and made much use of the Fabian tracts as sources of ammunition for his attacks on capitalism and maldistribution of income. His Socialism was, indeed, essentially moderate, though it was often expressed fiercely when his indignation had been moved by actual examples of suffering or flagrant injustice. In *Merrie England* and later in *Britain for the British* and in his Socialist romance, *The Sorcery Shop*, he hammered home the gospel of collective ownership as the necessary means to fair distribution and high production ; but he had very little to say about the future administration of socialised services, except that some would need to be controlled on a national scale, but most would be best managed locally — which was precisely the view put forward in *Fabian Essays*. With the Fabians, he built high hopes on the extension of municipal enterprise, and was confident that publicly managed services would be easily able to undersell capitalist competitors because they would be rid of the burdens of interest and profits, would enjoy all the economic benefits of large scale, and would have no motive to employ restrictive methods in order to keep prices high. He felt no doubt that the 'John Smiths' would work more contentedly and better when they were working for themselves collectively : he had nothing to say about such matters as industrial self-government by the producers. He was indeed a very simple collectivist, in no doubt that low production was the consequence of the wastes of competition and the restrictiveness of capitalist monopoly, or that it was easily possible to produce amply enough for all within the limits of a working day of eight hours at most — and ere long many fewer.

Blatchford had, however, some views of his own which set him at loggerheads with Socialists who had carried over from Liberalism a belief in the virtues of Free Trade. He held fervently to the view that every country ought to be able to feed its own population and to supply most of its needs out of its own production, and that foreign trade ought to be reduced to quite small dimensions. He hated big industrial towns, loved the beauty of the countryside, felt sure that the factory system was destructive of health and happiness, as well as of beauty, and was entirely convinced that Great Britain could easily feed its whole population if the land were put to proper use and modern techniques of intensive agriculture applied. He never tired of quoting Kropotkin and other authorities now forgotten to this effect ; and when he was confronted with the argument that it was cheaper to import food than to grow more of it at home, he replied that the price of the food was not the final criterion, and that against its cheapness had to be put the bad conditions and ill-health of the industrial workers who had to toil at producing exports to pay for it. He railed, too, against the effect of competitive export trade in setting the industrial workers in each advanced country to beat down the wages of their fellow-workers in other countries, and against the tendency of capitalistic export trade to breed imperialism at the expense of the peoples of the less developed countries. Finally, he usually clinched the argument in favour of Britain feeding herself by pointing to the danger of starvation in the event of war — for he tended to think as a soldier long before Germany had become the subject of his particular fears.

Blatchford, in effect, thought of Socialism mainly in national terms of 'Merrie England', and of a Socialist world as made up of free, collectivist countries each able to live on its own resources and exchanging only surpluses or luxuries which it could afford to do without if need arose. His conception of the advantages of large-scale production tended to stop short at national frontiers : he thought of international trade as bound up with competitive rivalries and with exploitation of one nation by another, leading within each nation to exploitation of class by class. His very national outlook in this respect undoubtedly constituted part of his appeal to the 'John Smiths' whom he addressed ; for most of them were concerned much more with 'Britain for the British' than with setting the whole world straight, even if they were ready to cheer sentiments of international working-class fraternity.

In his earlier writings, including the early days of *The Clarion* and of *Merrie England*, Blatchford wrote much about the misdeeds of particular Christians, but little about Christianity itself and nothing against it. Later, however, he became involved in vehement religious controversies, and ranged himself definitely on the side, first of those who denied the *truth* of Christian theology, and then of those who attacked, on the basis of a strict determinism, the whole notion of human responsibility for evil-doing and of divine punishment of the transgressor. These doctrines were developed mainly in two books — *God and My Neighbour* (1903), and *Not Guilty: a Plea for the Bottom Dog* (1906). In both these books, he was concerned essentially with the social aspect of religion and of religious beliefs. In *God and My Neighbour*, though he began by saying that he did not believe Christianity to be *true*, what really concerned him most was to deny God's right to punish men for sins which were not their fault, but that of a world God was alleged to have created in his omnipotence.

1. As to God. If there is no God, or if God is not a loving Heavenly Father, who answers prayer, Christianity as a religion cannot stand.

   I do not pretend to say whether there is or is not *a* God, but I deny that there is a loving Heavenly Father who answers prayer.

2 and 3. If there is no such thing as Free Will men could not sin against God, and Christianity as a religion will not stand.

   I deny the existence of Free Will, and the possibility of men's sinning against God.

4. If Jesus Christ is not necessary to Man's 'salvation', Christianity as a religion will not stand.

I deny that Christ is necessary to men's salvation from Hell or Sin.

5. I do not assert or deny the immortality of the soul. I know nothing about the soul, and no man is or ever was able to tell me more than I know.[1]

Blatchford's argument was simplicity itself. He found the world around him full of misery and injustice, and he heard men who professed to be good Christians announcing that these evils must be accepted as God's will. He heard them extolling God's fatherly mercy and proclaiming God's omnipotence. He asked why God, if he was in truth both merciful and omnipotent, had made the world to contain such suffering and injustice, and why God, if he was aware of them, did not remove them at once. He heard Christians denouncing sin, and asked why God, if omnipotent, had made men with a propensity to sin, instead of giving them only impulses to do good. To these questions he could find no satisfying answers ; and he came to the conclusion, first that there was no valid reason for believing in God's existence, or in his omnipotence or mercy if he did exist. He denied that good men stand in any need of divine pardon, and that God could justly punish or pardon sinners, if it was his doing that they had natures which disposed them to sin. Finally he asserted, as Robert Owen among others had done before him, that men were not responsible for their actions, because their behaviour was determined by their social environment, and that as the universe was ruled by laws and man a part of nature, human actions must be no less determined than the actions of other natural objects. Free will, then, was an illusion : men behaved as their circumstances compelled them to behave.

From all this Blatchford drew the moral of wide, friendly toleration — which was in fact the attitude with which he had set out long before he had rationalised it into a philosophy. In the army he had taken his fellow-soldiers as he found them, had liked them though their ways were not his, had tried to befriend them when they got into trouble, but not to preach to them or to reform them. He had felt already at that stage that what they were nature and nurture had made them, and that when they went wrong and got into trouble nurture more than

[1] *God and My Neighbour*, p. 122.

172

nature was at fault. He had wanted to amend the environment in order to amend the behaviour of its victims. Just as the great *philosophes* of the eighteenth century had blamed all evil on the unnatural arrangements of society and had imagined that all would come right if men would but order their social institutions in accordance with the dictates of nature, so Blatchford came to believe that everything would come right under Socialism.

This, of course, brought him face to face with the inconsistency of thinking that it could be of any use to exhort men to adopt Socialism, if their actions were strictly determined by an unsocialist environment. He tried to get round the difficulty by proclaiming that men's actions were determined by self-interest and that the self-interest of the workers pointed clearly to Socialism as soon as they could be made to understand its advantages. This involved holding that men's actions were not determined apart from their understanding of what was good for them, and could be influenced by enlightening them about their common interests. But Blatchford, no more than other necessarian optimists, could see this point. He was made blind to it by his desire to exculpate those who acted amiss by proclaiming that they were not responsible for their doings ; and he allowed himself to accept a completely necessarian doctrine which made nonsense of his own efforts to persuade his fellow-men to mend their ways.

In defending this doctrine of necessity Blatchford, in the spirit of his time, made much use of Darwinism and of the appeal to science against theological and idealistic conceptions. But his determinism and his use of rationalistic arguments in fact grew upon him as his earlier optimism waned. The less hopeful he became of persuading the 'John Smiths' to behave sensibly in their common interests — and at the outset he was very hopeful about this — the more he comforted himself for the ill-success of his appeals by asserting that the unresponsiveness of the main body of the workers was not their fault, but their misfortune. *God and My Neighbour* and *Not Guilty* were written only after Blatchford had ceased to be able to think of himself as the destined saviour of society, who would have the working class fully converted to Socialism within a few years by the sheer power of his pen.

Before this vision faded, he worked closely, in the 1890s, with John Trevor (1855–1930), the creator of the Labour Church movement which spread rapidly over Northern England during the years which brought a flock of ardent newcomers to the Trade Union and Socialist movements. Trevor had been an Unitarian minister, and had worked as assistant to the economist-minister, Philip Wicksteed, in London before he received a call to a chapel at Manchester. There the new currents of Labour sentiment took hold of him, and caused him to abandon his Unitarian faith and to open a freethinking Labour Church where converts to Socialism could find a community and a service near enough to those of the Nonconformist chapels they had abandoned to fill the void left by the breaking of the familiar ties. In place of Bible lessons, he gave them readings from great humanitarian thinkers ; in place of sermons, long addresses by protagonists of Socialism and New Unionism ; in place of the old hymns, ethical songs and chants mostly fitted to the familiar tunes. Soon there were other Churches founded on Trevor's model : Wicksteed and other well-known progressives helped with money as well as by coming to address the new congregations. Sunday Schools were started for the children : the 'Churches', which at first had mostly to use hired halls, acquired buildings of their own, which provided meeting-places for many other Labour bodies. Trevor started a paper, *The Labour Prophet* (1892–8), as the organ of the movement ; in 1893 a Labour Church Union was set up to co-ordinate the local Churches. For a few years it flourished greatly, especially in Lancashire and Yorkshire. Then it began to die down : new Labour Churches ceased to be founded, and a number perished. Some survived for a long time, even into the 1920s : perhaps there are a few left even now. Of that I am not sure ; but I think the movement lost its impetus after the first few years mainly because the new converts to Labour and Socialist ideas no longer needed it with the same poignancy as in the 1890s. When Socialism and New Unionism had once become well-established movements, most of those who joined them no longer underwent a spiritual experience which involved a sharp break with their previous associations. Many stayed in the chapels of the various Dissenting sects, and found a bridge between politics and religion in the Pleasant Sunday Afternoons and Brotherhoods which these sects organised as a means to holding their working-class following. Others, of the younger generation, drifted away from religious observances without feeling the need for a substitute. The Labour Church movement was essentially a part of the ferment which accompanied the sudden emergence of the New Unionism and of the Independent Labour Party; and at that stage Blatchford was able to work in close association with Trevor, on the basis of a common humanitarian gospel. The followings of the Labour Churches and of *The Clarion* largely overlapped for a time. Both receded as the first enthusiasm of the years after 1889 died down : the Clarion movement, however, proved the more enduring, because its sociable appeal continued to attract young people long after the need for a substitute Socialist religion had lost most of its force.

The Clarion, as we saw, began in the December of 1891. In May of the following year Blatchford, already President of the Manchester Fabian Society, and John Trevor joined forces to form the Manchester District I.L.P., which merged into the national I.L.P. after the Bradford Conference. At this stage *The Clarion* had no separate organisation of its own. The paper was still feeling its way, making friends with its readers, and building up the collective personality of the group that produced it. The appearance of the Clarionettes as an organised element in the Socialist movement followed the publication of *Merrie England* in 1894. That same year the Clarion Scouts were founded, and the first of many Clarion Cycling Clubs was started in Birmingham. The first Clarion Van appeared on the roads in 1895, copying a method of itinerant propagandism that had been used already by the followers of Henry George ; but the main Clarion Van campaign came only a good deal later, in the early years of the new century.

The Clarion's group of writers included, besides Robert Blatchford, his elder brother Montagu Blatchford (1849–1910), who composed verses and was the principal inspirer of Clarion Glee Clubs for community singing; Alexander Thompson, who bore a very large part of the editorial burden and kept a cool head through all the troubles ; and Edward Francis Fay, an irresponsible Irish bohemian, who might write funnily about almost anything, and was entirely incapable of doing anything in an orderly way, but could be relied upon to insult and scarify respectability in all its forms. It was Fay, not Blatchford or Thompson, who during the early years chiefly earned *The Clarion* the shocked disapproval of the puritans in the Socialist ranks. A fifth member of the group, R. B. Suthers, began as a mere clerk, but soon made his place as a writer. Soon there were further recruits : Julia Dawson (d. 1947), who ran the women's page and made the paper a force among women despite the excessive masculinity of its originators ; Tom Groom, the leader of the Cyclists and of other auxiliary organisations which spread rapidly over the industrial areas ; and, presently, Albert Neil Lyons (1880–1940), with his excellent stories of low life (the best is *Arthur's*, about an East London coffee stall). Robert Blatchford himself liked best to write about books rather than about politics, except when he was making his direct appeals to 'John Smith of Oldham' ; and even these did not satisfy him for long. He much preferred writing his soldier stories, some of which are very good indeed (for example, *The Scrumptious Girl*) or reminiscences of his life in the army, or later his attacks on the doctrines of human responsibility and on the illogicalities of Christian belief.

Altogether, the Clarionettes were a highly individual group, who could never settle down to a defined place in the new Labour movement. One important element in their divergence from Hardie and the I.L.P. leadership was that, whereas the I.L.P. tended from the first towards internationalism and pacifism, Blatchford always thought mainly in national terms and largely as a soldier. When he argued that Great Britain could feed its own people and urged it not to depend on imported food, he stressed from the first the danger of starvation in the event of war. This annoyed pacifists and internationalists, who thought such talk liable to increase the danger and to aggravate nationalist sentiment, as well as Free Traders, who were outraged by his brusque dismissal of the claims of the international division of labour. At first, Blatchford's nationalist and soldierly outlook did not greatly affect — indeed it may have aided — his appeals to 'John Smith'. But when, in the South African War, he took sides against the Boers, there was a sharp rift among *The Clarion's* rank-and-file supporters, many of whom regarded the war against the Boer Republics as an example of economic imperialism, and took the side of its Radical-Labour opponents. There were similar rifts in the Fabian Society, from which Bernard Shaw's *Fabianism and the Empire* caused a number of important secessions. These rifts were largely healed after the return of peace ; and in the new century *The Clarion* regained and for a time greatly extended its influence as public opinion shifted over in preparation for the Liberal victory of 1906. But a much more serious dissension was to come when Blatchford, having been sent to Germany to report the German army manœuvres for *The Daily Mail*, came back convinced of that country's aggressive intentions and of Great Britain's unpreparedness to meet them. His articles, reprinted as a pamphlet, *The Truth about Germany* (1910), had a very wide sale, and met with very strong criticism in the working-class movement. The I.L.P. and a large section of the Labour Party attacked him fiercely for backing the Tory side and taking no account of the international Socialist and Trade Union movements as means of preventing war. The German Social Democrats were at that time still the leading group in the Socialist International, looked up to as the world's foremost and best organised Socialist Party ; and Blatchford's 'Anti-Germanism' was the more resented because he had been paid for giving expression to it in Alfred Harmsworth's jingo *Daily Mail*.

Blatchford and *The Clarion* never recovered from the blow to their influence delivered by this controversy. Whether Blatchford was right or wrong about Germany, the circulation of *The Clarion* and the influence of the Clarion Fellowship and the other auxiliaries that had grown up round the paper depended on attracting support from the left rather than the right of the Labour movement. But the left was predominantly internationalist, if not positively pacifist ; and though the *Clarion* magic was powerful enough to retain the inner group of enthusiasts, the paper lost heavily among its less devoted readers. The Clarionettes still carried on with their social activities and commanded a substantial following ; but Blatchford practically ceased to write about Socialism and his political influence disappeared. *The Clarion* lasted under the control of the original group, or such of them as remained, through the 'twenties. Ernest Davies, Fabian and Labour politician, then took it over and attempted to carry it on as a serious journal for the discussion of Socialist policy, but failed to restore its circulation. Finally, Odhams Press, the publishers of the *Daily Herald*, took it over, turned it back into a popular journal aiming at a wide appeal, and when it failed to sell, killed it dead in 1935. Long before then it had ceased to count.

Blatchford himself lived on until 1943, dying at the ripe age of 92. But his work for Socialism belongs almost entirely to the years between 1889 and the return of the Liberals to power in 1906, and mainly to the 1890s. At that time he supplied far better than anyone else one of the two appeals to which the new recruits to Socialism were most ready to respond — the gay as against the grave. Keir Hardie and presently such men as Ramsay MacDonald and Philip Snowden supplied the other. There were some Socialists, such as F. W. Jowett, who could respond to both ; but the leading personalities in the two groups never could have got on together. In the event the puritans won, largely because, when the Liberal-Labour alliance against which both groups had revolted came back in a new form in 1906, the I.L.P. fitted much more easily into the new pattern than the Clarion Fellowship, which was at bottom a movement of revolt against the drabness of life and an appeal for justice on behalf of the 'bottom dogs' rather than an heir of Victorian Nonconformity or a partisan of the Trade Union claims of the organised workers.

CHAPTER IV

GREAT BRITAIN—THE LABOUR PARTY AND THE GREAT UNREST

(i) THE RISE OF THE LABOUR PARTY : SOCIALISTS AND LIBERALS : H. G. WELLS

WE have seen in a previous chapter of this volume how the Independent Labour Party, pushing Hyndman's Social Democratic Federation aside, became the principal rallying-point for the New Unionists and for the growing number of former Liberals who were breaking away from the Liberal Party and basing their politics on the 'social question'. The I.L.P. claimed, equally with the S.D.F., to be a Socialist body ; but its Socialism did not rest on Marxian foundations. It was definitely ethical in its appeal ; and it based its propaganda mainly on the demand for collective action to do away with preventable human suffering and waste of human lives and to ensure that, as far as means could be found, everyone from birth to old age should get a fair chance of a decent and happy existence. Its most frequent slogans were the eight hours' day, the minimum wage, and the right to work ; and with them it coupled the demands for better housing and sanitation, better and more equal education, and full equality between men and women.

This I.L.P. type of Socialism was part of a much wider movement, for the most part not Socialist at all, of revulsion against the manifest evils of industrial society and, in particular against the sharp contrast between the rapidly growing wealth of British society, regarded as a whole, and the appalling squalor and wretchedness of a large section of the population in London and other great cities. These conditions were nothing new : nor was it a new thing to expose them. Charles Kingsley and other Christian Socialists, the brothers Mayhew, and many others had done so in the 1850s and 1860s with very little effect. During that period, two factors had made against any widespread arousing of the social consciences of the well-to-do, as well as against any movement of revolt from below. One factor was the actual improvement that was taking place as a result, for the most part, not of State intervention, but of higher productivity and of Great Britain's remarkably favourable position in the world market. The continuing misery of the 'bottom dogs' was to a great extent concealed by the improvements in the economic conditions of the more skilled workers, by the increase in the size of the middle and lower-middle classes, which were necessarily recruited largely from below, and by the withdrawal from revolutionary, or near-revolutionary activities of the leaders of the very groups which had formed the backbone first of Owenism and then of the Chartist movement. The Hungry 'Forties were over; and with the skilled workers too busy building up their Trade Unions and Co-operative Societies to pay much attention to the plight of the unskilled, the potential rebels among the middle classes no longer felt the challenge of a hunger-revolt demanding their sympathy and support. Things seemed to be getting on well enough to make it unnecessary to go to extremes in the hope of advancing faster; and complacency replaced the social questioning of the preceding decades.

The second factor was the dominance of a religious outlook which, in sharp contrast to both Owenism and Christian Socialism, put the main emphasis on each man's individual responsibility for his own salvation, and made the religious all too willing to see misery as the god-ordained punishment for individual sin. Where so many were getting materially better-off and therewith improving their social habits, it was only too easy to blame those who fell behind in the race towards prosperity and respectability as the authors of their own misfortunes and, wherever the facts evidently failed to fit this diagnosis, to fall back on the comfortable conclusion that it would all be somehow made up to the virtuous poor in the next world. Moreover, it was a simple matter, according to the prevalent economic notions, to demonstrate that helping the poor often did more harm than good by undermining their self-reliance and their will to produce, on which the national prosperity depended.

The question we have to ask ourselves here is not why this

mood arose, but why by the 1890s it was so rapidly changing. One factor was the decline of the Radical impulse in the Liberal Party after Chamberlain's defection. Another part of the answer is to be sought in the undermining of confidence in continually increasing economic prosperity by the heavy unemployment which occurred in the late 'seventies and in the 'eighties; for this served to bring to notice the exceedingly depressed and precarious conditions under which a considerable proportion of the town populations were living, and presently set the statisticians, such as Charles Booth, to work producing facts and figures which convincingly refuted the notion that the main cause of poverty was sin and brought into relief especially the sufferings on the one hand of the children and on the other of the aged poor. The exposure of these conditions carried with it a sharp revelation of the estrangement of a large part of the urban population from the churches, and indeed from all friendly contact with the more comfortable classes; and in a deeply religious society the sense of this estrangement counted for at least as much as the revelations of physical privation in arousing the social consciences of a section both of the well-to-do and of the better-off part of the working class. The effect was to make slumming fashionable enough to affect a part of the university population, and at the same time to set a number of working-class 'agitators' attempting to organise the unskilled and to raise again the old cries for a minimum wage, a limited working-day, and the right to work. The same impetus lay behind the establishment of missions and settlements in the poor districts of the great towns and behind the organisation of the New Unions by such men as John Burns, Will Thorne, Keir Hardie, Havelock Wilson, and Tom Mann. The impetus was the same — a powerful ethical drive towards remedying a state of affairs that was felt to be humanly intolerable in a society not only calling itself Christian, but also priding itself on being the world's foremost in the art and science of creating wealth.

The impulse was fundamentally the same; but the ideas and policies that arose out of it were widely different. For the most part the middle-class idealists who helped to arouse the social conscience of their fellows had no thought of establishing Socialism or a classless society. On the contrary, most of them aimed not at *fusing* the classes but at *reconciling* them by rebuilding the human relations which had been destroyed by the growth of industrial, urbanised ways of living. It seemed to them — for example, to the founders of Toynbee Hall and other settlements — a terrible thing that in the slums there were no gentlefolk to provide natural leadership to the people. They saw each slum as a village deprived of its squire — or, if that is too hard a saying, deprived of men and women of superior culture and education, able to stand above the daily struggle for mere existence and to make themselves responsible for tasks of succour and organisation which the poor could not undertake for themselves. Just as, in Russia, the early Narodniks had tried to bridge a social gulf by going among the peasants, these idealists, inspired by Arnold Toynbee and Thomas Hill Green, wanted to go among the slum-dwellers; but because the British State was a constitutional State already heading towards political democracy and allowing freedom of speech and organisation, they saw no need to go as revolutionaries. They went as reconcilers, hoping in most cases, though not in all, to find in religion — in some sort of *social* Christianity — the means of recreating human relations across class-barriers. Politically, they were of all opinions — from Tory Social Reformers to various kinds of ethical Socialists. In fact, most of them were Liberals, of that wing of Liberalism which hoped to persuade the party seriously to take up the social question and to constitute itself the champion of the depressed. The curious tangle of ideas that lay behind this movement can be studied nowhere better than in Sir Walter Besant's once popular social novel, *All Sorts and Conditions of Men* (1882).

So far I have been speaking mainly of the new drive towards social ethics and social reform as it took shape in the older universities. But, of course, this was only one manifestation of a much more widespread tendency. All over the country similar impulses were being felt by groups of middle-class people, chiefly young, who felt the call to some sort of social service. Some of these threw themselves into philanthropic activities of one sort or another, or into service on local public bodies, which were still mostly elected on a non-party basis. Some found scope inside the local agencies of the Liberal Party, which they sought to bring over to fuller endorsement of a far-reaching social programme; and a smaller number became 'Tory Democrats'. But in the provinces, or at any rate in the industrial areas, a substantial minority, despairing of both the great parties, went over to Socialism and became members of the local branches of the I.L.P. For many of these converts the break with the old parties was accompanied either by a loss of religious faith or, more often, by a weakening of it which still left the ethical promptings of religious sentiment intact while shaking them loose from the associations of church or chapel. Such half-unbelievers felt, as we have seen, the need for a continuance of the kind of fellowship which their membership of a religious community had hitherto supplied. Some became members of Labour or Ethical Churches: others sought in the I.L.P. itself or in the *Clarion* movement the satisfaction of their gregarious ethical impulses. There arose a mingling of classes in the new Independent Labour bodies which was quite different from, and yet akin to, the movement for class-reconciliation *de haut en bas* which was emanating chiefly from the older universities. For in the I.L.P. and the *Clarion* organisations members of different classes — but chiefly of the lesser middle-classes, the professions, and the upper strata of the working classes — met on an equality and, far from seeking class-reconciliation, met as advocates of a classless society resting on a basis of social ownership and of a recognition of need as the most important title to a share in the product of communal effort.

Of course, the line between these two kinds of coming together across class barriers was not sharply drawn. There were some who experienced both impulses, and were torn between them, and some who failed to see the difference. But, broadly, the distinction holds good.

To those who came over to Socialism, it usually appeared that nothing was to be hoped for from the Liberals, because they constituted the party of *laissez-faire* capitalism in its most extreme form. But this feeling was much stronger, as a rule, in the industrial centres, and in the coalfields where the Liberal employer and his Trade Unionist workers were often at open variance, than in London or in mainly residential towns or rural areas, in which Liberalism much more often constituted the main opposition to a strongly entrenched Conservative ascendancy. In such places, and similarly in the universities, Liberals and Socialists tended to hang together because neither group had much hope of winning, at any rate alone. London was, in certain respects, a special case, because Liberals and Socialists had been drawn together into a combined movement for the reform of metropolitan government and, when this was achieved in 1889 by the establishment of the London County Council, there were powerful inducements for the groups which had co-operated in pressing for it to hold together in an attempt to reap the fruits. London's new government was bound, from the outset, to be conducted on party lines ; and the only question in that connection was how many parties there were to be. If Liberal and Labour were to fight each other, Tory rule was almost certain to be the result ; whereas a combined Progressive Party, could it but hold together, stood an excellent chance of ruling the roost, but was also certain, in that event, to find itself sharply disliked by the Government when the Conservatives were in power nationally. This largely explains why, while the local I.L.P. branches in the provinces set to work to secure the election of independent Labour councillors and members of other public bodies, in London, as far as the County Council was concerned, most of the Labour support went into the Progressive Party. It also largely explains the Fabian policy of permeation ; for in the 1890s the body which the Fabians — mainly a London organisation — were chiefly engaged in permeating was the Progressive Party on the L.C.C.

In most of the industrial areas a substantial fraction of the younger men and women who were active in the Trade Unions and in other local working-class bodies were in process of being converted to the causes of Independent Labour representation and ethical Socialism ; and they were everywhere being joined by a sprinkling of men and women of other classes. But the case was different with the older people, most of whom clung to the Liberal associations of their younger days and were much less affected by the decline in the hold of church or chapel. As the Trade Unions and, still more, the Co-operative Societies were largely officered and led by these older people, the attempts of Socialists and New Unionists to bring them bodily over to the side of Independent Labour representation did not meet with much success. It became evident that the only hope of bringing either the Trade Unions or the Co-operatives into the movement for Indndeepence *as organised bodies* lay in not asking for any profession of Socialist faith and in not pushing the demand for independence to the point of demanding a complete break with Liberalism. There were, of course, Socialists who were entirely unprepared to make such concessions and regarded the making of them as treason to the Socialist cause. But most of the I.L.P. leaders were so well aware of the immense difficulties in the way of establishing a Socialist, or indeed an effective Labour, parliamentary party without organised Trade Union backing, and were also so much ethical and evolutionary rather than Marxist revolutionary Socialists in their basic ideas, as to regard what Keir Hardie called the 'Labour Alliance' as worth a great many concessions. Year after year, Hardie and his group had been hammering away at the Trades Union Congress in an effort to persuade its affiliated Unions to create, not an explicitly Socialist Party, but a Labour Party independent of Liberalism ; and it would have been grossly illogical on their part if, when they had at length persuaded the Congress to tell its Parliamentary Committee to summon a conference with the Socialists for this purpose, they had attempted to use the occasion to set up a definitely Socialist Party or to insist at the outset on the acceptance of a Socialist ideology. Besides, had they done this, only a few of the New Unions would have joined such a party, and the majority of the Unions might well have been thrown back right into the arms of Liberalism.

As it was, though the Conference of 1900, which established the Labour Representation Committee, was fairly well attended by Trade Union delegates, the Co-operative Movement, which had also been invited, held obstinately aloof, and a good many Unions whose delegates voted for setting up the L.R.C. thereafter failed to join it. In particular the Miners abstained and kept their Liberal connections through their local associations, largely because they had been partly successful in forcing their nominees on Liberal and Radical Associations in the coalfield areas which they dominated, but also because the tie with Liberalism through the Dissenting chapels was particularly strong in the mining population. It has often been said that the turning-point in the fortunes of the L.R.C. was the Taff Vale

Judgment, which convinced the Unions of the need to have their own men and their own party to plead their case in Parliament. This legal judgment, in which heavy damages were awarded against the Amalgamated Society of Railway Servants for damage done to the Taff Vale Railway Company during a strike, manifestly jeopardised the whole structure of collective bargaining based on the final right to withhold labour; and the Trade Unions were bound to take whatever action they deemed most likely to be effective in getting it reversed. There were, however, two ways of setting about this — one the creation of a separate Labour Party, and the other an intensified campaign within the Liberal Party to secure the adoption of candidates who would pledge themselves, on this matter, to support the Trade Union demands. In practice, the Unions made use of both methods, with remarkable success; and there can be no real doubt that, for this immediate purpose, the combination of the two served them best. What is not true is that, confronted with the Taff Vale Judgment, the Trade Union movement had no alternative to coming over to the L.R.C. in order to get it upset. Where the Taff Vale Judgment did help in rallying support to the L.R.C. was in strenghtening the body of opinion that held the scales of the law and of the existing social order to be unfairly weighted against the workers and regarded the creation of an independent Labour Party as an indispensable part of the process of getting this bias removed.

The L.R.C. of 1900 was in fact set up with only very limited Trade Union support. At the end of its first year of existence its affiliated Trade Union membership was only 353,000, out of nearly two million Trade Unionists in all, of whom about 1,400,000 belonged to the Trades Union Congress. The 'New' Unions joined it almost as a matter of course; but their membership was not very large, only the Amalgamated Society of Railway Servants, with 60,000, and the Gasworkers, with 48,000, having more than 20,000. The only other Union with more than this number to join the L.R.C. in its first year was the National Union of Boot and Shoe Operatives, with 32,000. The Miners, the Textile Factory Workers, the Engineers, and the Boilermakers remained outside, though the Engineers and the Textile Factory Workers were already

considering the question of affiliation, and both actually came
in during the next two years. By 1903 the affiliated membership had risen to 873,000, with the Miners still holding aloof
and running their own candidates, usually under the auspices
of the local Liberal and Radical Associations. Only then could
the new vessel be considered to have been fairly launched.

Even so, it was still a long way off constituting a party.
It was no more than a committee, each of whose constituents
kept the full right to manage its own affairs. Each affiliated
body — Socialist Society or Trade Union — put forward and
paid for its own candidates. There was no central fund for
financing candidates or even for engaging in any propagandist
or organising activities. There was not even a Programme —
only an affirmation of willingness 'to co-operate with any party
which, for the time being, may be engaged in promoting
legislation in the direct interest of Labour'. Nor was there any
local organisation at all under the party's control. Although
Local Labour Representation Committees or Labour Parties
existed in a number of areas, they were not admitted to affiliation
to the national party or represented at its Conferences. Only
in areas where the local Trades Councils had joined the party
had it any formal local machinery. This was partly because
the L.R.C. was open to Trades Councils and the Trade Union
section preferred to work through them rather than through
local L.R.C.s which would more easily pass under Socialist
control; but it was also because the I.L.P. saw the establishment of local L.R.C.s as a threat to the influence of its own local
branches: so that right and left combined to block the growth
of any effective constituency organisation.

It soon became clear that the L.R.C. could make little
progress until it had some assured income behind it. This issue
had already been raised in 1901, when the Fabian Society had
moved for the establishment of a central fund. The I.L.P.,
fearful for its own position, combined with the Trade Union
right wing to vote the proposal down. It was raised again the
following year, on the motion of the Gasworkers and the Dock
Labourers, and this time a committee was appointed to draw
up a scheme. In 1903 this Committee reported, and the conference agreed to a levy of one penny a year from each member
of each affiliated body. Arthur Henderson, soon to become

the principal architect of the party structure, wanted the levy to be fourpence, and Paul Weighill, of the Stonemasons, moved that it should be one shilling; but neither of them got much support.

Even one penny, however, was better than nothing. It did not enable the L.R.C. to finance any candidates of its own; but it did make possible the payment of £200 a year towards the maintenance of each M.P. elected under L.R.C. auspices; and the granting of this subvention was made the occasion for introducing a 'Party Pledge', binding L.R.C. candidates, if elected, to vote in accordance with majority decisions of the Labour Parliamentary Group, or to resign their seats. Members of Parliament at that time received no salaries, and had to depend on what the organisations sponsoring their candidatures chose to allow them. The Trade Unions could solve the problem either by keeping them on the Union payrolls or by making them allowances out of specially established Political Funds; but the I.L.P. and the other Socialist bodies were very short of money, and would have found it difficult to get suitable candidates unless some provision had been made. The new arrangement was, however, even more important as the first step towards binding the elected L.R.C. representatives together as a party, though a sequence of attempts to persuade the 1903 Conference to commit itself to a programme was voted down. The Electrical Trades Union wanted a declaration making recognition of the class-war and advocacy of the socialisation of the means of production the basis of the L.R.C.'s activities; Jack Jones, on behalf of the West Ham Trades Council, tried an alternative proposal committing the movement to the overthrow of capitalism and to public ownership of the means of production. The Conference would have neither of these; and when Jones moved for the setting up of a committee to work out an agreed programme Keir Hardie opposed him, and that too was rejected. The most the Conference would accept was that the L.R.C. Members of Parliament should constitute themselves a separate 'group' — not yet 'party' — in the House, with its own Whips.

Even these mild advances towards making the L.R.C. into a party cost it the loss of one of the two Members elected in 1900 — Richard Bell of the Railway Servants, who persisted in supporting Liberal candidates at by-elections, even against Labour men, and finally broke with the L.R.C. on this issue in 1904. By this time the Labour Group had been reinforced by three new M.P.s — David Shackleton of the Weavers, Will Crooks of the Fabian Society and the Coopers' Union, and Arthur Henderson of the Ironfounders. The advent of Henderson, who became Treasurer of the L.R.C. in 1903, was of great importance. He had been a Liberal Party agent in the constituency for which he was elected ; and when the Liberal caucus jockeyed him out of the succession on the sitting member's retirement he managed to carry over with him a substantial part of the following of the Liberal Association. This following he made the nucleus of a local L.R.C. based on wide individual membership, thus in effect inaugurating the method of building up behind the nascent party a structure of individual supporters working directly for it and not merely for one of its affiliated organisations. Will Crooks, in Woolwich, adopted a similar method ; but in face of I.L.P. and Trade Union opposition it was not taken up over most of the country until Henderson completely reorganised the Labour Party during the first world war and at last secured full recognition of the local Labour Parties as an integral part of the party structure. This change was impracticable up to 1914 because it was opposed both by many Trade.Unions and by the I.L.P., and also by the Trades Councils in a number of areas — all three groups fearing, from their different standpoints, the growth of a powerful party machine.

The Social Democratic Federation, as we saw, had joined the L.R.C. at the outset. But it had seceded the following year, after failing to get the doctrine of the class-war accepted as the basis of unity. Thereafter, it acted alone, under Hyndman's leadership. In 1903 a part of its membership in Scotland seceded to form a Socialist Labour Party modelled on Daniel De Leon's American organisation and advocating, like the De Leonites, an extreme form of Industrial Unionism which would set out to unite all workers in one big departmentalised Union resting on the principle of the class-war and seeking to wage it, under a common control, in both the industrial and the political fields. The S.L.P. obtained a considerable hold in Glasgow, and in some other Scottish towns ; but it remained almost entirely a Scottish movement. It lasted on to play a considerable rôle in the Clyde engineering factories during the first world war and to contribute much of the leadership of the rebel Clyde Workers' Committee of 1915. After the war most of its members passed over into the Communist Party.

Two years after the S.L.P. secession, the S.D.F. suffered a further breakaway. A group headed by C. L. Fitzgerald, mainly in London and Lancashire, seceded to form the Socialist Party of Great Britain. The S.P.G.B. stood for a policy of complete Socialist intransigence. It regarded industrial action as useless for the achievement of Socialism and, while asserting the necessity of political action, rejected all palliative programmes and insisted that no parliamentary candidate could be worth voting for unless he stood for the complete immediate establishment of a Socialist system. As it was not strong enough to put up candidates of its own and as no Labour or Socialist candidate who was put up met S.P.G.B. requirements, the S.P.G.B. leaders urged their supporters not to vote, but to carry on active Socialist propaganda and education in the hope of creating popular support for the Socialist revolution. The S.P.G.B. remained a tiny group, active chiefly in London. The S.D.F., weakened by these secessions, lost ground in most areas to the I.L.P.; but up to 1906 the I.L.P. itself made but slow progress.

The Fabian Society too was in the doldrums during these years. It had lost ground considerably at the turn of the century because it supported the South African War, to which both the I.L.P. and the S.D.F. were opposed. Its support of the war was expressed mainly in Bernard Shaw's tract, *Fabianism and the Empire*, in which he took the line that the Boer Republics were thoroughly reactionary, that neither side cared a rap about the welfare of the native inhabitants of South Africa, and that, as there was no World State or Federation that could take the Republics over and compel them to manage their affairs in the common interest of mankind, the best thing that could be done to them was for the British Empire to annex them and force them to become more efficient agents of civilisation. 'The problem before us is how the world can be ordered by Great Powers of practically international extent. . . . The partition of the greater part of the globe among such powers is, as a matter of fact that must be faced approvingly or deploringly, now only a question of time.' And again, 'The notion that a nation has a right to do what it pleases with its own territory, without reference to the interests of the rest of the world, is no more tenable from the International Socialist point of view — that is, from the point of view of the twentieth century — than the notion that the landlord has a right to do what he likes with his estate without reference to the interests of his neighbours'. And yet again 'The State which obstructs international civilisation will have to go, be it big or little'.

Shaw was arguing, in effect, that the world should be regarded as a common possession of mankind, and that the efficient exploitation of its resources in the common interest of all peoples should take precedence over all limited national claims. He was arguing that in the twentieth century nationalism should be regarded as obsolete, and that men should direct their attention to the creation of a world order based on Socialist principles. But he was also taking up the standpoint of *realpolitik* and contending that, whether one liked it or not, the future lay with the Great Powers, which were bound to sweep the lesser powers aside in their development of the world market; and he was reassuring himself with the conviction that 'a Great Power, consciously or unconsciously, must govern in the interests of civilisation as a whole'. In relation to the Boer Republics, he contended that 'it is not to those interests that such mighty forces as gold-fields, and the formidable armaments that can be built upon them, should be wielded irresponsibly by small communities of frontiersmen. Theoretically, they should be internationalised, not British-Imperialised; but until the Federation of the World becomes an accomplished fact we must accept the most responsible Imperial Federations available as a substitute for it.' By implication, Shaw defended the partition of China — then a lively issue — by the same arguments, as he was later to oppose Irish independence. He spoke admiringly of German imperial policy in the pushing of foreign trade; and he concluded with the statement that 'The moral of it all is that what the British Empire wants most urgently in its government is not Conservatism, not Liberalism, not Imperialism, but brains and political science'.

Naturally, Shaw's argument shocked a number of people,

including some Fabians. Half a century later, it deeply shocks me : indeed, the entire Fabian position in this matter strikes me as deplorable. But Shaw was strongly supported by the Webbs, and his policy was endorsed by a very large majority at the Fabian meeting which was called to pronounce on his draft. A few Fabians, headed by H. W. Massingham, seceded from the Society ; but they were lonely voices. Robert Blatchford and most of the leaders of *The Clarion* group took much the same line, and forfeited much more support by doing so ; for *The Clarion*'s following belonged by instinct to the left and sided by instinct against the apostles of empire. The Fabians, who had up to this point paid very little attention to international affairs and were for the most part temperamentally reformists, were much readier than the working-class Socialists to accept Shaw's 'efficiency first' line of argument. Most of them were disposed to regard the case for Socialism largely in terms of more efficient organisation for welfare, and to apply to international affairs the notion of a planned and orderly world society guided by the skill and knowledge of the expert. The Webbs in particular, in their attempts to permeate the existing parties with Socialist ideas, found more response among Conservative and Liberal Imperialists than among either old-fashioned Conservatives or old-fashioned Liberals of the *laissez-faire* school. Their friends among the Liberals were Grey and Haldane rather than the Gladstonians ; and among Conservatives they had most in common with such men as Milner. They agreed with Shaw in regarding nationalism as an obsolete nuisance, and in looking to the large State as the necessary instrument of progress.

Whereas Shaw and most of the Fabians appeared in relation to the South African War as opponents of the 'reactionary nationalism' of the Boer Republics, the great economist and sociologist, John Atkinson Hobson (1858–1940), who was at that time still a supporter of the Liberal Party, entered the lists on the other side with his important study of *Imperialism* (1902). Hobson, who had already proclaimed his 'under-consumptionist' theory of economic crises in his early work, *The Physiology of Industry* (1889), written in collaboration with A. F. Mummery, was an upholder of nationalism, which he regarded as the foundation on which world internationalism would have to be built. The Imperialism which he denounced was, in his eyes, a perversion of nationalism : it arose wherever a national State set out to extend its rule or supremacy over other peoples who had different traditions, or whose ways of living were different from its own. Hobson distinguished sharply between Colonialism, taking the form of emigration to unpeopled areas in which the immigrants reproduced the way of living of the country they had left — as in the British colonies in Australasia and parts of Canada — and Imperialism such as was to be found in Asiatic and African 'colonies', where the settlers established themselves as a ruling caste among populations whose traditions and ways of life were essentially other than their own. He drew attention to the immense expansion of this second kind of colonial development during the closing decades of the nineteenth century, to the rapid increase in the area and population of the subject territories and dependencies of the British and other empires, and to the essentially competitive character of this type of imperialist aggrandisement. In Nationalism, he argued, there was nothing that need prevent the peoples of the earth from living together in peace and building up friendly collaboration through mutual trade and intercourse ; but Imperialism was in its nature aggressive and predatory and favoured both the concentration of capitalist economic power and the alliance of this power with the ruling class in each imperialist country. Both directly and through the rivalries it engendered, Imperialism led to the piling up of armaments and to ever-increasing threats of war for the possession of spheres of influence and for keeping rival imperialist States away from them. It brought with it the will to subject the less powerful States to domination by the great powers ; and it aroused the spirit of nationality among the peoples threatened by it, especially in the less developed parts of the world. Imperialism, in Hobson's view, was quintessentially predatory. The product mainly of advanced capitalist techniques and of the insatiable search for fresh markets arising out of the limitation of consuming power among the peoples under capitalist domination, Imperialism was leading the world towards an internecine struggle which threatened to destroy the victories of nineteenth-century liberalism by plunging the world into immensely destructive wars.

Hobson thus linked together his under-consumptionist critique of the capitalist economy and his denunciation of imperialist expansion. Yet he was not, at this stage, a Socialist. He was a Radical, who continued to hope that the Liberal Party could be brought over to an advanced social policy of income redistribution that would counteract the under-consumptionist tendencies of modern capitalism, and therewith to a reversal of the imperialist drive as the need to conquer fresh markets was removed by the increase in domestic consuming power. In relation to the South African War he was a 'pro-Boer'; but he was also the most persistent advocate of a thoroughgoing Radical policy in home affairs. It is common knowledge that his book on *Imperialism* had a profound influence on Socialist thought, not only or even mainly in Great Britain, but in all the parties of the Second International and most of all on Lenin, whose own work on *Imperialism, the Highest Stage of Capitalism* (written in 1916) was largely based on Hobson's study.

Later on, Hobson was to oppose the great war of 1914 and to renounce his Liberalism and join the Labour Party. But up to 1914 he continued to count as a Radical. The further development of his under-consumptionist doctrine in *The Industrial System* (1909) and in other works stirred up a great controversy among the Liberal economists, most of whom rejected his theory with contumely. Only with the severe economic crisis of the 1930s did his economic ideas win increasing acceptance, even among Socialists, when they were partly taken up and re-stated by J. M. Keynes. Even then, Hobson was seldom given the credit he deserved as the pioneer of the 'New Economics'. Modest and retiring by nature, he played no active part in the Socialist movement except through his writings; but he has quite as good a claim as the Fabians to be regarded as the pioneer philosopher of the 'Welfare State', and over and above this the supreme distinction of being the first to subject the economics and politics of capitalist Imperialism to thorough and devastating exposure.

In 1903 Joseph Chamberlain launched his crusade for Tariff Reform and Empire Preference; and the Fabian Society again invoked Shaw's aid to define its attitude. The result was the tract, *Fabianism and the Fiscal Question* (1904), in which Shaw attacked both Free Trade and Tariff Reform, advocating instead of either a plan for the development of empire trade through the nationalisation of railways, the provision of free shipping services for pushing exports and consolidating imperial economic relations, the organisation of improved consular services, and an extensive system of technical education in order to improve industrial efficiency. This plan too was adopted by the Fabians with very little opposition, though it led to the secession of a few leading members, including Graham Wallas. In retrospect what is most remarkable about Shaw's tract is that he evidently expected Chamberlain's crusade to sweep the country and had no anticipation at all of the coming Liberal electoral triumph or of the advent of the Labour Party, in half-alliance with Liberalism, as a real political force. The Fabians were indeed, under his and the Webbs' influence, singularly blind to the signs of the times. They showed no great interest in the Labour Representation Committee, and put no substantial hopes in it — which was a not unnatural mistake — but they were also blind to the renascence that was going on within the Liberal Party and to the general leftward swing of opinion in the country as a whole.

This leftward swing had, at the outset, a good deal to do with the conflict of attitudes over the South African War. Later in the same year as the L.R.C. was set up, *Reynolds' Newspaper*, then edited by W. M. Thompson, took the initiative in summoning a Democratic Convention, made up of anti-war elements. The Convention launched a National Democratic League, which was supported by a variety of elements drawn from both the Socialist and the Liberal camps. Thompson was President, Lloyd George Vice-President, Tom Mann Secretary ; and among the active proponents were John Burns, Robert Smillie of the Scottish Miners, and John Ward of the Navvies' Union, together with such old 'Lib-Labs' as George Howell, and Sam Woods of the Miners' Federation, then Secretary of the Trades Union Congress. The National Democratic League was definitely a Radical, and not a Socialist, body. It demanded universal suffrage, payment of M.P.s, abolition of the House of Lords, and the rest of the traditional Radical programme, together with an extensive programme of social reforms. For a time, it had much more of the limelight than the L.R.C. But the main bodies of organised Socialists — the I.L.P. and the S.D.F. — stood aloof from it because of its Liberal connections and its refusal to accept a Socialist programme; and as the issues raised by the South African War receded it gradually lost its importance, but not without playing a highly significant part in the leftward reorientation of the Liberal Party and thus checking considerably the movement towards Labour independence. It was undoubtedly a factor in the great Liberal victory of 1906, which carried the L.R.C. along with it and resulted in the appearance of a Labour Party numerous enough to count as a factor in politics, but still bound tightly to the Liberals despite its profession of independence.

The Liberal landslide of 1905–6 took many people besides the Fabian leaders by surprise. Liberalism, which the Socialists had been denouncing as a decaying and obsolete doctrine, suddenly re-emerged, under the influence of a resurgence of Radical sentiment, with an extensive social programme. The Liberal Ministry, with a very large parliamentary majority behind it, included a number of Radicals in key positions. The Labour Party, thirty strong, had no voting importance in the House of Commons: the Liberals were amply strong enough, as far as voting went, to dispense with its support. It was, however, tied firmly to the Liberals because the great majority of its members had been elected with the support of Liberal voters and would have stood no chance of being elected without that support. Only three of them, F. W. Jowett in West Bradford, J. W. Taylor in Chester-le-Street, and G. N. Barnes in Glasgow, had won in three-cornered fights against both Liberal and Conservative opponents. One more, C. W. Bowerman at Deptford, had defeated a Tory and an unofficial 'Lib-Lab'; and Keir Hardie had won in a two-member constituency, Merthyr, against one official and one unofficial Liberal, with no Tory in the field. The rest had all been elected with the backing of Liberal voters, though without any open pact with the Liberal Party. As against this, of course, a great many Liberals had been elected with the aid of Labour votes, either in two-member constituencies where each party had put forward only one candidate or in ordinary constituencies in which no Labour candidate took the field. Many of these Liberals had given pledges to support particular measures favoured by the Labour Party, especially the reversal of the Taff Vale Judgment. Both parties stood for Free Trade, for Irish Home Rule, against Chinese Labour in South Africa, and for a settlement of the South African question by a federal solution designed to reconcile the Dutch and British settlers; and both expected, and were prepared to meet, the obstructive opposition of the House of Lords. There was much to hold them together, and not a great deal, in terms of practical politics, to drive them apart, in view of the fact that the Labour Party was not committed to Socialism and had not fought the election on a Socialist programme. The majority of the Labour men elected were Trade Unionists — most of them, no doubt, Socialists of a sort, but many of them by no means sharply marked off from the still considerable 'Lib-Lab' contingent, among whom the Miners' representatives predominated.

In the first year of the new Parliament, the Labour Party secured two notable successes. It was able to force the Liberals to withdraw their own compromise measure for dealing with the Taff Vale Judgment, and to enact a Trade Disputes Act which fully conceded the Trade Union demands; and it persuaded the House of Commons to pass F. W. Jowett's Bill empowering local authorities, if they wished, to provide school meals for needy children. The success over Taff Vale was due to the pledges given by most Liberal candidates during the election — pledges on which the Government felt unable to go back. Jowett's Act got through because it was only permissive. After these initial achievements the Labour Party, which had formally adopted that name after the election, found itself practically limited to the rôle of supporting the measures of the Liberal Government, which covered an extensive field of social reforms — an improved Workmen's Compensation Act, Trade Boards in sweated trades, medical inspection of school-children, old age pensions subject to a means test, the eight hours' day and improved safety regulations in the coal-mines, the establishment of Labour Exchanges, and so on, as well as South African Federation and payment for Members of Parliament. It also found itself presently lined up behind Lloyd George in his famous 'Land Tax' budget of 1909 and in the ensuing struggle with the House of Lords. In addition, there was in the background the impending battle over Irish

Home Rule, in which it would be bound to rally to the Government's side.

As against these factors making for Labour support of the Government there were no very urgent matters in Parliament to divide the two parties; but there was a considerable body of Socialist feeling against the policy of Liberal-Labour co-operation. The Labour Party was to a great extent the creation of Keir Hardie's I.L.P., which had made its way largely by denouncing the Liberals and calling on the workers to sever connections with them and build up an independent party of their own; and it went much against the grain to accept as the fulfilment of this design a party which was doing hardly more than swell the Liberal majority. Moreover, trouble soon began to develop over by-elections. The triumphant Liberals were in no mood to cede more seats to Labour men by refraining from putting forward their own candidates; and the leaders of the Labour Party did not want to jeopardise the seats they held by antagonising Liberal support. Where the Labour Party did fight a three-cornered contest, it usually came off badly, whereas in straight fights with the Tories two Lib-Lab miners won seats. In one case, a Labour man, Pete Curran of the Gasworkers' Union and the I.L.P., got in at Jarrow as the result of a four-cornered fight against Liberal, Conservative and Irish National-ist opponents. At Leicester, when the old Lib-Lab, Henry Broadhurst, died in 1907, his seat, in this two-member con-stituency, was allowed to go to a Liberal without Labour opposition, presumably because fighting the Liberals there would have endangered the other seat, held by James Ramsay MacDonald. By far the most significant by-election of that year was fought at Colne Valley, in Yorkshire, where a young independent Socialist, Victor Grayson (1881– ?), stood without official party endorsement and was elected largely on the issue of better treatment for the unemployed, but on a far-reaching and aggressive Socialist programme.

This was, indeed, a highly significant contest. Employ-ment, which had been good in 1906, had seriously worsened in the following year; and the efforts of Keir Hardie and other Labour men in Parliament to push the Government into action had met with scant success. The Labour Party had its Right to Work Bill, but could get no facilities for it; and left-wing

Socialist opinion fastened on this issue to accuse the Party of
supineness in pressing working-class claims. Grayson was
adopted at Colne Valley against the wish of the I.L.P. leaders
as well as of the other leaders of the Party. He was a young
theological student, aged 25, with a powerful gift of oratory
and an attractive personality, but without much stability or
character. He belonged to the I.L.P., but was in rebellion
against its leadership. Of the I.L.P's prominent parliamentary
representatives only Philip Snowden went to Colne Valley to
support him. When he had been elected, as 'Labour and
Socialist' candidate, trouble at once arose over his position in
Parliament. He refused to sign the 'Party Pledge', which
would have compelled him to vote as a majority of the parliamentary party decided, and was thereupon refused recognition;
and he proceeded to defy the standing orders of the House by
making a scene when he demanded that priority should be given
to considering the claims of the unemployed. Suspended for
the rest of the session, he was set free to tour the country,
raising up opposition to the Labour Party's subservience to
the Liberals.

At this point the House of Lords, in its capacity as a law
court, administered a heavy blow at the Labour Party by
deciding, in the Osborne Judgment, that Trade Unions had no
legal right to engage in political activities or to spend money on
them. This legal decision knocked the bottom out of the Labour
Party's finances, and also out of those of the Miners' Federation,
with its separate parliamentary group. With payment of M.P.s
not yet in force, the sitting Labour Members were faced with
disaster; and it was clear that the Party would be in a bad way
when it had to contest a general election. One result of the
Osborne Judgment was to lead the Miners' Federation to join
the Labour Party as a body in order to fight for its reversal; but
the outlook was serious for all that. Trade Unions had been
actually spending money on political activities for many years
past, without having their right questioned. The Lords'
decision, which rested mainly on a narrow construction of the
powers conferred by the Trade Union Acts, but also in part on
the judges' view that Trade Union political action was contrary to 'public policy' — a view based partly on the existence
of the Party Pledge, as running counter to the Member's

duty to his constituents — took the Labour Party and the Trade Unions by surprise. The 'Party Pledge' was formally abolished; but that did not mend matters — for the Judgment stood. At this point, in 1910, the dispute over Lloyd George's budget plunged the Labour Party into two successive general elections the same year, fought under conditions which made it both financially unable to contest any large number of seats and compelled to woo Liberal support for getting the Judgment reversed by legislation. The policy of electoral collaboration had to be continued on penalty of virtual annihilation of the Party; and at the same time feeling against collaboration was rising among the Party's supporters.

From these two elections the Labour Party emerged nominally stronger, because it had been joined by the Miners in 1909, but actually a little weakened by the loss of a few seats, and in a condition of severe financial distress. Payment of M.P.s, enacted in 1911, alleviated the difficulties, but did not remove them. In one respect, the Labour Party's position should have been strengthened; for the Liberals had lost enough seats to make them dependent for the future on Labour and Irish support. But in practice this only increased the Labour Party's dependence; for it could not let the Liberal Government be defeated until legislation to reverse the Osborne Judgment had been enacted, and it was also tied to support legislation to curtail the powers of the House of Lords and to concede Home Rule to Ireland, as well as to franchise reform.

At the two general elections of 1910 the Labour Party again fought in informal alliance with the Liberals. Of the 40 M.P.s returned in January, 39 had no Liberal opponents, and the fortieth only an unofficial Liberal. In December, out of 42 returned, three were unopposed, and the other 39 had only Tory opponents. Every Labour or Socialist candidate, official or unofficial, who fought a three-cornered contest went down to defeat. Victor Grayson lost his seat in January, and no new exponent of left-wing policy took his place. As long as the struggle with the House of Lords continued, it was impossible to force other issues to the front; and discontent with the Labour Party's doings and with the rising price-level had to find expression outside Parliament. It affected particularly the I.L.P., many of whose members were chafing at the failure to turn the Labour Party into a definitely Socialist organisation. These malcontents began to co-operate with the Social Democratic Party — the new name adopted by the S.D.F. in 1908. *The Clarion*'s supporters were also restive. In 1909 these elements formed in Manchester a Socialist Representation Committee and launched a campaign for Socialist Unity. Similar bodies were formed in other towns; and in 1911 a Socialist Unity Congress established the British Socialist Party, made up of the whole of the S.D.P., together with most of *The Clarion* group, headed by Blatchford, and a substantial body of seceders from the I.L.P. In practice, what happened was that the S.D.P. swallowed the others; for Blatchford soon broke with the new body and began his campaign for rearmament against Germany, and the I.L.P. group lacked any outstanding leader. Blatchford's new line, which he expounded in a series of alarmist articles published in the *Daily Mail* and then widely circulated in pamphlet form, involved a sharp break with the left wing, and wrecked *The Clarion*'s influence within the Labour movement; and the B.S.P. at once became sharply divided over the new issues raised by the outburst of strikes and industrial unrest which occurred simultaneously with its establishment.

During these years the Fabian Society also had been going through a period of crisis. H. G. Wells, who had joined it in 1903, had begun before the general election of 1906 to demand a new policy. He wanted the Society to go all out for a big membership, to refound its local branches throughout the country, and to come forward as the apostle of a new Scientific Socialism based on the assimilation of the lessons of modern science and on their application to the solution of social problems. In 1905 he published *A Modern Utopia*, in which he put forward the conception of a devoted order of Samurai who would constitute themselves the organisers and guardians of mankind; and for a time he seems to have cherished the hope of converting the Fabian Society into such an order under his own leadership. In some respects his ideas were akin to those of Shaw, who was also an apostle of government by the experts, and to those of the Webbs. But Wells's campaign involved the displacement of the Fabian 'Old Gang' by a new group of leaders; and a sharp conflict of personalities arose. Wells led off with a paper on *The Faults of the Fabian*, and followed this up by securing the appointment of a special committee to consider reforming the Society's basis and policy. Some of his proposals were accepted, including the development of local Societies; and as the scheme came at a moment when the Labour victories of 1906 had stimulated a wide interest in Socialism, Fabian membership, both national and local, shot rapidly up. But a large part of Wells's plan was sheerly impracticable. He wanted the Society to found a journal for mass-circulation, to set up in a large way as a publisher of books and pamphlets, and to undertake an organising campaign that would have been far beyond its financial strength. He was a poor speaker and allowed Shaw to make rings round him in debate; and presently he wearied of a campaign in which he was clearly not getting more than a small part of his own way, and flounced out of the Fabian Society while it was still in the middle of discussing his proposals. The 'Old Gang', in fact, had been very careful not to challenge him to a conclusive vote. It had consistently preferred to adopt some of his proposals, while adjourning a final decision on others, and then to take the sting out of those it adopted by modifying their execution. On many points the 'Old Gang' was helped in this by the vagueness of many of Wells's projects and by his frequent changes of front. When its leader shook the dust of Fabianism from his feet, the Wells party in the Society at once disintegrated, and its place was taken by a new Fabian Reform Movement, which met with no better success. One of the Wells proposals had been that the Society, having organised its own local branches, should convert itself into a Socialist Party and put up its own candidates for Parliament; and there had been talk of a 'Middle-Class Socialist Party', which would convert the middle classes to Socialism as a gospel of efficiency and ordered scientific government. The new Fabian Reformers who took Wells's place insisted, on the other hand, that the Society should rid itself of its Lib-Lab adherents, a few of whom were sitting in Parliament as Liberals, should identify itself fully with the Labour Party, and should give up altogether the traditional Fabian technique of permeation.

Both these Fabian rebellions, though defeated, left a considerable impression on the Society. Wells's incursion had greatly increased its membership; and the second group of reformers did much to develop closer collaboration between it and the I.L.P., especially in the fields of local government and Socialist educational work. A joint I.L.P.-Fabian Committee undertook some activity in these fields and helped to spread Fabian ideas and policies inside the Labour movement: so that the illusion grew up that the Fabians had been from the first the main inspirers of I.L.P. policies — which was far from being the case. No doubt, *Fabian Essays* and the *Fabian Tracts*, and also the travelling lecturers sent out by the Society under the Hutchinson Trust, had exerted a substantial influence in supplying British Socialists with facts, figures, and suggestions, and in weaning them away from dogmatic Marxism and from notions of revolution to gradualist doctrines and to advocacy of the extension of public enterprise under the auspices of the existing State and the organs of local government; but the concept of gradualism was implicit in the entire policy of the I.L.P. from the beginning. It was not the Fabian Society but the New Unionism that taught the I.L.P. to put its main stress on the minimum wage, the eight hours' day, and the right to work. Still less was it the Fabian Society that infused into the I.L.P. its strong ethical insistence on the claims of the 'bottom dog'. Blatchford and Hardie both did much more than Wells or Shaw to give the I.L.P. its strongly humanitarian quality. The Fabians were at that stage apostles of efficiency more than of brotherly love, and were inclined to regard the Blatchfords and Hardies as rather foolish sentimentalists. Only later, and especially under the influence of Beatrice Webb, who took little part in the Society's work before 1909, did the Fabians appear as the leading proponents of the 'national minimum standard of civilised life'.

Herbert George Wells (1866–1946) made his chief mark as a novelist; but he was also of great importance in the early years of the twentieth century as a populariser of Socialist ideas. As a novelist he excelled above all else in describing with insight based on personal experience the lives and thoughts of people born into the lower middle classes to which he had himself belonged, and especially of those who found their way to higher education through Polytechnics, Technical Colleges, and other institutions at which the main way of approach was through natural science. Although in his later years he wrote much about the rich and successful, he was never equally at home among them ; and his accounts of 'high life' always bear traces of his early upbringing with his mother, who was house-keeper at a great house in the south of England. Nor did he ever really understand the working classes or the Trade Union movement. He had a remarkable flair for the short story — and also for the story — short or long — with a scientific marvel as its central theme, as in *The Invisible Man* or *The Food of the Gods*. In his approach to Socialism he was dominated by the conception of a well-ordered Society that would make an end of the wastes and frustrations that he saw besetting the lives of 'little men'. He had a deep sympathy with the 'little man' who found himself mauled and badgered about by a complex society which his education gave him no chance of under-standing ; and this gave him an enthusiasm for popular education which found expression in such works as *The Outline of History* and *The Science of Life*. It also led him to his exaltation of the rôle of a devoted order of leaders, organisers, and educators who would set the world to rights, not by establishing any sort of dictatorship, but by making it a better place for ordinary people, with all their quirks and oddities, which he could so amusingly as well as understandingly de-scribe. The passion for order which runs through his writings contrasts curiously with the disorderliness of his own mind and behaviour. He had very little capacity for co-operating with any group : he was always getting exasperated with his colleagues and going off hopefully on a quite new tack. Never-theless, he was at the height of his powers an exceedingly influential maker of Socialists. His great period ran from 1896, when he created his hero — the 'little man' — in the excellent comedy of *The Wheels of Chance*, written when the fashion for country bicycling was reaching its height — to 1911, when he published *The New Machiavelli*, containing, along with a good deal of dross, his unkind but amusing satire on Sidney and Beatrice Webb. During these years he produced his main series of scientific Socialistic studies, from *Anticipations* (1901), *Mankind in the Making* (1903), and *A Modern Utopia* (1905) to *New Worlds for Old* (1908), which was certainly the most influential piece of Socialist propaganda in Great Britain since

Blatchford's *Merrie England*; and during the same period he wrote his best social novels — *Love and Mr. Lewisham* (1900), *Kipps* (1905), *Tono-Bungay* (1909), and — best of all — *The History of Mr. Polly* (1910). A new period, much less socialistic but still devoted to the idea of a world order, began with *The Outline of History* (1920) and continued with an unceasing stream of stories and educational studies almost to his death. To his later years belong his further 'utopian' story, *The Shape of Things to Come* (1933), and his revealing *Experiment in Autobiography* (1934). His educational ideas are expounded chiefly in *Joan and Peter* (1918), but run through a great deal of his work. One of the best of his shorter writings is his Fabian tract, *This Misery of Boots* (1907), in which he denounced the waste and deprivation involved in competitive capitalist production. It ran through many editions, and was one of his most influential contributions to Socialist propaganda.

Wells's best writings came at a time when large numbers of young people of the middle classes were turning to Socialism as a result of the spread of higher education, particularly through evening classes. He knew exactly how to address this public, and to a certain extent his influence upon it can be compared with Blatchford's on the public of the 1890s. Blatchford, however, though he too influenced many middle-class readers, wrote primarily for the more intelligent workers, whereas Wells's appeal, though it reached many workers, was primarily to the 'black-coats' and to the more educated classes that read his novels as well as his tracts. Wells, moreover, was primarily a writer of books, and not a journalist: he needed space to spread himself, and had no special talent for the short article, though a great one for the short story. Apart from his brief incursion into Fabian politics he played no part in the organised Socialist or Labour movement; he hovered round it, but was too much of an individualist ever to accept service in any organisation.

The duel in the Fabian Society between Wells and Bernard Shaw was a curious affair because it was a clash of personalities much more than of ideas. In it Shaw was not so much up-holding a principle as defending the Webbs against their assailant. Wells's opening attack, in his paper on *The Faults of the Fabian*, was devoted mainly to criticising the Fabian Society for being content to go on in its small way, without advertising itself or trying to attract a large membership. 'Make Socialists and you will achieve Socialism : there is no other plan', he exclaimed ; and the 'Old Gang', far from repudiating his projects, not only set to work to increase membership and establish local Fabian Societies, but also came out in support of the idea of creating 'a middle-class Socialist Party' — presumably quite distinct from the Labour Party, of which the Fabian Society was an affiliated member. No more was heard of this proposal when the entire episode ended with Wells's withdrawal from the Society in 1909.

During these years the Fabian Society, apart from its internal battles, had not been doing very much, largely because its most active spirit, Sidney Webb, had been giving most of his attention to the affairs of the London County Council and to working with Beatrice Webb in preparing the material for the Minority Report of the Poor Law Commission which had been set up in 1905. This famous Report, which appeared in 1909, embodied a comprehensive plan of social security which had been elaborated by the Webbs as a practical essay in 'permeation'. It was signed by Beatrice Webb, by the two Labour representatives on the Commission — George Lansbury and F. W. Chandler, Secretary of the Amalgamated Society of Carpenters and Joiners, and by H. Russell Wakefield, then a Prebendary of St. Paul's and later Bishop of Birmingham. In order to campaign on behalf of its proposals the Webbs set up a special organisation, called at first the 'National Committee to Promote the Break-up of the Poor Laws' and subsequently the 'National Committee for the Prevention of Destitution', in which they enrolled a large body of non-Socialist as well as Socialist supporters, including many active members of local government authorities. Their main proposal was that the Poor Laws, and with them the taint associated with 'pauper' status, should be abolished and the functions of the Boards of Guardians, first set up in 1834, transferred to the municipal and county Councils and merged with the public health and other services already in the hands of these authorities. On this basis the Report proposed that there should be built up a comprehensive range of social services for the care of the sick, the disabled, the aged, the children, and those unable to find work. All these services were to be organised so as to carry for the recipients no disqualification in respect of political or social rights : they were to be regarded as services which the community owed to its members as of right, and were to be controlled democratically by the elected local authorities and financed out of public funds, partly local but partly provided through grants in aid from the central exchequer. In relation to unemployment the Report proposed that maintenance at living wages should be provided for those out of work, subject to the right of the authorities to insist in suitable cases on retraining for alternative work, and that, in order to reduce cyclical unemployment, the Government and other public bodies should plan the execution of public works so as to hold back in good years and expand them when trade was bad.

The Majority Report of the Commission also proposed substantial reforms, but fell a long way short of the ambitious plan of the Minority. The Minority Report of the Poor Law Commission is indeed a landmark : it is the first full working out of the conception and policy of the Welfare State — more comprehensive, because covering a wider ground, than the Beveridge Report of 1942, which in many respects reproduced its ideas. The essential difference between the two is that, in between, Great Britain actually developed an extensive plan of social security based on the principle of compulsory contributory insurance, which the Minority Report rejected in favour of a plan financed entirely out of general taxation. This question of principle was to come almost at once to a head when Lloyd George, imitating Bismarck's German social legislation, introduced the National Insurance Bill of 1911 and carried it through in face of all the efforts of the Minority Report's supporters to prevent its passage.

Immediately, the Webbs' efforts met with considerable success. They published a cheap edition of the Report, which had a very wide sale ; and their National Committee started a journal, *The Crusade*, edited by Clifford Sharp (1883–1935), which served as a forerunner to the *New Statesman*, founded by them, again with Sharp as editor, in 1912. The National Committee also issued a large number of pamphlets and special reports ; and a great part of the activity of the leading Fabians was transferred to it. The President of the Local Government

Board under the Liberals was the old Socialist, John Burns;
and it had been hoped that he would support the Webbs' plan.
In fact, under the influence of his officials, he opposed it
strongly, and a sharp struggle developed between him and the
Webbs. Burns, who was chiefly concerned at the time with
his Housing and Town Planning Act of 1909 — the beginning
of modern town-planning legislation — argued that the desirable parts of the Webb plan could be carried through largely,
and at moderate cost, through improved administration of the
existing law; and he also favoured compulsory insurance as
against the financing of social security services entirely or
mainly out of general taxation. Despite the powerful support
which the Webbs managed to attract to their National Committee, the Liberal Government would have none of their
plan, which was much too Socialistic, as well as too expensive,
for its taste. Instead, it set to work on the preparation of an
alternative project of health insurance, coupled with an experi-
mental scheme of unemployment insurance confined to a few
selected industries; and when these projects had become law
under the National Insurance Act of 1911 it became clear that
the Webb plan had suffered defeat, at any rate for the time.

Lloyd George's plan of National Insurance — often spoken
of at the time as having 'dished the Webbs' — sharply divided
the Labour movement. Under it Trade Unions, as well as
Friendly Societies and capitalist Insurance Companies, could
set up Approved Society Sections to administer the benefits
provided, receiving grants to cover the costs of administration.
Many Trade Unions saw in this a possibility of extending their
influence and membership, and accordingly favoured the
scheme. The Trade Unions in the selected industries were
also entrusted, under a similar arrangement, with the administration of unemployment benefits, and Unions in other trades
were offered subsidies towards their own unemployment funds.
Thus, the main body of Trade Union opinion was brought
round to support the Government's proposals. Most of the
Socialists, on the other hand, roundly denounced them, and
were joined by a number of Liberals, headed by Hilaire Belloc
(1870–1953), who saw in the compulsory deductions from wages,
to be made by employers acting as the Government's agents, a
dangerous step in the direction of the 'Servile State'. Belloc's

book, *The Servile State* (1912) was an elaboration of the arguments he had used against Lloyd George's Bill. It was wrong in principle, he argued, for the State to make the employer its agent in forcing the workers to contribute out of their wages towards the cost of an essentially public service. The effect would be to give the employer a disciplinary right over the worker, and this first step could easily be used as a foundation for a general system of State regimentation of the workers and of compulsion to labour under the employer's control. Among the Socialists, Philip Snowden took the lead in opposing Lloyd George's Bill in Parliament; and the Fabian Society joined in the fray with a pamphlet on *The Insurance Bill and the Workers*, in which it re-argued the case for non-contributory provision. George Lansbury and his East End followers were also active in opposition; and several independent Socialists fought by-elections mainly on the insurance issue. But in face of the large measure of support given to the Bill by the Trade Union leaders the opposition was bound to be ineffective. The National Committee for the Prevention of Destitution lasted on into the war period; but it gradually petered out, and the Webbs transferred their main energies to establishing the *New Statesman* as a journal of informed Socialist opinion and to the setting up of a Fabian Research Department through which they embarked on an ambitious new enquiry into the Control of Industry. The record of these developments, however, belongs more properly to a later chapter; for it is closely bound up with the great industrial unrest which, from 1910 onwards, was facing the British Socialist movement with a new situation in the realms both of everyday practice and of Socialist ideas.

(ii) FABIAN SOCIALISM — THE WEBBS, SHAW, AND WALLAS

In a previous chapter some account has been given of the new policy of gradualist Socialism which was set forth by Sidney Webb, Bernard Shaw, and their collaborators in *Fabian Essays*. The point has now been reached at which it is necessary to attempt a more general appreciation of the work of the Webbs and of Shaw in the realm of Socialist thought. The triple partnership of these very dissimilar persons was, indeed, a remarkable thing. The two Webbs, closely as they worked together for many years, were very different in their approach to the problems of society; and Shaw, faithfully as he fitted in with them, was temperamentally of yet another, still more different, shape of mind. Sidney Webb's first thought, in dealing with any question that he took up, was to find an administratively workable solution; and apart from a very few essentially simple ideas he did not trouble himself much about any underlying philosophy. He was fully convinced that the trend of events in the modern world was towards Socialism, and that this trend would continue: so that he saw no need to put himself in revolutionary opposition to the main course of development. He saw his task rather as that of accelerating a tendency which he regarded as irresistible, but as capable of being speeded up or slowed down and of being guided for better or worse. He had what is sometimes called a 'civil service' mind — that is, a habit of translating every idea into terms of the machinery needed to give it effect; and, save concerning the trend, he was quite unaffected by doubts or spiritual hesitations. This does not mean that he rode rough-shod over other people: on the contrary, he was capable of great patience in dealing with them, when he saw a prospect of using them to serve his ends. He was, however, impatient of dreamers, and uninterested in theories which he could not turn into practical schemes.

Beatrice Webb had in her much more of the philosopher. She began, indeed, more as a sociologist than as a Socialist, and in her earliest writings she was concerned more with criticism of the inadequacies of orthodox Economics and of Spencerian Sociology than with any gospel for easing social ills. She was very insistent that Economics, as an abstract science, gave much too lop-sided a view of social problems and needed to be integrated into a more comprehensive 'Social Science' that would take full account of the non-economic factors in human behaviour. Moreover, whereas Sidney Webb thought instinct-ively in terms of state and municipal action and of public administration, Beatrice Potter, even after she had become Mrs. Webb, instinctively laid much greater stress on non-governmental action and organisation. She showed this in her early study of *The Co-operative Movement in Great Britain* (1891), written before her marriage; and she drew Sidney Webb into their joint studies of Trade Unionism (*The History of Trade Unionism*, 1894, and *Industrial Democracy*, 1897) and into their later work on Co-operation (*The Consumers' Co-operative Movement*, 1921). The massive series of studies of local government history which they produced together were the product of convergent interests; for whereas Sidney Webb regarded democratic local government as the necessary foundation for a Socialist structure of public administration, she tended to think of it rather as a bridge between the public and the private spheres of social action.

In some respects, Beatrice Webb was less amiable than Sidney. Coming out of the top-layer of capitalist business — her father was a railway chairman and a considerable financier, whereas Sidney was of the lower range of the professional intelligentsia — she had a considerable amount of inborn arrogance, and was apt to be disconcertingly rude to those whom she dismissed as stupid. Sidney, on the other hand, had no arrogance at all, and could bear with fools more easily. Beatrice in practice schooled herself to bear with them, subject to occasional lapses; but the strain was often visible.

Shaw, having fallen under Webb's spell, remained miraculously subject to it and accepted Beatrice's partnership scarcely less wholeheartedly. His attitude, however, remained throughout essentially different from theirs. He saw Socialism primarily neither as a problem of social administration nor as one of adapting society to the needs of human beings, but rather as a matter of efficiency and convenience. Webb was interested in administration, but insisted that the administrators must work under the salutary discipline of democratic control. Shaw, fundamentally, did not care a button about democracy : he wanted things to be run by experts, not merely as administrators, but also as makers of policy, and he was apt to admire dictators, if only they would give the experts a free hand. There was, however, in Shaw's Socialism a second strand — an all-or-nothingness that was far removed from the practical experimentalism of both Webbs. This came out in Shaw's insistence that the only allowable principle for the distribution of incomes in a Socialist society was absolute equality, involving a complete divorce of income from any form of remuneration for service rendered, and an entire reliance on non-economic incentives for getting the necessary labour done. Shaw did not propose this as an immediate measure — for he too had taught himself to be a gradualist; but as a matter of Socialist theory, until his conversion to Stalinist inequality, he was entirely uncompromising about it. Immediately, he wished to attack unearned income, which he described comprehensively as 'rent', and, by appropriating this social surplus, to transfer the means of production to public ownership. But he never really formulated any plans for carrying on the work of society during the transitional period, when rent had been socialised but the time had not yet arrived for putting the system of equal incomes, divorced from all connection with productive services, into effect. In practice he supported the Webbs' demand for a national minimum standard of civilised life, as a stage in the transition; but the transition interested him much less than it did the Webbs, and he never considered it in terms of the problem of social education for democracy, which was always in the front of Sidney Webb's mind.

Shaw, indeed, like many Socialists before him, held an exaggerated view of the immediate economic benefits to be derived from the confiscation of 'rent' and from the transference of the means of production to public ownership and control. He believed that the capitalist system was the cause not only of gross under-production but also of colossal waste through the production of the wrong things and through the useless consumption of the rich. It appeared to him that, if 'rent' were socialised and used for the re-equipment of industries and services for the benefit of the common people, there would be no difficulty in the way of producing enough to supply everyone with the means to the good life. Consequently he paid little attention to the problems involved in organising production under the changed conditions. He took it so much for granted that socialisation would put an end to scarcity that the problem of finding new incentives to effort appeared to him quite unimportant.

In *Industrial Democracy* the Webbs performed a most valuable service for the growing Trade Union movement, which had never before been scientifically studied as a problem

of social engineering. But they always studied the Trade
Unions as outsiders, and with more than a little suspicion of
the 'producer' approach. Beatrice in particular always regarded
the problems of industry from the 'consumer' end. She was
extremely critical of Producers' Co-operation as only a form of
more democratic profit-sharing, still under the domination of
the profit-motive. All her enthusiasm was reserved for the
Consumers' Co-operative Societies, as capable of expressing
the needs of the whole body of citizens as consumers, and not
those of a sectional interest. She saw the producers' need of
Trade Unions to protect their interests under capitalism, and
she had the imagination to foresee that this protection would
continue to be needed in a Socialist society; but both she and
Sidney were quite unsympathetic to the idea that under
Socialism the workers should be allowed to run their industries
under producer-chosen management. Industrial democracy
meant for them managerial responsibility to the whole people,
through their elected representatives in Parliament, in local
government, and in the Consumers' Co-operative movement.
Indeed, they thought of the State as primarily a great inclusive
consumers' organisation rather than a political body. In the
question of 'workers' control' they took little interest until it
was forced on them during the years of labour unrest before
1914; and then their first response in a pamphlet entitled
What Syndicalism Means (1913) was highly unfavourable.
They acutely disliked the Bergsonian and Sorelian aspects of
French Syndicalist doctrine, and they were no less hostile to
the entire philosophy of Direct Action. They coined a phrase,
of which they made frequent use in their arguments with the
Industrialists : they said that what was needed was 'a discreetly
regulated freedom' — an expression calculated to infuriate the
Direct Actionists, who flung back at them Hilaire Belloc's
charge that what they were really aiming at was the 'Servile
State'.

The Webbs did not believe that most workers wanted to
share in the management of their industries, or that they could
be trusted to participate in managing them efficiently in the
general interest. They were insistent on the need for the fullest
recognition of the Trade Unions as bargaining agencies; but
they wanted the Trade Unions to act as disciplined bodies and

not as insurgents. They had a great respect for Trade Union officials, and insisted on the need for adequate training for the work, especially in the light of changing industrial techniques which called for a revision of traditional Trade Union practices. Sidney Webb in particular stressed this point in his volumes, *The Works Manager To-day* (1917), and *The Restoration of Trade Union Conditions* (1918).

They also, despite their admiration for the achievements of Consumers' Co-operation, saw the danger of the Co-operative movement falling behind by failing to adapt its democratic machinery to the changes in scale that were the necessary consequence of its success. In *The Consumers' Co-operative Movement* they made many suggestions for bringing the Co-operative Societies' methods of government up to date; but they were never able to get much attention paid to their projects.

The Webbs, during the period before 1914, gained, perhaps rather undeservedly, the reputation of being the principal exponents of the virtues of bureaucratic nationalisation and municipalisation. This was largely because they appeared as leading critics of the doctrines of Syndicalism and workers' control, and also because the Fabian Society, of which they were rightly regarded as the leaders, was during this period actively pressing the case for public ownership. In fact, however, the Webbs did not play a large part in this phase of Fabian activity, which was more closely connected with the incursion of H. G. Wells and with the younger Fabians who were pressing against the 'Old Gang' for a more aggressive Socialist policy. The Webbs up to 1911 were too much occupied with the Poor Law campaign to spare a great deal of attention for anything else. Then they did actively take up the question through the Fabian Research Committee on the Control of Industry, which became the Fabian, and later the Labour, Research Department. Far, however, from approaching the matter with a dogmatic preference for nationalisation of industries under civil service control, they were eager to explore alternative possibilities and, particularly, to leave as large as possible a field for municipal, or regional, and for Co-operative enterprise. Nor had they any prejudice against the device of the Public Corporation, as Webb had shown in the cases of the Metropolitan Water Board and the Port of London Authority, provided only that such Corporations must be made finally answerable to democratic control by elected representatives and must be so organised as to fit in with a general pattern of economic planning under government control. These ideas were developed by Sidney Webb in the volume, *How To Pay for the War*, which he edited for the Fabian Society in 1916.

In stressing the need to develop municipal, as against national, enterprise to the fullest possible extent, the Webbs — and, indeed, the Fabian Society as a whole — were well aware that the existing areas of local government were in many cases unsuitable for the conduct of major services under modern technical conditions. The series of Fabian tracts issued in 1891 as the *Fabian Municipal Programme* had been almost entirely concerned with London affairs. They had included proposals for municipalising gas, tramways, water supply, docks, and markets, as well as for taking over the property of the City Guilds and for amending the rating system, and they had ended with a more general tract outlining *A Labour Policy for Public Authorities* generally. Thereafter the Society produced a steady stream of tracts dealing with various aspects of local government, some concerned with London, but others covering the work of almost every type of local authority. Among the special subjects dealt with were the municipalisation of the drink traffic (1898), of milk supply (1899), of pawnshops (1899), of slaughterhouses (1899), of bakeries (1900), of hospitals (1900), of fire insurance (1901), of the Thames steamboats (1901), and of electricity supply (1905), accompanied by a general tract on *Municipal Trading* (1908), and by Shaw's volume, *The Common-sense of Municipal Trading* (1904). As against this, until 1910, the only tract advocating the nationalisation of a particular service was *State Railways for Ireland* (1899). Then Emil Davies, the most ardent of the Fabian nationalisers, produced *State Purchase of Railways* (1910), Lawson Dodd *A National Medical Service* (1911) — at the time of the Insurance Act — and in 1913 H. H. Schloesser (subsequently Lord Justice Slesser) wrote for the Miners' Federation a tract containing the text of a Bill for nationalising the coal-mines on civil service lines, and C. Ashmore Baker produced a tract on *Public versus*

Private Electricity Supply (1913). This is hardly an output suggestive of an excessive concentration on national as distinct from municipal enterprise.

In 1905–6 the Fabians came forward with a series of tracts, collectively entitled the *New Heptarchy* series, in which they attempted to face the problem posed by the unsuitability of municipal areas for the conduct of major services. In Tract 125, *Municipalisation by Provinces*, they put forward a plan for the constitution of about seven elected regional authorities for this purpose, to be endowed by stages with large administrative functions and to exercise in respect of others a supervisory control over such activities of the smaller local authorities as might need co-ordination over wider areas. It was about this time that Sidney Webb, because of his support of the 1903 Education Act, had been ousted by the Progressives from his chief position of influence on the London County Council and that Beatrice Webb began her work on the Poor Law Commission, with the result that their energies were largely directed from the local government field. They played no major part in the Fabian struggle that centred round H. G. Wells, preferring to leave Shaw to do most of the fighting on behalf of the 'Old Gang'. It was Emil Davies (1875–1950), and not the Webbs, who, up to 1914, mainly pressed the case for nationalisation within the Fabian Society after the Wells episode, particularly in his book, *The Collectivist State in the Making*, subsequently renamed *The State in Business*, which appeared in 1913. Sir Leo Chiozza Money (1870–1944), whose *Riches and Poverty* (1905) was one of the most effective pieces of propaganda during this period, also contributed with his volumes, *The Nation's Wealth* (1914) and *The Triumph of Nationalisation* (1920).

Not until after 1918 did the Webbs set down in any comprehensive way their conception of the structure of the coming Socialist society. This appeared in *A Constitution for the Socialist Commonwealth of Great Britain* (1920), with its proposal that there should be two parallel Parliaments, both democratically chosen by the general body of voters, one dealing with political and the other with social affairs. With this went a curious proposal, closely resembling one put forward by César de Paepe in the 1870s, for a system of local government based on fixed local units which could be combined over different areas for the conduct of different services, so that the appropriate area for each service could be used — a single unit serving as big enough for some, a few units for others, and a large province, made up of many units, for yet others. The same representatives were to sit on all the combined bodies as the direct representatives of their constituents. This plan came under heavy criticism. It was argued that, in practice, no satisfactory way could be found of marking off the separate spheres of the two Parliaments, and that the body to which was assigned the ultimate power in finance — that is, in raising money and in controlling expenditure — would necessarily be all-powerful in relation to the other. Against the local government plan it was argued that bodies of constantly changing composition according to the service they were dealing with would never develop the habit of working together as a team, on which their effectiveness would necessarily depend, and that real power would fall into the hands of the officials who actually managed the services the elected members were supposed to control as representatives of the consuming public. The Webbs made little or no attempt to answer these criticisms : it seemed as if, having published their plan and found it ill-received, they had lost interest in it. Certainly they hardly ever referred to it in later years.

A Constitution for the Socialist Commonwealth of Great Britain was presumably meant as the Webbs' answer to the Guild Socialists and to the various advocates of some form of occupational representation. The notion of occupational representation, or of a separate House of Industry, perhaps replacing the existing Second Chamber, was, of course, by no means new. It came to the front again in Great Britain during the war years, when it was put forward, not by the Guild Socialists, but in answer to them by those who wanted some plan of industrial self-government based on the reconciliation of class-interests. It usually took the form of a demand for an Industrial Parliament representing employers and employed equally, in some cases with 'impartial persons' added to represent the 'public', whereas what the Guild Socialists wanted was a Parliament or Chamber representing the Guilds on the principle of 'one member, one vote'. The Webbs were equally against both these projects, and took their stand on the need to base both the proposed Parliaments on universal 'consumer' voting, which satisfied neither the Guild Socialists nor the class-reconcilers and was objected to by the Parliamentarians as undermining the indivisible sovereignty of Parliament. The Webbs' local government proposal seems to have been a bright idea of Beatrice's, which according to her diary came over her while she was listening to H. G. Wells.

The Webbs were undoubtedly influenced at this time both by Wells's semi-technocratic advocacy of public enterprise and by the Guild Socialist attacks on bureaucratic collectivism. They were aware of the dangers of bureaucratic industrial administration, and wanted to secure the largest practicable amount of consumer control over socialised industries and services. But, though they made some concession, they held firmly to their idea of the State as the proper guardian of the consumers' interests ; and they never worked out any clear plans of administrative control. It is somewhat curious, in view of Webb's long-standing interest in administrative problems, that they never did this. I think they tried, but failed, leaving it to others to devise in detail the form of nationalisation through Public Corporations which was actually adopted by the Conservatives in the 1920s and taken over from them by Herbert Morrison when he proposed his Bill for the socialisation of London Transport in 1930.

I do not propose in the present chapter to deal at all with the later development of the Webbs' thought, which centres round their vast tract, written in the 1930s, about Soviet Communism. The proper place for discussing both that startling marriage of Fabian thought and Leninist construction will be in the fourth volume of this work, where it will also be necessary to consider Shaw's reaction to the advent of the dictators. For the present we are concerned with the Webbs and with Shaw mainly in connection with the development of their ideas up to 1914, though it has been necessary to follow the Webbs into the early 'twenties in order to round off the account of their pre-war attitude. The conclusion must be that up to 1914 the Webbs at any rate were much more municipalisers than nationalisers, and that the Fabian move towards greater emphasis on nationalisation was mainly due, not to their influence, but to that of H. G. Wells, and, after him, of Emil Davies.

Shaw as a Socialist is a great deal harder to place. For many years he was the principal draftsman of Fabian publications, regarding himself as a faithful exponent of the Webbs' essential ideas, but always really advancing a quite distinct position of his own. As we have seen, Shaw's master ideas were, first, the will to confiscate and apply to public uses the income accruing from ownership of land and capital, to which he gave the comprehensive name of 'rent'; secondly, the desire to advance towards complete economic equality; and thirdly, the belief that no group or nation had any right to stand in the way of the full development in the interest of the whole world of any productive resources of which it stood possessed, and that accordingly higher civilisations had a complete right to work their will upon backward peoples and to override national or sectional claims, provided only that by doing so they increased the total wealth of the human race. This third idea led directly to his insistence that the final right to control events rested with those who knew best how to achieve this result. Shaw did not stop short at the wish that the experts should do the actual work of administration: he kept harping on the idea that politics should be a matter for experts, and that the right to take any part in them should depend on the possession of qualifications, and should not be extended to amateurs who would not go to the trouble of making themselves well-informed. Shaw was intolerant of stupidity, and found most people stupid: he had no sympathy at all with the slow or limited man's desire not to be driven along too fast, and not to be made the victim of the unco' clever.

If the Webbs influenced Shaw, so that he constituted himself the popular interpreter of many of their ideas, Shaw also influenced the Webbs, particularly in their attitude to questions of empire and nationality. They were not, for a long time, much interested in such questions, or, indeed, in anything outside Great Britain. The Webbs' brand of Socialism was peculiarly British, and they made little attempt to work out its bearings on the problems of other countries: nor were they ever much interested in the International. But this was not because they were conscious nationalists: emphatically they were not. It was rather because up to 1914 they were so much engrossed in the study of British institutions and of British problems as to have little attention to spare for anything else. Shaw, on the other hand, was always very conscious of being Irish and not British, and of being a sojourner in a strange land. But this, far from turning him into an Irish patriot, made him instinctively non-national in his approach. He had the greatest contempt for the priest-ridden politics of his own country and an intellectualist dislike for the mind of the peasant; and he tended to look upon all backward peoples as inferior Irishmen, who needed to be dragged out of their primitive superstitions and induced to adopt modern ways. The Webbs, when they did begin to attend to international problems, took a good deal of their colour from Shaw, first in relation to the South African War and later in relation to the wider problems of the empire. They, like Shaw, had no sympathy with nationalism as a senti-ment. They never went to the lengths to which he went in maintaining the rights of the advanced to ride rough-shod over the primitive; but on the whole in the conflict over imperialism they were on Shaw's side.

Shaw, as distinct from the Webbs, is not of real importance as a Socialist thinker. There was nothing original, save in the special meaning he gave to the word 'rent', in his desire to wipe out unearned incomes by taxation, and to use the proceeds for the development of public services. Nor was there anything particularly new in his *Case for Equality*, which differed from earlier versions of 'From each according to his capacities : to each according to his needs' mainly in retaining money incomes, and making them equal, instead of going right on to the anarch-istic conception of a society in which everyone would be able to take as much of anything as he wanted without being called upon to pay for it — a utopian vision which his common sense led him to reject as impracticable under any imaginable condi-tions. Nor was there very great originality in his insistence on the claim of those who knew best to call the tune : that was only the doctrine of the Saint-Simonians restated in different language. Shaw was a magnificent expositor and pamphleteer. He could put a case with the greatest clarity of style — when he had a clear case to put — and the Webbs, especially Sidney, were excellent at providing the materials for clear cases. But when, as in his *Intelligent Women's Guide to Socialism and Capitalism* (1928), he set out to state his own case, the effect was by no means clear, because he had no clear vision of his own beyond a limited number of very general ideas and a high capacity for debunking those of others.

Next to the Webbs and Shaw, the chief Fabian thinker was Graham Wallas, who presently dropped out of the Society when he found it becoming too dogmatic for his liking. Wallas, in his later years, became obsessed with a dislike of the egoism of vocational organisations, and came to regard them as the arch-enemies of freedom and progress. This attitude ran through *Our Social Heritage* (1921), which suffers, because of it, from a distinctive negativity characteristic of his later writing. Wallas's real contribution was made earlier, above all in *Human Nature in Politics* (1908), his first theoretical book. It has been often said that in that early work was the promise of a really great book which Wallas spent the rest of his life failing to write. In *The Great Society* (1914) there was some sign that he was settling down to write it; but even there he was wavering and failed to develop his ideas in a really constructive way. In *Human Nature in Politics* he had not simply recognised and acutely described the large irrational element in ordinary political behaviour : others had done that before him, if not so well. He had also, as a rationalist who believed that it was indispensable to strengthen the rational element in political practice, tried to see how this could be done, and to think out ways of making political and social education more effective. His standpoint was that of a Benthamite who held that the supreme purpose of politics was to make men happy, and that everyone had the right, within the general framework of society, to pursue happiness according to his own bent. That should have been a starting point for considering how much of a pattern of behaviour it was necessary for a twentieth-century society to impose on its individual members, how group patterns of behaviour could be given freedom to develop within the general framework, how education could be moulded to increase the element of rationality in the shaping of social action, and how all this could be done democratically, by the people themselves, rather than by subjecting them to the rule of superior persons or to the pressures exercised by vested interests. But

Wallas, instead of carrying out this magnificent research programme, stopped short at recommending that it should be done,
and never took any real step to carry it out. He was, I think,
for a single lecture, the most inspiring lecturer I have ever
heard ; but, when I attended a course by him, I came to the
conclusion that he could not keep it up because, in his first book,
he had exhausted his impulse to go and look at men as they
were, and had thereafter contented himself with chewing over
and over again the inspiration he had brought back from these
admirable, but insufficient, contacts.

Human Nature in Politics and *The Great Society* together
constitute the restatement of Utilitarianism in its Fabian form,
in which it turns from *laissez-faire* to state intervention for the
prevention of suffering and for the positive promotion of happiness by collective means. Neither the Webbs nor Shaw ever
clearly stated this conception, though it underlies a good deal
of their Fabian writing. Wallas had the great merit of being
both a collectivist and a libertarian. His misfortune was that
he lacked the persistence to carry through the immense intellectual enterprise of which he so clearly saw the need.

(iii) THE GREAT UNREST : THE LABOUR PARTY AND ITS LEADERS : SYNDICALISM AND GUILD SOCIALISM

The years between 1910 and 1914 in Great Britain have often
been referred to as the period of 'Labour Unrest'. They were,
indeed, marked by a series of strikes on an unprecedented scale,
by a rapid growth of Trade Union membership, and by a
ferment of new ideas and policies. The Labour Party, dragged
along behind the Liberals in the struggles with the House of
Lords over Lloyd George's budget and with the serried forces
of Toryism over Irish Home Rule, came in for a great deal of
abuse for its supineness in backing working-class claims ; and
the Trade Union leaders were also under constant attack on
account of their refusal to support the aggressive strike policy
of the Industrial Unionists and Syndicalists. There were loud
calls both for the amalgamation of Trade Unions into more
comprehensive bodies in order to bring all the workers in an
industry into one Union and for the linking up of these Unions
into a close federation or even into 'One Big Union'. At the

same time the policy of entering into sectional agreements with employers, expiring at different dates so as to prevent the Unions from taking common action, was roundly denounced, and the doctrine of the 'sympathetic strike' propounded. No worker, it was urged, should handle 'tainted goods' coming from or consigned to establishments involved in trade disputes. The entire working class should organise and act on the principle that 'an injury to one is an injury to all'.

With these demands went a preaching of the gospel of 'Workers' Control', adopted mainly from the French Syndicalists, but also from the Industrial Workers of the World. The Trade Union, it was proclaimed, or rather the Industrial Union that should take its place, should have as its purpose, not the mere protection of its members' interests under the wage-system, but the abolition of 'wagery' or 'wage-slavery' and the taking over of the control of industry from the capitalist class. Nationalisation was dismissed as inadequate, or was opposed altogether, on the ground that it would leave the worker as much as ever a wage-slave, merely substituting the State for the private employer as his master. The new gospel of 'the mines for the miners' was set forth defiantly, in opposition to nationalisation, in a famous pamphlet of 1912, *The Miners' Next Step*, prepared by an Unofficial Reform Committee of the South Wales Miners' Federation, which had been involved in a sequence of bitter conflicts with the colliery companies, and especially with the Cambrian Combine. Various bodies of Industrial Unionists and Syndicalists came forward with rival schemes, some putting their entire faith in revolutionary industrial action and scorning every sort of 'politics' short of revolution, while others, though giving the primacy to direct action, refused to turn their backs altogether on parliamentary methods, but wanted a revolutionary Socialist Party to replace the 'Lib-Lab' Labour Party, and yet others followed De Leon's lead and demanded a revolutionary party which would build up under its own leadership a revolutionary industrial movement. At the same time there appeared the National Guilds movement, with its plan for State-chartered guilds of workers, based on the Trade Unions, to take over the management of industry as the agents of the community under the auspices of a re-formed State set free from capitalist

223

domination. The National Guildsmen were at the outset a group of intellectuals, with A. R. Orage's *New Age* as their organ. Only from about 1912 did they begin to attract working-class followers; and the main growth of Guild Socialism as a widely influential movement came only after 1914.

This ferment of ideas and movements in Trade Union and Socialist circles was part of a wider ferment. It followed on the ebullition of militant suffragism under the leadership of Mrs. Emmeline Pankhurst's Women's Social and Political Union, which after instituting as early as 1903 a mildly militant policy of interrupting political meetings, set out in 1906 on a campaign of harrying Cabinet Ministers and party politicians and destroying property by way of protest against the continued refusal of women's political rights. The Labour ferment went on to the accompaniment of growing unrest in Ireland, and of announcements by Tory politicians and generals that they would be no parties to the subjection of Irish Protestants to Irish Catholics or to the rupture of the Union, and that, if Ulstermen rebelled, they would refuse to put them down and would even fight on their side. It was accompanied, moreover, by growing international tension and recurrent crises threatening war.

Rising prices, without corresponding wage-advances, played their part in causing the industrial unrest. Up to 1906, strike action had been inhibited and Trade Union bargaining power seriously weakened by the Taff Vale Judgment; and after the passing of the Trade Disputes Act of that year had restored the right to strike it took some time for the pent-up discontents to issue in large-scale disputes. Strikes had been increasing since 1906; but they had been held back by industrial recession in 1908-9, and only in 1910 did they take shape in widespread demands for improved conditions. 1911 was the critical year, with great strikes spreading like wildfire among seamen and waterside workers, with a national railway strike, and with the fiercely fought struggle in the South Wales coalfield. The following year came the great national strike of the mineworkers and the defeat of the London transport workers in a second struggle. In 1913 there was no one outstanding dispute in Great Britain; but in Ireland there was the great Dublin strike or lock-out, which symbolised the conflict in the ranks of Labour as well as the class-conflict between Labour and Capital. By 1914 the wave of industrial unrest seemed to be receding even before the outbreak of war ; but there was bitter struggle in the London building industry, and the three groups which had played the leading parts in the battles of 1911 and 1912 were taking steps to join forces in a Triple Alliance of Miners, Railwaymen, and Transport Workers in order to present simultaneous demands, under pledge not to return to work without a common agreement. This Alliance, however, came into operation only after the war, and then collapsed in the disastrous struggle of 1921.

The great unrest came at a time when the Liberal Government, having exhausted its first momentum in the struggle with the House of Lords, was working out a new social policy in the form of National Insurance and, as we saw, was driving a wedge between the Trade Union leaders and the Socialists by offering the Trade Unions the right to take part in the administration of the scheme. Not all Trade Union leaders favoured the Lloyd George plan, and many rank-and-file Trade Unionists besides the organised Socialists were against its contributory basis ; but there was enough support for it to make concentrated Labour opposition impossible, and only guerrilla warfare by the left wing was in fact waged against it. The 'ninepence for fourpence' which Lloyd George offered, mainly out of employers' and workers' weekly contributions, had its attractions ; and only the left wing took to heart Hilaire Belloc's prognostications that compulsory deductions from wages heralded the coming of the 'Servile State'. Nevertheless the Insurance Bill, by alienating the left, was a factor in turning the Trade Unionists towards industrial militancy.

The great strikes of these years were 'official' — that is to say, they were called by the Trade Unions under regular leadership. But they were accompanied by a host of smaller stoppages, a good many of which occurred suddenly and without official Trade Union authorisation in advance. In the big strikes, except in Dublin in 1913–14, the Unions were fighting for well-established objects — recognition of bargaining rights, higher wages, and improved conditions of work. Many of the smaller disputes turned on the same issues — for there were still a great many employers who refused to recognise Trade

Unions, and bargaining was still in most industries local and in many cases a matter of dealing with individual firms. But there were also many disputes which turned on less familiar issues — strikes against unpopular foremen or managers, or against acts of tyranny or victimisation of 'agitators', strikes called in sympathy by workers not directly involved; and strikes against the employment of non-unionists. There was even a strike, strongly denounced by most of the press as the 'Right to Get Drunk Strike', which arose out of the dismissal of an engine-driver for being drunk *off duty*. Commentators noticed the existence of a new spirit among the workers, of an assertion of personal and collective rights and claims to social equality which outraged the upholders of the established order. Employers complained that the workers were meddling with questions of discipline and management that were quite beyond their legitimate scope; and while some called for strong measures to put the upstarts down, others, encouraged by the Liberal Government, went in quest of devices for promoting 'industrial peace'.

We are here concerned with this unrest only as it affected Socialism and the Socialist movement. There had been, as we saw, a considerable spread of Socialist ideas during the earlier years of the Liberal Government's activity; and both the I.L.P. and the Fabian Society had profited by it. The Social Democratic Federation, reinforced by other left-wing groups, had blossomed out into the British Socialist Party; and the very small but energetic Socialist Labour Party was beginning to spread from Clydeside into a few English towns, especially in the North. The Labour Party, though still uncommitted to Socialism, was taking part in the work of the Socialist International, and was regarded by the public as at least a socialistic organisation. But there was nothing in Great Britain at all resembling the mass Socialist Parties of Germany and Austria or even France. All the Socialist bodies were small; and the Labour Party, though large in terms of affiliated membership, had still hardly any organisation of its own and carried on hardly any propaganda. In any area, the main tasks of Labour and Socialist propaganda fell on the local branches of the Socialist Societies — and mainly on those of the I.L.P., which was by far the strongest of them. Within the I.L.P., hardly less after the breakaway to the B.S.P. than before, there was much discontent with the conduct of the Labour Party in Parliament, and the new ideas that were abroad had an increasing influence. But the I.L.P. had been the real creator of the Labour Party and was bound to it by tight bonds; and the I.L.P. leaders who were also largely its leaders had a great prestige, which held most of their followers back from doing more than grumble.

The principal leaders of the Labour Party in the Parliaments between 1906 and 1914 and in the country were Keir Hardie, Ramsay MacDonald, Philip Snowden, and Arthur Henderson — all save the last leaders in the I.L.P. as well. In the second rank were F. W. Jowett of Bradford, and John Robert Clynes (1869–1949) of Manchester — also I.L.P. leaders — Will Crooks of Woolwich, and George Nicol Barnes (1859–1942) of the Engineers, also connected with the I.L.P. George Lansbury did not rank as a party leader; he became, after he had resigned his seat in Parliament in order to fight it as the women's champion and had lost, the point of focus for a rebel group connected with the *Daily Herald* — then by no means an official organ, but an irreverent and rebellious left-wing sheet. Among the women, the outstanding figure was Mary R. Macarthur (1880–1921) — in private life Mrs. W. C. Anderson — the energetic Secretary of the National Federation of Women Workers and, with her husband, active also in the I.L.P. Of the Trade Unionists who were mainly Trade Unionists rather than politicians John Hodge (1855–1937) of the Steel Smelters, Robert Smillie (1857–1940) of the Miners, Ben Tillett (1860–1943) of the Dockers, and the relative newcomer J. H. Thomas (1874–1949) of the Railwaymen were the most prominent — a mixed bunch, with Smillie and Tillett on the left and Hodge and Thomas on the right wing.

Of all these leaders, Keir Hardie (1856–1915) had much the greatest prestige. He had fought to make first the I.L.P. and then the Labour Alliance, and his devotion and singleness of purpose were beyond question. He had been the Labour Party's natural choice for the leadership in 1906; but he soon found himself thoroughly unhappy in the job. Parliamentary manœuvres and accommodations went against the grain with him: he was of a fighting disposition and was happiest when he was fighting the battles of the bottom dogs. Though he had been largely responsible for the compromise on which the Labour Party had been based, he had never really liked it. He deeply distrusted not only Liberals, but also old-style Lib-Labs who had been persuaded to call themselves 'Labour', and new-style politicians, who enjoyed the party game. Yet he had a high sense of loyalty to the Party he had made, and to his colleagues in it. He was a great deal happier when, in 1907, he was allowed to resign the leadership, which then passed in turn to D. J. Shackleton (1907), Arthur Henderson (1908–9) and G. N. Barnes (1910). In 1911 it was taken over by Ramsay MacDonald, who was re-elected annually till 1914, when Henderson replaced him because of his attitude to the war.

Hardie was essentially a preacher and propagandist, not a parliamentary leader. His simple eloquence suited the plat-form, but was out of place in Parliament except when he was free to give his indignation vent. He had a deep hatred of cruelty and oppression and a mind that saw all social issues in ethical terms. His Socialism, like Blatchford's, was a gospel of fellowship and justice, of sympathy with the wrongs and sufferings of common people, and of a simple faith that most men and women were good and decent at bottom and would be able to live happily ever after in a society in which they were not allowed to oppress or be oppressed. He differed from Blatchford, as we saw, in being also a Puritan, with a deep scorn for flamboyancy and Bohemianism, and with a 'chapel' mind — religious despite its discarding of theological dogma, and very ready to see bad behaviour as 'sin'. Hardie accepted the class-struggle as a fact; and he would probably have acquiesced in the regarding of it as an historical necessity. But, though he imbibed a number of Marxist ideas about Capitalism and historical development, his mind could never have taken a Marxist shape. He did not revel in the struggle; nor did he see it in terms of a scientific process, from which ethical considerations should be excluded. He wanted Social-ism because he believed it would promote human well-being, which was not to be had in a society in which the means of production were privately owned and used — or left unused, or misused — to serve the interests of profit-making. In the meantime, he wanted to do all that could be done to improve the position of those who were worst off — above all of the unemployed and their dependents. The right to work was the demand that roused him to the greatest vehemence, with the minimum wage and the eight hours' day — which he thought of as the right to leisure — not far behind. Colliery accidents enraged him ; and he was very ready to attribute them to the profit-makers' refusal to spend money on ensuring safe conditions of work.

Besides all this, Hardie was a devout internationalist, but one whose great passion was to prevent war rather than to stir up international revolt. His internationalism was not, like that of Rosa Luxemburg, primarily an appeal to world-wide working-class solidarity, disregarding national frontiers. It had that element in it, but less with a view to the world-wide revolution than to the prevention of war. War was, in his eyes, a sort of gigantic colliery disaster, no less the outcome of the greed of imperialist exploiters who sought their profit in it at the expense of human life. He was strongly anti-imperialist : his book on *India* (1909) is mainly an exposure of the destruction of Indian crafts by capitalist competition and of the harm done to the peasant by the tax-gatherer and the money-lender. He had an instinctive feeling for the wrongs of subject peoples, and a scorn for those who were prepared to uphold empire as a means of profiting by cheap colonial labour.

In the niceties of Socialist theory he was not much interested, nor did he ever attempt to make any clear picture of the Socialist society of the future. From the controversies that were rending the Socialist movement during his last years — except where they touched the great issue of war and peace — he stood largely aloof, continuing to preach the same gospel as he had preached in the 'nineties, save when he was inhibited from doing so by loyalty to his party — and preferring on such occasions to say nothing. In relation to the war danger, however, he had to speak out ; and his sense of the sheer betrayal that would be involved in doing nothing to prevent war made him an ardent advocate of the general strike against it. When war came in 1914 he was quite literally heart-broken, both at the disaster itself and at the collapse of the International in face of it. By then he was already a sick man, and could do but little : I think the sheer fact of war hastened his end.

The women's question troubled him deeply. He sympathised with the suffragists' fury at having their claims put off by a House of Commons the majority of whose members were pledged to support them. He felt about the women's case much as George Lansbury did ; but he could not bring himself to act like Lansbury because he felt tied down by loyalty to his I.L.P. and Labour colleagues. The women's case, in his eyes, was one of simple justice ; and it hurt him deeply when the militants accused him of betraying it.

Ramsay MacDonald (1866–1937), who led the Labour Party during the critical years before 1914, was in almost every respect a sharp contrast to Hardie. Though they were both illegitimate children of middle-class fathers and working women, they appeared as adults to belong to quite different social classes. Hardie remained essentially a working man, though he was earning his living as a journalist long before he became a national figure. MacDonald was quintessentially middle-class, in body and bearing as well as in mind. With his magnificent voice and his fine presence, he was in seeming every inch a leader, so that his vacillations and uncertainties often went unnoticed. He spoke so impressively, and looked so impressive, that the frequent woolliness of his utterances was often mistaken for profundity. He was, of course, by bent of mind an intellectual, but his intellect was not of the first grade. His book about the fundamentals of Socialism, as he understood them — *Socialism and Society* — is a thoroughly second-rate performance, dominated entirely by the organic analogy and indeed containing little else. It is a typical product of the period, full of echoes of Herbert Spencer and of popular scientific phraseology, all used to present the picture of society as an organism made up of functional parts contributing in their several ways to its common life. The trend of social action is represented as making irresistibly towards this organic unity — and there the thought stops, at an evolutionary theory of the crudest kind, and almost without any notion of hostile forces to be overcome in the process. The conception of Socialism is no doubt ethical, though it is cast into a quasi-scientific form. But it is altogether lacking in the passion for social justice and in the hatred for oppression that gave vitality to Keir Hardie's ethics.

MacDonald's later work on *Socialism and Government* is a much better book, because in it he was writing largely about the process of government rather than about fundamental ideas. He was undoubtedly a skilled parliamentarian and had, within the assumptions of his creed, an eye to discern what would work and what would not. He was at his most congenial tasks when he was attacking proportional representation or upholding the parliamentary method against critics, such as F. W. Jowett, who wanted to remodel it on the pattern of local government administration. But even at his best, from the standpoint of the quality of his thought, he was never good, because there was no sharpness or precision about his thinking. He preferred the ambiguous to the decisive commitment. Even his attitude to the war of 1914 was unclear. He attacked the diplomacy that had led up to it; but he shilly-shallied about what was to be done in face of the actual outbreak. Later, this quality of preference for vagueness and reluctance to reach a decision grew on him more and more. It was shown at its worst when he was Prime Minister from 1929 to 1931 in the second Labour Government.

MacDonald was a vain man and, because of his vanity, a bad colleague. When things went awry, he always found the fault in others; when they went well, he took the credit to himself. He loved admiration dearly, but found it difficult to appreciate the good qualities of those with whom he worked. These defects did not appear plainly, save to a few, until the qualities in which he excelled had raised him to the top of the tree. Then they came out very plainly, especially in his relations with Arthur Henderson. MacDonald had the further defect of being an incorrigible snob and a worshipper at the shrine of that aristocracy to which he somehow felt himself by rights to belong.

Arthur Henderson (1863–1935) was very different from both Hardie and MacDonald. He had no vanity; but equally he lacked Hardie's passion. He was a devoted, honest social reformer with great skill in organisation and great determination in pursuing his rather limited ends. Of working-class background and an important figure in his Trade Union — the Ironfounders — he was a very representative member of his class. A lifelong Nonconformist who never lost his religious faith, he

moved from Liberalism to Labour not because he was converted
to Socialism but because he became convinced that Labour
needed an independent party to press its claims. He was
never much of a Socialist, though with Sidney Webb he
devised the 'new model' Labour Party which from 1918 made
evolutionary Socialism its profession of faith. He saw the
future in terms, not of a Socialist Utopia or of a revolutionary
change in the basis of society, but rather of the gradual development of a Welfare State which would involve a great increase
in State intervention and control. He was deeply interested in
protective industrial legislation and in the extension of social
security : these concrete reforms interested him much more
than any visionary picture of the shape of things to come. In
later years he was to show his genuine internationalism ; but
this was never specifically Socialist. It was for him always
mainly a matter of disarmament treaties, of the acceptance of
international arbitration, and of appeals to reasonable men
rather than of any attempt to mobilise the workers of the world
against war. In Trade Union affairs he was a patient and
persistent advocate of industrial peace.

Henderson's great quality as a leader was his loyalty to the
Party and his preparedness to put self aside in working for it.
Unlike MacDonald, he was prepared to take his share of the
blame when mistakes were made, and to give others their full
share of the credit for success. What made him lose his temper
was most of all anything he felt to be disloyalty. Having
discarded his Liberal past, he gave himself entirely to serving
the new party of his adoption.

By temperament, Henderson fitted much the best of these
three into the environment in which he actually lived. He
wanted to lift up the bottom dogs and to give the main body of
the workers better living conditions and more security ; but he
did not even want radically to change their manner of life.
He had no social ambitions. He enjoyed the community of
the Dissenting congregation — and also the football crowd of
a Saturday afternoon. He did not want to be rich, or socially
distinguished, or anything very different from what he was ; and
what he wanted for himself was not, in his view, too good for
others or beyond their reach if social legislation were brought
to their aid. As a speaker he had no eloquence, but a good

capacity for stating a plain case and an effective way of trampling on foolish or unwary opponents. Personal magnetism he entirely lacked and, I think, distrusted. He got on excellently with Sidney Webb, who in these respects resembled him. With all his limitations, the Labour Party owed him an enormous debt, of which he would have been the last man to claim payment.

Philip Snowden (1864–1937) was different from all these three. He was a man of immensely strong will-power, fighting all the time against serious physical disablement, and embittered by the struggle. He was exceedingly dogmatic and sure of his own rightness, and all too ready to look on other men as fools. He enjoyed contention, and was unmerciful to weaker adversaries in debate; but his bitterness was relieved by an often sardonic humour, and this made him not an easy man to hate. His Socialism was of a somewhat narrow, doctrinaire kind. He had a firm belief in the virtues of nationalisation, and no perception of the human problems involved in it. In economic doctrine he remained an old-style Radical, with no use for unorthodox or new-fangled notions. He believed in Free Trade and in the gold standard with nineteenth-century fervour, and disbelieved strongly in the power of Trade Unions to achieve real gains by industrial action. Even during the years of the great labour unrest he continued to tell the workers that only legislation would do them any good. This made him seem a more determined Socialist than many of his colleagues; and, if Socialism is to be identified with Collectivism, he was. Moreover, until his last years he was more aggressively anti-capitalist than most of them, both because he abhorred fine shades and because he sincerely believed in the collectivist State. Beyond this belief he made no contribution to Socialist theory. But he was impressive in argument because he had a quick mind and his ideas were well arranged. He never gave away a point, or admitted himself beaten; and he often wore down opposition by sheer obstinacy. He and MacDonald worked long and closely together, but neither ever really liked the other. Snowden saw through MacDonald's shallowness and indecision: MacDonald often found Snowden's plain-speaking highly inconvenient. But the fates made them partners for life; and they could not afford to quarrel openly.

Fred Jowett (1864–1944) never took rank with this group of leaders ; but he cannot be ignored because he had a distinctive point of view which, though it never prevailed, had for a time a real influence on Socialist thinking. Hardie, MacDonald, Henderson, and Snowden were all essentially national figures ; but it is impossible to think of Jowett except as a man from Bradford. His deepest interests were local, in the affairs of his town and its people ; and when he considered the world he saw it as a series of Bradfords inhabited by human beings with similar capacities for happiness and unhappiness. For Bradford, he wanted better education, better-fed children, better houses, better conditions at work, and better provision for the use of leisure ; and what he sought for Bradford folks he sought for others as well. His ideal of government was a well-regulated city, dispensing welfare with an even hand. So, when he looked at Parliament, his first thought was to recreate it in the image of what he had helped to make of the Bradford City Council. Instead of time-wasting oratory in the Chamber, he wanted committee work : instead of a party system that reduced the back-bench member to little more than a voting machine, he wanted to divide up the House of Commons into a number of functional committees, each presided over by a Cabinet Minister, for business-like discussion of practical problems. When it was objected that such a system would undermine Cabinet responsibility and make each Minister the servant of his committee, he remained unmoved — for why not ? That was how local government worked, and, in Bradford at least, worked well. Of course, he wanted his reformed Parliament to be made up as far as possible of Socialists, and did not want to abolish parties. He was a strong Socialist, of the I.L.P. persuasion, and belonged in the I.L.P. to the left wing. But parliamentary procedures repelled him — most of all in their glamorous aspects which MacDonald loved. He was a humdrum Yorkshireman, with no nonsense about him, but a great deal of humility and good-will. To national leadership he did not aspire : he liked best to work in a team, and had no wish to be its master.

Will Crooks (1852–1921) was an East Londoner, much experienced in the local government of that area, and an orator with a strong emotional appeal. He had espoused the cause of the 'bottom dogs' and had worked closely with George Lansbury in attempts to humanise the working of the Poor Law and to secure better treatment of the unemployed. He represented the ethical appeal of Socialism in its most purely humanitarian form, and was at his best in arousing the sympathies of middle-class audiences. A cooper by trade and an active Trade Unionist, he associated himself politically with the Fabian Society and with its policy of working with the Progressives in London affairs. In 1906 he and Lansbury came under heavy official fire on account of their activities on the Poplar Board of Guardians. They were accused not only of improperly generous spending of the ratepayers' money, but even of lax administration and positive corruption. An official enquiry set up by the Local Government Board was manipulated to provide the press with a great deal of sensational material; and wild charges were flung at Crooks and Lansbury, though there was not even a Labour majority on the Board. In the event, their attempts to provide decent relief and retraining for alternative work for the unemployed were censured, but their financial integrity was completely upheld. The sensation died down; but the accusations that had been made in the press were never withdrawn. The entire episode helped to embitter relations between John Burns, the President of the Local Government Board, and the Socialists.

George Lansbury (1859–1940) himself cannot be included among the number of those who ranked as leaders of the Labour Party during these years. He was a great figure in East London, where he lived, and a greater fighter for advanced causes; but, though he belonged to the Labour Party, he was always a rebel against its compromising policies. From December 1910 he sat for nearly two years in the House of Commons as member for his beloved Bow and Bromley, in East London; but he was always at loggerheads with the party leadership, and in 1912 his keen sympathy with the suffragists led him to resign his seat in order to fight it — without party support — on the suffrage issue. He lost; and the following year he took over the editorship of the *Daily Herald*, which had begun in 1911 as a printers' strike sheet and had lived a precarious existence as an organ of left-wing opinion. It was the only Labour or Socialist daily newspaper until the Labour Party and the

Trade Unions brought out the *Daily Citizen* in direct opposition to it in 1913 ; and it became the home of every sort of left-wing cause, from militant suffrage to Syndicalism and Guild Socialism. It attacked not only the House of Lords, but also the monarchy — it had a habit of referring to the King as 'His Maj.', and thoroughly enjoyed cheeking the respectable of every sort. Its main importance lay in the steady encouragement it gave to industrial militancy and to movements for the reorganisation of Trade Unionism on a class-war basis. Ben Tillett, the Dockers' leader, played a large part in it. Its Australian cartoonist, Will Dyson (1883–1938), enjoyed himself most when he was attacking the orthodox Labour leaders or drawing pictures of the capitalist as the 'Fat Man'. Dyson also produced excellent cartoons against militarism and war : the *Daily Herald*, especially after Lansbury took it over, was vehemently pacifist. It gathered round it an impressive group of writers — the poet Gerald Gould (1885–1936), the lampoonist, C. Langdon Everard (b. 1888), the industrial correspondent, William Mellor (1888–1942), with whom I was then collaborating, G. K. Chesterton (1874–1936), who broke with the Liberal *Daily News* to join it, and a number more. It was often doubtful from day to day whether the next issue would ever appear ; for the paper had no solid financial basis, and was often saved only by a last-moment donation or by its compositors refusing to abandon it even when there was no money to pay their wages. Lansbury, in his history of it, called it *The Miracle of Fleet Street*, and so it was — a most annoying miracle not only to Labour's opponents but also to most of the leaders of the Labour Party and of the Trade Unions.

Lansbury himself was not a workman, though he had worked for wages, but a small timber-merchant. He was a Christian, though not of any orthodoxy, and saw Socialism as applied Christianity — the modern policy that expressed the spirit of the Sermon on the Mount. His social Christianity, which he shared with Will Crooks, made him a thorough-going pacifist as well as a Socialist. He abhorred war and violence, except that peaceful violence which was practised as a protest against oppression. He supported the militancy of suffragists and strikers on this ground, without modifying in any way his complete opposition to war. His Christian approach set him apart from many of those who were associated with him in the *Daily Herald* and in other left-wing movements, but did not prevent him from continuing to work with them. He had a great deal of friendliness and good-will, a great charitableness and belief in fundamental human decency, and an infinite persistence in doing what he believed to be right. During the war years after 1914, his *Herald*, reduced perforce to a weekly, was to be the main rallying-point for anti-war Socialists and internationalists of many schools of thought and was to give a friendly reception to Trade Union militants and unpopular causes in general. In 1917 it was to take firmly the side of the Russian Revolution, not only in its first but also in its Bolshevik phase, but at the same time to reject Communism as a doctrine. Lansbury had a great power of evoking devotion among those who worked with him. He was so clearly unself-seeking, so simply the friend of the oppressed, and so little in love with power that even when he exasperated his leftist friends by his pacifism, they were often ready to take from him what they would have scornfully rejected from anyone else.

Another outstanding figure on the extreme left was Tom Mann (1856–1941), who returned in 1910 from some years' absence mainly in Australia to take the lead in forming the Transport Workers' Federation. Mann, while in Australia, had played an active part in the left-wing Socialist and Trade Union movement; and he came back to England full of Industrial Unionist and Syndicalist ideas and eager to put himself at the head of the Trade Union militants in Great Britain. The transport workers, apart from the railwaymen, were ill-organised: the seamen had their national Union, but were unrecognised by most of the shipowners, who made extensive use of blackleg labour at the ports. The dockers, carters, and other port workers were divided among a large number of Unions, mostly local or regional. Casual labour was the rule; and working conditions and wages were very bad. Tom Mann joined forces with Ben Tillett, Harry Gosling (1861–1930) of the Lightermen's Union, James Sexton (1856–1938) the Liverpool Dock Labourers' leader, and others to form the Federation, which was meant to be a combined bargaining unit, superseding the separate Unions as the main instrument for winning both full recognition by the employers and improved conditions, including the decasualisation of labour.

Mann was a very effective mob-orator, and loved a fight. The new Federation was soon in action. The first to take the field in 1911 were the seamen, led by Joseph Havelock Wilson. The seamen's strike, spreading rapidly from port to port, took the shipowners by surprise; and the Union won a remarkable victory. From the seamen the stoppage spread to the port workers, who were also highly successful in winning concessions, though not without serious disturbances and clashes with the police in Liverpool, where Mann and Sexton were at the head of the movement. Then came the extension to the railwaymen, whose Trade Unions were still refused recognition by the railway companies, on the ground that railway work required a quasi-military discipline. The railway Trade Unions had already come near to a strike in 1907, when they had conducted an 'All-Grades Movement' for recognition and the establishment of effective bargaining machinery. They had been put off, after Government intervention, with a most unsatisfactory Conciliation Scheme under which the employees were allowed to elect representatives to sit on a number of sectional committees for particular grades, but the Trade Unions were still unrecognised and Trade Union officers were not eligible to sit on the committees or to put the men's case. By 1911 the dissatisfaction created by this scheme had risen to the height of promoting a national stoppage, which was hastily settled by Lloyd George by means of an amended Conciliation Scheme allowing Trade Union officials to become secretaries of the men's committees and to put their case, but still withholding recognition and maintaining the system of electing the committees quite apart from the Unions. One outcome of the railway strike of 1911 was that three of the railway Trade Unions amalgamated at the beginning of 1913 to form a National Union of Railwaymen open to all railway workers, and acclaimed as a great victory for Industrial Unionism. In practice, however, the refusal of the powerful Unions of Locomotive Engineers and of Railway Clerks to join the N.U.R. and the hot disputes with the craft Unions which organised the railway 'shopmen' prevented an effective 'all-grades' Union from being set up; and the N.U.R., under the cautious leadership of J. H. Thomas (1874–1949), by no means fulfilled the hopes of the left wing, though it did become a party to the decision, in 1913, to set up a Triple Alliance of Miners, Railwaymen, and Transport Workers on the basis already described.[1]

Tom Mann, not content with his point of vantage among the transport workers, had set out on a national campaign to bring the working-class movement over to militant industrial Syndicalism. In a series of pamphlets under the collective title of *The Industrial Syndicalist*, and in a journal, *The Syndicalist*, he preached assiduously the priority of industrial over parliamentary action and called on the workers to build up Industrial Unionism as a revolutionary force. He would never go quite to the length of repudiating parliamentary action altogether, as some of the Syndicalists and Industrial Unionists demanded; but he was altogether hostile to the compromising politics of the Labour Party and was soon in violent antagonism to most of the Trade Union, as well as to the political leaders. Soon 'rank and file' conferences of delegates from Trade Union branches were being held up and down the country under various auspices, from Mann's Industrial Syndicalist Education League to the two rival British bodies based respectively on the Chicago and the Detroit factions of the I.W.W. Rank-and-file Amalgamation Movements and Reform Movements were established in a number of industries, especially coal-mining and engineering; and many of the local Trades Councils became active on the side of the Syndicalists. The Syndicalist doctrine, as it appeared in Great Britain, was a mixture of French and American influences. Those who were under American influence usually stressed the idea of One Big Union, or of linked great Unions for the various industries, on a class-war basis and with the emphasis on centralised fighting discipline and on the day-to-day struggle; whereas those who were influenced chiefly by the French tended to insist on the need for spontaneity and local freedom and to give a larger attention to the need for 'workers' control' in the factories and work-places and to the vision of a future society in which free communes of producers would take over the control of industry from the capitalist class. These two groups sometimes fell out; but

[1] See p. 225.

Tom Mann, who was little concerned with niceties, made himself the popular apostle of both.

The policy laid down in *The Miners' Next Step* had a wide influence on the extreme left.[1] Its authors opposed the official policy of the Miners' Federation, which demanded the nationalisation of the mines, on the ground that the State would be a no less tyrannical master than the private coal-owner, and even more powerful. They called, instead, for a militant industrial policy designed, by ever-increasing exactions of higher wages and improved conditions, to make the mines unprofitable to the owners. When that had been achieved, the miners themselves would take over the industry and reorganise it under workers' control to serve the interests of the whole working class. Meanwhile, other bodies of workers were to follow a similar policy, and their combined action was to render the capitalist system unworkable and thus clear the road for the social revolution. *The Miners' Next Step* got a great deal of shocked attention in the anti-Socialist press, and was taken as representing a much bigger body of opinion than was ever really behind it ; but it did present, in an extreme form, a body of industrialist doctrine strong enough to rally behind it substantial minority groups in many of the Trade Unions, though not to come near capturing any of them for its full programme.

At this point came the great struggle in Dublin, led by James Larkin (1876–1947) and James Connolly (1870–1916), of the Irish Transport and General Workers' Union. Connolly, who was presently to take part in the Irish Easter Week Rebellion of 1916 and to be shot by a British firing squad after its defeat, had come first to the front in British affairs in connection with the formation of the Socialist Labour Party in Scotland. Like Larkin, he had worked in the United States, and had close connections with the left-wing Irish Republican movement. He had returned from America to join forces with Larkin in building up a fighting Union which gained a following in Belfast as well as in Southern Ireland. It spread from the transport workers to many other trades and made much use of the sympathetic strike by boycotting employers with whom it was in dispute. Larkin tried to apply as a weapon of militant Industrial Unionism the concept that no worker should handle

[1] See p. 223.

'tainted goods' by delivering supplies to or touching goods produced by firms against which the Union was pressing its demands. At that time many of the Irish workers belonged to Trade Unions which had their headquarters in England ; and these Unions took strong objection to having their members called on by the I.T. & G.W.U. to strike without their authorisation. Presently the Dublin employers, headed by William Martin Murphy, decided to hit back, and many firms announced that they would not only refuse to bargain with the I.T. & G.W.U., but would actually dismiss all workers who remained members of it. Thus began the famous Dublin lock-out of 1913, claimed by the left wing as a struggle against capitalist tyranny for the right to combine, but strongly objected to by many Trade Union leaders as the necessary consequence of Larkin's and Connolly's intransigent policy.

The British Trade Union leaders found themselves, however, in a serious dilemma. The Irish appealed to the British workers for help, and Larkin toured Great Britain making impassioned speeches against them as well as against the 'capitalist tyrants'. He was a very moving and effective orator, with a strong strain of mysticism in his revolutionary outlook, and he carried a very large body of British working-class support. The Trades Union Congress found itself compelled to send a food ship to Dublin to relieve the starving workers. A big campaign was set on foot for finding Irish children homes with British workers till the dispute was over ; and the left-wing groups set busily to work to collect funds for the support of the locked-out Irishmen. The *Daily Herald* played a large part in organising these campaigns ; but they did not avail to prevent the defeat of the Dubliners. The movement to receive Irish children in Great Britain aroused the vehement opposition of the Catholic Church : the British Trade Union leaders tried to mediate, but were snubbed by the Dublin employers. Gradually, in the early months of 1914, the affair petered out, to the accompaniment of many recriminations. Larkin, supported by the *Daily Herald*, had tried to bring about a sympathetic refusal by British Trade Unionists to handle Dublin goods ; but the attempt failed, and only worsened relations with the Trade Union leaders.

The two men who led the Dublin strike were both very

remarkable figures. James Larkin was a passionate giant, who combined a strongly revolutionary temper with a deeply felt nationalism that made him hate the British usurpers. He was an agitator and not a theorist : what theory he had he had taken from the traditions of Irish rebellion and from the I.W.W. Connolly, on the other hand, was a theorist as well as a fighter. He, too, was intensely Irish, and kept throughout his membership of the Catholic Church, despite his hatred of its hierarchy, because Catholicism seemed to him an inescapable part of the national tradition of revolt. He was, indeed, more anti-Protestant than positively Catholic in any theological sense. He had a deep sense of the wrongs of the Irish peasants, as well as of the urban workers ; and he wrote powerfully about the history of these wrongs in his book, *Labour in Irish History*. He was also a writer of stirring revolutionary songs — his *Rebel Song* is the best-known — and a journalist of parts. The son of a labourer, he worked at many unskilled jobs in order to keep alive and devote all the time he could to agitation. For some time he composed and printed off on a hand press, as well as wrote, his Irish Republican journal. He wrote, as he spoke, simply and directly : every speech and every article was, directly or by implication, an incitement to revolt. His, to a great extent, was the organising capacity behind the I.T. and G.W.U., though Larkin was the leader most in the public eye.

These two had, of course, only peripheral connections with British Socialism ; but they linked the extreme left in Great Britain to the extreme left in Ireland, at a time when civil war was threatened in connection with the Home Rule struggle. Connolly, as he watched the international situation and saw world war approaching, made no bones about his conviction that 'England's difficulty would be Ireland's opportunity'. In 1916 he hardly expected the Easter Week Rising to succeed ; but he believed that it was better to try and to fail than to hold back. The idea of conscripting Irishmen to fight England's battles roused him to passionate resentment. That at any rate should be resisted to the death. Connolly was an implacable rebel, with a strange blending of nationalism and proletarianism in his mental constitution.

While these various broths of revolutionism were brewing, Guild Socialism was developing side by side with them, and in part association with them, as an intellectual doctrine. The Guild movement, as we saw, began with a book by the Christian Socialist architect, Arthur Joseph Penty (1875–1937), called *The Restoration of the Gild System*. Penty, a mediaevalist and a good hater of modern industrialism, called for a return to handicraft and to a system of small-scale production under the supervision of regulative Trade Gilds. Following William Morris, he denied that the mass-production of 'cheap and nasty' products really benefited the consumers and argued that the production of such goods condemned the workers to lives of irksome labour, in which they could find neither pride nor pleasure. A little later, Penty answered H. G. Wells's *New Worlds for Old* in a counterblast entitled *Old Worlds for New* (1917), and he presently followed up his plans for the revival of craftsmanship with demands for the development of intensive agriculture. Great Britain, he believed, could easily grow, by intensive methods, all the food its people needed, and could at the same time, by producing durable works of craftsmanship, meet the consumers' other needs if only they would break away from the capitalist system, with its continual creation of fresh wants that could be satisfied only by an ever-increasing output of shoddy commodities.

Then the *New Age*, under the editorship of Alfred Richard Orage (1873–1934), took up Penty's ideas and turned them into something utterly different. The responsibility for the change lay mainly with Samuel George Hobson (1864–1940), a technical journalist and merchant who had been long associated with the Socialist movement and had been crusading in the Fabian Society for the establishment of an independent Socialist Party. Hobson, far from sharing Penty's mediaevalism, was favourable to, and well versed in, modern productive techniques. He had lived in the United States, and done much journalism there; and what he wanted was that the workers should make themselves the masters of the means of production and use them to abolish poverty by putting them to the most up-to-date technical use. Hobson conceived the idea of Guilds, not as regulative associations of independent craftsmen, but as vast democratically controlled agencies for the running of industry; and he envisaged these National Guilds as arising out of the Trade Unions through their extension to include all workers 'by hand or brain' and through a change in their objectives from mere bargaining about working conditions to the winning of industrial self-government. The way in which he saw this coming about was by a combination of industrial struggle with the conversion of the Government to the idea of 'industrial Socialism'. The Trade Unions, converted into inclusive Guilds and possessed of a 'monopoly of labour', were to demand of the State that it should accept their right to take over the management of industries and services; and the State was to issue to the Guilds Charters conferring this right and embodying the conditions of responsibility to the public. Thus, Hobson was not a Syndicalist: he did not contemplate that the State would disappear or wither away, to give place to a social structure based on working-class economic organisation. He regarded the State as an unsuitable agency for conducting industry; but he recognised it as an agency for representing the whole body of citizens in their collective capacity and expected it to continue, in a democratised form, to perform legislative and executive functions. He was a Socialist who accepted the fact of the class-struggle and the need for collective ownership of the means of production, but was strongly hostile to bureaucracy and held that men could not be really free as citizens unless they were also free and self-governing in their daily lives as producers. He agreed with the Syndicalists that 'economic power precedes political power'; but he did not deny either that politics had its rôle or that, in the last resort, the State, as representing the whole people, must have the last word.

The volume *National Guilds*, based on articles which had been previously published in the *New Age*, originally appeared under Orage's name. Hobson was out of the country at the time; but he protested, and his name was added in the second edition. Actually, he had drafted, and Orage revised, the text, for whose final form they were both responsible. The *New Age* was not a journal of large circulation; but it had a very intelligent public and a remarkable body of contributors, including Arnold Bennett, who wrote for it on books under the name of Jacob Tonson, G. K. Chesterton, Hilaire Belloc, and most of the leading members of the intellectual left. The articles, and the book which followed them, attracted little working-class attention, but much among Socialist intellectuals. The Guild proposals appeared to offer a bridge between Syndicalism and Industrial Unionism on the one hand and State Socialism or Collectivism on the other. They could, moreover, be interpreted at will in either a revolutionary or a moderate sense. Those who read them could envisage the Guilds as coming into being through a process of industrial struggle which would force the politicians to accept them; but they could also set out in the hope of converting the politicians of the Labour Party and the Socialist societies to 'industrial democracy' and of persuading a Labour or Socialist Government, in due course, to hand over the control of industry to the workers 'by hand and brain'.

Guild Socialism had a particular attraction for many Christian Socialists — especially for high Anglicans who were opposed to the 'Erastian' control of the State over the Church, and were demanding that the Church's liberty to govern its affairs should be restored. A leader in this movement was John Nevill Figgis (1866–1919), a political and social theorist whose writings were grist to the mill of the left-wing Christian Socialists — especially his *Churches in the Modern State* (1913). Another influential figure was the 'Red Vicar' of Thaxted, Conrad Noel (1869–1942), who wrote a Socialist *Life of Jesus* and took an active part in the Guild Socialist movement. Yet another was Maurice B. Reckitt, who was energetic both in the Guild movement and in the Church Socialist League — with which Penty was also connected. R. H. Tawney (b. 1880), too, linked Christian Socialism to the Guild Socialists; and William Temple (1881–1944), later Archbishop of Canterbury, was on the fringe of the movement.

Chiefly, however, the Guild Socialists rallied round them a small, but very energetic group of young intellectuals, largely from Oxford — among whom William Mellor (1888–1942), Maurice Reckitt, and I were numbered. Until 1915 they had no formal organisation. When I published my *World of Labour* in 1913, I did not yet call myself a Guild Socialist, though I was largely in sympathy with the ideas of the *New Age* group. By the end of that year, however, I had accepted the label. Orage, whose interests were centred upon the *New Age*, did not want any organisation to be set up. He preferred to let his ideas spread gradually through the paper. Not until the beginning of 1915 was his resistance overcome, and the National Guilds League launched. Its history, and that of the Guild Socialist movement beyond its early stages, therefore belong to a period beyond that which is meant to be covered in the present volume.

A little more, however, must be said about the Guild ideas, as they had developed up to 1914, and about their relation to the Socialist movement. Communist writers usually dismiss Guild Socialism as essentially a form of 'petty bourgeois' doctrine, afflicted with 'utopianism' and designed to obscure the realities of the class-struggle and to evade the necessary implications of Marxism. I can see what they mean. Guild Socialism was fundamentally an ethical and not a materialist doctrine. It set out, as against both State Socialism and what was soon to be called Communism, to assert the vital importance of individual and group liberty and the need to diffuse social responsibility among the whole people by making them as far as possible the masters of their own lives and of the conditions under which their daily work was done. Not poverty, but slavery and insecurity, the Guild Socialists urged, were the worst evils the workers needed to overcome. Freedom from the fear of unemployment, freedom at work, and the right to work under supervisors and managers of their own choosing and to rid the work-places of rulers appointed from above, whether by the capitalist employer or by the State, were the necessary foundations of industrial democracy, without which political democracy could be only a pretence. What a man was in his daily labour, that would he be in his leisure and as a citizen. 'Workers' control' must be built up from the bottom, on a foundation of workshop democracy and the 'right to work'.

It did not appear clearly until later how much the different advocates of 'workers' control' were at cross-purposes. To some of the Industrial Unionists, and subsequently to the Communists, it meant control by the workers *as a class*, to be exercised through the dictatorship of the proletariat as a whole, and was thus quite consistent with centralisation and imposed discipline provided the discipline was imposed by representatives of the class. The Guild Socialists, on the other hand, were strongly anti-authoritarian and personalistic: the 'workers' control' they stood for was, above all else, control by the actual working group over the management of its own affairs within the framework of a wider control of policy formulated and executed as democratically as possible, and with the largest diffusion of responsibility and power.

There were, indeed, differences of emphasis and doctrine among the Guild Socialists themselves. Hobson and Orage, as we saw, stood for a structure of Guilds controlling and organising production under Charter from the State. But this view met with increasing challenge among Guild Socialists, many of whom — myself among them — opposed the entire notion of State Sovereignty and universal authority. In its place we advanced a doctrine of Political Pluralism, based on the conception of function. This involved a challenge to the commonly accepted theory of democratic representative government. No man, we argued, could truly represent other men: all a man could do was to act as the representative of common purposes which he shared with others. Accordingly, all true representation must be functional; and there could be no single authority representing all the people in all their purposes. This led to the conception of a pluralistic society in which there would be no 'sovereign', but instead a distribution of power which would preserve the freedom of the individual by enabling him to invoke one functional group to protect him against the pretensions of another, the final decision emerging as a consensus between the different groups, and not as the dictate of an universal superior. It was, of course, objected that there must be somewhere a final authority of law if the unity of society was not to be dissolved into anarchy; but the pluralistic Guild Socialists retorted that they did not see the necessity, or agree that society could not be held together without this final acceptance of a single overlord. In that matter they agreed with the 'federalistic' Anarchists against the Marxists. They invoked Proudhon and Kropotkin and William Morris against the authoritarians, and rejected the view that all political issues must be thought of primarily in terms of concentrated power.

That this attitude was highly intellectualist, and in that sense 'petty bourgeois', is undoubtedly true. That it was the

worse for that is at all events not self-evident. That it appeared
when it did, and that it subsequently lost hold, was not merely
accidental. It emerged at a moment when, from a number of
different approaches, the idea of the creative rôle of social
groups was challenging both the atomistic concepts of Benthamite utilitarianism and the mass-doctrines of authoritarianism
underlying both the Hegelian and the Marxist attitudes. It
receded when, both in post-Czarist Russia and in the West,
war and its aftermath engendered a new tendency to think of
the problems of society in terms of mass-power and put
libertarian notions once more at a discount. In this respect
Syndicalism, Industrial Unionism, Guild Socialism, militant
feminism, and the various movements for religious independence of the secular power had common characteristics and, as
Sorel emphasised, fitted in with the Bergsonian philosophy and
its emphasis on the *élan vital*. They were all, moreover,
ambivalent tendencies, in that they could be combined either
with highly democratic or with hierarchical gospels, so that
their protagonists came to blows one with another in the post-
war period, and the whole movement broke up. These later
developments, however, we must leave to be considered in the
next volume of this study.

On the surface, what took place in Great Britain between
1910 and 1914 has been aptly described by George Dangerfield
in a book which he called *The Strange Death of Liberal England*.
Within a few years of the great electoral victory of 1906, which
appeared to have given Liberalism a new lease of life and a new
shape adapted to twentieth-century conditions, the ideological
basis of the new Liberalism had been undermined, not by the
rise of the Labour Party, but by the sudden upsurge of a number
of separate challenges to the conception of orderly social
evolution to which both Liberalism and Labourism were
deeply committed. These emergent forces did, indeed, accomplish the destruction of the Liberal Party ; but in doing so they
largely exhausted their own impetus, leaving a void which
between the wars Communism and Fascism staked out rival
claims to fill.

CHAPTER V

GERMANY: THE REVISIONIST CONTROVERSY

WITH the expiry of the Anti-Socialist Laws and the fall of Bismarck from power an epoch in the history of German Socialism ended, and another began. For twelve years the Social Democratic Party had been persecuted : its journals had been closed down, its organisation proscribed, its leaders harried by the police. Had Bismarck had all his will, it would have been unable to put up candidates for the Reichstag or for the Landtags of the various German States ; but the Reichstag itself had refused to interfere with the freedom of its own elections, and in some of the States considerable parliamentary liberties remained. The party, though sorely beset, was able to fight elections and to conduct electoral propaganda ; and its deputies, when elected, could speak freely in the Reichstag or in the State Landtags, and could even address their constituents provided they were careful not to give the police too easy a handle. Party gatherings of any size could be held only outside the country — in Switzerland ; and Switzerland also provided a place of publication for the party journal — *The Social Democrat* — which was smuggled successfully into Germany on a considerable scale.

At the first, the Socialist vote had suffered. In the Reichstag election of 1877, it had reached 493,000 : in 1881 it had fallen to 312,000. But thereafter it had risen sharply — to 550,000 in 1884 and to 763,000 in 1887. In 1890 the Social Democrats celebrated their new freedom with a vote of 1,427,000 — nearly 20 per cent of the total. They won 35 seats, as against 9 in 1878, and 24 in 1884. In 1887 they had been reduced to a mere 11 by a combination of the anti-Socialist parties against them ; but even then their total vote had risen, both absolutely and as a percentage of the whole.

German Social Democracy had won deep admiration abroad

by reason of its remarkable success in standing up to persecution. It was, indeed, during the period of its outlawry that it found imitators in one country after another, and appeared to be setting the line for European Socialism almost everywhere, if not for the whole world. The conditions of its existence necessarily affected its working. The open leadership had to be handed over to its parliamentary representatives, who alone could speak or act with any freedom. The party organisation proper had to go underground; and it was impracticable to carry on any system of branches belonging to a central body. Thus began the arrangement of choosing 'men of confidence' to maintain touch with small groups of members — a system which was kept up after 1890 and became an important element in the party's basic structure. The conditions required a high degree of centralised control and of leadership from above. It was impossible to hold a fully representative party Congress; and because of this the party programme adopted at Gotha in 1875 remained unchanged. Policy pronouncements were made at election times by the leading candidates and between elections by the members in the Reichstag or in the State Landtags. Wilhelm Liebknecht and August Bebel were the outstanding party spokesmen: Eduard Bernstein and Karl Kautsky were coming to be recognised as its principal theorists. All four were ardent Marxists: Bernstein was on terms of close friendship with Engels — his revisionist deviations were still unsuspected. He and Kautsky collaborated closely in expounding the party's new policy after the Erfurt Congress of 1891.

When the period of repression ended, the party made haste both to re-form its organisation and to equip itself with a new programme. Almost at the same moment, the Trade Unions, which had been almost destroyed after 1878 but had been allowed to creep back, under severe restrictions, during the later 'eighties, set about forming a new central organisation of their own; and a new Co-operative movement, based on the principles of Rochdale, began to grow up among the industrial workers. Both these movements were interested in winning freedom for development, securing legal recognition, and pressing for immediate economic reforms. The Socialists, if they were to hold the allegiance of the working class and to extend their influence over it, had to come to terms with both Trade Unionism and Co-operation, and to take up a constructive attitude in relation to the reforms which the adherents of these movements desired. This presented no small problem to the Socialist leaders. As long as their party had been proscribed, it had been natural for them to make use of the Reichstag as a forum for Socialist propaganda. There had been no question of their being able to influence the Government's policy : their task had been to fight it on every possible occasion. But with Bismarck dismissed and a new, young Emperor, Wilhelm II, playing with advanced notions of social reform ; with freedom to organise, and with lively expectations aroused by their electoral successes, they had to reconsider their attitude and to make up their minds how far they were still a revolutionary party. During their years of outlawry they could not well have been anything else ; but now — how far was the case altered by the return to legality ?

This question was none too easy to answer ; and almost from the first it received to some extent varying answers. For the situation differed considerably in different parts of Germany. For the Reichstag there was — and had been ever since its establishment in 1867 — manhood suffrage. There was not, however, any kind of responsible democratic government. The Reichstag had no control over the executive, and no share in executive power. The Emperor ruled, directly or through his Chancellor, at the executive level ; and the federal Bundesrat, dominated by Prussia, was much nearer to the keys of power than the popularly elected Chamber. Moreover, in Prussia itself — by far the largest and most powerful State — there was no element of democracy at all. The Prussian Landtag was elected under a three-class system of voting which made it practically impossible for the Socialists to win a single seat — at any rate unless they were prepared to enter into an electoral arrangement with the liberal bourgeois parties against the Conservatives. In the other States, the situation varied : some had wide electorates, so that the Socialists had been able to make headway in them even during the years of repression : others were virtually closed. In the States which possessed the more liberal constitutions, there had been some tendency for Socialists and Progressives to act together in Land and in municipal elections. But in Prussia and in some other States there had been bitter antagonism between Socialists and Liberals, who mostly stood for an extreme policy of *laissez-faire* in matters of industrial legislation and social welfare.

In the early days, before the followers of Marx and Lassalle had amalgamated to form a united party, one of the great points of contention between them had been whether or not co-operation with the more progressive bourgeois parties should be encouraged or allowed. The Lassallians had been in the habit of saying that all the non-Socialists formed a single reactionary mass against which it was the mission of Socialists to wage political war. The acceptance of this standpoint in the Gotha Programme of 1875 had been one of Marx's main objections to the draft; for Marx had again and again urged the necessity for acting with the progressive bourgeoisie for the purpose of winning advances towards constitutional democracy — even if he had usually added something about the need for the Socialists to turn on their erstwhile allies in their hour of success. Marx had accused the Lassallians of using their indiscriminate denunciations of all the non-Socialist parties as a cloak for their real preference for the reactionary imperialists over the liberal capitalists; but this ground of difference had been in effect removed during the years when Marxists and Lassallians were victims of a common persecution. There remained, however, a deeper difference, not unrelated to the original ground of quarrel. Was the German Reich, as established in 1870, to be regarded as the enemy, or was it to be accepted as a fact? Was Social Democracy to set itself in opposition, not only to the policy of the Reich Government, but also to the Reich itself? This question was closely connected in the minds of Socialists with that of the annexation of Alsace-Lorraine, which they had opposed. Were they now, twenty years later, to accept this act of militant imperialism as an accomplished fact; or were they to stand for restitution, and to oppose the Reich on that account? Later on, this question took shape in the further question whether Socialist deputies should on any occasion vote for the Government's budget, and became entangled with the much wider issues of national defence and colonial expansion. But we shall come to that in due course: for the present what concerns us is the problem which faced the Social Democrats immediately after the lapsing of the Anti-Socialist Laws.

In 1869 Wilhelm Liebknecht, in a speech which was reprinted as a pamphlet and became famous, had given expression to an extreme revolutionary standpoint in relation to parliamentary action. 'Socialism', he had said, 'is no longer a question of theory : it is simply a question of force which cannot be resolved in a parliament, but only in the street, on the field of battle, like any other question of force. . . . For the peoples as well as for the princes, it is violence that has the last word.' He had gone on to attack the illusion that universal suffrage was 'the miraculous key that would open the doors of public power to the disinherited'. He had added 'Certainly universal suffrage is a sacred right of the people, and a fundamental condition of the democratic State — of the democratic Socialist State. But taken apart, sundered from civil liberty, without freedom of the press, without right of association, under the domination of the sabre of policeman and soldier — in a word, within the absolutist State — universal suffrage can be only the plaything and the tool of absolutism.' What would happen, he had asked, in 'the almost inconceivable event of a Socialist majority being returned to the Reichstag ?' If such a majority were to attempt to transform the fundamental institutions of German society, 'a company of soldiers would disperse the Socialist majority, and if these gentlemen did not quietly accept their dismissal, a handful of policemen would conduct them to the public gaol, where they would have time to reflect on their quixotry'.

In 1891, at the Erfurt Congress, Liebknecht spoke in a different sense, when he was replying to the attacks of the left wing headed by the Berlin compositor, Wilhelm Werner. His attitude to parliamentarism had undergone a great change under the influence of the Social Democrats' electoral advance.

I hold — we all hold — that the centre of gravity for our party's activity is not to be found in the Reichstag, but outside it, and that our activity in the Reichstag, as long as we have not a decisive influence there, should have propaganda chiefly in view. But does it follow that, because we have not a decisive influence, we must condemn parliamentarism ? Parliamentarism is simply the system of representation of the people. If so far we have not achieved results in the Reichstag, that is not the fault of parliamentarism : it is simply the consequence of our not having yet in the country, among the people, the necessary power. If we had behind us as many votes, and as much force, as the bourgeois parties have, the Reichstag would be for us as little unfruitful as it is now for them. . . . To say this is not to maintain that every question can be solved by legislation ; but let someone show me any other road that leads to the goal! I know there is another road which, in the view of a few among us, is shorter — that of violence . . . but that road leads to Anarchism, and it is the great fault of the opposition not to have reckoned with this outcome. . . . In process of time brute power should yield to the moral factors, to the logic of things. Bismarck, the man of brute force, the man of the politics of blood and iron, lies prostrate — and Social Democracy is the strongest party in Germany. . . . The essence of revolutionism lies not in the means, but in the end. Violence has been for thousands of years a factor of reaction. Prove that our end is false, and then you will be in a position to say that the party is being led aside by its leaders from the path of revolution.

In effect, by 1891 the leaders of German Social Democracy, flushed by their successful resistance under the repression and by their notable electoral achievements, had come to believe that before long they would win a majority of seats in the Reichstag, and that it would no longer be possible for such a majority to be dispersed by the Government's soldiery, or its leaders, if they resisted, haled off to prison by a squad of police. They had become parliamentarians because they had come to believe, as they had not believed earlier — or rather as Liebknecht and the Eisenachers had not believed — that the Reichstag could be used as an instrument for bringing about the transformation of society from a capitalist to a Socialist basis. The Lassallians had taken up from the first an attitude of trying to use their position in the Reichstag for furthering social reforms. They had taken a full part in its debates, moving amendments and voting for the better and against the worse, even when the better was a long way short of what they wanted. They had been denounced for doing this — above all by Liebknecht himself — in the name of Marxist orthodoxy. But even among the Eisenachers there had been from the outset some hesitations about the merits of Liebknecht's intransigent attitude. Bebel had questioned it as early as 1869 ; and the matter had been brought up at the Stuttgart party Congress the following year. There a compromise motion, supported by both the protagonists, had been adopted. It had laid down that the Eisenach Party should take part in Reichstag elections, 'chiefly for propagandist reasons', and that 'it should take part in the work of parliament in the interest of the working classes, but in general should maintain a negative attitude towards the work of parliament'. Thus Liebknecht, in 1870, had got most of his way ; but now, in 1891, he appeared as the protagonist of the opposite cause.

After the Erfurt Congress the left opposition seceded from the Social Democratic Party and formed an Independent Socialist Party. But they carried with them only a small following ; and among these were not a few Anarchists of various complexions. The Independent Socialist Party soon fell to pieces : those who were not Anarchists rejoined the Social Democrats and accepted the parliamentary activity, seasoned with professions of revolutionary Marxism, which had become the official policy. Before long they found themselves allied with Liebknecht and Kautsky against the Revisionists.

In 1891, in preparation for the revision of the party's constitution at Erfurt, Engels published, in the *Neue Zeit*, Marx's suppressed letter attacking the Gotha Programme of 1875. This was a material factor in inducing the party to open the new programme with an uncompromising affirmation of its Marxist faith. But, as we saw, the Erfurt Programme was silent about such matters as the class-character of the State and the necessity of overthrowing it by force. It demanded universal suffrage, including women's suffrage, the secret ballot, proportional representation, biennial elections, payment of members, direct legislation by the initiative and the veto, and administrative autonomy at every level — Reich, States, provinces and communes. It also demanded popular election of public officials, and the responsibility of such officials before the law. In short, the Erfurt Programme embodied a radical demand for constitutional reform, but left open the question whether the changes demanded were to be brought about by parliamentary action, backed by the pressure of public opinion, or by revolutionary means.

The leaders of the party, however, were in no doubt concerning the right policy for the immediate future. This was to use its new freedom to win over a majority of the electorate and to confront the young Emperor and his advisers with a popular movement so strong that they would not dare to appeal to force against it. This seemed good sense ; but what was the best way of winning the required electoral support ? Was it by continuing to adopt in and towards Parliament the essentially *negative* attitude which Liebknecht had formerly recommended to the party ? That could hardly be ; for in the interval the Government of Bismarck had instituted social insurance laws which, it could hardly be denied, were of benefit to the working classes : so that it had to be admitted that even the existing State was capable of passing useful measures, and, if so, that vigilance by the Social Democrats in the Reichstag might be of use in making them better, or at any rate in getting dangerous provisions removed. Moreover, the developing Trade Unions were demanding industrial reforms and were looking to the Socialist members of the Reichstag for support. In these circumstances, a policy of constructive activity in Parliament appeared to offer the best prospect of getting increased support among the electorate.

Recognition of this, however, raised two further issues. Should the Social Democrats maintain the policy of complete independence of, and non-co-operation with, all other parties ; or should they be prepared to enter into arrangements either in Parliament, or for the purpose of electoral give-and-take ? Secondly, should the party continue to regard itself as the class-representative of the industrial workers ; or should it make an effort to enlist the support of the peasants, who formed a large fraction of the electorate in many parts of Germany ?

On the first of these issues, the Social Democratic leaders had taken up a decisive stand in 1890, when the future of the Anti-Socialist Laws was still at stake. Three years earlier it had been decided (at the St. Gall Congress of 1887) that Socialists should abstain from voting at the second ballot when their own candidate had been eliminated at the first. As the policy was to put up Socialists for every possible seat, this in effect meant that no electoral support was to be given to candidates of any other party. In practice, however, the members refused to obey the party decision, and voted in large numbers for Liberals or Progressives in the second ballot. In 1890, faced with an issue of overmastering importance for the party's future, the Social Democratic leaders took it upon themselves to declare the St. Gall decision inoperative, and issued positive instructions to their followers to vote for candidates who would pledge themselves to action against the renewal of the Anti-Socialist Laws. This policy paid handsome dividends ; and it became thereafter the regular party policy in subsequent Reichstag elections. A similar policy was followed elsewhere — in those States in which there was a fairly liberal franchise. But in Prussia, where, as we have seen, the 'three-class' system of voting remained in force, there was no possibility of following a similar line. The only chance of getting any representatives elected to the Prussian Diet lay in making an electoral pact with the bourgeois parties at the outset, so as to combine two of the three 'class' votes. To such a policy of electoral alliance the Social Democrats remained, after 1890, firmly opposed ; and as it was useless to contest the elections at all on any other basis, the official policy was one of entire abstention. In 1893, however, Bernstein, in an article in the *Neue Zeit*, attacked this policy and recommended his party to enter into a pact with the bourgeois Progressives in the Prussian elections. The question was discussed at the Cologne party Congress of that year, and, on Bebel's motion, Bernstein's proposal was unanimously rejected on the ground that it would 'demoralise' the party.

The State in which, thanks to a wide franchise and a large development of industry under very bad labour conditions, the Socialists made most progress in elections for the Diet was Saxony. In 1896, however, this progress was abruptly checked. Under Prussian influence, the other parties combined against the Socialists to alter the electoral law. A class-system of voting, akin to the Prussian, was reintroduced ; and the Socialist representation was wiped out in the Diet, though the Socialists continued to win more and more of the Saxon seats in the Reichstag. This and other developments appeared to suggest that the road to the peaceful conquest of political power was not so open as had been supposed on the morrow of the victories of 1890. If, in Saxony, the electoral advance of Socialism had been countered by a reactionary *coup*, might not the same methods be used to prevent the Socialists from winning a majority in the Reichstag itself? Was universal suffrage so firmly established that it could not be overthrown; or did Liebknecht's words of 1867 still hold good?

Under these conditions, the question of participation in the Prussian elections was reopened. Bebel declared himself a convert in face of the danger : Liebknecht was still strongly opposed. The party Congress at Hamburg in 1897 debated the issue fully, and decided that it must be left for the local party organisations to decide whether to take part or not, but that 'all compromises or alliances with other parties are forbidden'. This resolution was of no use to anyone; for participation without alliances was bound to be fruitless. At this point the party found itself faced with a threat from the Emperor of fresh repressive legislation; and at the Stuttgart Congress of 1898 the advocates of participation were able to make a real advance. It was still to be left to local party decision whether to take part in the Prussian elections or not; but where the local party decided for participation arrangements with other parties were allowed, subject to pledges that their candidates would support universal suffrage and vote against any repressive laws that might be proposed.

In Prussia it was a matter of seeking bourgeois aid against an absolutist régime. In some other parts of Germany a different situation arose. Bavaria, for example, was both a Catholic and predominantly a peasant country; and the Socialists saw no hope of winning a majority there unless they could get the poorer peasants as well as the industrial workers on their side. In pursuance of this object, the Bavarian Social Democrats entered, in 1898, into an alliance with the Catholic Centre Party. This was at once challenged as a defiance of the approved Social Democratic policy of independence, and at the Hanover Congress of 1899 there was an acrimonious debate, which ended with a lengthy resolution redefining the party's attitude.

> The party, in order to achieve its end, makes use of all means which, being in harmony with its fundamental principles, promise success. Without being under any illusion about the nature and essence of the bourgeois parties as representatives and defenders of the existing political and social order, it does not refuse, in this or that particular case,

combined action with certain of them, whether it is a matter of adding to the party's electoral strength, of extending the rights and liberties of the people, of improving seriously the social condition of the working class, of furthering the accomplishment of duties to civilisation, or of combating projects hostile to the working class and to the people. The party, however, preserves everywhere in its activities its entire autonomy and its independence, and regards each success it makes as but a step which brings it nearer to its final goal.

This resolution was a notable victory for the advocates of electoral alliances ; but it left untouched the issue of participation in the Prussian 'three-class' elections. Finally, at the Mainz Congress in 1900, it was decided that the Socialists should everywhere take part in the Prussian elections, but that they should present their own candidates at the primary elections and should enter into pacts with other parties only through their representatives elected at this stage. (The method of election to the Prussian Diet was indirect : the electors, by classes, chose their delegates, and the combined delegates then chose the actual representative in the Diet.) The Social Democratic Party thus travelled in the decade after 1890 a long distance towards a policy of electoral and parliamentary compromise. In effect, it completed its conversion from a revolutionary into a parliamentary party.

In this remarkable evolution the peasant problem played a highly significant part. In Social Democratic theory very great stress was put on the historical tendency towards large-scale enterprise and the concentration of capital in fewer and fewer hands. No other element in Marx's doctrine received so much emphasis : the process of 'socialisation' of production was the guarantee of the coming of Socialism. The word 'socialisation', as used by Marx in *Capital*, meant not nationalisation or social ownership, but the supersession of individual businesses by larger and larger capitalistic concerns, the co-operation of a horde of workers under unified direction in the making of final products, the increasingly 'social' or collective character of production under the influence of modern technology and concentrated financial organisation. This process constituted, in Marx's view, a necessary element in the evolution of society ; and it was leading irresistibly to a situation in which every product was the outcome of the combined labours of many co-operating individuals, who worked together willy nilly, despite the class-antagonisms that divided them. This growing 'socialisation' of productive processes, Marx held, was preparing the way for the time when, as capitalism was revealed as incapable of ordering its conduct or of preventing the recurrence of increasingly severe crises, the proletariat would be in a position to seize political power and to institute a rational 'socialisation' by transferring the means of production from private to public ownership, and thereafter planning the output of industry with a view to meeting the needs of the whole people.

Large-scale enterprise, trustification, and the concentration of ownership in fewer hands were thus regarded by the Social Democrats as necessary stages on the road to Socialism ; and small-scale enterprise was looked on with contempt, as a mere survival from an earlier epoch and as destined inevitably to decline and supersession as capitalistic achievement reached a higher stage. This contempt extended, not only to artisans, shopkeepers, and small industrial entrepreneurs, but also to the peasants who tilled their patches of land with none but the simplest implements, with only the most rudimentary division of labour, and with a foolish devotion to the ownership and transmission by inheritance of their wretched holdings. In the coming society, said the Social Democratic theorists, echoing Marx and Engels, the peasantry would be eliminated along with other obsolete relics of barbarism ; the land would be exploited by scientific methods of large-scale cultivation which would yield a much higher output at a greatly reduced cost ; and the dispossessed peasants, having been reduced to the status of proletarians by the 'industrialisation' of the countryside by capitalist farming, would share in the general emancipation that would follow the proletariat's conquest of political power.

There were two flies in this soothing ointment. In the first place, the peasantry obstinately refused to die out. Capitalistic farming did, no doubt, make some advances ; but so did peasant farming on land previously uncultivated or undercultivated by large landowners of the pre-capitalist feudal type. A number of Social Democratic theorists, including for some time Kautsky, made feverish attempts to interpret the available statistics as verifying their assumption that peasant farming must be giving way before the advance of capitalistic agriculture ; but the facts were too strong for them. Gradually, it had to be admitted that over a large part of Europe peasant agriculture was gaining, and not losing ground, and landownership becoming more diffused, instead of becoming concentrated in fewer and fewer hands. It was then argued that the peasant, even though he survived, was falling more and more a prey to money-lenders and financiers and was having his standards of living beaten down more and more by the competition of the industrial farm-entrepreneur as well as by the exactions of landowners, money-lenders, and merchants. But, even so, the facts were disconcerting to the party theorists — the more so because the rate of supersession of other forms of small-scale business was also seen to be much less rapid than they had confidently expected it to be.

The second fly in the ointment was that the refusal of the peasants to vanish from the scene, by conversion into prole- tarians working in the growing industries or on industrialised farming estates, made it much more difficult for the Socialists to win a parliamentary majority by acting as the spokesmen of the proletariat alone. This difficulty was, of course, most acute in the less industrialised parts of Germany, and especially in those parts of Western Germany in which peasant farming was predominant. In Eastern Germany it was possible to treat the exploited, half-serf labourers on the great feudal estates as akin to industrial workers, and to appeal to them with programmes of expropriation of the feudal proprietors of the soil. But no such appeal would serve to win over the peasants of Southern and Western Germany, who were not labourers but to an increasing extent small proprietors for whose support parlia- mentarians could angle most profitably by promising them reforms which would consolidate their rights of ownership and transmission and would make it easier for them to get capital and credit on not too onerous terms. Agricultural Co-operation, chiefly in the form of Credit Societies, had already made substan- tial progress in Western and Southern Germany ; but this was no thanks to the Social Democrats. Catholics and Liberals, not Socialists, had fostered Agricultural Co-operation of this type, and had used it against Socialism as a means of strengthening the peasant economy. Indeed, whereas the Liberals, hostile to State intervention, had for the most part limited their help to the encouragement of voluntary Co-operation, the Catholics had been prepared to invoke State assistance for the protection of the peasants against the encroachments of capitalistic agriculture and of the power of private finance.

In face of a large peasant electorate, full of many discontents but passionately devoted to private ownership and cultivation, what were the Socialists to do ? The Bavarians, as we have seen, tried to strengthen their electoral position by alliance with the Catholic Centre Party ; but this furnished no answer to the peasant problem. The Socialists wanted a means of winning the peasants over to Social Democracy ; but how could they even attempt this without denying their own principles ? In order to get peasant support they would have to offer something that peasants wanted ; and this was bound to be something that, instead of speeding up their supersession, would actually strengthen their hold on the land and help them to compete more successfully with large-scale farmers and with importers of agricultural produce. It would thus retard the very process of 'socialisation' on which the Social Democrats were relying for the means of victory.

Throughout the period after 1890 German Social Democracy was wrestling with this awkward dilemma. The Bavarians, headed by Georg von Vollmar (1850–1922) made themselves the protagonists of the doctrine that the poorer peasants at any rate ought to be regarded as in essence proletarians, even where they were tilling their own land with the labour of their families. Socialists, they urged, could by no means afford to wait until peasant agriculture and other forms of small-scale production had died out. To help the peasants and secure them as allies of the industrial proletariat, far from weakening the Socialist cause, would be of the greatest advantage when the time came for overthrowing capitalist society. It would lessen the birth-pangs of the new social order.

The Bavarian Socialists were conscious of the danger that the peasants might take the Socialists' help and pay them back by turning upon them from their strengthened position. Accordingly, they tried to work out a policy that would prevent this. They found their answer in demanding that the State should take over all agricultural mortgages, should establish a monopoly of agricultural credit and reduce the rate of interest on farm loans, should similarly nationalise the entire business of agricultural insurance, and should take into its own hands both the exploitation of the forests and the maintenance of all common rights in the use of land. The State should then use its powers to encourage Agricultural Co-operation in forms which, instead of solidifying individual farming, would lead to the development of large-scale collective cultivation, collective processing of agricultural products, and collective purchase of requisites and sale of products.

In Württemberg, Hesse, and Baden, the Social Democrats soon adopted agrarian programmes modelled on that of the Bavarians ; and the question was brought up for discussion at the Frankfurt-on-Main Socialist Congress of 1894. The opponents of the Bavarian policy charged its advocates with betrayal of the interests of the agricultural labourers — the proletariat's true allies. This argument was advanced chiefly by delegates from Eastern Germany — that is, from the area of the great estates. The Congress swept it aside, though it insisted that special measures must be taken to help the agricultural wage-labourers, who should be granted the full right to organise and should have their hours and conditions of work regulated by statute. A special committee was set up to work out a considered policy for submission to the next Congress ; and both Liebknecht and Bebel, as well as Vollmar, were given seats upon the committee.

In due course the committee produced a report which, broadly, accepted the policy of the South German Socialists. But Karl Kautsky, in the *Neue Zeit*, thereupon delivered a violent attack on the entire policy of appealing for the support of the peasants by the adoption of proposals designed to strengthen their position by invoking the aid of the State. The committee, in attempting to give its proposals a socialistic turn, had stressed the need for public exploitation of forests and for widened powers for public acquisition of land ; but Kautsky attacked it as fiercely for this part of its proposals as for its measures designed to aid the peasant cultivators. On the latter issue he indignantly repudiated the notion that peasant cultivators could be regarded as having anything in common with the industrial workers. They were, he asserted, merely a section of the classes that lived by exploiting the workers and deserved no consideration save in their capacity as consumers — in which they stood to benefit by the parts of the Erfurt Programme that would improve the position of the whole consuming public, and not of the workers alone. Kautsky asserted with vehemence that, despite all demonstrations to the contrary, the peasant cultivators were being crushed out, because they were fighting a losing battle against the highly capitalised agriculture of the United States and of other 'prairie' countries; and he said that Socialists should welcome their decline as part of the 'increasing misery' which was bound to accompany the passing of capitalism into its final phases of crisis and collapse. There was no need, Kautsky argued, for the Social Democrats to base themselves on any class except the proletariat, which could be assured of coming victory as the difficulties of capitalism increased. It would be a sheer betrayal of the principles of the party and an abandonment of fundamental Marxist doctrine to convert Socialism from a class-doctrine resting on the historic mission of the proletariat into an amalgam of petit-bourgeois radicalism and political opportunism.

Although Kautsky thus strongly opposed any concessions to the peasants that would help to reinforce their position against the competition of capitalist farming and of imported food products, he did not hold that even after 'the revolution' the class of peasants would or should immediately disappear. Moreover, in his book on *The Agrarian Problem*, written after the controversy over Social Democratic agrarian policy in 1893–4, he appeared as the advocate of a number of measures which would in his view help to relieve peasant poverty and to secure peasant backing for the Social Democratic Party, without being open to the danger of entrenching the peasant more firmly on his small farm. These measures were mainly designed to ease taxation on the rural communes and to increase their revenues, rather than to give direct assistance to the peasants as a special group. Bernstein, criticising these proposals of Kautsky, pertinently remarked that in practice they would be of much more help to the wealthier peasants than to the poorer, and of little or none to the hired agricultural labourer. He favoured, as against Kautsky, a policy of direct help to the peasants, who were, he said, so numerous as to hold the deciding vote in many constituencies between the capitalist parties and the Socialists. Social Democracy, Bernstein contended, should commit itself to measures which offered an immediate improvement in the condition of the small peasants, without troubling itself about their consequences in strengthening the peasant sector of the economy. Why not, as, unlike Kautsky, he believed the peasants as a class to be increasing over most of Europe, and by no means destined to speedy eclipse ?

Kautsky attacked the report of the party's agrarian committee for a further reason, besides its tendency to enable the peasantry to survive. He was no less vehement in denouncing the committee for proposing a series of measures whose effect would be to add to the powers of the State. Socialists, he argued, far from increasing the authority and functions of the existing State, should regard it as the central representative of the exploiting classes, and should do everything possible to undermine its power. Some of the measures which the committee recommended would be admirable if the proletariat were already in control of the State ; but it would be disastrous to concede to the capitalist State functions which could well be entrusted to its proletarian conqueror and successor. The proletariat's first task was to win political power : that done, it could afford to undertake the tasks of agricultural reorganisation. But, while the capitalist State remained, such measures would necessarily work against Socialism. Moreover, their adoption at Socialist instance would entangle the Social Democratic Party in responsibility for the success of profit-seeking enterprise, would thrust on the party the blame for the losses that would necessarily be incurred through bolstering up an obsolete form of productive organisation, and would alienate the true proletarians in the rural areas by allying the Socialists with their exploiters.

Kautsky's articles caused a great stir. When the committee's report came up at the Breslau Congress of 1895, his view prevailed. The report was rejected by a majority of three to one ; and the Party went on record as repudiating all attempts to bolster up peasant agriculture or to represent peasant and proletarian interests as having anything in common. It also adopted Kautsky's view that nothing must be done to increase the power of the 'exploiter-State' and thus to put further obstacles in the way of the proletariat's victory. True, it also decided to institute a full enquiry into the agrarian problem and to publish a series of reports based on this enquiry. But in fact this last proposal was quietly dropped; and the agrarian problem disappeared from the agenda of subsequent party Congresses. The controversy, however, continued, though the party took care not to press its internal differences again to an issue. In 1898 Kautsky published a lengthy volume on *The Agrarian Problem*, restating and amplifying his views; and five years later Eduard David, who had been a member of the committee of 1894-5, retaliated in his *Socialism and Agrarian Economy*. The South German Socialists were overborne, but not convinced; and in practice they continued to advocate in their own States a considerable part of their rejected programme.

Karl Kautsky (1854–1938) had by this time won for himself an assured position as the principal expositor of orthodox Marxism. Born in Prague, and thus Austrian by birth, he was educated at Vienna University and, turning to Socialist journalism, worked mainly in Switzerland 'and London during the 1880s. In 1883 he founded the *Neue Zeit* at Stuttgart, but was soon driven into exile, continuing to publish his journal at Zürich and later at London. In 1890 he returned to Stuttgart, but moved to Berlin in 1897 and later to Vienna. The *Neue Zeit*, which remained under his editorship until 1917, soon established itself as the leading Marxist review, and is an invaluable source for students of Marxist controversies. In 1892 Kautsky published his book expounding the new Erfurt Programme of the German Social Democratic Party. He had already written several books, including a study of More's *Utopia*; but his *Erfurt Programme* was the first of a long series in which he defended his conception of Marxism against a varied series of opponents, among whom Eduard Bernstein and Nikolai Lenin stand out. After 1914 he took a strong line against Germany in the first world war, and was thereafter associated with the Independent Socialist group in the German Social Democratic movement. After 1918 he was made editor of the archives of the German Foreign Office and was responsible for publishing the secret documents relating to the origins of the war.

In 1887 Kautsky published *The Economic Doctrines of Karl Marx*, a text-book expounding the basic conceptions of Marxism. This became in effect the official popular exposition : it was translated into a number of languages, and retained its popularity for many years. His *Erfurt Programme* acquired a hardly less recognised status as the best guide to the policy of German Social Democracy ; and during the 1890s his articles in the *Neue Zeit* had a large influence on the making of party policy. When the Revisionist controversy took shape near the end of the century, it was natural that Kautsky should appear as the principal champion of Marxist orthodoxy against Bernstein's attack. Both Wilhelm Liebknecht and August Bebel stood higher in the party hierarchy, and were opposed to Bernstein's views ; but they were active politicians as well as iournalists, whereas Kautsky was pre-eminently a theorist and played little part in politics except through his writings.

As we shall see, Kautsky took his stand on the complete correctness of Marx's social diagnosis. His book on Marx's economic doctrines is a stringent exposition of the Marxist theory of surplus value, with no critical element. He accepted entirely the Marxist account of the distinction between productive and unproductive labour, and between paid and unpaid labour. He also endorsed without qualification Marx's account of the 'contradictions' of capitalism, including the view that crises were bound to recur with increasing severity and to lead up to the 'final crisis' in which the capitalist system would be overthrown. He took over from Marx the doctrine of the 'increasing misery' of the workers, and of the inevitable casting down of the small bourgeoisie into the ranks of the proletariat. Most of all he stressed the notion of capitalist 'concentration' — of the inevitable growth of big business at the expense of small, of the accumulation of wealth in fewer and fewer hands, and of the progressive 'socialisation' of production as preparing the way for Socialism. But, far from seeing in the existence of this tendency a reason why Socialists should support nationalisation and an increase in the power of the State, he drew a sharp distinction between the policy which Socialists should follow before and after their conquest of political power. He echoed

Marx's view that the existing State must be regarded as an instrument of class-oppression, and therefore as the enemy of the workers; and he argued that, for this reason, Socialists should do their utmost to weaken its authority, and should by no means seek to use it as a constructive instrument of social reform. In face of the evident difficulty of resisting demands from the Trade Unions that the Socialists in the Reichstag and in the State Landtags should support measures which would ameliorate the condition of the workers, he was prepared to qualify his attitude a little, but only to the extent of agreeing to Socialist support of legislation that would strengthen the workers' movement without adding to the State's power. In his view, the time for constructive use of the State could come only when the workers had seized it, including its executive as well as its legislative branch; and he insisted that this seizure must be made by the workers as a class and that the Social Democratic Party must fight its way to power as the class-representative of the workers and must not in any way dilute its class-war doctrine in order to enlist the support of other classes. He denied that there was any need for such dilution: in his view the other classes which might be induced to rally to a diluted form of Socialism were doomed to destruction in any event and would come over to the side of the proletariat as they were reduced to proletarian status by the development of capitalist concentration. If Socialists made any compromise in attempting to attract them, the inevitable result would be that the Socialist doctrine would lose its logical coherence and degenerate into mere opportunism.

Kautsky thus appeared, in the 1890s, to be the defender of revolutionary Marxism against every sort of compromise. But, though he insisted on the proletarian basis of the party, and often used phrases which seemed to rank him with the advocates of proletarian dictatorship, he in fact envisaged the overthrow of the existing State and the proletarian conquest of political power mainly in terms of a peaceful advance by propagandist and parliamentary action, and agreed with Liebknecht in regarding the essence of revolution as consisting rather in the end accomplished than in the means. When he spoke of a coming 'workers' State' he had in mind a State in which the workers' party would have won a clear majority of the popular vote and would have used its power in the legislature, backed by its influence in the Trade Unions and among the people generally, to insist on a transformation of all the key institutions of society. This he envisaged as coming about, not by a gradual accumulation of piecemeal reforms, but as the sudden sequel to the attainment of sufficient power, inside and outside Parliament, to enforce a revolutionary change which the upholders of capitalism would be too weak to resist. He foresaw this as certain to come to pass because the historical tendencies of capitalism would necessarily bring it about through the sharpening of class-antagonisms as the 'contradictions' of capitalism became more and more acute.

This explains how it was that, later on, Kautsky appeared, in his controversy with Lenin and Trotsky, as the leading theoretical opponent of the 'dictatorship of the proletariat', as it was conceived by the Bolsheviks in and after 1917. It was Kautsky, more than any other thinker, who insisted that the time could not be ripe for the establishment of Socialism in any country until the development of capitalism had gone far enough to bring the majority of the people over to the Socialist side, and that any attempt to establish Socialism before the conditions were ripe would necessarily lead to a betrayal of democracy and to a perversion of Socialism into a form of Blanquist tyranny.

Kautsky, then, was essentially a centrist, rather than a man of the extreme left. He appeared, in the 1890s, as a leftist (though even then he was strongly opposed to the extreme leftists, such as Werner) because he was the opponent of the right — first of the Bavarian deviationists headed by Vollmar, and then of the Revisionists led by Bernstein.

Kautsky's emphasis on the historical tendency towards concentration of economic power led him inevitably towards a belief that the Socialist society of the future would inherit this tendency and carry it a great deal further. He was the advocate of a highly centralised and planned economy — but not until after political power had passed into Socialist hands. There were for this reason always two aspects of his thought which appeared to be contradictory and led to misunderstandings. He admired centralisation and discipline : he envisaged the future in terms of thorough planning centrally conceived and controlled. But he was also the determined opponent of every form of centralised planning that would involve, before the 'revolution', an increase in the power of the capitalist State ; and because of this he was often mistaken for a supporter of anti-Statism and found himself in temporary alliance with libertarian Socialists who were against centralisation on principle and regarded it as inconsistent with real democracy. Kautsky had no such libertarian views : centralisation seemed to him an essential element in progress, a necessary feature of the determined evolution of human society, a fundamental postulate of Socialist thought. This attitude, which he derived from his interpretation of Marx's conception of 'socialisation', fitted in with the state of mind of the German Social Democratic leadership. A strong centralised discipline had been forced on the party during the years of repression, and was felt to be still necessary when it was able to resume open activity. There were lively memories of the inconveniences that had resulted in the 1870s from the existence of two rival Socialist parties, which the authorities could play off against each other. Unity had been achieved at Gotha in 1875 — at a doctrinal price ; and this unity had been consolidated by the enactment of the Anti-Socialist Laws. It appeared to Liebknecht and Bebel, as well as to Kautsky, that unity, not merely in organisation but also in policy, was indispensable for the conquest of political power — the more so because even after 1890 Social Democracy was still subject, especially in Prussia, to considerable police oppression and had to face a State in which the feudal and militaristic elements remained very strong.

But there was more than this in it. The *idea* of unity had a powerful hold on the German mind — including the minds of the leading German Socialists. The Germans were then, as they remain to-day, a disciplined people, who prefer to be told — or to tell one another — dogmatically what to do. It was not difficult for the most part to induce Social Democratic Congresses to accept the view that minorities ought to be prepared to toe the line and to accept the obligation of loyal obedience to majority decisions. There were, indeed, deviationist tendencies, especially in South Germany, that were too strong to be altogether repressed ; but even in Bavaria the Social Democrats on the whole accepted the party line when a national Congress had given a decision against them. Generalisations about national character are usually suspect; but it will hardly be denied that the Hegelian philosophy and the drive towards national unification worked together to give German Socialism, as well as other aspects of German thought, a strong tendency to emphasise solidarity and disciplined action that differentiate it sharply from the Socialism of the Latin countries or of Great Britain. Moreover, the Germans are a systematic people : they like to feel that what they do rests on a firm basis of philosophical principle : they like dogma. In the hands of Kautsky, Marxism became a much more rigidly dogmatic creed than it had ever been for Marx himself. Marx, with his Hegelian background, supplied the essential ingredients for this dogmatism : Kautsky rigidified Marxism by leaving out all Marx's subordinate clauses. On the whole, German Social Democrats preferred Kautsky's version to the original : it was more systematic — not to say more flat-footed and easier to learn by rote.

Finally, there was in Kautsky a strong element of pacifism that was alien to Marx's thought. He hated war and violence. This led him to a strong emphasis on the internationalism of the Socialist doctrine. In his internationalism he was at one with Liebknecht and Bebel, who had both proved their devotion to it at the time of the Franco-Prussian War, and had continued to stand out against the imperialistic tendencies of the unified Reich. Kautsky, however, was not only a proletarian internationalist, but also a lover of peace. He believed war to be, in the modern world, the direct outcome of capitalism; and accordingly his pacifism reinforced, instead of weakened, his Socialism. But it also made him wish to believe in the practicability of a conquest of power by the workers without civil war.

Such was the leading theorist of Marxism at the time when Eduard Bernstein launched his 'revisionist' onslaught upon it. Bernstein, indeed, professed to be attacking, not Marxism itself, but only some parts of the master's doctrine that were in no way essential to its main significance. He attempted to draw a distinction between the central core of Marxism, which he accepted as true — and indeed took for granted — and certain excrescences upon it which had arisen out of a mistaken reading, by Marx himself, of the movement of contemporary historic forces. Had he attacked Marxism as a whole, he would no doubt have been drummed out of the Social Democratic Party almost without a hearing ; but there is no reason to suppose that he limited the area of his attack for this reason. Bernstein did believe in Marxism, as a general system of thought — or believed that he believed in it. Nevertheless, the 'revisions' which he proposed went a very long way towards undermining the particular interpretation of Marxism that had been embodied in the Erfurt Programme and made an article of faith for Social Democrats in accordance with their sense of need for a common underlying philosophy and for a policy resting directly on that philosophy.

Eduard Bernstein (1850–1932) was born in Berlin, of Jewish parents. After leaving achool he went to work in a bank, where he served from the age of 16 to that of 28. He then became private secretary to Karl Höchberg, a wealthy supporter of the Social Democratic Party. Three years later, after the passing of the Anti-Socialist Laws, he had to leave Germany, and settled in Switzerland, where he edited *The Social Democrat*, the organ of the party which was smuggled into Germany in large numbers. Expelled from Switzerland in 1888, he went to London ; and there he remained until 1901, as the correspondent in England of the newspaper *Vorwaerts*. In London, he was on terms of intimacy with Engels in his later years. He was much influenced both by the Fabians and by the Independent Labour Party, which enjoyed Engels's favour against the professedly Marxist Social Democratic Federation. Bernstein was consulted concerning the drafting of the Erfurt Programme, and was thanked by Kautsky for the help which he gave in the shaping of Kautsky's book expounding it. At that time the two do not appear to have been aware of any sharp disagreement. But in 1896 Bernstein contributed to Kautsky's journal, the *Neue Zeit*, the first of a series of articles which stirred up an acute controversy within the party and presently brought their author under official rebuke. Bernstein replied in a volume *Die Voraussetzungen des Sozialismus und die Aufgaben der Sozialdemokratie* (1899 — translated into English under the title *Evolutionary Socialism*). In the course of the ensuing controversy, Kautsky replied on behalf of the orthodox Marxists in his *Bernstein und das Sozialdemokratische Programm*

(1899), and Rosa Luxemburg in her *Sozialreform oder Revolution?* (1899). The Revisionists were duly voted down at a party Congress held at Hanover the same year ; but they were not expelled from the party. Bernstein, after the decision had been taken, continued to press his point of view, and to find substantial minority support. Two years later the matter was brought up again at the Lübeck Congress. Bernstein was accused of having offended against party loyalty by the exclusive manner in which he had continued to argue his case 'to the neglect of all criticism of bourgeois society and its defenders'. Bebel was again the proposer of the motion against him. When it had been adopted, Bernstein rose and said that a vote by the Congress naturally could not modify his convictions, but could never be to him a matter of indifference. 'My conviction is that this resolution is objectively unjust to me and rests on false suppositions. But, now that Comrade Bebel has declared that this resolution does not contain a vote of no confidence, I declare that for the future I will tender to the vote of the majority of this assembly all the esteem and all the respect that are due to such a decision of Congress.'

Far from being expelled from the party, Bernstein, who since 1900 had been living in Germany, was soon afterwards elected to the Reichstag with the united support of those who had been on opposite sides in the great Revisionist controversy. He remained active in the party, and found himself, during the first world war, reunited with Kautsky in the anti-war minority.

The reformist movement within the German Social Democratic Party after 1890 began well before Bernstein played any part in it. The first shot was fired in a speech delivered by the Munich deputy, Georg von Vollmar, in 1891. 'There have', said Vollmar, 'no doubt been on occasions great crises in which history has made, or appeared to make, a leap. But what occurs in general is a slow organic evolution. . . . all political and social situations are of a relative character, are forms of transition. To make use of the form which exists in order to exert an influence on that of tomorrow — therein lies our proper rôle.' Vollmar went on to urge the importance of immediate reforms, and of programmes adjusted to immediate conditions : he singled out protective labour laws, full rights of combination, legal regulation of business cartels, abolition of taxes on subsistence goods, and a few other secondary reforms. In a second speech, replying to critics who had denounced his reformist attitude, Vollmar asserted that the recent history of advanced countries showed plainly that the workers' condition could be improved, and had in fact been improved, by such measures of reform. But desirable reforms could not be got by standing aside from the work of legislation and refusing to have any dealings with other parties or with the State, except those of outright hostility. In order to get concessions it was necessary to negotiate and to compromise, as well as to fight.

Vollmar repeated his ideas at the Erfurt Congress, and was duly voted down after Bebel had declared, in an impassioned oration, that if they were adopted nothing could save the party from degeneration into sheer opportunism. It was the function of Social Democracy, said Bebel, to put forward not those demands which other parties could be most easily induced to support, but on the contrary those which no other party *could* support, because they struck at the roots of the class-system.

The following year Vollmar returned to the charge in an article on 'State Socialism', published in France in the *Revue Blanc*. After attacking the reactionary 'State Socialism' of Bismarck, he went on to say that the words could be used to apply not only to such a system, but also 'to a number of measures which we ourselves ought to demand'. 'One can call "State Socialism" all *étatisation*, every transfer of a branch of exploitation from private enterprise into the hands of the existing State.' Socialists, he pointed out, had voted for the nationalisation of the railways and for the establishment of various new forms of public enterprise; and they had been right to do so, because it was a necessary step on the road to improved social conditions. It was impossible, he argued, for Socialists to oppose extensions of State activity which they knew to be desirable in themselves, simply because they objected to the class-character of the existing State. In the ensuing controversy Vollmar argued that the State, despite its class-character, was in practice forced to take account of certain responsibilities towards the public which private capitalism wholly ignored. 'The motive of immediate personal interest which is operative in private industry to a great extent disappears in state enterprise.'

Vollmar, who had urged in 1891 that the Socialists should constitute themselves the party of immediate social reform, was now adding the contention that it should become the party of nationalisation. This roused the greater storm because in Germany there had long been a body of academic State Socialists who repudiated the class-struggle and denied the need for a revolutionary change in the character of the State ; and this group, which had exercised some influence on Bismarck's social policy, was held in particular execration in Social Democratic circles. When the question came up at the Berlin party Congress of 1892, Liebknecht vehemently repudiated Vollmar's doctrine. 'When the existing State takes over (*étatises*)', he said, 'it does not change its nature. It takes the place as employer of the private entrepreneurs : the workers gain nothing, but the State reinforces its power and its capacity for oppression.' 'This so-called State Socialism', he declared, 'is in truth State Capitalism, and under it economic slavery would increase and intensify political slavery, and *vice versa*.' Yet only three years later, at the Breslau party Congress, Liebknecht himself was saying, in connection with the demand that the State should take over agricultural mortgages,[1] that if the proposals of the party's agrarian committee were accepted, and put into practice,

> Undoubtedly the power of the State would be extended, but it would not be reinforced. It is in this case as it is with the army : the bigger this grows, the more popular elements enter into it, and the weaker it becomes as an instrument against the people. Similarly, the more numerous those whose existence depends on the State become, and the more numerous the obligations it incurs, the less can the Junker dominate the State.

This was most unrevolutionary language ; and, as we saw, it was too much for the Congress, which rejected the committee's report, despite the fact that both Liebknecht and Bebel were members and urged its acceptance. I mention Liebknecht's change of front on this issue because it helps to bring out the point that the acknowledged leaders of the party were not nearly so sharply separated from Vollmar's opportunism as they supposed. Kautsky, on the other hand, took up a

[1] See p. 263.

consistent line throughout the controversy, and would have nothing to do with any projects for extending the authority and powers of the existing State. For him, nationalisation was essential; but it had to come after the conquest of political power, and not before.

A study of the party Congress reports makes it clear that, up to the point at which Bernstein threw down his challenge, both Liebknecht and Bebel were moving rapidly towards the right. Then the challenge pulled them back sharply to a reaffirmation of their basic Marxist beliefs; but when Revisionism had been duly voted down, they had no wish at all to drum its advocates out of the party. On the contrary, they resumed their interrupted rightward movement.

Bernstein began his attack with an article, the first of a series entitled *Problems of Socialism*, which was published in 1896 in the *Neue Zeit*. His opening article was entitled 'Utopianism and Eclecticism': it accused the party of being 'utopian' because, although it rigorously excluded speculations about the future organisation of society, it allowed itself to be dominated by the notion of a coming sudden leap from capitalism to Socialism. Everything that was done before this leap was regarded as mere palliative: on the conquest of power, the new Socialist society was expected to solve all problems, 'if not in a day, at all events in a very short time'. This was to 'suppose miracles without believing in them'. In subsequent articles he combated above all the idea that capitalist society was near the point of collapse — was approaching a 'final crisis' which would usher in the epoch of the proletarian conquest of power. He did not deny that this belief rested on Marx's teaching: he argued that Marx had been mistaken. But if there was to be no speedy collapse of capitalist society, what became of the accepted Social Democratic policy of putting off all constructive reform until after 'the revolution'? Were the workers expected to wait for an indefinite time without pressing for reforms that could be obtained within the capitalist system, and from the capitalist State? Would not the party, if it required them to do this, merely forfeit their support and surrender to other parties the kudos of bettering the condition of the people?

It was in this connection that Bernstein wrote the famous

sentence in which he declared that to him the 'movement' meant everything and what was usually called 'the final aim of Socialism nothing'. His critics fastened particularly on this sentence as implying an abandonment of the Socialist faith. Bernstein was unable to attend the Stuttgart party Congress of 1898 at which his article was discussed, because he was then an exile debarred from setting foot on German soil. He sent a long letter, in which he explained his meaning. He was not, he said, at all indifferent about 'the final carrying out of Socialist principles', but only 'about the form of the final arrangement of affairs'.

> I have at no time had a too great interest in the future, beyond general principles : I have not been able to read right through any picture of what is to come. My thoughts and efforts are concerned with the duties of the present and the immediate future, and I busy myself with mere distant perspectives only as far as they guide me to a line of conduct for appropriate action now.

In these words Bernstein was saying in effect that he shared the party's disbelief in utopianism and in all attempts to construct in advance any picture of the coming Socialist society. But he really meant much more than this, as his book *Evolutionary Socialism*, published the following year, made abundantly clear. He was really arguing that Socialism would come, not as a system constructed by Socialists on the morrow of their conquest of power, but by an accumulation of piecemeal changes which would be brought about by social action within the limits set by the sheer necessities of economic development. There would be, in his view, no sudden transition from capitalist to Socialist society, but rather a gradual transformation of the one into the other ; and it would not be possible to say that the great change had occurred at any one point in this evolutionary process.

This was, of course, precisely what the Fabians — above all, Sidney Webb — had been saying for more than a dozen years before Bernstein wrote his opening article. The Fabian philosophy of history, as we saw, was hardly less determinist than Marx's in relation to the general course of social evolution, and hardly less economic in its stress on the primary importance of the economic factors. But where Marx saw history proceeding from epoch to epoch by sudden leaps, Webb and his disciple Bernstein saw an evolutionary process in which sudden leaps were exceptional and the general rule was that of gradual, cumulative change. For Marx, the *method* of change, as distinct from its underlying cause, was to be found in the class-struggle, and in the revolution in which the rising class overthrew the declining class that could no longer effectively exploit the powers of production. For Webb and Bernstein, on the other hand, the class-struggle, though not denied as a fact, was not the really important instrument of change. Things changed because the underlying conditions of social life changed, and because the changes in these conditions caused men (rather than classes) to adapt their institutions to meet new needs. Class might be one of the factors involved; but it was not the one essential factor — which was rather the human capacity for adaptation of social institutions to the service of human wants.

In the eyes of the orthodox leaders of German Social Democracy, Bernstein's principal offence was that in denying that capitalist society was about to collapse and in doing so to present the proletariat with the occasion for the conquest of power, he was also in effect denying the primacy of the class-struggle, which was the very foundation of the entire programme of working-class action laid down by Marx and Engels in the *Communist Manifesto*. Marx had reconciled economic determinism with revolutionary activity — as against merely waiting for things to happen of themselves — by including the revolutionary activity of the working class as a part of the determined evolutionary process. He had said that the proletariat, by organising and planning aright in accordance with the historical trend, could 'shorten and soften' the birth-pangs of the new society. This implied that, although Socialism was bound to come, the manner and date of its coming were not determined apart from the skill and courage with which the proletarian party faced its tasks; but it was also left to be understood that no mistakes on its part could involve it in final failure. The proletariat was bound to win in the end; and its victory was bound to be that of a class achieving its own emancipation in an historic moment of social revolution. There was inconsistency in this doctrine; for if the rule of nature, including mankind, was that of strict necessity, must it not follow that every class, and indeed every person, was fully necessitated to act precisely as they did ? But the discrepancy was covered up by contending in one breath that what men, and still more what classes, did could affect the course of history, at any rate in secondary ways, and in the next that what classes, and what men in the mass, did was inexorably determined by the laws of social growth.

Bernstein was in the same dilemma ; but his way of escape from it was to discard determinism. 'Philosophic materialism, or the materialism of natural science, is deterministic in a mechanistic sense. The Marxist conception of history is not. It allots to the economic foundations of the life of nations no unconditional determining influence on the forms this life takes.'

In supporting this contention, Bernstein quoted from Marx, and still more from Engels, passages in which it was allowed that non-economic forces could exert an influence on the course of history, as well as passages which asserted that men could by their actions affect the manner and the pace of social adaptation. Such passages were easily found ; for it is indisputable that Marx did believe that 'man makes his own history', and Engels, in defending the materialist conception against its critics, went a long way in admitting the influence of non-economic factors, including ideas, and agreed that he and Marx had exaggerated and over-simplified in their earlier presentations of their theory. There was nothing unorthodox in Bernstein's reiteration of what Engels had said already : the unorthodoxy lay, not in the admittance of the non-economic factors to a place among real historical forces, but in the denial of the central doctrine of social determinism. It was legitimate within the Marxist school to admit ideas among the *secondary* forces, provided that it was left unquestioned that the *general* course of social evolution was determined by economic forces, working themselves out in the class-struggle. This, however, was precisely what Bernstein denied, though he paid homage to the economic factors as very important. He did not put his case very clearly : nor was he, probably, very clear what precisely he meant. But there was no doubt that he was challenging the entire notion of the inevitability of Socialism, even if he would not quite admit that he was doing so.

To whatever extent other forces besides the purely economic influence the life of society, so much the more does the rule of what we call, in an objective sense, historical necessity also change. In modern society we have to distinguish in this connection two great currents. On the one hand there appears an increasing insight into the laws of evolution and particularly of economic evolution. With this knowledge goes hand in hand — partly as its cause, and also partly as its effect — an increasing capacity to *direct* economic evolution. Natural economic force, like physical, changes from being man's master to being his servant as its nature is understood. In theory, society gains greater freedom than ever before in respect of economic change; and only the antagonism of interests among its elements — only the power of private and group elements — hinders the full transition from freedom in theory to freedom in practice. The common interest, however, increasingly gains in power as against private interest, and the elemental rule of economic forces is superseded to the extent that this is the case, and whenever it is the case. The development of these forces is anticipated, and is therefore all the more quickly and easily effected. Individuals and nations thus withdraw an ever greater part of their lives from the sway of a necessity that compels them, without or against their will.

This passage was a blow right at the heart of Marxism, not only because it denied the rule of necessity, but also because it invoked against it not the consciousness of the proletariat, but that of the 'common interest', implying the very conception of 'social solidarity' which Marx had so often denounced. Bernstein gave further offence when he went on to say

Modern society is much richer than earlier societies in ideologies which are not determined by economics and by nature operating as an economic force. Science, the arts, a whole series of social relations are nowadays much less dependent on economics than formerly they were; or let us say, in order to leave no room for misunderstanding, the point of economic development that has now been reached leaves the ideological, and especially the ethical, factors greater scope for independent activity than used to be the case. Consequently, the interdependence of cause and effect between technological, economic evolution and the evolution of other social tendencies is becoming continually more indirect; and accordingly the necessities of the former are losing much of their power to dictate the form of the latter.

This was rank heresy, though Bernstein professed still to accept a broadly 'economic', if not a 'materialist' conception of history. It was a reinstatement of ideologies and of ethics, and a denial of 'scientific' Socialism, or at any rate of its adequacy. This was the issue round which the battle raged mainly in its opening phases. But when Bernstein had produced his complete argument there were many other issues to be fought over. What he claimed to do was to distinguish the essential conceptions of Marxism from those which were only secondary and inessential, and to save the former by jettisoning many of the others. But how much was left when he had done ?

To begin with, Bernstein questioned the soundness of Marx's conception of surplus value. But it seems unnecessary to enter into this part of his argument beyond saying that the gist of his contention was that the notion was of no practical help because on Marx's own showing the rate of surplus value bore no constant relation to the high or low standard of wages of the workers whose exploitation it was supposed to measure. The whole conception was abstract : it was an intellectual construct not in any way verifiable from the facts of daily life. The worth of such constructs should be measured by their utility ; and Bernstein's verdict was that the theory of surplus value, as stated by Marx, was not needed in order to explain exploitation, did not in fact explain it, and served only to confuse the issue.

I say no more on this point because it did not in fact figure at all largely in the Revisionist controversy. It was swept aside in favour of other issues. Bernstein's next main point was a denial that the tendency towards capitalist concentration — which he admitted as existing — actually operated with anything like the rapidity or the force which Marx had attributed to it. He accused Marx, in stating what was true, of having ignored all the forces making the opposite way. In particular, he brought up against Marx the great diffusion of shareholding which had accompanied the rise of joint stock business. There were not fewer and fewer owners of capital : on the contrary there were more and more. Business concerns were no doubt getting bigger ; but the great businesses had many owners, most of whom held only a small capital interest. This meant that the middle class of small capitalists was not dying out even where the scale of enterprise was getting bigger : the middle class was only changing its form. The shareholder was replacing the small entrepreneur ; and the consequence was that there were more exploiters than ever. Moreover, big business was driving out small business only in some branches of enterprise, and not in all. There were many small businesses left, even in production ; and in commerce their number had greatly increased. Nor was it true that the land was passing into fewer hands ; on the contrary, though there were local exceptions, the general tendency in Europe was towards a multiplication of small peasant holdings. It followed that the middle classes were by no means being flung down into the ranks of the proletariat : indeed, account had to be taken of the advent of an ever-growing middle class of managers and supervisors attached to large-scale industry. It was significant, Bernstein said, that Marx had left unfinished the chapter of *Capital* in which he had started out to analyse the composition of classes.

Bernstein turned next to the statistics of income, which showed that the numbers of middle incomes had been increasing fast. He next enquired whether the workers were actually being plunged into a condition of 'increasing misery' and concluded that they were not. Who, if not they, consumed the vastly greater quantities of necessary goods that were admittedly being produced ?

On all these issues the orthodox Marxists challenged Bernstein's conclusions, and sometimes his statistics as well. But on the statistical facts there was really no denying the truth of what he said. Even Kautsky was driven in the end to modify what he had asserted about the decay of the peasants, though he continued to argue that they were bound to be reduced to 'increasing misery' by the growingly efficient competition of more highly capitalised farming. On the question of capitalist concentration in general, the orthodox were driven more and more to argue that, even if the *ownership* of capital was not getting into fewer hands, the *control* was, as the small shareholder had no control over the use made of his capital, and the small businesses were falling more and more under the domination of financial capital and of the great concerns which controlled the market. This, however, true though it largely was, did not meet Bernstein's main point, which was that the middle class was not being crushed out of existence, but rather rejuvenated in new forms, with the consequence that the class-struggle, instead of growing more acute, was being blurred by the rise of intermediate classes and groups.

As for the 'increasing misery' of the workers, some of Bernstein's critics tried to argue that the workers, despite all appearances, were getting poorer. Others, realising that this thesis could not be sustained at any rate for either Germany or Great Britain, fell back on the contention that they were being *relatively* impoverished, in the sense that their share in the total national product was falling, even if their consumption was rising to some extent. This, however, was at best very doubtful, as a generalisation ; and even if it were true, would *relatively* increasing misery, accompanied by an absolute rise in living standards, necessarily accentuate the class-war ? Yet others argued, more plausibly, that the workers' standards in the advanced countries were being maintained, or even improved, temporarily by the growing exploitation of colonial labour. Finally, this line of argument was often combined with another, in which it was asserted that advancing capitalism was passing into a period of more and more intense recurrent crises, aggravated by imperialist rivalries, and that these crises would soon usher in the period of 'increasing misery', even if it had not yet arrived.

Bernstein challenged this last view by an outright denial that capitalism showed any tendency to move rapidly towards a 'final crisis'. In the late 'nineties, when he was writing his book, men could look back on more than a decade during which there had been no capitalist crisis comparable in severity with those of earlier decades. After the boom of the late 'eighties there had been recessions, but not crises. The years of the 'Great Depression' (which had not then been whitewashed as it has been since) had been left behind. Production had been increasing fast ; and unemployment had not been nearly so bad, even in the years of recession, as it had been in the 'seventies and 'eighties. Trade had expanded : new areas were being opened up : there was no real sign that capitalism had reached the zenith of its expansion, and was in decline — certainly no ground for anticipating its speedy collapse. Accordingly, those who counselled postponing all constructive action till after the revolutionary crisis had brought the workers to power were in effect counselling a delay, not of a few years, but of indefinite and certainly long duration. This raised the question whether it was really advisable to wait. Might it not be better to consider what gains could be made, short of the overthrow of capitalism, and to go all out to secure the largest concessions that could be won within this limiting condition?

This, of course, was the heart of the matter practically; for Bernstein's argument demanded a fundamental change in the Social Democratic Party's practice, as well as in its theory. It involved not only a preparedness to recognise that good could come of the existing State, as an author of desirable social legislation, but also a change of attitude towards Trade Unionism and collective bargaining. The German Social Democrats had from the first been disposed to look on Trade Unions mainly as recruiting-grounds for Socialism and as aids to the development of working-class-consciousness, and to belittle the possible achievements of collective bargaining with capitalist employers backed by the power of the State. They had told the Trade Unionists that Trade Unionism could never be enough, because it would always have to face the combined economic and political power of the ruling classes — an alliance which could be broken only by the overthrow of the capitalist State. Bernstein was now questioning the inevitability of this alliance, and was urging the workers to use their power of collective action to secure protective legislation from the State, as well as to bargain with their employers for improved conditions. If he were right in arguing that the road to Socialism lay through piecemeal gains, rather than through revolution, his argument would hold good for gains made by Trade Unions, as well as through political action. The Trade Unions would thus be elevated to a status of equal partnership with the party, and would no longer be mere auxiliaries. This was by no means a pleasing notion to the orthodox leaders, who were inclined to suspect the Trade Unions of a desire to put their several sectional interests above those of the working class as a whole. The Trade Unions, in their view, stood for only some of the workers: the party was the embodiment of the class-mission of the entire proletariat.

German Trade Unionism had to a large extent shared in the

repression imposed on the Socialists after 1878. In the 1890s it was gaining ground rapidly, but was still not strong, and was weakened besides by the division into three contending movements — the 'Free' (in practice almost wholly Social Democratic), the Christian (mainly Catholic), and the Hirsch-Duncker (liberal). Of these, the Free' Unions were much the strongest ; but in 1898 they had only about 400,000 members ; the Christian Unions had about 100,000, and the Hirsch-Duncker a still smaller number. Two years later the 'Free' Unions had risen to 680,000, and the Christian Unions to about 150,000 : the 'liberal' Unions were declining. As we saw, the 'Free' Unions had formed a central body, the General Commission, in 1890, under Social Democratic leadership. There was a small group, influenced by contemporary Trade Union developments in France, which advocated 'syndicalist' policies of workers' control and direct action, and demanded independence of Social Democracy ; but it had little influence. The German working class was politically minded, rather than industrialist : except in the Catholic areas the urban workers were almost solidly Social Democratic. That, however, did not mean that they were prepared to defer their hopes of better conditions until after 'the revolution'. They looked to the Social Democratic Party to help them, not only in getting the remaining restrictions on the right of combination — mainly in respect of federal, inter-union activities — removed, but also by backing their demands for labour legislation, including the recognition of collective bargaining rights and the enforcement of arbitration in industrial disputes. In practice, the Social Democrats had to include such measures in their immediate programme, though they continued to tell the Trade Unions that nothing much could be accomplished without the conquest of political power.

From the rejection of the notion of an impending 'final crisis' of capitalism, Bernstein passed on to a consideration of the reasons why a severe crisis was unlikely in the near future. The International Socialist Congress of 1896 had passed a resolution urging the workers in all countries, in view of the probable nearness of such a crisis, to make themselves masters of the techniques required for the successful exercise of governmental power. Bernstein took the Congress to task for its utopianism. Engels, he pointed out, had said that the repeated enlargements of the market through the economic development of new countries had eased the situation of capitalism for the time being, though he had also insisted that in the long run the effect would be to make crises more severe. Bernstein agreed with the first of these points, but held the second to be unproven. At all events, there was no sign, he considered, that the expansionist phase was near its end.

This was one of the main points on which Rosa Luxemburg took the field against him, stressing the huge advances made by finance capital as leading to intense imperialistic rivalries and conflicts, accompanied by increasing exploitation of cheap colonial labour and by its use to beat down labour standards in the more advanced countries. Rosa Luxemburg's argument put emphasis on the likelihood of economic rivalries leading to war, and on the opportunities for revolutionary action that would be presented by the strains imposed by war on the governing classes of the capitalist countries. This was a line of argument somewhat different from the traditional Marxist argument concerning the inherent tendency of capitalism to breed crises through a multiplication of capital instruments beyond those whose products the available markets could absorb. It was indeed far from clear what Marx's doctrine concerning crises had really been. In the then recently published third volume of *Capital* he had stated that the final cause of crises was the inability of the consumers to buy the growing product — an 'under-consumptionist' doctrine. But Engels had repeatedly denied that Marx was an 'under-consumptionist': that, he had said, was the doctrine of Sismondi and of Rodbertus rather than of Marx. In the second volume of *Capital* Marx had repudiated the 'under-consumptionist' theory, pointing out that 'crises are always preceded by a period during which wages rise and the workers actually receive a greater share than is usual of the annual produce destined for consumption' — which appeared to indicate that raising wages — even real wages — was no way of averting a crisis. He had moreover formulated in this volume a theory which related the occurrence of crises to the period of turnover of fixed capital equipment. The passage about under-consumption in the third volume had actually been written at an earlier date than the second volume,

though it appeared in print later. Bernstein agreed with
Engels that Marx had not attributed crises to 'under-consumption', save in the special sense that the low consumption of the
masses caused a struggle between rival capitalist groups to
increase their control of the limited market. But, whereas
Marx and Engels had both held that crises, whatever their
cause, were destined to grow more intense, Bernstein, as we
have seen, regarded this as unproven, and as resting on *mystique*
rather than on scientific diagnosis.

Indeed, it was an essential part of Bernstein's argument
that a good deal of Marx's doctrine was not scientific at all, in
the sense of being based on a study of facts, but was part of a
vast theoretical construction into which the facts were subsequently fitted — or, where they could not be fitted, ignored.
He was, I think, unconscious how fatal such an admission must
be to the entire structure of Marxism, of which he professed
himself as still accepting the fundamental part.

In the third chapter of his book, Bernstein went on to
attack the idea that the workers, even if they were able to seize
power, would be capable as yet of exercising it effectively. It
was part of the orthodox Social Democratic view that the
centralisation and trustification of industry were preparing the
way for Socialism by creating economic institutions which the
victorious workers could easily take over and administer in
the common interest. Bernstein did not question this ; but he
pointed out how enormous still was the number of separate
businesses which it would be necessary to take over and administer, and he ridiculed the notion that this could be done all
at once, on the morrow of a successful revolutionary *coup*. It
was, he said, obvious that, even if the workers did achieve
political power, the vast majority of these enterprises would
have to be left for the time being in the hands of the persons
who knew how to conduct them, and that their transfer to
public ownership and administration would be bound to be a
long and gradual process. This led him to a consideration of
the possibilities of Co-operative enterprise, as an alternative to
State operation ; and he came down strongly on the side of
consumers' Co-operation and against the forms of producers'
Co-operation which had traditionally found greater favour
among Socialists. He cited with approval Beatrice Webb's

book — *The Co-operative Movement* — in which she had treated producers' Co-operation as a demonstrated failure and had emphasised the large success achieved by consumers' Co-operation on the Rochdale model. Following Beatrice Webb, Bernstein lauded consumers' Co-operation as a truly democratic solution of the problem of 'production for use', and decried producers' Co-operatives as examples of group profit-seeking — and unsuccessful examples at that. Bernstein wanted the party to give serious support to the German consumers' movement, which was still in its infancy, and to recognise it as providing an alternative form of social ownership and control. But he did not suggest that this would solve the problem of controlling industry after a sudden assumption of political power. That problem he regarded as insoluble ; and accordingly he dismissed the whole idea, advancing in its place that of a gradual development of democratic capacity for the exercise of power through Trade Unions and consumers' Co-operative Societies, as well as through the experience of political activity both at the municipal and regional and at the State levels.

In this part of his book Bernstein, still following Beatrice Webb, dismissed the idea of workers' self-government in industry. 'It is simply impossible', he wrote 'that the manager should be the employee of those whom he manages, that he should depend for his position on their favour or their ill-temper. It has always proved impossible to maintain this arrangement, and it has always led to a change in the form of the associative factory.' He added that, the larger an undertaking was, the less was the desire of the workers to take part in managing it. His conclusion was that State, regional and municipal administration should be extended, and that they should be supplemented by consumers' Co-operatives. But he said that such Co-operatives could not be created artificially to fill a gap : they must be left to grow spontaneously. 'What the community itself cannot take in hand, whether by the State, or the region or the municipality, it would do far best, especially in stormy times, to let alone.' Thus Bernstein argued in favour of leaving a large part of business enterprise in private hands, until some agency representing the collectivity was in a position to manage it effectively and could achieve some real advantage by acquiring it. He was advocating, at any rate for a long period to come, what is now called a 'mixed economy'.

Bernstein proceeded next, in his book, to a discussion of the relation between Socialism and democracy. He attacked the notion of the 'dictatorship of the proletariat' as inconsistent with democratic principle. Democracy, in his view, connoted the idea of equal justice for all. It accordingly involved limitations on the right of the majority to ride rough-shod over the minority. Even if the proletariat constituted the majority of the people, that would not give it a right to disregard the rule of justice. Democracy meant the suppression of class-government, not the substitution of one form of it for another. 'Social Democracy cannot do better than take its stand unreservedly on the theory of democracy — of universal suffrage, with all the consequences to its tactics which follow.' In practice, this was what Social Democracy had done, demanding not only universal suffrage but also proportional representation and the right of direct legislation by popular vote. Such demands were wholly inconsistent with 'dictatorship': so what sense was there in clinging to the outmoded phrases? Having thus discarded yet another dogma of Marxism, Bernstein rounded off his argument by recommending Socialists to moderate their attacks on 'liberalism'. It was true, he said, that modern liberalism had arisen for the advantage of the capitalist bourgeoisie, and that the Liberal Parties had become simply 'guardians of capitalism'.

> But in relation to liberalism as a great historical movement, Socialism is its legitimate heir, not only in sequence of time, but also in its qualities of spirit, as is shown in every matter of principle on which Social Democracy has had to take up an attitude.

Bernstein went on to declare, 'I consider the middle class, not excepting the German, to be in the main fairly healthy, not only economically, but also morally'. This was the prelude to a section dealing with the dangers of bureaucracy and the need for decentralised administration within the general framework of nationally unified planning. Bernstein quoted not only Marx's *Civil War in France* but also Proudhon in favour of a federal structure of society, and extolled the virtues of municipalisation. He spoke of the task of Socialism as that of 'organising liberalism', and added that 'if democracy is not to exceed centralised absolutism in the breeding of bureaucracies, it must be built up on an elaborately organised self-government with a corresponding economic, personal responsibility of all the units of administration as well as of the adult citizens'.

The practical upshot of this defence of liberalism was that Socialists ought to set out, not to destroy the whole structure of capitalist society, but rather to amend it.

> Feudalism, with its inflexible organisations and corporations, had to be destroyed almost everywhere by violence. The liberal organisations of modern society are distinguished from those of feudalism precisely in being flexible, and capable of change and development. They need, not to be destroyed, but only to be further developed. For this we need organisation and energetic action, but not necessarily a revolutionary dictatorship.

Bernstein then quoted similar sentiments from Pablo Iglesias, the Spanish Socialist leader, and from *The Labour Leader* and *The Clarion*, as representing the British Socialist standpoint. 'Democracy', he went on to say, 'is a condition of Socialism to a much greater extent than is commonly assumed : it is not only the means, but the substance also'.

There was yet more to come in criticism of Marx's doctrine. In his next section Bernstein quoted from the *Communist Manifesto* the statement that 'the workers have no country' and commented as follows :

> This sentence might perhaps to some extent apply to the worker of the 1840s, without political rights, excluded from political life. Nowadays, in spite of the very great increase in international intercourse, it has already lost a large part of its truth ; and it will continue to lose more and more as the worker, through the influence of Socialism, moves from being a proletarian to being a citizen. The worker who has equal rights as a voter in state and local elections and is thereby a co-owner of the common property of the nation, whose children the community educates, whose health it protects, whom it secures against injury, has a fatherland without ceasing on that account to be a citizen of the world, just as the nations draw closer together without ceasing to live lives of their own.

This passage was the prelude to the contention that German Socialists could no longer be indifferent to the fortunes of their country, or refuse to take any responsibility for its defence.

> As little as it is to be desired that any other of the great civilised nations should lose its independence, so little can it be a matter of indifference to German Social Democracy whether the German nation, which has performed, and is performing, its honourable part in the work of civilising the world, should be kept down in the councils of the nations.

This passage naturally exposed Bernstein to the charge of chauvinism. He answered that, the larger the German army became, the more it had to be made up of workers, and the less able would the Government be to use it for offensive war upon other nations.

> But Social Democracy is not called upon to speak in favour of renunciation of the safeguarding of German interests, present or future, if or because English, French or Russian chauvinists take umbrage at the measures adopted. . . . I consider it a legitimate task of German imperial politics to secure the right to have a voice in the discussion of such cases [international issues affecting the balance of power]; and to oppose, on principle, steps requisite for that purpose falls, I hold, outside the sphere of Social Democracy's tasks.

These were dangerous words ; and Bernstein went on to aggravate their meaning by relating them specifically to German colonial policy. He defended the acquisition by lease of Kiaochow Bay in China and in effect came forward as a supporter of colonial expansion.

> The assumption that colonial expansion will hinder the achievement of Socialism rests at bottom on the utterly outmoded notion that this achievement depends on the steady narrowing of the circle of the wealthy and on the increasing misery of the poor.

He denied that colonial expansion could be used to protect capitalism against crises, or that it would have adverse effects on political conditions in Germany. He admitted that 'naval chauvinism' had some connection with colonial policy, but asserted that it had existed before colonialism came to the fore.

> There is some justification, when colonies are being acquired, for careful examination of their value and prospects,

and for controlling the settlement and treatment of the natives as well as other matters of administration ; but that does not amount to a reason for considering such acquisition, *a priori*, as something reprehensible.

For the present, indeed, Bernstein denied that Germany needed colonies ; but he said it was also necessary to consider the future, when it might become desirable for Germany to derive some of its imported products from its own colonies. He denied that the occupation of tropical countries by Europeans had usually harmed the natives, and said roundly that 'only a conditional right of savages to the land they occupy can be recognised. The higher civilisation can in the last resort claim a higher right. Not the conquest, but the cultivation of the land gives the historical legal title to its use.' [1] He even quoted Marx in support of this view, taking the citation from the third volume of *Capital*, as follows :

> Even a whole society, a nation, nay all contemporary societies taken as a whole, are not owners of the earth. They are only tenants, usufructuaries, and must leave it improved as *boni patres familias* for succeeding generations.

This part of Bernstein's book, more than any other, made certain the rejection of his entire programme by the Social Democratic Party. He had supporters, even for his defence of German national rights and colonial policy. But his nationalist doctrine offended against the deeply rooted Social Democratic tradition of hostility to the militaristic character of the Reich. It awakened memories of Marx's charges against the Lassallians of being the abettors of Bismarck and the Junkers. Of course, in truth Bernstein had no intention of supporting German militarism : far from being disposed to take sides with the Junkers against the bourgeoisie, he was exceedingly well-disposed to the latter and a great hater of militaristic swagger and authority. He had, however, a belief in the civilising mission of the German people which he sublimated into an acceptance of the right of the 'great civilised nations' to extend their culture, even by compelling the 'lesser breeds' to develop their territories under the rule of the more advanced. It must be said in extenuation of his attitude that he was writing before

[1] This was, of course, Bernard Shaw's argument. See pp. 190 ff.

nationalism had made much impact on the less developed peoples and while the partition of Africa by Great Britain, France, and other colonising powers — to the exclusion of Germany — was still in full swing. As we have seen, Bernard Shaw in Great Britain took a line against the Boer Republics not greatly different from Bernstein's argument that a people had no right to its land unless it made proper use of it for production. Nevertheless, Bernstein's defence of colonial annexations and of Germany's right to assert by armed strength its place in the councils of Europe offended against a deep anti-imperialist sentiment in the German Social Democratic Party of the 1890s. The Social Democrats had but recently emerged from their long period of persecution and suppression by the imperial Government. Even if they had strong nationalist feelings, they were not yet prepared to allow these feelings to carry them over into identifying the German people with the Bismarckian German Empire.

Bernstein went too far for his views on these matters to stand any chance of being accepted by the party at the time when he put them forward. His own later record showed that he was in truth no chauvinist and that he had not abandoned his internationalism in accepting a part of the nationalist outlook. Nor was what he was saying so very different, in certain respects, from what was being said by more orthodox Marxists. German Social Democracy was animated, as Marx had been before it, by an intense feeling of danger from Russia. Its leaders regarded Czarism as an infinitely worse form of government that even Prussian imperialism, and the Russians as a barbarous eastern people threatening Western civilisation, of which Eastern Germany (from which Bernstein came) was the frontier-guardian and outpost. August Bebel himself had declared that it would be right for German Socialists to rally to the defence of the fatherland against a Russian attack ; and the guilty conscience which many German Socialists had over the annexation of Alsace-Lorraine aggravated their fears of Franco-Russian alliance. This fear of Russia lay behind the unwillingness of many Social Democrats to maintain the policy of voting steadily in the Reichstag against the military estimates. Bernstein put his case in a form which made its rejection certain ; but there were many among his opponents who sympathised with a good deal of it, though they were not prepared to draw the theoretical conclusions with which he had bound it up.

In the final chapter Bernstein gave further offence to the orthodox by appealing from Hegel to Kant and by invoking the memory of the moderate Socialist, Friedrich Albert Lange (1828–75) as a progenitor of Social Democracy. In Lange he found 'the distinctive union of an upright and intrepid championship of the struggles of the working class for emancipation with a large scientific freedom from prejudice which made him always ready to acknowledge mistakes and to recognise new truths'. He agreed that 'perhaps so great a broadmindedness as we meet with in Lange's writings is to be found only in persons who are lacking in the penetrating acuteness that is the mark of pioneer spirits such as Marx'. But he accused Marx of being at bottom unscientific as well as dogmatic.

> He [Marx] erected a mighty structure within the framework of a scaffolding which he found already in existence ; and in its construction he kept strictly to the laws of scientific architecture as long as they did not collide with the conditions which the shape of the scaffolding prescribed, but he neglected or evaded them when the scaffolding did not allow them to be observed. When the scaffolding put limits in the way of the building, instead of pulling down the scaffolding, he altered the building at the cost of correct proportions and so made it depend all the more on the scaffolding. Was it the awareness of this irrational relation that caused him again and again to turn aside from finishing his work to amending particular parts of it ?

This is acute criticism of the Marxist system, with its Ricardian and Hegelian framework. Bernstein termed the Hegelian dialectic 'cant', and appealed against it to Immanuel Kant (the pun is his own). 'Social Democracy', he said, 'needed a Kant who would judge the received opinion and examine it critically with the utmost acuteness, who would show where its apparent materialism was the highest — and therefore the most easily misleading — ideology, and would warn it that contempt of the ideal, magnifying of material factors until they became omnipotent evolutionary forces, is self-deception, which has been and will continue to be exposed as such on every occasion by the actions of those who proclaim it'. He appealed to Social Democracy to emancipate itself from outworn shibboleths and 'to make up its mind to appear what it in fact now is — a democratic, socialistic party of reform'.

Bernstein thus enrolled himself among the Neo-Kantians, against whom Lenin among others was later to launch so furious assaults. And he had thrown over the revolutionary conception of Socialism with dramatic completeness.

> As soon as a nation has reached a position in which the rights of the propertied minority have ceased to be a serious obstacle to social progress and in which the negative tasks of political action are less pressing than the positive, appeal to revolutionary force becomes meaningless talk.

To this sentence Bernstein attached a footnote, in which he cited the British Independent Labour Party as saying, in its monthly *News*, 'Fortunately, "revolution" in this country has ceased to be anything more than an affected phrase' (January 1899). But it was startling to German Social Democrats to be told that in their country 'the right of the propertied minority' 'was no longer a serious obstacle to social progress'. Moreover, it was certainly untrue.

Such, then, was the substance of the 'Revisionist' case which Bernstein presented to the German Social Democratic Party. He can hardly have expected that it would be accepted as a whole, or even in its main outlines, at any Congress of the party. It raised far too many issues, involved the abandonment of far too many cherished dogmas, and handled the 'Master' far too roughly not to give deep offence. In the event, the party, after immense and often acrimonious argument, decided to say nothing as a party on the questions Bernstein had raised, and to confine itself to passing a mild censure on him for the manner in which he had pressed his case. It was made clear that this censure did not mean exclusion from the party, or even the banning of further discussion on any of the questions which had been raised. Bebel, who moved the official resolution, was very definite that Bernstein, despite all his heresies, was not regarded as a 'bad comrade' or a renegade. That this was so showed the leaders' awareness of the extent of support within the party, not so much for Revisionism as a whole, as for many of Bernstein's criticisms of Marxist orthodoxy. In effect, the

Congress voted Revisionism down, but did not vote it out ; and thereafter the party as a whole moved steadily and rapidly in the direction in which Bernstein had wished it to move. Wilhelm Liebknecht died in 1900, well before the final vote on Revisionism had been cast at the Lübeck Congress of the following year. New party leaders, most of them less devoted to the Marxist tradition than their forerunners, were coming into prominence. Kautsky's theoretical influence was declining. Rosa Luxemburg, the big new force on the left of the party, was in a minority among the younger generation. Revisionism failed to alter the official dogma ; but it had an increasing influence on the party's mode of action and on the practical thinking of those who directed it.

CHAPTER VI

GERMANY AFTER THE REVISIONIST CONTROVERSY: APPEARANCE AND REALITY

THE German Social Democratic Party, during the period between the defeat of the Revisionists and the outbreak of the first world war, occupied a curious position of uncompromising independence in theory combined with an increasing tendency towards timidity in practice. It was indeed to a great extent the victim of its own success. It had succeeded in building up a very strong body of electoral support as the leading antagonist of the autocratic, militarist régime which still dominated the affairs of the German Reich ; and it cherished the hope that steady persistence in its propagandist and organising activities would in due course bring it the backing of a clear majority of the electorate and would even enable it, despite the unfavourable distribution of seats, which favoured the rural areas, to elect a clear majority to the Reichstag. It was not under the illusion that the mere winning of such a majority would automatically give it the control of the State ; but it did believe that the Kaiser and his ministers would find it impracticable to govern against the Reichstag, and that, given this point of vantage, it would be in a position to enforce a great transformation in the entire system of government, whether or not it were forced to make use of unconstitutional means in bringing the change about. This caused it to postpone the possible need for acting unconstitutionally until after it had won over a majority of the people and got the authority of the Reichstag into its hands. Moreover, it was clear that this could not be achieved without the support, not only of the great majority of the industrial workers, but also of other elements drawn from the countryside and from the small trading and professional classes ; and the Party was accordingly very anxious not to antagonise such possible backers and to appear simultaneously as a revolutionary Socialist Party and as a reforming party which was essentially moderate in its immediate political objectives.

In the political situation which existed in Germany up to 1914, the Kaiser's Government was far from commanding an assured majority in the Reichstag. It had to get its laws through and its budgets voted with the support of a succession of parliamentary coalitions among the anti-Socialist parties, from the Conservatives to the Radical Progressives and to the predominantly Catholic Centre Party. The Radicals, who united in 1910 under Friedrich Naumann to form a Progressive Party, were usually, but not quite always, in opposition; the Centre Party was sometimes in the coalition and sometimes outside it; the Liberals usually, and the Conservatives always, were on the Government side. There were moments when the Social Democrats, by allying themselves not only with the Progressives but also with either the Liberals or the Centre, could have put the Government in a minority, and perhaps have induced the majority to vote for social reforms which were on their programmes but were unobtainable without the support of other parties, and even to press for electoral and structural reforms that would have gone some way towards democratising the State machine. The bourgeois parties all wanted in varying degrees a liberalisation of the State system, especially by the establishment of constitutional government with Ministers responsible to the Reichstag instead of to the Crown; and the Liberals and Progressives also favoured some measure of redistribution of seats in order to reduce the influence of the landed interests. But the Social Democratic Party held firmly to the view, not only that it must not co-operate in the Reichstag with any other party, but also that it must never vote for the budget of any non-Socialist Ministry, even when the purposes for which the money was wanted were such as it approved or the methods proposed for raising it such as to put the burden on the wealthier classes. It was laid down as a matter of principle that the Social Democrats, being opposed to the existing system and to the State which stood for its maintenance, must refuse to take any action that would sustain the Government upholding such a régime.

This attitude made sense on the assumption that the Social Democratic Party was already well on the way to winning an independent majority in the Reichstag and would before long be in a position to prevent the continued functioning of the existing régime. There was a strong case for refusing to make alliances with any other party if it could be reckoned on that the refusal would hasten the withering away of the middle parties and would put the reactionaries, even when they had been driven to combine against the Socialists, into a minority unable to carry on the Government. But there were many in the Social Democratic ranks who doubted this diagnosis of electoral prospects; and there were others who argued that, if such a situation ever looked like arising, the Kaiser and his reactionary supporters would not scruple to alter the conditions of election to the Socialists' disadvantage, or even to resort to a military *coup d'état* in order to prevent them from taking political power. There were accordingly partisans of co-operation with the bourgeois parties in order to win a more liberal constitution, on the ground either that, under the existing constitution, a majority was not to be had without their aid, or that it would be much more difficult for the militarists and reactionaries to stage a *coup d'état* against an alliance of bourgeois and Socialists than against the Socialists alone.

The whole position was greatly complicated by the big differences, within the Reich, between the constitution of Prussia and those of some of the lesser German Laender. In Prussia, the class system of voting made it utterly out of the question for the Socialists to win a majority, or even any effective representation at all, in the Landtag; whereas in some other Laender the electoral system was similar to that of the Reich, and in some of them it often depended on what line the Socialists followed whether right-wing or progressive bourgeois Governments should hold the power. This latter situation existed particularly in Bavaria and in Baden; and in these Laender and in some others the Social Democrats had long been resistant to the intransigent line of the Party as a whole. We saw in an earlier chapter [1] how the Bavarians, under Vollmar's leadership, fell into dispute over this issue well before Bernstein launched his Revisionist campaign, and how they supported Revisionism because it fitted in with their desire to enter into

[1] See p. 273.

electoral and parliamentary arrangements with the parties representing mainly the peasants. Revisionism, as a primarily theoretical doctrine, must not be identified with Reformism arising out of considerations of political expediency : nevertheless, it is a plain fact that Bernstein's main support came either from the Reformists who wanted to be free to enter into political alliances or from the moderate wing in the Trade Unions.

In the Reichstag, at any rate after the big electoral victory of 1912, the Social Democrats, had they wished, could have been the largest party in an alliance against the system of irresponsible government. In Bavaria, on the other hand, the Catholics were too strongly entrenched for the Socialists to be able to hold the dominant position ; and, in general, the bourgeois Liberals and Radicals were a good deal stronger in other Land legislatures than in the Reichstag : so that coalitions would have needed to be made on fairly equal terms. Of course, in the Laender except Prussia and Saxony, though powers and functions were limited, some degree of responsible government did exist ; and coalitions, had they agreed on common programmes within these limits, would have been in a position to carry them out, whether the Socialists were in the Government, or only giving it their support. In effect, Social Democrats, in some such cases, did support, though not join, progressive Land Governments and did secure, through them, a certain amount of progressive legislation. But even such support was frowned upon by the national leadership, on the grounds that it comprised the Social Democratic Party's independence and postponed the winning of the hoped-for Socialist majority.

Thus the paradoxical situation developed that, the more the Social Democratic Party insisted on its revolutionary objective and on the need for complete independence in order to conquer the State machine, the more moderate it had to be in practice in order to win over bourgeois and peasant voters from the other parties. It had to soft-pedal, for electoral purposes, not only its social programme, but also its antagonism to the Catholic Church, and to appear as the leader of the people in the struggle against autocratic government and aristocratic militarism even more than as the champion of the proletariat or of Socialism. In practice, it could not escape the necessity of supporting measures of social reform which a majority of its adherents, especially in the Trade Unions, desired. But it had at one and the same time to join with the Centre Party and the Progressives in speaking in favour of such measures, and to vote against them because an affirmative vote would have meant a vote for the existing régime. This applies particularly to Reich politics, as against the politics of the separate Laender. But, even in the Laender, the central policy of the party was one of opposing the final stages of measures which it approved, in order to avoid commitment to the existing system.

One great continuing weakness of the German Social Democrats was their failure to arrive at any agreed agrarian programme. One reason for this failure lay in the immense difference between the conditions of land-tenure and rural employment in different parts of Germany. Western and Southern Germany were, broadly speaking, areas of peasant cultivation on small farms, with a proportion of well-to-do peasants ; whereas Eastern Germany was, again broadly speaking, an area of great feudal estates, with a large and much oppressed population of landless agricultural labourers working under very bad conditions. The dividing line was the Elbe. In the peasant areas the Social Democrats had to decide whether to try to come to terms with the peasant cultivators and their political representatives, or to oppose them in the expectation that they would gradually die out as a class because of their inability to compete with the products of large-scale agriculture and, more especially, with the imports from the prairie farms of the New World. This, of course, raised the issue of agricultural protection, which was supported by the landowning classes, but opposed by most of the Socialists both because it raised living costs and because it strengthened the feudal elements in German society. A few Socialists nevertheless went over to it ; but many more, especially in the south, favoured public help to the peasants through the provision of cheap credit and the lowering of rent and tax burdens. Against this view the orthodox Marxists objected that such help would benefit chiefly the wealthier peasants, who would be best able to take advantage of it, and also that it would perpetuate an obsolete system of small-scale cultivation, which ought to be superseded by the application of capitalist methods. This became an issue first between Vollmar's Bavaria and the

Northerners and then between Bernstein and Kautsky. As we saw,[1] in 1894, the party Congress had adopted the outline of an agrarian programme which favoured the peasants, but offered nothing to the landless labourers of Eastern Germany; but this programme, elaborated by a special committee, had been rejected at the following Congress. Thereafter, the Party appointed a long succession of committees to draw up an agrarian programme; but no agreement was reached, and a decision was again and again postponed. The orthodox Marxists stressed the importance of appealing to the rural wage-labourers, rather than to the peasants; but neither in the peasant nor in the feudal parts of the country did they actually succeed in building up any substantial organisation among them. They were an urban-minded party, except in parts of the South; and, in face of all the evidence to the contrary, most of them clung to the dogma that the small-scale cultivator was economically doomed, and was only being kept alive by the governing classes and the Churches as a bulwark against Socialism.

In general, except in their agitation for electoral reform in Prussia, the Social Democratic Party was careful to avoid any action that might involve it in a direct conflict with the police or the courts of law. The more revolutionary it was in theory, the more moderate it felt itself forced to be in practice. Somewhere ahead of it loomed a new kind of State and a new social system that was to be brought into being when it had 'conquered political power' by winning a majority in the Reichstag and compelling the Kaiser and the reactionaries to give way. Until this victory had been won, the Socialists were still confronted with a State power hostile to them and recognising no responsibility to the people; and because this was the character of the existing State it was regarded as wrong and dangerous to do anything that would increase its power. Nationalisation could not be advocated because it would mean handing over yet more power to the existing State: the Socialists opposed nationalisation of the Reichsbank on this ground. They were not precluded from advocating industrial and social legislation to safeguard the workers' interests; but even the case for this had to be argued by showing that it would not add to the power of the enemy State. The Social Democratic Party, largely under

[1] See p. 285.

Trade Union pressure, in fact put more and more emphasis on social legislation; but it could not advance from this to any programme of constructive socialisation in advance of the conquest of the public power. All its Socialist eggs were in the electoral basket; and this meant trying to rally behind it the largest possible volume of electoral support. It had to win the middle groups over to voting for Socialists; and this meant in practice even more dilution of its doctrine than if it had been prepared to enter into temporary alliance with the left-wing bourgeoisie.

It was a further complication that liberalism, except in South Germany, was so feeble and wanting in independence. The National Liberals, as distinct from the Progressives, were essentially the party of large-scale capitalism — of bankers, merchants, and industrialists — and these classes were reaping immense economic advantages from the rapid industrial development of the German Reich. Accordingly, though they wished to modify the autocratic structure and especially to decrease the influence of the landowning interests which supported agricultural protection, they were in no mind to take strong action against the régime, and on the whole were behind it in its aggressive imperialist policies. A strong Germany, with the Reich Government favouring the expansion of trade and industry and the development of colonialism, served their interests; and they were prepared to back Prussian militarism in its external policies even while they criticised the constitutional structure. Consequently, there was no liberal-capitalist movement capable of playing the part on behalf of parliamentary government that liberalism played in other economically advanced countries; and the Social Democrats found themselves having to take the place of the Liberals as the principal advocates of liberal democracy, and to attempt to combine this rôle with their mission of establishing a Socialist society. This, in practice, meant uttering Socialist slogans, but subordinating Socialist policies to agitation for liberal reforms.

Above all, the policy of Socialism after the constitutional revolution of 1871 meant that the party must at all costs be held together and wielded as a completely unified electoral and propagandist machine. Dissensions leading to splits would have destroyed all prospect of the hoped-for Reichstag majority;

and accordingly there had to be a united front and a centralised party discipline. This discipline, however, could never be taken to the point of expelling any considerable section of the party; for, had that been done, rival Socialist parties might have arisen, as they had in other countries. Therefore, in practice, dissentients had to be allowed a great deal of rope, even if their dissent was on fundamental issues. Bernstein could not be expelled; Vollmar and his Bavarians, and later Ludwig Frank and his Baden followers, had to be kept in the party and allowed to interpret its decisions with a large amount of latitude; and so, on the left, had Rosa Luxemburg and Karl Liebknecht to be barely tolerated, lest they should become the point of focus for a more revolutionary and internationalist party. Over and above this, the national feeling for unity was exceedingly strong, and the fact that the rebels against the established policy were largely concentrated in certain regions — notably South Germany — was an additional reason against allowing them to break away, so as to endanger the unity of Socialism as an expression of the unity of the nation.

The German Social Democratic Party prided itself on being internationalist, and on waging war on militarist imperialism in Germany as well as elsewhere. In this, its outstanding leaders, except a few, were not insincere; but most of them failed to realise how very nationalist they also were. Their nationalism, as far as it was directed outside Germany's frontiers, was indeed mainly anti-Russian, though it had also a considerable element of hostility to British imperialism, which barred Germany's way in so many areas. It rested most of all on the fear of Czarist Russia as a barbarous power threatening the eastern frontiers of the Reich and contending with German ambitions in South-Eastern Europe; and Russia was regarded as no less dangerous as an ally than as an enemy, because it could be the ally only of the most objectionable elements in the Reich — of Prussian reactionism against the more liberal forces of the West. When the question of national defence was posed in German Socialist debates, it was always defence against Russia that was uppermost in the minds of the debaters. The one occasion on which the German Social Democrats moved abruptly leftwards in their international attitude — even to the extent of voting, in principle, in favour of the general strike — was when they had been stirred by the news of the Russian Revolution of 1905 ; and when that Revolution failed, they reverted promptly to their previous attitude.

In general, the German Social Democratic Party, despite its reiterated affirmations of belief in a coming revolution, was a stickler for constitutional action. It was constantly afraid of having its remarkable electoral progress interrupted by a renewal of the legal repression to which Bismarck had resorted against it. Even after the Anti-Socialist Laws had been allowed to lapse, the German Socialists had to submit to continual supervision of their meetings by the Prussian police, who could stop a meeting at any moment if they considered that seditious or subversive sentiments were being expressed. There was also a repressive press law which bore hard on Socialist editors and journalists ; and it was always doubtful where the borderlines of legality lay. To some extent the Socialists defied the authorities ; but they were kept continually looking over their shoulders at them, and this undoubtedly influenced their conduct. Indeed, the more the party built up its organisation and became the possessor of printing presses, clubrooms and offices, and other valuable property, the more the fear of falling foul of the law weighed upon it. These fears haunted the Trade Union leaders even more than the politicians, as the Unions accumulated funds and developed extensive benefit services ; and as the Trade Unions grew stronger and wealthier, their influence on the party increased, and was thrown more on the side of a scrupulous observance of legality.

With this fear of suppression or legal persecution went the fear of having the electoral system changed to their disadvantage. In Prussia, of course, the situation was quite different as between Reichstag and Landtag affairs. In Reichstag elections there was the same need as in other parts of Germany to woo the marginal voters, and a better prospect of winning their support on account of the exceedingly reactionary character of the whole Prussian system. Progressive Liberalism was weak in Prussia ; and the Social Democrats were the head and forefront of the opposition to an even greater extent than in the rest of the country. But in Landtag politics the Prussian Constitution allowed the Social Democrats no chance of appreciable electoral successes even if they allied themselves with

non-Socialist groups. Not until 1906 did they succeed in electing
any members at all to the Prussian Landtag. Then there were
three, with the aid of bourgeois voters; but this small group
could do nothing in face of the immense preponderance of the
reactionary parties. Accordingly, Socialist politics in Prussia
turned almost exclusively on the demand for constitutional
reform. In 1906 an Act was passed increasing the size of the
Diet and making certain very minor reforms in the system of
election by redistributing seats; but Radical amendments
proposing manhood suffrage and the ballot were rejected by large
majorities. In 1908 the Radicals in the Diet again moved for
franchise reform, but were met by von Bülow with a sharp
refusal, and were again voted down. The Social Democrats
resorted to an extensive campaign of street demonstrations,
which led to serious clashes with the police. Such was the
state of feeling that, despite the obstacles put in their way by
the narrow franchise and the class-system of voting, seven
Social Democrats were elected with the support of Radical
voters antagonised by the Government's attitude. The reform
resolution was reintroduced into the Diet in 1909, again to the
accompaniment of great demonstrations and disturbances; and
it was again thrown out by the dominant parties. Four of the
seven Social Democrats were unseated on technical grounds
only to be re-elected; and the disturbances spread from Berlin
to other Prussian towns. In 1910 the Kaiser, under this
pressure, announced that the franchise would be reformed; but
when the Government produced its proposals it was seen that
no real change was meant. The class-system of voting was to
remain, voting was still to be open. The only amendments
were the substitution of direct for indirect voting in certain
cases and an increased representation of the professional classes
at the expense, not of the landowners, but of the wealthy
bourgeoisie. The announcement of this plan caused a renewal
of the demonstrations on a bigger scale than ever. Finally,
the Government got the Bill passed by the votes of the Conservatives and the Centre Party after it had conceded vote by
ballot to the Centre, but withdrawn its direct voting proposals
on the demand of the Conservatives. Although the agitation
continued, no further change in the Prussian Constitution had
been secured when war broke out in 1914.

In other Laender the position was better; but in Saxony, which was a Socialist stronghold, the reactionary electoral law of 1896 remained in force to remind the Social Democrats that the forces of reaction had then successfully countered the advance of their party by altering the electoral law and re-instating a system of class-voting which gave them no chance of reproducing in the Landtag their immense success in the elections for the Reich Parliament. What had been done in Saxony, the Socialists feared, might be repeated elsewhere. The best safeguard their leaders could see was to make their party as numerically strong as possible under the existing constitutional arrangements, except where these were such as to allow them no scope.

In Prussia and Saxony, as far as the Landtag elections were concerned, little or nothing could be done without constitutional revision; and accordingly in both these Laender the Socialists launched mass campaigns for electoral reform, conducting their agitations mainly outside the elected Chambers but invoking the aid of such progressive elements as were to be found inside them. In both cases, as the outcome of these campaigns, they received promises of constitutional changes; but the proposals, when they were produced, proved to be almost useless. In Saxony the Social Democrats were able to win a few additional seats; but in Prussia the autocratic system and the class-arrangements for voting made it impossible for them to make any headway right up to 1918. As Prussia dominated the Federal Upper Chamber of the Reich Parliament, this was enough to put an unsurmountable obstacle in the way of a constitutional advance towards responsible government.

German Socialism had thus a difficult row to hoe; and its difficulties were increased by the growing economic prosperity of the country, which made possible a rapid rise in the standards of living and enabled the Trade Unions to win substantial victories in respect of wages and conditions without having to encounter very obstinate resistance. It was, moreover, part of the Government's policy to improve social services and industrial legislation as a counter to Socialist propaganda; and this policy, though it was unsuccessful in detaching the workers from their allegiance to Social Democracy, did appreciably affect the attitudes which they, and the Trade Unions on their behalf, took up within the Socialist movement. In 1906, when the defeat of the Russian Revolution had become clear, a secret conference was held between the leaders of the Trade Unions and the party, which as we saw had been moved the previous year to pass a resolution contemplating the possibility of resort to the general strike. The party leaders, under Trade Union pressure, agreed that on no account would they attempt to call a general strike without the prior consent of the Trade Union movement; and this agreement was subsequently endorsed by the party Congress. It was generally regarded as marking the beginning of a period of increasing Trade Union influence on party policy — an influence wielded by the central Trade Union leadership rather than by the body of Trade Union members, and thrown consistently on the side of Reformism.

After the death of Wilhelm Liebknecht in 1900, the leadership of the party passed without question into the hands of August Bebel (1840–1913), who had been, with him, the founder of the Eisenach Party out of which the existing party had grown. Bebel was a fine speaker and a pillar of Marxist orthodoxy as understood among German Social Democrats of the old school. He was generally regarded, until his last years, as belonging to the left wing of the party; and this was broadly correct. He was a strong opponent of those South German Reformists who wished to come to terms with the bourgeois Progressives and to support Progressive Governments in the Laender; and when the Revisionist issue arose he sided strongly against Bernstein and made common cause with Kautsky in repelling both the economic heresies of the Revisionists and Bernstein's attempt to restate Socialist philosophy on Kantian rather than on Hegelian-Marxist foundations. He was a convinced materialist, who found complete mental satisfaction in the Marxist system he had learnt from Wilhelm Liebknecht in his early days; and in the party he carried on Liebknecht's tradition. He was, however, by no means so leftish in practice as he appeared in theory; and though he combated the Reformists and Revisionists he had no wish to carry opposition to the length of expulsion from the party. He believed whole-heartedly in the need for unity, and was prepared to allow such dissenters and deviationists as Frank and Bernstein to carry on their propaganda unmolested, on condition of their submitting to an occasional rebuke. His chief contribution to the literature of Socialism was his book, *Woman*, in which he reviewed the history of the relations between the sexes and pleaded for equal rights. His three-volume autobiography, *Mein Leben*, is a rich quarry for information about the inner history of the German Party.

Close to Bebel throughout these years was the Austrian, Karl Kautsky, generally acclaimed as the leading theorist of Marxism after the death of Engels, and, like Bebel, a great upholder of the orthodox tradition. He, too, was regarded, up to a few years before 1914, as belonging to the left wing, on the ground of his vehement opposition to Revisionists and Reformists and of his assurance that Socialism would emerge necessarily out of the increasing concentration and trustification of capitalist enterprise. We have already considered the essentials of Kautsky's doctrine, and there is no need to go over the ground again. What concerns us here is that, from the moment when a militant left wing made its appearance under the leadership of Rosa Luxemburg, Karl Liebknecht, Georg Ledebour, and Franz Mehring, Kautsky occupied a centrist position between the Reformists and the Revolutionaries, and fell increasingly foul of the latter as they attempted to swing the party back from its growingly Reformist tendencies during the years before 1914.

Kautsky was a theorist and not a practical leader in party affairs. Of the men round Bebel, who ran the party machine, the most important included Ignaz Auer (1846–1907), a veteran Eisenacher who had become Secretary of the party as far back as the Gotha Congress of 1875, and held the post till his death, and Paul Singer (1844–1911), who had become Chairman in 1890. Auer was a South German, originally a saddler. He had fought, and been wounded, in the war of 1870. He took an active part in the Second International, but was notable chiefly as an organiser and an adroit tactician, rather than as a thinker. He wrote little : his one notable work, published in 1889, is valuable for its account of the fortunes of German Socialism in exile under Bismarck's Anti-Socialist Laws. Paul Singer was an abler man. A Jewish merchant and industrialist of Berlin, he made a considerable fortune in business, and later devoted most of it to the Socialist cause. He had been elected to the Reichstag from Berlin in 1884, and in 1887 he became a member, and in 1890 Chairman, of the Central Committee of the party. He too was notable as an organiser : he and Auer between them were largely responsible for the very high degree of organisation which the party achieved. At the International, he was often in the chair on important occasions ; but he was no great orator. Nor did he make any substantial contribution to Socialist thought : he was usually prepared to take his lead from Bebel in matters of policy and from Kautsky in doctrine. He was indeed by instinct a centrist, with a strong desire to hold the party together, come what might.

The death of three of these four in quick succession — Auer, Singer, and Bebel — left a void in the central direction of the Social Democratic Party ; and new men came rapidly to the front during the years immediately before 1914. Bebel's successor as leader of the party was Hugo Haase (1863–1919), who was to break away from the war party with Bernstein and Kautsky in 1915 and to join them two years later in founding the Independent Socialist Party. Haase was by profession a lawyer : he came from East Prussia and represented Königsberg in the Reichstag. He took an active part in the peace movement in the Second International and in various movements for Franco-German understanding, and in 1914 opposed the voting of war credits at the party meeting, though for the time being he accepted the majority verdict. But he was always a moderate, and never a leftist.

The other new leaders were Friedrich Ebert (1870–1925) and Philip Scheidemann (1865–1939). Ebert, son of a Heidelberg tailor and himself a saddler and harness-maker, had been long active in the Social Democratic Party before his election to the Reichstag in 1912. He belonged definitely to the right wing of the party, and became the leader of its pro-war majority after 1914. The German Revolution of 1918 was to carry him to the presidency of the Weimar Republic. Philip Scheidemann, his principal coadjutor during the war years, had gained something of a reputation for leftism before the war, when he had been ousted from the vice-presidency of the Reichstag because of his refusal to pay a visit of ceremony and homage to the Kaiser. But he was always nearer to the right than to the left. In 1918 he became Prime Minister in the first German Republican Government, only to resign the following year in disapprobation of the Peace Treaty, and to abandon politics to become Burgomeister of his native Cassel. His *Memoirs of a Social Democrat* (English translation, 1929) are an important source for the history of the party, especially during the war years.

Another outstanding figure of the period before 1914 was the leader of the Baden Socialists, Ludwig Frank (1874–1914), who was definitely on the right wing of the party. Frank was the principal spokesman and practitioner of the policy favoured in South Germany, of electoral alliance between the Social Democrats and the bourgeois Progressives ; and he with his followers persisted in this policy, and in sustaining bourgeois left Governments by their votes, despite the reiterated disapproval of Social Democratic Congresses and in face of Bebel's rebukes. Frank was active in the Second International and took a leading part in a number of movements designed to promote Franco-German understanding and to procure joint action against war by the French and German workers. He held that the best hope of breaking Prussian autocracy and liberalising the institutions of the Reich lay in building up a democratic bloc based on the South German Laender, France, and Alsace-Lorraine ; and he campaigned for the introduction of manhood suffrage in Alsace-Lorraine (which was conceded in 1912) as a means to this end. Noted for his pacific opinions, he nevertheless insisted on enlisting in the army in 1914, saying that Prussia would become liberalised as an outcome of the war. Before the year's end he fell in battle.

Still further to the right was Eduard David (1863–1930). David, who came from Hesse, joined the Social Democratic Party as a student, and became the exponent of an agrarian policy in sharp conflict with orthodox Marxist teaching. In his most important book, *Socialismus und Landwirtschaft* (1903) he controverted the opinion that economic development was necessarily leading to the supersession of peasant agriculture by large-scale capitalist farming, and called for a policy designed to maintain the peasant class and to expand it further by breaking up the great estates. He regarded peasant proprietorship as both desirable in itself and fully consistent with Socialism. This brought him into keen controversy with Kautsky. In the Revisionist controversy he was naturally on Bernstein's side. In the Reichstag, to which he was first elected in 1903, he was an influential member of the right wing. He became Under-Secretary for Foreign Affairs in Prince Max of Baden's Government in 1918 and then Minister of the Interior under the Republic. He played a considerable part in the drafting of the Weimar Constitution.

Another right-wing figure was Georg von Vollmar (1850–1922) of Bavaria, whose views on the agrarian question and on collaboration with non-Socialist parties have been considered in an earlier chapter. Vollmar, however, after a series of sharp conflicts with Bebel, culminating in a famous dispute at the Dresden Social Democratic Congress of 1903, became much less active in the party. He was in ill-health and, without altering his opinions, left the contest to others.

Finally, among the leaders of the right wing, mention must be made of the Trade Unionists. Foremost among them was Carl Legien (1861–1920), the formidable President of the German Trade Union Commission and Secretary of the Trade Union International. Legien, a Hamburg woodworker, was largely responsible for creating the central organisation of the Trade Unions after the expiry of the Anti-Socialist Laws in 1890. He was an active Social Democrat, but one who strongly resisted any attempt to subordinate the Trade Unions to the party or to make use of them for political ends. A determined opponent of the mass-strike, he believed that the Trade Unions should stick to their task of improving wages and conditions, and should be prepared to enter into friendly relations with employers for this purpose — when the employers were prepared to follow a reasonable line. His ideal was the 'constitutional factory', in which the workers would share the control with the employers, until at a later stage the private employers were superseded by the Socialist State. Similarly, in the political field he looked forward to a gradual transition through constitutional monarchy to a democratic Republic, which would build up Socialist institutions. In the party, he was on the extreme Reformist side. In his Trade Union capacity, he was a vigorous disciplinarian, addicted to strong language and to strong measures against left-wing militants, and never happier than when he was lecturing his opponents about their duty to obey orders. He took a firm stand against the Trade

Union International even considering the question of the general strike, which he also fought against in the Socialist International. More than anyone else, he was responsible for the increased Trade Union influence on the German Party after 1905. Paradoxically, it fell to him to issue in 1920 the general strike call against the Kapp Putsch.

A close co-worker of Legien was the cigar-maker, Adolf von Elm (1857–1916), who was a prominent figure in both the Trade Union and the Co-operative movement, as well as in the Social Democratic Party. Von Elm had worked in the United States before he became the leader of the Cigar Sorters' Union in Hamburg in 1883. Eight years later he took on the management of the Hamburg Tobacco Workers' Co-operative Society, which prospered; and in 1899 he played a leading part in setting up the Hamburg Consumers' Co-operative, Produktion, which was the pioneer of the modern German Consumers' movement. He became Chairman of the Central Union of Consumers' Societies, and was largely responsible for inducing the Social Democratic Party to give active support to the movement and to urge all Socialists to assist its development. At the same time von Elm continued to play a very active part in the Trade Union movement. In the party he supported the Revisionists, and in the Reichstag, till he retired from it in 1906, he belonged to the right wing. His chief preoccupation, however, was with the building up of strong Trade Unions, backed by ample funds, and of Consumers' Co-operatives which, while remaining entirely independent of the Social Democratic Party, would work in association with it.

The left wing which took shape in the Social Democratic Party, especially after 1905, was headed by Rosa Luxemburg, Karl Liebknecht, Clara Zetkin, Franz Mehring, and Georg Ledebour. The controversy between the left and the centre, which during the years before 1914 largely replaced that between the left-centre and the right, turned chiefly on two issues — anti-militarism and the general strike, which the Germans usually called the 'mass strike' in order to distinguish it from the general strike of the Anarchists and the Syndicalists. Karl Liebknecht (1871–1919), son of Wilhelm Liebknecht, was the protagonist in the demand that the German Socialists should carry on active anti-militarist propaganda, including direct appeals to the armed forces. In 1907 he published his tract, *Militarism and Anti-militarism*, which cost him a sentence of eighteen months in a fortress and was promptly repudiated by the Social Democratic Party. In 1912 Potsdam elected him to the Reichstag; and he was the first member who defied the majority and voted against the war credits in 1914. After organising the Spartacus movement during the war, he was to be murdered in 1919 with Rosa Luxemburg as the victim of the Weimar Republic. Karl Liebknecht was a man of great courage and inflexible revolutionary opinions. Sent to the front as a soldier during the war, he had done his best to stimulate revolt among the armed forces; and when he was out of the army and of prison, he devoted himself to building up an organisation of revolt among the factory workers. He was not, however, a theorist of originality: he was a fighter, with a detestation of war, who was prepared to act on his principles without compromise.

Among the leaders of the left wing of Social Democracy Franz Mehring (1846–1919) occupied an important position as the historian of the party and one of its most active writers. Originally a liberal journalist and an opponent of Bismarck, Mehring had come over to Socialism in 1890 and had at once associated himself with its most advanced section. His *History of German Social Democracy*, originally published in 1897–8, was in effect a study of the entire background out of which the Socialist movement had arisen, with emphasis on the cultural as well as on the economic and political factors. He was remarkable in doing justice to Lassalle and his followers as well as to Marx and the Eisenachers, and in approaching Marxism, while accepting its essential doctrines, in a critically objective spirit. He was one of the few Socialists in the Prussian Diet before 1914. During the years before 1914 Mehring worked closely with Rosa Luxemburg; and this collaboration was strengthened during the war years. Mehring was one of the inspirers of the Spartacus movement: his biography of Marx remains by far the best.

No less close to Rosa Luxemburg was the leader of the women's section of German Social Democracy, Clara Zetkin (1857–1933), who for many years from 1892 edited *Gleichheit* as the organ of Socialist feminism and was active in every field of the party's educational and cultural work. An ardent internationalist and a believer in international working-class revolution, she shared Rosa Luxemburg's hostility to the party's increasing nationalist tendencies. She was a strong opponent of Revisionism and a believer in the mass-strike as the forerunner of social revolution. In 1914 she actively opposed the war; and in 1917 she ranged herself with the Independent Socialist Party. After the war she joined the Communists, but soon became associated with Paul Levi's opposition group. When, however, Levi was expelled from the Communist Party, she was allowed — or persuaded — to remain within its ranks, and during her latter years she lived chiefly in the Soviet Union.

Georg Ledebour (1850–1947) stood less far to the left than either Mehring or Clara Zetkin; but he belongs rather with them than with the centre. He was associated with the Reichstag group that opposed the war in 1914, was the leading German delegate at the Zimmerwald Conference of 1916 and, after joining the Independent Socialist Party at its foundation and remaining with it to its end, refused to return to the Social Democratic Party when the Independents agreed to fuse with it in 1922.

Rosa Luxemburg (1871–1919), too, was an apostle of anti-militarism. But whereas Karl Liebknecht concentrated on this issue, it was for her only part of a much wider question — that of Revolution versus Reform. Her conflict with the leaders of the Social Democratic Party — with the centre as well as with the right — began by turning largely on the mass-strike, and on its essentially revolutionary character. As her views will be discussed fully in a subsequent chapter [1] there is no need to expound them in detail here. She stood for the use of the mass-strike not as a glorified political demonstration designed to extract a particular concession, such as manhood suffrage, but as a revolutionary weapon which would bring the masses into action and lead to the overthrow of the existing order. The German Trade Union leaders, when they were brought reluctantly in 1905 to face the bare possibility of being called on to declare a mass-strike, were quite unprepared to contemplate anything of this sort. They assumed that the most that

[1] See pp. 459 ff.

could happen would be a strike of their own members, who included only a fraction of the working class. They excluded the public servants and the railway workers, who were not allowed by the State to organise, the large bodies of workers in the mines and heavy industries that were prevented by their capitalist masters from joining the Free Trade Unions, and also the members of the Christian Unions connected with the Centre Party, of the Catholic Trade Associations run under the direct auspices of the Church, and of the Liberal (Hirsch-Duncker) Unions. They showed to their satisfaction that the effects of a mass-strike limited to their own members would be very restricted, and would fall a long way short of paralysing the country ; and they ended by saying that to attempt it would be to invite the Government to confiscate their funds and buildings and to destroy their movement. The Social Democratic leaders, for their part, although under the influence of the excitement caused by the Russian outburst of 1905 they had accepted a resolution at the party Congress contemplating a possible resort to the mass-strike, had by no means endorsed the kind of strike that Rosa Luxemburg had in mind. They had accepted the mass-strike only as a weapon that might have to be invoked in face of action by the Government to destroy existing constitutional rights ; and even so Bebel, in speaking to the resolution, had emphasised the point that success could be hoped for only if such a strike had been very carefully prepared for and organised in advance — which was precisely what Rosa Luxemburg argued it could never be. She and Bebel were in fact thinking of two quite different kinds of strike — he of an orderly demonstration taking the form of a cessation of work and designed to achieve a particular, limited object, and she of a mass-dislocation of the working of the social structure, joined in by the masses and serving as the starting-point for an insurrection.

But even the very cautious approach of the Social Democratic Party to the possibility of using the mass-strike as a weapon of defence was enough to raise the fears of the Trade Union leaders. In order to placate them the party leaders promised, not only to consult them in advance, but also to take upon the party the actual responsibility for issuing the call to strike, should it ever be decided to use the mass-strike for political purposes. In this way the Trade Unions would be freed from responsibility for it, and the Government, it was said, would have no ground for taking legal action against them. On this understanding the matter was patched up : it was declared that there was no inconsistency between the decision of the 1905 Trade Union Congress against the mass-strike and the qualified decision of the Socialist Congress of the same year in its favour. At the Mannheim Socialist Congress of 1906 the 'mass-strike' policy was effectually buried by the undertaking not to resort to it without Trade Union consent.

Yet there was nothing essentially revolutionary about the 'mass-strike', though there was about Rosa Luxemburg's version of it. The Austrians and the Belgians had both used it in the cause of franchise reform ; and it had been used successively in the Scandinavian countries. None of these were strongholds of revolutionary Socialism. But the German Trade Unions and most of the German Socialists were against its use, even in its most limited and pacific form — except possibly as a retort to a reactionary coup that would take away the existing right to vote or to organise. They had a strong feeling that the German Government would not hesitate to shoot if they tried it ; and the last thing they wanted was to give the Prussian army a chance of shooting them down. They scouted Rosa Luxemburg's notion that if the right moment were chosen for calling out the workers — not only the Trade Union members, but *all* the workers — the non-Unionists would join in — railwaymen, miners, workers in the heavy industries, public employees, and all — in a great spontaneous uprising that would spread to the armed forces and leave the reactionaries helpless. That, they felt strongly, was not how Germans would behave ; and I think they were correct in this opinion.

The German Social Democrats had indeed in 1907 an experience of what happened when they allowed themselves to be put in the position of fighting a Reichstag election on an issue which set them directly in opposition to the State as the champion of nationalist feeling. In 1906 the Social Democrats, the Centre Party, and the Poles had combined to refuse the credits needed by the Government for intensifying its repression of the Herreros in German South Africa. The Chancellor, von Bülow, had retaliated by dissolving the Reichstag, and the bourgeois parties had leagued themselves against the Social Democratic candidates. At the elections, early in 1907, the Social Democratic Party had lost 38 seats out of 81 previously held, though its aggregate vote had slightly increased. This result had been arrived at because at the second ballot, held when at the first no candidate had a clear majority, the other parties had lined up as patriots against the Socialists, who had been represented as the enemies of national defence and colonial expansion. In reporting to the Stuttgart International Socialist Congress the Social Democratic Party evidently considered that it had been most unfairly treated. So, indeed, it had ; for it had explicitly recognised not only the duty of national defence but also the justifiability of colonial enterprise and had refused to take its stand with the out-and-out opponents of colonial imperialism. It had not at all meant its challenge to the war being waged against the Herreros to be taken as a general attack on colonialism or as a rejection of the duty of national defence. It had found itself manœuvred into a position which its leaders did not at all wish to occupy ; and a study of the election results showed that, while increasing its working-class vote, it had lost the support of a large body of black-coated and middle-class electors who were the deciding factor in many urban constituencies. Large majorities in the industrial areas could not, under the existing distribution of seats, which had remained unaltered since 1871, make up for the defection of the marginal voters at the second ballot. The lesson, as it was learnt by the Social Democratic leaders, was that, in their quest for the majority that was to put them into a position to transform German society, they must on no account antagonise the democratic elements in the middle class. On this presumption they set to work to rebuild their forces ; and in 1912 they had their reward in the election of no fewer than 110 deputies as against 43 in 1907, and in polling four and a quarter million votes as against three and a quarter, with the aid of a greatly increased contingent of middle-class electors. On that occasion they were able to play down their internationalism, such as it was, and to fight mainly on domestic issues, which suited them a great deal better.

The plain truth was that national expansion was popular

with the majority of the electorate, and that support for it was growing in the Social Democratic Party itself, at any rate among the leaders, and in the Trade Unions. Since 1906 the party had been moving steadily to the right ; for the centre had been shifting rightwards since the defeat of the Russian Revolution and the electoral disaster of 1907. Not only Kautsky and Haase, but also Bernstein and some other Revisionists, were to show after 1914 that they retained their internationalist outlook ; but that did not prevent them, for the time being, from moving rightwards in order to maintain the unity of the party, which could afford much better, electorally, to quarrel with its left than with its right wing. Increasingly, during the years before 1914, the Social Democratic centrists became the prisoners of the right : the nearer war came, the less could they maintain their position. The Stuttgart resolution of the International nominally required the party both to take drastic action against the threat of war and, if war came, to make it the opportunity for overthrowing the capitalist system. But few of the leaders took this seriously, and most of the German leaders least of all. After 1914 even the left centre whittled it down to the pursuit of a negotiated peace. The Luxemburg-Liebknecht faction was left in an exiguous minority till after 1917.

Yet, right up to 1914, German Socialism continued to present an imposing face to the world. It had not only the numerically strongest, but also the most elaborately organised, Socialist movement. Its Trade Union movement, closely allied with the party, was growing rapidly, and was also very highly organised. The Co-operative movement, especially among consumers, was also developing fast, and was largely under Socialist influence. The Socialists had a most formidable array of newspapers and journals, and a large output of books and pamphlets. Their educational activities were widespread ; and they had set up their own training school for party officials and leaders. They were very active too in cultural fields ; they had their own theatres and concert halls, as well as fine meeting-places and clubs. The Social Democratic women's organisations were strong, despite the heavy restrictions imposed by Prussian law on female participation in politics. The party possessed an extensive sports organisation, and its youth sections were very active — though these had been brought under strict party control when they showed signs of leftist deviation. Up to 1907 Karl Liebknecht had been at the head of the party's Youth Organisation : when he published his pamphlet on Anti-militarism he was deprived of his office, and Friedrich Ebert was put in his place. At the same time the Youth Organisation was recast, and brought under the firm control of the party machine. In fact, whatever could be done by sheer efficiency of organisation the German Social Democratic Party and the Trade Unions had done — to the admiration of themselves as well as of the rest of the world.

And yet — what was wrong with them ? Above all else, a refusal to face facts. They had put all their faith in the prospect of winning so large a body of electoral support as not merely to become a majority in the Reichstag, but also to be able to use that majority to win responsible government in the Reich and to force a reform in the Prussian constitution that would place them in power there too and give them full freedom to reshape the State according to their will. They had assumed that these things could be accomplished by sheer voting solidarity and disciplined organisation. They had never really faced the difficulty that the majority they hoped for could hardly be secured without the support of a large body of marginal voters who would vote for them only if they diluted their positive programme to meet its wishes, and could not be relied on to back them if it came to a show-down with the armed might of the Imperial Government. They were too much addicted to counting heads and too little to asking themselves how many of those who voted for them would be prepared to act for them in a decisive struggle against the power of the State. Though they were Republicans, they never ventured to put the Republic into their programme : though they were in theory revolutionists — by majority vote against the Reformists and Revisionists — their revolution was post-dated to electoral victory. If they had really been revolutionists, they would have known that revolutions need the backing of a revolutionary spirit at least among a significant fraction of the people ; but, far from encouraging their followers to develop a revolutionary spirit, they did their best to damp it down wherever it appeared. They were in truth Reformists, but would not admit it, and were for that reason disabled from making the most of the reformist policies which they followed in practice. They fell between the two stools of Marxism and Revisionism, unable to renounce the one, or to escape in practice from the other.

Why was this ? It was, I think, largely because the German Reich, under Prussian leadership, had made itself the symbol of national unity and greatness in a form which they could neither accept nor whole-heartedly oppose. They could not accept it, because it was autocratic, half-feudal, militaristic, and hostile to all their social aims. But equally they could not quite reject it, because it embodied their desire for national unity and their taste for co-ordinated power. They loved bigness, as appeared very plainly in their vision of the coming Socialist society as the heir of trustified capitalism, in their instinctive dislike of the peasants, and in their revulsion from anything at all un-disciplined or anarchical. In one aspect, this love of centralisation held them fast to Marxist theory : in another it caused them to admire, even while they hated, the Prussian State. It has often been said that they were at bottom Lassallians rather than Marxists, and that, at the Gotha Congress, not the Eisenachers but the Lassallians really got their way. There is something in this ; but it is not the case that, after 1871, the Marxian and the Lassallian influences were still pulling opposite ways. The unification of the Reich had established the Prussian ascend-ancy, and Marxism had to come to terms with it as an accom-plished fact. The orthodox Marxists did this a great deal more easily than the Reformists and Revisionists. It was among the Reformists of Southern Germany that the process was most difficult of all. Lassallianism mingled with Marxism in the making of the orthodox Social Democratic creed.

These contradictions at the very heart of German Social Democracy were, of course, observed and commented upon by many critics from outside Germany — above all, in France. Nevertheless, the achievements of the German Social Demo-cratic Party, in terms of organisation and electoral success, were massive enough to make a profound impression on the Socialists of other countries which had much less to show. They deeply impressed Engels, watching from England ; they impressed Guesde in France, Iglesias in Spain, Branting in Sweden, Hyndman in England, Hillquit and Berger in the

United States, Adler in Austria, Turati in Italy, Troelstra in Holland, and a great many more; and they also impressed Plekhanov in Russia — and not only Plekhanov, but Lenin as well. The edifice was indeed imposing; and great was its fall.

CHAPTER VII

FRANCE TO 1905

GERMAN Socialism, despite internal differences, formed from 1875 onwards a massively united party, and was drawn more closely together by the repression which Bismarck practised against it. French Socialism, on the other hand, coming to life again after its almost complete eclipse in 1871, soon showed itself as fissiparous as ever, and maintained its multiplicity of contending factions right up to 1905, when, at the behest of the Socialist International, the Unified Socialist Party was brought into existence by the fusion of at least six national groups, besides a number of regional organisations. Even then the French working class did not achieve unity ; for the Trade Unions, themselves but recently unified in the Confédération Générale du Travail (in 1902) maintained their entire independence of the Socialists and of all political parties, and proclaimed against the parliamentary policy of the Unified Socialist Party their creed of Syndicalism and Direct Action.

In the second volume of this work the revival of Trade Unionism and Socialism in France after the eclipse of the 1870s was briefly described. We there saw that the Marseilles Labour Congress of 1879 decided, at the very moment when the amnesty to the Communards was being approved, to set up a Fédération des Ouvriers Socialistes de France, which it proclaimed as the 'workers' party'. Jules Guesde, whose journal, *Égalité*, started in 1877, had helped to prepare the way, was the moving spirit. Exiled after the Commune, he had settled in Switzerland, and had there been associated with a variety of Socialist groups, including the Anarchists ; but he had also been impressed by the development of the German party, and when he returned to France and started his paper he enlisted the support of Wilhelm Liebknecht as well as of César de Paepe. In 1878 there was an International Exhibition in Paris ; and the Paris Trade Union and Socialist groups decided to call an

International Labour Congress to meet in connection with it. The Government banned the Congress ; and most of the groups which had joined in convening it accepted the ban. Guesde and some others refused and attempted to hold the Congress in defiance of the police. The meeting was dispersed ; and the leaders were sent to prison. From prison they issued a manifesto, demanding the establishment of an effective national Labour and Socialist organisation. This helped to prepare the way for the decision of the Marseilles Congress the following year. From this point Guesde moved steadily in the direction of Marxism : he wanted to create in France a united, centralised Socialist Party on the German model ; and after the Marseilles Congress he visited Marx in London, in 1880, to seek his advice. Back in Paris, he drew up in collaboration with Marx's son-in-law, Paul Lafargue (1842–1911) a draft constitution and statement of objects for the proposed new party ; and these, based largely on the Gotha Constitution of the German Social Democrats, were approved by a Congress held in Paris in June 1880. This was a regional gathering : the Marseilles Congress had set up a number of regional Federations, which were to meet and prepare the way for a national Congress to be held later in the year at Le Havre. When this gathering met, there were lively disputes. The delegates, drawn from working-class bodies of every sort and kind, represented many conflicting tendencies. The Mutualists — that is to say, the right wing which favoured social peace and class-co-operation — broke away on one side, and the Anarchists on the other. The Mutualists founded a national organisation of their own : the Anarchists decided to hold an International Congress, which duly met in London the following year.[1] But these secessions left those who remained by no means united. The Marseilles Congress had declared that 'Before all else, the proletariat should break completely with the bourgeoisie' and had pronounced in favour of making 'land and minerals, machines, transport agencies, buildings, and accumulated capital' collective property. The organising committee, in its report, had represented these demands as the reaction to the banning of the International Congress planned for 1878 and to the refusal of the bourgeois Radicals to

[1] See Vol. II, p. 322 ff.

give support to the workers' claims. The Congress had rejected Co-operation as an adequate means of emancipating the proletariat, and had adopted a definitely 'class-war' standpoint. But the Socialist majority which endorsed these views was made up of mixed elements. Apart from the Anarchists, who rejected political action, there were Blanquists, who wished to organise a revolutionary *émeute*, Guesdists, who wished to build up a powerful Socialist Party with a massfollowing, Trade Unionists who held that the political party should play second fiddle to the industrial movement, and 'integralists', who believed in the combined use of all methods, political and industrial, without ruling out either reformist activities or revolution. There were, moreover, among those who wished to create a workers' party to contest seats in Parliament and on other public bodies, rival views concerning the line of action which the elected working-class representatives were to follow. The Guesdists, taking their line from the Germans, stressed the use of Parliament as a means of making Socialist propaganda and fighting against the Government, and made little of the notion of attempting to use it for the achievement of immediate reforms — which indeed was hardly possible without collaboration with the left bourgeois parties. But there were others, soon to rally under the leadership of Paul Brousse, who held that, if not in Parliament, at any rate in local government working-class representation could be used for the achievement of positive reforms, and were not really averse, despite the Marseilles resolution, to all bargaining and co-operation with the bourgeois groups, at all events in local and provincial affairs.

Nor were the Guesdists themselves disposed to rest their hopes entirely on the industrial proletariat. The Guesdist manifesto of 1878 laid great stress on the wrongs of the peasants and of the petite bourgeoisie, who were being exploited by finance capital and unfair taxation. The Guesdists hoped to win the support of these classes for a workers' party, arguing, like the German Social Democrats, that they were being ground out of existence by the rapid advance of big business and finance and could be brought over to Socialism by an appeal to their sense of grievance and frustration. The Guesdists were thus at one and the same time preachers of class-war and advocates of a combined pact of the left ; and their central position antagonised on the one hand the more moderate political Socialists and on the other the left-wing Trade Unionists who wished to have nothing to do with the petite bourgeoisie and were in favour of rallying the agricultural wage-workers to the Trade Unions rather than seeking any accommodation with the peasants.

In 1881 Paul Brousse put himself at the head of Guesde's opponents by coming forward as the advocate of 'Possibilism'. By this was meant a policy of working for immediate reforms under capitalism, instead of postponing all constructive action until after the conquest of political power. In particular, Brousse urged strongly the need for active participation in local politics, in order to capture control of as many as possible of the local communes (local councils) in the industrial areas and to secure representation on the councils of the départements (counties). The situation in France differed from that of Germany, where the local electoral system still made it almost impossible for the workers' party to become an effective force in local government, whereas it was relatively easy to win seats in the Reichstag. In France, there was a good chance for work-ing-class leaders to be elected as maires of industrial communes, or as councillors ; and a fair sprinkling of workers already held such offices, though many of them came from the right-wing groups which had broken away at the Havre Congress of 1880. Brousse wanted to build up a workers' party nationally by beginning mainly at the local level ; and he argued that this could be done only by making the party the spokesman of immediate claims, as well as the advocate of a complete social transformation. With this in view, he stood for a good deal of local autonomy as against the Guesdist policy of strong cen-tralisation on the German model ; and this aspect of his policy won him support on the left as well as the right.

The dispute came to a head at the St.-Étienne Congress of 1882. There was a split, from which two rival parties emerged. The Possibilist majority retained control of the Fédération des Ouvriers Socialistes de France, and gave it the new second name of Parti Ouvrier Socialiste Révolutionnaire : the Gues-dists held a separate Congress, and formed the Parti Ouvrier Français on the centralised, Marxist model. This split has often been described as if it had been a straight separation of the left from the right; but it was not. It was a separation of the Marxists who wanted a closely knit party of the German type from both the more moderate politicians and the advocates of local autonomy. These latter included considerable left-wing elements — especially those who gave a high place to industrial as against parliamentary action and wished the Trade Unions to have a large, independent voice in the shaping of Socialist policy.

Paul Brousse (1854–1912) was a doctor of medicine. Leaving France after the Commune, he went first to Spain and then to Switzerland, where he met Bakunin and worked with the Federation of the Jura. After a sojourn in England he returned to France when the amnesty was proclaimed, and joined forces with Guesde and Lafargue. He made his journal, *Le Prolétaire*, the organ of the Possibilist movement and in 1883 expounded his policy in a booklet, *La Propriété collective et les services publics*. From near-Anarchism he had passed over to a gradualist Socialism which laid stress on local control. He held that industries and services became gradually ripe for socialisation as they passed under large-scale control, and that the first step should be the taking over by municipal, regional, or national public bodies, as might be appropriate in each case, of the essential public services. He was antagonistic to Guesde's ideas both because of his insistence on local initiative and auto-nomy and because he believed that it was necessary to take over industries and services as they became ripe, without waiting for a new 'workers' State' to administer them. His hostility to centralisation gave him the support of many Socialists who did not endorse his gradualist views.

Jules Guesde (1845–1922) and Paul Lafargue, upon the split with the Broussists, founded, as we have seen, the Parti Ouvrier Français. Lafargue, who married Marx's daughter, Laura, was born in Cuba, and became, like Brousse, a doctor. He took an active part in the First International as the leading figure in the Marxist Section which he founded in Madrid, in opposition to the Anarchism of the main Spanish sections. In 1882 he took up permanent residence in France, and played a leading part in building up the Parti Ouvrier. He was an active writer, as well as a propagandist.

Hardly had these two parties taken shape when the strike

at Montceau-les-Mines and the alleged Anarchist plot at Lyons led to the trial and imprisonment of many of the leaders of French Anarchism.[1] The following year, however, the French Government changed its policy, and, under the influence of Pierre Waldeck-Rousseau (1846–1904) passed a law giving greater freedom of combination to Trade Unions, coupled with requirements that they should register, and deposit the names of their officers, with the police. In connection with the new law, Waldeck-Rousseau, as Minister of the Interior, circularised the prefects of the départements telling them to encourage the formation of Trade Unions, in the hope of persuading them to adopt a pacific policy, including arbitration in trade disputes. The purpose of this policy was to drive a wedge between the revolutionary Trade Unionists and Socialists, on the one hand, and the moderates on the other, and to alienate as much working-class sympathy as possible from the former, against whom the Government would then be more easily able to continue its measures of repression. But one of the effects of the law was to make it lawful to establish a central Trade Union organisation, as distinct from mere occasional congresses ; and the Lyons Congress of 1884, dominated by the Guesdists, proceeded to set up a Fédération Nationale de Syndicats. This was necessarily a very loose grouping ; for in France at that date national Trade Unions hardly existed. Each trade had its own local syndicat, and these were grouped mainly in local unions or circles combining the syndicats of the various trades. In 1884 only the printers had a really effective national organisation, headed by Auguste Keufer (1851–1924), who was to become the outstanding leader of the moderate group in the French Syndicalist movement. The hatters and the leather workers too had national federations ; but the Fédération du Livre stood alone as a national body possessed of substantial funds and closely knit organisation. Consequently, the Fédération Nationale de Syndicats was necessarily made up mainly of local syndicats of particular trades, or of loose local groupings. To save expense, a Congress delegate often represented a number of syndicats ; and the financial weakness of the whole movement made it difficult to secure representative delegations or even a representative committee or council to

[1] See Vol. II, p. 327 f.

act between Congresses. This exposed the Fédération to the danger of capture by an active minority; and in fact the Guesdists managed to get control of it.

The Lyons Congress took strong objection to the registration provisions of the new law; but its effects on the growth of Trade Unionism were undoubtedly favourable. The Broussists and the Guesdists alike urged their adherents to join Trade Unions, and to play an active part in their work; but the attitudes of the rival parties towards Trade Unionism showed a significant difference. The Guesdists, like a section of the German Marxists, were uninterested in the day-to-day work of Trade Unions and were inclined to deny that they could be productive of any real economic benefit to the workers. Dominated by the idea that capitalism was fated to bring about conditions of 'increasing misery' and that only the conquest of political power could improve the workers' position, they regarded Trade Unionism as simply a school in which the workers could learn the lessons of the class-war and become converts to political Socialism. The Broussists, on the other hand, included both 'possibilists' who wished to strengthen the Trade Unions for effective collective bargaining under capitalism and revolutionaries who saw in the Trade Unions a potential instrument of revolutionary working-class action. Accordingly, the Broussists were ready to help the Unions to develop in their own way, rather than to attempt to dominate them; whereas the Guesdists were continually trying to force their brand of Marxism down the Trade Unionists' throats.

In the long run, the Guesdist policy produced its Nemesis; but in the short run, because of good organisation, it had considerable success. The Fédération Nationale de Syndicats held its first Congress in 1886. It declared that political differences were to be set aside in the interest of class-unity; but it also adopted an essentially Guesdist series of resolutions. It declared in favour of public ownership of the means of production, and gave its support to the programme of the Parti Ouvrier. Even at this stage, however, there came up an issue which disconcerted the Guesdists — that of the general strike.

The idea of the general strike was by no means new. It had been advocated by William Benbow and by the Owenite National Regeneration Society in England in the 1830s, and

had been adopted, under the name of 'Sacred Month', by the
Chartist Convention of 1839.[1] It had been much talked of
thereafter in France and Belgium, and had become an element
in Anarchist conceptions of the way in which the Social Revolution would begin. But in the early 1880s it had come to the
front again in the United States in connection with the movement for the eight hours' day. The Owenites had proposed in
1834 that the workers should win the eight hours' day by a
concerted and general refusal to continue work beyond eight
hours ; and a similar proposal was now being canvassed in the
United States. From the Americans the Parisian Anarchist
carpenter, Joseph Tortelier (1854–1928), who was a renowned
mob-orator, took up the idea, advocating a general strike
to secure the eight hours' day ; and this proposal was developed
by French Anarchists and revolutionary Trade Unionists into
that of a general strike which would turn of itself into a revolution leading to the overthrow of capitalism and the assumption
of power by the victorious proletariat. The Guesdists denounced this project as sheer nonsense. Guesde said that
workers who could not even be persuaded to vote for Socialist
candidates would be most unlikely to take part in a revolutionary
strike for Socialism. But he could ·not persuade the Trade
Union Federation to dismiss the idea, which, first discussed by
it in 1885–6, thereafter haunted each successive Congress.

At this point a new political group made its appearance on
the Socialist side. In 1885 Benoît Malon (1841–93), who had
fled to Switzerland after taking part in the Paris Commune,
had gone thence to Italy, where he had a considerable influence
in Socialist development, and on his return to France had
worked with Guesde in founding the Parti Ouvrier, started the
Revue Socialiste and, leaving the Guesdists, founded a Société
pour l'Économie Sociale which was intended to serve as an
independent agency for Socialist research on lines similar to
those of the Fabian Society, which had just been set up in
London. Malon, as a resident in Italy, as well as in Switzerland,
during his exile, had established contacts with a great many
foreign Socialists. From 1882 to 1885 he had been publishing
the successive volumes of his massive *Histoire du socialisme*, in
which he had embodied many contributions from Socialists

[1] See Vol. I, p. 146 f.

describing the movements in their own countries. From revolutionism he had passed through semi-Marxism to an evolutionary position, to which he gave the name of *le socialisme intégral*, meaning thereby to indicate that the movement towards Socialism was one not of economic forces alone but of the whole society, and was as much a matter of legal and ethical as of economic factors. This doctrine allied him closely to some aspects of Possibilism ; but he was not a Broussist. He took up a position of independence of the rival Socialist factions and endeavoured to create a body of Socialist thinkers and philosophers who would embrace in their vision, without partisanship, all the aspects of the contemporary Socialist movement. In his hands, the *Revue Socialiste* became an outstanding journal of Socialist theory ; and his Society for Social Economy soon attracted the support of a number of men of high ability — among them both Alexandre Millerand, the future Minister whose entry into the Waldeck-Rousseau Government in 1899 was to lead to a world-wide crisis in the Socialist movement, and Jean Jaurès, the future leader of the Unified Socialist Party.

Malon's society never had either a large membership or a wide appeal. It was essentially a group of intellectuals ; and it attracted especially ambitious young lawyers and other professional men who were repelled by the rival orthodoxies of the Socialist parties and wished to maintain freedom of action while accepting Socialist principles. It proved to be particularly attractive to men who sought entry to Parliament as Socialists without accepting the discipline of any of the organised parties. Accordingly, its adherents developed rather as a parliamentary group than as an organisation. They became the Independent Socialists, a group of deputies who had no formal organisation until they were forced to create one during the crisis which arose out of the *affaire Dreyfus*. Meanwhile, the *Revue Socialiste* was an open forum for the discussion of Socialist ideas and policies.

Malon had begun to develop his essential ideas in a book, *La Question sociale*, which he published at Lugano in 1876. In 1882–3 he published, in two volumes, *Le Nouveau Parti*, in support of Guesde's attempt to create a Socialist Party on a broad basis. His views after his rift with Guesde were set down in *La Morale sociale* (1886) and, more fully, in his principal theoretical work, *Le Socialisme intégral*, which appeared in two volumes in 1890 and 1891.

For the moment, Benoît Malon's initiative in founding his review and his society had little influence on the course of events. In 1886 President Grévy ordered the release of the Anarchist prisoners, and a milder régime set in. This accentuated the differences within the Possibilist Party, in which, as the Broussists moved towards a policy of gradualist advance, a left wing, headed by the former Communard, Jean Allemane (1843–1935) differentiated itself as the advocate of a policy of direct, Trade Union action, decrying parliamentary methods and calling for complete proletarian independence of the bourgeoisie. The quarrel came to a head in 1890, when Allemane's followers broke away from the Broussists and founded a new Parti Ouvrier Socialiste Révolutionnaire. (The Possibilists had dropped the word 'Révolutionnaire' from their title some time before.) The Allemanist party took over most of the Trade Union connections of the Possibilists and became a strong advocate of the revolutionary general strike.

While the Possibilists were quarrelling among themselves, France had been diverted temporarily from attending to *la question sociale* by the Boulangist movement. General Boulanger had first come to the front as an army reformer and a supporter of the common soldier's claims to better treatment. He had been backed by Clemenceau, and had acquired wide popularity by his strong hostility to the German Empire and his advocacy of a policy of *revanche*. His jingoism made him for the moment a national hero; and despite his radical connections he was enthusiastically urged on by Bonapartists, Royalists, and indeed by all the enemies of the Third Republic. Under these influences he came forward with a demand for revision of the constitution to provide for a stronger executive authority — a programme which won the more support because the position of the Republic had been shaken by a series of financial scandals involving leading political personalities. Elected as deputy for the Nord, and later for Paris, he pressed his demands on the Chamber and began to threaten a *coup d'état*. So great were the forces that had rallied round him out of hostility to the existing régime that it was widely believed he had the strength, whenever he pleased, to overturn the constitution and place himself in power by means of a plebiscite. But he delayed, and his opportunity passed. When the Government finally determined on his arrest, instead of calling on the country to rise in his support, he fled to Brussels, and the entire movement collapsed. He was tried for treason and convicted in absence. This was in 1889 : two years later he committed suicide in Brussels on the grave of his dead mistress.

The Boulangist affair caused considerable turmoil in the ranks of the Socialists, as well as elsewhere. A sprinkling of Socialists, including a number of leading followers of Blanqui, supported Boulanger on the strength of his radical record. The Guesdists attempted to stand aside from the whole affair, as an internal squabble among the bourgeois, of no direct concern to revolutionary proletarians. Their unwillingness to rally to the side of the bourgeois Republic, especially in face of the financial scandals that had recently been exposed, helps to account for this attitude, which nevertheless cost them a good deal of working-class support. The Broussists, on the other hand, came closer to the defenders of the bourgeois Republic ; and this helped to precipitate the split in the Possibilist Party, and to gain recruits for the advocates of the general strike, as the instrument with which the proletariat could assert its power in independence of the corrupting influence of parliamentarism and without entangling itself in alliances with the Liberal bourgeoisie.

We have seen that in 1889, when the *affaire Boulanger* was drawing to its ignominious close, two rival International Socialist Congresses were held in Paris — one called by the Guesdists and the other by the still undivided Possibilist Party.[1] What concerns us here is the decision of both these Congresses to institute the celebration of May Day as a Labour festival, and to connect it specially with an international demand for the establishment of the eight hours' day. The immediate occasion for this decision was the action taken by the American Trade Unions, which had been using May Day for this purpose. But at Paris the initiative was taken by the Guesdist, Raymond Lavigne (1851–1930), supported by Liebknecht and Bebel on behalf of the German Social Democratic Party — the dominant

[1] See Chapter I, p. 6 ff.

group at the Marxist Congress. It was decided that May Day should be celebrated in 1890 by national demonstrations in all the countries represented at the Congress, with the eight hours' day as the principal immediate objective. It was left unclear what the precise form of the celebration was to be. Some wanted an entire cessation of work — a one-day general strike ; but the Germans insisted that each national movement should be left free to adopt its own measures, in accordance with the circumstances in each country.

Thus, one group was left free to associate the idea of the May Day celebration with that of the revolutionary general strike, while another group eagerly took up the idea as a means of combating that very proposal. The Guesdists, backed by the German Social Democrats, came out more strongly than ever against the general strike : their opponents in the French Trade Unions set to work to make the new celebration a preparation for it. Actually, the May Day demonstrations which were held all over industrial France in 1890 led to a number of serious clashes with the police ; and the following year at Fourmies, in the Nord, near the Belgian frontier, soldiers who had been called in by the employers fired on the workers' demonstration, killing a girl of 18. This affair caused a sensation, and helped to strengthen the militant wing in the Trade Unions. The annual Congresses called by the Fédération Nationale de Syndicats, which were in fact open to all Trade Union groups that cared to send delegates, became more than ever a battle-ground between the Guesdists and their opponents, with the general strike as the principal issue. As early as 1888, the Bouscat Congress of the F.N.S. had adopted a resolution urging the syndicats to 'separate themselves from the politicians who deceive them' and had declared that, whereas partial strikes could serve as no more than means of agitation and organisation, 'the general strike alone — that is, the entire cessation of all labour and the revolution — can lead the workers towards their emancipation'.

Soon after this resolution, a powerful new advocate of the general strike appeared in Aristide Briand (1862–1932), later its bitter enemy but at this time on the extreme left of the workers' movement. In 1892 Briand produced for the Mar-seilles Labour Congress a full report on the general strike and the way in which it could be brought about, and in the same year the future leader of French Syndicalism, Fernand Pelloutier, also took up its advocacy. Moreover, from 1892 dates the real beginning of Syndicalism, with the foundation of the Fédération des Bourses du Travail, of which Pelloutier became the Secretary the following year.

The first Bourse du Travail had been founded in Paris in 1888, as a sequel to the freedom of organisation conferred by the Trade Union Act of 1884. It was a federal grouping of Parisian Trade Unions, designed to act primarily as a Labour Exchange under Trade Union control, in opposition to the private employment bureaux (*bureaux de placement*) organised in the employers' interests. These agencies not only charged the workers fees for finding them jobs, but also discriminated against known Trade Unionists : they were regarded with intense hostility by the militant workers. As part of the policy of encouraging moderate Trade Unions and industrial conciliation, Waldeck-Rousseau had urged the prefects and the local authorities to help the Trade Unions to develop machinery for collaborating in such matters as vocational training and the filling of jobs, in the hope of diverting them from militant action. The Paris Bourse du Travail, then, was intended to be a means of guiding Trade Unionism into more peaceable ways ; and before long similar Bourses were set up in a number of other towns, usually aided by subventions from the local authorities in respect of their work in organising the supply of labour and the conditions of industrial training. The Possibilists, who, as we saw, were active in local government affairs, strongly supported the new movement.

Up to 1892 the Bourses remained isolated one from another, except that some of them sent delegates to the national and regional Congresses called by the Fédération Nationale de Syndicats. It was as a representative of the Saint-Nazaire Bourse that Pelloutier moved his resolution in favour of the general strike at the Tours regional Congress of 1892. For by this time most of the Bourses, far from carrying out the Government's hopes, had been captured by the Trade Union militants. They were becoming in effect the principal rallying point for those Trade Unionists who objected to the Guesdist domination of the F.N.S. When, in 1892, they set up their separate

Federation and broke away from the F.N.S., they had the good fortune to find in Pelloutier a leader who knew precisely what he wanted to do and had a genius for organisation.

Fernand Pelloutier (1867–1901) came of a middle-class family and received a classical education. His life was one of constant ill-health : he died at the age of 34. Beginning as a Radical, he worked first for Briand as a journalist, and then joined the Guesdist party, with which he retained his connection until in 1890 he was incapacitated by serious illness for two years. He emerged from convalescence to break with the Guesdists and announce his entire disillusionment with all political parties. Instead of politics, which disunited the workers, he called for industrial action to establish the new society. He accepted the general strike as the objective, the instrument of the coming revolution ; but, unlike many of its advocates, he did not believe that it would come about of itself when the right moment arrived, or succeed unless the workers had prepared themselves in advance for the assumption and exercise of power. Nor did he share the view, common to the Guesdists and to many of the Trade Union militants, that it was idle utopianism to speculate about the institutions of the new society that would rise upon the ruins of capitalism. On the contrary, he had a clear vision of the nature of the society he wanted the workers to establish and of the necessary means of preparing the way for it. This vision was in effect a new kind of Anarchist-Communism, transmuted by the central place which he assigned to Trade Unionism, not only in bringing it about, but also in administering it after the revolution. In effect, Pelloutier invented Syndicalism and, as Secretary of the Fédération des Bourses du Travai! from 1895 to his death in 1901, laid the foundations for the Syndicalist phase of French Trade Unionism which reached its culmination only after he had been prematurely removed from the leadership by his last illness and death.

Pelloutier's vision of the future society had as its central point the local community of producers. Whereas the Anarchist-Communists had envisaged the commune as a general grouping of free citizens, he envisaged it as a federal grouping of producers. Each industry, organised in a local syndicat embracing all the occupations within it, would be managed by the local producers on behalf of the commune, which would own the means of production — as far as any concept of ownership would survive. The delegates of the various syndicats would form the communal agency for the administration of the general affairs of the local community ; and such larger administration as was needed would be undertaken by the federated communes of producers. These ideas had much in common with those which César de Paepe had advocated in the days of the First International ;[1] but Pelloutier differed from de Paepe in putting the entire stress on the syndicat — the local Trade Union — as the basic social institution of the coming free society. He was a thorough-going advocate of 'workers' control', believing in the workers' capacity for industrial self-government and rejecting the view that, in the interests of efficient management, the workers at the factory level must continue to work under managers not of their own choosing. He was, however, well aware that the workers were by no means ready or equipped to assume these responsibilities ; and accordingly he regarded as the great immediate mission of the Trade Unions the education of their members for the tasks of 'self-emancipation'. For this purpose the Bourse du Travail appeared to him to be the destined instrument. It was essential, he urged, for the Trade Unions to take over completely the work of *placement* — of supplying labour — and thus to establish a monopoly of the labour factor of production. Equally, they must take over the control of apprenticeship and of all forms of vocational training, and must develop out of their own ranks men capable of holding technical and managerial positions. Furthermore, they must instruct themselves in social and economic knowledge. Every Bourse must have its library and its study-circles, of which every active Trade Unionist should regard it as a duty to make good use. If support for the Bourses could be got from municipal funds, so much the better : they would be able to do all the more to prepare the workers for the Revolution and for the exercise of power. But the Trade Unions must not moderate their aims or tactics in order to secure municipal subventions : they must be fighting organisations, because only the pursuance of militant and energetic immediate policies would put them in the right state of mind for

[1] See Vol. II, Chapter VIII.

the conquest of power. There must be strikes, as preparations for the general strike which would come when they were ready for it.

Pelloutier's best-known work is his *Histoire des bourses du travail*, published in 1902 — the year after his death. He there told the story both of the movement which he had created and of his own ideas. He also collaborated with his brother, Maurice Pelloutier, who later wrote his biography, in a remarkable descriptive work, *La Vie ouvrière en France*, which appeared in 1900 ; and he wrote a number of booklets and manuals for use in the Bourses in furtherance of his educational schemes. By the spring of 1899 his health had become so bad that he had to retire into the country and confine himself to writing, leaving the tasks of organisation to others ; but his influence continued to dominate the Fédération des Bourses until his early death.

Such was the inspirer of the French Syndicalist movement — no proletarian agitator, but a studious intellectual with an intense belief in education and self-mastery as the necessary conditions of the good exercise of power, and in that 'capacity of the working class for self-government' of which Proudhon, in his *Capacité politique des classes ouvrières*, had made himself the exponent a generation earlier. After Pelloutier's death, the Syndicalist movement was to pass under the leadership of a very different person, Victor Griffuelhes — a dour proletarian much more concerned with the revolutionary struggle than with the nature of the new society which was to arrive after the workers' victory. But Pelloutier's utopianism remained alive in the Syndicalist movement after its great inspirer had been removed. It was one element in a doctrine which came to be compounded of a number of influences when, after Pelloutier's death, the Fédération des Bourses du Travail ceased to exist as a separate body and became a constituent part of the reorganised Confédération Générale du Travail.

The year 1892, when the Fédération des Bourses du Travail was established, was also that of the *affaire Ravachol*,[1] which opened up a new series of Anarchist assassinations. But this did not prevent the Socialists, of a variety of colours, from winning considerable successes, nationally and locally, at the

[1] See Vol. II, p. 333.

elections held in 1893. That same year the Paris Labour Congress recommended the fusion of the Fédération Nationale de Syndicats and the F.B.T., after the Government had closed the Paris Bourse du Travail. The following year Pelloutier, in collaboration with Henri Giraud, published his manual, *Qu'est-ce que la grève générale?* (What is the general strike?), and took office as Assistant Secretary of the F.B.T. A few months later, in 1895, he became General Secretary. Meanwhile the Nantes Labour Congress of 1894 had decided to set up a special committee, with independent finance and powers of action, to take over the task of preparing the workers for the general strike. By this time the Guesdists had definitely lost control of the F.N.S., in which they gradually ceased to take any part. The new elements which controlled the F.N.S. and the Committee for the General Strike included Allemanists and some Blanquists, but there was also a strong contingent of Anarchist-Communists, headed by Émile Pouget. It might have appeared natural for the Fédération des Bourses du Travail to take the advice of the Paris Congress and accept amalgamation with the F.N.S. But the Bourses, under Pelloutier's leadership, refused. Pelloutier and his group regarded the F.N.S. with some suspicion and objected to its inefficiency ; and Pelloutier saw his way to develop his educational plans through the Bourses and felt they would probably be wrecked if the F.B.T. gave up its independence. In face of this refusal, the F.N.S. decided to reorganise and to appeal to the individual Bourses to transfer to it from the F.B.T. At the Limoges Labour Congress of 1895 the F.N.S. was transformed into the Confédération Générale du Travail, subdivided into two sections, of which one represented national and local syndicats, or federations of local syndicats in particular trades or industries, and the other Bourses du Travail and local Unions de Syndicats (Trades Councils) or similar bodies. The F.B.T. was again invited to affiliate, but again refused. The two bodies thus became rivals ; and their rivalry continued, with a short interval during which the F.B.T. first joined and then seceded from the C.G.T., until 1902. Up to 1896 there was a third body, called the Secrétariat National du Travail, which was also attempting to act as a co-ordinating agency. This had been set up on the initiative of the International Labour

Congress of 1891, which recommended the establishment of such agencies in all countries with the idea of using them as the means of linking the various national movements together. This move had no success : the French National Secretariat never commanded much support. It expired in 1896, leaving the C.G.T. and the F.B.T. to share the field.

That same year the Allemanist Party split, and the seceders, who demanded a more revolutionary policy, formed the Alliance Communiste Révolutionnaire. There were thus no fewer than six national Socialist parties — Guesdists, Broussists, Allemanists, Blanquists, Communists, and Independents — all fighting one another, though some of them sometimes combined on particular occasions and most of them reached in 1896 an agreement that, though they might oppose one another at elections in the first ballot, they would all vote in the second ballot for the surviving Socialist candidate. Besides the parties, and overlapping them in varying degrees, there were a number of Anarchist groups, the Trade Union militants of the C.G.T., and the Fédération des Bourses du Travail. The moderate Mutualist group which had seceded at the Marseilles Congress of 1879 had faded away, and its leader, Barberet, had become a government official in charge of labour information services. The mantle of moderation had passed over to a section of the Independent Socialists — the successors of Malon's group — headed by Alexandre Millerand. In 1896, at a Socialist banquet held at Saint-Mandé and attended by many of the Socialist leaders, including Guesde, Jaurès, and even Vaillant, the Blanquist leader, Millerand delivered an oration, which became famous, in support of a reformist policy. The banquet was organised to celebrate the municipal successes of the Socialists and to promote a better understanding between the Socialist parties ; and the purpose of Millerand's oration was to define what the various groups of Socialists had in common.

Alexandre Millerand (1859–1943) had been a deputy since 1885, and was a leading member of the Independent group. In 1896 he was editing *La Petite République*, in which he and Jaurès were earnestly advocating Socialist unity. Only three years later he was to accept office in a Radical Cabinet ; but at this time no such development was expected. Millerand was, however, already well on the right of the Socialist movement.

In his oration he scoffed at the idea that Socialists should seek to reach their objectives by other than constitutional means, or without winning the support of a majority of the people. He spoke enthusiastically of the virtues of manhood suffrage and, with obvious reference to General Boulanger, denounced *coups d'état* and would-be dictators. He proclaimed as the objects of Socialism the general diffusion of liberty and property, and declared his devotion to the Republic. He spoke, moreover, in an entirely gradualist strain, disclaiming the notion that Socialism could be introduced all at once, and representing it as an inevitable tendency which Socialists could do nothing to make, but could only guide by co-operating with the necessary forces of social evolution. In this part of his speech, though the language was that of Marxism, the meaning was much closer to the Fabian evolutionism of Sidney Webb. Millerand put the development of public ownership of the means of large-scale production right in the forefront of his account of the essentials of Socialism ; and he clearly meant this process of gradual socialisation to take place under the existing State, and not to be postponed, as Kautsky would have had it, until after the workers' conquest of power. Like the Fabians, he laid much stress on municipal enterprise, beginning with the taking of essential services into public hands. He spoke of industries and services being taken over, nationally or locally, one after another, as they became ripe ; and, like the German Social Democrats and the Fabians, he rested his case on the inevitable tendency towards capitalist monopoly as preparing the way for public ownership and administration. He asserted that the small property owners had nothing to fear from Socialism, because their enterprises would not be taken over. Of the peasant problem he made no special mention.

In the closing section of his speech, Millerand proceeded to discuss the question of internationalism. He declared himself a believer in the international solidarity of the working class ; but at the same time he proclaimed himself a nationalist and ready to rally at need to the defence of *la patrie*. He thus repudiated entirely the anti-militarist internationalism which was the doctrine of the leaders of the C.G.T., and agreed with Bernstein in regarding as nonsense Marx's assertion in the *Communist Manifesto*, that 'the workers have no country'.

It is a remarkable fact that the Saint-Mandé oration, far from provoking outraged protests from Millerand's hearers, seems to have been enthusiastically received and to have helped to promote closer unity of action between the main Socialist parties, including the Guesdists and even a section of the Blanquists, who can hardly have agreed with it. It has to be remembered that it was delivered at a time of Republican crisis, only a few years after the very life of the Republic had seemed to be menaced by Boulanger and a section of the Blanquists had given their support to the Boulangist movement and had thus helped to drive the rest into a stronger sense of the need to rally round the democratic political structure of the Republic. But, even so, the acquiescence of the men who listened to the Saint-Mandé oration is remarkable; and it helped to strengthen the distrust of politicians which was already very great in a large section of the French working class, and therewith to reinforce the Syndicalist tendency in the growing Trade Union movement.

Millerand's speech was delivered not long before the new crisis of the Republic, arising out of the *affaire Dreyfus*, came to a head and gave a further impulse to the movement for Socialist unity. Towards the end of 1897, the battle over the Dreyfus case was fairly joined with the publication of Émile Zola's *J'accuse*. Captain Alfred Dreyfus, a Jewish officer in the French army, had been charged with betraying military documents to agents of a foreign power, and had been convicted and sent to Devil's Island on evidence which was shown to have been trumped up. The affair went back to 1894; but the protest movement which was launched by his supporters took time to gather force, and at first the Socialists seem to have paid little attention to it. It provoked, however, a violent campaign of Anti-Semitism masquerading as patriotism. Anti-Semitism was already strong in French reactionary circles, and had been fanned by an organised group led by Édouard Drumont (1844–1917), whose scandalous book, *La France juive*, had appeared in 1886. From 1892 Drumont had been editing an anti-Semitic journal, *La Libre Parole*, in which he attacked particularly those Jews who had been involved in the financial scandals that were all too frequent during these years — notably the Panama Canal scandal of 1892. When the Dreyfus case occurred, Drumont made full use of it to arouse patriotic feeling against the Jews. Zola, who took up the defence of Dreyfus, was prosecuted and convicted for his charges against the army authorities, and had to flee the country. But presently the Dreyfusards were able to prove that the documents alleged to show Dreyfus's guilt had been forged and that persons high up in the army and the Ministry of War had been parties to the fraud. The Government was compelled to order an investigation, much to the fury of the opponents of Dreyfus, who persisted in asserting his guilt. A group of fanatics, headed by Paul Déroulède, even planned an anti-Republican rising. So persistent and powerful were Dreyfus's enemies that, when he was retried, he was again convicted, despite the clear proof of the forgeries. By this time, however, the counter-feeling on his side was so strong that President Loubet immediately pardoned him and set him free. Even then, his innocence was not admitted and he was not reinstated in the army, from which he had been expelled with public ignominy. Not until 1906 was a new trial held before the Court of Cassation, a complete acquittal secured, and Dreyfus restored to his military rank.

This extraordinary and disgraceful affair had, in relation to Socialism, two main effects. It caused, on the one hand, a rallying of the Socialist politicians to the cause of the threatened Republic and a *rapprochement* between most of the Socialist groups, and, on the other hand, a sharp anti-political, anti-state revulsion among many Frenchmen, leading among the workers to a strengthening of Syndicalism in its revolutionary form. It thus drove a fresh wedge between the Socialist parties and the Trade Unions. The Socialist parties formed in 1898 a Joint Vigilance Committee to protect the Republic; and the Blanquists transformed themselves formally into a political party, in place of their Comité Central Révolutionnaire. (They took the name of Parti Socialiste Révolutionnaire; but in practice their revolutionism became considerably diluted.)

During the same year, 1898, the Trade Unions suffered a serious set-back. They had been affected by the general excitement that attended the *affaire Dreyfus*, but had taken no part in it, beyond using it to illustrate the rottenness of politics and politicians. Since 1894 the Committee for the General Strike, set up at the Nantes Labour Congress, had been undertaking propaganda and trying to familiarise the workers with the idea of a revolution to be accomplished with the initial aid of a general cessation of work. The prevailing idea was that the general strike could not profitably be planned for, or arranged for, any definite date. It would happen when the right moment arrived, provided only that the working class had been educated to expect it and to put it to revolutionary use. The general view was that it would begin with a big strike in a particular industry, or perhaps in a particular area, and that the workers in other industries or areas would then leave work of their own accord, stimulated in all probability by some incident between the original strikers and the police or the soldiery who would be called in to aid the employers in breaking their resistance. Sorel had not yet put forward his conception of the general strike as a 'social myth' : it was expected actually to occur, and to begin the Revolution. But in the view of the leaders of the movement, a general strike prepared and organised in advance would be bound to fail : the cessation of work and the ensuing mass demonstrations must occur spontaneously, as the expression of working-class feeling, or the requisite mass-enthusiasm would be wanting.

In 1898 the leaders of the C.G.T. believed that their moment had come. An extensive building strike was in progress ; and the Railwaymen's Federation had formulated a programme of demands and was preparing to strike for their achievement. A national strike of railwaymen, involving public employees of the State Railways, raised a big legal issue ; for the rights of combination and strike action conceded in 1884 had been ruled not to apply to public employees. A railway strike was thus of doubtful legality, and was certain to provoke strong Government action against the strikers. The advocates of the revolutionary general strike anticipated that the Government's counter-measures against the strikers, who were expected to resort to vigorous action in order to prevent the running of blackleg services, would rouse working-class feeling and bring workers in other industries streaming out on strike in the railwaymen's support. The Central Committee of the Confédération Générale du Travail decided to send out a secret letter urging all the Trade Unions to stand ready to rally to the railwaymen's aid ; but the Government got wind of the letter and intercepted it. When the moment came, the railway strike was a complete fiasco. Threatened with dismissal and the suppression of their syndicats, the railway workers, save a handful, remained at work; and the entire movement collapsed. In the ensuing inquest on what had gone wrong, the Secretary of the C.G.T., Lagailse, came under strong suspicion of having betrayed that body's plans to the Government, and was deposed from office. The C.G.T. set to work to reorganise its forces under stronger left-wing leadership; but it had suffered a serious blow.

It was still licking its wounds when, in 1899, the crisis over the Dreyfus case brought to power a ministry of Republican defence headed by Waldeck-Rousseau. The new Prime Minister, wishing to bring the Socialists into a general rally of the Republican forces, offered the Ministry of Commerce and Industry to the Independent Socialist, Alexandre Millerand, who accepted without consulting either the joint Socialist Vigilance Committee or even his own party colleagues. This was the first instance since 1848 of a Socialist being offered Cabinet office — and of course Louis Blanc's office in the Republican Government of 1848 had been the outcome of revolution and not of a parliamentary shift of power. Millerand's acceptance at once provoked a storm in the Socialist movement. He himself defended his action as necessary to save the Republic and professed his continued adherence to the principles he had laid down in his Saint-Mandé oration. Jean Jaurès and the rest of the Independents — some with misgivings and some whole-heartedly — rallied to his support. Socialist unity was broken: the Guesdists and Blanquists denounced Millerand's action as a betrayal of Socialism, and formed a Socialist Revolutionary Union in opposition. The Independent Socialists, the Broussists, and the Allemanists (shorn of their left wing by the split of 1896) drew together in a league which took the name of Parti Socialiste Français, but left the separate parties in independent existence. On a similar basis, the Guesdists and Édouard Vaillant's Blanquist followers joined forces and took the name of Parti Socialiste de France.

This breach was not made complete until the Lyons Congress of 1901 had shown the incompatibility of the rival points of view. In the meantime, Millerand had brought forward a programme of labour reforms and had proclaimed himself as the apostle of *le socialisme réformiste*. Millerand wished to alter the status of the syndicats by constituting them legal persons capable of suing or being sued at law ; to endow them with the power to engage in commercial operations and to encourage the practice of 'collective labour contracts', under which the syndicats would undertake collectively to provide and organise the labour needed for carrying out jobs at an agreed price ; to introduce compulsory arbitration in labour disputes ; and to provide that strike action should be taken only with the sanction of a majority of the workers affected, to be given by ballot vote, and to be renewed at short intervals — failing which, the strike would become illegal. He wished to establish Councils of Labour in the various industries ; to reorganise, with fuller Trade Union representation, the Conseil Supérieur du Travail already founded in 1891 ; and also to set up in all considerable establishments Works Councils for the promotion of better relations between employers and employed.

This policy of social peace was vehemently denounced by the Trade Union leaders both in 1899–1900, when it was first advanced, and when it was renewed by Millerand in 1906. 'They want to tame us' (*nous domestiquer*) said Victor Griffuelhes, the militant spokesman of the C.G.T. It was pointed out that making the Trade Unions legal persons would expose them to actions for damages arising out of strike action (as happened in Great Britain almost at the same time in the Taff Vale case), and that the proposed regulation of strike action would outlaw the sudden strike, which was the Syndicalists' favourite weapon. The Fédération des Bourses du Travail, equally with the C.G.T., denounced Millerand's projects as a wholly illegitimate interference with the right of the Trade Unions to order their affairs as they pleased.

For the time being, nothing much was done ; but Millerand's attempt to tame the Trade Unions was an important factor — Pelloutier's death was another — in inducing the two central labour organisations at length to join forces. In 1902 the C.G.T. and the F.B.T. amalgamated into a single body, with the Trade Unions and the Bourses as equal partners and a central committee representing the two sections on a basis of equality. The Bourses had by this time mostly lost their municipal subsidies and ceased to work with the municipalities, even where these were under Socialist control; and in a number of cases the local Bourses had become sub-sections of Unions de Syndicats covering whole départements or groups of neighbouring centres of industry. Pelloutier had made great efforts to extend their influence into the agricultural districts, chiefly by organising the craftsmen in the small towns and villages and setting them to work as missionaries to the agricultural wage-workers. But outside some of the wine-growing districts this policy had not made much progress.

One section of the amalgamated C.G.T. consisted of Bourses du Travail and local or departmental Unions de Syndicats. The other was made up of craft or industrial national Fédérations de Syndicats and of detached local syndicats for which no national federation existed. Local syndicats, except in such cases, were no longer admitted: membership was twofold, through adherence to a Bourse or Union and to a national, or in a few cases a regional, Fédération. The policy of the C.G.T. was to encourage the grouping of the syndicats in Fédérations on a basis of industry rather than of craft — for evidently this was the right basis if the workers were presently to take over the control of industry. But in practice it was not possible to enforce industrial unity in all cases; and craft Fédérations 'had to be allowed to remain in the C.G.T., under continual pressure to amend their ways.

Before the amalgamated C.G.T. came into being, its predecessor had started, in 1900, an official organ, *La Voix du Peuple*, edited by the former Anarchist Émile Pouget (1860–1932), who had earlier secured a considerable success with his hard-hitting and vivid journal, *Le Père Peinard*.[1] The leader of the C.G.T. was the former Blanquist, Victor Griffuelhes (1875–1922), a workman, militant, class-conscious, blunt to rudeness, and strongly suspicious of intellectuals who aspired to leadership. Unlike Pelloutier, Griffuelhes did not trouble his head with theories about the coming society: what interested him was the daily struggle, which he regarded as a means of educating the workers in hostility to capitalism and in militant action that would culminate one day — not very distant — in the revolutionary general strike. But this did not mean that

[1] See Vol. II, p. 327 ff.

Griffuelhes cherished illusions about the capacity or will to power of the ordinary workman. He continually denounced the 'mutton-headed stupidity' of the majority, and rested his faith, not on their will to act but rather on their mass-suggestibility. They could, he believed, be led into revolutionary action by the determined leadership of a 'conscious minority' — an idea which he took over from Blanqui and made an essential part of the Syndicalist gospel as it developed in the C.G.T. under his leadership. Griffuelhes was also largely responsible for the strong anti-militarist line which the C.G.T. adopted and for the prominence given by it to the conception of the international general strike as a means of preventing war. His chief lieutenant, Pouget, became Secretary of the department of the syndicats within the C.G.T.: Georges Yvetot (1868–1942), Pelloutier's second-in-command, took over the department of the Bourses du Travail. The C.G.T., strengthened by the cessation of its rivalry with the F.B.T., took on a fresh militancy, and entered upon what Édouard Dolléans has called its 'heroic age'.

But before we deal with the development of Syndicalist doctrine after 1902, we must turn back to consider what happened to French Socialism after Millerand's entry into the Waldeck-Rousseau Ministry. The Guesdists, the Blanquists, and the Communist Alliance which had broken away from the Allemanist Party at once issued a manifesto against Millerand's action, and announced that he could commit no one but himself, and that they had withdrawn from the Socialist Union in the Chamber of Deputies. They persuaded the Federation of Socialist Workers to convene a Congress open to all working-class bodies which accepted the class-struggle as the basis of international Socialism: the Congress was to pronounce on the legitimacy of Socialist participation in a bourgeois Government. But when the 800 delegates met, representing 1400 organised groups, no clear lead was given. By 818 votes to 634, the Congress declared that the class-struggle did not allow of Socialists taking part in a bourgeois Government; but it went on to pass, by 1140 votes to 240, a second resolution recognising that exceptional circumstances might induce the Socialist Party to envisage 'the expediency of such participation'. It further resolved that 'in the existing state of capitalist society, exclusive consideration should be given to the winning of electoral positions, as the political expropriation of the capitalist class ought to be accomplished before the revolution'.

Having delivered these ambiguous judgments, the Congress proceeded to constitute itself as a 'party', not by fusing its constituent organisations, but by forming a loose federal organisation in which the separate groups were represented. The Guesdist Labour Party, as the largest group, was given 12 seats on the General Committee, the Blanquist Revolutionary Socialist Party 6, the Federation of Socialist Workers 3 ; and there were also 4 Trade Union delegates, 1 from the Socialist Co-operative Societies, and 7 from the autonomous regional Federations which had attended the Congress. These together constituted the Parti Socialiste de France ; but as each body continued its separate organisation, the effect of their union was not great, except in the Chamber of Deputies and in other elected public bodies, in which their members worked together as a group. On the other side, the Independents, the Broussists, the rump of the Allemanists, and a number of other groups, similarly united in a loose federal Parti Socialiste Français, supported the Waldeck-Rousseau Government in its struggle to preserve the democratic Republic and exonerated Millerand on account of the commanding necessity of this defence.

From the national level the question was transferred to the International Socialist Congress which met in Paris in 1900. There, as we have seen, the celebrated Kautsky resolution, drafted by Kautsky but actually moved at the Congress by Émile Vandervelde, attempted to formulate an answer to the problem posed by Millerand's action in such a way as to make clear the disapproval of it by the great majority of Socialists, without actually closing the door to Socialist participation in all circumstances. The text of the resolution has already been given.[1]

This resolution, drawn up by the leading theorist of German Marxism, then in the midst of his contest with the Revisionists, came down on the whole against Millerand, who certainly had not the support of 'the great majority' of the French Socialists, and was assuredly not acting as the 'mandatory' even of the parties which were prepared to endorse his participation. It

[1] See p. 39 ff.

did not, however, give the unequivocal decision on the question of principle which the Guesdists and their allies wanted : nor did it involve the expulsion from the International of the parties which had endorsed, or refused to condemn, what Millerand had done. Jaurès, who had defended Millerand in the debate, announced at the end that he accepted the International's verdict. But the rift in French Socialism was not healed : it took three more years of pressure from the International to bring unification about, and when it came the differences were scaled over rather than reconciled.

In France, the rival groups of parties held from 1901 to 1905 their separate Congresses ; and each formulated its own programme. The Parti Socialiste de France proclaimed itself 'the party of the Revolution' and took its stand on the class-struggle, national and international, for the conquest of political power and the expropriation of the possessing class. It rejected 'all compromise with any section of the bourgeoisie' and demanded the 'socialisation of the means of production and exchange', which it characterised as the 'transformation of capitalist society into a collectivist or communist society'. It declared that, though it was part of its task to enforce (*arracher*) 'such reforms as might better the working class's conditions of struggle', it would under no circumstances 'by participation in the central power, by voting for the budget, or by alliance with bourgeois parties, provide any of the means that might prolong the domination of the bourgeois enemy'.

The Parti Socialiste de France, at its Tours Congress of 1902, also formulated a declaration. This began by asserting the connection between Socialism and the development both of democracy and of the forms of production. 'Between the political régime, which is the outcome of the [French] Revolution, and the economic régime, contradiction exists. The evolution of the means of production has put the world under the domination of capitalist forces. Only proletarian action can cure the universal disorder. But it is the right course neither to discard the hypothesis of revolutionary occurrences, nor to neglect the great potentialities of legal pressure. Socialism is republican : it is the very Republic, because it is the extension of the Republic to the régime of property and labour.' The programme then declared in favour of international solidarity against war, and proceeded to outline a series of reforms to be worked for within the existing political structure. These included democratisation of the State, *laïcité* (secularity), educational development, tax reform, labour protection, and social insurance laws.

At the general election of 1902, the rival groups polled almost the same aggregate vote — 400,000 each. But whereas the Parti Socialiste de France won only 12 seats, the Parti Socialiste Français, thanks to electoral coalitions with bourgeois groups, won 37. In 1904 the former had about 18,000 subscribing members, and latter about 10,000. Each side had its press ; but the moderates were soon to be the better served : *Humanité* was founded in 1904, and at once became the outstanding Socialist newspaper.

Millerand's participation in the Waldeck-Rousseau Government did not end his connection with Socialism. He continued to regard himself as belonging to the 'Socialist Party' — a phrase which Frenchmen habitually used to describe the whole complex of parties and groups of which the political Socialist movement was made up. In 1903, when he was no longer in office, he gathered together into a volume a number of his speeches, beginning with the Saint-Mandé oration of 1896 ; and to this collection he gave the title *Le Socialisme réformiste français*. In an introduction to this volume, Millerand summed up his point of view. He echoed the sentiment that identified the cause of Socialism with that of the Republic and with the democratic electoral system. He declared the imperative need for Socialists, instead of isolating themselves from the Republic and from the life of contemporary France, to play an actively constructive part in contemporary affairs both nationally and in local government, and not to be afraid of alliances with the bourgeois parties of the left wherever such alliances were needed to safeguard or extend democracy, or to secure the enactment of useful reforms. He affirmed his support of Trade Unions and Co-operative Societies ; but he said that, in place of the existing chaos of economic affairs, he wanted to see industry organised to play a proper part in the life of the nation. He wanted the workers to share in the responsibility for productive efficiency and, instead of bickering continually with the employers, to come to terms with them. For this purpose, he

351

reiterated his belief in the value of works councils (conseils d'usine) to negotiate with factory managements and enter into collective contracts for the execution of the work. He declared again his belief in arbitration and in industrial peace. Regarding Socialism as an inevitable tendency rather than a preconceived system, he attacked those who believed it could be set up suddenly by a proletarian conquest of power. He envisaged as Bernstein did, rather a gradual movement towards Socialism than even a distant arrival at a Socialist goal. This gradual advance would be marked not only by the taking of one essential service after another into public hands but also by the development of a wide range of protective measures for the workers and of social legislation, including better provision for health and education and the institution of social insurance. With such legislation would go an advance in local government activity — the Parti Socialiste Français adopted an extensive municipal programme in 1904.

Millerand laid great stress on the duty of Socialists to extend personal liberty and to promote the distribution of property in the means of enjoyment. The Socialists, he said, far from wishing to abolish private property, stood for its extension to all : far from wishing to curtail liberty, they were ardent devotees of the rights of man. In these respects they had a great deal of common ground with the bourgeois Radicals ; and they should seek to make the most of what they had in common, in order to facilitate the adoption of their ideas. He argued that in practice Socialists in Parliament and on local governing bodies, whatever the principles on which they professed to act, had owed such successes as they had achieved to working with other progressives instead of isolating themselves on the basis of class-war doctrine.

Finally, turning to international questions, he restated with much greater emphasis the view he had expressed at Saint-Mandé that there was no inconsistency between nationalism and internationalism. Repudiating chauvinism, he asserted the necessity of national defence. Describing France as 'the foremost soldier' of the ideal which Socialists professed, he said that unilateral disarmament would be a crime against this ideal. Then, in his peroration, he called on French Socialists to discard the ambiguous and misleading term 'revolutionary' and to proclaim themselves openly as 'reformists' — 'since reformists we are'.

These principles, as Millerand applied them, were soon to lead him out of the ranks of the Socialist movement and back into office as a leading personage in a bourgeois Government which was not, like that of Waldeck-Rousseau, based on an immediate and imperative need to rally to the defence of the threatened Republic. His plea for working with the bourgeois parties, not merely in an exceptional crisis but as a settled policy, was not at all acceptable to most of the supporters of the Parti Socialiste Français. They had been prepared to defend his action in 1899 as an unpleasant necessity ; but most of them were quite unprepared to endorse his thoroughgoing programme of class-reconciliation and of friendly collaboration between employers and employed. He was not without distinguished supporters among the Independent Socialists : René Viviani (1863–1925), who was to be Prime Minister when war broke out in 1914, went with him all the way, and Aristide Briand (1862–1932), until recently the vociferous advocate of the general strike, soon made his great *volte-face* and became the partner of Millerand and Viviani in bourgeois office. But Jaurès carried the majority of the adherents of the Parti Socialiste Français with him into the unified Socialist Party of 1905 ; and *le socialisme réformiste* lived on only as the creed of a parliamentary faction — a group of prominent politicians without an organised following in the country. The French Socialists, even if they largely practised Reformism, were no more prepared to swallow the name than the German Social Democrats were to espouse Bernstein's Revisionism as their admitted creed. The French situation, however, differed sharply from the German. In Germany, the Trade Unions were, and remained, the docile followers of the Social Democratic Party, despite their personal independence of it. In France, the Trade Unions found in Syndicalism a philosophy and a programme of their own, which reinstated the 'revolution' as the objective and lumped all the politicians together as 'fakers' because they attempted to operate by parliamentary methods and were thus driven to 'class-collaboration', instead of conducting the class-struggle on its natural ground, the economic — *sur le terrain de classe*.

CHAPTER VIII

FRANCE AFTER 1905. THE UNIFIED PARTY AND THE SYNDICALISTS. JAURÈS AND SOREL

THERE were some who hoped, when the French Socialists unified their political forces in 1905 under the leadership of Jean Jaurès, that the new situation would lead to unification between the political and the industrial wings of the working-class movement as well. The 'anti-politicals' in the Trade Unions had often argued against any association with the Socialist parties on the ground that the effect would be to split the workers up, industrially as well as politically, into warring factions and thus to render them impotent either to protect the immediate interests of their members or to pursue their wider objectives with any hope of success. This argument lost its force when the Socialists agreed to form an unified party — except, of course, among those who believed that the union would speedily dissolve. It was indeed evident that unification had not removed the differences between right and left, and that it would not be an easy matter to hold the conflicting elements together. But the same could be said of the Confédération Générale du Travail, which had equally its revolutionary and its reformist wings and, between them, a shifting body of opinion which inclined now to one side and now to the other. There were, no doubt, even more imperative arguments for unity in the industrial than in the political field ; for Trade Unions do not stand much chance of success in either negotiations or strikes unless they can present an united front ; whereas, under the second ballot system in force in France, it was quite possible for rival Socialist candidates to fight one another at the first ballot and for their supporters then to join forces for the second. Nevertheless, the achievement of political unity did bring a good deal of fresh support to the Socialist Party ; and it could be argued that the logical sequel to it was a concordat between the united party and the Trade Union movement.

No such thing occurred, or came near occurring. On the contrary, the C.G.T. at its Amiens Congress of 1906 adopted by an overwhelming majority the Charter in which it proclaimed the complete independence of the Trade Union movement and its repudiation of all political party alliances. A small section, headed by V. Renard of the Textile Federation, attempted to persuade the Congress to ally itself to the Socialist Party ; but it was brushed aside by the combined opposition of the revolutionary Syndicalists and the Reformists. The Reformists, whose chief spokesman was Auguste Keufer of the Fédération du Livre, wanted to keep the Trade Unions strictly to economic activities, and to avoid any entanglement of them with political issues. The Revolutionaries, on the contrary, wanted the Trade Unions to act politically, but to do so by direct action and not by taking any part in parliamentary affairs. 'On peut arracher directement les lois utiles', they exclaimed ; for they did not at all object in most cases to attempts to secure legislation in the workers' interests, even within the capitalist system. What they insisted on was that the workers must win such legislation by their own strength — by demonstrations and strikes — and not by relying on the politicians, of any party, to secure it for them. Thus moderates and revolutionaries were able to join forces to vote down the proposal that there should be any alliance between the C.G.T. and the Socialist Party ; and many members of the Socialist Party supported this view, because they feared that any attempt to enforce an alliance would disrupt the unity of the Trade Union movement. Jaurès himself always took good care to present himself as an upholder of *l'autonomie syndicale*.

Within the C.G.T. the Revolutionaries held a majority over the Reformists ; but the minority was considerable. Moreover, the majority was by no means homogeneous. It was made up of advocates of aggressive strike action, based on the doctrine of the class-war ; but it was divided into Anarchists, pure Syndicalists, and Socialists who were not opposed to parliamentary action, even if they gave pride of place to direct action and held that the Trade Unions, as organised bodies, should keep out of the electioneering field. Many of them belonged to the

Socialist Party; and it was made clear at Amiens that they had a perfect right to do so, and to be active politicians if they pleased, as long as they did not try to draw the Trade Unions into party politics. The C.G.T. was never Anarchist, though some of its leaders were : nor was it even anti-parliamentary, in the sense of requiring its members to be so. Even less was it Sorelist, in the sense of taking its doctrine or its policy from that highly undependable philosopher of violence. It developed its basic doctrine, that the workers must rely on their own efforts and must fight their main battles for themselves, without relying on anyone else's help, quite apart from Sorel, as an inheritance from a revolutionary past reinterpreted by Fernand Pelloutier, but going back through Eugène Varlin and the days of the Commune to the traditions of 1848 and even of 1796.

The years between 1902 and 1909 have often been described as the 'heroic period' of French Syndicalism. Its outstanding figure during this period was Victor Griffuelhes (1874–1923), who became Secretary of the C.G.T. in 1902. Griffuelhes was a remarkable person. By trade a ladies' shoemaker, he persisted in carrying on his skilled craft in such time as he could spare even while he was conducting the affairs of the C.G.T. He was rude to coarseness and exceedingly blunt of speech even to those with whom he had to work most closely — so that he made many enemies in the C.G.T. as well as outside it. By faith he was not an Anarchist, but a Blanquist, with a deep contempt for the stupidity of the common man ; and he never hesitated to denounce the feebleness and mutton-headedness of his own followers. With this attitude he combined a strong dislike of intellectuals who attempted to poke their noses into working-class affairs. He was acutely class-conscious, but thought of his class mainly in terms of an élite of revolutionary proletarians whose task it was to lead the masses by espousing their immediate grievances and thus training them in action for revolutionary behaviour. At the outset he was somewhat scornful of Pelloutier's insistence on the need for working-class education and spoke contemptuously of the danger of turning the Trade Union movement into an affair of study-circles instead of leading it into the fray. Later, after he had ceased to hold office in the C.G.T., he was converted by Alphonse Merrheim (1871–1925), the leader of the Metalworkers'

Federation and, next to him, the outstanding figure in Revolutionary Syndicalism, to the view that it was after all necessary for the workers, or at any rate for their activists, to understand the ways of capitalism and to train themselves for the task of running industry in the coming society, and that there was no inconsistency between education and action. But by temperament he was not an educator but an agitator, with a belief that, the more trouble there was between the workers and their masters, the more revolutionary and the less 'muttonish' they would both become. For he welcomed militant masters as well as militant workers : the more unreasonable employers were, the better was he pleased ; the more they invoked the Government to send in soldiers to blackleg or to shoot down demonstrators, the nearer he felt the revolution to be. In effect, he remained throughout a Blanquist, but one who had come to conceive of the social revolution in terms of industrial action as the harbinger of insurrection.

In the eyes of Griffuelhes and Merrheim, of Émile Pouget, and of Georges Yvetot and of Paul Delesalle (1870–1948) — to name the principal leaders of the C.G.T.'s left wing during the 'heroic years' — the great danger facing the working-class movement was that of 'domestication'. They saw the Reformist Socialists as having deliberately set out, from the time of the Waldeck-Rousseau Ministry of 1899, to tame the Trade Unions by the offer of specious concessions and fraudulent social reforms.

This, of course, was precisely what Alexandre Millerand was attempting to do. In his view, revolutionism was folly, and the right course was for the workers to break away from the revolutionary tradition and adopt the policy of Reformism which he had outlined in his Saint-Mandé oration of 1896. Millerand wanted the Trade Unions to stop their mass-demonstrations and calls to strike action and to enlist the aid of the State in inducing the employers to bargain with them, to enter into binding collective agreements, and, where they could not come to agreement, to accept arbitration sponsored by the State. At the same time he wanted the State to enact protective legislation for the improvement of industrial conditions, and also to introduce forms of social insurance — especially old age pensions — based on contributions from employers and workers. The Syndicalists would have none of this policy of industrial peace, which they regarded as mere deception. For them the capitalist State was an enemy agency, incapable of being converted into an instrument of welfare, and the employer no less an enemy to be combated and not come to terms with, except by way of occasional truce in a continuing class-war. They were against any collective agreements that would tie the workers to capitalism, and turn the Trade Unions into agencies for disciplining their members in the interests of capitalist production.

There was thus a sharp conflict of principles, which was speedily translated into a positive conflict of forces. For when the workers, in pursuance of their policy of 'direct action', struck work and refused to respond to the offers of the Government or the local public authorities to act as impartial mediators, these same authorities were invoked by the employers to take action against the strikers' unreasonable behaviour, to preserve the peace, and to ensure the maintenance of production by enabling blacklegs to work or, in the case of essential services, themselves to supply blacklegs by sending in soldiers from the corps of engineers to take the strikers' places. One violent clash followed another : demonstrators and strikers were shot down or bludgeoned, and quite a number killed : the Trade Unions issued proclamations of protest, in which they incited the soldiers not to shoot : the authorities arrested the leaders responsible for these placards and there were further protest demonstrations, in which more killing and wounding occurred. There was, indeed, nothing new in this kind of violence, which had a long history behind it. What made the difference was that in the period after 1900 it was being carried on largely under the auspices of men who were, or had recently been, Socialists, and still called themselves Socialists, though they had become Ministers in bourgeois Governments. To the *affaire Millerand* succeeded the *affaire Viviani*, when René Viviani, following his lead, became Minister of Labour in the Clemenceau Cabinet of 1906. Then came the much more sensational *affaire Briand*, when Aristide Briand, who unlike Millerand and Viviani had been, as we saw, an outstanding figure on the extreme left and a leading advocate of the general strike, abruptly changed sides and as Prime Minister in a

Radical Cabinet broke the railwaymen's strike of 1910, not only by occupying the stations with soldiers and sending in engineers to take over strikers' tasks, but also by calling the railwaymen who were army reservists to the colours and setting them to work to break their own strike. Briand had already been expelled from the unified Socialist Party in 1906, for taking office in Clemenceau's Government; and round him, Millerand, and Viviani there had grown up in the Chamber of Deputies an informal group of 'coalition' Socialists at sharp issue with the unified Socialist Party. In 1910, before Briand became Prime Minister, this faction had become formally organised as a Republican Socialist Group in the Chamber, standing for a policy of 'republican concentration' and alliance with the bourgeois Radicals, and vigorous in its denunciations of the anti-social attitude of the C.G.T.

Apart from the question of industrial peace, there were two other great issues between the Syndicalists and the Reformist Socialists — anti-militarism and the right of association and strike action in the public services. The Act of 1884 legalising Trade Unions was not extended to public employees, who were regarded as outside the proper range both of collective bargaining and of strike action because the State was treated as a superior power. In practice association among public servants had achieved a certain measure of toleration; but this had not involved any recognition of the right to bargain collectively, as distinct from sending deputations to Ministers or endeavouring to influence the Chamber by stating grievances. The Government had maintained its right to dissolve as unlawful any association of public servants which transgressed the permitted limits; and during these troubled years, as the C.G.T. began to get a hold on such groups as the postal workers and the elementary teachers, this power of dissolution was repeatedly invoked. This matter came to a head in 1909. In March of that year the postal workers came out on strike, mainly for the removal of the exceedingly unpopular Minister who presided over them. Clemenceau, taken by surprise, made half-promises on the strength of which the strikers returned to work. When what had been taken for promises were not carried out, and the unpopular head of the postal department remained in office, the strike broke out again, but with much less widespread support. The C.G.T. called on other Unions to support the strikers; but the response was poor. Clemenceau felt strong enough to break the postal workers' organisation by mass dismissals of its activists. The C.G.T. could do nothing: the bitter feelings left behind prepared the way for the still greater bitterness created by Briand's handling of the railway strike the following year.

During these events the C.G.T. itself was in a state of crisis. In 1908, in connection with serious clashes with police and soldiers arising out of industrial disputes at Draveil and Villeneuve - Saint - Georges, Clemenceau's Government had arrested and gaoled Victor Griffuelhes, Émile Pouget, Georges Yvetot, and other leaders of the C.G.T., and a new group of second-line leaders had taken temporary charge of the organisation. Griffuelhes, as we saw, had made many enemies both by his militant policy and by his rough way of handling opposition. While he was in prison charges were brought against him of irregularities in the administration of the funds of the C.G.T., and his opponents were able to insist on an investigation being held. Griffuelhes resigned his position in anger. The result of the investigation was to exonerate him completely from any taint of dishonesty, and to prove that nothing worse than some slackness in account-keeping had occurred. But though, after his release, the C.G.T. Congress affirmed its entire confidence in his integrity, he was not reinstated as General Secretary, a member of the right wing, by name Louis Niel, being elected in his place. That was in 1909; and Niel was in office during the critical phase of the postal struggle of that spring. He handled the affair so weakly that the left wing promptly reasserted itself and procured his dismissal. Léon Jouhaux (1879–1953), who was a close associate of Merrheim and belonged to the Syndicalist left, replaced him, and thus began his long career as the outstanding figure in the French Trade Union movement.

The railway strike of 1910 involved a fresh issue. As we saw, Briand broke it by bringing in soldiers and by recalling the strikers to the colours. Now, of the French railway lines only one was State-owned, and the Nord line, on which the strike began, was owned as well as conducted by a private joint stock company. The strikers were not public employees; but the

Government argued that the law did not extend to authorise strike action in a vital public utility service and that it was fully entitled to take exceptional measures to break it in the public interest. The Socialists in the Chamber, as well as the Trade Unions, protested vigorously against this view, and above all against the calling of the strikers to the colours; but Briand, overriding their opposition, re-formed his Government and carried on with his repressive policy. The string of defeats at the hands of the Government seriously shook, but did not break, the C.G.T.'s power. After 1910 Trade Union militancy declined while the C.G.T. set to work to rebuild its organisation on a firmer basis. What has been called the 'heroic period' of Syndicalism was at an end : it had provoked not only strong action by the Government, but also a great consolidation of the employers' organisation through the drawing together of the Comité des Forges and other associations representing mainly the heavy industries. The C.G.T. attempted to meet the new situation by persuading its constituent craft Unions to amalgamate on industrial lines, so as to meet the employers on more equal terms; and it also revised its local structure by linking up the local Bourses du Travail, which had greatly increased in number, into Unions Départmentales, one for each Department of France, with the local Bourses remaining as constituent elements of the Unions, but no longer entitled to separate representation on the Confederal Committee. This was an important change; for the Bourses, as their numbers grew, had increasingly dominated the Confederal Committee at the expense of the National Trade or Industrial Federations. These latter, which were becoming rather more centralised, wanted greater control over C.G.T. policy; and the new C.G.T. Constitution, in shifting the balance in their favour, weakened the left wing to the advantage of the more moderate groups. The final authority in the C.G.T. remained, however, with the Congress, which was made up of one delegate from each local syndicat, irrespective of size, without any provision for card voting or for representation of either the Bourses or Unions or the National Federations as such. There were repeated attempts to change this system of voting so as to give each syndicat a vote proportionate to its numbers : they were all rejected on principle, on the ground that each local productive unit, large or small, made a necessary contribution to the life of the community and should receive direct representation in final decisions on policy. It was further agreed that there would be great difficulties in the way of deciding on what membership each syndicat should be allowed to vote. French Trade Unionists were notoriously bad at paying regular contributions, and the effective following of a syndicat often greatly exceeded its paying membership. Moreover, some Trade Unionists believed in the desirability of keeping together regularly as members only the class-conscious militants and relying on their influence to draw the majority after them when positive action was required.

As the National Federations increased their strength, and particularly where they developed benefit services and built up central *résistance* funds, the national leaders naturally began to press for higher membership and more regular contributions. But the official tradition of the C.G.T. was against any development of the syndicats into friendly benefit societies, and on the extreme left there was even an objection to centralised strike funds. Only a few bodies, such as the Fédération du Livre, developed friendly benefits ; and for the most part even strikes were conducted without the aid of regular strike pay, at any rate on a scale adequate to cover even basic needs. The C.G.T. continued, for the most part, to rely on emergency funds raised to support a particular struggle and on 'soupes communales' — that is, on direct provision of meals and other necessaries for the strikers and their dependants. They were seldom able to sustain a long contest. Unless they could win quickly, they usually called a strike off, and at once began preparation for calling it on again at the first opportunity. That was one reason why they objected to binding agreements and to regular procedures of collective bargaining. They were essentially guerrilla fighters, waging jungle warfare against the capitalists and their agents, the public authorities. During the years before 1914 this attitude was being gradually modified as the *patronat* built up its counter-organisation and as the Fédérations tried to meet this with more centralised Trade Union methods. But the localism persisted in the majority of the C.G.T.'s sections ; and even among the centralisers there were many who, while regarding more centralisation as necessary, were determined not to let it undermine the militancy of the movement. The Metalworkers and the Builders were the chief exponents of this view, against the moderates of the 'Livre' and the Textile Workers on the one hand and the extreme localism of the Anarchists, well entrenched in some of the Bourses du Travail, on the other.

The remaining great issue in the C.G.T. — and also in the Socialist Party — during these years was that of anti-militarism. This had several interrelated aspects. In the first place there was the growing threat of European War, marked by a sequence of crises arising out of the rivalries of the great powers. To the French working-class leaders this threat presented itself primarily in two guises — most fundamentally as arising out of the contest between Germany and Great Britain for economic domination, and to a less extent as the outcome of conflicting Russian, Austro-Hungarian, and German ambitions in South-Eastern Europe and in the Middle East, complicated by British-German rivalries and British-Austrian and British-Russian claims in the Eastern Mediterranean. Much the most lively fear in the minds of the French anti-militarists was that France might be drawn into war with Germany as the ally of Great Britain, and to serve British imperialist ends; and accordingly their first preoccupation was to secure an understanding with the German working-class movement for a common front against war and war-preparations. They wished, of course, to draw other working-class and Socialist movements, including the British, into this common front. But they tended to think of it as depending most of all on the combined action of the French and German movements, and to look with more than a little suspicion on the British, who had neither a powerful Socialist Party nor a Trade Union movement firmly committed to Socialism or to the doctrine of class-war. They looked mainly to the French and German workers to make it impossible for the governing classes of the two countries to plunge them into war against each other, and they felt that, if they could reach a clear understanding for common action with the Germans, the working-class movements of other countries would in all probability come in.

There was, however, the big question of the form which Franco-German understanding was to take, and of the methods that were to be employed in face of the threat of war. The Syndicalists of the C.G.T., in pursuance of their policy of entire independence of the political parties, wanted to negotiate a common policy with the German Trade Union movement and to get this policy confirmed and extended through the International Trade Union Secretariat which had been set up at the International Trade Union Conference of 1903. The first of these international, purely Trade Union, Conferences had been held, on German initiative, at Copenhagen in 1901 ; and at the third, held in Dublin in 1903, Karl Legien, the General Secretary of the German Central Trade Union Commission, had been charged with the function of acting as International Secretary. What had been created, however, had been in effect no more than an international correspondence bureau : there had been no definition of the precise functions of the new International or of its relations to the International Socialist Bureau set up two years earlier ; nor had there been, on the part of most of the participants, any intention of endowing it with policy-making attributes. This, however, was what the C.G.T. leaders wanted to do. In their eyes the Trade Union movement, and not the Socialist parties, constituted the supreme embodiment of the working-class spirit, and should be the main agent in creating the spirit of international class-solidarity and in wielding it as a weapon both against war and for the overthrow of capitalist society. Their chosen weapon was, of course, the general strike, which was to be used by the workers to prevent war and, if the occasion served, to clear the road for insurrection and for the establishment of a new social order. They wanted to induce the Trade Union movements of other countries, and particularly the Germans, to pledge themselves to meet the threat of war with an international general strike — and to do this without bringing in the Socialist politicians, who, it was felt, were too tied up with the parliamentary régimes of their various States to be capable of taking the unconstitutional action which the situation required.

Accordingly, the C.G.T. put down a motion for discussion at the next International Trade Union Conference, advocating anti-militarist activities and the use of the general strike to prevent war. Legien, as International Secretary, refused to put the motion on the agenda, on the ground that it raised political issues that were quite outside the functions of the Trade Unions and ought to be dealt with by the International Socialist Congress, if at all. The French, failing to shake his determination, absented themselves from the International Trade Union Congress of 1905, held at Amsterdam. Early the following year, Griffuelhes made a special journey to Berlin to interview Legien and other German leaders, in the hope of inducing them to come to an agreement about anti-militarist and anti-war activities, and to allow the matter to be raised at the next meeting of the Trade Union International. He found Legien and his colleagues quite immovable. In their view, Trade Unions, though they should act as allies of Social Democracy in an informal way, should confine their activities to the strictly industrial field and should leave political questions to be dealt with by the Socialist parties. They insisted that the French, if they wished to raise the issues of anti-militarism and the general strike, should do so through the French Socialist Party and at the Socialist International — at which the German Trade Unions would be represented as part of the Social Democratic delegation. This, of course, did not at all satisfy Griffuelhes or his C.G.T. colleagues, who were on the point of reaffirming, in the Charter of Amiens, the complete independence of the Trade Unions in relation to political parties and the essentially revolutionary, and therefore 'political', character of the Trade Union movement. It was made clear that the Germans were opposed, not only to having the general strike discussed by the Trade Union International, but also to the general strike itself, under whatever auspices it might be invoked. Legien and his colleagues particularly annoyed Griffuelhes by affirming the need for the Trade Unions to confine themselves within the limits of legality in order to avoid suppression and to serve their members' immediate economic interests. Trade Unions were, in the view of the German leaders, essentially bargaining bodies for the protection of their members' interests under whatever economic system they had actually to face. They had no revolutionary function : the social revolution was a matter for the Social Democratic Party, which they would help and encourage their members to join, but of which they would remain independent the better to pursue their day-to-day work within the limits set by law. Griffuelhes, while he was in

Berlin, saw some of the Social Democratic leaders as well as the Trade Unionists ; but he got no better response from them. They would continue in Parliament to combat militarism and war and to vote against the war credits, and they would campaign in the country on these issues ; but they would have nothing to do with the notion of a combined pledge of the French and German working classes to resort to the general strike as a means of meeting the threat of war.

The French Trade Unionists did not, after this rebuff, renounce their attempts to persuade the Germans to change their minds. They returned to the Conferences of the Trade Union International and attempted, at Paris in 1909, to get its structure changed in the hope of altering its attitude. They wanted it to become, instead of a meeting-place of representatives chosen by the national Trade Union Centres, a Congress of delegates directly elected by the Trade Unionists of the various countries and endowed with policy-making powers. But this proposal was voted down ; and right up to 1914 the Trade Union International remained no more than an occasional Conference of the leaders of the various national movements and a secretariat for the exchange of information. It was, moreover, weakened by the refusal of the British Trades Union Congress to become connected with it. Great Britain was represented, not by the T.U.C., but by the much smaller General Federation of Trade Unions, to which many of the larger Unions did not belong. The T.U.C. had not yet assumed the character of a central, co-ordinating industrial body : it was still rather an agency of the Trade Unions for bringing pressure to bear on Parliament. Actually it preferred to send delegates to the International Socialist Congress rather than to the Trade Union gatherings, because it was at the former that such matters as industrial legislation were chiefly discussed.

In the Trade Union International the C.G.T. formed a frustrated left wing. At the Budapest Conference of 1911 its representatives tried in vain to secure the admission of the Industrial Workers of the World on a parity with the American Federation of Labor. Attempts were also made to form a Syndicalist International, with representatives from the Syndicalist and Industrial Unionist minorities from Italy, Holland, America, and other countries, together with the C.G.T. and the Spaniards ; but no effective body resulted.

Meanwhile, the question of anti-militarism and the general strike against war had been in effect transferred from the Trade Union to the political plane, and was being ardently debated at successive Congresses of the Socialist International. An account of these debates has already been given in the chapter dealing with the whole question of the International's action in relation to the continual war danger.[1] Here, it is more appropriate to consider the other aspects of the anti-militarist campaign as it was carried on in France.

The C.G.T., in its attempts to secure international Trade Union action against war, was seeking to extend to other countries the Syndicalist policy to which it committed itself in the Charter of Amiens — that is to say, the policy of reliance on direct working-class action without any invocation of the aid of any political party. But by no means all the apostles of anti-militarism in France were supporters of the C.G.T. line. To the left of the C.G.T. leadership there was a body of pure insurrectionists, who contended that the answer of the workers to the threat of war should be not merely a general strike but out-and-out rebellion ; and this group largely overlapped with the preachers of an extreme anti-patriotic doctrine, headed by Gustave Hervé (1871–194 ?). These latter pressed to an extreme the dogma that 'the workers have no country', and that national frontiers are of no account to the exploited and dispossessed. They advocated positive resistance to compulsory military service and a complete rejection of all conceptions of nationality. The C.G.T. leaders, while mainly in agreement with their theoretical position, were not prepared to push matters so far. What they did introduce, under the pressure of their left wing, was the '*sou du soldat*' — the small subvention sent to the serving conscript by his Trade Union to remind him of his solidarity with the rest of his class, and to reinforce the admonition that he should not allow himself to be used as a strike-breaker or to shoot down workers who were demonstrating in support of their class-claims. The C.G.T. and its associated organisations and journals engaged actively in propaganda addressed to the soldiers in these terms, and were often brought up against the law by doing so. They did not, however, attempt

[1] See Chapter II.

to stir up the conscripts either to resist military service or to refuse to obey orders, except when the orders required them to take action against their fellow-workers. It was none the less clear that success in calling a general strike against war would necessarily involve calling upon the soldiers not to take action to break the strike, and therefore to disobey the orders they were certain to be given. Indeed, the whole conception of the general strike against war really involved a readiness to turn it into an insurrection unless the Government promptly gave way. What was to happen if the workers of one country struck, whereas those of another belligerent did not, was never at all clearly stated, though this objection was, of course, made much of by those who were hostile to the entire policy.

The French Socialists, meanwhile, had been working out their own solution of the problem of anti-militarism. Under the influence of Jaurès they made their central point of policy the supersession of conscript regular armies by non-professional citizen armies — that is, by a people in arms, trained to the use of weapons, not by years of continuous service, but by short periods devoted to martial exercises that would not take them away for long from their regular environments. Under this system, it was argued, the army would become, instead of an instrument the Government could use against the workers, the possession of the people themselves, who would be able to turn it against a Government that was pursuing militaristic or other anti-social objectives. Moreover, such an army would be strong in defence, if the country were attacked, but practically unusable for aggressive war. This was the line of argument adopted by Jaurès in his book, *L'Armée nouvelle*, which appeared in 1910.[1] The French Socialist Party was by no means prepared to accept the anti-patriotism of Hervé and his followers, or to reject the claims of national defence if France found itself attacked. What it wanted was to find a solution that would preserve the means of defence, but would exclude both aggressive war against another State and the kind of colonial warfare that was a necessary part of policies of imperialist expansion. The kind of army it proposed could not have been used either to conquer colonies or to garrison them when they

[1] It was also the policy of the Socialist International, reaffirmed at successive Congresses. See pp. 31, 63 ff.

had been conquered ; and the Jaurès plan accordingly seemed to meet the political requirements, though it was, of course, exposed to the objection of the military technicians that such an army would be in reality incapable of effective resistance to a heavily equipped modern mechanised professional army. The idea for this reason, if for no other, could not hope to meet with much acceptance outside Socialist circles unless it could be 'sold' to other Socialist movements, and especially to the Germans. It had therefore to be pressed at the international level.

Anti-colonialism and anti-imperialism, to which reference has just been made, played an important part in the French discussions about militarism and war. In the eyes of Socialists and Syndicalists alike the war danger arose mainly out of imperialist rivalries which were at bottom quarrels concerning the right to appropriate and exploit the national resources of the less developed countries, and to exploit their peoples both as consumers and as cheap labour for the benefit of the great capitalists of the imperial States. For the French the question of North Africa loomed largest, in relation successively to Egypt, Tunis, Algeria, and Morocco. They were, however, as we saw, inclined to regard the whole matter as one primarily concerned with the imperialist conflicts of Great Britain and Germany, and to look for a solution, first and foremost, in promoting common action between the French and German working-class movements against imperialist tendencies in both countries, in the hope that such an entente would strengthen the hands of the anti-imperialists in Great Britain and elsewhere. In this matter, as in most, the Syndicalists were well ahead of the Socialist Party in denouncing 'colonialism' not only as involving the danger of war, but also because of its effects in facilitating the economic exploitation of the colonial peoples.

The question of military service and of the attitude of the working-class movement towards it became particularly acute when, in 1912, the proposal to extend the period of military service from two to three years became an immediate political issue. The Brest Congress of 1913, meeting after the three years' law had been voted, reasserted its demand for the substitution of a national militia for the standing army, decided to conduct a campaign against the three years' law and in favour of international arbitration and an entente with Germany, and expressed particular satisfaction at the action taken by the French and German Socialists and Trade Unionists at the time of the Agadir crisis. On that occasion, after an attempt by the C.G.T. to organise a joint French-German-British Trade Union demonstration had failed, the German Trade Union Commission invited a French delegation of 45 to visit Berlin, where its members spoke to vast and fervent anti-war demonstrations. In return the Germans Molkenbuhr and Gustav Bauer came to Paris, where they addressed a similar demonstration. The Socialists of Alsace-Lorraine at the same time declared their hostility to any war of *revanche* designed to restore the provinces lost to France in 1871 ; and the French Socialists vigorously applauded this attitude. The Germans were, indeed, very ready to demonstrate and entirely sincere in their opposition to the war which they saw approaching ; but this did not make them any the more prepared to pledge themselves to meet the threat with a general strike arranged in concert with the French Syndicalists, whose ability to conduct such a movement with success they strongly doubted — no less strongly, in effect, than their own ability to take mass action against a war in which Russia, as well as France and Great Britain, might be involved.

Long before this, of course, the Stuttgart Congress of the Socialist International had adopted the well-known resolution in which the various delegations had attempted to formulate a collective policy for action in face of any immediate threat of war and also in face of failure to prevent war from breaking out. In 1911 the French and German delegations which visited each others' countries were acting, they believed, in the spirit of this resolution, of which the ineffectiveness had not yet become plain, though many Frenchmen were already aware of it.

Throughout the period between 1906 and 1914 the French Socialist Party had been troubled by the question of the general strike, not only as a weapon to be invoked against the threat of war, but also generally. Confronted with the overwhelming majority in favour of the Charter of Amiens, with its assertion of complete Trade Union independence of party politics, the Socialist Party had to make up its mind what attitude to take up towards this declaration of independence. The 'Charter' began with two preliminary affirmations, concerned respectively with the action to be taken by individuals and organisations. The first of these asserted that the individual adherent should be left entirely free to take part, outside his Trade Union group, in whatever form of struggle corresponded to his philosophical or political outlook, but should be required not to introduce into his Trade Union the opinions he professed elsewhere. The second laid down that, 'in order that Trade Unionism might reach the greatest possible strength, economic action should be taken directly against the employing class (*patronat*), and that the confederated organisations should not, as Trade Union groups, concern themselves with parties or sects, which are free outside and apart from the Trade Unions to work for social transformation as they think fit'.

As a preamble to these declarations, the Charter of Amiens laid down that the C.G.T. brought together, independent of all political schools of thought, 'all workers who are conscious of the need to struggle for the abolition of the wage system'. It then asserted that this declaration involved 'a recognition of the class-struggle, which, on an economic foundation, puts the workers in revolt against every form of exploitation and oppression, material and moral, that is operated by the capitalist class against the working class'. It went on to say that it made this theoretical affirmation more precise by adding to it the following points :

> In respect of everyday demands, Trade Unionism (*le syndicalisme*) pursues the co-ordination of the workers' efforts, the increase of the workers' welfare through the achievement of immediate improvements, such as the shortening of the hours of labour, the raising of wages, etc.
>
> This, however, is only one aspect of its work : it is preparing the way for the entire emancipation that can be realised only by the expropriation of the capitalist class. It commends the general strike as a means to this end and holds that the Trade Union, which is at present a resistance group, will be in the future the group responsible for production and distribution, the foundation of the social organisation.
>
> The Congress declares that this double task of day-to-day activity and of the future follows from the actual situation of the wage-earners, which exerts its pressure on every worker

and renders it an obligation for all workers, whatever their opinions or their political or philosophical tendencies, to be members of their Trade Union (syndicat — *i.e.* local union) as the basic group.

The Charter of Amiens thus committed the C.G.T. to the class-struggle as the basis of Trade Union action, to complete independence of political parties and philosophical sects, and to the general strike as a weapon. It further affirmed that in the coming society the Trade Unions would take over the control of production and distribution, without saying explicitly whether the State would disappear or continue in being, or what, if it did continue, its relation to the Trade Unions would be. This vagueness was necessary because the Charter had to get the support of both Anarchists and Socialists, as well as of the central group of Syndicalists who were attached neither to Anarchism nor to the Socialist Party.

The Socialist Party, in face of the adoption of the Charter by an overwhelming majority, had to decide whether to accept it and make the best of it, or to challenge it by counter-asserting the need for an alliance between the political and industrial wings of the movement. At the Limoges Socialist Congress of 1906 the Fédération du Nord, which was the Guesdist stronghold and one of the two largest sections of the party, proposed the second of these courses. Almost all the outstanding leaders, except the Guesdists, took the opposite view and spoke and voted for the alternative resolution, moved on behalf of the Fédération du Tarn, represented by Jaurès. Jaurès, the former Independent Socialist, Vaillant the Blanquist, Jean Allemane, and Gustave Hervé the extreme anti-militarist joined forces to support the Tarn resolution, which ran as follows :

> The Congress, holding that the working class cannot fully emancipate itself except by the combined force of political and trade union action — by Trade Unionism going to the length of the general strike, and by the total conquest of political power with a view to the general expropriation of capitalism ;
> Convinced that this double action will be all the more effective if the political and the industrial organisms enjoy full autonomy ;
> Taking note of the Amiens resolution, which asserts the independence of Trade Unionism in relation to all political

parties and at the same time assigns to Trade Unionism an objective which only Socialism, as a political party, recognises and pursues ;

Holding that this fundamental concordance between the political and the economic action of the proletariat will necessarily bring about, without confusion or subordination or mistrust, a free coordination between the two organisms ;

Invites the militants to use their best endeavour to dissipate all misunderstanding between the C.G.T. and the Socialist Party.

The vote was close. The Tarn resolution was adopted by 148 votes against 130 cast for the Guesdists, who stood, broadly speaking, for the same point of view as the German Social Democrats. The French Socialist Party thus committed itself not only to acceptance of Trade Union independence but also to support of the general strike as a form of Trade Union action, without specifying what sort of general strike, or what use of it, the party had in mind. This acceptance was, beyond doubt, partly tactical. The last thing the Socialist Party, or at all events Jaurès, wanted was to be plunged, on the morrow of unification, into a sharp conflict with the C.G.T. Such a conflict could hardly have failed to resplit the party, whereas the Guesdists, put in a minority, could not afford to break away and involve themselves in a battle on two fronts against both the C.G.T. and the Socialist majority. The Guesdists therefore stayed inside the party, and constituted within it a large enough minority to impose considerable limitations on its ability to carry out the spirit as well as the letter of the majority decision. Throughout the ensuing debates concerning the general strike, both in France and at the Socialist International, the French delegation remained under the handicap of sharp disagreement within its ranks ; and it took all Jaurès's genius for compromise to hold the contending factions together.

From the unification of 1905 to his assassination in 1914, on the eve of the war, Jaurès was the outstanding figure in the French Socialist Party, and also the greatest single figure in the Congresses of the Second International. He was a magnificent orator, with a great mastery of phrase and voice ; a distinguished writer, especially in the historical field, and — what is most of all to the point here — a most cunning draftsman of resolutions and reports designed to secure the adhesion of contending groups and factions. He knew better than anyone else how to intervene in an acrimonious discussion with a proposal which, by bringing in each faction's favourite phrases, got them all to sign an agreed report or to vote for a common resolution. He was often accused on these occasions of using mere verbal jugglery to induce a false harmony, and so patching over differences instead of reconciling them. That, indeed, he did again and again ; but he did it, not to display his own cleverness or to exalt his own power, but because he deemed it essential that the French Socialists should become and remain a unified party and, internationally, that the parties of the International should be held together rather than divided into warring ideological camps. This concept of unity among Socialists and of good relations between the Socialist parties and the Trade Unions was the first principle of his own Socialist doctrine, and he was prepared to subordinate almost everything else to it. Thus, he first defended Millerand and the Reformists, at any rate to the extent of not wishing to see them excluded from the party, and then accepted their exclusion and took sides against collaboration in bourgeois Ministries when he had become convinced that nothing less would avail to bring the main body of the party together. Thus, when the Trade Unions adopted the Charter of Amiens and rejected alliance with the Unified Socialist Party, he not merely accepted their decision but went out of his way to induce the party to pronounce unequivocally in favour of it, because he saw in such endorsement the only hope of the two wings of the movement being able in fact to get on amicably together. Similarly, he induced the party, against the Guesdists, to give its endorsement to the policy of the general strike, because he saw that to oppose it would mean tearing the working class asunder. These, it may be said, are the attitudes of an opportunist rather than of a man animated by clearly conceived principles ; but it must be answered that opportunism *was* Jaurès's principle, in the sense that, within very wide limits, he was prepared to do whatever he thought the 'common sense' (not the commonsense) of the working class indicated as the best way of maintaining it as a united force. He had, of course, deep convictions which set limits to what he could bring himself to do. He was an ardent humanist liberal, in the best sense of both words. He believed that it was the mission of Socialism to continue the work of the great French Revolution — to complete rather than to destroy its achievement. He saw the Republic, not as an enemy, but as an institution to be defended for what it embodied of the great 'idea of the Revolution'; and, though he was a revolutionary, he was so rather in the spirit of one carrying on a revolution already well on its way than in that of one seeking to make a new revolution — so that his revolutionism was fully consistent with Reformism, and quite inconsistent with any doctrine of destructive violence resting on a repudiation of bourgeois values. He was in fact by instinct a moderate in action; but he refused to be more moderate than the workers he was setting out to lead, or than the need to make them militant required — militant enough, that is, to force their enemies to take notice of them. He set a high value on immediate reforms; but he was not prepared to accept them on terms which would mean the 'domestication' of the workers' movement, because he was fully alive to the fact that 'domestication' would destroy its power.

Above all else, Jaurès was a great humanist. When such men as Gustave Hervé told him that the workers had no country, he replied with passion that this was utterly untrue. The French worker had as his 'patrie' the whole cultural life of France, based not only on great traditions of revolutionary achievement but also on the precious possession of the French language and of the grand procession of French literature and French self-expression in all the arts. Not for nothing had Jaurès begun his career as a professor of philosophy. Even as politician and journalist he remained the philosopher of an embracing humanism and set out to make the workers fully masters of society in all its aspects, and not merely of the State or of economic affairs. In this spirit he edited *Humanité*, seeking to make each issue not merely a means of giving the news of the day but also the conveyer of a greater message of social and cultural emancipation. His front pages were quite astonishingly good, carrying especially in his brilliantly conceived leading articles much more than a narrowly political message. Under his control, *Humanité* became a great educational force, of particular influence among teachers and Socialist 'militants', but so simply written as to reach a wide circle of readers with an appeal they could understand and accept. Of course, Jaurés did not achieve all this alone : he was brilliantly helped by Édouard Vaillant, no less an enthusiast for Socialist education, and by the less frequent contributions of great writers such as Anatole France (1844–1924). The main inspiration, however, came from Jaurès, and was sustained year after year up to his untimely death.

These qualities did not make Jaurès a great constructive political thinker. His main positive contributions to Socialist policy were his working out of the conception of the new army based on an armed people and his attempt to solve the problem of applying Socialist doctrine to the peasantry. On the first of these issues he carried his party along with him and won extensive support in the International. On the other the French Socialist Party, after repeated Congress debates, was still in 1914 unable to make up its mind ; but in that respect it was no worse off than other Socialist parties that were facing the same problem, and Jaurès's attempt was at any rate a great deal more realistic than Kautsky's, which has been discussed in a previous chapter.

It may be doubted whether the policy set forth in *L'Armée nouvelle*, for all the support it secured, was equally realistic ; but it was not necessarily the worse for that. It enabled Jaurès to keep down the size of the extreme anti-patriotic minority led by Gustave Hervé, which repudiated all forms of loyalty to the nation, including any form of national defence, and advanced in its place a policy of workers' insurrection irrespective of national frontiers. Jaurès, equally with the leaders of the German Social Democratic Party, upheld the right of national defence against foreign aggression : his problem was to find means of giving effect to this right without either arming the existing State with weapons that it could turn against the workers or equipping it with forces that it could use aggressively against other States, or in imperialist colonial wars. The citizen army, keeping its own weapons in readiness for the call of national defence and not isolated in camps or barracks but pursuing its daily avocations of civil life, seemed to furnish the answer. The example of Switzerland had, no doubt, shown that even a citizen militia could be used for breaking strikes;[1] but against this danger was to be set the fact that the strikers, in common with the rest of the people, would be armed, so that the army would be the people's as much as the State's, and might, if revolution came, act on the people's side as well as against it. The plan, of course, involved a democratisation of the officer cadres as well as of the non-commissioned ranks ; and Jaurès tried to work out the means of achieving this. His plan appeared most promising when it was envisaged, not in isolation, but as part of an internationally agreed Socialist proposal for reducing armaments to a purely defensive level and for the general acceptance of arbitration as a means of settling international disputes. The difficulty was that to envisage it in this way involved, as a prior need, the victory of Socialism, or at any rate of anti-imperialistic pacifism, in all the leading countries, and not merely in France. If it was put forward as a proposal for unilateral action by the French, its compatibility with successful national defence was doubtful, even in 1909, and became increasingly doubtful as each great power increased its armaments and made them more technically advanced. That was partly why, in the minds of the French Socialists, there was a close connection between the army proposals and the promotion of an entente with the German working-class movement.

On the agrarian issue Jaurès was never able to accept the orthodox Social Democratic view that the peasants were a class destined to be speedily swept away by the advance of large-scale capitalist farming. He understood the tenacity with which those of them who owned their land clung to it and the desire to possess the land they tilled that was widespread among cultivators under the *métayer* system. He was not prepared to range himself with those Socialists who, regarding the peasants, as distinct from the rural wage-labourers, as a reactionary class, contended that nothing must be done to strengthen their position and thus raise up fresh obstacles to the advance of Socialism. On the contrary, he was insistent not only that nothing must be done to dispossess the peasant owner against his will, but also that the State should intervene to reduce agricultural rents and to alter to the *métayer*'s advantage the terms on which he shared the produce of the land. He wished to take over the

[1] See p. 612 ff.

ownership of land farmed by large proprietors, or hired out to tenants, or worked under *métayage*, and to use the reduced rents or shares in the produce to form a capital fund for the improvement of agriculture under public auspices. He thought that large-scale farming would increase and that it would come to be organised on a Co-operative system under public ownership, but that small-scale cultivation would persist side by side with it — including very small-scale cultivation by workers who laboured for part of their time on the collective farms. He emphasised the extent to which already peasant farmers worked together without formal organisation, helping to get in one another's crops and lending one another beasts and carts and implements. These customs he took as signs of a natural co-operativeness, which would develop much further in a friendly social environment, in which the cultivator would no longer be either exploited by landlord or usurer or able to exploit the rural labourer for his own profit. Envisaging the future of industry under Socialism in terms of workers' self-government and not of bureaucratic State administration, which he disliked, he saw the future of agriculture as lying in a combination of worker-controlled Co-operative cultivation with a survival of individual farming reinforced by Co-operative methods of supply and marketing. He worked out these ideas early in his career as a Socialist, and never departed from them. But the French Socialist Party never either accepted or rejected them. It could not make up its mind; and at one Congress after another the decision was adjourned.

There was clearly an opportunistic element in Jaurès's views on the agrarian question, as on most other matters of practical policy. He did not want to make an enemy of the peasant class; and he was very much aware that, although peasant owners constituted only a minority of the agricultural producers, being outnumbered by the rural labourers, the *métayers*, and the tenant farmers, they were capable of opposing powerful obstacles to the advance of Socialism if the Socialist Party set itself against them. But his attitude was by no means solely opportunistic. As a firm believer that the task of Socialism was to complete, and not to overturn, the achievements of the great Revolution, he would have felt it treason to attack the peasantry, instead of giving them a fair chance to adjust themselves to the conditions of a Socialist society; and, as an opponent of bureaucracy and centralisation, he did not want them to be dispossessed, but only brought within a framework of Co-operative planning within which they could be given freedom to manage their own affairs.

Jaurès, up to a point, used the phraseology of Marxism, which was the *lingua franca* of the parties of the Second International, and he accepted a substantial part of Marx's economic doctrine. But he was never really a Marxist. He always stressed both the ethical elements in Socialism and its roots in a democracy which he conceived as a completion of existing democratic tendencies and not in terms of any sort of class dictatorship. He was strongly hostile to Blanquism as well as to the Marxist form of dictatorship doctrine. By disposition he was a parliamentarian, and he was by no means prepared to regard the State as simply the executive committee of the ruling class. Yet this did not mean that he belonged to the constitutionalist right wing: he insisted that the workers, in their struggle for power, could not allow themselves to be shut up within the confines of bourgeois legality. They might, he agreed, have to act unconstitutionally, to flout the law, or to rise in rebellion; but he regarded such a prospect, not with the jubilation of the instinctive revolutionary, but as an unpleasant necessity to be avoided as far as possible, because he was very anxious that the growing pains of the new society should not destroy the human and cultural values that were worthy of being taken over into it.

The second outstanding figure in the French Socialist Party of the years after 1905 was Jules Guesde who, having begun as a Radical and passed through a semi-Anarchist phase in Switzerland and Italy after the Paris Commune, became, with Paul Lafargue, the architect of a Workers' Party (Parti Ouvrier) following faithfully in the steps of German Social Democracy. Guesde was an entirely unoriginal thinker: his strength lay in organisation and in fidelity to Marxist orthodoxy as it was then understood. He believed strongly in centralisation and in the subordination of the whole working-class movement to the guidance of a party based on strict discipline and conformity to a determined line. He also shared the conviction, strong among the German majority, that the coming of Socialism was inevitable as an outcome of the economic development of capitalism towards greater and greater concentration of power. He favoured parliamentary action, and the use of Parliament for achieving immediate partial reforms ; but he always stressed the narrow limits to the real advantages that could be got in this way as long as capitalism remained in being, and insisted that the primary task — that of overthrowing capitalism — could not be accomplished without the use of revolutionary means. Sharing Marx's conception of the State as a class-agency, he strongly opposed the Possibilists, led by Paul Brousse, in their attempts to advance towards Socialism by developing municipal enterprise and public operation of utility services ; for he held that such forms of public enterprise would fall under the control of the bourgeois State and be turned by it against the workers. He was no less hostile to Syndicalism, which, he held, would divide the workers in the pursuit of corporative interests instead of uniting them to pursue the Socialist goal of distribution in proportion to services rendered to society.

All this, of course, was commonplace of German centrist Social Democratic doctrine ; but it was much less acceptable in France. It went down best in the north of France, which was always the chief Guesdist stronghold. For a time, before the rise of Syndicalism, the Guesdists had established a considerable control over the Trade Union movement ; but they never regained it, except in a few areas. In 1914 Guesde, despite his Marxism, rallied at once to the national cause and became a Minister in the war coalition. His writings, except his reminiscences, *Çà et là* (1914), are not of importance : they are chiefly pamphlets giving a popular exposition of Marxist doctrine. He was, however, a very active journalist, from the days of *Égalité*, which he started in 1877, before his full conversion to Marxism, to his long period as director of *La Voix du Peuple* and other journals devoted to the theory and practice of his strictly orthodox Social Democratic ideas.

The third leading figure was the former Communard and follower of Blanqui, Édouard Vaillant, who had led the Blanquist Socialist Party up to the unification, and was thereafter a member of the unified party. Vaillant (1840–1915), who had received a medical and scientific training, had been allied with

Guesde against Jaurès at the time of the *affaire Millerand* : he was a firm opponent of collaboration with the bourgeois parties. But he was not, like Guesde, under the spell of German Social Democracy. He thought much less in terms of a disciplined mass party than of a revolutionary élite, and he thus came nearer in his attitude to the Syndicalist militants than the other parliamentary leaders. He was strongly anti-militarist and anti-imperialist, and played an active part in the Second International during its discussions of the problem of Socialist action against war — for example, as the associate of Keir Hardie in the Hardie-Vaillant resolution of 1910.[1] His strong-hold was Paris. He had been elected to the Paris Municipal Council as far back as 1884, nine years before he became a deputy ; and his best constructive work was done in the development of education in Paris. He was the Socialist Party's leading educational expert. After the unification, despite his theoretical revolutionism, he worked very closely and amicably with Jaurès — much more so than Guesde, who resented Jaurès's pre-eminence. Despite the fading of his revolutionary ardour he was very popular among the Parisian left wing.

Of the other Socialist leaders, Paul Lafargue, Marx's son-in-law and co-founder with Guesde of the Parti Ouvrier, committed suicide in 1911, together with his wife, Laura. He had been born in Cuba in 1842, trained in France as a doctor and, on account of his political activities, had taken refuge in England, where he met Marx. Marx had sent him to Spain, where he had attempted to build up a Marxist section of the First International[2] against the Bakuninists. He was away from France until 1882, when he returned and joined forces with Guesde, with whom he drafted the programme of the Parti Ouvrier. He became a leading French exponent of Marxist doctrines, writing a series of books on various aspects of Socialism and in criticism of capitalist ideologies, especially in relation to property and religion. But, except as Guesde's ally, he was not an active figure of any great influence after the early years of the Guesdist Party.

Paul Brousse, the Possibilist leader, born in 1854, who had moved from semi-Anarchism to the advocacy of Socialist

[1] See p. 83 f. [2] See p. 327.

municipal enterprise and the building up of Socialist strength through active participation in local government, died in 1912, and no new leader appeared to take his place. Jean Allemane, another Communard, born in 1843, whose party had been, up to the unification, nearest to the Trade Union left, ceased to count for a great deal after 1905.

The remaining figures to whom it is necessary to give some consideration are the theorists most closely associated with Syndicalism — especially Georges Sorel and Hubert Lagardelle. As we saw, it is quite a mistake to suppose that Sorel had any considerable influence on the development of the Syndicalist movement, or even on the growth of its ideology. The Syndicalist leaders never accepted Sorel's conception of the general strike as a 'social myth'. Though they agreed with much that he said on behalf of their movement, they rightly considered that he had taken his ideas from the movement, rather than imposed them upon it.

Georges Sorel (1847–1922) was, indeed, a highly idiosyncratic thinker, whom it is quite impossible to pin down except in negative terms. There were a number of things that he most emphatically did not believe, or believe in; and such consistency as is to be discovered in his writings is made up mainly of these negatives. He did not believe in democracy, or in progress, or in the validity of reason as a basis for social action, or in the value of trying to reach agreement. He was much more against the bourgeoisie than for the workers, or, indeed, for anybody; and if there was anything he really enjoyed, it was being a pessimist. In many of these respects he bore a considerable resemblance to Proudhon, whom he admired greatly and often invoked. But what he found most congenial in Proudhon's thought was the acceptance of contradictions, not as evils to be transcended, but as the very stuff of living, for the individual and for society alike. For a long time he admired Marx too, and fancied himself a Marxist, which he neither was nor could have been. What he liked in Marxism was the conception of class-war and revolution, the defiant proclamation of the proletariat's historic rôle. But it was quite alien to his attitude to regard the proletariat as being carried onwards to inevitable victory by the advance of the powers of production. He liked to think, in his Marxist days, of the proletariat as engaged in a heroic conflict, of which the issue was altogether in doubt — a conflict waged in a world which might at any moment collapse upon the combatants and whelm them in a common disaster. What attracted him was the struggle, not the prospect of victory — except when he was thinking of the latter, not as victory, but as the defeat of the other side.

I have said that Sorel did not believe in progress ; but that is not quite true. In a strictly technical sense he did believe in it. He had been trained as an engineer and had spent the formative years of his manhood practising his profession at the Ponts et Chaussées before he set up as a prophet ; and he had the engineer's outlook on progress as a technical fact. What he added was that, from the human and moral point of view, this progress was an illusion. It did not add to man's stature, except as far as it provided continually fresh issues for men to fight about, and thus stimulated their heroic qualities — if they had any. He incited the working class to organise for battle ; but he wanted the capitalists to improve their organisation too, in order to provide the workers with an enemy capable of testing their resources. His scorn for politicians, of all parties, was based mainly on his view of them as persons who were out for a quiet life and were always trying to compromise and reach agreed settlements, or at least agreements to differ, instead of enjoying a good scrap. He detested 'reasonable' people, whom he saw as always blurring the issues, instead of turning every difference into a point of principle on which there could be no giving way. But when politicians became doctrinaire he denounced them no less roundly as makers of procrustean beds for confining the human spirit.

Sorel, in his earlier social writings, was affected by Antonio Labriola[1] and by Benedetto Croce in his brief Marxist phase.[2] For a number of years he wrote as a Socialist, and did not dissociate himself from the main trend of Marxist thought. His Syndicalist period began only with the publication in 1898 of *L'Avenir socialiste des syndicats*, in which he proclaimed that 'the proletariat should set to work, from this moment, to free itself of all direction that is not internal to itself. It is by movement and action that it should win juridical and political capacities. The first rule of its conduct should be to remain

[1] See p. 737.   [2] See p. 742.

exclusively working class (*ouvrier*), that is to say, to exclude the intellectuals, whose direction would have the effect of restoring hierarchies and of dividing the body of the workers. The rôle of the intellectuals is that of auxiliaries.' The use of the word 'capacities' in this passage is a plain echo of Proudhon. Sorel went on to declare : 'To sum up my whole thought in a formula, I will say that the entire future of Socialism lies in the autonomous development of the workers' Unions'.

Two years later, Sorel was writing that 'Socialism is finished' — that is, as a political movement. He then published in quick succession, *Introduction à l'économie moderne* (1903), *Les Illusions du progrès* (1906), *La Décomposition du marxisme* (1908), *Réflexions sur la violence* (1908), and *La Révolution dreyfusienne* (1909) — all these works falling within the period of the C.G.T.'s most militant activity under the leadership of Griffuelhes, Pouget, and Merrheim. Then, with the ending of the 'heroic period', the flow ceased ; and Sorel went off in search of fresh heroes ready to accept his gospel of 'violence'. He found them, for the time being, among ultra-conservatives and royalists, and fell foul of the Action Française group for being 'unduly democratic'. When the Bolshevik Revolution occurred, the fighting quality of Lenin caused him to add an appendix in praise of him to *Réflexions sur la violence* ; but that did not prevent him from being cited by Mussolini as one of the chief inspirers of his conception of Fascism.

Among Sorel's chief hatreds was that of the eighteenth-century enlightenment, which he was apt to credit with all the errors of the modern world. The eighteenth-century 'philosophers', in his view, had led the world astray into a false optimism, a misguided rationalism, and a dogmatic belief in the virtue of counting heads, which they called 'democracy'. They had committed the fatal error of regarding the intellect as an instrument for inspiring men to agree, when what they needed was the stimulus of disagreement to call out their moral qualities in action. Sorel saw those who, with Jaurès, treated the eighteenth-century enlightenment as the ideological foundation of a continuing impulse to social progress as misinterpreting it utterly and as perverting it into liberalism. He insisted that the task of the present was not to complete the liberal revolution by socialising it, but to break right away from the liberal tradition. In his Syndicalist phase, he was continually adjuring the proletariat not to be misled into taking over the ideas of the bourgeoisie and trying to adapt them to its own requirements, but to break right away from the bourgeois tradition and to create, by acting, a totally new ideology on foundations which could be built up only on the experience of the daily struggle. The character of this new ideology — or rather, new way of life, for he did not expect or wish the proletariat to formulate it in theoretical terms — was never made clear : indeed, it could not be, for it would arise only as it was practised. When the C.G.T. failed to live up to the promise he had seen in it during the 'heroic years', he lost interest. What he would have made of Communism if he had lived on to watch its development I do not pretend to know. Probably, from the side-lines, he would have urged on both Stalin and Trotsky to combat, without caring which won, and indeed, enjoying the combat and regarding both the 'permanent revolution' and 'Socialism in one country' as excellent examples of the 'social myth'.

The book of Sorel's that is best known — indeed, the only one that has been widely read — is *Réflexions sur la violence*, in which both his notion of the creative function of 'violence' and his conception of the 'social myth' are set forth. What did Sorel mean by this 'violence' that he defended and exalted ? Not necessarily physical violence, though that was included in it, but essentially a refusal to compromise and a determination to act that was made stronger by opposition. Mere argument he despised : he required action, and he was emphatic that what spurred men to action was not intellectual conviction but a faith that was in essence non-rational, though it cloaked itself in what appeared to be reasoned aspirations and projects. In his Syndicalist period he was greatly influenced by Bergson's conception of the *élan vital*, and regarded himself as the exponent of a social version of Bergsonian philosophy. This *élan*, which was in men's natures, had to be expressed in terms of projects of action, and not of ideals. For the working class of the twentieth century its specific formulation was in terms of the general strike, but not of any sort of general strike — only of the general strike as an instrument for the complete overthrow of the existing social order. For the 'political general strike', used as a means to the winning of universal suffrage, as the Austrians, the Belgians, and others attempted to use it, he had the greatest contempt as a politicians' perversion of a noble revolutionary aspiration. The general strike, as it existed in the minds of the class-conscious workers, was in essence an insurrectionary act, a defiance of all authority. What matter if it never in fact happened ? The importance of it lay, not in the event, but in the stimulus to militant action which it supplied. Under that stimulus, a great deal of action would occur ; and it was of minor importance what form the action took, provided it was undertaken in the right spirit — that of a militant morality, which would give it the character of a crusade — of a war. Sorel was exceedingly fond of warlike metaphors : he repeatedly insisted that the class-struggle was a war. He extolled the military virtues, and regarded war as an ennobling experience — especially war for a 'cause'. An important count in his indictment of capitalism and of the bourgeoisie was, not that they waged wars, but that they were always patching things up instead of fighting them out.

The reader will have perceived some time ago that I acutely dislike Sorel as a thinker, though I have a great deal of sympathy for the Syndicalism which for a time he espoused. It may be, on occasion, necessary to fight, and cowardice not to ; but fighting is always, at best, a necessary evil, and there is nothing ennobling about it. Quite the contrary. It is perfectly possible to admire initiative, *élan* and determination without falling into the evil position of admiring combativeness in its own right. It is also perfectly possible to accept 'contradictions' as a necessary element in the life of society, as Proudhon did, without regarding each 'contradiction' as the occasion for a struggle leading to mutual extermination, in the Hegelian manner, or as an opportunity for the purposeless exercise of heroic virtues, as I think Sorel, despite all his 'moralism', came in effect to do. Griffuelhes also suffered from this vice, of which the outcome usually is that its advocates, instead of training their devotees for more and more heroic actions, end by tiring them out, as happened to both the American I.W.W. and the C.G.T. But Griffuelhes and Haywood at any rate believed that they were going somewhere : they were chasing, not a 'social myth', but what they held to be a realisable objective. They were not, like Sorel, pessimists moaning for blood.

Sorel's pessimism was, of course, closely connected with his irrationalism, which links his social thought to that of Vilfredo Pareto, and made them both grist to the Fascist mill. Pareto traced all men's social activities back, in the final resort, to what he called 'residues' — non-rational drives which impelled societies this way or that, according as particular types of drive dominated the ruling élites. He saw this domination as taking shape in a cyclical process in which one type of residue, or rather one combination of residues, gave place to another in endless succession, as new men of initiative and imagination, and new bureaucratic intriguers with a talent for 'combination', seized hold of the social structure. Meanwhile, Robert Michels was exposing in his writings — especially in his work on *Political Parties* (1912) — the corrupting tendencies of political action and the processes of manipulation by élites which made democratic action of the type accepted as normal by political 'liberals' a farce — a mere cover for bureaucratic management of gullible human material. Michels, who worked and wrote in Switzerland and Italy as well as in Germany, was one of the group which gathered round Hubert Lagardelle's *Mouvement Socialiste* and made it during the early years of the twentieth century the outstanding theoretical organ of the Syndicalist conception of Socialism. Like Sorel, he was an acute critic of Marxian Social Democracy. Above all, he attacked the German Social Democratic Party, which he described as a 'great automaton' . . . 'congealed in a sullen, stiff nationalism . . . dumb, blind and deaf to the cry of men'. To him, as to all the Syndicalists, political Marxism appeared to be in decomposition and decay, afraid to summon its massive following to action for fear of offending popular sentiment and letting loose forces it would not be able to control.

Hubert Lagardelle, who founded *Le Mouvement Socialiste* in 1899 and carried it on until 1914, was the central figure in the group of intellectuals who, during this period, rallied to the side of Syndicalism against the parliamentary Socialists. He wrote exceedingly well; and his writings, though intransigent in tone, were largely free from Sorelian 'myth-making' and from the sheer exaltation of violence. He was a keen student of movements as well as of ideas, with many international connections and much deeper roots in the Socialist movement than Sorel ever had; and he made his journal the point of focus for a great deal of exciting controversy at a period when Benoît Malon's *Revue Socialiste* had lost much of its drive in the hands of his successors. Its chief intellectual rival was *L'Humanité*, the daily newspaper founded by Jean Jaurès in 1904 and adopted, after the unification, as the Socialist Party's official organ, still under Jaurès's direction. At the outset, Jaurès made *L'Humanité* at least as much a journal of theory and opinion as a newspaper, including in it long articles after the manner of the Vienna *Arbeiter Zeitung*. This policy was fairly soon modified in quest of a large circulation; but *L'Humanité* kept a good deal of its original character and was a powerful force in building up the unified party. It was naturally the target of constant attack from the militants of the Syndicalist camp.

The best expression of Lagardelle's outlook is contained in his volume of studies, *Le Socialisme ouvrier*, which was published in 1911. He also edited several symposia, in which he brought together contributions from a number of countries — among them *Syndicalisme et socialisme* (1908), including studies by Michels, Griffuelhes, Arturo Labriola and B. Krichevsky, and *La Grève générale et le socialisme* (1904). Lagardelle differed from some of the Syndicalists in not being an out-and-out opponent of the Socialist Party, which he considered to be necessary as a working-class instrument for the time being, though destined to be superseded as the Trade Unions built up their power and rendered parliamentary action, and, indeed, 'politics' as a whole, unnecessary. 'Incontestably', he wrote, 'working-class democracy has need for its constitution and development, for a while yet, of political democracy. But it uses political democracy only the better to destroy it.' And again: 'The task of a Socialist Party in Parliament can be only to aid by legislation the work of the proletariat in organising itself autonomously'. 'Syndicalism', he said, 'does not deny parties, but only their ability to transform the world.' He insisted that 'Syndicalism has always laid it down as a principle that bourgeois institutions will be eliminated only in proportion as they are replaced by working-class institutions', and that the great task of the workers was that of creating their own institutions and through them building up their own ideology based on the conception of Co-operative production for common use. In this attitude Lagardelle was strongly supported by Alphonse Merrheim, the leader of the metalworkers in the C.G.T., who continually emphasised the need for Trade Union consolidation and for the acquisition and diffusion among the workers of an exact knowledge of the actual working of capitalist industry and finance, as necessary not only for success in the day-to-day struggle for better conditions, but also as a preparation for taking over the control. Lagardelle, who had a constructive mind, also differed from many of the Syndicalists in insisting on the need for the Trade Unions to equip themselves with more full-time officials and a stronger organisation of committees with a more assured tenure of office. Though he was a most vigorous critic of reformist tendencies in the Trade Unions, he realised that they could be built up as the controlling agencies of a new society only if their organisation were greatly strengthened and many of their notions of spontaneous activity modified. He believed in the value of winning reforms, with or without the aid of the law : his opposition to the Reformists was based on the criticism that 'the Reformists see in Reformism nothing but the reform', whereas reforms should be regarded from the standpoint of their contribution to the building up of the structure of working-class control 'within the womb of capitalist society'. He gave to Syndicalism the name 'Socialism of Institutions', as an expression of this idea, which runs through all his work.

The remaining member of the *Mouvement socialiste* group who deserves a mention is Édouard Berth, whose *Les Méfaits des intellectuels* appeared in 1914. Berth had been for many years a regular contributor to the *Mouvement*. He was the protagonist of the view that the new society must be built entirely round production and on the basis of a 'producer' ideology. He attacked Marxism in its Social Democratic form as a 'half-bourgeois philosophy', as a doctrine of 'political, parliamentary, dogmatic Socialism, which saw in the proletariat a material weapon to be wielded by the thought incarnated in a general staff of bourgeois intellectuals'. He wanted the proletariat to develop a philosophy entirely its own ; but, in common with Sorel, he fell foul in this matter of the C.G.T.'s use of sabotage as a weapon in the industrial struggle. An indispensable part of the new proletarian ideology, he insisted, must be a pride in doing good work ; and to train the workers in habits of bad work and deliberate sabotage as weapons of the class-war would inevitably make them unfit to take over the control of industry. It would cause their character to degenerate and would lead to a decline instead of an advance in human civilisation. This same argument was used by Sorel ; but it had no effect on Griffuelhes or Pouget, who regarded any weapon as legitimate in the struggle against capitalist exploitation. Griffuelhes cared little about the future society : his entire attention was concentrated on the struggle. Pouget did care ; but he was an apocalyptic Anarchist, who believed that the Revolution would change men's natures, so that there would be no danger of bad habits contracted under the existing social system being carried over into the new.

French Socialism, though it held together as a political movement after the unification of 1905, was much hampered by the continuing quarrel between the parliamentarians and the Syndicalists. The conduct of Millerand, and still more that of Briand, after their defection from the movement, put powerful arguments at the disposal of the anti-parliamentarians ; and Jaurès, though he entirely shed his support of collaborationism, had much to live down. He had to face, not only the Syndicalists, with their insistence that 'la lutte de classe ne peut être menée que sur le terrain de classe' — that is, in the industrial field — but also the Guesdists, who wished to challenge the principle of Trade Union autonomy and disliked his complaisance towards the industrialists ; and he was also constantly harried by the extreme anti-militarists led by Gustave Hervé. Hervé's *Leur Patrie* (1905) and *Mes Crimes* (1912) made a great stir, and his journal *La Guerre Sociale*, founded in 1907, had a wide public. Hervé's violent insurrectionist notions never came near to gaining a majority at the party Congresses, where the followers of Jaurès and of Guesde united to vote them down. But the complete denial by Hervé and his group that the workers had any country to defend or any reason at all to make concessions to the spirit of nationality was always a thorn in the side of the more discriminating internationalists. In 1914

Hervé changed sides abruptly, becoming as intransigent a patriot as he had been previously a denouncer of patriotism in all its forms. But up to 1914 he set Jaurès a problem, by arousing the fears of the right-wing Socialists and making it more difficult to uphold the right of national self-defence without falling into the support of increased armaments and renouncing the attempt to reach an understanding with the German Socialists and to build up the International as a constructive influence on the side of peace.

CHAPTER IX

RUSSIA TO 1905

THE Second International was throughout its history primarily a meeting place for West European Socialists whose main preoccupation was the building up of Social Democratic Parties for participation in the political struggle for parliamentary power. In some countries this involved, as a necessary preliminary, the winning of the right to vote — for example in Belgium and in Austria-Hungary. But in all the countries which played leading parts in the International and supplied its outstanding spokesmen, some form of parliamentary representation already existed, and the immediate preoccupation of the Socialist parties was with the means of getting the key representative institutions into their hands. It was, indeed, often unclear what use was to be made of parliamentary power when it had been won : revolutionaries and reformists held different views about the possibility of using Parliaments as instruments for Socialist construction and about the nature and extent, as well as about the value, of the reforms that could be secured by parliamentary means. But they agreed in wanting to win control of Parliament, whatever they might wish to do after control had been won. This was the issue over which they fought their running battle against the Anarchists, who were driven out of the International precisely because they rejected this form of political action. Even Spain had its Cortes, to provide an objective for the efforts of an orthodox Socialist Party.

In Russia, on the other hand, there was no Parliament for the Socialists to set out to conquer. The Czarist political structure was autocratic to an extent that the autocracy of Prussia or of Austria-Hungary did not approach. It was, of course, possible for Russians to demand the establishment of a Parliament on the Western model and to believe that some day constitutionalism would come to Russia as it had come in various forms and degrees to other countries as they advanced in civilised ways of living. But there was no existing institution resting on any representative principle through or upon which the Russian Socialist could attempt to work. The Russian Socialist was a revolutionary perforce, not merely in the sense of having to envisage the road to Socialism as passing necessarily through revolution, but also in the further sense that the only form of action open to him in the present, outside the realm of pure thought, was revolutionary. Indeed, he could hardly think, or at any rate express or exchange his thought, without exposing himself to the dangers of being treated as a revolutionary and being turned into one even against his will.

Because of this, it was impossible for the Russians to become assimilated to the climate of the Second International or to play more than a peripheral part in its doings and debates. They were outsiders, facing problems of their own which were immensely different from those of the Western Socialists even when they made use of the same words and philosophical concepts. No doubt, because many of them spent long periods in exile in the West and picked up a great many Western habits and ideas, the fundamental differences were partly hidden both from themselves and from the Westerners with whom they conversed and held debate. But they were apt to get false notions about the Westerners even when they had lived long among them. In particular, the Russian Marxists, who were strong westernisers in their own imagination as well as in fact, were apt to cherish deep illusions about the real character of that German Social Democracy which dominated the thought of the Second International and purported to be carrying on the revolutionary traditions of the Communist Manifesto of 1848. These illusions were to have results of the highest importance after 1917, because they fostered the belief that Western Europe *must* be on the point of Socialist revolution, with the Germans leading the way. Lenin, fully as much as Trotsky, was the victim of this mistaken belief, as he showed when he tried in 1920 to force his way through Poland in order to link up with the German Revolution he believed to be ripe. The fury with which Lenin assailed Kautsky in the war of pamphlets after 1917 was largely due to his bitter awakening to the true character of the ideology of the leaders he had mistaken for revolutionaries like himself.

In Russia, the Socialist *had* to be a revolutionary : there was nothing else for him to be, at any rate after the brief period during which it had seemed possible that Alexander II might assume the rôle of reforming Czar, as Herzen, in *Kolokol*, had demanded of him at the time of the emancipation of the serfs. After the middle 'sixties there was never any hope of ending the autocracy save by revolution : the only real question was whether the immediate task was to set about making the revolution at once — or, if that was impossible, to resort to terrorism as the next best thing — or whether priority should be given to the work of intellectual and social preparation for it. The immediate and violent repression met with by those intellectuals who, in the early 'seventies, attempted to make contact with the people by going and living among them showed that the autocracy would allow nothing to be done by open means to break down the barriers between the enlightened few and the main body of the people. It was highly dangerous even to discuss political matters at a 'highbrow' level, unless every subversive implication was carefully concealed. Chernyshevsky, though he refrained from any direct attack on the established system, paid in prison and then in Siberia the penalty for his advanced opinions ; and the very moderate Peter Lavrov wrote his works in exile. Among major figures in the development of Narodnik thought only Mikhailovsky managed to get his writings past the censorship without falling a victim to the political police. He did so by casting what he had to say mainly in the form of philosophical and sociological commentary on the great respectable authors of the West ; but even so it is something of a miracle that he was let alone.

One consequence of the intensity of the repression in Russia was that, in the absence of contacts between the main body of the intellectuals and the 'people', thought was effectively divorced from all forms of action save the most extreme. In the underground terrorist organisation it was possible for a few intellectuals to join hands with a few revolutionary workers, and to act; but such groups were inevitably very small and very secret. Local peasant risings and such strike movements as occurred in the towns arose, for the most part, without any participation by the intellectuals ; and most of the groups of students and other intellectuals which met to talk politics had no contact with either peasants or urban workers, and could only talk. In these circumstances it was inevitable that discussion should proceed in a social vacuum, and should take on a highly speculative tone; for there was nothing to bring it down to earth. The conditions for the creation of a popular movement on any organised basis were not yet ripe; and this left all the more room for falling out concerning the kind of organised movement the revolutionaries — that is, in effect, the intellectuals — ought to be setting out to create.

The great question posed much earlier by Herzen was still unanswered. Must the Russians, on the way to emancipation, tread the road the West was treading, through capitalism and industrial development to a Socialism founded on the power of the industrial working class, or could they, profiting by the lessons of the West, advance by a different route to a predominantly agrarian Socialism, based on the village commune, without needing to become industrialised or to accept that 'capitalist dictatorship' which had gone along with industrialisation elsewhere? On the answer given to this question turned the nature of the appeal Socialists needed to make and the social groups to whom it should be addressed. If the only road to Socialism were by way of industrial development under capitalist auspices, the Socialist should presumably do all he could to foster the growth of capitalism and industry, even if he hated both; and his principal appeal should be to the industrial workers, even though they were few and evidently still too weak to accomplish much by themselves. If on the other hand there was a real possibility of utilising the communal elements of the old Russian village organisation as foundations for an agrarian Socialism in which the moujiks would play the part assigned to the industrial proletariat in the West, the great need was to oppose the growth of capitalism, which was rapidly destroying the old village structure, and to create among the peasants a nucleus of Socialist sentiment to give coherence and direction to the mass discontents of the rural population. Even so, it might remain necessary to conduct propaganda largely in the towns, because of the almost insuperable difficulties in the way of carrying the message to the villages; but the purpose would be to convert town-dwelling industrial workers into missionaries to the moujiks when they went back, as they often did, to the villages from which they had been drawn in to work on the railways or in other urban pursuits.

In practice, however the fundamental questions were answered, the rival groups of Socialist intellectuals carried on their propaganda and made their contacts with the 'people' mainly in the towns because the villages were unapproachable. But they agitated as rivals, with different conceptions of Socialism and of the Russian destiny in their minds. Moreover, until the 1890s, even these urban contacts were very difficult to make in view of the backwardness of Russian industry and of the vigilance of the authorities in breaking up workers' combinations almost as soon as they appeared. In the 'seventies and 'eighties the intellectuals had mostly to rest content with arguing among themselves, and with studying such written matter as got past the censorship or was smuggled in from groups of refugees who had either gone abroad of their own motion or escaped from exile at home.

After the imprisonment of Chernyshevsky and the exile of Lavrov in the 1860s the first place among writers of the left inside Russia was taken by Nikolai Konstantinovich Mikhailovsky (1842–1904), who from 1869 wrote for the legally published *Otechestvenniya Zapiski* (Memoirs of the Fatherland) continuously till 1883 and then from 1890 to his death edited the monthly *Russkoe Bogatstvo* (Russian Fortune). From 1879 to 1883 he also wrote frequently for the illegal journal of Narodnaya Volya (People's Will), the terrorist organisation which was responsible for the killing of Alexander II in 1881. Through all this period he contrived to escape arrest and to get what he wrote past the censorship, though not, of course, without some mutilation of his articles and a great deal of subterfuge and deliberate avoidance of dangerous subjects. His social thought is buried in a vast number of articles cast mainly into the form of literary criticism and general sociological discussion and is nowhere formally put together. It is not easy at all points to make of it a consistent body of doctrine ; but its main drift is clear.

In the expositions which have been made Mikhailovsky is usually ranked, with Lavrov, as the founder of the Russian school of 'Subjective Sociology' ; and in order to appreciate his influence and the controversies which gathered round his doctrines it is essential to get as clear as we can about the meaning of this description. 'Subjective' is, of course, here contrasted with 'Objective'; and Marxist Sociology is contrasted as 'Objective' with the Subjectivism of Lavrov and of Mikhailovsky. Marxism is 'Objective' because it attributes the determining influence in social development to objective forces — primarily the 'powers of production' — and not to the subjective ideas of individual thinkers. Mikhailovsky is a Subjectivist, not because he denies the influence of these objective forces, but because he asserts the correlative importance of individual creative activity and of ideas formed in the minds of men. Moreover, when he is dealing with the factors he regards as objective, he insists on treating the economic as no more than a single element in the objective environment which impresses its character on man's social institutions and behaviour. Beyond this there is a further sense in which Mikhailovsky is a Subjectivist: he lays great stress on the fact that the only sentient beings to be found in society are individual men and women and that all social groups are, in the last resort, only so many individuals acting together. He denies that groups have any objective reality apart from that of the individuals who make them up, and at any rate by implication he therewith denies the reality of social classes as objective factors in historical development. This indeed is, from the Marxist standpoint, the very crux of his offence.

And yet Mikhailovsky speaks at other times as if social groups do possess an objective reality distinct from that of their members. This occurs when he is writing about the biological foundations of man's social life and is making use of Ernest Haeckel's biological classification, which treats what he calls the 'cormen', or 'colony', that is, the social group, as the highest stage of organic development — as an 'organism' transcending the individual man (or animal) as the man or animal transcends the hierarchy of organs which he unifies under a common control. Elsewhere Mikhailovsky again and again denies that society, or any group, is an 'organism'; but here he appears to be saying just the opposite. The explanation is that Mikhailovsky does not deny that society, regarded biologically, can have the characteristics of an organism transcending its individual members. He regards this, however, as a horror, and as a fate which society, regarded from a psychological standpoint, is in a position to avoid by the exercise of creative will to sustain the independence of the individual man. Mikhailovsky sees the individual in modern society under the menace of being robbed of his sovereign individuality by being made into a mere organ of the supraindividual 'cormen' which imposes on him a division of labour denying to him the integral satisfaction of his natural propensities. He sees it as the function of the individual to fight against this tendency and to bring about a reconciliation between his own claims and those of the society which is necessary to him ; and, as he thinks of society as becoming essentially a psychological rather than a merely biological structure, because it is influenced in its development by the creative wills of men, he finds in individual man's reasoning and creative powers the way of escape from mere subjection to the forces making for biological integration at the individual's expense.

All this is, of course, from the Marxist standpoint, deadly error. It is true that Marx's conception of economic determinism did not at all, in his mind, exclude the action of men, who, he insisted, 'make their own history.' ; but Marx makes the creative individual the representative of a class and assigns the creative rôle to the class itself as an objective historical force. By doing this he seeks to reconcile economic materialism with human activism. Mikhailovsky, on his side, also professes a sort of determinism and a 'scientific', anti-metaphysical approach to the theory of history ; but for him the conception of necessity is subjective. Psychological, not economic, necessity governs social development : the great driving force in history is the individual's striving to satisfy his mental, as well as his physical, wants.

This psychological approach is bound up with another which Marxists equally dislike — an insistence on the creative importance of ethical aspirations. Mikhailovsky, like Lavrov, contends again and again that the idea of progress is meaningless unless it is based on ethical valuation. He develops this point especially in the course of his criticisms of Herbert Spencer and of the Darwinians — that is, of those who attempted to make Darwinian conceptions of evolution the basis of social doctrine.

The increasing complexity of an organism — or of a society — he argues, is no evidence of its superiority; nor is fitness to survive in a given environment at all equivalent to worthiness to survive. The better is that which enlightened individuals think better — not that which 'nature' favours; for 'nature's' preferences do not coincide with human aspirations. Man's task is to conquer nature, to subdue nature to his purposes; and these purposes have in them an ethical element. They rest on values which have been conceived in the minds of individual men. Admittedly, such valuations are only relative, and are greatly influenced by the particular environments in which those who make them are living; but this subjective relativity does not invalidate them, or prevent them from being the motive forces in history.

Mikhailovsky, and to an even greater extent Lavrov, finds evidence of these psychological drives, and of their ethical content, in primitive as well as in advanced societies, and among animals as well as men. But he regards them as destined to take much more comprehensive shape in the societies of the future. The rôle of the thinking individual in society, as he sees it, is to find ways of social living and organisation that will reconcile the claims of the whole and of the groups within the whole with the need of the individual to live his own life as a rounded person. In the more primitive societies, he holds, the social division of labour takes mainly forms which involve the co-operation of numbers of people in the performance of similar tasks, each task remaining enough an integrated means of self-expression to be compatible with the sense of free co-operative effort. As against this, the effect of the subdivision of tasks in large-scale industrial society is to rob work of its expressive value to the individual, and therewith to rob the individual himself of his integrated personality. The notion of 'task' is here to be understood as including not only industrial employment, but also a much more widespread tendency of the modern world towards undue specialisation. For example, Mikhailovsky invokes the same idea in his consideration of the problem of sex relations. The desire to love and be loved, he says, is one of the fundamental drives, and in the more primitive societies it finds satisfactory expression in a family group within which the functions of the two sexes are not unduly differentiated.

The more sharply differentiated they become, the less husband and wife have in common in the way of shared tasks and the more each has to look for in the other in order to find a satisfactory relationship. Hence the prevalence of disillusionment and conjugal infidelity among the most advanced groups in contemporary societies — an evil to be cured only by reducing the artificial differentiation of functions and making men and women once more, but on a higher plane, partners in social activity as well as in their sexual relations. This is all part of Mikhailovsky's 'individualism': it leads him to a strong preference for social co-operation in small groups within the larger society, to a sharp opposition to those who mistake differentiation as such for progress, and to a refusal to accept industrialism as lying on the road to human emancipation. He prefers agriculture to industry and handicraft to factory production because agriculture and handicraft are compatible with division of labour without the disintegrating subdivision which large-scale operations involve.

Hostility to the worship of differentiation as the criterion of progress is not the only basis for Mikhailovsky's quarrel with the contemporary apostles of evolution. He objects strongly to their misuse of biological analogies in describing and evaluating social phenomena. Psychology, he insists — this time in his criticism of Comtism — is not a branch of Biology but a science in its own right ; and Sociology, as the evaluative study of society, must rest on psychological foundations. There are, he agrees, biological laws which can be discussed by the positive, inductive methods that are appropriate for the ascertainment of hard facts, and such laws are fully valid within their appropriate fields. But as soon as we come to study human beings either as individuals or in their social relations we move into a realm in which subjective values as well as objective facts have to be considered, and in which 'ought' is fully as important as 'is'. Darwinian conceptions of biological development in terms of natural selection and chance variation therefore become inappropriate, or at least inadequate. Mikhailovsky, like most of his contemporaries, including Spencer, held the evolutionary theory in its Lamarckian rather than its Darwinian form. He believed in the inheritance of acquired characteristics and in the power of the individual organism to adapt itself by effort to changes in its environment. But even if he had not believed this to be true biologically, he would have maintained none the less its psychological and sociological truth. His essential point was not biological : it was that men possess a mental power to adapt themselves to, and to shape their social environment and to impose upon society their own ethical conceptions of the criteria of fitness to survive and flourish.

From the Marxist standpoint, to attack the Darwinian conception of evolution and to prefer Lamarck was a further deadly offence, not because the Marxists favoured the 'survival of the fittest' to survive under the conditions of competitive capitalism. but because they thought of the Materialist Conception of History as the social correlative of Darwinism in the biological field. Engels repeatedly claimed that Marx had done for Social Science what Darwin had done for Biology ; and the deterministic aspect of the Darwinian doctrine seemed to fit in with the Marxist conception of the class-struggle, and with the study of history in terms of the 'origin of economic species'. It was unethical and unidealistic : it stressed the formative power of the objective environment as against the creative capacity of the individual mind. It appeared to square with the view that 'things' came first and ideas afterwards as derivations from them. Moreover, though Darwin himself was illogical enough not to be an atheist, it provided an account of nature's doings that left the universe free of God and made it easy to treat religion as an expression of class-attitudes — the 'opium of the people' supplied by the ruling class as an auxiliary to its temporal power. Whereas Mikhailovsky, from his psychological starting-point, approached religion as a mental fact, meeting a real, because factual, need of the human individual and therefore not to be explained away as mere ideological 'superstructure' on the basic realities of economic relations.

Mikhailovsky was not a 'believer'. His view of religion was nearer to Comte's, which was in turn derived from Saint-Simon's, who got the negative part of it from Condorcet. On the one hand he saw the supernatural element in religion being driven back continually by the advance of scientific knowledge ; but on the other he regarded the religious impulse as deeply rooted in men and as continually seeking new means of expression corresponding to changing forms of social relations. Historically, he said, every new form of social relationship has been accompanied by the spread of a new religious idea. He explained this by saying that religion serves as the 'inseparable bond between the things that are and those that ought to be'. In other words, he looked on religion as the means of unifying scientific knowledge with the ethical principles guiding conduct. 'These *disjecta membra* of the life of the spirit', he wrote, 'must be brought into unity, and to do this is the function of religion'. Naturally, the Marxists would have none of this:[1] they altogether refused to recognise the independence of the ethical imperative. But this view of the function of religion fitted in neatly with Mikhailovsky's belief in the function of the individual in the continual discovery of ethical values.

This process of discovery Mikhailovsky regarded as the work of individuals who were able to conceive ideas in advance of their age and to get these ideas imitated and adopted by their fellow-men. He laid great stress on the creative capacity of the individual in arriving at new ethical conceptions and on the suggestibility of the main body of men to the exhortations of the 'hero' — who corresponds closely to Max Weber's later notion of the 'charismatic' leader. But his conception of the 'hero' is not limited to the leader who influences men for good. ' "Hero" ', he writes, 'is the name we give to the man who by his example captivates the mass for good or for evil, for noble or for degrading, for rational or for irrational actions.' He explicitly denies that in saying this he is attempting to revive the 'great man' theory of history as it was taught by Thomas Carlyle and others. 'Heroes', or 'great men', he says, do not fall from the sky: they grow out of the earth under the influences of their contemporary environment. They are 'heroes' because they incarnate in a high degree feelings, thoughts, and desires which are implicit in the social situation and to which the mass is ready to respond. 'An evil-doer, an idiot, or a lunatic may be as important as a world-famous genius, if only the mob has followed him, has verily subjected itself to him, has imitated and worshipped him.' Mikhailovsky then goes on to explain how mobs choose their 'heroes', for good or ill, by

[1] Though Lunacharsky's group said something rather like it later.

affirming that in each man there exists a craving for an ideal, which seeks embodiment in an individual, and that, the more drab or unsatisfactory the life of the ordinary man is, the more readily will he yield himself to anyone who has the gift for making himself into a representative figure. He discusses the hypnotic influence of oratory, and attempts a quasi-mathematical explanation of the intensity of crowd emotion. He illustrates his general thesis particularly from the susceptibility of the mass in the Middle Ages to the influence of dancers, flagellants, and other whippers up of mass excitement.

'Heroism', then, in Mikhailovsky's sense of the word, is a source of evil as well as of good. His hopes for its beneficient working rest on the capacity of men to respond to ethically rational as well as to irrational influences and on the spread of enlightenment as a factor making for the success of the ethical innovator against his rivals. But he thinks that the good 'hero' will stand the best chance where the mass upon which he has to work consists mainly of individuals whose own lives are integrated by the habitual performance of meaningful, co-operative tasks, and the least chance where the undue subdivision of labour has turned the individual into a mere 'hand', performing only a detailed process meaningless in itself, and deprived of direct co-operation with his fellows in a rounded task intelligible to them all. This, of course, fits in with his hatred of industrialism and with his belief that the peasant and the artisan, however poor they may be, have yet the satisfaction which comes of integrated, meaningful activity.

Evidently, too, Mikhailovsky's conception of the 'heroes' — whom we should nowadays call the 'élites' — fitted in with the situation in which the Russian intellectuals of his day found themselves. They were the providers of new ideas ; and it was their task to make themselves into ' heroes ' — if they could — by presenting these ideas in forms which would make them acceptable to the mass of the people. If Mikhailovsky was right about the effects on men's minds of subdivided labour and specialisation of social tasks, the intellectuals were likely to find a better response for their advanced ideas among peasants and artisans than among workers employed in large-scale enterprise, save to the extent to which the latter were still peasant-minded and had kept their contacts with the villages from which they came. Even if, because of the sheer difficulty of carrying on village propaganda, the Socialist intellectuals had to work chiefly in the towns, they should appeal rather to the handicraftsman and to the peasant still lurking in the industrial worker than to the industrial proletarian as such, and, far from helping forward the process of industrialisation in Russia, they should do all they could to prevent it.

Thus, Mikhailovsky's doctrines led directly to the conclusion that the best hopes for Socialism in Russia lay not in the growth of an industrial structure modelled on Western capitalism, but in the creation of an élite of revolutionaries bent on leaping directly to agrarian Socialism without any intervening capitalist stage and without the capitalisation of agriculture itself. This meant retaining peasant property, but seeking to transform it by putting new life into the decaying communal institutions of the peasant village — the mir — and at the same time encouraging by every possible means the growth of peasant Co-operation, which would need to be developed through the free action of the peasants from below, and not imposed on them by authority from above. In order to achieve these things, the intellectuals required to make contacts with the more intelligent individuals among the 'people' and thus to build up a wider élite which would be in a position gradually to leaven the great lump of peasants, whose acceptance of the new ideas was the condition of the Revolution's success.

Evidently, these general notions of the advance towards Socialism admitted of widely different practical interpretations. At the one extreme, they could be interpreted as justifying terrorist action designed to shake the confidence and undermine the efficacy of the Czarist autocracy, and therewith to encourage spontaneous peasant revolts. Those who took most to heart Mikhailovsky's emphasis on the creative rôle of the individual could regard individual acts of terrorism as complying with the conditions for the good kind of 'heroism'; and, as we have seen, Mikhailovsky himself was a regular contributor to the clandestine journal of Narodnaya Volya. But only a few of the advocates of terrorism took this extreme view. Most of them justified terrorism only as forced upon the movement by the denial of other outlets, or only by way of reprisal against the torture or execution of arrested revolutionaries or against particularly brutal Czarist officials. Many, indeed, were actually opposed to terrorism as a policy, but refused to condemn it outright because they were not prepared to go against its idealistic practitioners or to join in the counter-revolutionary hue and cry against them.

At the other extreme, it was possible to draw the conclusion that the right course was to be patient, to use every opportunity which Government repression left open for the building up of social tissue that would help to develop a new spirit of co-operative activity among the peasants, to work in with the more liberal landowners in keeping alive the communal elements in the village, to seek to promote local government in the country-side through the Zemstvos,[1] to work for the extension of popular education, and to do what could be done to obstruct the growth of large-scale industry and financial enterprise.

Between these two extremes lay many intermediate possibilities ; and the main body of the Narodniks consisted neither of practising terrorists nor of evolutionary collaborationists. The main body consisted of men and women who wanted to use every chance of developing a revolutionary mass movement based mainly on the peasants, and saw the Revolution's only hope in the growth of agrarian discontent and the creation of an organised élite large and energetic enough to provide a co-ordinating leadership.

Peter Lavrov (1823–1900), writing in exile, became the outstanding theorist of this central type of Narodnism, with Prince Peter Kropotkin, the exponent of Anarchist-Communism, standing further to the left, but not at the terrorist extreme. Some account of Lavrov has been given in the second volume of this work.[2] We there saw that after his escape abroad in 1870 he settled in Paris and founded *Vpered* (Forward), which became the principal intellectual journal of the Narodnik movement. Lavrov at the outset stood for gradualism. He wanted a long period of education and ethical propaganda as the necessary preparation for revolution. But when the Czarist despotism closed all the avenues to peaceful agitation his views underwent a gradual change. Though he took no

[1] The Zemstvos were the organs of rural local government, dominated by landlords and officials, but including a substantial 'liberal' element, as appeared in 1905.
[2] See Vol. II, p. 53 ff.

part in the activities of Narodnaya Volya during its terrorist campaign against the Czar, he supported the attempt to rebuild it from abroad after 1881, and joined Leo Tikhomirov in editing from London the journal *Vestnik Narodnoy Voli* from 1884 to 1886. His main importance, however, lies in his historical writings, from his *Historical Letters*, written before he left Russia, to his *Principal Moments in the History of Thought*, published in 1900. Lavrov wrote these books under a number of pseudonyms — Myrtov for the *Historical Letters*, A. Dolengi for the *Principal Moments*, and Arnoldy and Shchukin for other works. He planned to put his essential ideas together in a comprehensive *History of Thought*, to which all his actual works were meant as introductory, but this encyclopaedic study was never written.

Lavrov, like Mikhailovsky, is particularly concerned with the relations between facts and values, that is, between science and ethics. He insists on the absoluteness of many truths, which are true whether men have knowledge of them or not and remain true even if they are wholly forgotten. But he contrasts these truths with others which contain a subjective element and are truths only as being correct answers to questions which can be formulated only at certain times and in certain social situations; and he regards the attempts to formulate laws of history as belonging to this class of relative truths containing a large subjective element. The historians — by which term he means the formulators of theories of history — do not merely ascertain facts : they select and group them in particular ways in order to answer particular questions, and ignore facts which do not seem to them significant in relation to the questions they ask. Thus, they arrive at truths which are in essence selective rather than comprehensive; and in the selections they make they are guided by their ethical concepts. The historian, he argues, cannot escape from this necessity unless he is content to be merely an annalist; for he cannot impute meanings without selection or without introducing the ethical notions which shape his questions. But this process ought to be entered upon not capriciously, but on the basis of objective study of those facts which belong to the category to which absolute truth can be assigned.

This distinction leads Lavrov into the never-ending argument about free will and determinism. He regards the universe as a mechanistically determined structure which is open to scientific investigation directed to the ascertainment of verifiable laws. But he holds also that not everything can be studied in this way and in especial that social phenomena cannot be understood unless they are considered in relation to their historical development and to the increasing extent to which men reflect upon their own conduct and in doing so modify it. He sees the problem of sociology, which he considers to be a normative study aiming at the promotion of human well-being, as the discovery of the right balance between solidarity of the social group and freedom of expression in action for the individual — a balance which has to be continually rediscussed and adjusted as the environing conditions change. The instinct of solidarity, the urge to form groups, he considers to be universal among men and to be shared by men not only with the higher animal types, but even with the lower. Biologically, he regards all organisms as having developed out of 'colonies' of like units, loosely connected together; and he differs from Mikhailovsky in regarding societies as organisms, possessing a psychic solidarity based on pleasure or satisfaction in holding together. The characteristic of human societies is to be found in their capacity to develop this primitive pleasure in solidarity into higher forms of co-operation, which take shape in customs and acquire the sanction of ritual observances. But men not only form customs to reinforce their solidarity: they also change their customs — paradoxically, for it is of the very nature of a custom to be resistant to change. How then do changes come about? By the largely unconscious accumulation of small deviations, which are gradually accepted in practice and are then given the status of old customs in men's minds. For though the need for adaptation to changing conditions stirs men to practical protests which result in modifications of behaviour, the instinct for solidarity causes the changes to be accepted as part of the traditional way of life. This instinct also causes the critical mind to endeavour to weave the whole way of living of a people into a system free from contradictions — as was done by the Greeks in the realm of philosophy, by the Romans in that of law, and by the mediaeval church in terms of scholasticism. The modern world, or at any rate the

West, has sought to achieve an all-embracing idea of solidarity on the basis of the nation State; and with the rise of the bourgeoisie this has shaped itself into a concept of class solidarity, which has prepared the way for democracy as the final expression of solidarity at the conscious level.

But this historical tendency to establish social solidarity is only one aspect of the process of social evolution. Side by side with it proceeds the struggle for individual freedom, of which the biological and psychological foundations are to be discovered in a need for nervous excitation that is a common property of living organisms and leads to different behaviour by individuals belonging to the same species or group. In this lies the whole basis of individuality and of the higher life of men. The higher a species is, the less will the individuals in it consent to be mere units yielding to the pressure of society. The individual emerges out of the group and is moulded by it; but he also asserts his personal likes and dislikes against its dominance. Thus, the individual, by asserting himself against society and by modifying society in doing so, comes to be a social force playing a rôle in history. At this point Lavrov's thought meets Mikhailovsky's; for he claims that upon the critically enlightened individual lies the responsibility of innovation and of instructing and persuading his contemporaries. It is an essential part of Lavrov's doctrine that the enlightened owe this duty to society: they must innovate and preach, not only in order to satisfy their own needs, but also for the benefit of their fellow-men.

Historically, this spirit of innovation has indeed, Lavrov holds, often done harm as well as good, because it has been perverted into promoting the interests, not of society as a whole, but of a limited class. But it is the sole source from which progress can proceed; and the problem accordingly is to develop its use for desirable social ends. This involves that the innovator shall be aware of the practical limits within which innovation can work successfully — that is, shall understand the laws which determine the general course of social change and shall seek to work within the room allowed by these laws, and not arbitrarily. Secondly, it involves that the innovator shall recognise the need for social solidarity and the threat to his own well-being that would develop if this solidarity were destroyed, or if he failed to work in common with a group of his fellows. He has to find his place, and to work, within a group largely like-minded with himself ; and, in common with the rest of this group, he has to recognise the need to work within the wider unity of the whole society, and generally in harmony with it, even when he is trying to change it in certain respects. Lavrov denies that there is any inconsistency between a strong bond of solidarity binding a whole society together and the existence within it of a lively mental activity making for change. Indeed, he thinks that history shows as the only progressive societies those in which solidarity and social criticism have been reconciled.

This summary account of Lavrov's social doctrine should be read in conjunction with what has been written about him earlier in the second volume of this book. Here I have been trying to bring out his conception of the creative rôle of the individual and his attempt to reconcile this with a modified acceptance of social determinism. His great offence in the eyes of Marxists was that his theory gave no importance to class as the instrument of social innovation — or rather that, when he did speak of class in this connection, he treated it as tending to pervert innovation from furthering the general welfare of society and to divert it to the furtherance of sectional interests. Lavrov's entire conception of the importance of solidarity in the life of society was, of course, anathema to Marxists, who saw in it a petit bourgeois repudiation of the creative function of social classes. This rejection of the class outlook was to become a marked characteristic of much Narodnik and, later, Social Revolutionary thinking.

Russia, up to the 1870s, had little knowledge of Marxism. Herzen had published a Russian translation of the *Communist Manifesto* in *Kolokol* in the 1860s, and Russian Socialists had become aware of Marx's continued activities in connection with the International Working Men's Association chiefly in connection with his epic contest with Bakunin. Bakunin himself had done something to advertise Marx to his disciples in Russia and, as we saw, had actually begun to translate *Das Kapital* into Russian after its appearance in 1867. Marx had certain contacts with Russian exiles, notably with Nicholas Utin and his small anti-Bakuninist group in Geneva. But there was in Russia not only no Marxist movement, but no group that had been much affected by Marx's ideas. As for Marx himself, we have seen how violent was his antipathy to Russia — and not only to Czardom but to the Russian temperament as well. He was taken quite aback when, in 1870, Utin's group at Geneva invited him to serve as the representative of Russia on the General Council of the International. He accepted the commission, and persuaded the General Council to admit Utin's group to affiliation. In his letter of acceptance, which was published in *Narodnoye Dyelo* (The People's Cause) he adjured Russian Socialists to direct their efforts to the liberation of Poland from the Russian yoke. 'The violent seizure of Poland by Russia', he wrote, 'forms the pernicious support and the actual cause of the military régime in Germany and consequently over the whole continent. Therefore, in bending their efforts towards smashing the chains of Poland the Russian Socialists impose upon themselves the noble task of destroying the military régime, a task that is essential as a preliminary condition for the general emancipation of the European proletariat.'

In reporting this correspondence to Engels he recorded more of his real thought.

> A funny position for me to be functioning as the representative of young Russia. A man never knows what he may come to or what strange fellowship he may have to submit to. In the official reply I . . . emphasise the fact that the chief task of the Russian section is to work for Poland (*i.e.* to free Europe from Russia as a neighbour). I thought it safer to say nothing about Bakunin. . . .

The connection thus begun was developed by the publication in 1872 of a Russian translation of Volume I of *Das Kapital* made by Nikolai F. Danielson (1844–1918), better known as Nikolai-on, who became one of the leading Narodnik economists. He also became one of Marx's regular correspondents and continued to correspond with Engels after Marx's death. Undoubtedly Marx was influenced by him when, after learning Russian in order to study the Russian agrarian problem from the original sources, he wrote the well-known passage in his introduction to Vera Zasulich's translation of the *Communist Manifesto* concerning the possibility of a direct transition to Socialism in Russia, without an intervening capitalist stage, by means of a transformation of the *mir* into a higher form of village community.

Danielson wrote extensively about economic conditions in Russia : his major work, which has been translated into French, is his *History of the Economic Development of Russia since the Emancipation of the Serfs* (1893). He there reached the pessimistic conclusion that the development of capitalism in Russia was fast destroying what was left of the traditional peasant community, but that capitalism stood no chance of successfully establishing itself as a substitute because of the narrow limits of its home market and its unavoidable inferiority to the countries of the West as an industrial producer. He argued that the growth of capitalist production would undermine the peasant and artisan economy, which often rested on a co-ordination of handicraft with agriculture, and would thus destroy the only market in which it could hope to sell mass-produced goods ; and he believed that at the same time the development of capitalist banking and the infiltration of capitalist methods into the countryside would create mere enclaves of high production in an otherwise impoverished countryside. He stressed the tendency of factory production to replace male artisans by low-paid female and child labour, thus swelling urban unemployment and depressing the standards of urban living. His conclusion was that industrialisation would act only as a disintegrating force, and that the best hope lay in this disintegration leading to a predominantly peasant revolution and to the rebuilding of the Russian economy on the shaken, but still undestroyed, foundations of the village commune.

These views, which represented the predominant outlook of Narodnik Socialism, at first impressed Marx and Engels enough to induce Marx to write, in 1877, that, 'If Russia continues to pursue the path she has followed since 1861 (*i.e.* industrialisation) she will lose the finest chance ever offered by history to a nation, in order to undergo all the fatal vicissitudes of a capitalist régime'. Later, in 1882, in his Preface to the Russian version of the *Communist Manifesto*, he put the matter thus :

> The question now is whether the Russian village commune — a form of primitive collective communal property which has indeed already been to a great extent destroyed —

can pass immediately into the highest communist form of landed property, or whether on the contrary it must go through from the beginning the same process of disintegration as that which has determined the historical development of the West. The only possible answer to this question to-day is as follows :—If the Russian revolution becomes the signal for the workers' revolution in the West, so that the one supplements the other, then the present form of land ownership in Russia may be the starting-point of an historical development.

Engels, in his correspondence with Danielson, both amplified Marx's answer and modified it in the light of the further growth of Russian capitalism during the ensuing ten years. Engels argued that the Russians, if they made their revolution, could succeed in building the required communist structure of the Russian village only if the victory of the Revolution in the more advanced West had already provided a model of communistic village agriculture for them to imitate. He also contended that the actual course of events did not bear out Danielson's conclusions concerning the narrow limits to the expansion of capitalism in Russia ; and that the growth of capitalist production, aided by protective tariffs, was creating markets for the absorption of its products. Engels further emphasised the long steps that had been taken by the 1890s towards the destruction of the old village community as having put additional obstacles in the way of the Narodnik solution.

Danielson had by this time found other antagonists, with the growth of Marxism in Russia itself. He was attacked both by the 'legal Marxist' economist, Peter Struve, and by Plekhanov, as well as by Lenin in his early work on the development of capitalism in Russia. Danielson's views were influenced by the impoverishment of the Russian peasants on account of falling agricultural prices during the latter decades of the nineteenth century and because of crushing tax burdens. He saw this impoverishment of the peasantry as a 'law' of economic development which prevented the growth of a sufficient market for capitalist industry, and also as the generating cause of a peasant revolution which Russian capitalism would be much too feeble to resist. Actually, the trend of agricultural prices was reversed in the last years of the nineteenth century, and considerable capitalist expansion did take place. Moreover,

Danielson, in his hostility to industrialism, over-estimated its disintegrating effects, as was pointed out by his fellow-Narodnik, Vassily Pavlovich Vorontsov (1847–1918), whose book on *The Fortunes of Capitalism in Russia* appeared as early as 1882. Vorontsov in general took the same line as Danielson in arguing that capitalism could not be successfully developed in Russia because of its inherent tendency to generate too little home demand for its products to enable it to subsist without export markets, into which Russian industry would be unable to penetrate in face of the competition of better-established capitalist countries. Vorontsov did not deny that capitalism could develop up to a point in Russia ; but he held that it would remain a sickly growth, sustained by high protection and, even so, dependent on an intense exploitation of cheap labour and subject to severe recurrent crises. The Marxists, including Plekhanov and Lenin, denounced these views as a mere revival of the exploded, petit bourgeois, underconsumptionist theories of Sismondi.

Vorontsov, besides his work on capitalism, wrote extensively about Russian agriculture and about the Russian handicrafts-men and their artels. He was a leading advocate of Co-opera-tion, and believed that the co-operative tendencies inherent in Russian agricultural methods would serve as a foundation for technical advances that would ensure economic and social development without the need for capitalist intervention. He thought the village would be able to achieve a high level of balanced production and consumption without the need to depend on a market economy or on capitalist marketing and finance. His book on *Progressive Techniques in Peasant Economy* (1892) set forth his hopes in this respect, on the basis of an extensive survey of actual developments. Politically, he stood on the right wing of the Narodniks. Trained as a physician, he became first a Zemstvo official and then a professional statistician. He contributed to Lavrov's *Vpered*, but broke away from the main body of the Narodniks when they gave their endorsement to terrorist methods, which he regarded as futile.

Danielson and Vorontsov were the two Narodnik economists who were most to the fore when Marxism began to develop seriously as a movement in Russia. Its development is none too easy to trace in its earlier phases both because it appeared in a number of different forms and at first more as an influence than as a separate movement, and also because its early history has undergone a good deal of rewriting in order to adjust it to the correct party line. It is now commonly traced back as a movement to the split in Zemlya i Volya when a section which included Georgy Plekhanov decided against Zelyabov's policy of terrorism and set up the organisation called Cherny Peredyel (Black-earth Distribution) with a programme of handing over to the peasants, without compensation, the land which had been given over to the landlords at the time of the emancipation of the serfs. This, which was, of course, regarded only as a first step, was to be made the basis of propaganda among peasants and peasant-minded workers in the towns. There was clearly nothing Marxist in such a programme; and the only reason for connecting Cherny Peredyel with the rise of Marxism is that Plekhanov later became the leading Russian exponent of Marxist views. In any case, it did not last long; in 1880 Plekhanov passed into exile and, coming into direct contact with Western Marxism, speedily became a full convert to the Marxist gospel and especially to the central importance of the industrial proletariat and of its organisation under the leadership of a party devoted to active participation in the struggle for political power.

Georgy Valentinovich Plekhanov (1857–1918), who speedily constituted himself the principal Russian interpreter of Marxism and soon became the best-known exponent of Russian Social Democracy among the Socialists of Western Europe, had begun his career as a Narodnik in 1875, while he was a student at the University of St. Petersburg. He at once became active in the underground movement and acted as editor for various clandestine publications. He had left Russia before Zelyabov's group succeeded in killing Alexander II, and he remained in exile until 1917, when he returned after the February Revolution. Essentially a theorist, rather than an organiser or a revolutionary leader, he came to be regarded as the arch-priest of Marxist orthodoxy and the principal left-wing champion of Marxism against not only the Narodniks but all kinds of enemies within the gates, from 'legal Marxists' of the type of Peter Struve to philosophical deviationists such as

Bogdanov and Lunacharsky. He vigorously assailed the sociological theories of Lavrov and Mikhailovsky; the so-called 'Economists' such as Martynov, who wished to concentrate on the day-to-day fight of the workers for better pay and conditions; the Russian admirers of Bernstein's Revisionism; the Anarchists and Anarchist-Communists, such as Kropotkin — indeed, every opponent of, or deviationist from, the strict version of the Marxist gospel, which he understood mainly in the sense in which it found expression in the theory and practice of German Social Democracy. The Germans, it must be remembered, were still, at the time when Plekhanov got to know them, working under the repressive conditions of Bismarck's Anti-Socialist Laws, which had forced them to establish their party headquarters abroad in Switzerland and to organise inside Germany as an underground party, though they were able to fight Reichstag elections and to speak freely in Reichstag debates. Though conditions in Germany in the 1880s were very different from conditions in Russia, they had in common the denial of the right to organise openly for Socialism; and this gave the German party a misleadingly revolutionary look and made its theorists, such as Kautsky, use revolutionary phrases which were only half-meant and were easily misunderstood. Plekhanov himself was to show later that his own revolutionism, which had appeared so uncompromising in the 'eighties and 'nineties, was in fact much nearer to Kautsky than to what came to be known as Bolshevism. But up to the quarrel which rent the Russian Social Democratic Party from 1903 onwards, his status as the apostle of left-wing Marxism went unquestioned.

In exile, in the early 'eighties, Plekhanov joined hands with a number of fellow-exiles, who included Pavel Borissovich Axelrod (1850–1925) and Vera Zasulich (1851–1919). Axelrod, son of a Jewish innkeeper, had been in his youth a follower of Bakunin, but after passing through a Narodnik phase, had come strongly under the influence of Lassalle's ideas. He had been with Plekhanov in Cherny Peredyel. The third member of the trio, Vera Zasulich, as we saw earlier, had been acquitted by a jury after shooting at Trepov, the Governor-General of St. Petersburg, in 1878, as a reprisal for the corporal punishment administered to the political prisoner, Bogolyubov. After her acquittal, which caused the Czarist Government to make an end of trial by jury for political prisoners, she prudently left Russia. In 1883 these three, with Lev Grigorevich Deutsch (1855–1941), V. I. Ignatov (1854–85), and a few others, founded the Labour Emancipation Group, which issued the following year a programme based largely on the Gotha Programme of the German Social Democratic Party. Before this Plekhanov had begun, in 1883, the long sequence of works in which he expounded the Marxist gospel. This series opened with *Socialism and the Political Struggle*, followed the next year by *Our Differences*, in which he sought to settle accounts with the Narodniks. In these works Plekhanov combated both terrorism and Anarchism and set himself in opposition to the 'Jacobins' who thought of revolution in terms of the seizure of power by an armed minority without the backing of a conscious and organised working class. He insisted that, as long as the mass of the workers remained unawakened, such a coup would be bound to end in fiasco. He had become fully converted to the need to build up a powerful working-class party under Socialist leadership, on the model of what the Germans were doing, in preparation for the coming revolution.

In 1887 the Labour Emancipation Group issued a revised version of its programme, in which it attempted to face the problem of the relation of the industrial workers to the peasantry. This showed traces of the continuing influence of Narodnik doctrine, and of the attempt of the group to escape from it. 'The main bulwark of absolutism', they declared, 'lies in the political indifference and intellectual backwardness of the peasantry'. The hope of ending this situation lay, according to Plekhanov, in the continuing links between field and factory. 'Cast out of the village as an impoverished member of the commune, the proletarian returns to it as a Social Democratic agitator. His appearance in this rôle brings about a change in the hitherto hopeless lot of the commune. Its disintegration is inevitable only to the point where that very disintegration creates a new popular force capable of putting an end to the domination of capitalism.'

From the early 'eighties onwards Russian Marxism took shape both inside Russia and abroad as an organised movement in opposition to the Narodniks. But its character was still by no means clearly defined; and the groups of which it was composed came and went with bewildering rapidity both among the exiles and at home, where they were constantly being broken up and re-formed. The 'eighties were in Russia a period of very rapid capitalist development, financed largely from French sources; and wherever industry took on large-scale forms the Socialists were soon at work forming small groups of militants, some under Marxist and some under Narodnik leadership, but many with no clearly defined doctrinal affiliation. We saw earlier that Trade Unions had already begun to spring up in the 'seventies — the South Russian Workers' Union, with its centre at Odessa, in 1875, and the Northern Union of Russian Workers, led by Stepan Khalturin and Victor Obnorsky at St. Petersburg in 1878.[1] A new League of South Russian Workers was organised by Shchedrin and Kovalskaya at Kiev about 1880. All these bodies were short-lived: the police were able to break them up by arresting most of their leaders. But despite the repression strikes grew more frequent in the 1880s. Between 1881 and 1886 there were 48 strikes, involving 80,000 workers, the biggest being the strike in the Morozov textile mill at Orekhova-Zuyevo in 1885, led by Peter Moiseyenko, a former member of the North Russian Workers' Union. Soldiers were called in to suppress this strike, and more than 600 arrests were made. During these years the strikes were mainly against wage-cuts made during the depression that had set in towards the end of the 'seventies.

The strikes of this period were led mainly by Socialists, but no one school of Socialists had any monopoly of them, nor had the ephemeral Trade Unions which sprang up any clear political allegiance. Politically, the clandestine groups which existed in most of the towns were unable to build up any regular connections one with another, though most of them had some contacts with the groups of exiles abroad, which were continually smuggling in illegal journals and pamphlets. The most active centres were Kiev in the Ukraine, Odessa on the Black Sea, Moscow and the region round it — the main centre of the textile industry — and above all St. Petersburg, which was beginning to develop as a centre of heavy industry. The building of railways did something to make communications easier

[1] See Vol. II, p. 320.

and also to scatter Socialist agitators over the country; but St. Petersburg was more closely in touch with the outside world than other towns, and became the principal centre of Social Democratic propaganda. In 1885 N. V. Vodovozov formed what is said to have been the first definitely Social Democratic group in that city; and the following year another group appeared under the leadership of Tochissky, who survived to take part, and to perish, in the October Revolution of 1917. But the most important groups inside Russia during the 'eighties were those led by Blagoev and Brusnev. Dimiter Blagoev,[1] whose group was broken up by the police in 1887, published an illegal journal, *Rabochy*: he escaped to Bulgaria when his group was destroyed and became a leader in the Bulgarian Socialist movement. He died in 1924. His place was taken by the engineer, Mikhail Ivanovich Brusnev (1866–1937), whose organisation lasted from 1888 until 1892. Both these groups were in contact with Plekhanov's Labour Emancipation Group in Geneva.

The 1890s opened evilly, with widespread famine and a serious epidemic of cholera in 1891, and with much unrest in the starving villages as well as in the towns. A section of intellectuals attempted the same year to form a Party of National Right, to unite liberals and revolutionaries in a common struggle for constitutional reform: they published a newspaper and a number of pamphlets, but were suppressed in 1894. The Narodniks also formed, about 1892, a new organisation in North Russia, which circulated a series of clandestine leaflets entitled *Flying Leaves*; but there was a much more rapid growth of Social Democratic groups. From 1893 a new strike movement began, culminating in the great strikes of textile workers in St. Petersburg in 1896. Lenin now first entered the field as a Social Democratic agitator.

Vladimir Ilyich Ulyanov (1870–1924), better known as Lenin, had become a Marxist during his student days at Kazan University. His elder brother, Alexander Ulyanov, had been executed in 1887 for his part in an abortive attempt to kill Alexander III, and this had set his younger brother off on his revolutionary career. Expelled from Kazan University, he moved first to Samara, where he set up a Marxist circle, and

[1] See p. 592.

then at the end of 1893 to St. Petersburg. Two years later he had succeeded in linking up the twenty or so Marxist groups he found there into a League of Struggle for the Emancipation of the Workers, which was soon in close touch with Plekhanov's Emancipation Group abroad and with other groups of exiles in Germany, France, and England. Meanwhile he published his first substantial pamphlet, *Who the Friends of the People Are* (1894), a sharply controversial statement of the Social Democratic case against the Narodniks. In the same year appeared Peter Struve's *Critical Notes on the Economic Development of Russia*, the beginning of a long controversy between the revolutionary Social Democrats and the group of intellectuals who came to be known as the 'Legal Marxists'. The following year, Lenin was arrested in St. Petersburg and exiled to Siberia, where he remained until 1900, studying and writing hard and building up connections with other Socialist exiles, while he watched as closely as he could the fortunes of the revolutionary movement in European Russia.

The speedy removal of Lenin from the leadership of the movement in St. Petersburg did not destroy its activity. It had begun under his influence to establish connections with the factory workers and to support strikes with specially written leaflets as well as with the spoken word. After his arrest, Lenin wrote in prison a pamphlet, *On Strikes*, in which he urged the Social Democrats to take the lead in organising the workers and championing their economic claims in an endeavour to bring them over to Socialism. After his removal, the League played its part in the great strikes of 1896, which led to the passing of the Factory Act of the following year, limiting the working day for adult males to $11\frac{1}{2}$ hours and making other reforms. The strike movement, both in St. Petersburg and elsewhere, continued during the next few years on a considerable scale; and the Social Democrats played a growing part in it. There arose, however, among them, partly as an outcome of Witte's Factory Act of 1897, sharp differences of opinion about policy. One section, later known as the 'Economists', held that the correct course was to concentrate on the economic struggle, to build up Trade Unions and organise strike movements for improved wages and conditions, and to subordinate political campaigning to these efforts until a mass working-class movement had been created in the economic field. Political agitation, it was said, not only failed to enlist mass support : it also divided the workers between rival schools instead of uniting them. As against this view the main body of Marxist Social Democrats protested hotly, insisting on the need for definitely revolutionary propaganda and for the creation of an organised Socialist Party to lead the working class and prepare for revolution. The argument was at this stage somewhat confused ; for the 'Economists' included both revolutionaries who hoped to give a revolutionary turn to industrial action and moderates who hoped to get the right of combination legally recognised, to establish forms of regular collective bargaining, and to induce the Government to pass further protective labour legislation. The latter group was headed by the 'Legal Marxists' Peter Struve (1870–1934) and Mikhail Ivanovich Tugan-Baranovsky (1865–1919) : the former found expression in the St. Petersburg journal *Rabochaya Misl* (Workers' Thought), founded in 1897 with Takhtarev and Lokhov as editors.

The rival views of the Social Democratic factions were represented among the exiles as well as in Russia. Among those who left Russia in the early 'nineties was B. N. Krichevsky (1866–1919), who, after connecting himself with Plekhanov's Labour Emancipation Group for a time, in 1895 joined hands with a number of others to form the League of Russian Social Democrats as a rival foreign centre. This body in 1898 began to publish a journal, *Rabocheye Dyelo* (The Workers' Cause), for which it sought recognition as the principal organ of Russian Marxism — A. S. Martynov (1865–1935), later a leading Menshevik, and V. P. Akimov (1875–1921), with Krichevsky, were its editors.

A lively dispute immediately developed between Krichevsky's group and the Plekhanov faction, which accused it of giving too much space to 'Economist' and other compromising doctrines, and set out to found a more thoroughgoing journal to express the views of the Labour Emancipation Group. Both groups were, of course, eager to win support in Russia, and neither was as yet prepared to excommunicate the other. Both in fact claimed to be sections of a common Social Democratic Party, which had not yet achieved a formal existence. Meanwhile, inside Russia, Leagues modelled on Lenin's St. Petersburg organisation had been developing in many towns out of the small, clandestine Social Democratic circles; and plans were being made for a secret Congress, at which a national organisation was to be constituted. There was also great Socialist activity in Russian Poland and in Lithuania, especially among the Jewish workers. A Polish Social Democratic Party, in sharp opposition to Pilsudski's nationalistic Polish Socialist Party, which was in close touch with the Austrian Poles, was established in 1895; and two years later a Jewish Socialist Party, known as the 'Bund', was founded to organise the Jewish workers over the whole area included in the Jewish 'Pale' — that is, in White Russia as well as in Poland and Lithuania. Both the Polish S.D.P. and the Bund, which was responsible for extensive strike movements during this period, regarded themselves as belonging to the Social Democratic movement which had its centre in Russia and were involved in the negotiations for a constituent Congress. In 1898 a small Congress, since regarded as the First Congress of the Russian Social Democratic Party, assembled secretly at Pskov. There were in all only nine delegates, including those from the Bund; and none of them was a person of outstanding importance. They met for three days, and decided to issue a manifesto to the workers of Russia; and they appointed a committee of three to undertake the work of organisation. But all the delegates and a great many other leaders of the Social Democratic groups throughout Russia were arrested almost immediately after the Congress. The manifesto, drafted by Struve, who was not present at the Congress, was issued; but the organisation disappeared, leaving behind it only certain resolutions, of which the most important asserted the right of every nation to self-determination in accordance with the decision of the London International Socialist Congress of 1896.

The destruction of the central organisation of the new party inside Russia left the groups abroad to continue their rivalries. The 1898 Congress had decided to make the *Rabochaya Gazeta*, which was published inside Russia at Kiev, the central organ of the party; but, this having become impracticable, the groups inside the country now decided that they must create a central organ abroad. Krichevsky's *Rabocheye Dyelo* set out to take this position; but most of the groups in Russia were not prepared to accept it, and discussions began among them about the possibility of a journal in which the group round Plekhanov could play the leading part.

At the beginning of 1900 Lenin was set free from his exile in Siberia, and returned to European Russia, where he at once became actively engaged in the plan to found a new journal and to refound the Social Democratic Party. At Pskov, where he settled when he was forbidden to live in St. Petersburg, he met a number of representatives of Social Democratic opinions, including not only Martov and Potresov but also Struve and Tugan-Baranovsky, to discuss plans for the proposed journal; and thereafter he travelled secretly to a number of places to consult the local groups. In July he went abroad to meet Plekhanov and his Emancipation Group, and secured their participation on terms which would make the new publication an independent journal, not under the control of any group except its own editorial committee. In Germany, he secured the help of Adolf Braun, of the German Social Democratic Party, in arranging for the journal to be printed by J. H. W. Dietz, the Social Democratic publisher, at Stuttgart.

There were by this time to be two journals, one informative and propagandist, the other 'scientific'. The first was to be called *Iskra* (The Spark), because, as its motto declared, 'the spark will kindle a flame'; the second was to be *Zarya* (The Dawn) and was to be devoted to longer articles dealing with theoretical issues. Up to a late stage in the preparations, Lenin was negotiating with groups and individuals covering a very wide range of Social Democratic opinion; but gradually the range was narrowed down. It can be seen from his letters how suspicious he was, not only of Struve and the 'Legal Marxists', but also of the groups of exiles in Paris and London, including the League of Russian Social Democrats. In the end, the *Iskra* group came to consist essentially of six persons, three old-stagers from the Labour Emancipation Group, together with three who had taken part in the discussions inside Russia. The three Emancipationists were Plekhanov, Vera Zasulich, and P. B. Axelrod: the other three were A. N. Potresov (1869–1934), Martov, and Lenin himself. Of the latter, Potresov, who also went by the name Starover, had been active in the St. petersburg Liberation League with Lenin, and had been banished to North Russia in 1898 : he now went abroad with Lenin. Martov (1873–1923), whose real name was Yuly Osipovich Zederbaum, had also worked with Lenin during and after his removal at St. Petersburg. Both were to take the Menshevik side in the Social Democratic Congress of 1903, as were Axelrod and Vera Zasulich ; but in 1900 they all appeared to stand well on the left of the movement, of which the ' Legal Marxists ' represented the extreme right and the main body of the 'Economists' the right centre, with Krichevsky and the Paris group headed by D. Ryazonov (1870–1945) holding a central position.

The first number of *Iskra* appeared in December 1900, that of *Zarya* following in March 1901. Well before either of them came out, the doctrinal disputes had reached a height among the *émigrés* who formed the Union of Russian Social Democrats. In March 1900 the fraction in this body which strongly opposed 'Economism' split away and set up a rival group of Revolutionary Social Democrats, which entered into relations with the *Iskra* group. The quarrel had been brought to a head partly by the disputes over the foundation of *Iskra*, but even more by the publication of Plekhanov's tract, *Vade Mecum* (1900), an edited collection of documents in which he went to work to expose the tactical manœuvres, as well as the doctrinal errors, of the Economists and their sympathisers. In 1898 had appeared a manifesto, *Credo*, in which I. D. Kuskova (b. 1869) set forth the gist of the Economists' programme ; and during the same year Tugan-Baranovsky had published his book, *The Russian Factory, Past and Present*, supporting the Economists' attitude. A sharp controversy had followed in the Russian Socialist press, both at home and abroad ; and there was much confusion of opinion in the local groups. Demands began to come in for the summoning of a full Social Democratic Congress to settle the party's policy ; but it was by no means clear who had the authority to call it together. The League of Russian Social Democrats was one possible claimant ; the Labour Emancipation Group was a second ; and there were several groups inside Russia which hoped to make themselves the nucleus for a general movement. Lenin, in agreement with the *Iskra* group, was against an early meeting of a full Congress. He argued that such a gathering would only make the confusion worse, and that it was desirable to allow a period for further clarification of opinion before a binding decision was reached. What he was really aiming at was a settling of conclusions with the Economists and their exclusion from the Congress and also the use of *Iskra* to formulate and put the case for a programme which the Congress could then be asked to endorse.

Something, however, had to be done, if only to prevent the League of Russian Social Democrats from calling a Congress which might be packed by the supporters of Economism. Accordingly, in 1901, the *Iskra* group got together two small preparatory meetings at Geneva and at Zürich to discuss the question of a Congress. At the second of these meetings there were sharp disagreements; and the split with the majority section of the Union of Social Democrats became wider. The Union then attempted to take the lead and, in conjunction with some of the groups in Russia, got together at Belostok in 1902 a preparatory conference which proceeded to issue instructions for the summoning of a full Congress and appointed an Organising Committee. This Committee, however, was arrested by the police, and the arrangements fell through. The *Iskra* group then resumed the lead. A draft programme, drawn up by Plekhanov with amendments by Lenin, was published in *Iskra* and in *Zarya* and became the main item for discussion at the forthcoming Congress; and, after much more manœuvring for position, the Second Congress of the Russian Social Democratic Party finally assembled in London in July 1903.

Thus Russian Social Democracy, before the meeting of what was in reality its first, though nominally its second Congress, was already at war on a number of fronts, quite apart from its main battle against the Czarist autocracy. It was united against the Narodniks by a common belief that Russia was destined to go through the process of industrial development and that there were no valid reasons, objective or subjective, why capitalist industrialism should fail to take root and grow in Russian soil. It was at one in resting its hopes of Socialism mainly on the industrial proletariat which this development would bring into being and would expose to conditions of exploitation and insecurity and thus lay open to Social Democratic propaganda. It was at one, too, in believing that industrial capitalism was a system involving 'contradictions' which would in due course lead it to destruction, and that by 'socialising' the processes of production it was preparing the way for the social ownership of the means of production and for their collective administration in the interests of the whole society. But it was not in agreement either about the form which the transition would take, or about the speed with which it would come about : nor was it at one about the part to be played in the transition, or in the working-class movement, by the peasantry, or by the intellectuals. As against the Narodniks, who thought in terms of 'the people' rather than of classes and regarded the peasants and the intellectuals as the key factors — with the intellectuals serving as the spark to influence the popular mass movement with Socialist ideals — the Social Democrats were at one in believing both that the main burden of constructing the new society must fall upon the industrial workers, aided by those intellectuals who were ready to identify themselves with them, and drawing the peasants — or at any rate the poorer peasants — along with them under their leadership. But they put widely different interpretations on this doctrine ; nor were they even fully agreed that the transition would necessarily take the form of a revolutionary uprising of the industrial workers against the capitalist class.

The difficulty was, in fact, that there was more than one 'revolution' in their minds. There was, in the first place, the revolution that was destined to overthrow the Czarist régime ; and in this the enemy was autocracy — an enemy common to every sort of Socialist and shared with many who were not Socialists. Secondly, there was the economic revolution, which was to put an end to the exploitation of the poor by the rich and powerful, who included landowners, financiers, bureaucrats, militarists, traders, and industrial employers — that is to say, a number of elements often at odds one with another, and perhaps including potential allies at some stages of the struggle. Even if a political revolution was necessary for the overthrow of the autocracy, it did not follow that it would be an economic revolution as well, or, at any rate, a Socialist revolution. It did not even follow that there would have to be an economic revolution in at all the same sense as there would have to be a political revolution. It was possible to hold that the political revolution would render it practicable to achieve the economic 'revolution' by peaceable means under the new political régime. Thus, at one extreme were those who argued that the two revolutions must be accomplished together, in one and the same act, by the immediate installation of a Socialist economic régime by the victors in the political revolution; while at the other extreme were those who wanted the political revolution to go only to the length of establishing constitutional government and looked thereafter to a gradual advance towards Socialism by the legislative action of the new Government, nationally and locally, and through the progressive activities of Trade Unions, Co-operative Societies, and other working-class agencies, aided by the constructive talents of the advanced sections of the intelligentsia, including the technicians who would come over to the Socialist camp.

Revisionism, as preached by Bernstein to the Social Democrats of the West, was, indeed, by no means without influence on the Russian Social Democrats. But under Russian conditions it was bound to take somewhat different forms, both because of the much greater degree of autocracy, which almost ruled out the idea of a gradualism in politics until the first step had been achieved by revolution, and also because of the backwardness of Russian industry, which excluded the possibility of a proletarian party backed by a majority of the people and seemed also to rule out the early advent of a predominantly socialised economy, such as Bernstein, as well as Kautsky, anticipated in the West. The Western Social Democrats took industrial capitalism for granted as the predominant structure of the economic system and were concerned only with the means of socialising it. The Russian Social Democrats, on the other hand, wanted industrial capitalism to develop, and had therefore to consider whether, and if so how, they could reconcile their hostility to it as exploiting the workers with positive support for it as the means of economic advance and of developing the proletariat and preparing it for the conquest of power. The 'Legal Marxists', headed by Peter Struve, were those who were prepared to side positively with capitalism, while at the same time pressing it to accept economic reforms in the workers' interests and to ally itself with the workers against autocracy and landlordism. They were politically on the side of the revolution, as a means of establishing constitutional government, and they contemplated that the political revolution would clear the way for a rapid growth of capitalist enterprise, accompanied, as it had been in the West, by a parallel development of working-class organisation which would exert an ever-increasing pressure on the capitalists and in due course become strong enough to bring about the transition to Socialism.

Lenin, as we have seen, met and negotiated with Struve and Tugan-Baranovsky while he was busy about the preparations for *Iskra* in 1900; and, in doing so, he recognised that the 'Legal Marxists' were still a part of the Russian Social Democratic movement — though he was, of course, determined to edge them out. They were in effect edged out well before the Second Congress met. But this left well inside the movement the much larger group of Economists who did not desire, as Struve did, an alliance with the capitalists, but held that, for the time being, the political should be subordinated to the economic struggle and the main attention given to building up Trade Unions, encouraging strike action, and persuading the workers to put forward demands for such industrial concessions as the eight hours' day, the enforcement of improved sanitary conditions in the factories, better housing, and the granting of bargaining and consultative rights to elected factory committees. The supporters of 'Economism' were not necessarily right wingers, or reformists as against revolutionaries, though some of them were. Their essential purpose was to build up a mass workers' movement by appealing through immediate grievances without prejudicing this mass appeal by bringing in Socialist ideology or arousing antagonism by direct attacks on the Czar or on religion. They held that the first task was to get as many as possible of the workers organised in Trade Unions and factory committees for which the Social Democrats would supply the leadership, rather than to establish a large Socialist Party which could hope, at best, to enrol only a minority.

The desire of the Economists to concentrate on building up Trade Unions was reinforced when, upon the renewed outburst of strikes in 1901 and 1902, the police authorities in a number of areas set to work to foster the establishment of workers' Unions under the leadership of police spies and *agents provocateurs*. The methods varied from place to place — from the deliberate provocation of disturbances which gave an opportunity for the arrest of agitators and the violent disruption of the workers' movements to the promotion of tame Unions which were allowed to give expression to real grievances, provided they did not pass beyond what the police regarded as legitimate limits. This latter form of police-inspired Union annoyed employers as much as the other gratified the more reactionary of them. But the police were not necessarily moved by the opposition of employers who were in many cases themselves opponents of the autocracy and demanding constitutional reform. The principal inspirer of the tame type of Trade Union was Zubatov, head of the Moscow political police — the Okhrana — and after him the manœuvre came to be known as 'Zubatovism'. At the beginning of 1902 Zubatov founded the Society for the Mutual Help of Workers in the Engineering Industry, under strict police supervision ; and this body went to the length of organising strikes against particularly unpopular employers, including some firms owned by foreign capitalists. The French Government protested ; and the employers attempted a counter-measure by organising factory committees or 'house Unions' under their own control. Zubatov was dismissed towards the end of 1903 ; but the abandonment of his methods in Moscow did not prevent the use of similar methods elsewhere, as in the case of Father Gapon's St. Petersburg organisation in 1905.[1]

Zubatovism and the more extreme methods employed by the police in other areas stimulated the desire of Socialists to organise real Trade Unions in order to win the workers away from the police-sponsored bodies. But apart from this there was an evident case for doing all that could be done to promote Trade Unions among the factory workers, transport workers, and other industrial groups in the hope of winning them over to Socialism later on. The main body of Social Democrats was not opposed to this, but insisted that the Trade Unions could not be brought under effective Socialist leadership without a strong Social Democratic Party to direct them and to supply the leaders. They were, however, divided between those who put their main hopes in the revolutionary development of industrial action, and were thus akin in thought to the Syndicalists of the

[1] See p. 446.

West, and those who held that Trade Unionism was incapable of being more than an auxiliary to the action of a Socialist Party, as it was in Germany and Austria. Moreover, there were fears among the more left-wing Social Democrats that Economism would lead in practice to the organisation only of the skilled workers and to the creation of a type of Trade Union that would limit itself to serving the economic interests of a minority and would develop into a counter-revolutionary force. The record of the British and American Trade Unions was held out as an awful warning of the dangers of such a development.

Lenin, in addition to translating Sidney and Beatrice Webb's *History of Trade Unionism* and completing his work on *The Development of Capitalism in Russia* (published in 1899) during his Siberian exile, had begun his attack on the Economist tendency as early as 1898, when Kuskova's *Credo* appeared. He had also written in exile his pamphlet, *The Tasks of the Russian Social Democrats* (1897), in which he formulated his conception of a centralised revolutionary party. In addition to his writings in *Iskra* and *Zarya* he went on, after his experiences of the forces at work within the Social Democratic movement in 1900, to launch a full-scale attack on the Economists and on the right wing generally in his book *What is to be done ?*, which was published in 1902 as part of his propaganda in preparation for the coming Congress. He there argued that to concentrate on the economic struggle was to condemn the workers to eternal slavery because they needed to destroy capitalism, and not merely to fight for improvements under it and could not do this as long as the autocracy barred the way to the struggle against capitalism. He went on to attack the notion that mere Trade Union organisation would lead the workers on to a spontaneous acceptance of Socialism as an objective, arguing that Trade Unionism could achieve nothing without the impulsion of revolutionary theory to stiffen it and inspire the workers' consciousness. 'Without a revolutionary theory', he wrote, 'there can be no revolutionary movement. . . . The rôle of vanguard can be filled only by a party that is guided by the most advanced theory.' Socialist ideology, he said, arguing against the 'Syndicalists', was a matter of scientific knowledge, not of spontaneous class-ideology : if the Socialists failed to teach the workers Scientific Socialism, bourgeois ideology would usurp the vacant place. He drew the sharpest possible contrast between Socialist and bourgeois ideology, and denied that there was room for any middle doctrine or for any realm of neutrality between them. Economism, he argued, was bound to end up in mere reformism, and to destroy the revolutionary spirit. He denounced the Economists as the Russian equivalents of the Revisionists who were doing their best to destroy Marxism in the West.

In 1902 there were not only great industrial strikes in Russia, including a violently fought general strike in Baku and Odessa, but also many signs of growing peasant unrest. These, of course, were grist to the mill of the Narodniks, who had by this time reorganised themselves in a loosely knit Social Revolutionary Party in active opposition to the Social Democrats. It is impossible to date at all precisely the foundation of the Social Revolutionary Party. It seems to have begun with a Conference of Narodnik groups in Central Russia in 1898, where a loose Union was established and a journal, *Our Task*, started as the organ of the movement. Parallel movements developed in other parts of the country, especially in North Russia, where the journal, *Revolutionary Russia*, began publication in 1900. That year a more widely representative secret Congress was held and decided to establish a national Social Revolutionary Party. At the same time an Agrarian School for training agitators was set up abroad; and the S.R.s sent two delegates to the International Socialist Congress at Paris. I. A. Rubanovich (1860–1920) became their regular representative in the affairs of the Socialist International. They remained, however, a very loose organisation, embracing many tendencies and insisting on a large autonomy for their local and regional groups. Their adherents ranged from terrorists of the old school to moderates intent on building up peasant Co-operatives and collaborating with the more progressive elements in the rural Zemstvos. Outstanding figures among them, at this stage, besides Rubanovich, were Victor Chernov (1876–1952), Katherine Breshkovskaya (1844–1934) in exile in Siberia — and, on the right wing, Felix Volkhovsky (1846–1914) and Nikolai Vasilievich Tschaikovsky (1850–1926), both of whom were to become active counter-revolutionaries in 1914.

The establishment of the Socialist Revolutionary Party,

otherwise called the 'Social Revolutionaries', was followed immediately by a revival of terrorist activities, to which all wings of the Social Democrats were opposed. It was also followed by a rapid spread of peasant disturbances, not so much stirred up by the S.R.s as affording them an opportunity to gain peasant support. The Social Revolutionaries had by this time lost most of their hold on the industrial workers in the bigger towns ; but they retained a substantial following among the handicraftsmen and among the more scattered industrial workers in small towns and country areas. Their leadership still came almost exclusively from intellectuals ; and in the villages they tended to recruit mainly the more prosperous peasants, especially those to whom some form of Co-operation made an appeal. Their policy was unclear, even in relation to agrarian questions ; but so, up to 1903, was that of the Social Democrats, who had, indeed, tended to ignore the peasants. They demanded, of course, land reform and the handing over to the peasants of more land — especially of the land which had been given to the landlords at the time of the emancipation of the serfs. In general, they stood for peasant cultivation within the framework of a revived and reformed village commune, within which they hoped to see a large development of Co-operative enterprise. But they were not mere reformers : they stood for political revolution as the necessary prelude to the establishment of the village community ; for decentralised administration ; and in some cases for an almost Bakuninist type of Federalism. They included near-Anarchists of the Kropotkinite persuasion as well as Socialists who saw the need for some sort of political government. And beyond them was an Anarchist fringe, which had its following in the towns as well as in the country and its connections with the extreme Syndicalistic group among the Economists.

Advocacy of peasant Co-operation was not confined to the S.R.s. It was also favoured by a section of liberal landowners and officials connected with the Zemstvos and by a number of liberal economists who were on the side of agrarian reform. This last group had connections with the 'Legal Marxists', who, however, looked to the development of capitalist methods in agriculture and therefore favoured the growth of larger agricultural holdings and the establishment of credit banks to assist agricultural investment. As against these groups, which favoured the more prosperous and progressive peasant farmers, the S.R.s sought to appeal to all sections of the peasantry, whereas the Social Democrats were inclined to draw an increasingly sharp line between 'kulaks' and poor peasants whose land did not provide them with a living unless they found auxiliary employment. The S.R.s, too, were well aware that it often paid the capitalist farmer better to employ small peasants at low, part-time wages than to engage full-time workers; but they were unwilling to draw within the village sharp class lines that might help to destroy what was left of the old village community.

In 1902 Struve, after his definitive break with Lenin and Plekhanov, set up his own journal outside Russia. It was published at Stuttgart, and was called *Osvobozdenie* (Liberation). From this point the 'Legal Marxists' had their own groups quite apart from the Social Democratic Party. They held in 1903 a conference of their own, in which they joined forces with the liberals from the Zemstvo movement. Before long most of them were to go over, in the course of the 1905 Revolution, to the Cadet (Constitutional Democratic) Party.

Accordingly, when the Social Democratic Congress met in 1905, this element was no longer represented; and the Economists had also ceased to exist as an organised group within the party. We have seen that the draft party programme for submission to the Congress had been drawn up in advance by Plekhanov, whose first draft had been heavily cut about by Lenin. In revised form, it had been published in *Iskra* well ahead of the Congress, and its contents had been expounded in many articles as well as in Lenin's *What is to be done?* At the Congress it went through with surprisingly little opposition, backed by the joint authority of the *Iskra* group, which included those who were soon to become the outstanding leaders of the Menshevik faction. It was not over the programme but over the question of party organisation that the historic split into Bolsheviks and Mensheviks arose. But behind this apparent consensus of opinion lay a great deal of earlier disputation behind the scenes.

The full account of these discussions was published only in 1924 — in the *Lenin Miscellany*. The largest single issue in the controversy was that of the dictatorship of the proletariat, which Lenin successfully insisted on against Plekhanov's reluctance as a cardinal point. This was also the most contested point at the Congress itself; but it was accepted in the following apparently unequivocal form:

> An essential condition for the social revolution is the dictatorship of the proletariat — that is, the conquest by the proletariat of such political power as will allow it to suppress all attempts at resistance on the part of the exploiters.

There followed demands for universal, direct, and equal suffrage, for a Constituent Assembly to draw up a constitution, for freedom of speech and of assembly, and of the press, for the right to organise Trade Unions and to strike, for abolition of arbitrary arrest, and so on; and some delegates found an inconsistency between these demands and the assertion in favour of dictatorship. It was Plekhanov who answered the objectors by saying—

> The success of the Revolution is the supreme law; and if the success of the Revolution should require the temporary limitation of one or another democratic principle it would be criminal to refrain from such limitation. In my opinion, even the principle of universal suffrage has to be considered from the point of view of the fundamental principle of democracy to which I have referred. Hypothetically, one can envisage a situation in which Social Democrats would be opposed to universal suffrage. There was a time when the Italian bourgeois Republics deprived persons belonging to the nobility of political rights. The revolutionary proletariat might restrict the political rights of the upper classes, just as the upper classes restricted the rights of the proletariat.

This passage makes it clear that Plekhanov was thinking of exclusive dictatorship as an exceptional measure, to be resorted to in emergency, and not as the form of government which the workers would normally adopt or persist with as a durable form of government. Lenin, no doubt, had more than this in mind, though he, too, as he was to show later, thought of a Constituent Assembly elected by universal suffrage as the natural sequel to the Revolution. He preferred to leave it to Plekhanov, at the Congress, to put his own gloss on the text, happy enough to get the declaration in favour of dictatorship accepted as part of the Social Democratic Programme.

Next to this issue the most hotly contested parts of the programme were those which dealt with the agrarian question and with the problem of national self-determination. The agrarian question had also been in dispute in connection with Plekhanov's draft. It was a matter of agreement that the *otrezki* — the peasant-tilled lands given over to the landlords in 1861 — should be placed in the hands of the peasants for redistribution through the communal committees; and, as we saw, the Social Revolutionaries also made this demand. Lenin insisted, against opposition on the *Iskra* committee, that the programme should also call for the nationalisation of all land, not merely after the Socialist Revolution, but as part of the minimum demands to be made on any Government holding office after the first stage of the Revolution, which was expected to place the bourgeoisie in power. Here again Lenin successfully insisted on his point, which coincided with a similar demand in the programme of the S.R.s. The S.R.s, however, did not draw the distinction between the two stages of the Revolution — bourgeois and Socialist — which Lenin firmly impressed on the Social Democratic Programme.

The First Social Democratic Congress of 1898, as we saw, had passed a resolution affirming the right of national self-determination, and this was reproduced in the draft programme. This was a matter of agreement among the *Iskra* group, and, indeed, among most of the delegates; but it was strongly opposed by the delegates of the Polish Social Democratic Party, headed at the Congress by Adolf Warski.[1] The Polish Social Democrats, as we saw, were at bitter feud with the rival Polish Socialist Party, led by Pilsudski, against which they insisted on the need for the Polish workers to throw in their lot with the Russian workers in a common struggle for emancipation. At the Congress their objections were swept aside: Rosa Luxemburg, their most powerful spokesman, was not present. They were, however, supported by the Jewish Bund.

At a later stage in the Congress proceedings, when the programme had been disposed of and the party rules were under debate, the Bund again fell foul of the majority by demanding

[1] See p. 490 ff.

recognition as the sole representative of the Jewish workers throughout Russian territory. By this time it had been agreed that the party should be constituted on a centralised foundation, with territorial sections acting under central direction. The Congress rejected the Bund's claim as inconsistent with this structure; and the Bund's five delegates thereupon quitted the meeting. Three other delegates also left when, on similar grounds, the majority refused to recognise the League of Russian Social Democrats as the Foreign Section of the party. As we shall see, these secessions, by altering the balance of the Congress, had momentous consequences.

The great discussion which, before the Congress ended, had divided the remaining Social Democrats into what soon became virtually two opposing parties arose, not over the programme, but in the first place over the basis of party membership and then over the persons who were to be put in charge of the party's affairs. The first great battle was joined between Lenin and Plekhanov on the one hand, and Martov and Trotsky on the other, over the wording of the clause defining eligibility for membership. Lenin wanted to lay down that membership should be open to 'those who accept the programme of the party and support it both materially and by personal participation in one or other of the party organisations'. Martov wished to omit the reference to 'participation in one or other of the party's organisations'. The point at issue is by no means clear from the wording; but behind the words lie deep differences in the conception of the party. What Lenin wanted was a disciplined party consisting of picked individuals who were prepared to work under orders which they were to receive from the particular party organisation to which they were attached. He wanted these organisations to be definite local branches of the party, acting under instructions received from the central directing bodies. That is to say, he wanted to do away with the existing practice, which left any handful of Social Democrats free to constitute their own group and then attach themselves to wider groupings built up from below. For this structure he wished to substitute one in which authority would flow downwards from the centre, so as to exclude the existence of contending factions claiming equal rights. He wished also to curb the tendency of intellectuals to act on their own, and to merge the groups of intellectuals into branches including proletarians as well, as a check on bourgeois idea-chopping — which he regarded as something entirely different from the inculcation of the correct Marxist ideology of 'Scientific Socialism'.

At the Congress Lenin, who had the support of Plekhanov, was narrowly beaten on this particular issue, and Martov's draft was adopted, Trotsky taking a prominent part in the debate on Martov's side. It was, however, clear that the course actually taken by the party would depend much less on the precise phrasing of its membership rule than on its programme, over which Lenin had his own way, and on the persons chosen to direct it when the Congress was over. This question of personnel was difficult; for there had in practice to be two bodies, one in charge of the organisation of the party inside Russia and the other of its periodicals edited abroad. Over and above this there was the question which of these two bodies was to have the last word between Congresses in the event of differences arising between them. There was also to be considered the claim of the League of Social Democrats abroad, which was in hands hostile to the Lenin group, to have some general supervision over the work outside Russia, including the journals published abroad. This last claim, as we have seen, was pushed aside at the Congress, which decided to entrust the general control of the party to a Central Commission mainly composed of members inside Russia and the control of the journals published abroad to a specially elected *Iskra* Committee, or editorial board, made up of members living outside Russia, with provision for a joint Council composed of two members from each of these bodies, *plus* a Chairman directly elected by the Congress, to deal with disputes between them and to settle policy between Congresses in case of need.

The great controversy which followed the endorsement of this plan turned on the composition of the *Iskra* board. The old board, which had been quasi-independent, had consisted of Plekhanov, Vera Zasulich, and Axelrod — the old-stagers — with Lenin, Martov, and Potresov, who had been newcomers from inside Russia when *Iskra* was founded. Lenin proposed to drop Vera Zasulich, Axelrod, and Potresov, who had largely opposed his views at the Congress, and to reduce the board to

Plekhanov, Martov, and himself, on the assumption that this would give him and Plekhanov a clear majority over Martov. Thanks to the departure of the delegates from the Bund and from the League of Social Democrats he was able to carry his proposal. The offended supporters of Zasulich and Axelrod, including Trotsky, thereupon refused to have anything to do with the nominations for the Central Committee of the party; and a Committee, consisting entirely of Lenin's supporters, hereafter to be called Bolsheviks, was elected. The Congress thus ended, leaving the minority — henceforth to be called Mensheviks — in a furious temper, and many of the majority, including Plekhanov, in a state of deep mental distress at what they feared would mean the break-up of Social Democracy into impotent warring factions. Trotsky shared this feeling of distress. During the year preceding the Congress he had been closely associated with Lenin and the *Iskra* group and had been living with Axelrod and Vera Zasulich on terms of intimacy. He had escaped from Siberia only in the summer of 1902, and in the autumn had been summoned by Lenin to London to report on the position of the groups inside Russia which he had been visiting since his escape. Lenin had taken to him, and had introduced him to *Iskra* in face of opposition from Plekhanov, who had taken a dislike to him ; and he was shocked when Lenin and Plekhanov joined hands to oust their associates from the board, and repelled by Lenin's attempt to construct a narrow party under rigid central discipline. These feelings drew him into the Menshevik camp, though he was in most matters much nearer to the Bolsheviks, and was soon to react no less strongly against Menshevik sectarianism than he had against Lenin.

For the moment, however, what counted most was Plekhanov's attitude. When he saw that the effect of the Congress had been not to create the unified party which he had in mind, but to split it from top to bottom, he quickly altered his attitude, and set out to play the part of conciliator by inviting the Mensheviks back into the fold. He tried to persuade Lenin to agree to restore the deposed members to the *Iskra* board ; but Lenin stood fast on the Congress decision. Martov had already resigned from the board in protest, leaving only Plekhanov and Lenin in office ; but Plekhanov had also been made Chairman of the joint Council and held a position of greater authority in the party than Lenin. He took it on himself to invite the four old members to rejoin the board, from which Lenin thereupon resigned. Thus *Iskra* passed out of the control of the Bolshevik faction, and became the organ of the Mensheviks, with whom Plekhanov was thereafter fully associated. Lenin was co-opted to the Central Commission of the party, which remained under Bolshevik control. The joint Council simply disappeared.

Thus, from 1903 onwards there were in effect two rival Social Democratic Parties — Bolshevik and Menshevik — with a number of would-be conciliators, including Trotsky, hovering unhappily between them. But, bitter though the quarrel was, neither faction was prepared to admit that there were two parties instead of one. It was for both a cardinal part of the faith that there could be only one Social Democratic Party, which was the vanguard of the proletariat and not a 'sect'. Accordingly, each faction claimed to be the true representative of the one party, and a shadowy unity remained. They were to be driven together again for a time under the impact of the Revolution of 1905, only to fly apart again almost at once and to carry their dissensions right on to 1912, still as nominal co-members of a single party. From 1903 to 1905 they quarrelled furiously, much to the bewilderment of many of their supporters up and down Russia, who had much difficulty in understanding what the fight was about. Before long the Central Commission in Russia began to waver. Some of its members were arrested; and the new members co-opted in their place included a number who wished to heal the quarrel and some who inclined to the Menshevik side. Lenin's supporters in Russia then created a new Organising Committee, which challenged the authority of the Central Committee; and there was a constant exchange of angry letters between Lenin and the warring Social Democratic groups. Almost from the beginning of the split Lenin had been angrily demanding a new Congress to fight the dispute out afresh; but he was also determined to make sure of a majority. In effect, neither side was prepared to attend a Congress called by the partisans of the other; nor could they agree to let the conciliators call one open to both. When the next Congresses did meet, they were rival gatherings under the auspices of the contending factions.

438

In 1904 Lenin published his famous tract, *One Step Forward, Two Steps Back*, in defence of the policy he had advocated at the previous year's Congress. He opened with an attack on the Menshevik conception of a party open to all who professed agreement with its principles, and with an attempt to define the essential difference between class and party and between the Social Democratic Party in particular and other claimants to the title. The distinction between class and party, he said, was fundamental. The party was the advance guard of the class, marked out for leadership by its clear conception of the road to be travelled and by its possession of a scientific ideology. The party should not set out to enrol the entire working class : not even the Trade Unions were able to do that. Still less should it set out to enrol all and sundry who professed to agree with it, irrespective of class : such a method would only open the door to cranky and unreliable intellectuals who, in the name of 'freedom', would defy all discipline and ruin the party with sectarian squabbles. Intellectuals were welcome in the party, but only on condition that they were prepared to accept its discipline by becoming members of one of its recognised organisations and obeying whatever orders they received from that organisation, which would in its turn obey the orders it received from the central directing agencies of the party — that is, from the Congress and from the body or bodies set up by Congress to exercise its authority. Lenin insisted that the party must be an 'organised whole', exercising a proletarian discipline equally upon all its members. There must be no preferences for intellectuals : the workers, Lenin insisted, understood the need for discipline and would readily accept it. The intellectuals must do the same, or stay outside the party. Lenin was very scornful of what he called the 'anarchistic' predilections of the petit bourgeois intellectuals who were entrenched in the League of Russian Social Democrats — by now a Menshevik stronghold. They were, he said, entirely out of touch with what was going on inside Russia. They did not appreciate that the party, while essentially different from the class, must have its roots in the class and must work within the class in order to be able to lead it.

On the other side, Martov and his friends, to whom Plekhanov as well as Trotsky had rallied, regarded Lenin's conception of the party as altogether wrong. They did not, of course, as he professed to believe, identify the party with the class or suppose that the whole working class could be drawn into the party; but they did uphold the idea of a mass-party, such as had been created in Germany, which should be open to any worker or, indeed, to anyone who was prepared to join, to accept its stated principles, and to subscribe to its funds. They saw in such a party the only means of ensuring that there should be only one Social Democratic Party that counted, rather than a number of contending factional parties. Unity of action, they argued, must be achieved, as it had been in Germany, not by excluding those who held divergent views, but by allowing all such views to be argued out inside the party and insisting that the minority should accept the majority decision, or get out of their own accord. Martov, and still more Plekhanov, wanted a disciplined party; but their conception of discipline, modelled on the German example, was different from Lenin's, as it was bound to be if the party was thought of as a mass organisation rather than as an élite, and if there were, in fact, as well as ideologically, to be only one Socialist Party and not several standing for different policies, as there were, for example, in France. I think it was above all else Plekhanov's deep admiration of the Germans and his horror at the notion of there being two rival Social Democratic parties that carried him over so swiftly from the Bolshevik to the Menshevik camp.

Martov's view was not quite the same as Plekhanov's. He was, in the ideological realm, a much more tolerant person, and much less sure than either Lenin or Plekhanov that there was only one true way and that he knew it beyond a doubt. Like Trotsky, he was a Jew and an internationalist by instinct as well as by rational conviction. He had much less of the Russian all-or-nothingness than Lenin or Plekhanov, and was much more affected by current trends in Western Socialist thought. Plekhanov did not object to Lenin's extreme centralism, as such: indeed, he sided with Lenin on that issue at the Second Congress. He revolted only when he saw that the effect of Lenin's policy was not to enforce organic unity in the party, but to split it and destroy its unity. Lenin, of course, did not consciously wish to split the party: he hoped to enforce his view upon it, with only individuals seceding, not in sufficient strength to form a rival party. When, however, the Mensheviks proved strong enough to constitute what was in effect a rival party, he was undeterred. He believed that he would be able to get behind him the main body of proletarian Social Democrats and most of their intellectual supporters inside Russia and that with this support he could reduce the Menshevik exiles to impotence and constitute himself the real leader of the part of the movement that really counted — the part that was inside Russia and would have to make the Revolution if it were to be made at all. He became seriously worried — though he was still undeterred — when he found that the Mensheviks had a following inside Russia, and, still worse, that many of the groups and individuals inside Russia on whom he had relied wished to compromise with the Mensheviks or to wash their hands of what appeared to them an unnecessary sectarian squabble. This is shown clearly in his letters, written in 1904 and 1905, before the split had reached the point of two rival Congresses, each claiming to represent the Social Democratic Party.

Meanwhile, inside Russia, events were moving fast. Count Sergius Witte, who had been trying to follow a mildly liberal policy, was dismissed by the Czar in August 1903. A year before this Nicholas III, after the assassination of the Minister of the Interior, Sipyagin, by the student Balmashov, had appointed as his successor the former police chief, Viatscheslav Plehve, a violent anti-Semitic reactionary. Plehve, instead of going on with the Zubatovist policy of encouraging tame Trade Unions, adopted a policy of violent provocation and set to work to divert the growing unrest from strikes and peasant revolts to anti-Jewish pogroms. Under his direction the police deliberately organised anti-Semitic secret societies, demonstrations, lootings of Jewish shops and places of worship, and actual pogroms involving murder and much physical maltreatment of the Jewish population. From the time of his appointment Plehve steadily pushed Witte out of power and favour, and followed a policy of intensified repression almost unchecked. He was not able to prevent a rapid growth of the liberal movement based on the Zemstvos, which had come together in a Union, were beginning to pass resolutions pressing for political as well as agricultural reforms, and were strongly supported by

Struve's Liberationist group, which as we have seen, published its journal, *Liberation*, abroad, but had become organised as a Liberation League inside Russia. But he intensified the campaign against the Socialists — Social Democrats and Social Revolutionaries alike — at the same time as he carried on his pogroms. In July 1904 he paid the penalty : he was assassinated by a group of Social Revolutionaries, that extraordinary character, Azev, who was both a police spy and the principal member of the central terrorist organisation of the S.R.s, playing a leading part in the plot. The fatal bomb was actually thrown by the Social Revolutionary, Sazonov, who was seriously wounded by the explosion.

By that time the disasters of the Russo-Japanese War had gone far enough to shake Czarism to its foundations, and the Revolution of 1905 was already well on the way. In August 1904 Lenin got together in Switzerland a preliminary conference of his supporters inside Russia to prepare for the full Bolshevik Congress which was to meet the following year, and also to complete the preparations for launching his new journal, *Vperod* (Forward), which was to replace *Iskra*, now in the hands of the Mensheviks, as the organ of Bolshevik Social Democracy. The first issue appeared in January 1905. Actually, the Bolshevik organising committee issued invitations to the Mensheviks as well as to its own groups to attend the Congress of 1905, which met in London in April. But the Mensheviks refused the invitation and held a Congress, or Conference, of their own at the same time in Geneva. But as, by the time these meetings took place, the Revolution in Russia had already begun, it seems best to defer consideration of their proceedings.

CHAPTER X

THE FIRST RUSSIAN REVOLUTION

THE Russian Revolution of 1905 was a direct outcome of the Russo-Japanese War. Had the Czarist Government kept out of war, there would no doubt have been a continuance of the ferment of the previous few years ; but it is most unlikely that there would have been anything that could properly be called a revolution. There would have been strikes, but nothing approaching a general strike spreading from end to end of the country ; and the strikes would have followed the familiar pattern and have been ended speedily either by military and police action or because the strikers, who had no funds behind them, could not stay idle for more than a few days. There would have been peasant uprisings, but they would have been seasonal, as the peasants could not afford to miss either the sowing or the harvest ; and the authorities would have been easily able to put them down — though not to prevent their recurrence at the next convenient season. There would have been a continuance, and perhaps a rising tide, of both Social Democratic and Social Revolutionary agitation and of liberal protests and demands for constitutional reform ; but had there been no war, or rather no defeat in war, the main groups of liberal reformers would certainly not have dreamt of any direct challenge to the authority of the Czar's Government. It was first war and then defeat which for a time roused almost the whole population except the landlords, the bureaucracy, and the devotees of the Orthodox Church to demand insistently that something drastic should be done.

Something drastic ! But it was by no means clear what : nor did the various groups all ask for, or want, the same things. The peasants wanted not to be taken away from their fields to serve in the army, and, when they had been taken, to get back. They wanted less burdensome taxes, lower prices for consumers' goods, more personal freedom, and more land. They wanted to be set free from the compensation payments that were still being levied on them as an outcome of emancipation in the 1860s ; and they wanted the government-appointed headmen who were continually interfering in the affairs of the villages removed. But, whereas some of them wanted more freedom in order to make an end of the village communes and turn themselves into prosperous and credit-worthy individual farmers, others wanted to restore the powers of the commune and to bring about a levelling process in the village rather than to clear the way for the further development of a class of *kulaks* for whose benefit the rest would have to work.

On the agrarian question, liberals as well as Socialists found it difficult to agree. Most of the liberals demanded that the lands handed over to the landlords at the emancipation should be given to the peasants and that the compensation payments under the emancipation laws should cease. But some wished to compensate the landlords for the loss of the additional land, whereas others stood for no compensation ; and some wanted a continuance of peasant farming, aided by Co-operative Credit and Marketing Societies, whereas others wanted to develop capitalist agriculture and to break up the traditional peasant structure. The Socialists, too, were divided, not only as between Social Revolutionaries and Social Democrats — that is, between agrarian Socialists and industrialisers — but also within each of their parties. Some wished to demand immediate expropriation of all the landlords' estates : others wished to stop short for the time being at socialising the lands handed to the landlords as their share when the serfs were emancipated. All liberals and all Socialists demanded land reform ; but even such words as socialisation and expropriation meant very different things in different contexts.

On the constitutional issue, again, all the liberals and all the Socialists called for the ending of autocratic government. But, up to 1905, most of the liberals were only calling on the Czar to reform his Government, and were not going to the length of demanding an elected Constituent Assembly to decide upon the future form of government — much less to that of demanding a Republic. The Socialists, of course, did all demand a Republic ; but they were divided between those who made this an outright immediate objective and those who were prepared to help the liberals to get a form of constitutional government, even if this meant, for the time being, the retention of the Czar, or some other member of the royal family, as a constitutional monarch. The great majority both of S.R.s and of Social Democrats called for a Republic; but both wings of Social Democrats were quite prepared for the Revolution to result in the setting up of a 'bourgeois Republic' and not of a Socialist State. Indeed, Bolsheviks as well as Mensheviks were readier for this halting-place than most of the S.R.s: naturally so, for the S.R.s did not consider that Russia's economic backwardness made it unripe for a Socialist Revolution. Quite the reverse: they were set on making the Socialist Revolution *before* capitalism had developed too far for agrarian Socialism to be based on the communal institutions of the village and on the small-scale enterprises of the handicraftsmen's artels. While Bolsheviks denounced Mensheviks for their willingness not merely to support the capitalists in establishing the bourgeois Republic, but also to become their allies in running it, and while Mensheviks denounced Bolsheviks for refusing to make common cause with the bourgeois revolutionaries, both groups of Social Democrats united to attack the Social Revolutionaries for actually opposing the bourgeois Revolution and thus serving the interests of reaction even in fighting against it.

The war transformed this situation, first of all, by provoking violent protests against the call-up for military service — most violent of all in Poland and in other non-Russian areas, and extending, especially in Poland and White Russia, to the industrial workers as well as to the peasants. The brutal suppression of the Poles was an important factor in stirring up revolutionary feeling even before the effect of military defeats had been felt; and, of course, as long as the war lasted and the Government continued to pour more and more troops into the Far East in the hope of retrieving the situation, the call-ups went on and provoked more and more local disturbances. The state of sheer unpreparedness in which the Czarist State had entered upon the war aggravated its effects, both by causing the call-ups to be rushed on at a prodigious pace and by adding greatly to the dislocations they involved. It is clear that the Czar and his advisers had not at all expected the Japanese to offer armed resistance to the drive into Korea and the building up of Russian control over Manchuria. The sudden swoop of the Japanese fleet on the Russian fleet at Port Arthur in February 1904 took them utterly by surprise.

Thereafter disasters followed one another swiftly, on both sea and land. By August 1904 the entire Russian fleet in Far Eastern waters had been sunk, dispersed, interned, or shut up in Port Arthur. By January 1905 Port Arthur itself had sur-rendered. By March, after a series of sanguinary battles, the vast Russian armies had been thoroughly defeated and forced to withdraw from Mukden into the interior. By May the relief fleet which had been despatched from Europe after the earlier naval defeats had been overpowered and the war was virtually over. In October 1905 it was formally ended by the signing of the Treaty of Portsmouth, on terms forced on Japan by the great powers, which had no wish to see the Japanese, any more than the Russians, undisputed masters of the Far East.

The Russian Revolution of 1905 opened in January with 'Bloody Sunday', when the great unarmed procession led by Father Gapon to appeal to the Czar for redress of popular sufferings was fired on and dispersed, with hundreds of casual-ties, at St. Petersburg outside the Winter Palace. It reached its height in October, in the great general strike which spread over the country and, with the railwaymen and postal workers joining in, brought the life of the towns almost to a standstill and, for a time, made it impossible for the Government to move its soldiers against the rebels. Thereafter, the counter-revolution asserted itself, and amid ferocious repressions the upheaval gradually subsided as Stolypin's hangmen did their work. It left behind a hand-picked Duma dominated by reactionary groups and a measure of land reform which de-stroyed what had remained of the old village community and rapidly created a large class of individual farmers using improved methods as a bulwark against agrarian revolution.

'Bloody Sunday' — January 9th, old style, 1905 — was the outcome of a renewal of the Zubatovist police policy in a revised form. The priest, Father Georgiy Apollonovich Gapon (1870–1906), had been encouraged by the authorities in St. Petersburg to establish, in February 1904, his Assembly of Russian Factory Workers as an instrument for drawing the people away from the seductions of the Socialists and from underground Trade Unions under their influence. The Assembly was designed to provide various benefit services and also to organise educational activities for the St. Petersburg workers; and for this purpose it received substantial subsidies from public funds. But it soon began to develop also as a Trade Union. After the outbreak of war prices rose sharply, whereas wages for a time actually fell. The workers joined the Assembly in great numbers, and branches were formed in most of the bigger factories. But the subsidies were not withdrawn; nor were these activities interfered with by the authorities, even when employers began to demand that Gapon's movement should be suppressed. The police did not interfere even when the Assembly started talking about political matters, or when a number of adherents of the Socialist parties began to take an active part in its work. Whatever its origins, it was not a counter-revolutionary body, but one which was allowed to put forward quite extensive demands in a non-revolutionary way. Gapon himself was not a reactionary, but up to a point a sincere reformer who hoped that the Czar could be induced to dismiss his reactionary ministers and make real concessions to the people. The petition which his huge demonstration wished to present to the Czar included not only a statement of the workers' economic grievances with a request for redress, but also demands for land settlement and for constitutional reform. It had been under preparation for a number of months; and there had been consultations about it with Struve's Liberationist group, but not apparently with the police authorities, who were at this time standing aside and letting the more moderate reformers have their head, in the hope of using them against the more revolutionary elements.

On January 9th, 1905, Gapon led his monster procession to the Winter Palace to present his petition. There were some disturbances on the way, in one of which Gapon himself was thrown from his horse and injured, so that he took no further part in the proceedings. But the main body of the demonstrators were allowed to reach Palace Square without interference. The Square, however, had been surrounded in advance by large bodies of troops; and when it was full these suddenly opened fire on the vast crowd, causing hundreds of casualties. The crowd fled and dispersed ; but there were many scattered fights in the city between soldiers or police and demonstrators who broke open gunsmiths' shops in the search for arms, and many isolated officers and policemen were attacked and manhandled. Barricades were thrown up in some working-class quarters, and it took some days for the police and soldiers to regain complete control.

These proceedings can be explained only on the assumption that the authorities were at cross purposes. One section of the Government wished to follow a conciliatory policy in face of the intensity of popular feeling, whereas another saw in Gapon's demonstration a splendid opportunity to teach the workers a lesson. On the fatal day the Czar was absent from St. Petersburg, and final authority was vested in the Grand Duke Sergius, who was an extreme reactionary and seems to have been personally responsible for the massing of troops and for the order to fire. He paid the penalty the following month, when he was assassinated by the Social Revolutionary, Kaliaev. Undoubtedly the Social Revolutionaries had infiltrated strongly into Gapon's movement and had helped to swell the demonstration ; but the crowd appears to have been at the outset entirely unarmed, and the resort to violence clearly came from the soldiers' and not from the demonstrators' side.

Gapon, who fled from Russia after the massacre and published abroad his *Story of My Life* (1905), remains a somewhat enigmatic figure. He did not attempt to conceal that he had been in close relations with the police and had been helped by them in building up his organisation ; but he held himself out as a sincere Christian reformer who had hoped to induce the Czar to put himself at the head of the movement for constitutional and economic reform. He received a great ovation abroad, but his behaviour speedily disgusted the exiled revolutionaries who had welcomed him. In the autumn of 1905 he went back to Russia and, astonishingly, resumed his relations with the police, apparently promising to give them information about the conspiratorial activities of the Social Revolutionaries. He approached a leading S.R., Pinkas M. Rutenberg, and attempted to enlist his collaboration. Rutenberg pretended to agree and arranged a meeting with Gapon, in such a way that their conversation was overheard by other members of the

Party hidden in an adjoining room. These revolutionaries then killed him as a spy.

In attempting to reach any judgment on Gapon, it is necessary to consider his case in connection with that of Evno Azev (1870–1918), who, as we saw, played to an even greater extent a double part. Azev was undoubtedly a police spy who was at the same time actually chairman of the Social Revolutionaries' central terrorist organisation and played an active part in its work. He was undoubtedly one of the persons chiefly responsible for the assassination of Plehve, the reactionary head of the Ministry of the Interior, which controlled the police. He appears, in fact, to have combined the rôles of revolutionary and police spy with equal sincerity, or insincerity. The explanation may be, in fact, that, as a Jew, he hated Plehve as the chief instigator of the campaign of pogroms ; but this can hardly be the whole explanation of his conduct. He appears to have been a true case of divided personality. Gapon may have been the same ; but it seems more likely that he was merely a half-demented demagogue who believed in his own destiny as a leader of the people, and was quite prepared to betray rival leaders in order to get money for building up his own influence. Such characters as Azev and Gapon are difficult to understand in the atmosphere of countries unused to either terrorism or the more extreme forms of police espionage and provocation. But they are less unintelligible to-day in the West than they were half a century ago, when the revelation of Azev's exploits in particular struck astonishment into men's minds. The exposure of Azev in 1908 was the work of the exiled Russian Social Revolutionary, Vladimir L. Burtzev (1862–1936), who was then at the head of the League of Left Social Revolutionaries in Paris and made a speciality of unmasking police spies and *agents provocateurs*. His revelations about Azev's doings brought to a head the dispute concerning terrorist activities inside the Social Revolutionary Party.

When Gapon's demonstration was held, St. Petersburg was already the scene of a great strike which had begun among the metal workers employed in the huge Putilov works, on account of the dismissal of three men who were members of the Assembly and had fallen foul of the management. The strike had spread from the Putilov to other engineering works in the city.

After January 9th it spread to other centres in a great wave of strike action in which economic and political grievances and mass protests against the massacre all played a part, but feeling against the war probably counted for most of all. Already in November 1904 the mounting hostility to the Government among the middle classes had begun to provoke open organisation for the presentation of demands for reform. The more advanced members of the Zemstvos, working with the Liberationists, had held an open Conference and had decided to present a petition to the Czar calling for constitutional government and for increased powers of local government for the Zemstvos and municipalities. In connection with this movement political banquets, imitated from France, were held in many places, and an extensive movement of professional organisation began. The professional classes flocked into organisations which, established nominally for the reading of learned papers and the discussion of technical questions, openly debated political matters and passed resolutions in favour of constitutional and agrarian reform. Scared by these manifestations, the Czar in December 1904 issued an extraordinary *ukase* in which, without making any definite promises, he spoke of his will to establish 'legality' and held out vague hopes which induced the liberals to believe that constitutional government was well on the way. But the affair of January 9th and the assassination of the Grand Duke Sergius changed his mind, and, under pressure from the reactionaries who surrounded him, he issued in February 1905 a further manifesto declaring his intention to maintain autocracy intact. At the same time the police invaded and closed the sessions of a number of the professional societies and ordered many of them to disband. There followed a further *ukase*, drawn up by the minister, Bulygin, announcing the Czar's intention to constitute a Duma, or assembly, to be chosen by a very restricted electorate, designed to ensure the predominance of landowning interests, and to be given only consultative functions and no power to legislate or to control the ministers. These proceedings led to sharp disagreements among the liberal reformers, many of whom had been scared by the strikes and by the suppression of the professional bodies. Struve's Liberationists held a Conference, at which there was a split. The left wing broke away

from the majority, which joined forces with many of the
Zemstvo liberals to form a new party — the Constitutional
Democrats, or Cadets, under the leadership of Paul Milyukov
(1859–1943). Milyukov and his group, though not, of course,
satisfied with the proposed consultative assembly, were prepared to welcome it as a first step and to take part in its proceedings; whereas the left-wing liberals wished to boycott it,
above all because of the exceedingly undemocratic form of
election on which it was to be based.

The full plan for what came to be called the 'Bulygin Duma'
was not published until August; and before then the situation
had changed considerably. After January the strike movement
among the workers had died down, and for a time the middle-
class agitation for reform had occupied the centre of the
political stage and was being watched eagerly by the Socialists,
who set great hopes upon it as heralding the collapse of the
absolutist régime, but were divided about the line they should
take in relation to it. Inside Russia both the Social Revolutionaries and the Social Democrats were eagerly expectant of
revolution; and one effect of this was to drive the rival factions
within each party closer together. Leonid N. Krasin (1870–
1926), the Kiev technical engineer who was later to be one of
the chief organisers of Soviet industry, was at this time the
outstanding leader of the Bolshevik underground inside Russia.
He disagreed with Lenin's intransigence towards the Menshevik faction and was doing his best to bring about united
action by the two factions. Indeed, there had been no such
complete separation between these in the Russian underground
as among the émigré leaders abroad. Trotsky, though he was
working with the Mensheviks and writing regularly for *Iskra*,
at once joined forces with Krasin when he returned secretly to
Russia in February 1905, and soon began writing manifestoes
and leaflets for the Central Committee, which was under
Krasin's direction. Trotsky's judgment of the situation in the
early months of 1905, as shown in his *Iskra* articles, was that
an insurrection was well on the way, and that the proletariat
was the only force capable of taking hold of it and guiding it to
a successful issue. Martov, on the other hand, at the head of
the Mensheviks in exile, though he expected a revolution, held
that it would be carried through under bourgeois direction and

that the task of the Social Democrats was to help the middle-class groups to power and to act as their ally. Trotsky was thus nearer to the Bolsheviks than to the Mensheviks : indeed, he went beyond the group of which Lenin was the head in antici-pating that the Revolution would pass straight from its bourgeois into its proletarian phase. Trotsky, in fact, had already formu-lated in his own mind, largely under the influence of Parvus, his conception of the 'permanent Revolution', which we shall need to discuss later in this volume.[1] The Social Democrats inside Russia, Mensheviks as well as Bolsheviks, were mostly more inclined to his view than to Martov's and were ready to work together in the coming revolutionary struggle. Meanwhile, the Social Revolutionary Party had undergone some dislocation as a result of the arrest of the whole of its Central Terrorist Committee after the assassination of the Grand Duke Sergius, and was busy reorganising its forces and disputing whether to carry on with the terrorist campaign.

The rival gatherings of Bolsheviks and Mensheviks met — the one in London and the other in Geneva — in May 1905, during the lull which followed the excitements of January and February. The Bolshevik Congress, which was much the larger, was attended by a number of delegates who were later to take a prominent part in the Revolutions of both 1905 and 1917 — among them Krasin, Kamenev, Rykov, Litvinov, Bogdanov, and Lunacharsky. Its general tone was exceedingly hostile to the liberal bourgeoisie and to the Mensheviks who were prepared to act with them, but much less so to the Social Revolutionaries, with whom the Bolsheviks recognised the need to make common cause in the coming revolutionary up-heaval. The Congress concerned itself largely with reformu-lating its policy in relation to the land question and to the peasants. It recognised that it was no longer enough, even as an immediate measure, to demand merely the handing over of the *otrezki* [2] and the discontinuance of the compensation payments exacted from the peasants, and called for the complete confiscation of the landlords' estates and for their redistribution by elected peasant committees under the auspices of a Pro-visional Revolutionary Government. It demanded that this redistribution should take place at once, without waiting, as

[1] See p. 956 ff. [2] See p. 460.

the Menshevik Congress advocated, for the step to be first authorised by the Constitutent Assembly which the Provisional Government would convoke. In addition, the Bolsheviks now declared that the peasants must be the partners of the proletariat in carrying through the Revolution and that peasant organisations must be created in the villages for this purpose, based especially on the poorer peasantry and on the wage-earning elements in the countryside. There was, in the resolution on this matter, the adumbration of the idea of a class-war in the villages between the quasi-proletarian elements and the *kulaks*, corresponding to the class-war between industrial workers and capitalists in the towns, and of the simultaneous conduct of two wars — one on the same side as capitalists and *kulaks* against the Government, and the other against capitalists and *kulaks* for the economic emancipation of workers and peasants alike. It was made clear that the delegates expected the bourgeois revolutionaries to come to terms with Czarism rather than to overthrow it, and to endeavour to halt the rural, as well as the urban, revolution half-way, and held that it was the task of the Socialists to see to it that there should be no compromise with the Czarist system, and that the revolution should not be thus arrested. The Mensheviks, as well as the liberals, were accused of wishing to halt it.

The policies advocated by the rival factions were, however, not simply intransigence on the one side and a willingness to compromise on the other. The Bolshevik Congress contemplated that it might become necessary for Social Democrats to enter a Provisional Government with the bourgeois groups in order to prevent the latter from halting the Revolution, whereas the Mensheviks opposed such participation on the ground that it would make Social Democrats responsible for predominantly capitalist policies and would lose them the confidence of the workers. The Mensheviks, in effect, held that the Provisional Government would have to follow a capitalist policy because Russia was not ripe for Socialism, and that Socialists should support it from outside in carrying through such a policy; whereas the Bolsheviks held that participation in office might be needed for the purpose of carrying the Revolution to the full length to which it was practicable to carry it, above all in two respects — the overthrow of Czarism and the establishment of a Republic, and the complete destruction of the landlords' power.

The Bolshevik Congress dealt also with the problems of party organisation and preparation for the insurrection it held to be imminent. It rescinded the rule adopted at the previous Congress on Martov's motion concerning eligibility for membership and substituted Lenin's wording;[1] and it also laid down that there must, for the future, be a much larger proportion of actual workers on the party's committees — Lenin proposing a four-to-one preponderance as a minimum. Such a change had become practicable because of the great increase in working-class members during the past few months, largely as a result of the strikes. It was also urged because so many of the intellectuals had been co-operating with the professional groups in their reform agitation, and because this had strengthened suspicions of them as potential compromisers with Czarism.

The strong anti-Menshevik tone of the Bolshevik Congress seems at first thought difficult to reconcile with the tendency of the two factions to fraternise inside Russia. It was due partly to the failure to agree on terms for the holding of a common Congress — at which the Mensheviks knew they would be outvoted — and to the domination of the Menshevik Conference by the Menshevik exile group headed by Martov, Martynov, and Krichevsky; but it was also largely the outcome of Lenin's personal influence over the delegates. It was above all Lenin who used the Congress to secure a complete endorsement of his ideas : those who voted with him at the Congress did not always follow his line at all completely when they got back to Russia and found there Social Democratic organisations which still included, if not absolute Mensheviks, at any rate many who still believed in the need for a united party and felt it to be greater than ever in face of imminent revolutionary upheaval. There was no break between Krasin and Trotsky when Krasin got back from London. They continued to work together, though the formal agreement between the Bolshevik and Menshevik groups inside Russia had been brought to an end by disagreements over the Congress.

Spring — after the sowing — brought a fresh outburst of

[1] See pp. 439 ff.

peasant troubles and some renewal of industrial strikes. In May a general strike at Ivanovo-Voznesensk, the great textile centre 200 miles south of Moscow, led to the establishment of what is regarded as the first Soviet in Russia — that is, the first general body made up of delegates from factory and similar groups in all types of industry. In June, after Cossacks had fired on a workers' demonstration at Łódź, in Russian Poland, there was an attempted insurrection, which was quickly suppressed. Almost simultaneously a great strike was raging in Odessa and spreading to other towns in South-East Russia ; and, while the strike was in progress, the battleship *Potemkin*, manned chiefly by newly recruited conscripts, mutinied, and was joined a little later by a second vessel, the *St. George*, which was part of a squadron sent against the mutineers. This mutiny occurred only a few days after the annihilation of the last Russian fleet in the Far East at the battle of Tsushima, which virtually ended the Japanese War.

The news of the naval mutiny spread fast, and led to further strikes and disturbances. But the mutineers, with no leadership and no technical capacity to manage the ships, did not know what to do. Food and coal began to run short. The *Potemkin* put in at the Rumanian port, Constanza, but was refused supplies. After some further aimless cruising about, it returned to Constanza and surrendered to the Rumanians. The *St. George* had surrendered earlier, to the Russian admiral : the leaders among its mutineers were executed.

What had been hoped and planned for was a much more extensive naval mutiny and the turning of the strike in the Black Sea ports into an insurrection. But these things failed to happen. The mutiny was, however, enough to strike terror into the heart of the Czar and to make him more double-minded than ever about his course. On the one hand, he allowed the reactionaries their head by encouraging a fresh round of pogroms organised by the reactionary leagues known as the 'Black Hundreds', while on the other hand he temporised with the more moderate liberals. The professional associations were allowed to reorganise and to form a Union of Associations, which renewed the demand for constitutional reform. A second Congress of Zemstvos was allowed to meet : it decided to present a reform petition to the Czar. The tight control which had been put on the Universities was relaxed ; and they joined in the demand for reforms. The Czar, however, was still set on pursuing his plan for a carefully picked consultative assembly without any real powers ; and Bulygin's scheme was definitely proclaimed in August. It was too manifestly useless even for most of the constitutional liberals. In September a further Congress of Zemstvos rejected the Bulygin plan and reiterated its demands for a Constitution ; and the following month the Cadet Party held its constituent Congress.

Well before this, big industrial troubles had recurred. In August there was a general strike at Warsaw : martial law was proclaimed, and the repression was violent. At the beginning of September there was a big strike in the Baku oilfield. The Black Hundreds were mobilised against the strikers ; and there was civil war throughout the area. Oil wells were burnt ; many Jews were killed in pogroms. Later in the month a printers' strike began in Moscow, and presently other trades joined in. There were great strike demonstrations, which the police were unable to repress. There was street fighting : gunsmiths' shops were looted : the university students joined in the fight. The strike movement began to spread to other areas, and took on a new character when the railwaymen, who had formed a Union earlier in the year, left work, paralysing communications between Moscow and St. Petersburg. Railwaymen on other lines came out, followed by postal workers and other public employees. In October the movement spread to St. Petersburg, where a Soviet of Workers' Delegates was formed to take control. Swiftly the strike movement extended over most of Russia, spreading consternation among the governing classes. Troops could not be moved : letters were undelivered : the work of administration was brought almost to a stand. The peasants, who in August had formed an All-Russian Union mainly under Social Revolutionary leadership, launched a new offensive against the landlords ; and in a number of areas their revolt took a new form. Many country houses were burnt down, especially in the 'black earth' areas ; and there were great struggles in Latvia between the 'Baltic barons' and the exploited rural labourers.

In St. Petersburg working-class and Socialist newspapers began to be published openly. The Soviet was not quite an alternative government; but in some respects it began to behave almost as if it were. The Czar seriously considered fleeing from Russia; he hovered between the alternatives of abdication, granting a constitution, and mobilising all his resources to put the movement down. At one point he decided on this last course but was dissuaded by his brother, the Grand Duke Nicholas, who reported that the army, which had so far remained under orders, might revolt at any moment. He decided to make concessions and sent for Count Witte to advise him. Later in October, on Witte's advice, he issued a new *ukase*, in which he definitely promised to introduce constitutional government. The Bulygin plan was given up: there was to be an elected Duma, with legislative powers, not a merely consultative body, and the electorate was to be widened to include peasants and the entire middle class. The details were not filled in; but the proposal split the middle-class reformers. At a fourth Zemstvos Congress in November 1905 the Cadets rejected the new plan, and called for a Constituent Assembly, whereas the right wing, based mainly on business and financial interests, accepted it and formed a new party — the Octobrists — to fight the coming elections. Meanwhile the reactionaries drew together in a 'patriotic' Union of the Russian People, which set to work to organise the Black Hundreds on a greatly extended scale.

The general strike reached its highest point towards the end of October. It had become by then mainly political, with the demand for a Constituent Assembly as its principal slogan, though other cries were also raised, including a widespread demand for the eight hours' day. But it was not in the nature of things that a general strike should endure for long: either it had to develop into an insurrection or the strikers were bound to be driven back to work for want of food. The workers were not yet ready for insurrection: the Czar's promise of a Duma with legislative powers helped to send them back to work. Almost immediately after they had gone back there was a mutiny among the sailors at Kronstadt. It was put down; and when its leaders were sentenced to execution, the workers of St. Petersburg struck again in protest, and the proposed executions were postponed. A second mutiny took place in the Black Sea fleet, and was crushed; and then the Rostov regiment, stationed in Moscow, mutinied too, with the same sequel. Before this the Government had plucked up courage to arrest Khrustalev-Nosar, the lawyer who had been made Chairman of the St. Petersburg Soviet, and Trotsky had been elected in his place. By mid-December it had become bolder still ; it arrested the entire Soviet in session, including Trotsky. The activists who were left tried to call a further general strike in protest ; but the workers were leaderless and tired out and the response was meagre. In St. Petersburg the revolutionary wave had passed its peak, and the expected rebellion had not quite broken out.

In Moscow, however, the climax was still to be reached. There a Soviet had been set up at the end of November, and the Social Democrats and Social Revolutionaries had formed a joint organisation to direct the struggle. The Moscow Soviet in mid-December decided to call a general strike ; and the joint Socialist body determined to make this the starting-point of an actual insurrection. Already the Socialist parties had procured small quantities of small arms : barricades were erected and there were pitched battles in the streets, most of the city being in the hands of the revolutionaries for several days. But only a fraction of the workers had arms, and the Government had been able by this time to bring considerable forces to the spot — mainly drawn from other parts of the Empire, in order to lessen the danger of fraternisation with the rebels. After heavy fighting the revolt was put down, and with its suppression the prospect of successful revolution virtually disappeared. The independent Republic which had maintained itself in Georgia through the greater part of the year was conquered almost at the same moment ; and the Government forces also began to get the upper hand against the peasant risings in the Baltic provinces. The advent of severe winter conditions caused the peasant movements in other parts of Russia to die away. Everywhere the reaction was in a position to take the counter-revolutionary offensive.

This indeed it had begun to do from the very moment of the Czar's proclamation promising a Duma with legislative powers. A great fresh outburst of pogroms had immediately followed the proclamation, and the Black Hundreds had been organised on a very extensive scale. But from December the repression could also take legal forms. In the wake of the soldiers, punitive commissions were sent through the provinces and exacted stern reprisals on strikers and rioters and on anyone they could catch who was suspected of revolutionary activities. Many Socialist leaders escaped abroad, or went into hiding, in many cases in Finland, which was still outside the jurisdiction of the Russian police organisation. The persecution drew together those who were left at liberty, especially as in the last stages of the strikes and in the Moscow rising Bolsheviks and Mensheviks had acted together. In December a Bolshevik Conference held in Finland decided in favour of the re-establishment of a single Social Democratic Party, including both Bolsheviks and Mensheviks; and a Menshevik Conference reached a similar decision. Negotiations followed concerning the basis of union, and it was agreed that delegates to a joint Congress should be elected by the rank-and-file membership and not by the local party committees, as Lenin would have wished. This enfranchised a large body of new members, and resulted in the Mensheviks and the middle groups winning a majority in the delegation : so that, when the Unity Congress met at Stockholm in April 1906 the Bolsheviks found themselves outvoted on the outstanding issues. For the time being they were compelled to admit defeat and to accept a Menshevik majority on the new governing organs of the party ; but they at once proceeded to re-establish a distinct organisation of their own to work for a reversal of the position. The victory of the Mensheviks at the Unity Congress was due largely to the fact that the prospect of successful revolution had for the time being receded. In the changed circumstances it seemed essential to hold what was left of the party together and not to weaken the movement in Russia by stressing doctrinal differences which most of the rank-and-file members did not understand. The Bolsheviks were, indeed, successful in retaining Lenin's form of the rule governing eligibility for membership ; for in face of the revolutionary situation most Mensheviks were prepared to agree on the need for a large measure of party discipline. On the other hand, the Mensheviks were able to carry a resolution which favoured the building up of Trade Unions on a non-party basis, against the Bolsheviks' wish to declare explicitly in favour of party leadership over them. On this issue the Bolsheviks finally withdrew their own proposal and voted for the Menshevik resolution, which was so phrased as to recognise the need for close ideological, though not formal, connections between the Trade Unions and the party.

The longest discussion at the Stockholm Congress turned on agrarian policy and on the relations between the proletarians and the peasants. At this distance of time much of the discussion seems rather unreal; for in the main both factions now agreed on the necessity of establishing an alliance between the proletariat and the peasantry in order to make possible the success of the Revolution. They agreed too in wishing to include in their new programme the complete expropriation of the landlords and not merely of the *otrezki*. But the Mensheviks wished to 'municipalise' the landlords' estates by handing them over to the local Zemstvos for redistribution, whereas the Bolsheviks wanted to 'nationalise' them — that is, to hand them over to the new revolutionary Government which the hoped-for uprising was to install in power, and to declare in favour of direct occupation under the auspices of revolutionary peasant committees. On this issue the Mensheviks got their way over 'municipalisation', arguing that in practice 'nationalisation', as an immediate policy, would mean handing the landlords' land over to a capitalist-controlled State which would use its power to transfer large parts of it to exploitation by capitalist farmers at the peasant tenants' expense. The Bolsheviks, however, were successful in insisting that the programme should declare for confiscation of the landlords' holdings without compensation to the dispossessed owners.

There were also, behind the apparent agreement on the need for urban-peasant partnership in making the Revolution, large differences about the nature of this partnership. Neither faction had a large rural following, and each was eager to acquire this. But whereas Lenin thought in terms of a joint dictatorship of workers and peasants under the ideological leadership of the Bolsheviks, most of the Mensheviks, rejecting the idea of dictatorship and favouring a wide party built up from below and organised on a basis of popular voting, were afraid that the admission of the peasants to an equal position with the proletariat might lead to the swamping of the party by unenlightened rural members, and therefore turn the party against industrialisation and towards the agrarian Socialism favoured by the S.R.s.

There were also pronounced differences over tactics. One big question was whether to regard the Revolution as over for the time being, and to plan for a gradual rebuilding of the revolutionary forces, or to retain the hope of an early renewal of the mass-movement, despite the fact that the ferment caused by defeat in war was subsiding now that a peace treaty had been signed. Tangled up with this question was that of the attitude to be adopted towards the new Duma, which was shortly to open its session. Both wings of Social Democrats had actually boycotted the elections to the extent of not putting up candidates, though probably a great many voted, either for Labour or Peasant candidates or for Cadets against reactionaries. But there had been opposition to this policy among the Mensheviks ; and a number of unattached Socialists, mostly connected more nearly with the S.R.s than with the Social Democrats, had been elected and were soon to form a Labour Party on a rather ill-defined basis. Lenin, for his part, wanted to boycott the Duma mainly as a means of preventing the Social Democrats from being led into a position in which they would have to make common cause with the Cadets — that is, with the bourgeois liberals from whom he was trying to hold them apart ; whereas those Mensheviks who advocated a boycott did so mainly because of the conditions under which the elections were held, and in many cases urged their followers, if they had votes, to give them to the Cadets against the more reactionary parties. The majority at the Congress decided against continuing the boycott, and some Social Democrats from Georgia were elected to the First Duma after the Congress had dispersed.

The remaining big issue at the Stockholm Congress had to do with the attitude of the reunited party to national self-determination and to the question of cultural autonomy raised by the Jewish Bund. The Polish Social Democrats, as we saw, had broken away from the Russian Party in 1903 because they refused to accept its decision in favour of national self-determination, which, they held, would hamper them in their fight against the nationalism of the rival Polish Socialist Party. Since then, new Social Democratic Parties had appeared in Latvia and in the Ukraine, and also in Georgia, and had played a large part in the revolutionary movements of 1905, while the

Bund had considerably extended its following in White Russia as well as in Poland and Lithuania. The Stockholm Congress agreed, in its desire for a comprehensive unity, to admit the national parties to membership on a basis of wide autonomy, and also to admit the Bund as a separate organisation catering for Jewish workers, though not with any monopoly in enrolling such workers. These decisions involved a very wide departure from the conception of a centralised disciplined party advocated by Lenin, who, even if he had to accept them temporarily, was not in the least likely to rest content until he had overturned them and reinstated his own ideas, even at the cost of splitting the party over again.

The new Central Party Committee elected at Stockholm consisted of seven Mensheviks and only three Bolsheviks — Krasin, Rykov, and Desnitsky-Stroev. This was the body that was to operate inside Russia. Abroad there was to be an Editorial Committee independent of the Central Committee; and this consisted entirely of Mensheviks — Martov, A. S. Martynov, Potresov, F. I. Dan, and P. P. Maslov (1867–1946), the chief exponent of Menshevik agrarian policy. Thus, for the time being, the Bolsheviks entirely lost hold of the Party organisation.

Trotsky, who had been the outstanding figure in St. Petersburg during the critical months of the 1905 Revolution, did not attend the Stockholm Congress. He was in gaol, and was soon to be sent to Siberia, whence he escaped soon after his arrival early in 1907. Belonging to neither of the Social Democratic factions, and highly critical of both, he might have played an important part in influencing policy in the fluid condition of the party in 1906. He was indeed able to go on writing after his arrest; but his absence left leaderless those who were hovering between the rival factions — probably a clear majority of the rapidly swollen membership, which leapt from a few thousands in 1904 to well over 150,000 early in 1906. Up to 1905 the Social Democratic organisation in Russia had been based on local committees which were nominated from above and not elected from below. Under these committees there had been factory cells, student groups, and a variety of special groups; but all these had been, at any rate in theory, subject to the local committees, which received their orders from the

Central Committee chosen at Congress. Even this Central Committee had been recruited by co-option to fill vacancies when members of it were arrested or had to flee abroad. During 1905, however, appointed local committees had given place to committees made up of delegates from the cells, and thus elected from below; and both in the cells and in the local committees many more questions had been settled by open voting. Moreover, some matters of high importance had been referred to the whole membership for decision, either in large meetings or through the cells. Lenin's conception of a central-ised party organised from above had in practice largely gone by the board; and the great increase in the number of journals circulated, some of them quite openly, had provided a forum for continual discussion on party matters. At the height of the Revolution the Czarist censorship had completely broken down because the printers refused to print any journal which was submitted to the censor; and the Socialists had made up for their lack of printing presses by forcibly occupying those of their opponents and using them to print their own papers, moving from one office to another from day to day. The changes thus wrought in the character and organisation of the party largely account for the victory of the Mensheviks at the Stockholm Congress: it was not only that most of the new-comers preferred a democratic to a centralist structure, but also that many old Social Democrats were led by the experience of mass action in the Revolution towards the idea of a mass-party, enrolling any 'comrade' who cared to join and seemed willing to play his part.

When the Bolshevik Conference of December 1905 voted in favour of unity with the Mensheviks its members had different conceptions of what unity involved. Some, the 'conciliators', as they were called, believed that unity could last, and that there was room for large differences within an united, demo-cratically organised Party. Others, above all Lenin, regarded this as mere illusion, and were prepared to accept unity only because it would allow them to carry on their propaganda for centralism and for their conception of the Revolution and of dictatorship among the whole body of Social Democrats and not merely as a faction. In the actions of the Bolsheviks after the Unity Congress this latter attitude prevailed: they at once formed a committee of their own to rally their forces and had no compunction about defying the discipline of the Menshevik-dominated Central Committee chosen at the Congress. Lenin's will prevailed; and he had no use at all for formal democracy as it was understood in the West. Centralism meant in his view obedience to the central decision of a party which took the correct general line — it did not mean yielding to a majority of 'deviationists' from the true faith.

Among the Social Democrats of 1905 there existed much confusion about the correct relation between the party and the class. When the St. Petersburg Soviet of Workers' Delegates was first set up the Mensheviks and the Social Revolutionaries took part in it; but the Bolsheviks at first refused, and had to be talked round into participation. Some of them continued to say that they could see no reason for the Soviet's existence, that the party should provide the unifying leadership of the working class, and that the Soviet might become a dangerous rival, and might easily fall into the wrong hands. Such critics usually stood for a mass-party, based on factory and similar cells and either taking over such Trade Unions as existed or sub-ordinating them entirely to itself. Against them were ranged those who, with Lenin, wanted a small party of determined revolutionists, and emphasised the need for the party to main-tain contact with, and leadership of, the mass by helping to build up and to direct mass-organisations such as Trade Unions. Such Bolsheviks supported participation in the Workers' Soviets and hoped to create similar Soviets among the peasants and in the armed forces, but also insisted that the Bolsheviks should keep the final power in the hands of the party by placing them-selves at the head of the campaign for those things which most directly and immediately appealed to the mass of the workers. Against both of these groups was ranged a third, mainly sup-ported by Mensheviks, which held that an attempt should be made to create a broadly based Labour Party, wide enough to bring in the Social Revolutionaries and the Trade Unions and other Socialist or left-wing groups, and demanded an all-in Workers' Congress to set up such a comprehensive organisation. The principal advocates of this third policy were Axelrod and Y. Lavrin (1882–1932), whose pamphlet, *A Broad Labour Party and a Labour Congress*, appeared in the autumn of 1906.

Soviets were by no means a Bolshevik invention : nor did the Bolsheviks, in 1905, attach any special importance to them. They appeared to most Bolsheviks as *ad hoc* groupings of factory committees and Trade Unions which came into existence chiefly to co-ordinate strike movements, and were obviously needed to carry on general strikes in order to bring in workers who were not organised under party control. This attitude persisted to some extent even after the St. Petersburg Soviet, and to a less extent the Moscow Soviet, had played outstanding parts in the revolutionary outbreaks of 1905. Dislike of Trotsky, who was its outstanding figure, also aggravated Bolshevik suspicions of the St. Petersburg Soviet in particular : in retrospect Bolsheviks preferred the Moscow Soviet, which had been much more under their control, whereas in St. Petersburg the Mensheviks had played a prominent part. Few, if any, of them foresaw the rôle the Soviets were to play in 1917, or paid much attention to them, save as forms of Trade Union federation, in shaping plans for the next revolutionary outbreak. Indeed, later Bolshevik historians, in their desire to discredit Trotsky, have become more and more critical of the doings of the St. Petersburg Soviet of 1905, though no sign of such criticism is to be found in the utterances of Lenin, or of any other Bolshevik leader I know of, at the time.

The St. Petersburg Soviet was, indeed, a very remarkable body. It developed out of the organisation formed to conduct the printers' strike, was joined by fresh groups as the strike movement spread from industry to industry, and became a widely representative agency of the local working-class movement, with participation from the Socialist parties and from various other groups. During the great general strike of October it became in effect a local executive authority largely replacing the municipal authority and even, in some matters, the police. It issued permits for indispensable work to be done, countersigned municipal orders, and maintained its own discipline. As we have seen, it virtually abolished the press censorship by instructing the printers not to print periodicals submitted to it ; and it requisitioned printing offices to print its own journals and those of the Socialist parties and groups. It did all this for a short period virtually unmolested, because the authorities did not dare to attack it. It was even able to prevent the summary execution of the leaders of the Kronstadt mutiny and, before that, to secure an amnesty under which a large number of political prisoners, chiefly Social Revolutionaries, were released from gaol. Only in mid-December, when the St. Petersburg workers had become exhausted, did the authorities venture to close it down and to arrest its members, after they had tried their power out by arresting its first President, Khrustalev-Nosar, and had made sure that the danger of insurrection had gone by.

The later attacks on Trotsky's leadership have been mainly based on the notion that he and the Soviet ought to have made the general strike the beginning of an insurrection, but did not. The praise of the Moscow Soviet has been based on the fact that it did in the end attempt an insurrection, whereas St. Petersburg failed to rally to its support. Clearly, by the time of the Moscow rising there was no real possibility of a parallel large-scale movement in St. Petersburg. The movement there had already worn itself out. If St. Petersburg should have risen at all, it should have done so earlier, at the time of the October general strike, or at any rate in early November. But at that time neither Moscow nor St. Petersburg made the strike the occasion for an insurrection. In both cities the leaders of the movement who were preparing for an insurrection held the time to be unripe. They were waiting hopefully for signs of sufficient disaffection in the army to give them a chance ; for they could not hope to succeed unless a fair proportion of the soldiers either came over to their side or at least refused to shoot. Trotsky repeatedly counselled patience, in the hope that the situation would develop in that way ; but it never did. No doubt the left-wing groups in St. Petersburg, with the support of the Soviet, could have launched an insurrection on a small scale ; but to do so would have been to invite a massacre. It seemed best to play for time and, while waiting, to prevent the workers from frittering away their strength in too frequent general strikes. That was what Trotsky did, and for doing it he was subsequently denounced as an anti-revolutionary Menshevik, who had really been against an insurrection in any event — which is certainly not true.

The plain fact is that the situation in 1905 never did develop quite to the point that would have made successful insurrection possible, because the revolutionaries, though fairly strong in the navy, had not nearly enough hold on the army, which was made up mainly of peasants and had been carefully dispersed so that most of the regiments were serving far away from their own people, whom they probably would have refused to shoot. The authorities were, even so, much afraid of mutiny; and both S.R.s and Social Democrats were doing their best to carry their propaganda into the barracks and to form military cells. It may have been touch and go; but neither party was sure enough of its strength to put the matter to the test in October. Each then hoped that time was on its side; and time turned out to be on the side of the Government.

There was, of course, throughout the critical months also the doubt whether the Czar might not make large real concessions, or even abdicate, without an insurrection. When Nicholas issued his October Manifesto, promising a Duma with legislative powers, liberal hopes ran high, and with them the hopes of the Mensheviks who were looking not for a proletarian revolution but for a bourgeois Government, headed by the Cadets, to which the Socialists would then play the rôle of constitutional opposition through a mass party on the German Social Democratic model. This was what Lenin most feared: hence the violence of his language about the Cadets and the Mensheviks who wished to put them in power. Lenin by no means ruled out the possibility of a bourgeois Government, or even of helping to put it in power *against* the Czar: what he objected to was the prospect of the Cadets coming to power by agreement with the Czar, with the support of the Mensheviks for such agreement, and with the Mensheviks abandoning the Revolution for the rôle of constitutional opposition. Lenin wanted to overthrow Czarism, not to come to terms with it. He was prepared to join a coalition Government with the Cadets, provided that it took power by revolution and not by agreement; whereas the Mensheviks were against coalition government because they were thinking in terms of a Government which would retain the Czar as a constitutional monarch, and which it would be inconsistent with their republican principles to join. That was how it came about that the Mensheviks often sounded as if they were to the left of the Bolsheviks, because they denounced coalition government; but the coalition they denounced and the coalition Lenin contemplated as legitimate were two quite different things.

In October, when the fake Bulygin Duma was abandoned, and a rather more real Duma offered, liberals and right-wing Mensheviks had high hopes. These were badly dashed when the actual proposals were made known by stages, not only because the reconstituted Council of the Empire — a completely reactionary body — was to have equal powers with the elected Duma, but also because the system of election for the Duma was to be heavily weighted to give landowners and peasants an assured preponderance. The elections were to be indirect, through electoral colleges in each area; and the colleges themselves were to be chosen on a class basis, by separate voting in three classes — landowners, city dwellers, and peasants, — and in such a way as to give both the greater landowners and the rich citizens a privileged position, to cause the peasant delegates to be chosen by a further process of indirect election, and to place the industrial workers in a special inferior category. In addition, the Russian areas were to be much over-represented in relation to the areas inhabited by non-Russians; and, to crown all, the Czar reserved the power to disallow any decision of the Duma that he disliked. There was to be no responsibility of the Czar's ministers to the Duma; nor was the Government to emanate in any way from the Duma, which could be at any time dissolved by the Czar and was to be left hanging with a very indefinite status.

As we have seen, in October 1905 the Cadets and their allies were demanding the convening of a Constituent Assembly to make a new constitution, but when this was refused decided to fight the elections, despite the reactionary character of the plan of election, which was made known in December, and despite the further restrictive conditions, most of which became known only just before it took place. The Social Democrats — both wings — and the Social Revolutionaries, who had split into rival Maximalist and Minimalist factions before the end of the year — decided to boycott the Duma. This left the Cadets with almost a clear run in the towns, and in the villages there was no effective leadership. The landowners, in any case, were bound to elect either sheer reactionaries or Octobrists, with some Cadets who had been active in the Zemstvo movement.

In the event, in the first Duma the Cadets were much the strongest party, though not in a clear majority. This was unexpected; for the parties further to the right had been expected to win. Witte, who had been largely responsible for the plan, was forced to resign his position as minister. He had done what the Czar required of him by procuring a large French loan on the score that Russia was being made safe for capitalist investment by the introduction of constitutional government; and when the loan was safe, the Czar's reactionary entourage, which cordially disliked Witte, had no further use for his services in view of his failure to procure a Duma subservient to official wishes.

Accordingly in mid-July there appeared a *ukase* dissolving the Duma. At the same time Stolypin was made Prime Minister; and he at once instituted sterner measures against the revolting peasants, who were sentenced by field court martial, some to execution and others to lesser penalties. The Cadets, refusing to admit the Czar's right to dissolve the Duma, adjourned with such members as would follow them to Viborg in Finland, where they attempted to continue their sessions. From Viborg, with the support of the left parties, they issued a further appeal, in which they called for a new Duma and urged the people to refuse payment of taxes and recruitment to the armed forces unless this were done, but carefully refrained from any appeal to revolution in arms. Actually, the dissolution of the Duma provoked not only a fresh crop of peasant disturbances, but also a further naval mutiny at Kronstadt and some small army revolts. But these were successfully suppressed. The Socialists issued a call for a general strike; but it was not nearly so extensive as that of the previous autumn, and there was no attempt to make it the starting-point for an insurrection. The workers' movement had definitely receded; and though peasant uprisings were on a bigger scale than ever, they were unco-ordinated and could be crushed one after another if they were unaccompanied by sustained movements in the towns or by a stoppage of the railways. Stolypin's field court martials, reinforced in September, made short work of the rural revolution of 1906.

In November Stolypin published the Government's proposals for agrarian reform. There was, he asserted, plenty of land available for those who needed it without confiscation of private estates. The Government would provide land out of the holdings belonging to the Crown. But the real problem was not so much shortage of land as the poor use made of it. The way to improve its use was to set it free from traditional restrictions, to consolidate holdings, to allow land to be freely bought and sold, and to make funds available through a Credit Bank for its development. Stolypin set out to encourage the growth of a large class of progressive farmers (*kulaks*) with access to capital and credit, who would be in a position to give wage-employment to a much larger body of poor peasants and landless labourers. His law swept away what was left of the old village commune and instituted free trade in land. Its aim was both to increase agricultural output by encouraging better farming and to create in the villages a class of farmers who would become a bulwark against Socialist agitation and would join the landlords in defending the established order against the poorer peasants. His measures were remarkably successful in both respects. They did, during the next few years, bring about considerable improvements in agricultural methods ; and they did, in many places, successfully divide the village against itself.

Immediately, however, the most apparent part of Stolypin's programme was his drastic action against the peasant movement and its inspirers. 'Stolypin's Necktie' gained an infamous world notoriety for the inventor of the field court martials which carried the counter-terror over the country. Protests flowed in from horrified groups in the Western countries.

There was, however, still the question of the Duma's future to be faced. Stolypin decided to try a new election, in the hope that the terror would give him a more amenable majority. The Socialists had again to make up their minds what line to take in the elections. The Social Democrats had already decided at their April Congress to reverse the policy of boycott. They definitely meant to put up candidates ; but the question remained whether they should fight alone or try to enter into some sort of coalition. In the latter event, two possibilities were open — to fight in alliance with the Cadets against the Government, or to form a left bloc with the Labour Party (Trudovics) and the S.R.s and fight against both the

Government and the Cadets. A special Social Democratic
Conference met in November 1906 to consider this issue, which
sharply divided the Menshevik majority from the Bolsheviks.
The Mensheviks wanted a coalition with the Cadets : the
Bolsheviks, supported by the Polish Social Democrats and by
some of the Latvians, demanded a Left Coalition against the
Cadets. The former policy carried the day, in face of violent
Bolshevik objections. But the Bolsheviks got enough backing
to be able to insist that, though this was to be the central policy,
it should not be forced on local committees which took the
opposite view. Thus, where the Mensheviks had the upper
hand, they and the Cadets gave each other mutual support ;
but in a minority of areas the Social Democrats came to terms
with the Trudovics and the S.R.s. In St. Petersburg there was
a split : the local party rejected coalition with the Cadets : the
Mensheviks nevertheless approached them, but the Cadets
refused. The majority of the party fought in a coalition of the
left : the Menshevik dissidents called on their followers to
abstain from voting. Lenin, in one of his most trenchant
pamphlets, attacked the Mensheviks over this affair.

During this period of intense debate, the Social Revolutionary Party also split asunder, into Maximalist and Minimalist
factions. Towards the end of 1906 a Congress of the party
decided by a majority to suspend terrorist action, largely because
of the discredit brought upon it by experience of the part
played in it by *agents provocateurs*. The dissentients, who were
excluded from the party, came to be called Maximalists because
of their refusal to agree to work for a minimum programme and
to postpone their more far-reaching demands. In addition to
their advocacy of continuing terrorism, they were the exponents
within the S.R. movement of the policy of direct action to
procure funds for revolutionary purposes, by robbing banks and
treasuries, by holding up State or business agents known to be
carrying money, and by extorting contributions by threats of
violence to persons or property. These methods, except
assassination, had been largely used by Bolsheviks as well as by
S.R.s ; and the question of their legitimacy was hotly debated
in Social Democratic as well as in S.R. circles. The main body
of the Mensheviks, when they gained control of the Social
Democratic Congress, declared against them ; but some of the

Menshevik groups, especially the Georgians, took the other view. Despite the decision of the Unity Congress, the practices continued in some areas among Social Democrats; and S.R.s used them to an even greater extent.

Maximalism, as the creed of the left wing of the Social Revolutionary movement, harked back to Narodnik extremism. It tended to attract young intellectuals and also especially embittered individuals from other social classes; and in its terrorist and bank-robbing aspects it had an obvious attraction for the criminal types. The money-raising part of it was obviously of special attraction to criminals; and some of the stolen money was always finding its way into private pockets. The left wing of the Social Revolutionary movement was always a mixture of idealists, half-mad fanatics, criminals, and *agents provocateurs*; and occasionally the same individual incorporated more than one of these personalities. The idealistic side of it is well brought out in Grigori Nestroev's *Pages from the Diary of a Maximalist*, published in Paris in 1910 with a preface by V. L. Burtsev. Nestroev's view of the Revolution was highly ethical and idealistic: he saw the danger to a man's character of engaging in criminal acts and associating with criminals even from the highest motives; but he could not on that account abandon work which he felt had to be done for the Revolution's sake. It seemed to him an essential part of the task of revolutionaries not only to spread class-consciousness and to promote class-organisation but also to uproot the fetishistic belief in the sacredness of private property and the respect for the law which so often paralysed the action of the exploited classes. Nestroev was far from being a Nihilist, or an Anarchist of the type of Nechaiev. He had a tender conscience and a ready condemnation for criminal acts done from motives of self-interest. But equally with Lenin he put the cause of the Revolution above all else, though for him it carried an individual ethical imperative rather than an historic necessity.

The elections to the Second Duma by no means turned out as Stolypin had hoped. The Cadets lost ground, sinking from 187 to 123. To the right of them were 34 Octobrists and 63 out-and-out reactionaries; to the left about 100 Trudovics, 14 Popular Socialists (to the right of the S.R.s), 34 Social Revolutionaries, and a Social Democratic contingent of 66, made up of 33 Mensheviks, 15 Bolsheviks, and 16 who cannot be assigned to either group. The Second Duma was definitely more radical in composition than the First; but it was equally powerless. By the time it met, in March 1907, the revolutionary wave had been definitely thrown back. The Government had given up all thought of compromising with the Cadets on the constitutional issue. Stolypin had his own solution of the agrarian problem, which he proposed to carry through without invoking their help. From March to June the Second Duma was allowed to go on talking, and the Socialists were allowed to use it as a platform for addressing the people. But Stolypin was only waiting for a convenient moment to get rid of it, and was already laying his plans to ensure that it should have no successor of the same temper.

Beside the large Cadet contingent there had appeared in the First Duma a substantial Labour (Trudovic) Party made up, because of the abstention of the Socialist parties, of a very mixed body of members elected chiefly from the peasant colleges, with a few from the urban workers. These, numbering nearly 100, coalesced into a party with no very clear programme or policy, which on constitutional issues mainly supported the Cadets, but pressed for thoroughgoing land reform and for social legislation. Most of its members were closer to the Social Revolutionaries than to the Social Democrats. There were also a few Social Democrats, mainly Georgians, from non-Russian areas where parties had taken part in the election.

The Trudovics were radical in their social ideas, urgent in demanding the redistribution of the land by locally elected bodies made up mainly of peasants rather than by central commissions from St. Petersburg, and in political matters extreme democrats, in many cases of a rather naïve kind. Among their leaders was Aleksei Aladyin (b. 1873), a former student of peasant origin who had been an exile and had become a professional revolutionary, and Stepan Anakin (1869–1946), a village school-teacher of peasant heritage. But they also included some left-wing intellectuals of non-peasant origin. They did their best to press forward the land question in the Duma; but in the earlier stages they could do but little: the Cadets made the running with their demand for universal suffrage and responsible parliamentary government of the Western type.

The First Duma lasted from April to July 1906. It began its work to the accompaniment of a widespread renewal of strikes — mainly with economic objects, and mostly successful — and of peasant disturbances. It was at once clear that the Government had no intention of giving way to the constitutional demands, though there were negotiations behind the scenes about including some Cadets in the Government, and the Cadets even had hopes at the outset of being invited to form a ministry under Milyukov's leadership. Before long, the Duma turned its attention to the other great pressing question — agrarian reform. On this issue considerable differences appeared, not only between the Cadets and the parties further to the right, but also between the Cadets and the Trudovics. The Cadets were in favour of a considerable alienation of landowners' land to the peasants, but not of wholesale expropriation, which most of the Trudovics demanded. While these two parties were trying to reach a compromise, the right-wing groups persuaded the Government, already dominated by Stolypin, to announce that, whatever the Duma decided, there would be no alienation of privately owned land — even of land which was left uncultivated. The Cadets thereupon made up their minds to issue a public 'Appeal to the People' protesting against the Government's action, but couched in moderate terms and including an injunction to the people to remain calm and to abstain from lawless action — this at a time when there had been a widespread occurrence of peasant uprisings, as well as increasing signs of disaffection in the army! When the Cadets' 'Appeal' was put to the vote, it was supported only by the Cadets' votes. The right-wing parties and the Social Democrats voted against it, and the Trudovics abstained. This rift in the Duma was seized on by the Government as the occasion for dissolving it : the division between the Cadets and the left parties seemed to make united action by them unlikely.

The Second Duma was in session when the Social Democrats held their Fifth Party Congress, which met ultimately in London after the delegates had wandered over a large part of Western Europe in search of a meeting-place and had run out of funds, so that they had to borrow money from Joseph Fels, the Henry Georgite naphtha man, in order to pay their bills. It was a large Congress, in which the Bolsheviks (105) slightly

outnumbered the Mensheviks (97), but the balance was held
by 44 Polish and 29 Latvian Social Democrats and 57 delegates
from the Jewish Bund. These latter groups took different sides
on different issues, but, on the whole, the majority supported
the Bolsheviks. The policy of alliance with the Cadets was
definitely condemned and electoral collaboration with the
Trudovics and S.R.s approved. The Axelrod-Lavrin proposal
to call an all-in conference to form an inclusive Labour Party
was rejected. The resolution on Trade Unions asserted the
need for the party to lead them and for definite organisational
links between them and the party. As against these Bolshevik
successes, the Congress condemned 'partisan' activities such
as robberies of public funds or raids on banks and ordered the
disbandment of the 'fighting' organisations — that is, of the
bodies which had been specially responsible for preparing for
insurrection, procuring arms, and training militants for street-
fighting. The question of insurrection did not figure on the
agenda and was not directly discussed. The majority had made
up its mind that the Revolution was out of action for the time
being, and that a new period of underground work lay ahead.
The Bolsheviks tried to induce the Congress to condemn the
Duma representatives of the party for collaborating too much
with the Cadets and not following a militant enough policy,
especially in relation to the land question. But they were voted
down. The Poles and the Bund, and also most of the Latvians,
were against anything that might split the party, and were also
at variance with the Bolsheviks about the correct relations
between the industrial workers and the peasants, to whom, like
the Mensheviks, they assigned only a subordinate rôle. To use
the parlance of later writers, the Poles, headed by Rosa Luxemburg, were guilty of 'Trotskyist deviations' towards the doctrine of 'the peasant revolution' and tended to regard the
industrial proletariat as the sole revolutionary force making for
Socialism.

Trotsky and Stalin were both at the London Congress ; but
Stalin said little, whereas Trotsky talked a great deal, attacking
both Mensheviks and Bolsheviks and seeking to hold them
together by abusing them both, so as to earn a great deal of
ill-will. He vigorously attacked the Menshevik 'Liquidators'
— the name given to those who wished to liquidate the fighting

organisation and to constitute the party as a mass-party on the German model; and he agreed with Lenin on the need for a workers' and peasants' alliance, though he assigned the main revolutionary rôle to the industrial proletariat. As against these views he attacked the Bolsheviks as well as the Mensheviks for looking only for a bourgeois Revolution, and insisted on his conception of a 'permanent Revolution' that would be carried through all its stages by the power of the organised working class. Trotsky also sided against the Bolsheviks on the issue of 'partisan' activities and defended the idea of a party organised on democratic lines from below against Lenin's centralism and insistence on strict discipline. But, as against this, he glorified the underground struggle and stressed the need to prepare for party leadership in a new insurrection when the occasion came. He voted now with the one group and now with the other, infuriating both by refusing to regard their disputes as really important, and by telling both sides not to build 'paper walls' between them. 'If you think a split unavoidable', he said, 'at any rate wait until events, and not mere resolutions, force you apart. Do not run ahead of events.'

This was unpalatable advice, and neither side took it. During the Congress, the rival factions kept on holding separate meetings to decide on their attitudes in advance of the full debates; and when it was over the Bolsheviks promptly reconstituted their separate Central Committee side by side with the Central Committee chosen at the Congress.

In June Stolypin acted. He first asked the Duma to agree to the arrest of a number of its members whom he accused of engaging in propaganda among the armed forces; then, when this was refused, he dissolved the Duma and arrested, among others, the whole of the Social Democratic group, except those who escaped abroad or went successfully into hiding. Those whom he caught were sent to Siberia, where most of them stayed till the Revolution of 1917 set them free. Having thus disposed of the Second Duma, Stolypin set to work to ensure that the Third, which he proposed to summon, should not be like it. By imperial *ukase* he altered the whole system of election in such a way as to ensure a preponderance of reactionaries. The Poles and other non-Russian populations were disfranchised; the gentry were given greatly increased weight in the electoral colleges; the city weight was reduced. The elections, held in late September and early October, reduced the Cadets to 53, as against 133 Octobrists and 145 members of the extreme right. The Social Democrats were reduced to 14, and the Labour group to the same : the S.R.s were wiped out. The residue of the opposition was made up of Poles, Moslems, and miscellaneous 'Progressives', numbering in all 65. The Fourth Duma, elected in 1912, was to be made up of much the same elements as the Third. In both the right, including the Octobrists, outnumbered the centre and left combined by more than two to one.

The Duma, then, was out of action after 1907 as a factor making even for moderate constitutional reform ; and Socialism, of all brands, had again to depend on underground propaganda. The Third Duma obediently endorsed Stolypin's policies : it met to an accompaniment of renewed pogroms. The Stolypin land reforms went ahead : many moderate reformers gave up their advocacy of constitutionalism and approved the Government's measures as fostering the healthy growth of capitalist enterprise and better farming, and therewith a new element of stability in the economic life of the country. Unrest and sporadic disturbances, and occasional acts of terrorism, continued. In 1911 Stolypin himself fell victim to an assassin. But the First Russian Revolution was over.

The years after 1907 saw the almost complete disappearance of the mass-movements inside Russia which had grown up during the revolutionary phase. The Social Democratic and Social Revolutionary Parties both shrank up almost to nothing : the Trade Unions maintained only a precarious hold. There were few strikes, and in face of Stolypin's combined policy of repression and reform of a sort, peasant disturbances also died down. Only small groups of Socialists remained in being, and among them arrests were frequent and deportations to Siberia numerous. Nevertheless there grew up, as a logical accompaniment to Stolypin's policy of working in with the rising capitalist class and the Octobrists in the Duma, and of developing the *kulak* elements in the villages, a substantial relaxation of the autocracy and of the police régime, except in relation to those groups which were regarded as definitely dangerous and as lying in wait to prepare for a fresh revolutionary attempt. For those who were prepared to accommodate themselves to the modified Czarist régime there was greater freedom of speech. Press censorship was relaxed, and the small left-wing groups remaining in the Duma could carry on some legal agitation. In these circumstances there were many Socialists belonging to the right wings of the Social Democrats and Social Revolutionaries who came to believe that the correct policy was to disband the underground organisations and to concentrate on making use of the opportunities for action within the limits of the law.

These limits were not, of course, at all clearly defined; for the authorities could swoop down at will on a group they suspected of subversive activities, could suppress an offending journal, and could in the last resort still act as repressively as they pleased. It was, however, part of Stolypin's policy to leave some scope for legal propaganda and to endeavour to split the 'moderates' away from the extremists. In the industrial field Trade Unions of a sort were allowed; but they were not permitted to form either national amalgamations extending beyond a single area or federal groupings of different trades and industries into Trades Councils or Soviets. Political organisations of workers or peasants were still banned; but the more moderate were to a great extent let alone.

In these circumstances a great dispute arose inside the nominally united Social Democratic Party. Indeed, the entire period from 1906 to 1914 was one of bitter faction fights, not only between Bolsheviks and Mensheviks, but also within these rival factions and between both and the so-called Centrists (not to be confused with Centralists), or 'Conciliators', who attempted to reconcile them. The most significant of these struggles were the following: (1) Bolsheviks and Centrists against 'Liquidators' — *i.e.* those Mensheviks and other right-wing groups which wished to liquidate the underground organisations and concentrate mainly on lawful propaganda; (2) Leninists against 'Left Deviationists', divided into 'Otzovists' and 'Ultimatumists' — who wished to withdraw the Social Democrats from the Duma and to concentrate on underground as against lawful activities; (3) Leninists against 'Empirio-Critics' and 'Empirio-Monists', who wished to revise the philosophical foundations of Marxism in a 'Neo-Kantian' sense ; (4) Leninists against the group round Lunacharsky, who were trying to work out a revised doctrine about the relation between Socialism and religion ; (5) Leninists and right-wing Mensheviks against Trotsky's central group, commonly known as the 'Conciliators', who stood for a broad party accepting differences of opinion as legitimate and not imposing a rigid discipline, but also refused to discard 'insurrectionism' or underground work ; (6) most Bolsheviks against cultural Nationalism, which had its main stronghold in the Jewish Bund, but was also represented among the Georgians and other national minorities inside the Russian Empire ; (7) most Bolsheviks *for* national self-determination against Rosa Luxemburg and the majority of the Polish Social Democrats, who had some support in the Baltic States as well.

The decline of mass-agitation and the disappearance of any immediate prospect of revolution threw the remaining activists in on themselves and gave them abundant time to fall out on matters of theory. The faction fights of these years were partly an outcome of thwarted desire to act ; but behind most of them lay the profound difference between Lenin's unbending centralism and hostility to every sort of liberalism and the more libertarian and popular democratic conceptions of the majority of his opponents. It was Lenin who deliberately and unflinchingly picked most of the quarrels and refused to compromise on any of them, though he had occasionally *reculer pour mieux sauter*.

It would be very tedious to trace out in any detail the course of these disputes at the various Conferences of the party groups. After the Unity Congress of 1906 there was only one further full Congress of the Social Democratic Party — the London Congress of 1907. Instead there were thereafter only Conferences, the difference being that a Conference was entitled only to debate and not to take binding decisions. It could advise ; but according to the constitution approved at the Unity Congress decisions on policy between Congresses rested with the Central Committee. Up to 1912 these Conferences at least purported to represent the Social Democratic Party as a whole ; but in that year the Bolsheviks called a Conference to which only a few picked Menshevik groups were invited, and this gathering arrogated to itself the powers of a Congress, expelled the right-wing Mensheviks, and made the split in Social Democracy final and complete. From 1908 the Mensheviks had been issuing a journal, *The Voice of the Social Democrat*, at Geneva; and Trotsky had been editing his own journal, *Pravda*, first at Lvov and then at Vienna. The chief Bolshevik organ for most of the time was *Proletary*, which purported to be the official organ of the party as a whole. Other journals came and went, including both clandestine and legal newspapers, as well as journals of opinion. In December 1908 a Conference met in Paris, attended by 16 delegates drawn from both the main factions. It recognised the changed situation in Russia — the *rapprochement* between the Government and the bourgeoisie, the decline of leftism among the intellectuals, the eclipse of the mass-movement, and the drift towards what Lenin called 'Liquida-tionism'. It asserted the right of the Central Committee to control the Social Democratic group in the Duma; and it voted for a return of the party to the centralism which had been given up during the revolutionary period. On these issues the Menshevik minority was outvoted: the Bolsheviks had matters all their own way. But the Otzovists were also voted down. The struggle against the 'Left Deviationists' was resumed at a meeting of the board of *Proletary* and of a number of Bolshevik delegates from local committees in the summer of 1909. Lenin persuaded the meeting to denounce the activities of the left groups — the Otzovists who wanted to withdraw the Social Democrats from the Third Duma, the Ultimatumists, headed by Bogdanov, who wanted to deliver to them — they were mostly Mensheviks — an ultimatum that they must obey the Central Committee or be expelled, and the 'Goddites', led by Lunacharsky, who were roundly condemned for representing Socialism as in essence a new religion.

The Deviationists did not take their condemnation lying down. All these groups combined to establish at Capri a Training School for propagandists, which lasted for several years. They also set up their own journal *Vperyod*, and conducted a lively controversy with *Proletary* and the Leninists who controlled it. The lecturers at the school included Maxim Gorky, the novelist (1868–1936), Anatoly Vasilievich Luna-charsky (1875–1933), A. Bogdanov (A. A. Malinovski, 1873–1928), G. A. Alexinsky (b. 1879) and M. N. Lyadov (b. 1872)

— all prominent figures in the Bolshevik movement.

Meanwhile the Mensheviks too were falling out among themselves. Most of the leaders abroad — Martov, Axelrod, and Dan among them — had moved sharply to the right. Indeed, they had moved so far that Plekhanov dissociated himself from them, retired from *The Voice of the Social Democrat*, and began to publish a rival paper. Plekhanov was still unwilling to see a final split in Social Democracy, or an abandonment of underground work in preparation for a new Revolution. He resumed his connections with the Bolsheviks and wrote a number of articles for the party journal. But before long he fell out with Lenin's reassertion of the policy of rigid centralism and exclusiveness in the conduct of the party, and thereafter till 1914 he hovered uneasily on the edge of the party battle, torn between his desire for a united party on a strictly Marxist basis and his dislike of authoritarian control.

As a contribution to the controversy with Bogdanov and his friends, Lenin wrote in 1908 his singular book, *Materialism and Empirio-Criticism*, in which he vehemently denounced those who departed from strict materialism and attempted to rebuild Marxist philosophy on neo-Kantian foundations. Lenin was no philosopher : he had no acquaintance with professional philosophy except through Marxism. But in his furious indignation against those who were trying to introduce into Social Democracy lessons learnt from the Austrian scientific philosopher, Ernst Mach (1838–1916), and from the German philosopher, Richard Avenarius (1843–96), he started reading philosophy, especially the English empiricists, in order to equip himself to demolish their heresies. The name Empirio-Criticism was actually that given by Avenarius to his system, which rested on an attempt to co-ordinate thought and action and to elucidate the relations between knowledge and experience derived from environment. Avenarius, like Mach, proclaimed the 'principle of economy' in thought, but his approach was through science rather than through philosophical speculation. Mach was primarily a physiologist ; but he was influenced at an early stage by reading Kant, whose doctrine of phenomena he interpreted as involving that sensation was the sole content of experience. From his physiological studies he went on to an elaborate survey of methods in all the sciences, in an attempt to eliminate all metaphysical elements. As against the crude materialists, he repudiated the whole conception of 'substance' as lying outside the range of possible knowledge. Entering the field of Psychology, he developed a purely sensationalistic theory of mental processes, closely akin to that of Avenarius. According to Mach, scientific laws were not final statements of fact but convenient instruments of investigation. In Russia Bogdanov and his group fastened on these ideas. Bogdanov developed a theory which he called Empirio-Monism, according to which the sensational content of experience, rather than material objects, constituted the knowable world and was to be regarded as reality.

To Lenin this doctrine seemed to be destructive of the materialist basis of Marxism, and particularly of the Materialist Conception of History. It seemed to involve a denial that men's history was determined by objectively real forces — the powers of production — and to carry with it a relapse into the 'Subjectivism' which had been the crowning offence of the Narodnik doctrines of Mikhailovsky and Peter Lavrov. Lenin could see little, if any, difference between Machism or Bogdanovism and the idealism of Bishop Berkeley. Idealism and Subjectivism were as red rags to a bull to Lenin: in reaction against them he came close to affirming the 'crude materialism' from which Marx had been at pains to dissociate his own doctrine. *Materialism and Empirio-Criticism* is indeed a very bad book, even from the standpoint of Marxism. It is flat-footed and amateurish, and shows no power at all to appreciate the finer issues. Nevertheless it was polemically successful in branding neo-Kantism, Empirio-Criticism, and Empirio-Monism as inadmissible heresies, involving a lapse into Idealism and opening the way to the intrusion of ethical concepts into the structure of Marxist Socialism. Neither Mach nor Avenarius had any connection with Marxism, or with any form of Socialism, though Mach carried his ideas into the field of the social sciences. Their concern was with the nature and content of human knowledge. But in Lenin's eyes the Materialist Conception involved an affirmation of the final reality of material objects; and any denial of this, or of the knowability of it, struck at the very root of Materialism and therefore of Marxism as a whole.

This controversy raged among the Bolsheviks throughout 1908 and 1909, and in part diverted attention from the dispute with the Mensheviks. No Social Democratic Congress or Conference was held in 1908 ; and in 1909 there was only the enlarged meeting of the *Proletary* board. In January 1910, however, a full meeting of the Central Committee was got together, and the 'Conciliators' made yet another attempt to reunite the factions. Surprisingly, this meeting managed to adopt a unanimous resolution, by using ambiguous phrases which each group could interpret as it chose. Even more surprisingly, the delegates agreed to wind up all the factional groups, to amalgamate *Proletary* with the right-wing Menshevik *Voice of the Social Democrat*, and to give a subsidy to Trotsky's *Pravda*. A new editorial board, consisting of Lenin, Zinoviev, Martov, Dan, and the Pole, Warski — a most unhopeful team — was appointed ; and a Foreign Bureau of the Central Committee was set up, representing all the main groups, including the Poles, the Latvians, and the Bund.

Not surprisingly, this plan never worked. A section of the Mensheviks refused to come in ; and *The Voice of the Social Democrat* continued to appear. In Russia the Mensheviks who were proposed mostly refused to serve on the new Central Committee. Plekhanov and a section of the Mensheviks tried to carry out the agreement ; but in effect the Mensheviks split — which was perhaps what Lenin had intended all along. For more than a year, however, there was no further definite move. The Poles and Latvians and the Bund gradually withdrew from participation in the Central Committee and in the other organisations of the party, and went off on their own. Then, in June 1911, the Bolsheviks decided to end the farce of unity. In conjunction with the Poles and Plekhanov's group, they repudiated the Foreign Organisation Committee set up the year before, and formed a new one in its place mainly from their own followings, and instructed it to call a Party Conference. This new body, however, split almost at once, as Plekhanov withdrew when he found that the Bolsheviks were set on a clean break with the right-wing Mensheviks. The Bolsheviks thereupon decided to proceed on their own, without either Plekhanov's group or the Poles. They set up yet another Organisation Committee, consisting largely of new men, and decided to call a Party Conference made up of their own supporters, with a few left-wing Mensheviks from inside Russia. This Committee summoned a Conference, which met in Prague during January 1912, and resolved to expel the right-wing Mensheviks from the party and to proclaim itself the sole true representative of Marxist Social Democracy. The Prague Conference then took to itself the powers of a full Congress and became in effect the founding Congress of the separate Bolshevik Party.

The Poles, the Latvians, and the Jewish Bund had all been invited to Prague, but refused to come. The Bund agreed mainly with the Mensheviks : the Poles favoured conciliation and accused Lenin's group of splitting the Party : the Latvians were engaged in a faction fight of their own. The Conference was definitely a Bolshevik affair. It denounced the Russian Government and the liberals for co-operating with it : denounced the right-wing Mensheviks for having abandoned the Revolution ; and reaffirmed its insurrectionary objectives. For the next stage it adopted a three-point slogan : it would lead the workers in the fight for a Democratic Republic, the eight hours' day, and the confiscation of the landlords' estates. The Conference also reinstated completely the pre-1905 structure of the party as a centralised, disciplined machine : it by no means repudiated legal activities — indeed it took measures for their development — but it strongly asserted the necessity of an underground, definitely revolutionary organisation.

Faced with this coup, the 'Conciliators', as well as the excluded Mensheviks, were naturally very angry. In January 1912 they got together a rival Organisation Committee with the function of summoning a 'general' Party Conference open to all groups. Plekhanov refused to join this body, and stood aloof. The Polish Social Democrats came, but withdrew almost at once. The Latvians, the Bund, and the *Vperyod* group agreed to take part. In the course of the Conference itself, however, this last group seceded, and went back to its Bolshevik allegiance, and a shift in the Latvian group caused it, too, to withdraw. Trotsky found himself, much to his discomfiture, left to deal with a Conference dominated by the centrist and right-wing Menshevik exiles — Martov, Axelrod, and Dan. The result was a programme drawn up within the framework of legality, the establishment of a new effectively Menshevik Party, and the recruitment into the Bolshevik Party of a good many Mensheviks who disapproved of 'Liquidationism' — of which Trotsky and the 'Conciliators' also disapproved.

By the time the Menshevik-Conciliators' Conference met, the situation inside Russia had begun to change dramatically. There had been a renewal of strike action, and unrest in the navy and army was reappearing. From 1909 trade and industry had been booming; and now at last the workers were organising to demand their share. In April 1912 a big strike broke out in the Lena goldfields, and demonstrating strikers were shot down. Protests spread over Russia, with many strikes. On May Day there were strikes and demonstrations in St. Petersburg and many other towns. The Bolsheviks at once took special measures to get control of the revived Trade Union movement and succeeded in planting their men in the key positions in most of the Unions, except the printers, who remained obstinately Menshevik. When the new system of State Insurance came into force the same year, the Bolsheviks succeeded in capturing the workmen's committees set up in connection with it. In April they had already founded in St. Petersburg a legal daily, *Pravda*, which secured a much wider circulation than the rival Menshevik *Luch* (The Ray of Light). After the Lena massacre the strikes began to take on a political aspect, with a renewal of demands for constitutional change. The strike movement continued during the following years, culminating in great strikes and demonstrations on May Day 1914. Then came the war, with which began a new phase beyond the ambit of this volume.

It remains to say a little about some of the internal controversies of the Social Democrats that have not been dealt with in the course of the preceding narrative. These turned mainly on two issues — Nationalism, and the conception of 'Permanent Revolution'. These, however, can best be discussed, not as specifically Russian problems, but in the wider context of European Socialism as a whole.

CHAPTER XI

POLAND — ROSA LUXEMBURG

WHEREVER a revolutionary movement existed, through most of the epoch that ended in 1918, Poles were in the midst of it. Poles helped the English Chartists and provided military leaders for the Paris Commune. Poles were active in the Socialist movements of most countries : there were Polish Socialist groups not only in most of the countries of Western Europe and in the United States, but also in Latin America and in India. Wherever there was fighting to be done, Poles fought manfully on behalf of the oppressed ; but unhappily they also fought one another — not only aristocrats against the lower classes, but also Socialists against Socialists.

Poland was a divided country — the largest part of it, the Kingdom of Poland, together with Lithuania, under Russian rule, Posen in the west under Prussia, and Galicia in the south as part of the Austro-Hungarian Empire. This division faced the Poles with a problem : the treatment they received differed considerably in the three areas ; and the three great powers to which they were subject were rivals for predominance in Central and Eastern Europe. In Russian Poland, the revolt of 1863 revealed the deep division between the Polish aristocracy and the people : the two could never come together into a common movement, and were crushed the more easily because of their antagonisms. Thereafter, Russian Poland lost its liberties, such as they had been. The policy of the Czars was Russification and the destruction of the Polish language and culture ; and this policy was pursued especially against the aristocracy. The emancipation of the serfs which immediately followed the suppression of the revolt was much more complete than in Russia because it was designed to reduce the power of the Polish landowners. Without abolishing the great estates, it made possible the rise of a substantial class of peasant farmers, who were allowed the chance of economic advancement, but under conditions of accepting the rule of the Czars and assimilating themselves to Russian education and Russian administrative control.

Meanwhile, the Poles under German rule were subjected to a process of colonisation, by the settlement of Germans on Polish lands ; and a prolonged struggle ensued between native inhabitants and settlers, with the Poles largely successful in pursuing their own ways of life despite all the Prussian Government could do to germanise the country. In Galicia the Poles under Austrian rule fared best, at any rate the upper classes. The Austro-Hungarian Empire, a medley of nationalities, could not set out to germanise its many peoples. Its German ruling class had to look for allies among Czech and Polish, as well as among Hungarian, aristocrats ; and after its defeat by Germany in the 'sixties it definitely wooed the Galician upper classes, who became, through their deputies in the Austrian Reichsrath, a bulwark of imperial rule, and got in return, not indeed that position of equal partners in a Triple Monarchy they would have liked, but at any rate a substantial measure of self-government in their provincial affairs. This suited them well enough ; for it enabled the Austrian Poles, as a superior race, to rule arbitrarily over a population made up largely of Ruthenian or Ukrainian peasants, with whose claims to national rights of their own even the more democratic Poles had no more sympathy than their compatriots across the frontier in the Ukrainian or Ruthenian areas of Russian Poland.

Polish nationalism remained indeed a living force ; but it was sharply divided not only between aristocrats and democrats but also between Austrian, German, and Russian subjects. Some indeed dreamed of an independent, reunited Poland — usually on the assumption of resumed Polish rule over subject peoples within the area they arbitrarily claimed for it. But for a long time after the defeat of 1863 there appeared to be no prospect at all of winning national freedom by fighting simultaneously against all the three great occupying powers ; and in consequence there were some who planned to win for Greater Poland a status of autonomy, or even of third partner, within Austria-Hungary, and others who planned for an autonomous Poland still attached to Russia, and yet others, though only a few, who looked to Germany as a possible liberator. The whole position was complicated by the intense rivalry between Austria-Hungary and Russia, and to some extent Germany, in the Balkans, for this was bound up with the Polish question and divided the Polish nationalists as well as their rulers.

Polish Socialism could not help being affected by these divisions. The Galician Socialists — that is, the Poles among them — were for the most part strongly anti-Russian — hardly less so than the Galician Polish aristocrats who shared power at Vienna with the ruling castes of Germans and Czechs. The Socialists in Russian Poland, on the other hand, were sharply divided between a strongly anti-Russian group which tended to co-operate with the Austrian Poles and a group which held that Poland's sole chance of freedom lay in making common cause with the Russian Socialists in order to overthrow Czarism. This latter group tended to look to the German as well as to the Russian Socialists to aid it in its work of liberation ; for its leaders were very doubtful of the possibility of successful revolution in Russia without the help of the proletariat of the West — by which they meant mainly Germany as the home of the most advanced and powerful Western Social Democratic movement. Polish Socialism was thus, almost from the moment of its emergence, a divided force, even apart from the further division within it that arose from the presence in Poland of a large Jewish population and of a strong anti-Semitic tendency even among many Polish democrats.

Socialism had no existence as an organised movement inside Poland until the 1870s. Long before that there were isolated leaders and even groups that were affected by Western Socialist ideas. Joachim Lelewel (1786–1861), the mediaeval historian who was a member of the Provisional Government of 1830–1, adopted many of the ideas of the early Socialists, notably Fourier. In exile after 1831, he settled down in Brussels and there wrote his *History of Poland*, founded a Democratic Society, and contributed to left-wing journals. His writings on communal land ownership and cultivation affected Belgian Socialist thought. But he created no movement in Poland. The Poles played little part in the revolutionary movements of 1848. The Poznanian area had exhausted itself in an abortive rising in 1846. The still independent Republic of Cracow was extinguished and occupied by Austria in 1848 ; and in Galicia the Austrians successfully staved off a Polish revolt by encouraging a *jacquerie* of the Ruthenian peasants against their Polish masters. Nor did Socialism, as an organised movement, play any rôle in the rising of 1863, which was mainly under aristocratic leadership. The first attempts to create a Socialist movement came in the 'seventies, under the leadership of Ludwig Wariński (1856–89) and Stanisław Mendelssohn (1857–1913). Wariński began his Socialist career as a student at St. Petersburg, went to work in an engineering factory in Warsaw in order to establish contact with the workers, fled to Galicia when he was in danger of arrest and there continued his revolutionary activities, was deported from Austria in 1879 and went to Geneva. In 1881 he returned to Warsaw and helped to form the underground organisation, Proletariat, which organised numerous strikes. He was arrested again in 1883, and died in prison six years later. Wariński was in touch with the Russian terrorist organisation, Naradnaya Volya, and sympathised with its ideals, but instead of assassination he favoured the stirring up of strikes designed to disorganise the economy and the processes of government. Though his active career was short, his ideas had a strong hold in the Polish Socialist movement till well into the 1890s, and indeed left a permanent mark.

By 1885 the Russian authorities had succeeded in breaking the power of Proletariat by arresting most of its leaders, four of whom were hanged. But a residue was left, and the following year received an outstanding new recruit in Rosa Luxemburg (1870–1919), then aged only 16. She at once became active. Two years later, Proletariat was reorganised, and began again to form Trade Unions and to stir up strikes. The following year, however, the economic and the political movements were separated. A Polish Workers' League was formed to take charge of the Trade Union side, while Proletariat concentrated on underground political action. That same year Rosa Luxemburg, threatened with arrest, escaped to Switzerland with the help of her fellow-Socialist, Martin Kasprzak, and settled down in Zürich as a student. In Zürich she met a group of Russian Socialist exiles, including Plekhanov, Axelrod, and Parvus, as well as a number of Poles, among them her future co-workers

Julian Marchlewski and Adolf Warski. From Plekhanov and his friends she imbibed the doctrine of Marxism; and the following year the group was joined by Leo Jogiches (1867–1919) (also known as Jan Tyszka), with whom she formed a lifelong association. Jogiches, who was well-to-do, had escaped from Poland after being imprisoned for his Socialist activities. He and Plekhanov made plans for a Marxist journal, but fell out over its control, and nothing came of the project. In 1892 there were great May Day strikes in Russian Poland — especially in Łódź and Warsaw; and at Łódź the demonstrating strikers were shot down by Cossacks. In connection with this movement Proletariat, the Polish Workers' League, and some other groups amalgamated to form a Polish Socialist Party, with Jogiches and Warski as its principal leaders. The new party started a journal, *Sprava Robotnicza* (The Workers' Cause), edited by Warski, which lasted till 1896.

Rosa Luxemburg, still living at Zürich, represented the new party at the International Socialist Congress which met there in 1893. But already a rift had appeared. In 1892 the Polish exiles in Paris had formed the Union of Polish Socialists Abroad, which was also represented at the Zürich Congress; and its delegates challenged the credentials of those sent by the Polish Socialist Party, among them Julian Karski (1866–1925), who was not allowed to take his seat. Rosa Luxemburg, however, was allowed to make a report to the Congress on the position in Russian Poland and made full use of the opportunity to expound the views which she and Jogiches had already worked out. She stood for a party, conspiratorial but democratically organised, which should endeavour to create a mass movement among the workers by taking up their economic grievances and organising strikes, and should at the same time struggle politically for the establishment of democratic liberties, but should maintain entire independence of all bourgeois parties.

The emphasis in this assertion of the need for strict independence was on the importance of dissociating the workers' movement from all connections with the nationalist movement for an independent Poland. The rival Union of Polish Socialists Abroad stood for nationalism, whereas Rosa Luxemburg, Jogiches, and Warski held that the right course for the Socialists in Russian Poland was to identify themselves with the struggle of the Russian workers and of all the national working-class groups inside the Russian Empire for the overthrow of Czarism in a revolution which they thought of as essentially international. This had been the programme of Proletariat and of Wariński, and it was carried over by his successors into the new Polish Socialist Party. It was not, however, a policy that appealed either to the Austrian Poles or to a good many Socialists in Russian Poland — among them some of Wariński's old associates, such as Mendelssohn and H. Yanowska. There was a split ; and the group round Jogiches founded a new party — the Social Democratic Party of the Kingdom of Poland, *i.e.* claiming to represent only the areas of the old Polish Kingdom under Russian rule. In 1899, however, it extended its claims to include Lithuania, where a separate Social Democratic Party had been formed under the leadership of Felix Edmundovich Dzerzhinsky (1877–1926), later to play a prominent part in the Russian as well as in the Polish movement.

The dispute among the Polish Socialists was renewed at the London International Congress of 1896. Charges were even made by the delegates of the Polish Socialist Party and in particular by the Galician Polish leader, Ignacy Daszyński (1866–1936), that Rosa Luxemburg and Warski were police spies and had been given the task of disrupting the movement. A committee of investigation, presided over by Peter Lavrov, had already dismissed the charges against Warski as unfounded; but that did not prevent their renewal. Even while Daszyński was renewing them, the Polish Social Democratic Party was being disrupted by numerous arrests of its militants. It was largely out of action until 1899, when a considerable revival took place. Meanwhile, Rosa Luxemburg was in France in 1896 and 1897, and in 1898 produced her first important book, a doctoral thesis on the development of industry in Poland. Soon afterwards, she married Gustav Lübeck, a family friend, for the purpose of acquiring German nationality instead of Russian in order to facilitate her work for Socialism. It was only a legal marriage, based on friendship and not on love. Her love had gone out much earlier to Jogiches ; but they did not marry. She was indeed a half-cripple from childhood, owing to faulty medical treatment ; throughout her busy career her health was always bad.

After her marriage Rosa Luxemburg took up her residence in Germany and became very active in the German Social Democratic Party. She worked particularly with the Russian, A. L. Helphand, better known as Parvus, who was then writing the leading articles for the *Sächsische Arbeiterzeitung* at Dresden, and was strongly attacking Bernstein's Revisionist proposals. She also wrote for Bruno Schönlank (1859–1901), who edited the *Leipziger Volkszeitung*. In 1898 Parvus was expelled from Saxony, and Rosa Luxemburg was made leader-writer of the *Sächsische Arbeiterzeitung* in his place. She continued his policy, which included great emphasis on the importance of the Trade Union struggle. But almost at once she found herself in trouble for delivering a vehement attack on the Dresden Socialist deputy, Georg Gradnauer, the editor in chief, who belonged to the right wing. She resigned her editorial position and moved to Berlin, still continuing to contribute to Schönlank's journal. In Berlin she became a close intimate of the Kautskys and a regular writer for Kautsky's *Neue Zeit*, the principal theoretical organ of German Social Democracy. She continued her vigorous attack on the Revisionists and in 1900 republished some of her articles in a small book, *Social Reform or Revolution?*, which raised her to the status of principal spokesman of the extreme left in the German movement. She also delivered lively onslaughts on those who defended Millerand on his entry into the Waldeck-Rousseau Ministry, including Jean Jaurès, who nevertheless remained a close friend, whose talents she deeply admired. At the same time she continued her interest in Polish and Russian affairs, seconding Lenin in his campaign against the Economists and contributing to Polish as well as to German journals. At the time of the unsuccessful Belgian General Strike of 1902 she assailed Émile Vandervelde, the Chairman of the International Socialist Bureau, for making the strike simply a demonstration in aid of the Labour Party and for his compromises with the Liberals, when in her view he ought to have appealed to the natural militancy of the workers and thus given the strike movement a much more revolutionary character. She was to develop this point much further during the controversies over the general strike which occupied the International during the ensuing years.

In 1903, after the defeat of the Revisionists at the German Party Congress, Rosa Luxemburg fell foul of the German leaders, including Kautsky as well as Bebel. Like Kautsky, she favoured drastic action against the Revisionists, to the point of expulsion if they refused to recant. But the party leaders believed above all in the need to keep the party united; and she and Kautsky found no support from them on this issue.

Rosa Luxemburg's dispute with Kautsky arose over a different, though related, issue. She held that it was the party's duty to prepare actively for revolution, instead of merely talking about it; and she was entirely against the notion that 'the Revolution' could be postponed until the party had won a parliamentary majority and then carried through without resort to violence by a negotiated surrender of the old régime. She did not believe there was a chance of such a surrender: she thought it much more likely that, if the Social Democrats seemed at all near to winning a majority, the party would be again outlawed, and the right of manhood suffrage perhaps be taken away, as it had been in Saxony. She therefore wanted the party to get itself definitely ready for illegal action, to undertake propaganda in the armed forces, and to defy the Government to put it down. But on these matters the party leaders were even less prepared to consider her advice. They had a strong respect for legality, and were determined, as far as they possibly could, to carry on their campaign within the law in order to win over the doubtful electors, and give the Government no excuse for renewing Bismarck's tactics of persecution.[1]

Before this, in 1902, Rosa Luxemburg had become leader-writer on the *Leipziger Volkszeitung*: but again her tenure was brief. She fell foul of the censorship and, rather than accept its deletions, resigned. Her fellow-leftist, Franz Mehring (1846–1919), the historian of German Socialism, took her place.

In 1904 Rosa Luxemburg served her first term of imprisonment on a charge of insulting the German Emperor. Early the following year, after her release, she joined the editorial staff of the leading Social Democratic newspaper, the *Vorwaerts* of Berlin. She was there when the Russian Revolution of 1905 broke out, and there she wrote two of her three pamphlets,

---

[1] For a further discussion of the German Party's 'revolutionism' see Chapter VI.

published under the collective title *The Revolution Has Struck : What Next ?* The outbreak excited her greatly, and she was itching to be in the thick of it ; but she was ill, and thought her first duty was to act as its interpreter to the Germans. Only in December 1905 did she make her way, with considerable difficulty, into Poland, arriving in Warsaw when the Poles had already lost the fight. Warsaw, indeed, had heralded the coming of the Revolution by a series of large-scale strikes and peasant disturbances during 1904, largely provoked by the calling up of Poles for service in the armed forces after the outbreak of the Japanese War. These movements, brutally repressed, had led to considerable scattered fighting with the Russian forces ; and in November 1904 the Polish Socialist Party had decided to resort to actual insurrection. In that month there had been heavy street fighting in Warsaw, and the rising had been ruthlessly put down. But in January 1905 great strikes again broke out in Łódź and a number of other towns, and these too developed in some cases into half-insurrections, which were bloodily suppressed. In order to conduct these conflicts, the Polish Socialist Party had been doing its best to collect arms. In 1904 Pilsudski, on its behalf, went to Japan on the outbreak of the Russo-Japanese War and endeavoured to persuade the Japanese Government to supply it with arms. He returned empty-handed ; but the Polish Socialist Party's journal, *Robotnik*, which he had founded in 1894, nevertheless continued to advocate concentration on the formation of fighting groups — a policy which Rosa Luxemburg and the Polish Social Democrats condemned as doomed to failure unless it were accompanied, or indeed preceded, by the creation of a mass workers' movement animated by revolutionary will. The Social Democrats' policy, as expressed by Rosa Luxemburg, was to use every possible effort to disorganise the Government by mass-strikes — to dislocate industry and transport, and by getting the workers into action to put them into a more revolutionary frame of mind. She pointed out that insurrection could succeed only if the soldiers refused to obey orders, and that in Poland, garrisoned by Russian troops, it was very difficult to conduct successful propaganda in the armed forces. She was not against insurrectionary tactics ; but she wanted to prepare the way for them and to wait in the hope that mutiny in Russia would spread of its own accord to the forces garrisoning Poland, and would thus create the conditions needed for success. She saw the Revolution in Poland, not as a national revolution against Russia — which was in the main how it was envisaged by the Polish Socialist Party — but as part and parcel of the Russian Revolution itself.

The Polish Socialist Party, as a party standing for a united independent Poland, claimed to represent not merely Russian Poland, but German and Austrian Poland as well. Its first leader had been Boleslau Limanowski (1837–1935) ; but he had passed into exile, first in Paris and then in Switzerland, and had given up active work. He actually returned to Poland, and was allowed to settle there unmolested, in 1908. His place in Russian Poland had been taken by Józef Pilsudski (1867–1935), who had become a Socialist as a student at Kharkov, and had been exiled to Siberia in 1887. In 1892 he had been allowed to return to Vilna, where he had helped to organise the Polish Socialist Party. Two years later he had founded the journal, *Robotnik* (The Workman), which he continued to edit till 1900. That year he was arrested, but escaped from prison and went first to London and then, in 1902, to Cracow in Austrian Poland, where he entered for a time into close relations with Daszyński. After the defeat of the 1905 Revolution he continued to lead the nationalist wing of Polish Socialism. His later adventures, during and after the first world war, belong to a later part of this story.

In Russian Poland, 1905 had opened with a mass-strike, to which the P.S.P., as well as the Social Democrats, had given support. But the big strike soon gave place to a sequence of small strikes concerned mainly with particular economic grievances ; and the P.S.P. would have nothing to do with these, as they did not directly serve its purpose of national insurrection. The Social Democrats, on the other hand, supported the continuing strikes as means of arousing the workers, and tried to co-ordinate them by putting forward the slogan of the eight hours' day ; and Rosa Luxemburg also did her best to stir up peasant troubles to reinforce the disorganising process which she believed to be the indispensable prerequisite of success. The Polish Socialist Party's leaders retorted by accusing the Social Democrats of strike-mongering and of encouraging the workers to dissipate their strength instead of conserving it for a national insurrectionary effort. Daszyński, from Galicia, went so far as to condemn the strikes altogether because they tended to identify the Polish workers' struggle with the struggle of the Russian workers, instead of rallying them behind a Polish national movement that would seize the opportunity afforded by Russia's internal troubles to accomplish its own ends. What Daszyński clearly had in mind was that, if the Revolution in Russia were to succeed, the Poles should seize the chance offered by the collapse of the Russian Government to proclaim their independence, not as partners in the successful Revolution, but even, if need were, against it. The hatred of Russia went too deep among the P.S.P. leaders for any thought of co-operation even with a revolutionary Russian Government to be entertained.

In June 1905, when a fresh general strike broke out in Warsaw, the P.S.P. opposed it. Up to this point the P.S.P. had undoubtedly enjoyed a much larger body of support than the Polish Social Democratic Party, which had been indeed very weak. But the Social Democrats' support of the strike movement gained them a great accession of followers, especially among the factory workers, whereas the P.S.P. continued to have a large backing among the handicraft workers as well as among the left-wing intellectuals and the tradesmen. These same groups, in which there were many Jews, were also strongly represented in the Bund, which in general sided with the Social Democrats and was naturally hostile to the strong Polish nationalism of the P.S.P.

The insurrectionary tactics favoured by Pilsudski's followers became steadily more impracticable as, over Russia as a whole, the revolutionary wave began to ebb. The P.S.P.'s armed bands had been using the same methods as the fighting groups in Russia — raiding banks, offices, and government buildings in order to seize funds, and harrying the administration wherever they saw a chance. As in Russia, the ebbing of the revolutionary wave led to a degeneration of this type of guerrilla warfare into something not easily distinguishable from mere banditry; and the Social Democrats, like the Russian Mensheviks, strongly denounced it. The consequence of all these disagreements was that in 1906 the P.S.P. split. One section dissociated itself from the demand for immediate national independence and accepted the need to act in close conjunction with the Russian revolutionaries. This section joined forces with the Social Democrats ; and the reorganised Social Democratic Party decided to affiliate to the Russian Social Democratic Party. The other section followed Pilsudski, and renamed its party the Revolutionary Polish Socialist Party, denouncing its rivals as apostates from the cause of national revolution.

At this point we must turn back for a moment to consider the situation in Austrian Poland. Up to 1911 the Galician Poles formed a group within the federal Austrian Social Democratic Party. They had their own self-governing organisation, like the other nationalities under Austrian rule : their representatives in the Reichsrath formed a group within the combined parliamentary Socialist Party. From 1911 onwards these federative arrangements ceased to exist. The Austrian-Polish Socialists became a separate party, merely exchanging fraternal delegates at Congresses with the other national parties. Their leader, both before and after the separation, was Ignacy Daszyński, who had been first elected to the Austrian Reichsrath in 1891. They were for a while in close touch with Pilsudski's Polish Socialist Party, though they fell out with it later : as we saw, Pilsudski transferred his headquarters to Galicia in 1907, after the defeat of the Revolution in Russian Poland. Daszyński and his followers, like Pilsudski, were strongly anti-Russian. They were on the side of Austria-Hungary in opposing Russian penetration into the Balkans, and some of them played with the idea of recruiting Poland as a third element in the Austro-Hungarian State. In Galicia they had their own problem. Many workers from other parts of Austria were employed there ; and a large part of the indigenous population consisted not of Poles but of Ukrainians, whom Poles were apt to look down upon as a naturally subject people. Although the Ukrainian part of Galicia was mainly agricultural, the Ukrainians in Austria had possessed from 1897 some sort of Socialist organisation of their own and had been from 1899 organised in a Ukrainian Social Democratic Party led first by Mikota Hankiewycz, and then by Simon Wityk and by Jacko Ostapzuk, a peasant — who all won seats in the

Austrian Reichsrath — and by Ivan Warsniak. This party collaborated with the Revolutionary Ukrainian Party across the frontier in the Russian Ukraine, and stood for the policy of working for liberation in conjunction with the Russian proletariat. It was, up to 1911, one of the sections of the Austrian Party.

From this digression we must now return to the position in Russian Poland.

In March 1906 Rosa Luxemburg and Leo Jogiches, who had been living in Warsaw under false names, were arrested and lodged in gaol. Rosa Luxemburg managed to write several pamphlets and smuggle them out of the prison; but her health broke down, and after some months the Russian authorities, who were troubled by her German nationality, released her under police supervision. A little later she was allowed to leave the country and went to Finland, where she wrote her next important pamphlet, *The Mass Strike, the Party, and the Trade Unions*, expounding her theory of revolutionary mass action and of the rôle of the party in relation to it. Jogiches, meanwhile, had been sent to Siberia, but speedily escaped and resumed his revolutionary work.

In 1907 Rosa Luxemburg, as we have seen, took part as a delegate of the Polish Social Democratic Party in the London Congress of the Russian S.D.P.[1] She was also a delegate at the Stuttgart Congress of the Socialist International, and took a leading part in the celebrated debate concerning the attitude of the Socialist parties in the event of war. As we saw, the final paragraph of the resolution finally adopted, dealing with the line to be followed after war had actually broken out, was drafted mainly by her and Lenin in close consultation with Kautsky, who was concerned that it should not be so worded as to cause the German Government either to close down the Congress or to take repressive action against the German Social Democratic Party.[2]

The following year Rosa Luxemburg was back in Germany as a lecturer at the Training School for party workers which the German S.D.P. had set up in 1907. She replaced Rudolf Hilferding, who had been displaced on Government orders because of his Austrian nationality. Her subject was Political

[1] See p. 491.   [2] See p. 67 ff.

Economy ; and largely out of her work at the School came the studies which led to her best-known work, *The Accumulation of Capital*. This appeared in 1913, and was followed by a great controversy among Marxists, provoked by her criticism of certain parts of Marx's economic doctrine — notably in connection with his theory of capitalist crises. In 1919 there appeared a second volume, in which she forthrightly answered her critics. Her unfinished *Introduction to Political Economy*, though based on the lectures she gave at the School, was not actually written until 1916, and was published, from an uncorrected draft, only in 1925.

Apart from her work at the Training School, Rosa Luxemburg continued, through the years up to 1914, to take an active part in the affairs of the Social Democratic Party, always as an exponent of the views of the extreme left. When the Social Democrats conducted, from 1908 onwards, their intensive campaign for the reform of the exceedingly reactionary class-franchise in force in Prussia, she strongly advocated more militant measures. When, in 1910, the German Chancellor, von Bethmann Hollweg, introduced his proposals for altering the system without in any way improving the position of the main body of working-class electors, she was among those who advocated a general strike in order to force the Prussian Government to make an end of the class-system of voting and to introduce universal and equal suffrage. She was by no means alone in this : the pressure of opinion inside the movement was great enough to compel the party and the Trade Union leaders to call a special Conference to consider the proposal. They decided against it ; the Trade Union leaders were even less prepared than the party leaders to run full tilt against the power of the autocratic Prussian State. Thereafter, Rosa Luxemburg found herself more and more at odds not only with the right wing of the German Social Democrats but also with the Centre and with much of what had been regarded as the left. In 1910 she had urged the party to declare openly against the monarchy and to put forward the slogan of the 'Democratic Republic'. Her relations with Kautsky became strained ; and finally he refused to print in the *Neue Zeit* an article of hers which had already been refused by *Vorwaerts*. It had been largely a reply to Kautsky's *Der Weg zur Macht* (The Way to

Power), published in 1909. She now broke with the *Neue Zeit*, and in conjunction with Franz Mehring and her old Polish associate, Julian Karski, founded a new journal, *Sozialdemokratische Korrespondenz*, to expound the policy of the left. Its first number appeared in 1913.

Early the following year Rosa Luxemburg was again in trouble with the law — for her speeches, not her writings. In February 1914 she was sentenced to a year's imprisonment for inciting soldiers to mutiny in the course of an anti-war oration; but on account of her health execution of the sentence was postponed. She repeated her offence, and was prosecuted a second time; but she was left at large until well after the beginning of the war. At length, in February 1915, she was gaoled, and except for a few months she remained a prisoner until the German Revolution released her late in 1918 — to enjoy only a few months of activity before she was murdered by reactionary officers early the following year. The story of these latter years belongs, however, not here, but to the closing volume of this work.

Rosa Luxemburg, as this narrative will have made plain, is essentially an international figure, who cannot be assigned to the Socialist movement of a single country. She was active in Poland, in Russia, in Germany, and in the Second International, in which she was one of the outstanding figures during the decade before 1914. She was more continuously active in German than in Polish Socialist affairs; but she undoubtedly played a very important part, in conjunction with Leo Jogiches, in orienting a large section of the Polish Socialist movement away from nationalism and towards a partnership with the Russian workers based on essentially internationalist notions. Being a Jew was no doubt an important factor in determining her attitude — especially in face of the strong current of anti-Semitism among the Poles — including many of the Polish Socialists. But she was not only a Jew, but also the child of parents whose culture was much more Western than Eastern; and she was intellectually more at home in Berlin or Paris than in either Warsaw or St. Petersburg. Like Trotsky, she could understand the Socialists of the West and get on with them intellectually, even if she disagreed with them. She found herself very often on Lenin's side against them; but she could never swallow Lenin's conception either of the party or of the dictatorship. In many respects she had a good deal in common with Trotsky; but despite their common association with Parvus, of whom more will be said later, she and Trotsky never established any close relations. Her closest associations were with Jogiches, who was with her to the end in the Spartakus movement, with Kautsky, till their quarrel in 1910, with Kautsky's wife, Luisa, to the last, with Clara Zetkin, and, in terms of intellectual intercourse, with Jaurès.

The chief contributions which Rosa Luxemburg made to Socialist thought fall under three heads — her view of the relations between Socialism and Nationalism, her conception of the rôle of the Socialist Party in relation to mass-action and the general strike, and her attempt to revise Marxist economic theory in *The Accumulation of Capital*. In relation to the first two she undoubtedly owed a great deal to Jogiches, whose mouthpiece, as well as her own, she was : in relation to the third she may have owed something to Hilferding, but her main contribution was essentially her own.

On the issues of nationality and nationalism, her attitude was obviously affected by her Jewish blood and by the exclusive character of Polish nationalism in regard not only to Jews, but equally to Ruthenians and to Germans in German Poland. She disliked heartily the pretensions of the Poles to superiority over other peoples, including Russians, and their tendency to regard themselves as a ruling caste. She took pleasure in pointing out to how great an extent, when put to the test, the Polish upper classes and capitalists, despite these pretensions, were ready to invoke Russian or Austrian or German help to suppress any movement for liberation emerging from the lower classes of their own people. Their attitude gave her a contempt for nationalism in all its forms. She was none the less ready, as her pamphlet *In Defence of Nationality*, published in 1900 in Polish, showed, to defend the Poles in German Poland against the germanising policy of the imperial Government; and she was of course equally hostile to the Russification measures of the Czarist Government in Russian Poland. But she had no use for the idea that each nation has a fundamental right to self-determination, or for Lenin's formulation of this right as including the right of secession, because she wanted to build an international workers' authority transcending national frontiers, and because she was very much alive to the problem of racial or linguistic groups within the traditional territory claimed by a particular nation as its own. Poland raised all these problems and more : Polish nationalism needed to define its attitude to Jews, to Ruthenian or Ukrainian peasants, and to the Lithuanians, as well as to its Russian, German, and Austrian rulers. She considered class-division to be much more fundamental and decisive than divisions of race or language ; and like Marx she regarded nationalism as a most powerful obstacle to the establishment of class-solidarity.

As we have seen, Rosa Luxemburg, was not the inventor of the brand of Polish Socialism which set its hopes on the united action of the peoples subject to the Czar to make an end of Russian absolutism. That doctrine had already been advanced by Wariński on behalf of Proletariat before she joined the movement and had been part of the basis of its association with Narodnaya Volya. For Wariński, as for Rosa Luxemburg, the enemy to be fought by the Poles was primarily Czarism, or for German or Austrian Poles, the autocracy of Prussia or of the Austro-Hungarian Empire. They both wanted to unite the workers, over the widest possible field, in a common struggle against the autocracies that were holding them apart, and also against the nationalist movements that were threatening to maintain their division into conflicting groups. But it was not possible to do this without being denounced as an enemy of the national struggle for liberation. Yet it was easier in Poland than in countries where a single national group was living in subjection to an alien ruling State, because in Poland a purely nationalist movement could not make common cause with either Jewish craftsmen and traders or Ruthenian peasants, whereas both could be called upon to join with Poles and Russians and the many other peoples of the Russian Empire in a common struggle against autocracy. The appeal to the peasants as well as to the workers, on the need for which Rosa Luxemburg continually insisted, could not be made effectively on a basis of Polish nationalism, but could be made on a class basis against the exploitation of the poor and against the police State which existed for the defence of the exploiters.

Rosa Luxemburg, then, fell out with Lenin on the issue of

national self-determination. Lenin was seeking means of rallying the subject peoples inside the Russian Empire for a common crusade against Czarism, and regarded the slogan of national self-determination and the right of secession as valuable for enlisting this support. He was as contemptuous as she was of 'bourgeois nationalism'; but he believed that the acceptance of its slogan, to the extent of the right of self-determination, was necessary in order to unite the subject peoples against the aristocracy. Lenin was no less aware than she was that, when it came to the test, nationalist aristocrats and large-scale capitalists would rally to the side of Czarism against the workers and peasants. But he believed that, if he could win over the popular following of the nationalists to take part in the struggle against Czarism, he would also be able, when the show-down came, to hold their allegiance against the aristocratic and bourgeois nationalists who would seek to betray them as soon as they began to endanger the rights of property. Lenin was thinking not only, or even mainly, of Polish nationalism : he was concerned even more with Ukrainians, Transcaucasians, Moslems of various Asiatic areas, and, last but not least, Finns. He was, moreover, influenced by his own internationalism. The International Socialist Congress had accepted the right of national self-determination ; and this put into his hands a powerful weapon when he wished to denounce imperialist tendencies in the Socialist parties of the great Western imperial countries and to make colonial nationalism, where it existed, an ally in the struggle against world capitalism in its final, imperialist phase. For Lenin these arguments were overwhelmingly strong ; and he found it difficult to keep his temper with those who opposed them. But he also saw why the Polish Social Democrats hated Polish nationalism, and sympathised with their hatred of it. Lenin, however, in upholding the right of self-determination, manifested a violent hatred of 'cultural nationalism'. It seemed to him practicable, while accepting the struggle for national self-determination, to pursue at the same time the objective of organising the proletariat of each nation against its exploiters, so that the Socialist Revolution would ensue as a sequel to the national revolution within each country. Cultural nationalism, on the other hand — that is, the claim of each racial or linguistic group to maintain its own cultural institutions within each area, or across State frontiers — he saw as something that would keep the working class divided against itself in every territory in which members of different races or language groups were working side by side. He therefore rejected absolutely the claim of the Jewish Bund to an exclusive right to organise Jewish workers apart wherever they were living, though he had to accept the lesser claim to a separate Jewish organisation, without exclusive rights, in predominantly Jewish areas. On this issue Rosa Luxemburg was at one with him. She was a Jew ; but her affiliation was to the Polish Social Democratic Party and not to the Bund.

Rosa Luxemburg's second great contribution to Socialist theory was in respect of the relations between the Socialist Party and the mass of the workers. It will hardly be denied to-day by any serious student of Lenin's writings — though it has been hotly denied in the past — that there was in his attitude a substantial element of what is sometimes called 'Blanquism' — that is to say, belief in the revolutionary rôle of a conspiratorial élite. I am not suggesting that Lenin was a Blanquist — only that, like Marx when he was writing the *Communist Manifesto*, he was influenced by certain Blanquist ideas. Lenin was certainly not a Blanquist ; for no one insisted more strongly than he did on the need for the party to keep in close touch with the mass-movement of the workers and to participate actively in their day-to-day struggles. The Blanquist element in his thought lay partly in his insistence on the necessity of a rigidly disciplined party, organised from a single centre and free to disregard democratic electoral procedures in the choice of its local committees and agents ; and the other part of it lay in his conception of the dictatorship as involving, at any rate for a considerable transitional period, its exercise by a centralised party acting in the name of the class, rather than by directly chosen representatives of the class.

These were the two points on which Rosa Luxemburg disagreed with him. She, too, wanted a strong and a disciplined party to act as the spearhead of the mass-movement and to play its full part in the daily struggles of the mass, economic as well as political. But she was strongly of opinion that the party would not be able to give the masses the right leadership, or to avoid the contaminations of irresponsible power, unless it were kept as democratic as possible in its internal structure and made continually responsible directly to its rank-and-file members and, through them, to the whole conscious mass of the working-class movement. She was, moreover, an upholder of dictatorship only on condition that it should be the rule not of a party over the mass, but of the mass represented by a party responsive to its desires. She was often accused by Bolsheviks — by Zinoviev, for example, in a famous polemic — of putting her trust in the 'spontaneity' of the working masses and of denying the need for leadership over them. She was charged with reviving Bakunin's notions of spontaneous national revolutionism only waiting to be unchained. But in fact this was not at all her thought. She did believe very firmly that revolutions could not be made to order by small bodies of determined revolutionaries out of touch with mass-opinion and mass-feeling, and that opportunities for successful revolution arose out of conditions which revolutionary leaders could only watch for, and not create. But she believed no less that these opportunities would be missed or frittered away in the absence of a well-organised party in close touch with the mass, and always alert to take advantage of them.

On this basis, she supported, in common with Lenin, participation by the party in the day-to-day struggles of the workers for partial reforms, with the proviso — equally his — that everything practicable should be done to give such demands a common character — for example, by generalising them round such common slogans as that of the eight hours' day. She agreed with Lenin in condemning Economism, which stopped short at reformist economic demands and refused to utilise them as stepping-stones towards more revolutionary objectives; and she stressed, even more than he did, the educative value of the purely economic struggle, especially when it provoked repressive government action, and taught the workers the difference between capitalists demanding constitutional government and the same capitalists faced with a strike and invoking the authorities to suppress it. But she assigned to strike action a nearer approach to a revolutionary function than Lenin did because she drew a less rigid distinction than he between the two kinds of revolution, bourgeois democratic and Socialist, and was less sure that there had to be a bourgeois revolution to clear the way for the Socialist revolution.

To this question of the 'two revolutions' we shall have to come back. I am concerned with it here primarily as it relates to the conception of strike action, and in particular to that of the general strike. Rosa Luxemburg is generally ranked among the powerful advocates of the general strike in the great debates of the years before 1914. So indeed she was; but at the Stuttgart International Socialist Congress of 1907 she appeared as a strong opponent of the proposal that the Congress should commit itself to a general strike against war. She pointed out, with her habitual vehemence, that such a proposal was utopian nonsense in the existing condition of working-class opinion in the countries concerned; that the call, if made, would not be answered; and that, if the workers were in a mood to answer it, the Governments would take good care to steer clear of war in face of such a mood. She took this line, not as an opponent of the general strike — far from it — but because she held that general strikes of a revolutionary kind, such as a strike against war would need to be, could not be produced to order, but could arise only out of a swell of mass-feeling which would come at its own time and not at the beck and call of a group of leaders or of a party, however strongly organised. She drew a sharp distinction between the kind of general strike, such as those which had taken place in Austria, in Belgium and elsewhere, on behalf of constitutional reform, and the social general strike, surging up out of mass-feeling, which could be made, under proper leadership, the starting-point of successful revolution. She was not against the former kind of general strike, which she regarded as only a highly organised form of mass-demonstration with a limited objective; but she denied its revolutionary potentiality. As for the other kind of general strike, she ardently desired it, but only when it was ready to come of its own accord and when the party had prepared itself to take hold of it and give it the right direction. This kind, she held, could not be manufactured from above, or ordered for a definite day: the workers would get it going of themselves, but would need the party to help them carry it to a successful issue.

This theory was not Syndicalist, though it has often been

represented as being so. The Syndicalist theory of the general strike, as we have seen, when it treated the strike as reality and not as social myth,[1] trusted everything to the spontaneity of the masses. Rosa Luxemburg, on the other hand, regarded this spontaneity as a condition of practicability, but by no means as an assurance of success.

Her third main contribution to Socialist thought is contained in her two volumes on *The Accumulation of Capital*. In these she was directly concerned with a revision of Marx's theory of the 'contradictions of capitalism', but her practical purpose was to answer Bernstein rather than to refute Marx. Her second volume, written in answer to her critics, was mainly produced while she was in prison during the war, which she regarded as a direct outcome of the capitalist process she had attempted to analyse. *The Accumulation of Capital* is not an easy book to understand, except for those who are deeply expert in the Marxist scriptures. It is concerned largely with the second volume of *Das Kapital*, which is the least read of the three and by far the most technical; and it sets out from Marx's attempt to show why capitalist production necessarily runs into recurrent crises and why these crises are bound to grow more intense and to end up in destroying the entire system. The gist of Marx's argument was that, as the techniques of production advanced, labour was continually displaced by machinery, so that into each commodity produced there tended to enter less direct labour and more utilisation (and of course wear and tear) of capital goods. Accordingly, even apart from increases in population, labour was being continually displaced and could be reinstated in employment only if the demand for commodities grew at a sufficient rate to make such employment profitable. The displaced workers, however, would lose their purchasing power; and demand for consumers' goods would therefore tend to fall unless the capitalists increased luxury consumption at a sufficient rate. This they would not do, because they would wish to employ a large part of their incomes, not in consumption, but in investment designed to secure them greater profits. But new investment, over and above what was needed to replace worn-out capital goods, could not be profitable unless markets could be found for the increased output

[1] See p. 382.

that would result from it. Technical progress was continually making higher production possible ; but it was also, by displacing labour, narrowing the market in which the products could be sold. Accordingly, capitalism was plunged into recurrent crises, from which it escaped only by discarding great masses of old capital goods which could no longer be used at a profit. The real nature of capitalist crises was that they were the means by which this destruction of redundant capital assets was brought about. When it had been accomplished, a new cycle began ; but the new, more productive capital goods that were now in use only aggravated the situation and in due course brought on a further crisis of a more destructive kind.

This analysis of course involved the assumption that the increased production could not be consumed by the workers as the result of wage increases. Marx, in his account of the matter, assumed *real* wages to be constant — which meant that the displacement of labour would decrease the total consumers' demand coming from that source. This, he thought, followed from the fact that the displacement would increase the workers' competition for jobs and thus reduce their bargaining power — indeed, elsewhere he argued that the advance of capitalism would necessarily create a tendency for real wages to fall because of this competition. His point, however, in his study of crises was that, even without falling wages to aggravate the discrepancy, capitalism was bound to run into increasing contradiction between its expanding productive power and its tendency towards increasing capital accumulation on the one hand, and on the other its tendency to narrow the market for consumers' goods — for of course, as the only final use of capital goods was to produce consumers' goods, and these were of no profit to the capitalist unless they could be sold, the expanded production of new capital goods would only drive more and more existing capital goods out of action.

Having thus demonstrated the inherent tendency of capitalism to destroy the market for its own products, Marx had to meet the argument that he was proving altogether too much. Why, if he was right, had not capitalism collapsed long ago ? Why did slumps give place to renewed advances ? Why did capitalists go on investing, when the additional investment could only make their difficulties worse ? On the last of these points Marx answered that the capitalists had to go on investing, partly because it was of the very nature of capitalism to seek to expand, but also because they were in competition one with another, so that they had to be continually buying the most up-to-date machines in order not to be left behind in the race. The other questions he attempted to answer partly by what he said about the destruction of capital assets during each crisis ; but there was also implicit in his argument the notion of capitalism as an expanding system continually finding new outlets by displacing more primitive forms of production and thus creating new markets in which it could dispose of its expanding products. This part of the argument, however, was not brought out in Volume II of *Das Kapital*, which was devoted to an examination of the inner contradictions of capitalism as a system. Marx had undoubtedly expected these contradictions to lead to a rapid sequence of worse and worse crises, and before long to a situation in which it would become possible for the workers to overthrow the system ; and he was trying in Volume II, which remained in a not finally revised draft at his death, to provide a scientific demonstration of the inevitability of this collapse.

Rosa Luxemburg, writing nearly thirty years after Marx's death, had to face the fact that this collapse had not occurred and that crises, instead of getting worse, had diminished in intensity. Moreover, real wages, instead of falling, had manifestly been rising in the capitalist countries, and there had been other improvements, including a diminution in the length of the working week. Many economists had been ridiculing Marx's prophecies, and foretelling illimitable progress of the capitalist system. Many reformists had been urging the workers, instead of chasing Socialist utopias, to concentrate on getting the best out of capitalism, by pressing for higher wages, shorter hours, improved working conditions, and social legislation. Many Socialists, and foremost among them Eduard Bernstein, had been arguing that it was an illusion to expect the capitalist system to collapse, that trusts and combines were well able to prevent collapse by regulating the processes of production and marketing, and that Socialism would come, not through the collapse or violent overthrow of the old order, but through a gradual transformation into collectivist institutions by means of legislation enacted by a Socialist Party backed by a democratic electorate.

Rosa Luxemburg, as we saw, had taken a strong line against Bernstein's Revisionism; and she had also entered the lists against the Russian Revisionists, Peter Struve and Tugan-Baranovsky. She was by no means prepared to discard Marx's prophecies concerning the inevitable collapse of capitalism on account of its inherent contradictions; but she felt the need to explain why, instead of collapsing long ago, it continued to advance from strength to strength. She found her answer in a development of what Marx himself had indicated — the enlargement of the market for capitalist products by finding outlets for them in the pre-capitalist sectors of the world. Capitalism, she held, had been able to surmount repeated crises and to go on expanding because it had been constantly invading new areas, superseding more primitive methods of production, crushing out the village craftsmen, opening up fresh lands by developing railways and shipping services, introducing capitalist methods into agriculture, exploiting new sources of raw materials, and in general dumping on the non-capitalist world both the surplus consumers' goods which it could not sell to its own employees at home and the capital goods which could find no sufficient outlet in home investment. To be sure, in the long run these ventures could only aggravate the contradictions; for as each new area passed over to capitalistic methods, the same problems of deficient demand and displacement of labour by machinery would be reproduced on an ever-increasing scale. Moreover, the existing capitalists, in industrialising new areas, would only be stirring up additional competition against themselves, and making the situation worse in the older capitalist areas by utilising the vast resources of cheap labour available in the less developed countries. The 'long run', however, might be very long; and in the meantime the capitalists who were in possession of the most advanced techniques would be netting huge profits and would be able to find outlets for the accumulation of more and more capital in the new regions that were being opened up. Rosa Luxemburg argued that Marx had been wrong, not in his demonstration of the contradictions of capitalism, but only in his timing: he had not made enough allowance for the possibilities of continued capitalist expansion as long as there remained new areas in which surplus products could be disposed of and new investments profitably made.

This line of argument joined on to the great controversy which had been going on about the possibilities of capitalist development in Russia. As we saw, the Narodnik economists had contended that capitalism could not be successfully established in Russia, save within a very limited field, because it would not be able either to find adequate markets at home in face of the poverty of the people or to export its products in competition with the more efficient capitalists of other countries which had entered earlier upon the race. It would be the less able to find markets at home because, by driving the handicraftsmen out of business, it would further impoverish the countryside; and no amount of high protectionism would enable it to do more than cater for a limited luxury market. The Russian Marxists, including both the moderates — Struve and Tugan-Baranovsky — and the Social Democrats, had rejected these views, and had contended that it was entirely possible for Russian industry to develop an internal market. There were vast opportunities for capital construction within Russia — for example, railway-building; and the destruction of handicraft production would provide markets for the products of the power-driven machines. The entire process of changing over from a subsistence to a capitalistic money economy could be gone through in Russia, just as it had been gone through elsewhere. The Russian industrialisers differed about what would then happen. One group agreed with Bernstein that capitalism was showing its power to overcome its contradictions by improved organisation of the market — including better wages. The Social Democrats, on the other hand, stood by Marx's doctrine, and expected Russian capitalism, like capitalism in the rest of the world, to become in due course a victim to the inherent contradictions he had exposed.

In relation to Russia, Rosa Luxemburg had of course taken sides with the industrialisers, but against those of them who adopted the Revisionist standpoint in its Russian form. She held the capitalist system to be doomed to break down — in the long run. But she saw that, in Russia, capitalism might prove quite capable of advancing a long way by doing, within the Czarist Empire, precisely what the capitalists of the more advanced countries had been doing by penetrating the markets and opening up the resources of undeveloped areas beyond their frontiers, by colonisation and conquest as well as by peaceful trade. Like Lenin, she saw modern Imperialism as the expression of these forms of capitalistic expansion.

This view of Imperialism of course included the thesis that modern wars were to be regarded as the consequence of economic expansionism. 'Colonial' wars were forms of capitalist penetration of undeveloped territories : the wars between great powers were the outcome of the clash between rival capitalisms disputing for the right to acquire and exploit such territories. As more and more of the world was exploited for the purpose of capitalist profit-making, the rivalries between the great capitalist powers were bound to become sharper and the danger of war to increase. Already, the sums spent on armaments were growing at a great pace ; and this expenditure, which Rosa Luxemburg treated as being paid for by the workers through higher taxation which the capitalist Governments were able to arrange should fall on the poor rather than on the rich, further impoverished the mass of the people, and sharpened the internal contradictions of the capitalist States.

Rosa Luxemburg's book was thus an attempt to demonstrate that capitalism had not collapsed in accordance with Marx's expectations because it had been able continually to expand by penetration of pre-capitalist areas and sectors of production, but also to validate Marx's prophecies as a correct account of what would occur when this penetration had passed a certain stage. She did not hold that it would continue until the whole world had been opened up and subjected to capitalist control : long before that, she argued, the rivalries of the capitalist groups would bring on wars in which capitalism would destroy itself and open up the possibility of Socialist revolution. But, although she upheld Marx's general conception of capitalist contradictions, she attacked certain parts of his exposition, and also all his timing, as wrong.

This is, I believe, the gist of Rosa Luxemburg's book. But a large part of it is given up to exposing the unsoundness of Marx's own account of the process of capital accumulation in Volume II of *Das Kapital*. Marx there discussed this process under the name 'expanded reproduction of capital' as contrasted with 'simple reproduction' as it is found in pre-capitalist economies. Where 'simple reproduction' prevails, the current output is devoted partly to consumption and partly to replacing the capital goods as they wear out, so that an identical set of productive processes is repeated from year to year — that is, on the assumption that the techniques of production and the employed population remain unchanged. But under capitalism production does not remain static : even apart from changes in techniques or population it increases, because the capitalists, instead of consuming their entire net incomes (net after replacement of worn-out or obsolete capital goods) save a further part for investment with a view to enlarged production for profit. This further part they spend partly on buying additional capital goods and partly on wages for additional workers. But how are they able to do this, and what induces them to do it ? In order to do it, they must find buyers for all the goods they have already produced, and they must be able to expect to find buyers for the additional goods which the new capital will enable them to produce. Where are these buyers to come from ? Up to a point, the capitalists can create a market for their extra products by buying them themselves — or rather by one capitalist buying from another. But if the capitalists go on buying more capital goods, and thus increasing total production, they must in the end come up against the difficulty that, as the sole final use of capital goods is to produce goods for consumption, the enlarged supply of them will only intensify competition unless consumers' demand increases enough to take the larger quantities off the market. In other words, a high rate of capital accumulation is self-stultifying unless it is accompanied by a sufficient rise in consumers' demand.

Unfortunately Marx, in the course of his analysis of the process of 'expanded reproduction', made use for illustrative purposes of a 'working model' in which he showed the process as continuing over a period of years, apparently without coming up against this problem of the limitation of the consumers' market. In this model he took for granted the continuance of the capitalists' will to invest and treated the production of consumers' goods as a simple derivative of the demand created for them by this investment. He thus appeared to be giving sanction to the familiar thesis of the orthodox economists, known as 'Say's Law', which lays down that every act of production creates a market for its products by distributing in connection with the productive processes the purchasing power needed to buy the product. Of course, Marx did not mean this. He was simply presenting a very abstract working model of what would happen as long as the capitalists' will to invest was maintained irrespective of the limitations of the final consumers' market. But he got entangled in his own argument, and went on to a series of attempts to explain where the funds for sustaining the process came from — explanations which, in the form in which he left them, explained nothing. I think he got himself into a thorough muddle and that, as I have suggested earlier,[1] his failure to publish the second volume of *Das Kapital* during his lifetime may have been due to his awareness that something had gone wrong with the argument — which was in fact left unfinished, with some of the questions he had set himself still undiscussed. His 'working model' was then seized on by certain of his successors, notably in Russia by Struve, S. N. Bulgakov, and Tugan-Baranovsky, as indicating that he had admitted the possibility of capitalist production continuing to expand indefinitely without being brought to a halt by the limitations of the market for consumers' goods.

Rosa Luxemburg saw, and exhaustively exposed, the weaknesses in Marx's exposition. She argued, indeed, that he had provided no answer at all to his own fundamental question. She insisted that capitalists could and would go on investing in additional means of production only if they could find markets, and that, as they were depressing instead of expanding the home market for consumers' goods and thus, indirectly, for capital goods to supply it, the only answer possible was that they sold to 'third parties'. This 'third party' argument had been advanced before, in a different form. Struve and others had contended that the surplus products were got rid off by selling them to persons who were neither capitalists nor workers — for example, to the professional classes. Rosa Luxemburg ridiculed the 'third party' argument in this form; for where, she asked, did the 'third parties' get their incomes except out of the surplus value accruing to the capitalists, which had already

[1] See Vol. II, p. 298.

been included in their part of the total demand? But she put forward a different 'third party' argument, by contending that the required additional demand came from areas outside the capitalist structure, and especially from non-capitalist countries and groups which were penetrated by the products of capitalistic production.

This argument too, as we have seen, was not wholly new. It had been met, for example by Bulgakov, with the contention that capitalists did not give away their products to the less developed peoples, but exchanged them for goods — chiefly foodstuffs and materials — produced by these peoples. These imported goods had accordingly to be added to the supply of home-produced goods seeking an outlet in the market: so that the limitation of the total effective demand for consumers' goods — and therewith for capital goods — remained as great a difficulty as ever. This rebuttal, however, was not valid in respect of goods sent abroad as investments, and not exchanged for imports. Rosa Luxemburg's main contention was that the export of capital had provided the required outlet for the capitalists' will to invest, and had thus staved off capitalist collapse at the cost of intensifying world capitalist rivalries and making the problem less solvable than ever in the long run.

Her book had a mixed reception. There was little time for her fellow-Socialists to digest its arguments before the outbreak of world war gave them other things to think about. Among Marxists her close friend Franz Mehring welcomed it cordially; but many of the leading theorists were unprepared to accept her revision of Marxist theory, and denied that the expansion of capitalist production could be fully explained by the dumping of the surplus products of capitalist industry in the non-capitalist sectors of the world economy. Some — for example, Otto Bauer — attributed the continued expansion largely to the rise in population, which had continually enlarged the market as well as the productive power: others tried to show that, despite appearances, the contradictions of capitalism had been increasing and the workers been getting worse off — so that the next economic crisis, or at any rate the next after that, could be expected to bring the matter to a head, and open the way to a Socialist victory. Others denied that there were any contradictions that could not be overcome by Trade Union and Socialist action to raise wages and improve working-class consuming power by means of social and industrial legislation.

There is, of course, a great deal more in *The Accumulation of Capital* than has been mentioned in this brief account, which has been necessarily simplified in the process of extricating the essential ideas from a mass of secondary argument tied up with Marx's text. It is to be observed that Marx's formulation of the question in his second volume was such as to put the emphasis in respect of capital accumulation on the process of investment in the industries producing capital goods rather than in those producing consumers' goods. The relative increase of investment in the first of these groups had been, indeed, a very marked feature of capitalist development in all the advanced countries; and it was natural to think of it as playing the dominant part in the process of capital accumulation, with investment in the consumers' goods industries following in its wake. In giving priority to the development of the heavy industries the Soviet Union was following the pattern of capitalist evolution as it had been characterised by Marx and by later economists, rather than that which it had actually taken in the earlier, textile phase of the English Industrial Revolution. But even at that stage there had been considerable investment in ironworks and coal-mines, and also in canals, as well as in textile factories using power-driven machines.

For Rosa Luxemburg two great practical issues were at stake in her attempt to restate the theory of capital accumulation. The first was whether capitalism, as a world system, was in danger of early breakdown from internal causes — for the strategy of revolutionists in relation to it must clearly be affected by its prospects of survival. On this matter, her conclusion was that, whereas the Revisionists had gone too far in one direction, orthodox Marxists were inclined to go too far in the other. Capitalism was destined to break down — some day; but its purely economic contradictions would not kill it yet, because it could still invest abroad. But the fact that it could continue to stave off economic breakdown did not mean that it would actually survive, but only that suicide was more probable than natural death — or rather that the Revolution's best chance of ending it soon lay in the outbreak of war between the contending capitalist groups. This opinion did not induce her, any more than other Internationalists who shared her opinion, to work for war; but it did cause them to regard the threat of war as a signal to the workers to intensify their revolutionary efforts. This was the significance of the final paragraph which she and Lenin got written into the 'war' resolution of the Stuttgart International Congress of 1907.

The second great practical issue was that of the policy to be followed after the Revolution in order to ensure a full and rightly balanced use of productive resources. Under Socialism fully as much as under capitalism it would be necessary to divide the current product of industry into three parts. Under capitalism these were, according to Marx's formula, $C + V + S$. Of these, C, the product of constant capital, was needed to replace the materials and instruments of production as they were used up, so as to keep the capital stock intact. V was the sum paid out in wages and used to pay for what the workers consumed. S was the surplus, which, after deduction of necessary expenses for the maintenance of non-productive workers, such as managers and clerks, provided the rent, interest, and profits of the exploiting classes. Under Socialism the third of these would cease to be paid to its former appropriators; the other two would remain, though their proportion to the whole product might change. There would, however, arise a new S, part of which would be needed to supply new capital, to maintain under social ownership the process of 'expanded reproduction', whereas another part would be payable not to landlords or capitalists but to the aged and the disabled, or for the care of the children, or for social services on behalf of the whole people. It was necessary to make sure that under a Socialist economy no such contradictions as existed under capitalism would reappear in new forms. Marx's 'working model' was relevant here: by giving 'S' its new meaning, it could be transformed into the working model of a Socialist society. With V and S both collectively controlled there would no longer be any need to seek outside markets for the purpose of counteracting the failure of internal demand. International trade would be able to assume its rightful shape as a fruitful exchange of complementary products.

Quite recently *The Accumulation of Capital* — but only the first volume — has been translated into English, accompanied by an introductory essay by Mrs. Joan Robinson. Mrs. Robinson's conclusion is that there is much more to be said for it than either Socialists or anti-Socialists appreciated at the time of its publication. Speaking of the present generation of economists, she writes that 'few would deny that the extension of capitalism into new territories was the mainspring of what an academic economist has called the "vast secular boom" of the last two hundred years, and many academic economists account for the uneasy condition of capitalism in the twentieth century largely by the "closing of the frontier" all over the world'. Mrs. Robinson criticises Rosa Luxemburg for ignoring in her analysis the rise in real wages that has occurred throughout the capitalist world and thus presenting an incomplete picture ; but she sees in her book a remarkable anticipation of conceptions that were to be widely understood only when the great inter-war depression had given fresh actuality to the discussions concerning the possibilities of early capitalist collapse and had induced further study of the alleged contradictions inherent in capitalist production.

END OF PART I